Visit the Web site for

A HISTORY OF
World Societies
bedfordstmartins.com/mckayworld

FREE Online Study Guide

GET INSTANT FEEDBACK ON YOUR PROGRESS WITH

- Chapter self-tests
- Key terms review
- Map quizzes
- Timeline activities
- Note-taking outlines

FREE History Research Writing Help

REFINE YOUR RESEARCH SKILLS AND FIND PLENTY OF GOOD SOURCES WITH

- A database of useful images, maps, documents, and more at *Make History*
- A guide to online sources for history
- Help with writing history papers
- A tool for building a bibliography
- Tips on avoiding plagiarism

THE CONTEMPORARY WORLD

Greenland
(Den.)

ICELAND

Alaska
(U.S.)

80°N

60°N

CANADA

UNITED
KINGDOM

IRELAND

FRANCE

SPAIN

40°N

UNITED STATES

ATLANTIC
OCEAN

Azores
(Port.)

PORTUGAL

MOROCCO

Bermuda (U.K.)

Canary Is.
(Sp.)

BAHAMAS

Western Sahara
(Mor.)

DOMINICAN
REPUBLIC

MEXICO

HAITI

MAURITANIA

CUBA

Puerto Rico (U.S.)

JAMAICA

ST. KITTS AND NEVIS

CAPE
VERDE

Hawaii (U.S.)

20°N

BELIZE

ANTIGUA AND BARBUDA

SENEGAL

MALI

GUATEMALA

HONDURAS

DOMINICA

GAMBIA

Guadeloupe (Fr.)

ST. VINCENT AND THE GRENADINES

GUINEA-BISSAU

EL SALVADOR

NICARAGUA

Martinique (Fr.)

BARBADOS

GUINEA

ST. LUCIA

COSTA RICA

GRENADA

SIERRA LEONE

TRINIDAD AND TOBAGO

PANAMA

GUYANA

LIBERIA

VENEZUELA

SURINAME

CÔTE D'IVOIRE

French Guiana (Fr.)

BURKINA FASO

PACIFIC OCEAN

COLOMBIA

GHANA

0°

Equator

Galápagos Is.
(Ec.)

ECUADOR

BRAZIL

PERU

SAMOA

20°S

BOLIVIA

TONGA

PARAGUAY

Easter I.
·(Chile)

CHILE

ATLANTIC
OCEAN

URUGUAY

N

W   E

S

ARGENTINA

0   1,500   3,000 miles

0   1,500   3,000 kilometers

40°S

Falkland Is.
(U.K.)

60°S

80°S

160°W   140°W   120°W   100°W   80°W   60°W   40°W   20°W

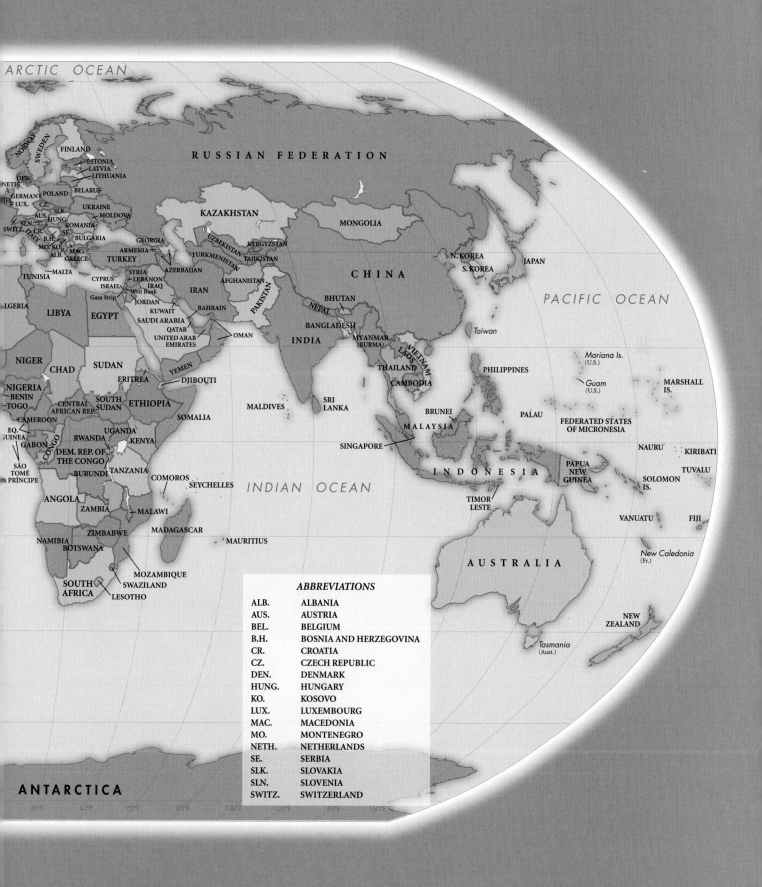

ARCTIC OCEAN

RUSSIAN FEDERATION

NORWAY
SWEDEN
FINLAND
ESTONIA
LATVIA
LITHUANIA
DEN.
NETH.
GERMANY POLAND
BEL. LUX. CZ.
B.FL. SLK.
AUS. UKRAINE
SLN. HUNG.
SWITZ. CR. SE. ROMANIA
ITALY B.H. BULGARIA
MO. KO. MAC.
ALB. GREECE
BELARUS
MOLDOVA
GEORGIA
ARMENIA
TURKEY
AZERBAIJAN
TURKMENISTAN

KAZAKHSTAN

MONGOLIA

UZBEKISTAN
KYRGYZSTAN
TAJIKISTAN

N. KOREA
S. KOREA
JAPAN

PACIFIC OCEAN

TUNISIA
MALTA
CYPRUS
ISRAEL
West Bank
Gaza Strip
SYRIA LEBANON
IRAQ
JORDAN
KUWAIT
SAUDI ARABIA
QATAR
UNITED ARAB
EMIRATES
IRAN
AFGHANISTAN
PAKISTAN
BAHRAIN
OMAN

CHINA

BHUTAN
NEPAL
INDIA
BANGLADESH
MYANMAR
(BURMA)
LAOS
VIETNAM
THAILAND
CAMBODIA

Taiwan

Mariana Is.
(U.S.)

Guam
(U.S.)

MARSHALL
IS.

LGERIA
LIBYA
EGYPT

NIGER
CHAD
SUDAN

NIGERIA
BENIN
TOGO
CENTRAL
AFRICAN REP.
SOUTH
SUDAN
ERITREA
DJIBOUTI
ETHIOPIA
YEMEN

CAMEROON
EQ.
GUINEA
GABON
CONGO
RWANDA
DEM. REP. OF
THE CONGO
BURUNDI
UGANDA
KENYA
TANZANIA
SOMALIA

SÃO
TOMÉ
& PRÍNCIPE

COMOROS
SEYCHELLES

MALDIVES

SRI
LANKA

BRUNEI

MALAYSIA

SINGAPORE

PHILIPPINES

PALAU

FEDERATED STATES
OF MICRONESIA

NAURU
KIRIBATI

TUVALU

SOLOMON
IS.

INDONESIA

PAPUA
NEW
GUINEA

INDIAN OCEAN

ANGOLA
ZAMBIA
MALAWI
ZIMBABWE
MADAGASCAR
MAURITIUS
NAMIBIA
BOTSWANA
MOZAMBIQUE
SWAZILAND
SOUTH
AFRICA
LESOTHO

TIMOR
LESTE

VANUATU
FIJI

New Caledonia
(Fr.)

AUSTRALIA

NEW
ZEALAND

Tasmania
(Aust.)

ANTARCTICA

ABBREVIATIONS	
ALB.	ALBANIA
AUS.	AUSTRIA
BEL.	BELGIUM
B.H.	BOSNIA AND HERZEGOVINA
CR.	CROATIA
CZ.	CZECH REPUBLIC
DEN.	DENMARK
HUNG.	HUNGARY
KO.	KOSOVO
LUX.	LUXEMBOURG
MAC.	MACEDONIA
MO.	MONTENEGRO
NETH.	NETHERLANDS
SE.	SERBIA
SLK.	SLOVAKIA
SLN.	SLOVENIA
SWITZ.	SWITZERLAND

20°E 40°E 60°E 80°E 100°E 120°E 140°E 160°E

A HISTORY OF
World Societies

Egyptian Mummy Mask, ca. 1295–1069 B.C.E.

NINTH EDITION

A HISTORY OF
World Societies

Volume A | TO 1500

JOHN P. McKAY | *University of Illinois at Urbana-Champaign*

BENNETT D. HILL | *Late of Georgetown University*

JOHN BUCKLER | *Late of University of Illinois at Urbana-Champaign*

PATRICIA BUCKLEY EBREY | *University of Washington*

ROGER B. BECK | *Eastern Illinois University*

CLARE HARU CROWSTON | *University of Illinois at Urbana-Champaign*

MERRY E. WIESNER-HANKS | *University of Wisconsin–Milwaukee*

BEDFORD/ST. MARTIN'S
Boston • New York

FOR BEDFORD/ST. MARTIN'S

Publisher for History: Mary Dougherty
Executive Editor for History: Traci M. Crowell
Director of Development for History: Jane Knetzger
Senior Developmental Editor: Laura Arcari
Senior Production Editor: Christina Horn
Senior Production Supervisor: Dennis J. Conroy
Executive Marketing Manager: Jenna Bookin Barry
Associate Editor: Lynn Sternberger
Editorial Assistant: Arrin Kaplan
Production Assistant: Laura Winstead
Copy Editor: Sybil Sosin
Map Editor: Charlotte Miller
Indexer: Leoni Z. McVey
Cartography: Mapping Specialists, Ltd.
Page Layout: Boynton Hue Studio
Photo Researcher: Carole Frohlich and Elisa Gallagher, The Visual Connection Image Research, Inc.

Permissions Manager: Kalina K. Ingham
Senior Art Director: Anna Palchik
Text and Cover Designer: Brian Salisbury
Cover Art: Mummy mask, New Kingdom, 19th–20th Dynasty (1295–1069 B.C.E.), painted cartonnage. Egyptian/Private Collection/Photo © Heini Schneebeli/The Bridgeman Art Library.
Composition: NK Graphics
Printing and Binding: RR Donnelley and Sons

President: Joan E. Feinberg
Editorial Director: Denise B. Wydra
Director of Marketing: Karen R. Soeltz
Director of Production: Susan W. Brown
Associate Director, Editorial Production: Elise S. Kaiser
Managing Editor: Elizabeth M. Schaaf

Library of Congress Control Number: 2011925869

Manufactured in the United States of America.

2 3 4 5 6   15 14 13 12

For information, write: Bedford/St. Martin's, 75 Arlington Street, Boston, MA 02116   (617-399-4000)

ISBN: 978-0-312-66691-0 (Combined edition)
ISBN: 978-0-312-57013-2 (Loose leaf)
ISBN: 978-0-312-56969-3 (High School edition)
ISBN: 978-0-312-66692-7 (Volume 1)
ISBN: 978-0-312-57014-9 (Loose leaf)
ISBN: 978-0-312-66693-4 (Volume 2)
ISBN: 978-0-312-57051-4 (Loose leaf)
ISBN: 978-0-312-66694-1 (Volume A)
ISBN: 978-0-312-66695-8 (Volume B)
ISBN: 978-0-312-66696-5 (Volume C)

☐ IN MEMORIAM

JOHN BUCKLER 1945–2011

John Buckler, who authored many of the chapters in earlier editions of this book, was born in Louisville, Kentucky, on March 16, 1945. John received his B.A. summa cum laude from the University of Louisville in 1967 and his Ph.D. from Harvard University in 1973. From 1984 to 1986, he held an Alexander von Humboldt Fellowship at the Institut für Alte Geschichte at the University of Munich. In 1980 Harvard University Press published his *Theban Hegemony, 371–362 B.C.* In 1989 his *Philip II and the Sacred War* was published, and he also edited *BOIOTIKA: Vorträge vom 5. Internationalen Böotien-Kolloquium.* During the 1990s he contributed articles to the American Historical Association's *Guide to Historical Literature, The Oxford Classical Dictionary,* and *The Encyclopedia of Greece and the Hellenic Tradition.* In 2003 he published A*egean Greece in the Fourth Century B.C.* In the following year his editions of W. M. Leake's *Travels in the Morea* (three volumes) and *Peloponnesiaca* appeared. Cambridge University Press published his *Central Greece and the Politics of Power in the Fourth Century,* edited by Hans Beck, in 2007. At the time of his sudden and unexpected death, he was writing a book on the history of Greek warfare and also contributing to revisions of *Die Fragmente der Griechischen Historiker* by Felix Jacoby. Known internationally for his work, John was a scholar of great stature who will be missed by all who knew him.

◻ BRIEF CONTENTS

☐ CONTENTS

1 The Earliest Human Societies
to 2500 B.C.E. 2

2 The Rise of the State in Southwest Asia and the Nile Valley

3200–500 B.C.E.   32

3 The Foundation of Indian Society

to 300 C.E.   64

6 The World of Rome

750 B.C.E.–400 C.E.   142

7 East Asia and the Spread of Buddhism

221 B.C.E.–800 C.E.   174

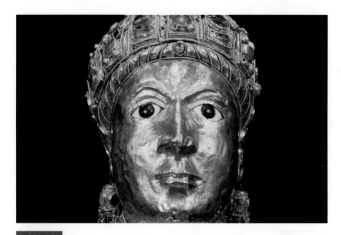

12 Cultural Exchange in Central and Southern Asia

to 1400   330

13 States and Cultures in East Asia

800–1400   364

FIGURES AND TABLES

□ SPECIAL FEATURES

The ninth edition of *A History of World Societies* has been particularly significant for us because it represents important changes with the author team and with our publisher. Our new publisher, Bedford/St. Martin's, gave us the opportunity to revisit our original vision and to revitalize the text and its scholarship in exciting and fulfilling ways. Sadly, founding authors John P. McKay and John Buckler retired from the book this year, but with Merry Wiesner-Hanks and Clare Haru Crowston, who joined as authors in the last edition, and Patricia Buckley Ebrey and Roger B. Beck, who joined in the fifth and seventh editions, respectively, we continue to benefit from a collaborative team of regional experts with deep experience in the world history classroom.

In this age of global connections, with its influence on the global economy, global migration patterns, popular culture, and global warming, among other things, the study of world history is more vital and urgent than ever before. An understanding of the broad sweep of the human past helps us to comprehend today's dramatic changes and enduring continuities. People now migrate enormous distances and establish new lives far from their places of birth, yet migration has been a constant in history since the first humans walked out of Africa. Satellite and cell phones now link nearly every inch of the planet, yet the expansion of communication networks is a process that is thousands of years old. Children who speak different languages at home now sit side by side in schools and learn from one another, yet intercultural encounters have long been a source of innovation, transformation, and at times, unfortunately, conflict.

This book is designed for twenty-first-century students who will spend their lives on this small interconnected planet and for whom an understanding of only local or national history will no longer be sufficient. We believe that the study of world history in a broad and comparative context is an exciting, important, and highly practical pursuit. It is our conviction, based on considerable experience in introducing large numbers of students to world history, that a book reflecting current trends in scholarship can excite readers and inspire an enduring interest in the long human experience.

Our strategy has been twofold. First, we have made social and cultural history the core elements of our narrative. We seek to re-create the lives of ordinary people in appealing human terms and also to highlight the interplay between men's and women's lived experiences and the ways they reflect on these to create meaning. Thus, in addition to foundational works of philosophy and literature, we include popular songs and stories. We present objects along with texts as important sources for studying history, and this has allowed us to incorporate the growing emphasis on material culture in the work of many historians. At the same time we have been mindful of the need to give great economic, political, and intellectual developments the attention they deserve. We want to give individual students and instructors an integrated perspective so that they can pursue — on their own or in the classroom — the themes and questions that they find particularly exciting and significant.

Second, we have made every effort to strike an effective global and regional balance. The whole world interacts today, and to understand the interactions and what they mean for today's citizens, we must study the whole world's history. Thus we have adopted a comprehensive regional organization with a global perspective that is clear and manageable for students. For example, Chapter 7 introduces students in depth to East Asia, and at the same time the chapter highlights the cultural connections that occurred via the Silk Road and the spread of Buddhism. We study all geographical areas, conscious of the separate histories of many parts of the world, particularly in the earliest millennia of human development. We also stress the links among cultures, political units, and economic systems, for these connections have made the world what it is today. We make comparisons and connections across time as well as space, for understanding the unfolding of the human story in time is the central task of history.

Textual Changes

In preparing the ninth edition of this book, we have worked hard to keep the book up-to-date and to strengthen our comprehensive, comparative, and connective approach. We carefully revisited and reconsidered every paragraph, rewriting and expanding sections for clarity and for stronger connections and comparisons and, most important, incorporating the latest scholarship, including a new first chapter on "The Earliest Human Societies, to 2500 B.C.E." informed by the most current research available. Moreover, we revised every chapter with the goal of readability and accessibility.

Several main lines of revision have guided our many changes. As in previous editions we added significantly more discussion of groups and regions that are often short-changed in general histories of world civilizations, and we have continued to do so in this new revision, including new material on the Minoans and Mycenaeans in Chapter 5; the Celts in Chapter 8; the Pacific Islanders and Easter Island in Chapter 12; Korea during the Koryŏ dynasty in Chapter 13; the American colonies in Chapters 17 and 22; Armenian traders in Chapter 20; the Congo Free State in Chapter 25;

the Palestinians, Kurds, and Lebanese in Chapter 32; and the countries of Latin America in Chapter 33. This expanded scope reflects the awareness within the historical profession of the enormous diversity of the world's peoples.

We have also continued to increase our coverage of social and cultural history, encouraging students to consider how life in the past was both similar to and different from our lives today. This increased emphasis is supported in every chapter by the use of artifacts that make history tangible. In addition, we enhanced the discussion of religion in many chapters, including both the central ideas and lived religious practices of world religions such as Judaism and Christianity and of local religions such as those of the Celts and Egyptians. So, for example, you will find new scholarship on Amon-Ra and Isis, Zoroastrianism, and Jewish religious beliefs in Chapter 2; expanded coverage of the Jewish background of Christianity along with new material on second- and third-century Christianity in Chapter 6; and an expanded discussion of Arian Christianity along with a new discussion of the development of the Bible as a text in Chapter 8. Students are increasingly interested in the diversity of religious practices in the world around them, and we hope these additions will help them better understand the wide range of religions in the past.

Other social and cultural additions include new sections on Life in Early India in Chapter 3, Life During the Zhou Dynasty in Chapter 4, and Life in Han China in Chapter 7; a new discussion of the *Iliad* and *Odyssey* in Chapter 5; more on Roman architecture and literature in Chapter 6; new coverage of the actual workings of the law and an expanded discussion of family structure and food in Chapter 14; a new section devoted to life in the colonies of the New World in Chapter 17; and a new in-depth section devoted to the social impact of the Atlantic world in Chapter 18, including an exciting new section on Identities and Communities of the Atlantic World, where we discuss the impact of colonization and world trade on the lives of ordinary people.

As mentioned above, in this edition we have continued to strengthen the comparative coverage within the narrative to help students see and understand the cross-cultural connections of world history. In addition, we have added an exciting **NEW Connections** feature to the end of each chapter. This feature's synthesis of main developments serves to conclude the chapter, and the connections and comparisons of countries and regions explain how events relate to larger global processes, such as the influence of the Silk Road, the effects of the transatlantic slave trade, and the ramifications of colonialism. This new feature also serves to guide students in their reading, introducing related events and cultures that they will encounter in chapters to come. In this way students are introduced to history as an ongoing process of interrelated events.

The importance of cross-cultural connections to the study of world history is reflected in new scholarship and information on the impact of writing on our understanding of the past, and the relationship between the development of writing and the growth of states in Chapter 2; attention to areas of the world in which there were significant encounters between groups, such as Nubia and Kush in eastern Africa in Chapter 2 and the Indo-Bactrian kingdoms in Chapter 3; the impact of European settlement on the lives of indigenous peoples in Chapter 16; a more global perspective on European politics, culture, and economics in the early modern period, including the global impact of the Seven Years' War and treatment of the American, French, and Haitian Revolutions as interrelated events in an Atlantic world of political debates, conflicts, and aspirations in Chapter 22; an emphasis on cross-cultural encounters along the East African coast in Chapter 19; expanded coverage of Korea in Chapter 21, allowing for more in-depth analysis of the similarities of and differences between Asian countries; coverage of early efforts at modernization and industrialization outside of Europe and a discussion of how slavery impacted worldwide industrialization in Chapter 23; connections between the early European contacts in Africa and those that occurred with the empires of Southwest Asia in Chapter 25; the worldwide effects of the Great Depression in Chapter 30; and a more global treatment of both World War I and World War II, with new coverage of the ways in which these wars affected colonial peoples, in Chapters 28 and 30.

These major aspects of revision are accompanied by the incorporation of a wealth of other new scholarship and subject areas. Additions, among others, include a new section on hieroglyphics and a discussion of gender as it relates to Mesopotamian politics in Chapter 2; a more in-depth treatment of Chinese military thought and technology in Chapter 4; new scholarship on mystery religions in Chapter 5; an updated discussion of sexuality and Christianity in Chapter 8; new scholarship on race in Chapter 10; an updated discussion of mound builders and a new discussion of environmental and political changes in Chapter 11; new coverage of China under Mongol rule in Chapter 12; new scholarship on the Crusades in Chapter 14; a revised discussion of humanism to include more about women, and an updated discussion of Machiavelli to reflect new scholarship in Chapter 15; new coverage of the Atlantic world and the ways in which Enlightenment ideas and debates circulated along with many different peoples and commodities in Chapter 18; increased attention to suffrage in Chapter 24; a new discussion of politically active emigrants and the ways in which some Asians rejected Western influence, while others embraced Western ideas and practice, in Chapter 26; and updates through 2011 in Chapters 31, 32, 33, and 34, including up-to-date coverage of the economic downturn and the 2010–2011 uprisings and protests in North Africa and the Middle East. In sum, we have tried to bring new research and interpretation into our global history, believing it essential to keep our book stimulating, accurate, and current for students and instructors.

New Chapters and Organizational Changes

To meet the demands of the evolving course, we took a close and critical look at the book's organization and have made several major changes in the organization of chapters to reflect the way the course is taught today. The most dramatic change is the addition of an entirely new first chapter, "The Earliest Human Societies, to 2500 B.C.E.," which reflects a growing awareness among world historians that the human story properly begins millions, not mere thousands, of years ago. In order to provide a more global perspective on European politics, culture, and economics in the early modern period, Chapters 17, 18, and 22 have been substantially reworked and reorganized. Chapter 17 on European absolutism and constitutionalism has been broadened in scope to include European expansion, and Chapter 18 on the scientific revolution and the Enlightenment now includes coverage of the Atlantic world. As a natural extension, Chapter 22, which used to focus on the French Revolution, now examines the age of revolution in the Atlantic world. Together, the enhanced global perspectives of these chapters help connect the different regions of the globe and, in particular, help explain the crucial period when Europe began to dominate the rest of the globe.

To increase clarity and to help students see the global connections between the events surrounding World Wars I and II, we dropped the chapter on Europe in the interwar years and integrated this material into the World War chapters. Chapter 28 now focuses on the Great War, the Russian Revolution, and the interwar years, while Chapter 30 begins with the Great Depression in order to better explain the global conditions that contributed to the outbreak of World War II. The post-1945 section has also been completely reworked. In addition to updating all of the postwar chapters through 2011, we substantially reworked the last three chapters, integrating the Epilogue on the Middle East into Chapter 32 to create a more tightly focused and accessible chapter, and moving the material on Latin America and Africa to create a new Chapter 33 on the Global South. In addition to these major organizational changes, we carefully scrutinized all chapters, reorganizing material and adding clearer heads throughout as needed for clarity and to highlight important material for students.

Features

We are proud of the diverse special features that expand upon the narrative and offer opportunities for classroom discussion and assignments. For the ninth edition we have augmented our offerings to include a new feature created in response to reviewer requests for more primary source materials. This **NEW** documents feature, **Viewpoints**, offers paired primary documents on a topic that illuminates the human experience, allowing us to provide concrete examples of differences in the ways people thought. Anyone teaching world history has to emphasize larger trends and developments, but students sometimes get the wrong impression that everyone in a society thought alike. We hope that teachers can use these passages to get students thinking about diversity within and across societies. The thirty-four Viewpoints — one in each chapter — introduce students to working with sources, encourage critical analysis, and extend the narrative while giving voice to the people of the past. Each includes a brief introduction and questions for analysis. Carefully chosen for accessibility, each pair of documents presents views on a diverse range of topics, such as Chinese and Japanese Principles of Good Government, ca. 650; Roman and Byzantine Views of Barbarians; Creation in the *Popul Vuh* and in Okanogan Tradition; Lauro Quirini and Cassandra Fedele: Women and Humanist Learning; Christian Conversion in New Spain; Ottoman Travelers in Mughal and Safavid Lands; Poetry of the Great War; Gandhi and Mao on Revolutionary Means; and Ghanaian and South African Leaders on Black Nationalism.

Each chapter also continues to include a longer primary source feature titled **Listening to the Past**, chosen to extend and illuminate a major historical issue considered in each chapter. The feature presents a single original source or several voices on the subject. Each opens with an introduction and closes with questions for analysis that invite students to evaluate the evidence as historians would. Selected for their interest and significance and carefully placed within their historical context, these sources, we hope, allow students to "hear the past" and to observe how history has been shaped by individuals. **NEW** topics include Paleolithic Venus Figures; Aristotle, On the Family and On Slavery, from *The Politics*; Cicero and the Plot to Kill Caesar; Sixth-Century Biographies of Buddhist Nuns; Felipe Guaman Poma de Ayala, *The First New Chronicle and Good Government*; A German Account of Russian Life; Denis Diderot's "Supplement to Bougainville's Voyage"; Katib Chelebi on Tobacco; Abbé de Sieyès, "What Is the Third Estate?"; Mrs. Beeton's Guide for Running a Victorian Household; Mary Seacole on Her Early Life; and Aung San Suu Kyi, "Freedom from Fear."

In addition to using documents as part of our special feature program, we have quoted extensively from a wide variety of primary sources within the narrative, demonstrating in our use of these quotations that they are the "stuff" of history. Thus primary sources appear as an integral part of the narrative as well as in extended form in the Listening to the Past and new Viewpoints chapter features. We believe that this extensive program of both integrated and separate primary source excerpts will help readers learn to interpret and think critically.

In our years of teaching world history, we have often noted that students come alive when they encounter stories about real people in the past. To give students a chance to see the past through ordinary people's lives, each chapter includes one of the popular **Individuals in Society** biographical essays, each of which offers a brief study of an individual or group, informing students about the societies in which the individuals lived. This feature grew out of our long-standing focus on people's lives and the varieties of historical experience, and we believe that readers will empathize with these human beings who themselves were seeking to define their own identities. The spotlighting of individuals, both famous and obscure, perpetuates the book's continued attention to cultural and intellectual developments, highlights human agency, and reflects changing interests within the historical profession as well as the development of "micro-history." **NEW** features include essays on the Iceman, Hatshepsut and Nefertiti, Lord Mengchang, Queen Cleopatra, Josiah Wedgwood, Henry Meiggs, Liu Xiaobo, and Eva Perón.

Rounding out the book's feature program is the popular **Global Trade** feature, two-page essays that focus on a particular commodity, exploring the world trade, social and economic impact, and cultural influence of that commodity. Each essay is accompanied by a detailed map showing the trade routes of the commodity and an illustration. Retaining the eight essays of the previous edition on pottery, silk, spices, tea, slaves, indigo, oil, and arms, we have added two **NEW** features on iron and silver. We believe that careful attention to all of these essays will enable the student to appreciate the complex ways in which trade has connected and influenced the various parts of the world.

With the goal of making this the most student-centered edition yet, we paid renewed attention to the book's pedagogy. To help guide students, each chapter opens with a **Chapter Preview** with focus questions keyed to the main chapter headings. These questions are repeated within the chapter, and again in the **Chapter Reviews**. For this edition, many of the questions have been reframed, and new summary answers have been added to the chapter reviews. Each chapter review concludes with a carefully selected list of annotated **Suggestions for Further Reading**, revised and updated to stay current with the vast amount of new work being done in many fields.

To promote clarity and comprehension, bolded **key terms** in the text are defined in the margin and listed again in the chapter review. **NEW phonetic spellings** are located directly after terms that readers are likely to find hard to pronounce. The **chapter chronologies**, each of which reviews major developments discussed in the chapter, have been improved to more closely mirror the key events covered in the chapter, and the number of topic-specific **thematic chronologies** has been expanded, with new chronologies on Major Figures of the Enlightenment, and Key Events of the American Revolution, among others. Once again we also provide a **unified timeline** at the end of the text. Comprehensive and easy to locate, this useful timeline allows students to compare developments over the centuries.

The consistently high-quality art and map program has been thoroughly revised and expanded. The new edition features more than 530 **contemporaneous illustrations**. To make the past tangible, and as an extension of our attention to social and cultural history, we include over 90 **artifacts** ranging from swords and coins to a spinning wheel and a phonograph. As in earlier editions, all illustrations have been carefully selected to complement the text, and all include captions that inform students while encouraging them to read the text more deeply. Completely redesigned and reconceptualized for the new edition, **100 full-size maps** illustrate major developments in the narrative. In addition, **82 NEW spot maps** are embedded in the narrative to show specific areas under discussion. **NEW** maps in the ninth edition highlight such topics as Human Migration in the Paleolithic and Neolithic Eras; The Settling of the Americas Before 10,000 B.C.E.; Settlement of the Pacific Islands; The Slave Coast of West Africa; The Atlantic Economy in 1701; The Muslim World, ca. 1700; Emigration Out of Asia, 1820–1914; The Spanish-American War in the Philippines, 1898; Cold War Europe in the 1950s; and Authoritarian Governments in Latin America, among others.

We recognize students' difficulties with geography and visual analysis, and the new edition includes **NEW Mapping the Past map activities** and **NEW Picturing the Past visual activities**. Included in each chapter, these activities ask students to analyze the map or visual and make connections to the larger processes discussed in the narrative, giving them valuable practice in reading and interpreting maps and images.

To showcase the book's rich art program and to signal our commitment to this thorough and deep revision, the book has been completely redesigned. The dynamic new contemporary design engages and assists students with its clear, easy-to-use pedagogy.

Acknowledgments

It is a pleasure to thank the many instructors who read and critiqued the manuscript through its development:

Alemseged Abbay, Frostburg State University
Funso Afolayan, University of New Hampshire
Maria Arbelaez, University of Nebraska
Eva S. Baham, Southern University, Baton Rouge
David S. Bovee, Fort Hays State University
Nancy Cade, Pikesville College
Stephen D. Carls, Union University
Steven Cassedy, University of California
Edward J. Chess, Pulaski Technical College
Erwin F. Erhardt III, Thomas More College
Matthew D. Esposito, Drake University
Angela Feres, Grossmont Community College
Sam Giordanengo, Hawai'i Community College
Randee Goodstadt, Asheville-Buncombe Technical
    Community College
K. David Goss, Gordon College

William W. Haddad, California State Fullerton

Susan M. Hellert, University of Wisconsin, Platteville

John S. Hill, Immaculata University

Ellen Kittell, University of Idaho

Donald McGuire, SUNY Buffalo

April Najjaj, Greensboro College

Sandra L. Norman, Florida Atlantic University

Edward Paulino, John Jay College

William E. Plants, University of Rio Grande/Rio Grande
    Community College

Carolee Pollock, Grant MacEwan University

Charlotte Power, Black River Technical College

Salvador Rivera, SUNY Cobleskill

Mark Schneider, Suffok University and Bridgewater
    State

J. M. Simpson, Pierce College

Carrie Spencer, Pikes Peak Community College

Pamela Stewart, Arizona State University

Steven A. Stofferahn, Indiana State University

Jason M. Stratton, Bakersfield College

Deborah A. Symonds, Drake University

George Watters, St. Johns River Community College

Robert H. Welborn, Clayton State University

Marc Zayac, Georgia Perimeter College

It is also a pleasure to thank the many editors who have assisted us over the years, first at Houghton Mifflin and now at Bedford/St. Martin's. At Bedford/St. Martin's, these include senior development editor Laura Arcari; freelance development editors Beth Castrodale and Arthur Johnson; associate editors Lynn Sternberger and Jack Cashman; editorial assistant Arrin Kaplan; executive editor Traci Mueller Crowell; director of development Jane Knetzger; publisher for history Mary Dougherty; map editor Charlotte Miller; photo researcher Carole Frohlich; text permissions editor Heather Salus; and senior production editor Christina Horn, with the assistance of Laura Winstead, Laura Deily, and Elise Keller and the guidance of managing editor Elizabeth Schaaf and assistant managing editor John Amburg. Other key contributors were designer Brian Salisbury, page makeup artist Cia Boynton, copyeditor Sybil Sosin, proofreaders Susan Moore and Angela Morrison, indexer Leoni McVey, cover image researcher Donna Dennison, and cover designer Brian Salisbury. We would also like to thank editorial director Denise Wydra and president Joan E. Feinberg.

Many of our colleagues at the University of Illinois, the University of Washington, the University of Wisconsin–Milwaukee, and Eastern Illinois University continue to provide information and stimulation, often without even knowing it. We thank them for it. The authors also thank the many students over the years with whom we have used earlier editions of this book. Their reactions and opinions helped shape our revisions to this edition, and we hope it remains worthy of the ultimate praise that they bestowed on it, that it is "not boring like most textbooks." Merry Wiesner-Hanks would, as always, like to thank her husband Neil, without whom work on this project would not be possible. Clare Haru Crowston thanks her husband Ali and her children Lili, Reza, and Kian, who are a joyous reminder of the vitality of life that we try to showcase in this book. Roger Beck is thankful to Ann for keeping the home fires burning while he was busy writing and to the World History Association for all past, present, and future contributions to his understanding of world history.

Each of us has benefited from the criticism of his or her coauthors, although each of us assumes responsibility for what he or she has written. In addition to writing an entirely new Chapter 1, Merry Wiesner-Hanks substantially reworked and revised John Buckler's Chapters 2, 5, and 6 and has written and revised Chapters 8, 11, 14, and 15; Patricia Buckley Ebrey has written and revised Chapters 3, 4, 7, 9, 12, 13, 20, 21, 26, and 27; Roger B. Beck took responsibility for John McKay's Chapters 24 and 25 and has written and revised Chapters 10, 19, and 28–34; Clare Haru Crowston has assumed primary responsibility for Chapters 16–18 and 22 and also built upon text originally written by John McKay to revise and expand Chapter 23.

◻ VERSIONS AND SUPPLEMENTS

Adopters of *A History of World Societies* and their students have access to abundant extra resources, including documents, presentation and testing materials, the acclaimed Bedford Series in History and Culture volumes, and much more. See below for more information, visit the book's catalog site at **bedfordstmartins.com/ mckayworld/catalog**, or contact your local Bedford/St. Martin's sales representative.

Get the Right Version for Your Class

To accommodate different course lengths and course budgets, *A History of World Societies* is available in several different formats, including three-hole-punched loose-leaf Budget Books versions and e-books, which are available at a substantial discount.

- Combined edition (Chapters 1–34) — available in hardcover, loose-leaf, and e-book formats
- Volume 1: To 1600 (Chapters 1–16) — available in paperback, loose-leaf, and e-book formats
- Volume 2: Since 1450 (Chapters 16–34) — available in paperback, loose-leaf, and e-book formats
- Volume A: To 1500 (Chapters 1–14) — available in paperback
- Volume B: From 800 to 1815 (Chapters 11–22) — available in paperback
- Volume C: From 1775 to the Present (Chapters 22–34) — available in paperback

The online, interactive **Bedford e-Book** can be examined or purchased at a discount at **bedfordstmartins.com/ ebooks**; if packaged with the print text, it is available at no extra cost. Your students can also purchase *A History of World Societies* in other popular e-book formats for computers, tablets, and e-readers.

Online Extras for Students

The book's companion site at **bedfordstmartins.com/ mckayworld** gives students a way to read, write, and study, and to find and access quizzes and activities, study aids, and history research and writing help.

FREE **Online Study Guide.** Available at the companion site, this popular resource provides students with quizzes and activities for each chapter, including multiple-choice self-tests that focus on important concepts; flashcards that test students' knowledge of key terms; timeline activities that emphasize causal relationships; and map quizzes intended to strengthen students' geography skills. Instructors can monitor students' progress through an online Quiz Gradebook or receive e-mail updates.

FREE **Research, Writing, and Anti-plagiarism Advice.** Available at the companion site, Bedford's **History Research and Writing Help** includes **History Research and Reference Sources**, with links to history-related databases, indexes, and journals; **More Sources and How to Format a History Paper**, with clear advice on how to integrate primary and secondary sources into research papers and how to cite and format sources correctly; **Build a Bibliography**, a simple Web-based tool known as The Bedford Bibliographer that generates bibliographies in four commonly used documentation styles; and **Tips on Avoiding Plagiarism**, an online tutorial that reviews the consequences of plagiarism and features exercises to help students practice integrating sources and recognize acceptable summaries.

Resources for Instructors

Bedford/St. Martin's has developed a wide range of teaching resources for this book and for this course. They range from lecture and presentation materials and assessment tools to course management options. Most can be downloaded or ordered at **bedfordstmartins.com/mckayworld/catalog**.

NEW *HistoryClass for A History of World Societies.* HistoryClass, a Bedford/St. Martin's Online Course Space, puts the online resources available with this textbook in one convenient and completely customizable course space. There you and your students can access an interactive e-book and primary sources reader; maps, images, documents, and links; chapter review quizzes; interactive multimedia exercises; and research and writing help. In History-Class you can get all our premium content and tools and assign, rearrange, and mix them with your own resources. For more information, visit **yourhistoryclass.com**.

Bedford Coursepack for Blackboard, WebCT, Desire-2Learn, Angel, Sakai, or Moodle. We have free content to help you integrate our rich content into your course management system. Registered instructors can download coursepacks with no hassle and no strings attached. Content includes our most popular free resources and book-specific content for *A History of World Societies*. Visit

bedfordstmartins.com/cms to see a demo, find your version, or download your coursepack.

Instructor's Resource Manual. The instructor's manual offers both experienced and first-time instructors tools for preparing for lecture and running discussions. It includes chapter review material, teaching strategies, and a guide to chapter-specific supplements available for the text.

Guide to Changing Editions. Designed to facilitate an instructor's transition from the previous edition of *A History of World Societies* to the current edition, this guide presents an overview of major changes as well as of changes in each chapter.

Computerized Test Bank. The test bank includes a mix of fresh, carefully crafted multiple-choice, matching, short-answer, and essay questions for each chapter. It also contains the Review, Visual Activity, Map Activity, Individuals in Society, and Listening to the Past questions from the text-book and model answers for each. The questions appear in Microsoft Word format and in easy-to-use test bank software that allows instructors to easily add, edit, re-sequence, and print questions and answers. Instructors can also export questions into a variety of formats, including WebCT and Blackboard.

PowerPoint Maps, Images, Lecture Outlines, and i>clicker Content. Look good and save time with *The Bedford Lecture Kit.* These presentation materials are downloadable individually from the Instructor Resources tab at **bedfordstmartins.com/mckayworld/catalog** and are available on *The Bedford Lecture Kit* Instructor's Resource CD-ROM. They include ready-made and fully customizable PowerPoint multimedia presentations built around lecture outlines with embedded maps, figures, and selected images from the textbook and with detailed instructor notes on key points. Also available are maps and selected images in JPEG and PowerPoint formats; content for i>clicker, a classroom response system, in Microsoft Word and PowerPoint formats; the Instructor's Resource Manual in Microsoft Word format; and outline maps in PDF format for quizzing or handing out. All files are suitable for copying onto transparency acetates.

Make History — Free Documents, Maps, Images, and Web Sites. *Make History* combines the best Web resources with hundreds of maps and images, to make it simple to find the source material you need. Browse the collection of thousands of resources by course or by topic, date, and type. Each item has been carefully chosen and helpfully annotated to make it easy to find exactly what you need. Available at **bedfordstmartins.com/makehistory**.

Videos and Multimedia. A wide assortment of videos and multimedia CD-ROMs on various topics in world history is available to qualified adopters through your Bedford/St. Martin's sales representative.

Package and Save Your Students Money

For information on free packages and discounts up to 50%, visit **bedfordstmartins.com/mckayworld/catalog**, or contact your local Bedford/St. Martin's sales representative.

Bedford e-Book. The e-book for this title, described above, can be packaged with the print text at no additional cost.

***Sources of World Societies,* Second Edition.** This two-volume primary source collection provides a revised and expanded selection of sources to accompany A *History of World Societies,* Ninth Edition. Each chapter features five or six sources by well-known figures and ordinary individuals alike. Now with visual sources and two more documents per chapter, this edition offers even more breadth and depth. Headnotes and questions supplement each document, while a new Viewpoints feature highlights two or three sources per chapter that address a single topic from different perspectives. Comparative questions ask students to make connections between sources and across time. Available free when packaged with the print text.

***Sources of World Societies* e-Book.** The reader is also available as an e-book. When packaged with the print or electronic version of the textbook, it is available for free.

The Bedford Series in History and Culture. More than one hundred titles in this highly praised series combine first-rate scholarship, historical narrative, and important primary documents for undergraduate courses. Each book is brief, inexpensive, and focused on a specific topic or period. For a complete list of titles, visit **bedfordstmartins .com/history/series**. Package discounts are available.

Rand McNally Historical Atlas of the World. This collection of almost seventy full-color maps illustrates the eras and civilizations in world history from the emergence of human societies to the present. Available for $3.00 when packaged with the print text.

The Bedford Glossary for World History. This handy supplement for the survey course gives students historically contextualized definitions for hundreds of terms — from *abolitionism* to *Zoroastrianism* — that they will encounter in lectures, reading, and exams. Available free when packaged with the print text.

World History Matters: A Student Guide to World History Online. Based on the popular "World History Matters" Web site produced by the Center for History and New Media, this unique resource, edited by Kristin Lehner (The Johns Hopkins University), Kelly Schrum (George Mason University), and T. Mills Kelly (George Mason University), combines reviews of 150 of the most useful and reliable world history Web sites with an introduction that guides students in locating, evaluating, and correctly citing online sources. Available free when packaged with the print text.

Trade Books. Titles published by sister companies Hill and Wang; Farrar, Straus and Giroux; Henry Holt and Company; St. Martin's Press; Picador; and Palgrave Macmillan are available at a 50% discount when packaged with Bedford/St. Martin's textbooks. For more information, visit **bedfordstmartins.com/tradeup**.

A Pocket Guide to Writing in History. This portable and affordable reference tool by Mary Lynn Rampolla provides reading, writing, and research advice useful to students in all history courses. Concise yet comprehensive advice on approaching typical history assignments, developing critical reading skills, writing effective history papers, conducting research, using and documenting sources, and avoiding plagiarism — enhanced with practical tips and examples throughout — have made this slim reference a bestseller. Package discounts are available.

A Student's Guide to History. This complete guide to success in any history course provides the practical help students need to be effective. In addition to introducing students to the nature of the discipline, author Jules Benjamin teaches a wide range of skills, from preparing for exams to approaching common writing assignments, and explains the research and documentation process with plentiful examples. Package discounts are available.

A HISTORY OF
World Societies

• **West African Man** Humans began to portray themselves on the surfaces of places where they lived and traveled as early as 50,000 B.C.E. Most of these paintings have vanished, but some have been redone, as in this rock painting from the region of Niger in Africa, which shows a person, perhaps a shaman, wearing a large headdress. (© David Coulson/Robert Estall Agency UK)

When does history begin? Previous generations of historians generally answered that question with "when writing begins." Thus they started their histories with the earliest known invention of writing, which happened about 3000 B.C.E. in the Tigris and Euphrates River Valleys of Mesopotamia, in what is now Iraq. Anything before that was "prehistory." That focus on only the last five thousand years leaves out most of the human story, however, and today historians no longer see writing as such a sharp dividing line. They explore all eras of the human past with many different types of sources, and some push the beginning of history back to the formation of the universe, when time itself began. This very new conceptualization of "big history" is actually similar in scope to the world's oldest histories, because for thousands and perhaps tens of thousands of years many peoples have narrated histories of their origins that also begin with the creation of the universe.

The Earliest Human Societies
to 2500 B.C.E.

Exploring the entire human past means beginning in Africa, where millions of years ago humans evolved from a primate ancestor. They migrated out of Africa in several waves, walking along coasts and over land, eventually spreading across much of the earth. Their tools were initially multipurpose sharpened stones and sticks, but gradually they invented more specialized tools that enabled them to obtain food more easily, make clothing, build shelters, and decorate their surroundings. Environmental changes, such as the advance and retreat of the glaciers, shaped life dramatically and may have led to the most significant change in all of human history, the domestication of plants and animals. •

Archaeologists at a Dig These researchers at a Native American site in the Boise National Forest in Idaho follow careful procedures to remove objects from the soil and note their location. The soil itself may also yield clues, such as seeds or pollen, about what was growing in the area, allowing better understanding of the people who once lived at the site. (David R. Frazier/Photo Researcher, Inc.)

Evolution and Migration

□ How did humans evolve, and where did they migrate?

Studying the earliest era of human history involves methods that seem simple — looking carefully at an object — as well as new high-tech procedures, such as DNA analysis. Through such research, scholars have examined early human evolution, traced the expansion of the human brain, and studied migration out of Africa and across the planet. Combined with spoken language, that larger brain enabled humans to adapt to many different environments and to be flexible in their responses to new challenges.

Understanding the Early Human Past

People throughout the world have developed systems of classification that help them understand things: earth and sky; seen and unseen; animal, vegetable, and mineral; past, present, and future. Among these systems of classification was one invented in eighteenth-century Europe that divided all living things on earth into groups. Each of these divisions — such as that between plants and animals — is further subdivided into smaller and smaller groups, such as class, order, family, and genus. The final important division is the species, which is generally defined as a group of organisms that can interbreed with one another and produce fertile offspring of both sexes.

In their natural state, members of a species resemble one another, but over time they can become increasingly dissimilar. (Think of Chihuahuas and Great Danes, both members of the same species.) Ever since humans began shaping the world around them, this process has often been the result of human action. But in the long era before humans, the increasing dissimilarity resulted, in the opinion of most scientists, from the process of natural selection. Small variations within individuals in one species allowed them to acquire more food and better living conditions and made them more successful in breeding, thus passing their genetic material to the next generation. When a number of individuals within a species became distinct enough that they could no longer interbreed successfully with others, they became a new species. Species also become extinct, particularly during periods of mass extinctions such as the one that killed the dinosaurs about 65 million years ago. Natural processes of species formation and extinction continue, although today changes in the biosphere — the living matter in the world — result far more from human action than from natural selection.

The scientists who developed this system of organizing the world placed humans within it, using the same means of classification that they used for all other living things. Humans were in the animal kingdom, the order of Primates, the family Hominidae, and the genus *Homo*. Like all classifications, this was originally based on externally visible phenomena: humans were placed in the Primates order because, like other primates, they have hands that can grasp, eyes facing forward to allow better depth perception, and relatively large brains; they were placed in the **hominid** family along with chimpanzees, gorillas, and orangutans because they shared even more features with these great apes. More recently, these classifications (along with many others) have been supported by genetic evidence, particularly that provided by DNA, the basic building block of life. Over 98 percent of human DNA is the same as that of chimpanzees, which indicates to most scientists that humans and chimpanzees share a common ancestor. That common ancestor probably lived between 5 million and 7 million years ago.

Genetic analysis is one of many types of technology used by scholars who study early humans. They often use chemical and physical tests to evaluate bones and other body parts left by humans and the animals they ate, and to study the material surrounding these remains. One of the most important of these tests is the analysis of the radioactive isotope of carbon, C-14, which appears in all things that were once alive. C-14 breaks down at a rate that is known, so that measuring the amount of C-14 that remains in an object allows scientists to determine how old the object is.

Physical remains were the earliest type of evidence studied to learn about the distant human past, and scholars used them to develop another system of classification, one that distinguished between periods of time rather than types of living creatures. (Constructing models of time is called "periodization.") They gave labels to eras according to the primary materials out of which tools that survived were made. Thus the earliest human era became the Stone Age, the next era the Bronze Age, and the next

☐ CHRONOLOGY

ca. 4.4 million years ago *Ardipithecus* evolve in Africa

ca. 2.5–4 million years ago *Australopithecus* evolve in Africa

ca. 500,000–2 million years ago *Homo erectus* evolve and spread out of Africa

ca. 250,000–9000 B.C.E. Paleolithic era

ca. 250,000 years ago *Homo sapiens* evolve in Africa

ca. 30,000–150,000 years ago Neanderthals flourish in Europe and western Asia

ca. 120,000 years ago *Homo sapiens* migrate out of Africa to Eurasia

ca. 50,000 years ago Human migration to Australia

ca. 20,000–30,000 years ago Possible human migration from Asia to the Americas

ca. 25,000 B.C.E. Earliest evidence of woven cloth and baskets

ca. 15,000 B.C.E. Earliest evidence of bows and atlatls

ca. 15,000–10,000 B.C.E. Final retreat of glaciers; humans cross the Bering Strait land bridge to the Americas; megafaunal extinctions

ca. 9000 B.C.E. Beginning of the Neolithic; horticulture; domestication of sheep and goats

ca. 7000 B.C.E. Domestication of cattle; plow agriculture

ca. 5500 B.C.E. Smelting of copper

ca. 5000 B.C.E. Invention of pottery wheel

ca. 4000 B.C.E. Wheel adapted for use with carts

ca. 3000 B.C.E. Earliest known invention of writing

ca. 2500 B.C.E. Bronze technology spreads; beginning of the Bronze Age

A note on dates: This book generally uses B.C.E. (Before the Common Era) and C.E. (Common Era) when giving dates, a system of chronology based on the Christian calendar and now used widely around the world. Scholars who study the very earliest periods of hominid and human history usually use the phrase "years ago" to date their subjects, as do astrophysicists and geologists; this is often abbreviated as B.P. (Before the Present). Because the scale of time covered in Chapter 1 is so vast, a mere 2,000 years does not make much difference, and so B.C.E. and "years ago" have similar meaning.

the Iron Age. They further divided the Stone Age into the Old Stone Age, or **Paleolithic era**, during which people used stone, bone, and other natural products to

- **hominids** Members of the family Hominidae that contains humans, chimpanzees, gorillas, and orangutans.
- **Paleolithic era** Period during which humans used tools of stone, bone, and wood and obtained food by gathering and hunting. Roughly 250,000–9,000 B.C.E.

make tools and gained food largely by **foraging**—that is, by gathering plant products, trapping or catching small animals and birds, and hunting larger prey. This was followed by the New Stone Age, or **Neolithic era**, which saw the beginning of agricultural and animal domestication. People around the world adopted agriculture at various times, and some never did, but the transition between the Paleolithic and the Neolithic is usually set at about 9000 B.C.E., the point at which agriculture was first developed.

On the scale of the universe or even of the earth, human eras are short. Geologists refer to the last twelve thousand years as the Holocene epoch, a period so short given the 4.5 billion years of the solar system that it often does not show up on geologic time lines. The entire history of the human species fits well within the Holocene and the previous geologic epoch, the Pleistocene (PLIGH-stuh-seen), which began about 2.5 million years ago.

The Pleistocene was marked by repeated advances in glaciers and continental ice sheets. Glaciers tied up huge quantities of the earth's water, leading to lower sea levels, making it possible for animals and eventually humans to walk between places that were separated by oceans during interglacial times. Animals and humans were also prevented from migrating to other places by the ice sheets themselves, however, and the colder climate made large areas unfit to live in. Climate thus dramatically shaped human cultures.

Genetic analysis can indicate many things about the human family, and physical remains can provide some evidence about how people lived in the distant past, but the evidence is often difficult to interpret. By themselves, tools and other objects generally do not reveal who made or used them (though sometimes this can be determined from the location in which they were found), nor do they indicate what the objects meant to their creators or users. Thus to learn about the early human past, scholars often also study groups of people from more recent times whose technology and way of life offers parallels with those of people in the distant past. They read written reports of conquerors, government officials, and missionaries who encountered groups that lived by foraging, and they directly observe the few remaining groups that maintain a foraging lifestyle today. Such evidence is also problematic, however. Outsiders had their own perspectives, generally regarded those who lived by foraging as inferior, and often misinterpreted what they were

seeing. Contemporary foragers are not fully cut off from the modern world, nor is it correct to assume that their way of living has not changed for thousands of years, particularly because adaptability is a key feature of the foraging way of life. Thus evidence from more recent groups must be used carefully, but it can provide valuable clues.

Hominid Evolution

Using many different pieces of evidence from all over the world, archaeologists, paleontologists, and other scholars have developed a view of human evolution whose basic outline is widely shared, though there are disagreements about details. Most primates, including other hominids such as chimpanzees and gorillas, have lived primarily in trees, but at some point a group of hominids in East Africa began to spend more time on the ground, and between 5 million and 7 million years ago they began to walk upright at least some of the time. Very recently, scientists have determined that skeletal remains from the genus *Ardipithecus*, which probably date from 4.4 million years ago, indicate a combination of two-limbed movement on land and four-limbed movement in trees. *Ardipithecus* also had smaller canine teeth than do modern chimpanzees, and male and female canine teeth were equal in size, which suggests that there was less male-male combat and perhaps closer male-female relations than among earlier hominids.

Over many generations the skeletal and muscular structure of some hominids evolved to make upright walking easier, and they gradually became fully bipedal. The earliest fully bipedal hominids, whom paleontologists place in the genus *Australopithecus*, lived in southern and eastern Africa between 2.5 and 4 million years ago. Here they left bones, particularly in the Great Rift Valley that stretches from Ethiopia to Tanzania. Walking upright allowed australopithecines to carry and use tools, which allowed them to survive better and may have also spurred brain development.

Sometime around 2.5 million years ago, one group of australopithecines in East Africa began to make simple tools as well as use them, evolving into a different type of hominid that later paleontologists judged to be the first in the genus *Homo*. Called *Homo habilis* ("handy human"), they made sharpened stone pieces, which archaeologists call hand axes, and used them for various tasks. This suggests greater intelligence, and the skeletal remains sup-

The Great Rift Valley

0   200   400 mi.

0   200   400 km

White Nile R.

GREAT RIFT VALLEY

Omo
Lomekwi
Ileret
Koobi Fora
L. Turkana
Nariokotome
Lothagam
Kanapoi
Tabarin
Baringo
Chesowanja
Chemeron

Peninj

Olduvai Gorge

L. Victoria

Laetoli

INDIAN OCEAN

Site of human fossils
🔺 Australopithecine
🔺 Homo habilis
🔺 Homo erectus

port this, for *Homo habilis* had a larger brain than did the australopithecines.

About 2 million years ago another species, called *Homo erectus* ("upright human") by most paleontologists, evolved in East Africa. *Homo erectus* had still larger brains — about two-thirds the size of modern human brains — and made tools that were slightly specialized for various tasks, such as handheld axes, cleavers, and scrapers. Archaeological remains indicate that *Homo erectus* lived in larger groups than had earlier hominids and engaged in cooperative gathering, hunting, and food preparation. The location and shape of the larynx suggests that members of this species were able to make a wider range of sounds than were earlier hominids, so they may have relied more on vocal sounds than on gestures to communicate ideas to one another, through which tasks could be planned and carried out more effectively.

One of the activities that *Homo erectus* carried out most successfully was moving (Map 1.1). Gradually small groups migrated out of East Africa onto the open plains of central Africa, and from there into northern Africa. From 1 million to 2 million years ago the earth's climate was in a warming phase, and these hominids ranged still farther, moving into western Asia by as early as 1.8 million years ago. Bones and other materials from China and the island of Java in Indonesia indicate that *Homo erectus* had reached there by about 1.5 million years ago, thus migrating over large landmasses as well as along the coasts. (Sea levels were lower than they are today, and Java could be reached by walking.) *Homo erectus* also walked north, reaching what is now Spain by at least 800,000 years ago and what is now Germany by 500,000 years ago. In each of these places, *Homo erectus* adapted gathering and hunting techniques to the local environment, learning about new sources of plant food and how to best catch local animals. Although the climate was warmer than it is today, central Europe was not balmy, and these hominids may have used fire to provide light and heat, cook food, and keep away predators. Many lived in the open or in caves, but some built simple shelters, another indication of increasing flexibility and problem solving.

Homo Sapiens, "Thinking Humans"

Homo erectus was remarkably adaptable, but another hominid proved still more so: *Homo sapiens* ("thinking humans"). A few scientists think that *Homo sapiens* evolved from *Homo erectus* in a number of places in Afroeurasia, but the majority think that, like hominid evolution from earlier primates, this occurred only in East Africa. The evidence is partly archaeological, but also genetic. One type of DNA, called mitochondrial DNA, is inherited through the maternal line and can be

Fossil Footprints from Laetoli in Tanzania About three and a half million years ago, several australopithecines walked in wet ash from a volcanic eruption. Their footprints, discovered by the archaeologist Mary Leakey, indicate that they walked fully upright and suggest that they were not solitary creatures, for they walked close together. (John Reader/Photo Researchers, Inc.)

traced far back in time. Mitochondrial DNA indicates that modern humans are so similar genetically that they cannot have been evolving for the last million or 2 million years. This evidence suggests that the evolution of *Homo sapiens* has instead taken place for only about 250,000 years. Because there is greater human

- **foraging** A style of life in which people gain food by gathering plant products, trapping or catching small animals and birds, and hunting larger prey.
- **Neolithic era** Period beginning in 9000 B.C.E. during which humans obtained food by raising crops and animals and continued to use tools primarily of stone, bone, and wood.

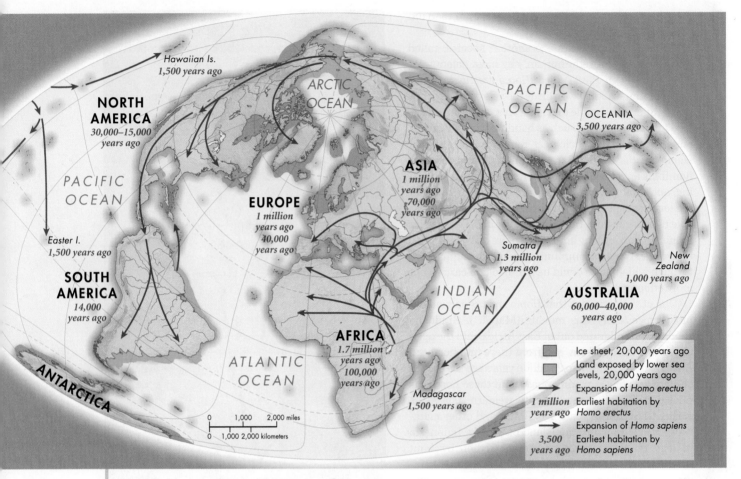

Hawaiian Is.
1,500 years ago

ARCTIC OCEAN

PACIFIC OCEAN

NORTH AMERICA
30,000–15,000 years ago

OCEANIA
3,500 years ago

PACIFIC OCEAN

ASIA
1 million years ago
70,000 years ago

EUROPE
1 million years ago
40,000 years ago

Easter I.
1,500 years ago

Sumatra
1.3 million years ago

New Zealand
1,000 years ago

SOUTH AMERICA
14,000 years ago

INDIAN OCEAN

AUSTRALIA
60,000–40,000 years ago

AFRICA
1.7 million years ago
100,000 years ago

ANTARCTICA

ATLANTIC OCEAN

Madagascar
1,500 years ago

0 1,000 2,000 miles
0 1,000 2,000 kilometers

■	Ice sheet, 20,000 years ago
■	Land exposed by lower sea levels, 20,000 years ago
→	Expansion of *Homo erectus*
1 million years ago	Earliest habitation by *Homo erectus*
→	Expansion of *Homo sapiens*
3,500 years ago	Earliest habitation by *Homo sapiens*

▢ Mapping the Past

MAP 1.1 Human Migration in the Paleolithic and Neolithic Eras

ANALYZING THE MAP What were the major similarities with and differences between the migrations of *Homo erectus* and those of *Homo sapiens*? How did environmental factors shape human migration?

CONNECTIONS What types of technology were required for the migration patterns seen here? What do these migration patterns suggest about the social organization of early people?

genetic variety today in Africa than in other parts of the world, the evidence also suggests that *Homo sapiens* have lived there the longest, so that Africa is where they first emerged. According to this hypothesis, all modern humans are descended from a relatively small group in East Africa. (Picking up on the biblical story of the first humans, some scientists have given the name Mitochondrial Eve to the most recent common matrilineal ancestor from whom all living humans are descended.)

Although there is some debate about where and when *Homo sapiens* emerged, there is little debate about what distinguished these humans from earlier hominids: a bigger brain, in particular a bigger forebrain, the site of conscious thought. The ability to think reflectively allowed for the creation of symbolic language, that is, for language that follows certain rules

and that can refer to things or states of being that are not necessarily present. Greater intelligence allowed *Homo sapiens* to better understand and manipulate the world around them, and symbolic language allowed this understanding to be communicated within a group and passed from one generation to the next. Through spoken language *Homo sapiens* began to develop collective explanations for the world around them that we would now call religion, science, and philosophy. Spoken language also enabled *Homo sapiens* to organize socially into larger groups, thus further enhancing their ability to affect the natural world.

The advantages of a larger brain seem evident to us, so we may not think to ask why hominids evolved this way. Large brains also bring disadvantages, however. They take more energy to run than other parts of the body, so that large-brained animals have to eat more than small-brained ones. Large brains create particular problems for bipedal mammals, for the narrow pelvic structure that works best for upright walking makes giving birth to a large-headed infant difficult and painful.

The question of why hominids developed ever-larger brains might best be answered by looking at how paleontologists think it happened. As *Homo habilis*, *Homo erectus*, and *Homo sapiens* made and used tools, the individuals whose mental and physical abilities allowed them to do so best were able to obtain more food and were more likely to mate and have children who survived. This created what biologists term selective pressure that favored better tool users, which meant individuals with bigger brains. Thus bigger brains led to better tools, but the challenges of using and inventing better tools also created selective pressure that led to bigger brains.

The same thing may have happened with symbolic language and thought. A slightly bigger brain, or a brain that kept developing rapidly after birth and was capable of learning more, allowed for more complex thought and better language skills (aided by anatomical changes in the vocal tract and larynx that allowed for a greater range of sounds). These thinking and speaking skills enabled individuals to better attract mates and fend off rivals, which meant a greater likelihood of passing on the enhanced brain to the next generation. As we know from contemporary research on the brain, learning language promotes the development of specific areas of the brain.

The growth in brain size and complexity may also have been linked to social organization. Individuals who had better social skills were more likely to mate than those who did not—this has been observed in chimpanzees and, of course, in modern humans—and thus to pass on their genetic material. Social skills were particularly important for females, because the combination of bipedalism and growing brain size led to selective pressure for hominid infants to be born at an even earlier stage in their development than other primate infants. Thus the period when human infants are dependent on others is very long, and mothers with good social networks to assist them were more likely to have infants who survived. Humans are unique in the duration and complexity of their care for children, and cooperative child rearing, along with the development of social skills and the adaptability this encouraged, may have been an impetus to brain growth.

All these factors operated together in processes that promoted bigger and better brains. In the Paleolithic period, *Homo sapiens'* brains invented highly specialized tools made out of a variety of materials that replaced the more general-purpose stone tools made by *Homo erectus*: barbed fishhooks and har-

poons, snares and traps for catching small animals, bone needles for sewing clothing, awls for punching holes in leather, nets for catching fish, sharpened flint pieces bound to wooden or bone handles for hunting or cutting, and slings for carrying infants. By 25,000 years ago, and perhaps earlier, humans in some parts of the world were weaving cloth and baskets, and by 17,000 years ago they were using bows and atlatls (AHT-lah-tuhlz)—notched throwing sticks made of bone, wood, or antler—to launch arrows and barbs with flint points bound to wooden shafts. The archaeological evidence for increasingly sophisticated language and social organization is less direct than that for tool use, but it is hard to imagine how humans could have made the tools they did—or would have chosen to decorate so many of them—without both of these.

Migration and Differentiation

Like *Homo erectus* had earlier, groups of *Homo sapiens* moved. By 200,000 years ago they had begun to spread across Africa, and by 120,000 years ago they had begun to migrate out of Africa to Eurasia (see Map 1.1). They most likely walked along the coasts of India and Southeast Asia, and then migrated inland. At the same time, further small evolutionary changes led to our own subspecies of anatomically modern humans, *Homo sapiens sapiens* (which literally translates as "thinking thinking humans"). *Homo sapiens sapiens* moved into areas where there were already *Homo erectus* populations, eventually replacing them.

The best-known example of interaction between *Homo erectus* and *Homo sapiens sapiens* is that between Neanderthals (named after the Neander Valley in Germany, where their remains were first discovered) and a group of anatomically modern humans called Cro-Magnons. **Neanderthals** lived throughout Europe and western Asia beginning about 150,000 years ago, had brains as large as those of modern humans, and used tools, including spears and scrapers for animal skins, that enabled them to survive in the cold climate of Ice Age central Europe and Russia. They built freestanding houses and decorated objects and themselves with red ochre, a form of colored clay. They sometimes buried their dead carefully with tools, animal bones, and perhaps flowers, which suggests that they understood death to have a symbolic meaning. These characteristics led them to be originally categorized as a branch of *Homo sapiens*, but DNA evidence from Neanderthal bones now indicates that they were a separate branch of highly developed *Homo erectus*.

> • **Neanderthals** Group of *Homo erectus* with brains as large as those of modern humans that flourished in Europe and western Asia between 150,000 and 30,000 years ago.

Cro-Magnon peoples moved into parts of western Asia where Neanderthals lived by about 70,000 years ago, and into Europe by about 45,000 years ago. The two peoples appear to have lived side by side for millennia, hunting the same types of animals and gathering the same types of plants. In 2010 DNA evidence demonstrated that they also had sex with one another, for between 1 and 4 percent of the DNA in modern humans living outside of Africa likely came from Neanderthals. The last evidence of Neanderthals as a separate species comes from about 30,000 years ago, but it is not clear exactly how they died out. They may have been killed by Cro-Magnon peoples, or they simply may have lost the competition for food as the climate worsened around 30,000 years ago and the glaciers expanded.

Until very recently Neanderthals were thought to be the last living hominids that were not *Homo sapiens*, but in 2003 archaeologists on the Indonesian island of Flores discovered bones and tools of three-foot-tall hominids that dated from only about 18,000 years ago. A few scientists view them as very small or malformed *Homo sapiens*, but most see them as a distinct species, probably descended from *Homo erectus* just as were Neanderthals. Nicknamed "hobbits," the Flores hominids or their ancestors appear to have lived on the island for more than 800,000 years.

Homo erectus migrated great distances, but *Homo sapiens sapiens* made use of greater intelligence and better tool-making capabilities to migrate still farther. They used simple rafts to reach Australia by at least 50,000 years ago and perhaps earlier, and by 35,000 years ago had reached New Guinea. By at least 15,000 years ago humans had walked across the land bridges then linking Siberia and North America at the Bering Strait and had crossed into the Americas. Because by 14,000 years ago humans were already in southern South America, ten thousand miles from the land bridges, many scholars now think that people came to the Americas much earlier. They think humans came from Asia to the Americas, perhaps as early as 20,000 or even 30,000 years ago, walking or using rafts along the coasts. (See Chapter 11 for a longer discussion of this issue.)

With the melting of glaciers sea levels rose, and parts of the world that had been linked by land bridges, including North America and Asia as well as many parts of Southeast Asia, became separated by water. This cut off migratory paths, but also spurred innovation. Humans designed and built ever more sophisticated boats

Polynesian Oceangoing Sailing Canoe This is a Hawaiian replica of the type of large double-hulled canoe in which Polynesians sailed around the Pacific as they settled many different island groups. This canoe, called the Hokule'a, has taken many voyages using traditional Pacific techniques of celestial navigation. The two hulls provided greater stability, and canoes designed like this sailed thousands of miles over the open ocean. (Photograph © Monte Costa)

and learned how to navigate by studying wind and current patterns, bird flights, and the position of the stars. They sailed to increasingly remote islands, including those in the Pacific, the last parts of the globe to be settled. The western Pacific islands were inhabited by about 2000 B.C.E., Hawaii by about 500 C.E., and New Zealand by about 1000 C.E. (For more on the settlement of the Pacific islands, see page 360.)

Once humans spread out over much of the globe, groups often became isolated from one another, and people mated only with other members of their own group or those who lived nearby, a practice anthropologists call endogamy. Thus, over thousands of generations, although humans remained one species, *Homo sapiens sapiens* came to develop differences in physical features, including skin and hair color, eye and body shape, and amount of body hair. Language also changed over generations, so that thousands of different languages were eventually spoken. Groups created widely varying cultures and passed them on to their children, further increasing diversity among humans.

Beginning in the eighteenth century, European natural scientists sought to develop a system that would

SIBERIA

Bering Sea

Bering Strait

Bering land bridge

NORTH AMERICA

0   200   400 mi.

0   200   400 km

Land Bridge Across the Bering Strait, ca. 15,000 B.C.E.

explain human differences at the largest scale. They divided people into very large groups by skin color and other physical characteristics and termed these groups "races," a word that had originally meant lineage. They first differentiated these races by continent of origin — Americanus, Europaeus, Asiaticus, and Africanus — and then by somewhat different geographic areas. The word *Caucasian* was first used by the German anatomist and naturalist Johann Friedrich Blumenbach (1752–1840) to describe light-skinned people of Europe and western Asia because he thought that their original home was most likely the Caucasus Mountains on the border between Russia and Georgia. He thought that they were the first humans and the most attractive. (His judgment about Caucasian attractiveness came from studying a large collection of skulls; he measured all other skulls against one from Georgia that he judged to be the most beautiful form of the skull.) This meaning of *race* has had a long life, though biologists and anthropologists today do not use it, as it has no scientific meaning or explanatory value. All humans are one species that has less genetic variety than chimpanzees.

Paleolithic Society, 250,000–9000 B.C.E.

☐ What were the key features of Paleolithic society?

Eventually human cultures became widely diverse, but in the Paleolithic period people throughout the world lived in ways that were similar to one another. Archaeological evidence and studies of modern foragers suggest that people lived in small groups of related individuals and moved throughout the landscape in search of food. Most had few material possessions, only what they could carry, although in areas where food resources were especially rich, such as along seacoasts, they built structures and lived more permanently in one place. (See "Viewpoints: Stone Age Houses in Chile and China," page 12.) In the later Paleolithic, people in many parts of the world created art and music and developed religious ideas that linked the natural world to a world beyond.

Foraging for Food

Paleolithic peoples have often been called hunter-gatherers, but recent archaeological and anthropological research indicates that both historical and contemporary hunter-gatherers have depended much more on gathered foods than on hunted meat. Thus it would be more accurate to call them "gatherer-hunters," and

most scholars now call them foragers, a term that highlights the flexibility and adaptability in their search for food. Most of what foragers ate were plants, and much of the animal protein in their diet came from foods gathered or scavenged rather than hunted directly: insects, shellfish, small animals caught in traps, fish and other sea creatures caught in weirs and nets, and animals killed by other predators. Pointed flaked stones, which were earlier viewed as hunting implements, may have been used for a wide variety of tasks such as chopping vegetables, peeling fruits, cracking open shells, and working leather. Gathering and hunting probably varied in importance from year to year depending on environmental factors and the decisions of the group.

Paleolithic peoples did hunt large game. Groups working together forced animals over cliffs, threw spears, and, beginning about 15,000 B.C.E., used bows and atlatls to shoot projectiles so that they could stand farther away from their prey while hunting. The final retreat of the glaciers also occurred between 15,000 and 10,000 years ago, and the warming climate was less favorable to the very large mammals that had roamed the open spaces of many parts of the world. Wooly mammoths, mastodons, and wooly rhinos all died out in Eurasia in this **megafaunal extinction**, as did camels, horses, and sloths in the Americas and giant kangaroos and wombats in Australia. In many places, these extinctions occurred just about the time that modern humans appeared, and increasing numbers of scientists think that they were at least in part caused by human hunting.

Most foraging societies that exist today or did so until recently have some type of **division of labor** by sex, and also by age, with children and older people responsible for different tasks

Paleolithic Hand Axes Like most Paleolithic stone tools, these two hand axes from Libya in northern Africa were made by chipping flakes off stone to form a sharpened edge. Although they are traditionally called axes, they were used for a variety of purposes, including skinning, cutting, and chopping. (Robert Harding/Masterfile)

- **megafaunal extinction** Die-off of large animals in many parts of the world about 15,000–10,000 B.C.E., caused by climate change and perhaps human hunting.
- **division of labor** Differentiation of tasks by gender, age, training, status, or other social distinction.

Viewpoints

Stone Age Houses in Chile and China

> • One of the central issues facing most human groups has been shelter from the elements. People's varying solutions to this issue reflect the environmental challenges and opportunities offered by their particular surroundings. Houses are not simply physical structures, however, but also reflect, communicate, and shape cultural and social values. The photographs on this page show the remains of houses built during the Paleolithic and Neolithic periods in two parts of the world very far from one another.

QUESTIONS FOR ANALYSIS

1. From the photographs and the descriptions, what similarities and differences do you see in the two types of houses?

2. Monte Verde was a Paleolithic community of foragers, and Banpo a Neolithic community of agriculturalists. How might the differences between the two houses have been shaped by the technology of food production? What other factors might account for the differences?

3. It is easy to see the vast differences between these houses and those of today, but what similarities do you find? What social and cultural values might lie behind these similarities?

Monte Verde Monte Verde in Chile dates from about 12,000 B.C.E. The archaeologists who have studied this site have concluded that here, along a creek, a small group of perhaps twenty to thirty people built a 20-foot-long structure of wooden poles covered by animal skins. Within the structure were smaller living quarters separated by skins, each with its own small fire pit, around which archaeologists have found stone tools, rope made of reeds, and many different types of foraged food, including wild potatoes and seaweed that came from coastal areas far away. (Courtesy of Tom D. Dillehay)

Banpo The village of Banpo near Xi'an in China dates from about 4500 B.C.E. Archaeologists have concluded that a group of several hundred people built fifty or so houses there, along with kilns for making pottery and cellars for storage. They built each house by digging a shallow hole as a foundation, surrounding this with walls made of stakes interwoven with branches and twigs, and plastering this with mud, which dried to become wind- and water-resistant. They made the roof out of thatch made from millet and rice stalks, grains they raised that formed the main part of their diet. (Courtesy of China Odyssey Tours)

than adult men and women. Men are more often responsible for hunting, through which they gained prestige as well as meat, and women for gathering plant and animal products. This has led scholars to assume that in Paleolithic society men were also responsible for hunting, and women for gathering. Such a division of labor is not universal, however: in some of the world's foraging cultures, such as the Agta of the Philippines, women hunt large game, and in numerous others women are involved in certain types of hunting, such as driving herds of animals toward a cliff or compound or throwing nets over them. The stone and bone tools that remain from the Paleolithic period give no clear evidence of who used them, and the division of labor may have been somewhat flexible, particularly during periods of scarcity.

Obtaining food was a constant preoccupation, but it was not a constant job. Studies of recent foragers indicate that, other than in times of environmental disasters such as prolonged droughts, people need only about ten to twenty hours a week to gather food and carry out the other tasks needed to survive, such as locating water and building shelters. The diet of foragers is varied and — especially compared to today's diet of highly processed foods loaded with fat, sugar, and salt — nutritious: low in fat and salt, high in fiber, and rich in vitamins and minerals. The slow pace of life and healthy diet did not mean that Paleolithic life spans approached those of the modern world, however. People avoided such contemporary killers as heart disease and diabetes, but they often died at young ages from injuries, infections, animal attacks, and interpersonal violence. Mothers and infants died in childbirth, and many children died before they reached adulthood.

Total human population thus grew very slowly during the Paleolithic. Scholars can make rough estimates only, but one of them proposes that there were perhaps 500,000 humans in the world about 30,000 years ago. By about 10,000 years ago this number had grown to 5 million — ten times as many people. This was a significant increase, but it took twenty thousand years. (By contrast, the earth's population today is approaching 7 billion; it was one-tenth this size a mere three hundred years ago.) The low population density meant

Finger Marks from Rouffignac Cave in France, 18,000–9000 B.C.E.**, and Handprints from Cueva de las Manos (Cave of the Hands) in Argentina, ca. 8000** B.C.E. Paleolithic hand markings have been found in many parts of the world. The finger marks of a young girl (right) are among those made by a group of adults and children who each left such finger flutings in the wet surfaces of the cave, far from the entrance, indicating that they would have used torches to see as they decorated the walls and ceiling. The handprints below, made by blowing colored clay around the hand through a bone pipe, are from different individuals. All are slightly smaller than adult hands, which suggests that this might have been some sort of ceremony involving adolescents. Most are left hands, which indicates that even in the Paleolithic, most people were right-handed, since they would have held the pipe for blowing in the hand they normally used for tasks. (finger marks: © Leslie Van Gelder; handprints: Hubert Stadler/Corbis)

that human impact on the environment was relatively small, although still significant. In addition to contributing to the extinction of some large animals, Paleolithic people may have also shaped their environments by setting fires, which encouraged the growth of new plants and attracted animals that fed on them, making hunting or snaring game easier. This practice was a factor in the spread of plants that thrived best with occasional burning, such as the eucalyptus in Australia.

Family and Kinship Relationships

Small bands of humans — twenty or thirty people was a standard size for foragers in harsh environments — were scattered across broad areas, but this did not mean that each group lived in isolation. Their travels in search of food brought them into contact with one another, not simply for talking and celebrating, but also for providing opportunities for the exchange of sexual partners, which was essential to group survival. Today we understand that having sexual relations with close relatives is disadvantageous because it creates greater risk of genetic disorders. Earlier societies did not have knowledge of genetics, but most of them developed rules against sexual relations among immediate family members. Thus people needed to seek mates outside their own group, and the bands living in large areas became linked by bonds of kinship. Mating arrangements varied in their permanence, but many groups seem to have developed a somewhat permanent arrangement whereby a man or woman left his or her original group and joined the group of his or her mate, what would later be termed marriage.

Within each band, and within the larger kin groups, individuals had a variety of identities; they were simultaneously fathers, sons, husbands, and brothers, or mothers, daughters, wives, and sisters. Each of these identities was relational (parent to child, sibling to sibling, spouse to spouse), and some of them, especially parent to child, gave one power over others. In many areas, kin groups remained significant power structures for millennia, and in some areas they still have influence over major aspects of life, such as an individual's job or marital partner. Paleolithic people were not differentiated by wealth, for in a foraging society accumulating material goods was not advantageous. But they were differentiated by such factors as age, gender, and position in a family, and no doubt by personal qualities such as intelligence, courage, and charisma.

Stereotypical representations of Paleolithic people often portray a powerful fur-clad man holding a club and dragging off a (usually attractive) fur-clad woman by her hair, or men going off to hunt while women and children crouched around a fire, waiting for the men to bring back great slabs of meat. Studies of the relative importance of gathering to hunting, women's participation in hunting, and gender relations among contemporary foraging peoples have led some analysts to turn these stereotypes on their heads. They see Paleolithic bands as egalitarian groups in which the contributions of men and women to survival were recognized and valued, and in which both men and women had equal access to the limited amount of resources held by the group. Other scholars argue that this is also a stereotype, overly romanticizing Paleolithic society as a sort of vegetarian commune. They note that although social relations among foragers were not as hierarchical as they were in other types of societies, many foraging groups had one person who held more power than others, and that person was almost always a man. This debate about gender relations is often part of larger discussions about whether Paleolithic society — and by implication, "human nature" — was primarily peaceful and nurturing or violent and brutal, and whether these qualities are gender-related. Like much else about the Paleolithic, sources about gender and about violence are fragmentary and difficult to interpret; there may simply have been a diversity of patterns, as there is among more modern foragers.

Whether peaceful and egalitarian or violent and hierarchical, heterosexual relations produced children, who were cared for as infants by their mothers or other women who had recently given birth. Breast milk was the only food available that infants could easily digest, so mothers nursed their children for several years. Along with providing food for infants, extended nursing brings a side benefit: it suppresses ovulation and thus acts as a contraceptive. Foraging groups needed children to survive, but too many could tax scarce food resources. Many groups may have practiced selective infanticide or abandonment. They may also have exchanged children of different ages with other groups, which further deepened kinship connections between groups. Other than for feeding, children were most likely cared for by other male and female members of the group as well as by their mothers during the long period of human childhood.

Cultural Creations and Spirituality

Early human societies are often described in terms of their tools, but this misses a large part of the story. Beginning in the Paleolithic, human beings have expressed themselves through what we would now term

- **animism** Idea that animals, plants, natural occurrences, and other parts of the physical world have spirits.
- **shamans** Spiritually adept men and women who communicated with the unseen world.

the arts or culture: painting and decorating walls and objects, making music with their voices and a variety of instruments, imagining and telling stories, dancing alone or in groups. Evidence from the Paleolithic, particularly from after about 50,000 years ago, includes flutes, carvings, jewelry, and paintings done on cave walls and rock outcroppings that depict animals, people, and symbols. In many places they show the outline of a human hand — often done by blowing pigment around it — or the tracings of the fingers, a simple art form that allowed individuals to say "I was here."

Some cultural creations had a larger purpose: they were created to honor and praise ancestors or leaders, help people remember events and traditions, or promote good hunting or safe childbirth. Some were easy to do, and everyone in a culture was expected to participate in some way: to dance in order to bring rain or give thanks, to listen when stories were told, to take part in ceremonies. Others of these creations required particular talents or training and were probably undertaken only by specialists.

At the same time that people marked and depicted the world around them, they also developed ideas about supernatural forces that controlled some aspects of the natural world and the place of humans in it, what we now term spirituality or religion. The Neanderthals' careful burial of their dead suggests to some scholars that they had ideas about an afterlife or at least something beyond the visible world, and there is no doubt that this was the case for Paleolithic *Homo sapiens*. Paleolithic burials, paintings, and objects indicate that people thought of their world as extending beyond the visible. People, animals, plants, natural occurrences, and other things around them had spirits, an idea called **animism**. The only evidence of Paleolithic animism that survives is physical, of course, but more recent animist traditions carry on this understanding of the spiritual nature and interdependence of all things, as in this contemporary Chinook blessing from northwestern North America:

> "We call upon the Earth, our planet home, with its . . . vitality and abundance of life, and together we ask that it *Teach us, and show us the Way.*"
>
> **CHINOOK BLESSING**

We call upon the Earth, our planet home, with its beautiful depths and soaring heights, its vitality and abundance of life, and together we ask that it *Teach us, and show us the Way.* . . .

We call upon the creatures of the fields and the forests and the seas, our brothers and sisters the wolves and the deer, the eagle and dove, the great whales and the dolphin, the beautiful orca and salmon who share our Northwest home, and ask them to *Teach Us and show us the Way.*[1]

Death took people from the realm of the living, but for Paleolithic groups people continued to inhabit an unseen world, along with spirits and deities, after death; thus kin groups included deceased as well as living members of a family. The unseen world regularly intervened in the visible world, for good and ill, and the actions of dead ancestors, spirits, and gods could be shaped by living people. Concepts of the supernatural pervaded all aspects of life; hunting, birth, death, and natural occurrences such as eclipses, comets, and rainbows all had religious meaning. Supernatural forces were understood to determine the basic rules for human existence, and upsetting these rules could lead to chaos.

Ordinary people learned about the unseen world through dreams and portents, and messages and revelations were also sent more regularly to **shamans**, spiritually adept men and women who communicated with the unseen world. Shamans created complex rituals through which they sought to ensure the health and prosperity of an individual, family, or group. Many cave paintings show herds of prey animals, and several include a masked human figure usually judged to be a shaman performing some sort of ritual. Objects understood to have special power, such as carvings or masks in the form of an animal or person, could give additional protection, as could certain plants or mixtures eaten, sniffed, or rubbed on the skin. (See "Listening to the Past: Paleolithic Venus Figures," page 16.)

Paleolithic Flute This flute, carved from the wing bone of a griffon vulture, was unearthed in a cave in Germany along with pieces of other flutes made from mammoth ivory and stone tools. Dating from at least 33,000 B.C.E., it is the oldest musical instrument ever found, and suggests that music has long been an important part of human culture. (H. Jensen/University of Tübingen)

Listening to the Past

Paleolithic Venus Figures

*Written sources provide evidence about the human past
only after the development of writing, allowing us to listen to
the voices of people long dead. For most of human history,
however, there were no written sources, so we "listen" to the
past through objects. Interpreting written documents is
difficult, and interpreting archaeological evidence about the
earliest human belief systems is even more difficult and
often contentious. For example, small stone statues of women
with enlarged breasts and buttocks dating from the later
Paleolithic period (roughly 33,000–9,000 B.C.E.) have been
found in many parts of Europe. These were dubbed "Venus
figures" by nineteenth-century
archaeologists, who thought they
represented Paleolithic standards of
female beauty just as the goddess
Venus represented classical
standards. A reproduction of one of
these statues is shown here. Venus
figures provoke more questions than
answers: Are they fertility goddesses,
evidence of people's beliefs in a
powerful female deity? Or are they
aids to fertility, carried around by
women hoping to have children — or
perhaps hoping not to have
more — and then discarded in the
household debris where they have
been most commonly found? Or are
they sexualized images of women
carried around by men, a sort of
Paleolithic version of the centerfold in
a men's magazine? Might they have
represented different things to
different people? Like so much
Paleolithic evidence, Venus figurines
provide tantalizing evidence about
early human cultures, but evidence
that is not easy to interpret.*

QUESTIONS FOR ANALYSIS

1. Some scholars see Venus figures as evidence that
   Paleolithic society was egalitarian or female-dominated, but
   others point out that images of female deities or holy figures
   are often found in religions that deny women official
   authority. Can you think of examples of the latter? Which
   point of view seems most persuasive to you?

2. As you look at this statue, does it seem to link more closely
   with fertility or with sexuality? How might your own situation
   as a twenty-first-century person shape your answer to this
   question?

**The Venus of Lespugue from
France, made from tusk ivory
around 25,000 years ago.**
(Ronald Sheridan/Ancient Art &
Architecture Ltd.)

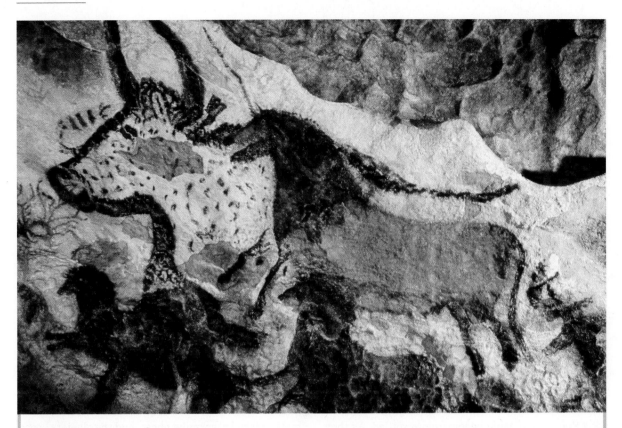

◻ Picturing the Past

Cave Paintings of Horses and a Horned Auroch from Lascaux Cave, Southern France, ca. 15,000 B.C.E. The artist who made these amazing animals in charcoal and red ochre first smoothed the surface, just as a contemporary artist might. This cave includes paintings of hundreds of animals, including predators such as lions, as well as abstract symbols. (JM Labat/Photo Researchers, Inc.)

ANALYZING THE IMAGE The artist painted the animals so close together that they overlap. What might this arrangement have been trying to depict or convey?

CONNECTIONS Why might Paleolithic people have made cave paintings? What do these paintings suggest about Stone Age culture and society?

Shamans thus also operated as healers, with cures that included what we would term natural medicines and religious healing. Because their spiritual and the material worlds appear to have been closely intertwined, Paleolithic people most likely did not make a distinction between natural and spiritual cures.

The rituals and medicines through which shamans and healers operated were often closely guarded secrets, but they were passed orally from one spiritually adept individual to another, so that gradually a body of knowledge about the medicinal properties of local plants and other natural materials was built up. By observing natural phenomena and testing materials for their usable qualities, Paleolithic people began to invent what would later be called science.

The Development of Agriculture in the Neolithic Era, ca. 9000 B.C.E.

◻ How did plant and animal domestication develop, and what effects did it have on human society?

Foraging remained the basic way of life for most of human history, and for groups living in extreme environments, such as tundras or deserts, it was the only possible way to survive. In a few especially fertile areas, however, the natural environment provided enough

Neolithic Tools from Lakes in Switzerland These highly specialized tools include arrow points, awls, chisels, scrapers, stone ax blades in antler sockets, sickle blades, and round spindle whorls, designed to twist fibers into thread. The people who made and used them lived in wooden houses on stilts over the water, and the mud of the lake bed preserved even the bone and antler. (Courtesy of Peter A. Bostrom)

food that people could become more settled. As they remained in one place, they began to plant seeds as well as gather wild crops, to raise certain animals instead of hunting, and to selectively breed both plants and animals to make them more useful to humans. This seemingly small alteration was the most important change in human history; because of its impact it is often termed the **Agricultural Revolution**. Plant and animal domestication marked the transition from the Paleolithic to the Neolithic. It allowed the human population to grow far more quickly than did foraging, but it also required more labor, which became increasingly specialized.

The Development of Horticulture

Areas of the world differed in the food resources available to foragers. In some, acquiring enough food to sustain a group was difficult, and groups had to move constantly. In others, moderate temperatures and abundant rainfall allowed for verdant plant growth; or seas, rivers, and lakes provided substantial amounts of fish and shellfish. Groups in such areas were able to become more settled. About 15,000 years ago, the earth's cli-

mate entered a warming phase, and the glaciers began to retreat. As it became warmer, the climate became wetter, and more parts of the world were able to support sedentary or semi-sedentary groups of foragers.

In several of these places, foragers began planting seeds in the ground along with gathering wild grains, roots, and other foodstuffs. By observation, they learned the optimum times and places for planting. They removed unwanted plants through weeding and selected the seeds they planted in order to get crops that had favorable characteristics, such as larger edible parts. For grain crops, people chose plants with larger kernels clustered together that ripened all at one time and did not just fall on the ground, qualities that made harvesting more efficient. Through this human intervention, certain crops became **domesticated**, that is, modified by selective breeding so as to serve human needs, in this case to provide a more reliable source of food. Archaeologists trace the development and spread of plant-raising by noting when the seeds and other plant parts they discover show evidence of domestication.

This early crop-planting was done by individuals using hoes and digging sticks, and it is often termed **horticulture** to distinguish it from the later agriculture using plows. In some places, digging sticks were weighted with stones to make them more effective (earlier archaeologists thought these stones were the killing parts of war clubs). Intentional crop-planting developed first in the area archaeologists call the Fertile Crescent, which runs from present-day Lebanon,

- **Agricultural Revolution** Dramatic transformation in human history resulting from the change from foraging to raising crops and animals.
- **domesticated** Plants and animals modified by selective breeding so as to serve human needs; domesticated animals will behave in specific ways and breed in captivity.
- **horticulture** Crop-raising done with hand tools and human power.

Israel, and Jordan north to Turkey and then south to the Iran-Iraq border (Map 1.2). About 9000 B.C.E. people there began to plant seeds of the wild wheat and barley they had already been harvesting, along with seeds of legume crops, such as peas and lentils, and of the flax with which they made linen cloth. They then modified these crops through domestication. By about 8000 B.C.E. people were growing sorghum and millet in parts of the Nile River Valley, and perhaps yams in western Africa. By about 7000 B.C.E. they were growing domesticated rice, millet, and legumes in China, yams and taro in Papua New Guinea, and perhaps squash in Mesoamerica. In each of these places, the development of horticulture occurred independently, and it may have happened in other parts of the world as well. Archaeological evidence does not survive well in tropical areas like Southeast Asia and the Amazon Basin, which may have been additional sites of plant domestication.

Nowhere do archaeological remains alone answer the question of who within any group first began to cultivate crops, but the fact that, among foragers, women were primarily responsible for gathering plant products suggests that they may also have been the first to plant seeds in the ground. In many parts of the world, crops continued to be planted with hoes and digging sticks for millennia, and crop-raising remained primarily women's work, while men hunted or later raised animals.

Why, after living successfully as foragers for tens of thousands of years, did humans in so many parts of the world all begin raising crops at about the same time? The answer to this question is not clear, but crop-raising may have resulted from population pressures in those parts of the world where the warming climate provided more food. More food meant lower child mortality and longer life spans, which allowed communities to grow. Naturally occurring and then planted foods included cereal crops, which were soft enough for babies to eat, so that women could stop nursing their children at a younger age. They lost the contraceptive effects of breast-feeding, and children may have been born at more frequent intervals, further speeding up population growth. Thus people had a choice: they could move to a new area—the solution that foragers had relied on when faced with the same problem—or they could develop ways to increase the food supply to keep up with population growth, a solution that the warming climate was making possible. They chose the latter and began to plant more intensively, beginning cycles of expanding population

The Fertile Cresent

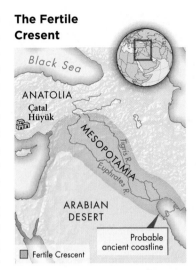

and intensification of land use that have continued to today.

In the Fertile Crescent, parts of China, and the Nile Valley, within several centuries of initial crop-planting, people were relying on domesticated food products alone. They built permanent houses near one another in villages with fields around them, and they invented new ways of storing foods, such as in pottery made from clay. Villages were closer together than were the camps of foragers, so population density as well as total population grew.

A field of planted and weeded crops yields ten to one hundred times as much food—measured in calories—as the same area of naturally occurring plants, a benefit that would have been evident to early crop-planters. It also requires much more labor, however, which was provided both by the greater number of people in the community and by those people working longer hours. In

Inca Farmers Planting Potatoes with a Digging Stick
Potatoes were a staple crop in the Andes for thousands of years. In this drawing from a sixteenth century C.E. book by the indigenous author Guaman Poma, the man at the left digs a hole while the woman in the middle puts in the seed potato, and the woman at the right stands ready to pound down the earth over it. (John Meek/The Art Archive)

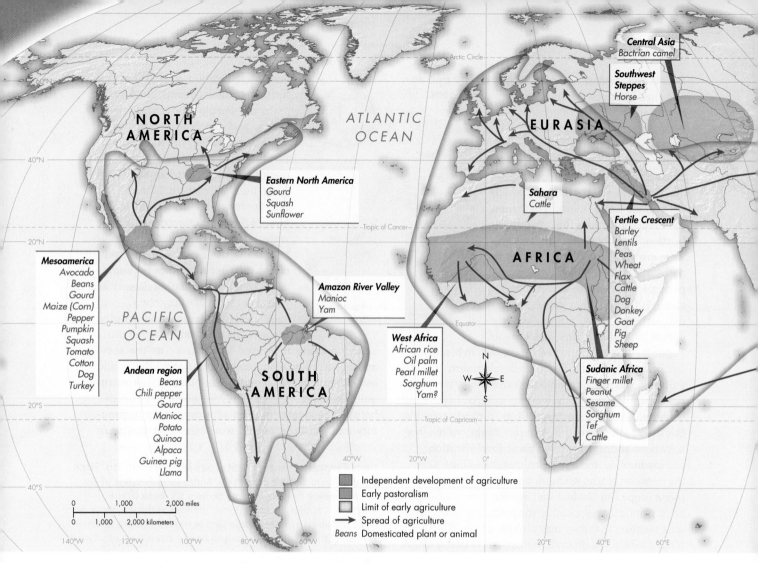

MAP 1.2 The Spread of Agriculture and Pastoralism Local plants and animals were domesticated in many different places. Agriculturalists and pastoralists spread the knowledge of how to raise them, and spread the plants and animals themselves, through migration, trade, and conquest.

Map labels:

NORTH AMERICA

ATLANTIC OCEAN

EURASIA

Central Asia
Bactrian camel

Southwest Steppes
Horse

Eastern North America
Gourd
Squash
Sunflower

Sahara
Cattle

AFRICA

Fertile Crescent
Barley
Lentils
Peas
Wheat
Flax
Cattle
Dog
Donkey
Goat
Pig
Sheep

Mesoamerica
Avocado
Beans
Gourd
Maize (Corn)
Pepper
Pumpkin
Squash
Tomato
Cotton
Dog
Turkey

PACIFIC OCEAN

Amazon River Valley
Manioc
Yam

West Africa
African rice
Oil palm
Pearl millet
Sorghum
Yam?

Sudanic Africa
Finger millet
Peanut
Sesame
Sorghum
Tef
Cattle

Andean region
Beans
Chili pepper
Gourd
Manioc
Potato
Quinoa
Alpaca
Guinea pig
Llama

SOUTH AMERICA

Independent development of agriculture
Early pastoralism
Limit of early agriculture
→ Spread of agriculture
Beans Domesticated plant or animal

contrast to the twenty hours a week foragers spent on obtaining food, farming peoples were often in the fields from dawn to dusk, particularly during planting and harvest time, but also during the rest of the growing year because weeding was a constant task.

Foragers who lived at the edge of horticultural communities appear to have recognized the negative aspects of crop-raising, for they did not immediately adopt this new way of life. Instead farming spread when a village became too large and some residents moved to a new area, cleared land, planted seeds, and built a new village, sometimes intermarrying with the local people. Because the population of farming communities grew so much faster than that of foragers, however, horticulture quickly spread into fertile areas. By about 6500 B.C.E. farming had spread northward from the Fertile Crescent into Greece and by 4000 farther northward all the way to Britain; by 4500 it had spread southward into Ethiopia. At the same time, crop-raising spread out from others areas in which it

was first developed, and slowly larger and larger parts of China, South and Southeast Asia, and East Africa were home to horticultural villages.

People adapted crops to their local environments, choosing seeds that had qualities that were beneficial, such as drought resistance. They also domesticated new kinds of crops. In the Americas, for example, by about 3000 B.C.E. corn was domesticated in southern Mexico and potatoes and quinoa in the Andes region of South America, and by about 2500 B.C.E. squash and beans in eastern North America. These crops then spread, so that by about 1000 B.C.E. people in much of what is now the western United States were raising corn, beans, and squash. In the Indus Valley of South Asia people were growing dates, mangoes, sesame seeds, and cotton along with grains and legumes by 4000 B.C.E. Crop-raising led to dramatic human alteration of the environment.

Certain planted crops eventually came to be grown over huge areas of land, so that some scientists de-

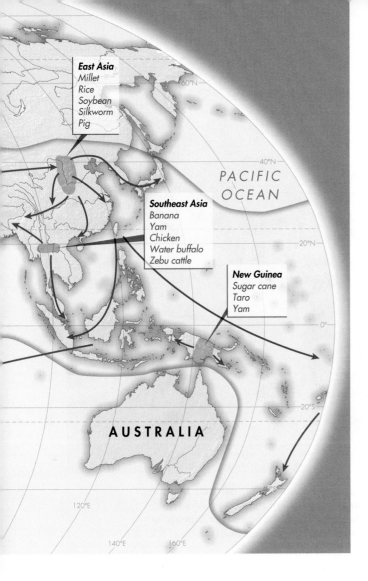

East Asia
Millet
Rice
Soybean
Silkworm
Pig

PACIFIC
OCEAN

Southeast Asia
Banana
Yam
Chicken
Water buffalo
Zebu cattle

New Guinea
Sugar cane
Taro
Yam

AUSTRALIA

another area and began the process again, perhaps returning to the first plot many years later, after the soil had rejuvenated itself. Groups using shifting slash-and-burn cultivation remained small and continued to rely on the surrounding forest for much of their food.

Animal Domestication and the Rise of Pastoralism

At roughly the same time that they domesticated certain plants, people also domesticated animals. The earliest animal to be domesticated was the dog, which separated genetically as a subspecies from wolves at least 15,000 years ago and perhaps much earlier. The mechanism of dog domestication is hotly debated: did it result only from human action, as foragers chose and bred animals that would help them with the hunt rather than attack them, or was it also caused by selective pressure resulting from wolf action, as animals less afraid of human contact came around campsites and then bred with one another? However it happened, the relationship provided both with benefits: humans gained dogs' better senses of smell and hearing and their body warmth, and dogs gained new food sources and safer surroundings. Not surprisingly, humans and domestic dogs migrated together, including across the land bridges to the Americas and on boats to Pacific islands.

Dogs fit easily into a foraging lifestyle, but humans also domesticated animals that led them to completely alter their way of life. In about 9000 B.C.E., at the same time they began to raise crops, people in the Fertile Crescent domesticated wild goats and sheep, probably using them first for meat, and then for milk, skins, and eventually fleece (see Map 1.2). They learned from observation and experimentation that traits are passed down from generation to generation, and they began to breed the goats and sheep selectively for qualities that they wanted, including larger size, greater strength, better coats, more milk production, and more even temperaments. The book of Genesis in the Bible, written in the Fertile Crescent sometime in the first millennium B.C.E., provides an early example of selective breeding. Jacob makes a deal with his father-in-law to take only those goats and sheep that are spotted, but he secretly increases the number of spotted animals in the flock by placing a spotted stick "before the eyes . . . of the strongest of the flocks . . . whenever they were breeding" so that more and stronger spotted animals were born (Genesis 30:41). This method was based on the idea — accepted for a very long time — that what a pregnant animal or woman saw during pregnancy would influence the outcome; although this has been firmly rejected in modern science, the Bible notes that it was successful, and that Jacob "grew exceedingly rich, and had large flocks."

scribe the Agricultural Revolution as a revolution of codependent domestication: humans domesticated crops, but crops also "domesticated" humans so that they worked long hours spreading particular crops around the world. Of these, corn has probably been the most successful; more than half a million square miles around the world are now planted in corn, and one-quarter of the nearly fifty thousand items in the average American supermarket contain corn.

In some parts of the world horticulture led to a dramatic change in the way of life, but in others it did not. Horticulture can be easily combined with gathering and hunting as plots of land are usually small; many cultures, including some in Papua New Guinea and North America, remained mixed foragers and horticulturists for thousands of years. Especially in deeply wooded areas, people cleared small plots by chopping and burning the natural vegetation, and planted crops in successive years until the soil eroded or lost its fertility, a method termed "slash and burn." They then moved to

A Goat Market in Mali Pastoral economies thrive in many parts of the world today, particularly in areas that are too dry for agriculture, including central Australia, Central Asia, northern and western Africa, and much of the U.S. West. As in early pastoralism, contemporary herders choose and breed their animals for qualities that will allow them to prosper in the local environment. (Ron Giling/Lineair/Photolibrary)

After goats and sheep, pigs were domesticated somewhat later in both the Fertile Crescent and China, as were chickens in southern Asia. Like domesticated crops, domesticated animals eventually far outnumbered their wild counterparts. For example, in the United States today (excluding Alaska), there are about 77 million dogs, compared to about 6,000 wolves. (Adding Alaska would add about 150,000 dogs and 10,000 wolves.) There are more than a billion and a half cattle, with enormous consequences for the environment. Animal domestication also shaped human evolution; groups that relied on animal milk and milk products for a significant part of their diet tended to develop the ability to digest milk as adults, while those that did not remained lactose intolerant as adults, the normal condition for mammals.

Sheep and goats allow themselves to be herded, and people developed a new form of living, **pastoralism**, based on herding and raising livestock, sometimes training dogs to assist them. In areas with sufficient rainfall and fertile soil, pastoralism can be relatively sedentary, and thus easily combined with horticulture;

people built pens for animals, or in colder climates constructed special buildings or took them into their houses. They learned that animal manure increases crop yields, so they gathered the manure from enclosures and used it as fertilizer.

Increased contact with animals and their feces also increased human contact with various sorts of disease-causing pathogens, including minor illnesses such as the common cold and deadly killers such as influenza, bubonic plague, and smallpox. This was particularly the case where humans and animals lived in tight quarters, for diseases spread fastest in crowded environments. Thus pastoralists and agriculturalists developed illnesses that had not plagued foragers, and the diseases became endemic, that is, widely found within a region without being deadly. Ultimately people who lived with animals developed resistance to some of these illnesses, but foragers' lack of resistance to many illnesses meant that they died more readily after coming into contact with new endemic diseases, as was the case when Europeans brought smallpox to the Americas in the sixteenth century.

In drier areas, flocks need to travel long distances from season to season to obtain enough food, so some pastoralists became nomadic. Nomadic pastoralists

• **pastoralism** An economic system based on herding flocks of goats, sheep, cattle, or other animals.

often gather wild plant foods as well, but they tend to rely primarily on their flocks of animals for food. Pastoralism was well-suited to areas where the terrain or climate made crop-planting difficult, such as mountains, deserts, dry grasslands, and tundras. Eventually other grazing animals, including cattle, camels, horses, yak, and reindeer, also became the basis of pastoral economies in central and western Asia, many parts of Africa, and far northern Europe.

Plow Agriculture

Horticulture and pastoralism brought significant changes to human ways of life, but the domestication of certain large animals had an even bigger impact. Cattle and water buffalo were domesticated in some parts of Asia and North Africa in which they occurred naturally by at least 7000 B.C.E., and horses, donkeys, and camels by about 4000 B.C.E. All these animals consent to carry people or burdens on their backs and pull against loads dragged behind them, two qualities that are rare among the world's animal species. In many parts of the world, including North America and much of South America and sub-Saharan Africa, no naturally occurring large species could be domesticated. In the mountainous regions of South America, llamas and alpacas were domesticated to carry packs, but the steep terrain made it difficult to use them to pull loads. The domestication of large animals dramatically increased the power available to humans to carry out their tasks, which had both an immediate effect in the societies in which this happened and a long-term effect when they later encountered societies in which human labor remained the only source of power.

The pulling power of animals came to matter most, because it could be applied to food production. Sometime in the seventh millennium B.C.E., people attached wooden sticks to frames that animals dragged through the soil, thus breaking it up and allowing seeds to sprout more easily. These simple scratch plows were pulled first by cattle and water buffalo, and later by horses. (Donkeys and camels were used primarily as pack animals, but occasionally for plowing as well.) Over millennia, moldboards—angled pieces that turned the soil over, bringing fresh soil to the top—were added, which reduced the time needed to plow and allowed each person to work more land.

Using plows, Neolithic people produced a significant amount of surplus food, so that some people in the community could spend their days doing other things, increasing the division of labor. Surplus food had to be stored, and some began to specialize in making products for storage, such as pots, baskets, bags, bins, and other kinds of containers. Others specialized in making tools, houses, and other things needed in village life, or in producing specific types of food, including alcoholic beverages made from fermented fruits and grains. Families and households became increasingly interdependent, trading food for other commodities or services. In the same way that foragers had continually improved their tools and methods, people improved the processes through which they made things. Sometime in the fifth millennium B.C.E. pot-makers in Mesopotamia invented the potter's wheel, which by a millennium later had been adapted for use on carts and plows pulled by animals. Wheeled vehicles led to road-building, and wheels and roads together made it possible for people and goods to travel long distances more easily, whether for settlement, trade, or conquest.

Stored food was also valuable and could become a source of conflict, as could other issues in villages where people lived close together. Villagers needed more complex rules about how food was to be distributed and how different types of work were to be valued than did foragers. Certain individuals began to specialize in the determination and enforcement of these rules, and informal structures of power gradually became more formalized as elites developed. These elites then distributed resources to their own advantage, often using force to attain and maintain their power.

Neolithic Pot, from China, ca. 2600–2300 B.C.E. This two-handled pot, made in the Yellow River Valley of baked ceramics, is painted in a swirling red and black geometric design. Neolithic agricultural communities produced a wide array of storage containers for keeping food and other commodities from one season to the next. (Palace Museum, Beijing)

Neolithic Society

☐ How did growing social and gender hierarchies and expanding networks of trade increase the complexity of human society in the Neolithic period?

The division of labor that plow agriculture allowed led to the creation of **social hierarchies**, the divisions between rich and poor, elites and common people that have been a central feature of human society since the Neolithic era. Plow agriculture also strengthened differentiation based on gender, with men becoming more associated with the world beyond the household and women with the domestic realm. Social hierarchies were reinforced over generations as children inherited goods and status from their parents; even the gods were increasingly understood to be arranged in a hierarchy, and assuring fertility became the most important religious practice. People increasingly communicated ideas within local and regional networks of exchange, just as they traded foodstuffs, tools, and other products.

Social Hierarchies and Slavery

Archaeological finds from Neolithic villages, particularly burials, show signs of growing social differentiation. Some people were buried with significant amounts of jewelry, household goods, weapons, and other objects, while others were buried with very little. How were some people able to attain such power over their neighbors that they could even take valuable commodities with them to the grave? This is one of the key questions in all of human history. Written sources do not provide a clear answer because social hierarchies were already firmly in place by the time writing was invented, so that scholars have largely relied on archaeological sources. (See "Individuals in Society: The Iceman," page 25.)

Within foraging groups, some individuals already had more authority because of their links with the world of gods and spirits, positions as heads of kin groups, or personal characteristics. These three factors gave individuals advantages in agricultural societies, and the advantages became more significant over time as there were more resources to control. Priests and shamans developed more elaborate rituals and became full-time religious specialists, exchanging their services in interceding with the gods for food. In many communities, religious specialists were the first to work out formal rules of conduct that later became oral and written codes of law, generally explaining that these represented the will of the gods. The codes threatened divine punishment for those who broke them, and they often required people to accord deference to priests as the representatives of the gods, so that they became an elite group with special privileges.

Individuals who were the heads of large families or kin groups had control over the labor of others, which became more significant when that labor brought material goods that could be stored. Material goods—plows, sheep, cattle, sheds, pots, carts—gave one the ability to amass still more material goods, and the gap between those who had them and those who did not widened. Storage also allowed wealth to be retained over long periods of time and handed down from one family member to another, so that over generations small differences in wealth grew larger. The ability to control the labor of others could also come from physical strength, a charismatic personality, or leadership talents, and this also led to greater wealth.

Wealth itself could command labor, as individuals or families could buy the services of others to work for them or impose their wishes through force, hiring soldiers to threaten or carry out violence. Eventually some individuals bought others outright. As with social hierarchies in general, slavery predates written records, but it developed in almost all agricultural societies. Like animals, slaves were a source of physical power for their owners, providing them an opportunity to amass still more wealth and influence. In the long era before the invention of fossil fuel technology, the ability to exploit animal and human labor was the most important mark of distinction between elites and the rest of the population. As we will see in later chapters, land ownership was often what distinguished elites from others, but that land was valuable only if there were people living on it who were required to labor for the owner.

Gender Hierarchies and Inheritance

Along with hierarchies based on wealth and power, the development of agriculture was intertwined with a hierarchy based on gender. The system in which men have more power and access to resources than women and some men are dominant over other men is called **patriarchy**. Every society in the world that has left written records has been patriarchal, but patriarchy came before writing, and searching for its origins involves interpreting many different types of sources. Some scholars see the origins of gender inequality in the hominid past, noting that male chimpanzees form alliances to gain status against other males and engage in cooperative attacks on females, which might have

---

• **social hierarchies** Divisions between rich and poor, elites and common people that have been a central feature of human society since the Neolithic era.

• **patriarchy** Social system in which men have more power and access to resources than women and some men are dominant over other men.

The Iceman

ON SEPTEMBER 19, 1991, TWO GERMAN vacationers climbing in the Italian Alps came upon a corpse lying facedown and covered in ice. Scientists determined that the Iceman, as the corpse is generally known, dates to the Neolithic period, having died 5,300 years ago. He was between twenty-five and thirty-five years old at the time of his death, and he stood about five feet two inches tall. An autopsy revealed much about the man and his culture. The bluish tinge of his teeth showed a diet of milled grain, which proves that he came from an environment where crops were grown. The Iceman hunted as well as farmed: he was found with a bow and arrows and shoes of straw, and he wore a furry cap and a robe of animal skins that he had stitched together with thread that he had made from grass.

The equipment discovered with the Iceman demonstrates his mastery of several technologies. He carried a hefty copper ax, indicating a knowledge of metallurgy. He relied chiefly on archery to kill game. In his quiver were numerous wooden arrow shafts and two finished arrows. The arrows had flint heads, a sign of stoneworking, and feathers were attached to the ends of the shafts with resin-like glue. He knew the value of feathers to direct the arrows; thus he had mastered the basics of ballistics. His bow was made of yew, a relatively rare wood in central Europe that is among the best for archers.

Yet a mystery still surrounds the Iceman. When his body was first discovered, scholars assumed that he was a hapless traveler overtaken in a fierce snowstorm. But the autopsy found an arrowhead lodged under his left shoulder. The Iceman was not alone on his last day. Someone was with him, and that someone had shot him from below and behind. The Iceman is the victim in the first murder mystery of Western civilization, and the case will never be solved.

QUESTIONS FOR ANALYSIS

1. What do these images demonstrate about the Iceman's knowledge of his environment?
2. What does the Iceman reveal about the society in which he lived?

• **The artifacts found with the body tell scientists much about how the Iceman lived. The Iceman's shoes, made with a twine framework stuffed with straw and covered with skin, indicate that he used all parts of the animals he hunted.** (discovery: Courtesy, Roger Teissl; shoes: South Tyrol Museum of Archaeology, http://www.iceman.it)

Egyptian Couple Planting Grain, ca. 1500–1300 B.C.E. In this wall painting from the tomb of an official, a man guides a wooden ox-drawn plow through the soil, while the woman walking behind throws seed in the furrow. The painting was not designed to show real peasants working, but to depict the well-to-do man buried in the tomb doing work viewed as worthy of an afterlife. Nevertheless, the gender division of labor and the plow itself are probably accurate. (Erich Lessing/Art Resource, NY)

also happened among early hominids. Other scholars see the origins in the Paleolithic, with the higher status of men in lineage groups.

Plow agriculture heightened patriarchy. Although farming with a hoe was often done by women, plow agriculture came to be a male task, perhaps because of men's upper-body strength or because plow agriculture was more difficult to combine with care for infants and small children than was horticulture. The earliest depictions of plowing are on Mesopotamian cylinder seals, and they invariably show men with the cattle and plows. At the same time that cattle began to be raised for pulling plows and carts rather than for meat, sheep began to be raised primarily for wool. Spinning thread and weaving cloth became primarily women's work; the earliest Egyptian hieroglyph for weaving is, in fact, a seated woman with a shuttle, and a Confucian moral saying from ancient China asserts that "men plow and women weave." Spinning and weaving were generally done indoors and involved simpler and cheaper tools than plowing; they could also be taken up and put

down easily, and so could be done at the same time as other tasks.

Though in some ways this arrangement seems complementary, with each sex doing some of the necessary labor, plow agriculture increased gender hierarchy. Men's responsibility for plowing and other agricultural tasks took them outside the household more often than women, enlarging their opportunities for leadership. It also led to their being favored as inheritors of family land and the right to farm communally held land when inheritance systems were established to pass land and other goods on to the next generation. In some of these systems all children inherited from both parents, but more often inheritance passed from father to son (or to other male family members if there were no sons) in a patrilineal inheritance system. In some places inheritance was matrilineal, that is, traced through the female line, but in such systems women themselves did not necessarily inherit goods or property; instead a man inherited from his mother's brother rather than from his father. Thus over generations, women's independent access to resources decreased, and it became increasingly difficult for women to survive without male support.

As inherited wealth became more important, men wanted to make sure that their sons were theirs, so they restricted their wives' movements and activities. This was especially the case among elite families. Among foragers and horticulturalists, women needed to be mobile for the group to survive; their labor outdoors was essential. Among agriculturalists, the labor of animals, slaves, and hired workers could substitute for that of women in families that could afford them. Thus in some Neolithic societies, there is evidence that women spent more and more of their time within the household, either indoors or behind walls and barriers that separated the domestic realm from the wider world. Social norms and ideals gradually reinforced this pattern, so that by the time written laws and other records emerged in the second millennium B.C.E., elite women were expected to work at tasks that would not take them beyond the household or away from male supervision. Non-elite women also tended to do work that could be done within or close by the household, such as cooking, cloth production, and the care of children, the elderly, and small animals. A special program set up under the third-century B.C.E. Indian emperor Ashoka, for example, supported poor women by paying them to spin and weave in their own homes.

Social and gender hierarchies were enhanced over generations as wealth was passed down unequally, and they were also enhanced by rules and norms that shaped sexual relationships, particularly heterosexual ones. However their power originated, elites began to think of themselves as a group apart from the rest with something that made them distinctive — such as connections with a deity, military prowess, and natural superiority. They increasingly understood this distinctive quality to be hereditary and developed traditions — later codified as written laws — that stipulated which heterosexual relationships would pass this quality on, along with passing on wealth. Relationships between men and women from elite families were formalized as marriage and generally passed down both status and wealth. Relationships between elite men and non-elite women generally did not do so, or did so to a lesser degree; the women were defined as concubines or mistresses, or simply as sexual outlets for powerful men. The 1780 B.C.E. Code of Hammurabi, for example, one of the world's earliest law codes, sets out differences in inheritance for the sons a man had with his wife and those he had with a servant or slave, while not mentioning daughters at all:

> If his wife bear sons to a man, [and] his maid-servant [has] also borne sons, [but] the father while still living . . . did not say to the sons of the maid-servant:

> "If . . . the father while still living . . . did not say to the sons of the maid-servant: "My sons," and then the father dies, then the sons of the maid-servant shall not share with the sons of the wife."

HAMMURABI'S CODE

"My sons," and then the father dies, then the sons of the maid-servant shall not share with the sons of the wife, but the freedom of the maid and her sons shall be granted.[2]

Relations between an elite woman and a non-elite man generally brought shame and dishonor to the woman's family and sometimes death to the man. (Early rules and laws about sex generally did not pay much attention to same-sex relations because these did not produce children that could threaten systems of inheritance.)

Thus along with the distinctions among human groups that resulted from migration and were enhanced by endogamy, distinctions developed within groups that were reinforced by social endogamy, what we might think of as the selective breeding of people. Elite men tended to marry elite women, which in some cases resulted in actual physical differences over generations, as elites had more access to food and were able to become taller and stronger. By 1800 C.E., for example, men in the highest level of the English aristocracy were five inches taller than the average height of all English people.

No elite can be completely closed to newcomers, however, because the accidents of life and death, along with the genetic problems caused by repeated close intermarriage, make it difficult for any small group to survive over generations. Thus mechanisms were developed in many cultures to adopt boys into elite families, to legitimate the children of concubines and slave women, or to allow elite girls to marry men lower on the social hierarchy. All systems of inheritance also need some flexibility. The inheritance patterns in some cultures favored male heirs exclusively, but in others close relatives were favored over those more distant, even if this meant allowing daughters to inherit. The drive to keep wealth and property within a family or kin group often resulted in women inheriting, owning, and in some cases managing significant amounts of wealth, a pattern that continues today. Hierarchies of wealth and power thus intersected with hierarchies of gender in complex ways, and in many cultures age and marital status also played roles. In many European and African cultures, for example, widows were largely able to control their own property, while unmarried sons were often under their father's control even if they were adults.

Trade and Cross-Cultural Connections

The increase in food production brought by the development of plow agriculture allowed Neolithic villages to grow ever larger. By 7000 B.C.E. or so, some villages in the Fertile Crescent may have had as many as ten thousand residents. One of the best known of these, Çatal Hüyük in what is now modern Turkey, shows evidence of trade as well as of the specialization of labor. Çatal Hüyük's residents lived in mud-brick houses whose walls were covered in white plaster and whose interiors were kept very clean, for all trash was taken outside the town. The houses were built next to one another with no lanes or paths separating them, and people seem to have entered through holes in the roofs; the rooftops may have also served as a place for people to congregate, for there is no sign of large public buildings. The men and women of the town grew wheat, barley, peas, and almonds and raised sheep and perhaps cattle, though they also seem to have hunted. They made textiles, pots, figurines, baskets, carpets, copper and lead beads, and other goods, and decorated their houses with murals showing animal and human figures. They gathered, sharpened, and polished obsidian, a volcanic rock that could be used for knives, blades, and mirrors, and then traded it with neighboring towns, obtaining seashells and flint. From here the obsidian was exchanged still farther away, for Neolithic socie-ties slowly developed local and then regional networks of exchange and communication.

Among the goods traded in some parts of the world was copper. Pure copper occurs naturally close to the surface in some areas, and people, including those at Çatal Hüyük, hammered it into shapes for jewelry and tools. Like most metals, copper occurs more often mixed with other materials in a type of rock called ore, and by about 5500 B.C.E. people in the Balkans had learned that copper could be extracted from ore by heating it in a smelting process. Smelted copper was poured into molds and made into spear points, axes, chisels, beads, and other objects. Smelting techniques were discovered independently in many places around the world, including China, Southeast Asia, West Africa, and the Andes region. Pure copper is soft, but through experimentation artisans learned that it would become harder if they mixed it with other metals such as arsenic, zinc, or tin during heating, creating an alloy called bronze.

Because it was stronger than copper, bronze had a far wider range of uses, so much so that later historians decided that its adoption marked the beginning of a new period in human history, the Bronze Age. Like all new technologies, bronze arrived at different times in different places, but by about 2500 B.C.E. it was making a difference in many places around the world. Techniques of copper and bronze metallurgy were later applied to precious metals such as gold and silver, and then to iron, which had an even greater impact than

Stone Circle at Nabta Playa, Egypt, ca. 4800 B.C.E. This circle of stones, erected when the Egyptian desert received much more rainfall than it does today, may have been a type of calendar marking the summer solstice. Circular arrangements of stones or ditches were constructed in many places during the Neolithic era, and most no doubt had calendrical, astronomical, and/or religious purposes. (Courtesy of Raymond Betz)

bronze. (See "Global Trade: Iron," page 54). It is important to remember that all metals were expensive and hard to obtain, however, so that stone, wood, and bone remained the primary materials for tools and weapons long into the Bronze Age.

Objects were not the only things traded increasingly long distances during the Neolithic period, for people also carried ideas as they traveled on foot, boats, or camels, and in wagons or carts. Knowledge about the seasons and the weather was vitally important for those who depended on crop-raising, and agricultural peoples in many parts of the world began to calculate recurring patterns in the world around them, slowly developing calendars. Scholars have demonstrated that people built circular structures of mounded earth or huge upright stones to help them predict the movements of the sun and stars, including Nabta Playa, erected about 4500 B.C.E. in the desert west of the Nile Valley in Egypt, and Stonehenge, erected about 2500 B.C.E. in southern England.

The rhythms of the agricultural cycle and patterns of exchange also shaped religious beliefs and practices. Among foragers, human fertility is a mixed blessing, as too many children can overtax food supplies, but among crop-raisers and pastoralists, fertility of the land, animals, and people is essential. Shamans and priests developed ever more elaborate rituals designed to assure fertility, in which the gods were often given something from a community's goods in exchange for their favor, such as food offerings, animal sacrifices, or sacred objects. In many places gods came to be associated with patterns of birth, growth, death, and regeneration. They could bring death and destruction, but they also created life. Figurines, carvings, and paintings from the Neolithic include pregnant women and women giving birth, men with erect penises, and creatures that are a combination of a man and a male animal such as a bull or goat. Like humans, the gods came to have a division of labor and a social hierarchy. Thus there were rain gods and sun gods, sky goddesses and moon goddesses, gods that assured the health of cattle or the growth of corn, goddesses of the hearth and home. Powerful father and mother gods sometimes presided, but they were challenged and overthrown by virile young male gods, often in epic battles. Thus as human society was becoming more complex, so was the unseen world.

CONNECTIONS

The human story is often told as a narrative of unstoppable progress toward greater complexity. The simple stone hand axes of the Paleolithic were replaced by the specialized tools of the Neolithic and then by bronze, iron, steel, plastic, and silicon. The small kin groups of the Paleolithic gave way to Neolithic villages that grew ever larger until they became cities and eventually today's megalopolises. Egalitarian foragers became stratified by divisions of wealth and power that were formalized as aristocracies, castes, and social classes, leading to today's vast divisions between wealth and poverty. Oral rituals of worship, healing, and celebration in which everyone participated grew into a dizzying array of religions, philosophies, and branches of knowledge presided over by specialists including priests, scholars, scientists, doctors, generals, and entertainers. The rest of this book traces this story and explores the changes over time that are the central thread of history.

As you examine what — particularly in world history — can seem to be a staggering number of developments, it is also important to remember that many things were slow to change and that some aspects of human life in the Neolithic, or even the Paleolithic, continued. Foraging, horticulture, pastoralism, and agriculture have been the primary economic activities of most people throughout the entire history of the world. Though today there are only a few foraging groups in very isolated areas, there are significant numbers of horticulturalists and pastoralists, and their numbers were much greater just a century ago. At that point the vast majority of the world's people still made their living directly through agriculture. The social patterns set in early agricultural societies — with most of the population farming the land, and a small number of elite who lived off their labor — lasted for millennia. You have no doubt recognized other similarities between the early peoples discussed in this chapter and the people you see around you, and it is important to keep these continuities in mind as you embark on your examination of human history.

CHAPTER REVIEW

□ How did humans evolve, and where did they migrate? (p. 4)

Scholars studying the natural world and the place of humans in it have devised various ways of classifying living creatures and organizing time. Through studying the physical remains of the past, sometimes with very new high-tech procedures such as DNA analysis, they have examined human evolution from earlier hominids in eastern Africa. Evolution involved a combination of factors, including bipedalism, larger brain size, spoken symbolic language, and longer periods of infancy. All these together led humans to invent ever more complex tools that allowed them to shape the world around them. They migrated out of Africa in several waves, adapting to many different environments and developing diverse cultures.

□ What were the key features of Paleolithic society? (p. 11)

In the Paleolithic period, people lived in small groups of related individuals, moving through the landscape in the search for food. They obtained food by foraging: gathering plants, seeds, nuts, and insects; trapping fish and small animals; and sometimes hunting large game. Most had few material possessions, and social and gender hierarchies were probably much less pronounced than they would become later. Beginning around 50,000 B.C.E. people in many parts of the world began to decorate their surroundings and the objects they made, often with vivid representations of animals and people, and sometimes with symbols. These, and careful burials of the dead, suggest that people had developed ideas about supernatural or spiritual forces beyond the visible material world.

□ How did plant and animal domestication develop, and what effects did it have on human society? (p. 17)

Beginning about 9000 B.C.E. people living in the Near East, and then elsewhere, began to plant seeds as well as gather wild crops, raise certain animals instead of hunt them, and selectively breed both plants and animals to make them more useful to humans. This domestication of plants and animals, called the Agricultural Revolution, was the most important change in human history. Crop-raising began as horticulture, in which people — often women — used hand tools to plant and harvest. Animal domestication began with sheep and goats, which were often herded from place to place so that they could eat the available vegetation, an economic system called pastoralism. The domestication of large animals such as cattle and water buffalo led to plow agriculture, through which humans could raise much more food. Agriculture required more labor than did foraging, but it allowed the human population to grow far more quickly.

□ How did growing social and gender hierarchies and expanding networks of trade increase the complexity of human society in the Neolithic period? (p. 24)

The division of labor that plow agriculture required led to growing social hierarchies between those who could afford the new tools and products and those who could not. These were reinforced over generations as children inherited goods and status from their parents, and as social norms and laws were developed that led members of the elite to marry one another. Plow agriculture also strengthened differentiation based on gender, and men became more associated with the world beyond the household and women with the domestic realm. Neolithic agricultural communities developed technologies to meet their needs, including pottery, cloth-weaving, and wheeled vehicles, and they often traded with one another for products that they could not obtain locally. In some parts of the world, production and trade included copper and bronze, although most tools continued to be made of stone, bone, and wood. Religious ideas came to reflect the new agricultural society, with fertility as the most important goal and the gods, like humans, arranged in a hierarchy.

SUGGESTED READINGS

Burenhelt, Goren. *People of the Stone Age: Hunter-Gatherers and Early Farmers*. 1994. Short articles and extensive illustrations of the transition to agriculture, presented as part of the American Museum of Natural History's excellent *Illustrated History of Humankind*.

Christian, David. *Maps of Time: An Introduction to Big History*. 2002. An elegant examination of the story of the cosmos, from the Big Bang to today.

Diamond, Jared. *Guns, Germs, and Steel: The Fates of Human Societies*, 2d ed. 2005. Extremely influential and wide-ranging examination of the long-term impact of agriculture, animal domestication, and the environment on differing rates of development around the world.

Ehrlich, Paul R., and Anne H. Ehrlich. *Dominant Animal: Human Evolution and the Environment*. 2009. By two of today's leading biologists, traces the impact of humans on the planet from the Paleolithic to today.

Fagan, Brian M. *People of the Earth: An Introduction to World Prehistory*, 13th ed. 2009. A thorough survey that presents up-to-date scholarship, designed for students.

Gamble, Clive. *Timewalkers: The Prehistory of Global Colonization*. 2006. A lively examination of how and why humans came to be everywhere in the world.

Hawkes, Kristen, and Richard R. Paine. *The Evolution of Human Life History*. 2006. A series of articles that examine the ways in which what makes humans distinct from other animals came to be.

Hrdy, Sarah Bluffer. *Mothers and Others: The Evolutionary Origins of Human Understanding*. 2009. Provides the new, more egalitarian perspective on evolution.

Lewin, Roger. *Human Evolution. An Illustrated Introduction*, 5th ed. 2004. A relatively compact and very readable introduction that includes the newest archaeological and chemical evidence.

Lewis-Williams, David, and David Pearce. *Inside the Neolithic Mind: Consciousness, Cosmos, and the Realm of the Gods*. 2005. An analysis of Neolithic belief systems and the cultural products that resulted from them.

McCarter, Susan Foster. *Neolithic*. 2007. An introductory survey of the development and impact of agriculture, with many illustrations.

Pinker, Steven. *How the Mind Works*, 2d ed. 2009. An insightful examination of how the mind evolved, along with a survey of modern brain science.

Pollan, Michael. *The Omnivore's Dilemma: A Natural History of Four Meals*. 2007. A witty and thoughtful look at the way food is produced today, and how this contrasts with our foraging past.

Smith, Bruce. *The Emergence of Agriculture*. 1999. Presents both the story of the early development of agriculture around the world and the ways in which scholars study this.

NOTES

1. Chinook Blessing Litany, in Wilma Mankiller, ed., *Every Day Is a Good Day: Reflections by Contemporary Indigenous Women* (Golden, Colo.: Fulcrum Publishing, 2004), pp. 170, 171. Copyright © 2004 by Wilma P. Mankiller. Used by permission of Fulcrum Publishing.
2. Code of Hammurabi, article 171, translated by L. W. King (1910), Internet Ancient History Sourcebook, http://www.fordham.edu/halsall/ancient/hamcode.html#text.

For practice quizzes and other study tools, visit the **Online Study Guide** at bedfordstmartins.com/mckayworld.

For primary sources from this period, see *Sources of World Societies*, **Second Edition**.

For Web sites, images, and documents related to topics in this chapter, visit **Make History** at bedfordstmartins.com/mckayworld.

• **Egyptian Lyre Player** Ancient Egyptians hoped that life after death would be a pleasant continuation of life on this earth, and their tombs reflected this. This wall painting from the tomb of an official who died about 1400 B.C.E. shows a female musician — for a good afterlife would surely include music. (Werner Forman/Art Resource, NY)

2

Five thousand years ago, humans were living in most parts of the planet. They had designed technologies to meet the challenges presented by deep forests and jungles, steep mountains, and blistering deserts. As the climate changed, they adapted, building boats to cross channels created by melting glaciers and finding new sources of food when old sources were no longer plentiful. In some places the new sources included domesticated plants and animals, which allowed people to live in much closer proximity to one another than they had as foragers.

The Rise of the State in Southwest Asia and the Nile Valley

3200–500 B.C.E.

That proximity created opportunities, as larger groups of people pooled their knowledge to deal with life's challenges, but it also created problems. Human history from that point on can be seen as a response to these opportunities, challenges, and conflicts. As small villages grew into cities, people continued to develop technologies and systems to handle new issues.

They created structures of governance not based on the kin group to control their more complex societies, along with military forces and taxation systems to support the structures of governance. In some places they invented writing to record taxes, inventories, and payments, and they later put writing to other uses, including the preservation of stories, traditions, and history. The first places where these new technologies and systems were introduced were the Tigris and Euphrates River Valleys of southwest Asia and the Nile Valley of northeast Africa, areas whose history became linked through trade connections, military conquests, and migrations. •

Writing, Cities, and States
□ How does writing shape what we can know about the past, and how did writing develop to meet the needs of cities and states?

Mesopotamia from Sumeria to Babylon
□ How did the people of Mesopotamia form the world's first states, and how did their institutions spread?

The Egyptians and Their Pharaohs
□ How did geography, leadership, and religion enable the Egyptians to build and maintain a cohesive,

prosperous society, and how did migrations and invasions shape Egypt's fate?

The Hebrews
□ How did the Hebrews create an enduring written religious tradition, and what was its significance?

The Assyrians and Persians
□ What were the strengths of and the major differences between the Assyrian and Persian Empires?

Writing, Cities, and States

□ **How does writing shape what we can know about the past, and how did writing develop to meet the needs of cities and states?**

The remains of buildings, burial sites, weapons, tools, artwork, and other handmade objects provide our only evidence of how people lived, thought, felt, and died during most of the human past. Beginning about five thousand years ago, however, people in some parts of the world developed a new technology, writing, the surviving examples of which have provided a much wider range of information. Writing was developed to meet the needs of the more complex urban societies that are often referred to as civilizations, and particularly to meet the needs of the state, a new political form that developed during the time covered in this chapter.

Written Sources and the Human Past

Writing is closely tied to the idea of history itself. The term *history* comes from the Greek word *historia*, coined by Herodotus (hi-ROD-duh-tuhs; ca. 484–ca. 425 B.C.E.) in the fifth century B.C.E. to describe his in-

Clay Letter Written in Cuneiform and Its Envelope, ca. 1850 B.C.E. In this letter (left) from a city in what is now southern Turkey, a merchant complains to his brother that life is hard and comments on the trade in silver, gold, tin, and textiles. Letters were often enclosed in envelopes (right) and sealed with a piece of soft clay that was stamped, just as you might use a stamped wax seal today. Here the sender's seal shows people approaching a king. (Courtesy of the Trustees of the British Museum)

quiry into the past. In fact, as Herodotus used them, the words *inquiry* and *history* are the same. Herodotus based his *Histories*, at their core a study of the origins of the wars between the Persians and the Greeks that had happened about the time he was born, on the oral testimony of people he had met as he traveled widely. Many of these people had been participants in the wars, and Herodotus was proud that he could rely so much on the eyewitness accounts of the people actually involved. Today we would call this methodology "oral history," and it remains a vital technique for studying the recent past. Following the standard practice of the time, Herodotus most likely read his *Histories* out loud at some sort of public gathering — one story of his life even has him doing this at the Olympic games. Herodotus also wrote down his histories, however, and consulted written documents. From his day until quite recently, this aspect of his methods has defined history and separated it from prehistory: history came to be regarded as that part of the human past for which there are written records. In this view, history began with the invention of writing — about 3200 B.C.E. in a few parts of the world and much later in others.

As we saw in Chapter 1, this line between history and prehistory has largely broken down. Historians who study human societies that developed systems of writing continue to use many of the same types of physical evidence as do those who study societies without writing. For other cultures the writing or record-keeping systems have not yet been deciphered, so our knowledge of these people also depends largely on physical evidence. Scholars can read the writing of a great many societies, however, adding greatly to what we can learn about them.

Much ancient writing survives only because it was copied and recopied, sometimes years after the writing was first produced. The oldest known copy of Herodotus's *Histories*, for example, dates from about 900 C.E., nearly a millennium and a half after he finished this book. The survival of a work means that someone from a later period — and often a long chain of someones — judged it worthy of the time, effort, and resources needed to produce copies. The copies may not be completely accurate, either, because the scribe made an error or because he (or, much less often, she)

□ CHRONOLOGY

ca. 7000–3000 B.C.E. Villages slowly grow into cities in Sumeria

ca. 3200 B.C.E. Invention of cuneiform writing

ca. 3000–2600 B.C.E. Establishment of city-states with hereditary kingship in Sumeria

2660–2180 B.C.E. Period of the Old Kingdom in Egypt

2331 B.C.E. Sargon conquers Sumeria and establishes an empire

ca. 1790 B.C.E. Hammurabi's law code

ca. 1600 B.C.E. Hittites expand their empire into Mesopotamia

ca. 1550–1070 B.C.E. Period of the New Kingdom in Egypt

ca. 1100–700 B.C.E. Phoenicians play a dominant role in international trade

ca. 1020–930 B.C.E. Period of united monarchy in the Hebrew Kingdom

ca. 800–612 B.C.E. Assyrian Empire

720 B.C.E. Assyrian conquest of northern Hebrew kingdom of Israel

727–653 B.C.E. Kushite rule in Egypt

ca. 600–500 B.C.E. Spread of Zoroastrianism

587 B.C.E. Conquest of southern Hebrew kingdom of Judah by the Babylonians

550 B.C.E. Creation of Persian Empire

538 B.C.E. Persian king Cyrus's conquest of Babylonia; Jewish exiles begin return to Jerusalem

decided to change something. Historians studying ancient works thus often try to find as many early copies as they can and compare them to arrive at the version they think is closest to the original.

Not surprisingly, the works considered worthy of copying tend to be those that, like the *Histories*, refer to political and military events involving major powers, that record religious traditions, or that come from authors who were later regarded as important. By contrast, written sources dealing with the daily life of ordinary men and women were few to begin with and were rarely saved or copied because they were not seen as significant.

Some early written texts survive in their original form because people inscribed them in stone, shells, bone, or other hard materials, intending them to be permanent. Stones with inscriptions were often erected in the open in public places for all to see, so they include things that leaders felt had enduring importance, such as laws, religious proclamations, decrees, and treaties. (This practice continues today, of course; the names etched in granite on the Vietnam Veterans Memorial in Washington, D.C., are perhaps the best-known recent example, but inscriptions can be found on nearly every major public building.) Sometimes this permanence was accidental: in ancient Mesopotamia (in the area of modern Iraq), all writing was initially made up of indentations on soft clay tablets, which then hardened. Thousands of these tablets have survived, the oldest dating to about 3200 B.C.E., and from them historians have learned about many aspects of everyday life, including taxes and wages. By contrast, writing in Egypt at the same time was often done in ink on papyrus sheets, made from a plant that grows abundantly in Egypt. Some of these papyrus sheets have survived—the oldest is an account sheet from about 2600 B.C.E.—but papyrus is a much more fragile material than hardened clay, so most have disintegrated. In China, the oldest surviving writing is on bones and turtle shells from about 1200 B.C.E., but it is clear that writing was done much earlier on less permanent materials such as silk and bamboo. (For more on the origins of Chinese writing, see page 97.)

However they have survived and however limited they are, written records often become scholars' most important original sources for investigating the past. Thus the discovery of a new piece of written evidence from the ancient past—such as the Dead Sea Scrolls, which contain sections of the Hebrew Bible, were written between 150 B.C.E. and 70 C.E., and were first seen by scholars in 1948—is always a major event. But reconstructing and deciphering what are often crumbling documents can take decades, and disputes about how these records affect our understanding of the past can go on forever.

Cities and the Idea of Civilization

Along with writing, the growth of cities has often been a way that scholars have marked the increasing complexity of human societies. In the ancient world, residents of cities generally viewed themselves as more advanced and sophisticated than rural folk—a judgment still made today. They saw themselves as more "civilized," a word that comes from the Latin adjective *civilis*, which refers to a citizen, either a citizen of a town or of a larger political unit such as an empire. In their view, those who lived outside cities were more backward and primitive.

This depiction of people as either civilized or uncivilized was gradually extended to whole societies. Beginning in the eighteenth century European scholars described those societies in which political, economic, and social organizations operated on a large scale, not primarily through families and kin groups, as "civilizations." Civilizations had cities; laws that governed human relationships; codes of manners and

social conduct that regulated how people were to behave; and scientific, philosophical, and theological ideas that explained the larger world. Generally, only societies that used writing were judged to be civilizations, for writing allowed laws, norms, ideas, and traditions to become more complex. By comparison, societies in which people were nomadic or lived in small villages without formal laws, and in which traditions and ideas were passed down orally, were generally not regarded as civilizations. They were often seen as inferior by those who lived in large-scale societies.

The idea of a civilization came to mean not simply a system of political and social organization, but also particular ways of thinking and believing, particular styles of art, and other facets of culture. Thus the boundaries between one civilization and another were not as easy to determine as those between one political unit and another, and places were often described as being part of many different civilizations at the same time. For example, when discussing the ancient city of Athens, some historians spoke of Athenian civilization and others of Greek civilization. Others came to view Athens as part of Western civilization, a very large division of human society, often set in opposition to Eastern civilization. In the era after World War I, "Western civilization" became a standard course at colleges and universities in the United States, designed by scholars who were upset that during the war many young Americans did not seem to appreciate the importance of the links between America and Europe.

Until the middle of the twentieth century, historians often referred to the earliest places where writing and cities developed as the "cradles of civilization," proposing a model of development for all humanity patterned on that of an individual person. However, the idea that all human societies developed (or should develop) in a uniform process from a "cradle" to a "mature" civilization has now been largely discredited, and some world historians choose not to use the word *civilization* at all because its meaning is so value-laden. But they have not rejected the idea that about 5,000 years ago a new form of human society appeared, first in the valley formed by the Tigris and Euphrates Rivers—an area the Greeks later called Mesopotamia—and then in other places around the world, often in river valleys. These societies all had cities with tens of thousands of people.

The Rise of States, Laws, and Social Hierarchies

Cities concentrated people and power, and they required more elaborate mechanisms to make them work than had small agricultural villages and foraging groups. These mechanisms were part of what political scientists call "the state," an organization distinct from a tribe or kinship group in which a small share of the population is able to coerce resources out of everyone else in order to gain and then maintain power. In a state, the interest that gains power might be one particular family, a set of religious leaders, or even a charismatic or talented individual able to handle the problems of dense urban communities.

However they are established, states coerce people through violence, or the threat of violence, and develop permanent armies for this purpose. Using armed force every time they need food or other resources is not very efficient, however, so states also establish bureaucracies and systems of taxation. States also need to keep track of people and goods, so they develop systems of recording information and accounting, usually through writing, though not always. In the Inca Empire, for example, a large state established in the Andes, information about money, goods, and people was recorded on collections of colored knotted strings called *khipus* (see page 305). Systems of recording information allow the creation of more elaborate rules of behavior, often written down in the form of law codes, which facilitate further growth in state power, or in the form of religious traditions, which specify what sort of behavior is pleasing to the gods or other supernatural forces.

Written laws and traditions generally create more elaborate social hierarchies, in which divisions between elite groups and common people are established more firmly. They also generally heighten gender hierarchies. Those who gain power in states are most often men, so they tend to establish laws and norms that favor males in marriage, property rights, and other areas.

Whether we choose to call the process "the birth of civilization" or "the growth of the state," beginning about 3200 B.C.E. some human societies began to develop into a new form. Neolithic agricultural villages

expanded into cities, where most people did not raise their own food but depended on that produced by the surrounding countryside and instead carried out other tasks. The organization of this more complex division of labor was undertaken by an elite group, which enforced its will by armed force, along with laws, taxes, and bureaucracies backed up by the threat of force. Social and gender hierarchies became more complex and rigid. All this happened first in Mesopotamia, then in Egypt, and then in India and China.

Mesopotamia from Sumeria to Babylon

☐ How did the people of Mesopotamia form the world's first states, and how did their institutions spread?

States first developed in Mesopotamia, where sustained agriculture reliant on irrigation from the Euphrates and Tigris Rivers resulted in larger populations, a division of labor, and the growth of cities. Priests and rulers developed ways to control and organize these complex societies, including armies, taxation systems, and written records. Conquerors from the north unified Mesopotamian city-states into larger empires and spread Mesopotamian culture over a large area.

Environmental Challenges, Irrigation, and Religion

Mesopotamia was part of the Fertile Crescent, where settled agriculture first developed (see pages 18–19). Beginning around 7000 B.C.E., more and more villages were built in the part of southern Mesopotamia known as Sumeria (soo-MAIRE-ee-uh), where the Tigris and Euphrates Rivers brought fresh soil when they flooded each spring. The area had more rainfall than it does now, but not enough for farming the ever-expanding fields. Thus villagers began to build and maintain irrigation ditches that took water from the rivers, allowing more food to be grown and the population to expand. By about 3000 B.C.E., some villages, including Ur and Uruk, had grown into true cities with populations of 40,000 to 50,000. These cities built

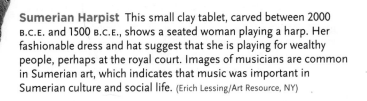

Sumerian Harpist This small clay tablet, carved between 2000 B.C.E. and 1500 B.C.E., shows a seated woman playing a harp. Her fashionable dress and hat suggest that she is playing for wealthy people, perhaps at the royal court. Images of musicians are common in Sumerian art, which indicates that music was important in Sumerian culture and social life. (Erich Lessing/Art Resource, NY)

Ziggurat The ziggurat is a stepped pyramid-shaped temple that dominated the landscape of the Sumerian city. Surrounded by a walled enclosure, it stood as a monument to the gods. Religious ceremonies for the welfare of the community were often performed on the top, and grain, animals, and equipment stores were within the outer enclosure. (Charles & Josette Lemars/Corbis)

defensive walls, marketplaces, and large public buildings. Because they ruled the surrounding countryside, they were really city-states, and the irrigation system they depended on required cooperation and at least some level of social and political cohesion.

The authority to run this system was initially assumed by Sumerian priests, who created many of the institutions that are essential parts of any state. How did these priests assume power? We cannot know for certain, as this happened before the invention of writing, but it appears that the uncertainties of life in Sumerian cities, in which the rivers often flooded uncontrollably and serious droughts threatened crops, convinced people that the gods were powerful, unpredictable, and vindictive. Humans thus needed to please and obey the gods in order to bring rain, prevent floods, and ensure good harvests. They saw the cosmos as a struggle between order and disorder; to ensure order, people believed they needed to serve the gods by obeying the rules set by religious leaders. Citizens of each city worshipped a number of gods but often focused

primarily on one who controlled the economic basis of the city, such as a god of the underworld who controlled the growing of grain or a god who had charge of sheep herds. Encouraged and directed by the priesthood, people erected a large temple in the center of each city, often in the form of a step-pyramid or **ziggurat** (ZIH-guh-rat), around which they built their houses. The best way to honor the gods was to make the temple as grand and as impressive as possible, for the size of the temple demonstrated the strength of the community, and gods who had a splendid ziggurat might think twice about sending floods to destroy the city.

Temples grew into elaborate complexes of buildings with storage space for grain and other products and housing for animals. To support these construction efforts, and to support themselves, temple officials developed taxation systems in which people paid a portion of their harvest to the temple or worked a certain number of days per year on land owned directly by the temple.

Sumerian Politics and Society

During times of emergencies, such as floods or invasions by other cities, a chief priest or sometimes a military leader assumed what was supposed to be temporary authority over a city. He established a regular army,

• **ziggurat** Temple in the form of a step-pyramid built in the center of a Mesopotamian city to honor the gods.

• **cuneiform** The wedge-shaped writing system that developed in Sumeria, the first writing system in the world.

trained it, and led it into battle, and he was given charge over the city's fortifications. Temporary power gradually became permanent kingship, and sometime before 2600 B.C.E. kings in some Sumerian city-states began to hand down the kingship to their sons, establishing hereditary dynasties in which power was handed down through the male line. The symbol of royal status was the palace, which came to rival the temple in its grandeur. Kings made alliances with other powerful individuals, often through marriage, and a hereditary aristocracy of nobles developed. These aristocracies were often different from those of the priests, but kings worked closely with religious authorities and relied on ideas about their connections with the gods, as well as their military might, for their power. Acting together, priests, nobles, and kings in Sumerian cities used force, persuasion, and threats of higher taxes to maintain order, keep the irrigation systems working, and keep food and other goods flowing.

The king and the nobles held extensive tracts of land that were, like the estates of the temple, worked by others — specifically, clients and slaves. Slaves were prisoners of war, convicts, and debtors. While they were subject to any treatment their owners might mete out, they could engage in trade, make profits, and even buy their freedom. Clients were free people who were dependent on the nobility. In return for their labor, they received small plots of land to work for themselves. Although this arrangement assured the clients of a livelihood, the land they worked remained the possession of the nobility or the temple. Some individuals and families owned land outright and paid their taxes in the form of agricultural products or things they had made. The city-states that developed later throughout Mesopotamia had similar social categories.

Each of these social categories included both men and women, but Sumerian society made clear distinctions based on gender. All Mesopotamian city-states were patriarchal — that is, most power was held by older adult men. Because other hierarchies such as those of hereditary aristocracy gave privilege to women connected to powerful or wealthy men, however, women saw themselves as either privileged or not, rather than as members of a single lower-ranking group. Therefore, they tended not to object to institutions and intellectual structures that subordinated them, or perhaps their objections were not recorded.

The Invention of Writing and Other Intellectual Advances

In the villages of Sumeria, people used small clay objects made into different forms to represent various types of goods that they owned, a simple system of record-keeping. By 3200 B.C.E. in the growing Sumerian cities, these objects had been replaced by tablets

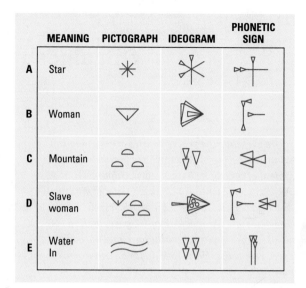

FIGURE 2.1 Sumerian Writing
(Source: Excerpted from S. N. Kramer, *The Sumerians: Their History, Culture, and Character.* Copyright © 1963 by the University of Chicago Press. Used by permission of The University of Chicago Press.)

marked with symbols standing for the goods, made either by rolling an engraved seal over soft clay or by making marks in the clay with a sharpened stylus. The stylus formed wedge-shaped marks, from which this style of writing took its name, **cuneiform** (kyoo-NEE-uh-form), the Latin term for "wedge-shaped." Initially cuneiform writing was pictographic, showing pictures of the objects, but gradually scribes simplified the system, creating stylized symbols called ideograms. These were used to represent actual objects but also came to represent ideas that were difficult to depict. Thus the sign for star (see line A in Figure 2.1) could also be used to indicate heaven, sky, or even god. Signs were also combined. For example, because many slaves in Sumeria came from mountainous regions far from cities, an inventive scribe decided to combine the sign for mountain with the sign for woman to indicate "slave woman" (see lines B, C, and D).

Certain things were still difficult to depict, and around 2700 B.C.E. scribes in some cities began to use signs to represent sounds rather than concepts. For instance, scribes drew two parallel wavy lines to indicate the word *a* or "water" (see line E in Figure 2.1). Besides water, the word *a* in Sumerian also meant "in." The word *in* expresses a relationship that is very difficult to represent pictorially. Instead of trying to invent a sign to mean "in," some clever scribe used the sign for water because the two words sounded alike. This phonetic use of signs made possible the combining of signs to convey abstract ideas.

The development of the Sumerian system of writing was piecemeal, with scribes making changes and additions as they were needed. The system became so

Listening to the Past

Gilgamesh's Quest for Immortality

The human desire to escape the grip of death appears in many cultures. The Sumerian Epic of Gilgamesh *is the earliest recorded treatment of this topic. In this story, Gilgamesh, a part-real, part-mythological king of Uruk who is not fulfilling his duties as the king very well, sets out with his friend Enkidu to perform wondrous feats against fearsome agents of the gods. Together they kill several supernatural beings, and the gods decide that Enkidu must die. Here, Enkidu foresees his own death in a dream.*

"Listen, my friend [Gilgamesh], this is the dream I dreamed last night. The heavens roared, and earth rumbled back an answer; between them I stood before an awful being, the somber-faced man-bird; he had directed on me his purpose. His was a vampire face, his foot was a lion's foot, his hand was an eagle's talon. He fell on me and his claws were in my hair, he held me fast and I smothered; then he transformed me so that my arms became wings covered with feathers. He turned his stare towards me, and he led me away to the palace of Irkalla, the Queen of Darkness [the goddess of the underworld; in other words, an agent of death], to the house from which none who enters ever returns, down the road from which there is no coming back."

After Enkidu sickens and dies, a distraught Gilgamesh determines to become immortal. He decides to journey to Utnapishtim and his wife, the only mortals whom the gods had granted eternal life in a beautiful paradise. Gilgamesh's journey involves the effort not only to escape from death but also to reach an understanding of the meaning of life. During his travels he meets with Siduri, the wise and good-natured goddess of wine, who gives him the following advice.

"Gilgamesh, where are you hurrying to? You will never find that life for which you are looking. When the gods created man they allotted to him death, but life they retained in their own keeping. As for you, Gilgamesh, fill your belly with good things; day and night, night and day, dance and be merry, feast and rejoice. Let your clothes be fresh, bathe yourself in water, cherish the little child that holds your hand, and make your wife happy in your embrace; for this too is the lot of man."

Ignoring Siduri's advice, Gilgamesh continues his journey until he finds Utnapishtim and puts to him the question that is the reason for his quest.

"Oh, father Utnapishtim, you who have entered the assembly of the gods, I wish to question you concerning the living and the dead, how shall I find the life for which I am searching?

Utnapishtim said, "There is no permanence. Do we build a house to stand forever, do we seal a contract to hold for all time? Do brothers divide an inheritance to keep forever, does the flood-time of rivers endure? . . . From the days of old there is no permanence. . . . What is there between the master and the servant when both have fulfilled their doom? When the Anunnaki [the gods of the underworld], the judges, and Mammetun [the goddess of fate] the mother of destinies, come together, they decree the fates of men. Life and death they allot but the day of death they do not disclose."

Then Gilgamesh said to Utnapishtim the Faraway, "I look at you now, Utnapishtim, and your appearance is no different from mine; there is nothing strange in your features. I thought I should find you like a hero prepared for battle, but you lie here taking your ease on your back. Tell me truly, how was it that you came to enter the company of the gods and to possess everlasting life?" Utnapishtim said to Gilgamesh, "I shall reveal

---

complicated that only professional scribes mastered it after many years of study. By 2500 B.C.E. scribal schools flourished throughout Sumeria. Most students came from wealthy families, and all were male. Each school had a master, a teacher, and monitors. Discipline was strict, and students were caned for sloppy work and misbehavior. One graduate of a scribal school had few fond memories of the joy of learning:

My headmaster read my tablet, said:
"There is something missing," caned me.
. . .
The fellow in charge of silence said:

"Why did you talk without permission," caned me.
The fellow in charge of the assembly said:
"Why did you stand at ease without permission,"
    caned me.[1]

Scribal schools were primarily intended to produce individuals who could keep records of the property and wealth of temple officials, kings, and nobles. Thus writing first developed as a way to enhance the growing power of elites, not to record speech, although it came to be used for that purpose.

Writing also came to be used to record religious traditions and stories of great heroes. These stories of-to you a mystery, I shall tell you a secret of the gods. . . . In those days the world teemed, the people multiplied, the world bellowed like wild bull, and the great god [Enlil, the warrior god] was aroused by the clamor . . . so the gods agreed to exterminate mankind."

Utnapishtim continues, telling Gilgamesh that one of the gods, Ea, had taken an oath to protect humanity, so he warned Utnapishtim to build a boat big enough to hold his family, various artisans, and all animals in order to survive the flood that was to come. The great flood killed all who were not on the boat. Although Enlil was initially infuriated by the Sumerians' survival, he ended up blessing Utnapishtim and his wife with eternal life. Gilgamesh wants this as well, but he fails two opportunities Utnapishtim provides for him to achieve it and returns to Uruk. The last part of the epic notes a different kind of immortality.

"The destiny was fulfilled which the father of the gods, Enlil of the mountain, had decreed for Gilgamesh: "In nether-earth the darkness will show him a light: of mankind, all that are known, none will leave a monument for generations to compare with his. The heroes, the wise men, like the new moon have their waxing and waning. Men will say, 'Who has ever ruled with might and power like him?' As in the dark month, the month of shadows, so without him there is no light. O Gilgamesh, this was the meaning of your dream [of immortality]. You were given the kingship, such was your destiny, everlasting life was not your destiny. Because of this do not be sad at heart, do not be grieved or oppressed; he [Enlil] has given you power to bind and to loose, to be the darkness and the light of mankind. He has given you unexampled supremacy over the people, victory in battle from which no fugitive returns, in forays and assaults from which there is no going back. But do not abuse this power, deal justly with your servants in the palace, deal justly before the face of the Sun."

● **Gilgamesh, from decorative panel of a lyre unearthed at Ur.** (Courtesy of the Penn Museum, Image #150108)

Source: *The Epic of Gilgamesh*, translated with an introduction by N. K. Sanders. Penguin Classics 1960, Third edition, 1972, pp. 89–116. Copyright © N. K. Sanders, 1960, 1964, 1972. Used with permission of Penguin Group Ltd.

QUESTIONS FOR ANALYSIS

1. What does the *Epic of Gilgamesh* reveal about Sumerian attitudes toward the gods and human beings?
2. What does the epic tell us about Sumerian views of the nature of human life? Where do human beings fit into the cosmic world?
3. At the end of his quest, did Gilgamesh achieve immortality? If so, what was the nature of that immortality?

ten took the form of **epic poems**, narrations of the achievements, the labors, and sometimes the failures of heroes that embody a people's or a nation's conception of its own past. Historians can use epic poems to learn about various aspects of a society, particularly its ideals. The Sumerians produced the first epic poem, the *Epic of Gilgamesh*, which recounts the wanderings of Gilgamesh, the part real–part mythological king of the Sumerian city of Uruk. The oldest surviving cuneiform tablets that record stories of Gilgamesh date from about 2100 B.C.E., but these tales were certainly told and probably first written down much earlier. In the epic, Gilgamesh, along with his companion, Enkidu, goes off

to fight monsters in a search for fame and glory. After Enkidu dies along the way, Gilgamesh is distraught and decides to search for eternal life, a quest that is unsuccessful. The *Epic of Gilgamesh* shows the Sumerians grappling with such enduring issues as life and death, people and the gods, and immortality. (See "Listening to the Past: Gilgamesh's Quest for Immortality," above.)

● **epic poems** Narrations of the achievements and sometimes the failures of heroes that embody a people's or a nation's conception of its own past. This type of writing first developed in ancient Sumeria.

Myths are the earliest known attempts to answer the question "How did it all begin?" and the story of Gilgamesh incorporates many of the myths of the Sumerians, including those about the creation of the universe. According to one myth (echoed in Genesis, the first book of the Hebrew Bible), only the primeval sea existed at first. The sea produced Heaven and earth, which were united. Heaven and earth gave birth to the god Enlil, who separated them and made possible the creation of the other gods.

The Sumerians did not spend all their time speculating about the origins of the universe. The building of cities, palaces, temples, and irrigation canals demanded practical knowledge of geometry and trigonometry. The Sumerians and later Mesopotamians made significant advances in mathematics using a numerical system based on units of sixty, ten, and six, from which we derive our division of hours into sixty minutes and minutes into sixty seconds. They also developed the concept of place value — that the value of a number depends on where it stands in relation to other numbers.

The Triumph of Babylon and the Spread of Mesopotamian Civilization

Judging by the fact that they had walls and other fortifications, the city-states of Sumeria regularly fought one another. Their battles were sometimes sparked by disputes over water, as irrigation in one area reduced or altered the flow of the rivers into other areas. During the third millennium B.C.E., the climate also became warmer and drier, which further heightened conflicts.

The wealth of Sumerian cities also attracted conquerors from the north. In 2331 B.C.E. Sargon, the chieftain of a group of loosely organized villages to the north of Sumeria, conquered a number of Sumerian cities with what was probably the world's first permanent army. He tore down their defensive walls and appointed his own sons as rulers, creating a new form of government, a state made up of several city-states, what we might think of as a small empire. The symbol of his triumph was a new capital, the city of Akkad. Sargon led his armies to the Mediterranean Sea, spreading Mesopotamian culture throughout the Fertile Crescent, and encouraged trading networks that brought in goods from as far away as the Indus River and the Nile (Map 2.1). Sargon spoke a different language than did the Sumerians, one of the many languages that scholars identify as belonging to the Semitic language family, which includes modern-day Hebrew and Arabic. However, Akkadians adapted Sumerian writing to their own language, a pattern followed by other groups that conquered the area.

Sargon's empire lasted about two hundred years and was then absorbed into the empire centered on the city of Babylon. Babylon was in an excellent position to dominate trade on both the Tigris and Euphrates Rivers, and it was fortunate in having a very able ruler in Hammurabi (hahm-moo-RAH-bee; r. 1792–1750 B.C.E.). He unified Mesopotamia using military force, strategic alliances with the rulers of smaller territories, and religious ideas. He encouraged the worship of Marduk, the all-powerful male god of Babylon, explaining that Marduk had been chosen by all the other Mesopotamian deities as their king. Thus the hierarchy among the gods reflected the hierarchy Hammurabi was establishing on earth, which gave his rule religious sanction. Under Hammurabi, Babylo-

Sargon of Akkad
This bronze head, with elaborately worked hair and beard, portrays the great conqueror Sargon of Akkad. The eyes were originally inlaid with precious jewels, which have since been gouged out. Made about 2300 B.C.E., this head was found in the Assyrian capital of Nineveh, where it had been taken as loot. (Interfoto/Alamy)

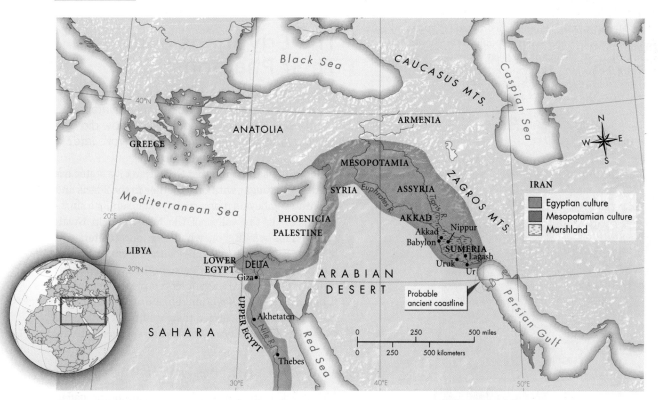

MAP 2.1 Spread of Cultures in the Ancient Near East, ca. 3000–1640 B.C.E. This map illustrates the spread of the Mesopotamian and Egyptian cultures through a semicircular stretch of land often called the Fertile Crescent. From this area, the knowledge and use of agriculture spread throughout western Asia.

nian ideas and beliefs traveled throughout Mesopotamia and beyond, with Babylonian traders spreading them farther as they reached the shores of the Mediterranean Sea and the Harappan cities of the Indus River Valley (see pages 66–69).

Hammurabi's Code and Its Social Consequences

Hammurabi's most memorable achievement was the code, introduced around 1790 B.C.E., that established the law of the land. Hammurabi claimed that divine authority stood behind the laws that promoted the welfare of the people. Laws regulating behavior and punishments set for crimes differed according to social status and gender.

Hammurabi's code provides a wealth of information about daily life in Mesopotamia. Because of farming's fundamental importance, the code dealt extensively with agriculture. It governed the duties and rights of tenant farmers, who were expected to cultivate the land carefully and to keep canals and ditches in good repair. Given that negligence in these duties could ruin or damage crops, tenants who were found negligent either bore the cost of losses or were sold into slavery.

Hammurabi gave careful attention to marriage and the family. The fathers of the prospective bride and groom legally arranged the marriage, with her father giving the bride a dowry that remained hers for the rest of her life. The groom's father gave a bridal gift to the bride's father. The wife was expected to be rigorously faithful. Adultery was defined as sex between a married woman and a man who was not her husband, and if a woman was found guilty, she could be put to death. But an accused wife could clear herself before the city council. If the investigation found her innocent, she could take her dowry and leave her husband. (Sex between a married man and a woman who was not his wife was not defined as adultery and carried no penalty.)

The husband technically had absolute power over his household. He could sell his wife and children into slavery for debt and disinherit his son, although the law made it very difficult for him to go to these extremes. Evidence other than the law code indicates that family life was not so grim. Countless wills and testaments show that husbands habitually left their estates to their wives, who in turn willed the property to their children. And though marriage was primarily an arrangement between families, a few poems speak of romantic love.

Law Code of Hammurabi Hammurabi ordered his code to be inscribed on stone pillars and set up in public throughout the Babylonian empire. At the top of the pillar Hammurabi is depicted receiving the scepter of authority from the god Shamash. (Réunion des Musées Nationaux/Art Resource, NY)

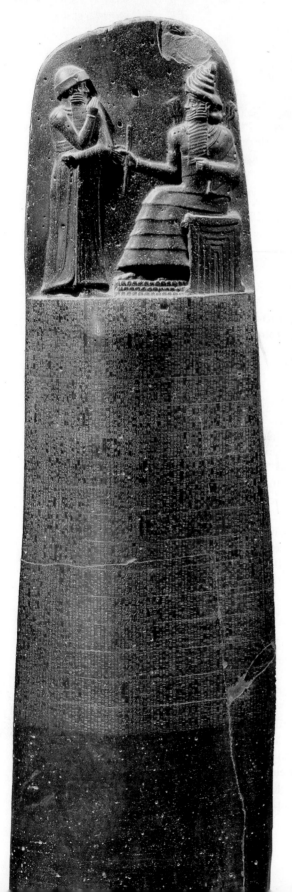

The Egyptians and Their Pharaohs

☐ How did geography, leadership, and religion enable the Egyptians to build and maintain a cohesive, prosperous society, and how did migrations and invasions shape Egypt's fate?

At about the same time that Sumerian city-states expanded and fought with one another in the Tigris and Euphrates Valleys, a more cohesive state under a single ruler grew in the valley of the Nile River in North Africa. This was Egypt, which for long stretches of history was prosperous and secure. At various times groups migrated into Egypt seeking better lives or invaded and conquered Egypt. Often these newcomers adopted aspects of Egyptian religion, art, and politics, and Egyptians also carried their traditions with them when they established an empire and engaged in trade.

The Nile and the God-King

The Greek historian and traveler Herodotus called Egypt the "gift of the Nile," and no other single geographical factor had such a fundamental and profound impact on the shaping of Egyptian life, society, and history as this river (see Map 2.2). The Nile flooded once a year, bringing fertile soil and moisture for farming. In contrast to the violent and destructive floods of the Tigris and Euphrates, Nile floods were relatively gentle, and Egyptians praised the Nile primarily as a creative and comforting force:

> Hail to thee, O Nile, that issues from the earth and
>   comes to keep Egypt alive! . . .
> He that waters the meadows which Ra created,
> He that makes to drink the desert . . .
> He who makes barley and brings emmer [wheat]
>   into being . . .
> He who brings grass into being for the cattle . . .
> He who makes every beloved tree to grow . . .
> O Nile, verdant art thou, who makest man and cattle
>   to live.[2]

The regular flooding of the Nile brought life back to the fields, which may have been why the Egyptians developed strong ideas about life after death. They saw both life on this earth and life after death as pleasant, not as the bleak struggle that the Mesopotamians envisioned. The Nile also unified Egypt, serving as a highway that promoted easy communication.

The political power structures that developed in Egypt came to be linked with the Nile. Somehow the idea developed that a single individual, a living god-king whom the Egyptians called the **pharaoh**, controlled the rise and fall of the Nile. This belief came about before the development of writing in Egypt, so, as with the growth of priestly power in Sumeria, the precise details of its origins have been lost. The Egyptians themselves told of a great pharaoh, Menes, who united Upper and Lower Egypt into a single kingdom around 3100 B.C.E. Thereafter, they divided their history into dynasties, or families, of pharaohs. Modern historians have combined the many dynasties into periods with distinctive characteristics (see page 46). The political unification of Egypt ushered in the period known as the Old Kingdom (2660–2180 B.C.E.), an era remarkable for prosperity, artistic flowering, and the evolution of religious beliefs. The focal point of religious and political life in the Old Kingdom was the pharaoh, who commanded the wealth, resources, and people of Egypt.

The pharaoh was only one of the many gods honored by the Egyptians, whose **polytheistic** religious ideas

> "Hail to thee, O Nile, that issues from the earth and comes to keep Egypt alive! . . . O Nile, verdant art thou, who makest man and cattle to live."

EGYPTIAN PRAYER

The Pharaoh Mykerinos and His Wife, ca. 2520

B.C.E. In this sandstone sculpture, the pharaoh and his wife look serenely toward the horizon. Stability and permanence were qualities prized by Egyptians in the Old Kingdom, and the sculptor captures them here. The figures are almost equal in size, suggesting the important role that the wives of pharaohs sometimes played. (Old Kingdom, Dynasty 4, reign of Mycerinus, 2532–2510 B.C.; Greywacke; H x W x D: 54 1/16 X 22 3/8 X 2 15/16 in. [139 x 57 x 54 cm]. Museum of Fine Arts, Boston. Harvard University–Museum of Fine Arts Expedition, 11.1738.)

evolved over thousands of years. Egyptians often adopted new deities that they learned about through trade or conquest, or combined the powers and features of these with existing deities. Originally the mightiest of the gods were Amon (AH-muhn), the sky-god, who created the universe by his thoughts, and Ra (rah), the sun-god, who brought life to the land and its people and commanded the sky, the earth, and the underworld. The similarities between Amon and Ra eventually led the Egyptians to combine them into one god, Amon-Ra.

Other powerful deities were Osiris (oh-SIGH-ruhs) and Isis (EYE-suhs). In what became one of Egypt's important religious stories, Osiris was killed and chopped apart by his brother Seth, who was jealous of his power. But Osiris was reassembled and resurrected for a brief period by his sister Isis, who was also his wife. (Siblings who marry each other are common in polytheistic religions, for the gods have to find divine spouses somewhere.) While he was resurrected, Osiris fathered Horus, who became associated with an earlier falcon-god. In some versions of the story, Osiris dies and Isis brings him back to life each year, just as the Nile brings Egypt back to life. Osiris eventually became king of the dead, and, according to Egyptian beliefs about the afterlife, he weighed people's hearts to determine whether they had lived justly enough to deserve everlasting life. The pharaohs came to associate themselves with both Horus and Osiris, and they were regarded as avatars of Horus in life and of Osiris in death. The pharaoh's wife was associated with Isis, for both the queen and the goddess were viewed as protectors.

During the Old Kingdom, the pharaoh was widely understood to be the power who achieved the integration between gods and human beings, and this integration was seen to represent the gods' pledge to care for their people (strikingly unlike the gods of Mesopotamia). The pharaoh's surroundings had to be worthy of a god, and only a magnificent palace was suitable for his home. In fact, the word *pharaoh* means "great house." Just as the pharaoh occupied a great house in life, so he reposed in a great pyramid after death, and the massive

- **pharaoh** The leader of religious and political life in the Old Kingdom, he commanded the wealth, the resources, and the people of Egypt.
- **polytheism** Belief in many deities.

□ PERIODS OF EGYPTIAN HISTORY

PERIOD	DATES	SIGNIFICANT EVENTS
Archaic	3100–2660 B.C.E.	Unification of Egypt
Old Kingdom	2660–2180 B.C.E.	Construction of the pyramids
First Intermediate	2180–2080 B.C.E.	Political chaos
Middle Kingdom	2080–1640 B.C.E.	Recovery and political stability
Second Intermediate	1640–1570 B.C.E.	Political disorder resulting from Hyksos migrations
New Kingdom	1550–1070 B.C.E.	Creation of an Egyptian empire
Third Intermediate	1100–653 B.C.E.	Political fragmentation and rule by outsiders

tomb contained everything he needed in his afterlife. The walls of the burial chamber were inscribed with religious texts and spells relating to the pharaoh's journeys after death. To this day the great pyramids at Giza near Cairo bear silent but magnificent testimony to the god-kings of Egypt.

As the story about Osiris's duties suggests, the pharaoh was not the only one with an afterlife. For all Egyptians, life after death depended both on how one had lived one's life on earth and on the conduct of proper funeral rituals, in which mummification of the physical body was essential. Osiris's care of the dead was shared by Anubis, the jackal-headed god of mummification who annually helped Isis resuscitate Osiris. Anubis's and Osiris's roles are described in the **Book of the Dead**, written to help guide the dead through difficulties they would encounter on the way to the underworld. This book explained that, after making the journey safely, the soul and the body became part of the divine.

To ancient Egyptians the pharaoh embodied justice and order—harmony among people, nature, and the divine. If the pharaoh was weak or allowed anyone to challenge his unique position, he opened the way to chaos. Twice in Egyptian history the pharaoh failed to maintain centralized power. During those two eras,

known as the First and Second Intermediate periods, Egypt suffered invasions and internal strife. Yet the monarchy survived, and in each period a strong pharaoh arose to crush the rebels or expel the invaders and restore order.

Social Divisions and Work in Ancient Egypt

Egyptian society reflected the pyramids that it built. At the top stood the pharaoh, who relied on a circle of nobles, officials, and priests to administer his kingdom. All of them were assisted by scribes, who used a writing system perhaps adapted from Mesopotamia or perhaps developed independently. Scribes wrote with a brush on papyrus sheets or on walls in characters called **hieroglyphs** (HIGH-ruh-glifs), not with a stick on clay tablets. Therefore their writing was more elaborate than that of the Sumerians. Like cuneiform, Egyptian hieroglyphs include both ideograms and symbols used phonetically, so that learning to write was a long process, generally open only to men from relatively well-off families or whose families had high aspirations. Aside from scribes, the cities of the Nile Valley were home to artisans of all types, along with merchants and other tradespeople. The wealthier lived in spacious homes with attractive gardens, walls for privacy, and specialized rooms for eating, sleeping, and entertaining.

Most people in Egypt were farmers. The regularity of the climate meant that the agricultural year was routine and dependable, so farmers seldom suffered from foul weather and damaged crops. Farmers sowed wheat and nurtured a large variety of trees, vegetables, and vines. They also tended cattle and poultry, and when time permitted they hunted and fished in the marshlands of the Nile. Their houses were small, which suggests that they lived in small family groups, not as large extended families. Marriage was arranged by the couple's families and seems to have taken place at a young age. Once couples were married, having children, especially sons, was a high priority, as indicated by surviving charms to promote fertility and prayers for successful childbirth. In terms of property rights within marriages, women in Egypt owned and controlled property more than they did in Mesopotamia, and they were especially active in doing so when they were widows.

As in Mesopotamia, common people paid their obligations to their superiors in products and in labor, and many may not have been able to easily leave the land of their own free will. Their labor obligations may have included forced work on the pyramids and canals, although recent research suggests that most of the people who built the pyramids were paid for their work. Slavery did not become widespread until the New

• **Book of the Dead** A book that preserved Egyptians' ideas about death and the afterlife.

• **hieroglyphs** Egyptian letters, including both ideograms and phonetic signs, written with a brush on papyrus sheets or on walls.

□ Picturing the Past

Egyptian Home Life This grave painting depicts an intimate moment in the life of an aristocratic family, with the father and mother in the center and their children around them. Often found in Egyptian tombs are statuettes of cats (inset), family pets and the symbol of the goddess Bastet. (family: Gianni Dagli Orti/The Art Archive; cat: Courtesy of the Trustees of the British Museum)

ANALYZING THE IMAGE What evidence do you find in the painting that Egyptian artists based the size of figures on people's status in the household?

CONNECTIONS Based on your reading, how might an image of a poor family differ from this depiction?

Kingdom (1570–1075 B.C.E.; see page 48). Young men were drafted into the pharaoh's army, which served both as a fighting force and as a labor corps.

Migrations and Political Revivals

While Egypt flourished behind its bulwark of sand and sea, momentous changes were taking place around it that would leave their mark even on this rich, insular civilization. These changes involved vast movements of peoples throughout the Fertile Crescent, as various groups migrated and then accommodated themselves to local cultures.

One of these groups was made up of speakers of a Semitic language whom the Egyptians called Hyksos (HIK-sahs), which means "rulers of the uplands." Looking for good land, bands of Hyksos entered the eastern Nile Delta about 1800 B.C.E. (Map 2.2). They brought with them methods of making bronze and casting it into tools and weapons that had been developed elsewhere in the Mediterranean world. Bronze tools made farming more efficient because they were sharper and more durable than the copper, stone, or bone tools they replaced (see Chapter 1). The Hyksos also brought inventions that revolutionized Egyptian warfare, including bronze armor and weapons as well as horse-drawn chariots and the composite bow, made of multiple materials for greater strength. The migration of the Hyksos, combined with a series of famines and internal struggles for power, led Egypt to fragment politically in what later came to be known as the Second Intermediate Period. During this time the Egyptians adopted bronze technology and new forms of weaponry from the Hyksos, while the newcomers

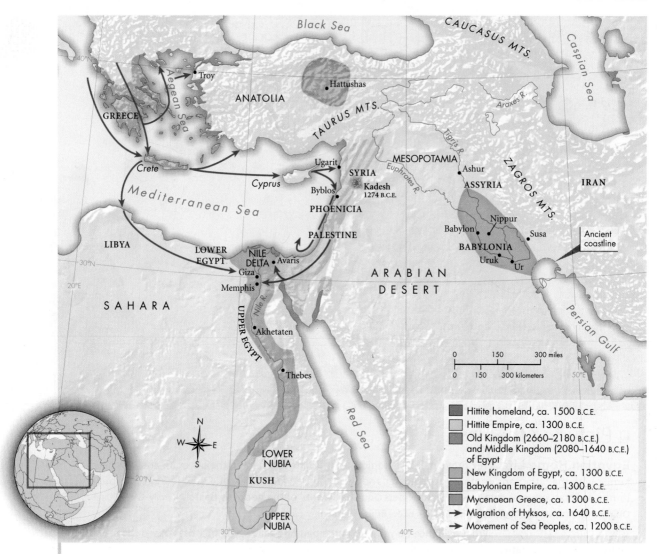

□ Mapping the Past

MAP 2.2 Empires and Migrations in the Eastern Mediterranean The rise and fall of empires in the eastern Mediterranean were shaped by internal developments, military conflicts, and the migration of peoples to new areas.

ANALYZING THE MAP At what point was the Egyptian Empire at its largest? The Hittite Empire? What were the other major powers in the eastern Mediterranean at this time?

CONNECTIONS What were the major effects of the migrations of the Hyksos? Of the Sea Peoples? What clues does the map provide as to why the Sea Peoples had a more powerful impact than did the Hyksos?

began to worship Egyptian deities and modeled their political structures on those of the Egyptians.

About 1570 B.C.E. a new dynasty of pharaohs seeking to unite Egypt sent armies against the Hyksos, pushing them out of the Nile Delta. These warrior-pharaohs thereby inaugurated what scholars refer to as the New Kingdom—a period characterized by enormous wealth and conscious imperialism. During this period the pharaohs expanded Egyptian power beyond the Nile Valley and created the first Egyptian empire, which they celebrated with monuments on a scale unparalleled since the pyramids of the Old Kingdom. Also during this period, probably for the first time, widespread slavery became a feature of Egyptian life. The pharaoh's armies returned home from conquests leading hordes of slaves who constituted a new labor force for imperial building projects.

One of the most extraordinary of this unusual line of pharaohs was Akhenaten (ah-keh-NAH-tuhn; r. 1367–1350 B.C.E.), who was more concerned with religion than with conquest. Nefertiti (nef-uhr-TEE-tee), his wife and queen, encouraged his religious bent. (See "Individuals in Society: Hatshepsut and Nefertiti," page 50.) Although the precise nature of Akhenaten's religious beliefs remain debatable, most historians agree that the royal pair were monotheists: they believed in only one god, Aton, a newer version of the sun-god. Akhenaten considered all the other deities of Egypt frauds and suppressed their worship. Yet this monotheism, imposed from above, failed to find a place among the people, and Akhenaten's religion died with him.

At about the same time that the Hyksos migrated into the Nile Delta, another group, the Hittites, established an empire in the eastern Mediterranean that would eventually also confront Egyptian power. The Hittites had long been settled in Anatolia (modern Turkey), and beginning about 1600 B.C.E. they expanded their empire east and south into Mesopotamia (see Map 2.2).

The Hittites were different from other peoples in the region in two significant ways. First, they spoke a language that scholars have identified as belonging to the **Indo-European language family**, a large family of languages that includes English, most of the languages of modern Europe, Greek, Latin, Persian, Hindi, Bengali, and Sanskrit, the sacred tongue of ancient India. (For more on Sanskrit, see page 69.) This suggests that their ancestors originated in central Asia, which historians of language see as the homeland of the Indo-European languages. (Language is one of the ways that what we now call ethnic groups are differentiated from one another, although this differentiation is also based on traditions, religion, politics, and other factors, and it is shaped by history.) The Hittites began to write only after they came into contact with the literate cultures of Mesopotamia.

Second, by the end of their period of expansion the Hittites used iron weapons to some degree. Techniques for smelting iron—which must be done at a much higher temperature than bronze — appear to have been invented first in Mesopotamia or Anatolia. (They were independently invented in other places as well, including India and West Africa; see "Global Trade: Iron," page 54.) Because iron weapons were very expensive, only the highest-ranking warriors could afford them, and most soldiers continued to use bronze swords and spear tips. Iron was the technology of the future, however, and by 1000 B.C.E. the much stronger iron weapons were the deciding factors in battles in southwest Asia and the eastern Mediterranean.

Around 1300 B.C.E. the Hittites and the Egyptians confronted each other, but decided to make an alliance, which eventually included the Babylonians as

Hittite Archer in a Chariot In this stylized stone carving made about 1000 B.C.E. in Anatolia (modern-day Turkey), a Hittite archer driven in a chariot shoots toward his foes, while a victim of an earlier shot is trampled beneath the horses' hooves. The arrows would probably have been tipped with iron, an important factor in Hittite military success. (Museum of Anatolian Civilizations, Ankara/Gianni Dagli Orti/The Art Archive)

well. The alliance facilitated the exchange of ideas throughout western Asia, and the Hittite kings and Egyptian pharaohs such as Ramses II (r. ca. 1290–1224 B.C.E.) used the peace to promote prosperity and concentrate their incomes. Peace was short-lived, however. Beginning about 1200 B.C.E. waves of foreign invaders, the most famous of whom the Egyptians called the Sea Peoples, broke the Hittite Empire apart and drove the Egyptians back to the Nile Valley for a long period of political fragmentation and conquest by outsiders that scholars of Egypt refer to as the Third Intermediate Period (ca. 1100–653 B.C.E.).

• **Indo-European language family** A large family of languages that includes English, most of the languages of modern Europe, Greek, Latin, Persian, Hindi, Bengali, and Sanskrit, the sacred tongue of ancient India.

Individuals in Society

Hatshepsut and Nefertiti

EGYPTIANS UNDERSTOOD THE PHARAOH TO BE the living embodiment of the god Horus, the source of law and morality, and the mediator between gods and humans. His connection with the divine stretched to members of his family, so that his siblings and children were also viewed as in some ways divine. Because of this, a pharaoh often took his sister or half-sister as one of his wives. This concentrated divine blood set the pharaonic family apart from other Egyptians (who did not marry close relatives) and allowed the pharaohs to imitate the gods, who in Egyptian mythology often married their siblings. A pharaoh chose one of his wives to be the "Great Royal Wife," or principal queen. Often this was a relative, though sometimes it was one of the foreign princesses who married pharaohs to establish political alliances.

The familial connection with the divine allowed a handful of women to rule in their own right in Egypt's long history. We know the names of four female pharaohs, of whom the most famous was Hatshepsut (r. 1479–1458 B.C.E.). She was the sister and wife of Thutmose II and, after he died, served as regent — as adviser and co-ruler — for her young stepson Thutmose III, who was the son of another woman. Hatshepsut sent trading expeditions and sponsored artists and architects, ushering in a period of artistic creativity and economic prosperity. She built one of the world's great buildings, an elaborate terraced temple at Deir el Bahri, which eventually served as her tomb. Hatshepsut's status as a powerful female ruler was difficult for Egyptians to conceptualize, and she is often depicted in male dress or with a false beard, thus looking more like the male rulers who were the norm. After her death, Thutmose III tried to destroy all evidence that she had ever ruled, smashing statues and scratching her name off inscriptions, perhaps because of personal animosity and perhaps because he wanted to erase the fact that a woman had once been pharaoh. Only within recent decades have historians and archaeologists begun to (literally) piece together her story.

Though female pharaohs were very rare, many royal women had power through their position as Great Royal Wives. The most famous was Nefertiti (ca. 1370–1330 B.C.E.), the wife of Akhenaten. Her name means "the perfect (or beautiful) woman has come," and inscriptions give her many other titles.

• **Granite head of Hatshepsut.** (Bildarchiv Preussischer Kulturbesitz/ Art Resource, NY)

Nefertiti used her position to spread the new religion of the sun-god Aton. Together she and Akhenaten built a new palace at Akhetaten, the present-day Amarna, away from the old centers of power. There they developed the cult of Aton to the exclusion of the traditional deities. Nearly the only literary survivor of their religious belief is the "Hymn to Aton," which declares Aton to be the only god. It describes Nefertiti as "the great royal consort whom he! Akhenaten! Loves, the mistress of the Two Lands! Upper and Lower Egypt!"

Nefertiti is often shown as being the same size as her husband, and in some inscriptions she is performing religious rituals that would normally have been carried out only by the pharaoh. The exact details of her power are hard to determine, however. An older theory held that her husband removed her from power, though there is also speculation that she may have ruled secretly in her own right after his death. Her tomb has long since disappeared, though some scholars believe that an unidentified mummy discovered in 2003 in Egypt's Valley of the Kings may be Nefertiti's.

QUESTIONS FOR ANALYSIS

1. Why might it have been difficult for Egyptians to accept a female ruler?

2. What opportunities do hereditary monarchies such as that of ancient Egypt provide for women? How does this fit with gender hierarchies in which men are understood as superior?

• **Painted limestone bust of Nefertiti.**
(Bildarchiv Preussischer Kulturbesitz/Art Resource, NY)

The political and military story of waves of migrations, battles, and the rise and fall of empires can mask striking continuities and exchanges. The basic social and cultural patterns of agriculture and polytheism survived the onslaughts. Disrupted peoples and newcomers shared practical concepts of shipbuilding and of metals and textile technology, as well as of methods of trade. Cuneiform tablets and papyrus scrolls testify to commercial exchanges and cultural accommodation, adoption, and adaptation.

New Political and Economic Powers

The decline of Egypt allowed new powers to emerge. South of Egypt along the Nile was a region called Nubia (NOO-bee-uh), which as early as 2000 B.C.E. served as a conduit of trade through which ivory, gold, ebony, and other products flowed north from sub-Saharan Africa. Small kingdoms arose in this area, with large buildings and rich tombs. As Egypt expanded during the New Kingdom, it took over northern Nubia, incorporating it into the growing Egyptian empire. The Nubians adopted many features of Egyptian culture, including Egyptian gods, the use of hieroglyphs, and the building of pyramids. Many Nubians became officials in the Egyptian bureaucracy and officers in the army, and there was significant intermarriage between the two groups.

With the contraction of the Egyptian empire, an independent kingdom, Kush, rose to power in Nubia, with its capital at Napata in what is now Sudan. The Kushites conquered southern Egypt, and in 727 B.C.E. the Kushite king Piye swept through the entire Nile Valley to the delta in the north. United once again, Egypt enjoyed a brief period of peace during which the Egyptian culture continued to influence that of its conquerors. In the seventh century B.C.E. invading Assyrians (see page 57) pushed the Kushites out of Egypt, and the Kushite rulers moved their capital farther up the Nile to Meroë, where they built hundreds of pyramids. Meroë became a center of iron production, which was becoming the material of choice for weapons. Iron products from Meroë were the best in the world, smelted using wood from the vast forests in the area.

Nubian Cylinder Sheath This small silver sheath made about 520 B.C.E., perhaps for a dagger, shows a winged goddess and the Egyptian god Amon-Ra. It was found in the tombs of the king of Kush and suggests ways that Egyptian artistic styles and religious ideas influenced cultures farther up the Nile. (Nubian, Napatan Period, reign of King Amani-natakelebte, 538–519 B.C.E. Findspot: Sudan, Nubia, Nuri, Pyramid 10. Gilded silver, colored paste inclusions. Height x diameter: 12 x 3.1 cm [4¾ x 1¼ in.]. Museum of Fine Arts, Boston. Harvard University–Museum of Fine Arts Expedition, 20.275)

They were traded to much of Africa and across the Red Sea and the Indian Ocean to India. Gold and cotton textiles also provided wealth to the Kushite kingdom, which in the third century B.C.E. developed its own alphabet. It was simpler than the Egyptian alphabet, but Meroitic script has not yet been deciphered.

While Kush expanded in the southern Nile Valley, another group rose to prominence along the Mediterranean. These were the **Phoenicians** (fih-NEE-shuhnz), a Semitic-speaking people who had long inhabited several cities along the coast of modern Lebanon and who took to the sea to become outstanding explorers and merchants. Phoenician culture was urban, based on the prosperous commercial city-states of Tyre, Sidon, and Byblos, each ruled by a separate king and council of nobles. Especially from about 1100 to 700 B.C.E., the Phoenicians played a predominant role in international trade. Their most valued products were purple and blue textiles, from which originated their Greek name, Phoenicians, meaning "Purple People." They also worked metals, which they shipped processed or as ore, and made and traded glass products. Phoenician ships often carried hundreds of jars of wine, and the Phoenicians introduced grape-growing to new regions around the Mediterranean, dramatically increasing the wine available for consumption and trade. They imported rare goods and materials, including hunting dogs, gold,

---

• **Phoenicians** People of the prosperous city-states in what is now Lebanon who dominated trade throughout the Mediterranean and spread the letter alphabet.

Phoenician Settlements in the Mediterranean

and ivory, from Persia in the east and from their neighbors to the south.

The variety and quality of the Phoenicians' trade goods generally made them welcome visitors. They established colonies and trading posts throughout the Mediterranean and as far west as the Atlantic coast of modern-day Portugal. In the ninth century B.C.E. they founded the city of Carthage in modern-day Tunisia, a city that would one day struggle with Rome for domination of the western Mediterranean (see pages 150–151). The Phoenicians' voyages brought them into contact with the Greeks, to whom they introduced many as-

pects of the older and more urbanized cultures of Mesopotamia and Egypt.

The Phoenicians' overwhelming cultural legacy was the spread of a completely phonetic system of writing—that is, an alphabet (see Figure 2.2). Cuneiform and hieroglyphics had both developed signs that were used to represent sounds, but these were always used with a much larger number of ideograms. Sometime around 1800 B.C.E. Semitic workers in the Sinai peninsula, which was under Egyptian control, began to use only phonetic signs to write, with each sign designating one sound. This system vastly simplified writing and reading and spread among common people as a practical way to record things and communicate. Egyptian scribes and officials stayed with hieroglyphics, but the Phoenicians adopted the simpler system for their own Semitic language and spread it around the Mediterranean. The Greeks modified this alphabet and then used it to write their own language, and the Romans later based their alphabet—the script we use to write English today—on Greek. Alphabets based on the Phoenician alphabet were also created in the Persian Empire and formed the basis of Hebrew, Arabic, and various alphabets of south and central Asia. The system invented by ordinary people and spread by Phoenician merchants is the origin of nearly every phonetic alphabet in use today.

HIEROGLYPHIC	REPRESENTS	UGARITIC	PHOENICIAN	GREEK	ROMAN
	Throw stick			Γ	G
	Man with raised arms			Ε	E
	Basket with handle			K	K
	Water			M	M
	Snake			N	N
	Eye			O	O
	Mouth			Π	P
	Head			P	R
	Pool with lotus flowers			Σ	S
	House			B	B
	Ox-head			A	A

FIGURE 2.2 Origins of the Alphabet List of hieroglyphic, Ugaritic, Phoenician, Greek, and Roman sign forms. (Source: A. B. Knapp, *The History and Culture of Ancient Western Asia and Egypt.* © 1988 Wadsworth, a division of Cengage Learning, Inc. Reproduced by permission, www.cengage.com/permissions.)

The Hebrews

☐ How did the Hebrews create an enduring
written religious tradition, and what was
its significance?

Another people took advantage of Egypt's collapse to
found an independent state, and their legacy has been
even more far-reaching than that of the Phoenicians.
For several centuries, a Semitic people known as the
Hebrews or the Israelites controlled a small state on
the western end of the Fertile Crescent. Politically unimportant when compared with the Egyptian or Babylonian empires, the Hebrews created a new form of
religious belief, a monotheism based on the worship
of an all-powerful god they called **Yahweh** (YAH-way,
anglicized as Jehovah). They began to write down their
religious ideas, traditions, laws, advice literature, prayers, hymns, history, and prophecies in a series of books.
These were gathered together to form the Hebrew
Bible (which Christians later adopted and termed the
"Old Testament" to parallel specific Christian writings
termed the "New Testament"). These writings are what
came to define the Hebrews as a people, and they are
the most important written record that exists from this
period. The reverence for these written texts was passed
down from Judaism — the religion of the Hebrews —
to the other Western monotheistic religions that grew
from it, Christianity and Islam.

The Hebrew State

Most of the information about the Hebrews comes
from the Bible, which, like all ancient documents, must
be used with care as a historical source. But archaeological evidence supports many of its details, and because it records a living religious tradition, extensive
textual and physical research into everything it records continues.

The Hebrews were nomadic pastoralists who probably migrated into the Nile Delta from the east seeking
good land for their herds of sheep and goats. There the
Egyptians enslaved them, but, according to the Bible,
a charismatic leader named Moses led them out of
Egypt, and in the thirteenth century B.C.E. they settled
in Palestine. There they encountered a variety of other
peoples, whom they both learned from and fought.
They slowly adopted agriculture and, not surprisingly,
at times worshipped the agricultural gods of their neighbors, including Baal, an ancient Semitic fertility god
represented as a golden calf. In this they followed the
common historical pattern of newcomers by adapting
themselves to the culture of an older, well-established
people.

The greatest danger to the Hebrews came from
a group known as the Philistines (FIH-luh-steenz),
whose superior technology and military organization at
first made them invincible. Sometime around 1020 B.C.E.
the Hebrew leader Saul, while keeping the Philistines
at bay, established a monarchy over the Hebrew tribes.
After Saul died fighting the Philistines, David of Beth-
lehem continued Saul's work and captured the city of
Jerusalem, which he enlarged and made the religious
center of the realm. His work in consolidating the monarchy and enlarging the kingdom paved the way for
his son Solomon. In the tenth century B.C.E. Solomon
launched a building program
that included cities, palaces,
fortresses, and roads. The
most symbolic of these projects was the Temple of Jerusalem, which became the home
of the Ark of the Covenant, the
chest that contained the holiest Hebrew religious articles.
The Temple of Jerusalem was
intended to be the religious
heart of the kingdom, a symbol of Hebrew unity and of
Yahweh's approval of the
state built by Saul, David, and
Solomon.

The Hebrew Exodus and State, ca. 1250–800 B.C.E.

Mediterranean
Sea

Samaria

Jerusalem

Dead
Sea

EGYPT

SINAI

Gulf of Suez

Possible
location
of Mt. Sinai

➤ Possible route of the Exodus,
ca. 1250 B.C.E.
☐ Solomon's kingdom, ca. 950 B.C.E.
■ Israel, ca. 800 B.C.E.
■ Judah, ca. 800 B.C.E.

The unified Hebrew state
did not last long. Upon Solomon's death his kingdom
broke into political halves. The
northern part became Israel,
with its capital at Samaria, and
the southern half was Judah,
with Jerusalem remaining its
center. War broke out between
the northern and southern halves, and the Assyrians
wiped out the northern kingdom of Israel in 720 B.C.E.
Judah survived numerous invasions until the Babylonians crushed it in 587 B.C.E. The survivors were sent
into exile in Babylonia, a period commonly known as
the Babylonian Captivity. In 538 B.C.E. the Persian king
Cyrus the Great conquered the Babylonians and permitted some forty thousand exiles to return to Jerusalem (see page 59 and "Viewpoints: Rulers and Divine
Favor: Cyrus the Great in the Cyrus Cylinder and Hebrew Scripture," page 60). They rebuilt the temple,
although politically the area was simply part of the Persian Empire.

• **Yahweh** All-powerful god of the Hebrew people and the basis for the
enduring religious traditions of Judaism.

Global Trade

Iron has shaped world history more than any other metal, even more than gold and silver. In its pure state iron is soft, but adding small amounts of carbon and various minerals, particularly at very high temperatures, transforms it into a material with great structural strength. Tools and weapons made of iron dramatically shaped interactions between peoples in the ancient world, and machines made of iron and steel literally created the modern world.

Human use of iron began during the Paleolithic era, when people living in what is now Egypt used small pieces of hematite, a type of iron oxide, as part of their tools, along with stone, bone, and wood. Beginning around 4000 B.C.E. people in several parts of the world began to pick up iron-nickel meteorites and pound them into shapes. Such meteorites were rare, and the objects produced from them were luxury goods, not things for everyday use. Jewelry, weapons, and occasionally tools from meteoric iron have also been found in China, Africa, and North and South America. These were traded very long distances, including thousands of miles around the Arctic, where indigenous peoples traded sharpened pieces from a gigantic iron meteorite that fell in Greenland for use as harpoon tips and knife blades.

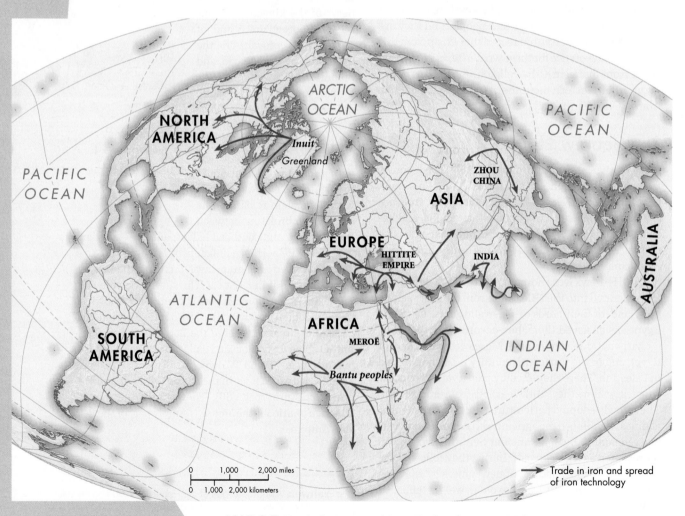

MAP 2.3 Trade in Iron and Iron Technology, to 500 B.C.E.

This Celtic iron helmet from the first century B.C.E. fit snugly over a warrior's head, with an attached iron flap protecting the forehead and cheekbones, and a ring that would have connected a leather chin strap. Found in France, it provides evidence of the spread of iron technology, as smelting techniques as well as iron products were traded over long distances. (Courtesy, Römisch-Germanisches-Zentralmuseum, Mainz)

Iron is the most common element in the earth, but most iron on or near the earth's surface occurs in the form of ore, which must be smelted to extract the metal. This is also true of copper and tin, but these can be smelted at much lower temperatures than iron, so they were the first metals to be produced to any great extent, and were usually mixed together to form bronze. As artisans perfected bronze metalworking techniques, they also experimented with iron. They developed a long and difficult process to smelt iron, using burning charcoal and a bellows (which raised the temperature further) to extract the iron from the ore. This was done in an enclosed furnace, and the process was repeated a number of times as the ore was transformed into wrought iron, which could be formed into shapes.

Exactly where and when the first smelted iron was produced is a matter of debate—many places would like to have this honor—but it was somewhere in Mesopotamia or Anatolia (modern-day Turkey) and occurred perhaps as early as 2500 B.C.E. The Hittites became a powerful empire in the eastern Mediterranean in part through their skills in making and using iron weaponry, and by 1200 B.C.E. or so iron objects were traded throughout the Mediterranean and beyond. Knowledge of smelting traveled as well. By 1700 B.C.E. artisans in northern India were making and trading iron implements. By 1200 B.C.E. iron was being produced and sold in southern India, though scholars debate whether smelting was discovered independently there or learned through contact with iron-making cultures to the north. Iron objects were traded from Anatolia north into Greece, central Europe, and western Asia, and by 500 B.C.E. knowledge of smelting had traveled these routes as well.

Smelting was discovered independently in what is now Nigeria in western Africa about 1500 B.C.E. by a group of people who spoke Bantu languages. They carried iron hoes, axes, shovels, and weapons, and the knowledge of how to make them, as they migrated south and east over many centuries, which gave them a distinct advantage over foraging peoples. In East Africa, the Kushite people learned the advantages of iron weaponry when the iron-using Assyrians drove them out of Egypt, and they then established a major center of iron production at Meroë and traded down the African coast and across the sea to India.

Ironworkers continued to experiment and improve their products. The Chinese probably learned smelting from central Asian steppe peoples, but in about 500 B.C.E. artisans in China developed techniques of making cast iron using molds, through which implements could be made much more efficiently. Somewhere in the Near East ironworkers discovered that if the relatively brittle wrought iron objects were placed on a bed of burning charcoal and then cooled quickly, the outer layer would form into a layer of a much harder material, steel. Goods made of cast iron were usually traded locally because they were heavy, but fine sword and knife blades of steel traveled long distances, and the knowledge of how to make them followed.

The Jewish Religion

During and especially after the Babylonian Captivity, the most important Hebrew texts of history, law, and ethics were edited and brought together in the Torah, the first five books of the Hebrew Bible. The exiles redefined their beliefs and practices, thereby establishing what they believed to be the law of Yahweh. Those who lived by these precepts came to be called Jews and their religion Judaism.

Fundamental to an understanding of the Jewish religion is the concept of the Covenant, a formal agreement between Yahweh and the Hebrew people. According to the Bible, Yahweh appeared to Moses while he was leading the Hebrews out of Egypt and made the Covenant with the Hebrews: if they worshipped Yahweh as their only god, he would consider them his chosen people and protect them from their enemies. That worship was embodied in a series of rules of behavior, the Ten Commandments, which Yahweh gave to Moses; these required certain kinds of religious observances and forbade the Hebrews to steal, kill, lie, or commit adultery. From the Ten Commandments a complex system of rules of conduct was created and later written down as Hebrew law.

The monotheistic Jewish religion contrasted sharply with the polytheism of most peoples of the surrounding area. Mesopotamian and Egyptian deities — and later Greek and Roman deities — were powerful and often immortal, but they were otherwise just like humans, with good and bad personal qualities. They demanded ceremonies in their honor but were relatively unconcerned with how people behaved toward one another. The Hebrews, however, could please their god only by living up to high moral standards as well as by worshipping him. In polytheistic systems, people could easily add new gods or goddesses to the group of deities they honored, and they often did so when they moved to a new area or learned about a god with particularly appealing qualities. Yahweh, by contrast, demanded that the Hebrews worship him alone. The first of the Ten Commandments expresses this demand: "I am the Lord your God . . . you shall have no other gods besides me" (Exodus 20:23). Like Mesopotamian deities, Yahweh punished people, but the Hebrews also believed he would protect them all, not simply kings and powerful priests, and make them prosper if they obeyed his commandments. A hymn recorded in the Hebrew Bible's book of Psalms captures this idea:

> Blessed is every one who fears the Lord, who walks
>   in his ways!
> You shall eat the fruit of the labor of your hands;
> you shall be happy, and it shall be well with you.
> Your wife will be like a fruitful vine without your
>   house;
> your children will be like olive shoots around your
>   table.
> Lo, thus shall the man be blessed who fears the Lord.
>   (Psalms 128:1–4)

Because Yahweh is a single god, not surrounded by lesser gods and goddesses, there is no female divinity in Judaism. Occasionally, however, aspects of God are described in feminine terms, such as Sophia, the wisdom of God. Religious leaders were important in Judaism, but not as important as the written texts they interpreted; these texts came to be regarded as the word of Yahweh and thus had status that other writings did not.

The Family and Jewish Life

Although the Hebrews originally were nomadic, they adopted settled agriculture in Palestine, and some lived in cities. These shifts affected more than just how people fed themselves. Communal use of land gave way to family or private ownership, and tribal identity was replaced by loyalty to a state and then to the traditions of Judaism.

Marriage and the family were fundamentally important in Jewish life; celibacy was frowned upon, and almost all major Jewish thinkers and priests were married. As in Mesopotamia and Egypt, marriage was a family matter, too important to be left solely to the

The Golden Calf
According to the Bible, Moses descended from Mount Sinai, where he had received the Ten Commandments, to find the Hebrews worshipping a golden calf, which was against Yahweh's laws. In July 1990 an American archaeological team found this model of a gilded calf inside a pot. The figurine, which dates to about 1550 B.C.E., is strong evidence for the existence of the cult represented by the calf in Palestine. (Harvard Semitic Museum, Ashkelon Excavations)

whims of young people. Although sexual relations were seen as a source of impurity that needed to be cleansed with specific rituals, sex itself was viewed as part of Yahweh's creation and the bearing of children as in some ways a religious function. Sons were especially desired because they maintained the family bloodline while keeping ancestral property in the family. A first-born son became the head of the household upon his father's death. Mothers oversaw the early education of the children, but as boys grew older, their fathers provided more of their education.

The development of urban life among Jews created new economic opportunities, especially in crafts and trade. People specialized in certain occupations, such as milling flour, baking bread, making pottery, weaving, and carpentry, but the most important task for observant Jews was studying religious texts, especially after the return from Babylon. Until the twentieth century this activity was limited to men. For their part, women were obliged to provide for men's physical needs while they were studying. This meant that Jewish women were often more active economically than their contemporaries of other religions, trading goods the household produced.

The Assyrians and Persians

☐ What were the strengths of and the major differences between the Assyrian and Persian Empires?

Small kingdoms like those of the Phoenicians and the Jews could exist only in the absence of a major power. In the ninth century B.C.E. one major power arose in the form of the Assyrians, who starting in northern Mesopotamia created an empire through often brutal military conquest. And from a base in what is now southern Iran, the Persians established an even larger empire, developing effective institutions of government, building roads, and allowing a variety of customs, religions, and traditions to flourish.

Assyria, the Military Monarchy

Assyria rose at the beginning of the ninth century B.C.E. and came to dominate northern Mesopotamia from its chief capital at Nineveh on the Tigris River. The Assyrians were a Semitic people heavily influenced by the Babylonian culture to the south. They were also one of the most warlike people in history, carving out an empire that stretched from east and north of the Tigris River to central Egypt.

Those who stood up to Assyrian might were often systematically tortured and slaughtered, but Assyria's success was also due to sophisticated, farsighted, and effective military tactics, technical skills, and organization. For example, the Assyrians developed a wide variety of siege machinery and techniques, including excavations to undermine city walls and battering rams to knock down walls and gates. Never before in the Near East had anyone applied such technical knowledge to warfare. The Assyrians even invented the concept of a corps of engineers who bridged rivers with pontoons or provided soldiers with inflatable skins for swimming. The Assyrians also knew how to coordinate their efforts both in open battle and in siege warfare. They divided their armies into different organizational units of infantry who fought with iron swords and spears, others who fought with slings or bows and arrows, and a third group who used chariots.

Not only did the Assyrians know how to win battles, but they also knew how to take advantage of their victories. As early as the eighth century B.C.E. the Assyrian kings began to organize their conquered territories into an empire. The lands closest to Assyria became provinces governed directly by Assyrian officials. In more distant parts of the empire, including Israel, the Phoenician cities, and Egypt, Assyrian kings chose local rulers whom they favored and required them to pay tribute.

Assyrians Besiege a City In this Assyrian carving from the ninth century B.C.E., archers shoot toward a tower, foot soldiers attempt to open a chained gate, and engineers undermine the foundations of the wall. Unfortunate defenders fall toward their fate, while at the very top, a woman from the besieged city raises her arms in horror at the scene. (British Museum. Photo © Michael Holford)

In the seventh century B.C.E. Assyrian power seemed firmly established. Yet the downfall of Assyria was swift and complete. Babylon won its independence in 626 B.C.E. and joined forces with a new group, the Medes, an Indo-European-speaking people from Persia. Together the Babylonians and the Medes destroyed the Assyrian Empire in 612 B.C.E., paving the way for the rise of the Persians. The Hebrew prophet Nahum spoke for many when he asked: "Nineveh is laid waste: who will bemoan her?" (Nahum 3:7). Their cities destroyed and their power shattered, the Assyrians seemed to disappear from history.

> **"Nineveh is laid waste: who will bemoan her?"**
>
> — NAHUM

Archaeology brought the Assyrians out of obscurity, however. In the nineteenth century archaeologists unearthed huge sculpted figures of winged bulls, human-headed lions, and sphinxes, along with cuneiform tablets that recounted everything from military campaigns to business relationships. Archaeologists also discovered reliefs that Assyrian artists carved for the kings' palaces. These showed scenes of war as a series of episodes that progressed from the time the army marched out until the enemy was conquered. The reliefs created a visual narrative of events, a form still favored by comic-book artists and the authors of graphic novels.

The Rise and Expansion of the Persian Empire

As we have seen, Assyria rose to power from a base in the Tigris and Euphrates River Valleys of Mesopotamia, which had been home to many earlier empires. The Assyrians were defeated by a coalition that included a Mesopotamian power—Babylon—but also a people with a base of power in a part of the world that had not been the site of earlier urbanized states: Persia (modern-day Iran), a stark land of towering mountains and flaming deserts with a broad central plateau in the heart of the country (Map 2.4).

Iran's geographical position and topography explain its traditional role as the highway between western and eastern Asia. Nomadic peoples migrating south from the broad steppes (grasslands) of Russia and Central Asia have streamed into Iran throughout much of history. (For an in-depth discussion of these groups, see Chapter 12.) Confronting the uncrossable salt deserts, most have turned either westward or eastward, moving on until they reached the advanced and wealthy urban centers of Mesopotamia and India. Cities did emerge along these routes, however, and Iran became the area where nomads met urban dwellers.

Among these nomads were various Indo-European-speaking peoples who migrated into this area about 1000 B.C.E. with their flocks and herds. They were also

MAP 2.4 The Assyrian and Persian Empires, ca. 1000–500 B.C.E. The Assyrian Empire at its height in ca. 650 B.C.E. included almost all of the old centers of power in the ancient Near East. By 513 B.C.E., however, the Persian Empire not only included more of that area but also extended as far east as western India.

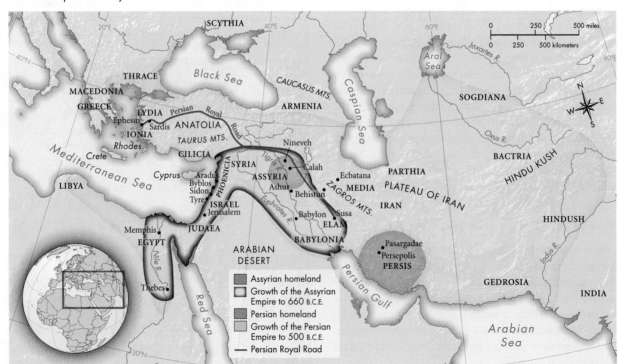

horse breeders, and the horse gave them a decisive military advantage over those who already lived in the area. One of the Indo-European groups was the Medes, who settled in northern Iran and built their capital city at Ecbatana, the modern Hamadan. With the rise of the Medes, marked by their union under one king and their defeat of the Assyrian Empire with the help of the Babylonians, the balance of power in western Asia shifted east of Mesopotamia for the first time.

The Persians were another Indo-European group, and they settled in southern Iran. In 550 B.C.E. Cyrus the Great (r. 559–530 B.C.E.), king of the Persians and one of the most remarkable statesmen of antiquity, conquered the Medes. (See "Viewpoints: Rulers and Divine Favor: Cyrus the Great in the Cyrus Cylinder and Hebrew Scripture," page 60.) The conquest resulted not in slavery and slaughter but in the union of the two peoples. Having united Iran, Cyrus set out to achieve two goals. First, he wanted to win control of the west and thus of the terminal ports of the great trade routes that crossed Iran and Anatolia (modern western Turkey). Second, he strove to secure eastern Iran from the threats of nomadic invasions. In a series of major campaigns Cyrus achieved both goals. He conquered the various kingdoms of the Tigris and Euphrates Valleys and swept into Anatolia, easily overthrowing the young kingdom of Lydia. His generals subdued the Greek cities along the coast of Anatolia and the Phoenician cities south of these, thus gaining him flourishing ports on the Mediterranean. Marching to the far eastern corners of Iran from Lydia, Cyrus conquered the regions of Parthia and Bactria in central Asia, though he ultimately died on the battlefield there.

With these victories Cyrus demonstrated to the world his benevolence as well as his military might. He spared the life of the conquered king of Lydia, Croesus, who came to be Cyrus's friend and adviser. He also allowed the Greeks to live according to their customs, making possible the spread of Greek culture farther east. Cyrus's humanity likewise extended to the Jews, whom he allowed to return from Babylon to Jerusalem, where he paid for the rebuilding of their temple.

Cyrus's successors continued the Persian conquests, creating the largest empire the world had yet seen (see Map 2.4). In 525 B.C.E. his son Cambyses (r. 530–522 B.C.E.) subdued the Egyptians and the Nubians. Upon Cambyses's death (the circumstances of which are disputed), Darius (r. 521–486 B.C.E.) took over the throne and conquered Scythia in central Asia, along with much of Thrace and Macedonia, areas north of the Aegean Sea. By 510 the Persians also ruled the western coast of Anatolia and many of the islands of the Aegean. Thus, within forty years the Persians had transformed themselves from a subject people to the rulers of a vast empire that included all of the oldest kingdoms and peoples of the region, as well as many outly-

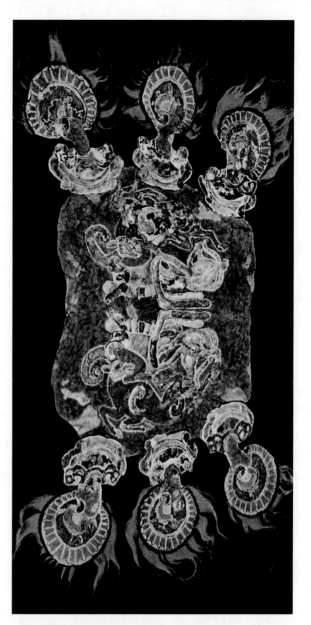

Persian Saddle-Cloth This elaborately painted piece of leather, dating from the fourth or third century B.C.E., shows running goats with huge curved horns. The fact that it survived suggests that it was not actually used, but served a ceremonial function. (© The State Hermitage Museum, St. Petersburg. Photo by Vladimir Terebenin)

ing areas (see Map 2.4) Unsurprisingly, Darius began to call himself King of Kings. Although invasions of Greece by Darius and his son Xerxes were unsuccessful, the Persian Empire lasted another two hundred years, until it became part of the empire of Alexander the Great (see page 131).

The Persians also knew how to preserve the peace they had won on the battlefield. Unlike the Assyrians, they did not resort to slaughter and torture to maintain order, preferring diplomacy instead. They created an efficient administrative system to govern the empire based in their newly built capital city of Persepolis,

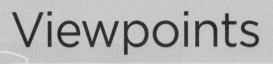

Viewpoints

Rulers and Divine Favor: Cyrus the Great in the Cyrus Cylinder and Hebrew Scripture

• *In Mesopotamia — and elsewhere in the ancient world — individuals who established large empires through conquest often subsequently proclaimed that their triumph was the result of divine favor, and they honored the gods of the regions they conquered. King Cyrus the Great of Persia appears to have followed this tradition. A text written in cuneiform on a sixth-century B.C.E. Babylonian clay cylinder presents Cyrus describing the way in which the main Babylonian god Marduk selected him to conquer Babylon and restore proper government and worship. Cyrus is also portrayed as divinely chosen in the book of Isaiah in Hebrew Scripture, probably written sometime in the late sixth century B.C.E. after Cyrus allowed the Jews to return to Jerusalem. Because Cyrus was not a follower of the Jewish God, however, the issue of divine favor was more complicated.*

The Cyrus Cylinder

"I am Cyrus, king of the universe, the great king, the powerful king, king of Babylon, king of Sumer and Akkad, king of the four quarters of the world. . . .

When I went as harbinger of peace i[nt]o Babylon I founded my sovereign residence within the palace amid celebration and rejoicing. Marduk, the great lord, bestowed on me as my destiny the great magnanimity of one who loves Babylon, and I every day sought him out in awe. My vast troops marched peaceably in Babylon, and the whole of [Sumer] and Akkad had nothing to fear. I sought the welfare of the city of Babylon and all its sanctuaries. As for the population of Babylon, . . . [w]ho as if without div[ine intention] had endured a yoke not decreed for them, I soothed their weariness, I freed them from their bond. . . . Marduk, the great lord, rejoiced at [my good] deeds, and he pronounced a sweet blessing over me, Cyrus, the king who fears him, and over Cambyses, the son [my]

issue, [and over] all my troops, that we might proceed further at his exalted command. "

The Book of Isaiah, Chapter 45

"Thus said the Lord to Cyrus, His anointed one—whose right hand He has grasped, Treading down nations before him, Ungirding the loins of kings, Opening doors before him, and letting no gate stay shut: I will march before you, and level the hills that loom up; I will shatter doors of bronze and cut down iron bars. I will give you treasures concealed in the dark and secret hoards—So that you may know that it is I the LORD, the God of Israel, who call you by name. For the sake of My servant Jacob, Israel My chosen one, I call you by name, I hail you by title, though you have not known Me. I am the LORD, and there is none else; beside Me, there is no God. I engird you, though you have not known Me. . . .

It was I who roused him [that is, Cyrus] for victory, and who level all roads for him. He shall rebuild My city, and let My exiled people go, without price and without payment—said the LORD of hosts. "

Sources: Cylinder inscription translation by Irving Finkel, curator of Cuneiform Collections at the British Museum, www.britishmuseum.org. Used by permission of The British Museum; "The Book of Isaiah" in *Tanakh: A New Translation of The Holy Scriptures According to the Traditional Hebrew Text.* Copyright © 1985 by The Jewish Publication Society. Used by permission of the Jewish Publication Society.

QUESTIONS FOR ANALYSIS

1. How would you compare the portrayal of Cyrus in the two texts?

2. The Babylonians were polytheistic, and the Hebrews were monotheistic. How does this shape the way divine actions and favor are portrayed in the texts?

3. Both of these texts have been very influential in establishing the largely positive historical view of Cyrus. What limitations might there be in using these as historical sources?

near modern Schiras, Iran. Under Darius, they divided the empire into districts and appointed either Persian or local nobles as administrators called satraps to head each one. The satrap controlled local government, collected taxes, heard legal cases, and maintained order. He was assisted by a council and also by officials and army leaders sent from Persepolis who made sure that he knew the will of the king and that the king knew what was going on in the provinces. This system was in line with the Persians' usual practice of respecting their subjects and allowing them to practice their native customs and religions, giving the Near East both political unity and cultural diversity. It also lessened opposition to Persian rule by making local elites part of the system of government, although sometimes satraps used their authority to build up independent power.

• **Zoroastrianism** The religion based on the teachings of Zoroaster, who emphasized the individual's responsibility to choose between good and evil.

Throughout the Persian Empire communication and trade were eased by a sophisticated system of roads. The main highway, the famous Royal Road, spanned some 1,677 miles (see Map 2.4). Other roads branched out from this main route to link all parts of the empire from the coast of Asia Minor to the valley of the Indus River. These highways meant that the king was usually in close touch with officials and subjects, and they simplified the defense of the empire by making it easier to move Persian armies. The roads also aided the flow of trade, which Persian rulers further encouraged by building canals, including one that linked the Red Sea and the Nile.

The Persians made significant contributions to art and culture. In art they transformed the Assyrian tradition of realistic monumental sculpture from one that celebrated gory details of slaughter to one that showed both the Persians and their subjects as dignified. Because it depicted non-Persians realistically, Persian art is an excellent source of information about the weapons, tools, clothing, and even hairstyles of many peoples of the area.

The Religion of Zoroaster

Originally Persian religion was polytheistic, with many deities under a chief god Ahuramazda (ah-HOOR-uh-MAZ-duh), the creator of all living creatures. Around 600 B.C.E., however, the alternative views of one prophet, Zoroaster (zo-roh-ASS-tuhr), became more prominent. A thinker and preacher whose birth and death dates are uncertain, Zoroaster is regarded as the author of key religious texts, later collected as a collection of sacred texts called the *Avesta*. He introduced new spiritual concepts to the Persian people, stressing devotion to Ahuramazda alone and emphasizing the individual's responsibility to choose between the forces of creation, truth, and order and those of nothingness, chaos, falsehood, and disorder. He taught that people possessed the free will to decide between these and that they must

rely on their own consciences to guide them through an active life in which they focused on "good thoughts, good words, and good deeds." Their decisions were crucial, Zoroaster warned, for there would come a time of reckoning. At the end of time the forces of order would win, and the victorious Ahuramazda, like the Egyptian god Osiris, would preside over a last judgment to determine each person's eternal fate.

Scholars — and contemporary Zoroastrians — debate whether Zoroaster saw the forces of disorder as a malevolent deity named Angra Mainyu who was co-eternal with and independent from Ahuramazda, or whether he was simply using this term to mean "evil thoughts" or "a destructive spirit." Forms of **Zoroastrianism** have followed each of these lines of understanding. Most Zoroastrians believed that the Ahuramazda and the Angra Mainyu were independent forces representing good and evil, respectively, who were locked together in a cosmic battle for the human race, a religious conceptualization that scholars call dualism. Others had a more monotheistic interpretation and saw Ahuramazda as the only uncreated god.

King Darius became a follower of Zoroaster's teachings and in many inscriptions proclaimed that he was divinely chosen by Ahuramazda. Continuing the common Persian pattern of toleration, Darius did not impose his religious beliefs on others, but under the protection of the Persian kings, Zoroastrianism won converts throughout Iran and the rest of the Persian Empire and spread into central China. It became the official religion of the later Persian Empire ruled by the Sassanid dynasty, and much later Zoroastrians migrated to western India, where they became known as Parsis and still live today. The religion survived the fall of the Persian Empire to influence Judaism, Christianity, Islam, and Buddhism, and its key tenets are shared by many religions: good behavior in the world, even though it might be unrecognized during one's life, will be amply rewarded in the hereafter. Evil, no matter how powerful in life, will be punished after death.

CONNECTIONS

"History is written by the victors," goes a common saying often incorrectly attributed to Winston Churchill. This is not always true; people who have been vanquished in wars or devastated by oppression have certainly made their stories known. But in other ways it is always true, for writing created records and therefore was the origin of what many people understand as history. Writing was invented to serve the needs of people who lived close to one another in cities and states, and almost everyone who could write lived in states. Because most history, including this book, concentrates on areas with states, the next two chapters examine the states that were developing in India and China during the period discussed in this chapter. In Chapter 5 we pick up on developments in the Mediterranean that link to those in Mesopotamia, Egypt, and Persia discussed in this chapter.

It is important to remember that, as was the spread of agriculture, the growth of the state was a slow process. States became the most powerful and most densely populated forms of human society, and today almost everyone on the planet is at least hypothetically a citizen of a state (or sometimes of more than one, if he or she has dual citizenship). Just three hundred years ago, however, only about a third of the world was governed by states; in the rest of the world, people lived in bands of foragers, villages led by kin leaders, family groups of pastoralists, chiefdoms, confederations of tribes, or other forms of social organization. In 500 B.C.E. perhaps only a little over 5 percent of the world's population lived in states. In his *Histories,* Herodotus pays primary attention to the Persians and the Greeks, both of whom had writing and states, but he also discusses many peoples who had neither. In their attempts to provide a balanced account of all the world's peoples, historians today are also looking beyond written sources. Those sources invariably present only part of the story, as Winston Churchill — a historian as well as a political leader — noted in something he actually *did* say: "History will bear me out, particularly as I shall write that history myself."

☐ CHAPTER REVIEW

> ### KEY TERMS
>
> ziggurat (p. 38)
> cuneiform (p. 39)
> epic poems (p. 41)
> pharaoh (p. 44)
> polytheism (p. 45)
> *Book of the Dead*
>   (p. 46)
> hieroglyphs (p. 46)
>
> Indo-European
>   language family
>   (p. 49)
> Phoenicians (p. 51)
> Yahweh (p. 53)
> Zoroastrianism
>   (p. 61)

☐ **How does writing shape what we can know about the past, and how did writing develop to meet the needs of cities and states? (p. 34)**

Beginning about five thousand years ago, people in some parts of the world developed a new technology, writing. Written sources provide a wider range of information about past societies than is available from physical evidence alone, which means that we know much more about the societies that left written records than about those that did not. Writing was developed to meet the needs of the more complex urban societies that are often referred to as civilizations and particularly to meet the needs of the state, a new structure of governance distinct from tribes and kinship groups. In states, a small share of the population is able to coerce resources out of everyone else, and leaders gain and maintain power through organized violence, bureaucracies, systems of taxation, and written laws. These laws generally created more elaborate social and gender hierarchies.

☐ **How did the people of Mesopotamia form the world's first states, and how did their institutions spread? (p. 37)**

States first developed in Mesopotamia, the land between the Euphrates and Tigris Rivers. Starting in the southern part of Mesopotamia known as Sumeria, sustained agriculture reliant on irrigation resulted in larger populations, a division of labor, and the growth of cities. Priests and rulers invented ways to control and organize these complex societies, including armies, taxation systems, and cuneiform writing. Conquerors from the north unified Mesopotamian city-states into larger empires and spread Mesopotamian culture over a large area. The most significant of these was the Babylonian empire, which under Hammurabi developed a written code of law and expanded trade connections.

☐ **How did geography, leadership, and religion enable the Egyptians to build and maintain a cohesive, prosperous society, and how did migrations and invasions shape Egypt's fate? (p. 44)**

During the third millennium B.C.E., a period known as the Old Kingdom, Egypt grew into a cohesive state under a single ruler in the valley of the Nile, which provided rich farmland and an avenue of communication. The Egyptians developed powerful beliefs in life after death, and the focal point of religious and political life was the pharaoh, a god-king who commanded the wealth, resources, and people of Egypt. For long stretches of history Egypt was prosperous and secure in the fertile Nile Valley, although at times various groups migrated in seeking better lives or invaded and conquered. Very often these newcomers adopted aspects of Egyptian religion, art, and politics, and the Egyptians adopted aspects of the newcomers' cultures, such as the techniques for making and casting bronze of the Hyksos. During the period known as the New Kingdom, warrior-pharaohs expanded their power beyond the Nile Valley and created the first Egyptian empire, during which they first fought and then allied with the iron-using Hittites. After the collapse of the New Kingdom, the Nubian rulers of Kush conquered Egypt, and another group, the Phoenicians, came to dominate trade in the Mediterranean, spreading a letter alphabet.

▢ How did the Hebrews create an enduring written religious tradition, and what was its significance? (p. 53)

For several centuries after the collapse of New Kingdom Egypt, a Semitic people known as the Hebrews or the Israelites controlled a small state on the western end of the Fertile Crescent. Their most important legacy was not political, but rather a new form of religious belief, Judaism, based on the worship of a single all-powerful god, Yahweh. The Hebrews wrote down their religious ideas, traditions, laws, advice literature, prayers, hymns, history, and prophecies in a series of books, which came to define the Hebrews as a people. This group of books, the Hebrew Bible, describes the Covenant between Yahweh and the Hebrew people and sets out laws and traditions that structured Hebrew society and family life. Reverence for these written texts was passed from Judaism to the other Western monotheistic religions that grew from it, Christianity and Islam.

▢ What were the strengths of and the major differences between the Assyrian and Persian Empires? (p. 57)

In the ninth century the Assyrians began a rise to power from northern Mesopotamia, creating an empire by means of often brutal military conquest. Assyria's success was also due to sophisticated, far-sighted, and effective military tactics, technical skills, and organization. From a base in what is now southern Iran, the Persians established an even larger empire, developing effective institutions of government and building roads. Though conquerors, the Persians, unlike the Assyrians, usually respected their subjects and allowed them to practice their native customs, traditions, and religions. Around 600 B.C.E. a new religion based on the teachings of the prophet Zoroaster grew in Persia. This religion emphasized the individual's responsibility to choose between good and evil.

SUGGESTED READING

Brosius, Maria. *The Persians: An Introduction.* 2006. Covers all of Persian history.

Edwards, David N. *The Nubian Past.* 2004. Examines the history of Nubia and the Sudan, using archaeological and written sources.

Gates, Charles. *Ancient Cities: The Archaeology of Urban Life in the Ancient Near East and Egypt, Greece, and Rome.* 2003. Provides a survey of ancient life, including society and culture, that relies primarily on archaeological evidence.

Hawass, Zahi. *Silent Images: Women in Pharaonic Egypt.* 2000. Blends texts and pictures to depict the history of Egyptian women.

Kuhrt, Amelie. *The Ancient Near East,* 2 vols. 1995. Covers the region from the earliest times to Alexander's conquest.

Leick, Gwendolyn. *The Babylonians.* 2002. Introduces all aspects of Babylonian life and culture.

Markoe, Glenn E. *The Phoenicians.* 2000. Presents these seafarers at home and abroad in the Mediterranean.

Niditch, Susan. *Ancient Israelite Religion.* 1997. A brief but broad interpretation of Jewish religious developments.

Redford, Donald B. *Egypt, Canaan, and Israel in Ancient Times.* 1993. A study of the political, cultural, and religious relationships among the peoples of Egypt and the Near East from 3000 B.C.E. to about 500 B.C.E.

Robinson, Andrew. *The Story of Writing: Alphabets, Hieroglyphs, and Pictograms.* 2007. A brief account of the scripts used in the major civilizations of the ancient world and of the major scripts we use today, with many illustrations.

Visicato, Giuseppe. *The Power and the Writing: The Early Scribes of Mesopotamia.* 2000. Studies the practical importance of early Mesopotamian scribes.

Vivante, Bella. *Daughters of Gaia: Women of the Ancient World.* 2008. Explores the political, religious, and economic activities of actual women, and also examines ideas about gender.

NOTES

1. From *The Sumerians: Their History, Culture and Character,* p. 238. Copyright © 1963 by The University of Chicago Press. Used by permission of The University of Chicago Press.
2. J. B. Pritchard, ed., *Ancient Near Eastern Texts,* 3d ed. © 1969 Princeton University Press. Reprinted by permission of Princeton University Press.

For practice quizzes and other study tools, visit the **Online Study Guide** at bedfordstmartins.com/mckayworld.

For primary sources from this period, see *Sources of World Societies,* **Second Edition**.

For Web sites, images, and documents related to topics in this chapter, visit **Make History** at bedfordstmartins.com/mckayworld.

• **Female Spirit from an Indian Stupa** Royal patronage aided the spread of Buddhism in India, especially the patronage of King Ashoka, who sponsored the construction of numerous Buddhist monuments. This head of a female spirit (called a *yakshini*) is from the stupa that Ashoka had built at Bharhut in central India. (India Museum, Calcutta, India/Giraudon/The Bridgeman Art Library)

3

During the centuries when the peoples of
ancient Mesopotamia and Egypt were developing
urban civilizations, people in India were wrestling
with the same challenges — food production, the
building of cities, political administration, and questions about human life and the cosmos. Like the
civilizations of the Near East, the earliest Indian

civilization centered on a great river, the Indus. From about 2800 to 1800 B.C.E. the Indus
Valley, or Harappan (huh-RAH-puhn), culture thrived and expanded over a huge area.

A very different Indian society emerged after the decline of this civilization. It was
dominated by the Aryans,
warriors who spoke an early
version of Sanskrit. The Indian caste system and the
Hindu religion, key features
of Indian society into modern times, had their origins
in early Aryan society. By
the middle of the first mil-

The Foundation of Indian Society
to 300 C.E.

lennium B.C.E. the Aryans had set up numerous small kingdoms throughout north India.
This was the great age of Indian religious creativity, when Buddhism and Jainism were
founded and the early Brahmanic religion of the Aryans developed into Hinduism.

The first major Indian empire, the Mauryan (MAWR-ee-uhn) Dynasty, emerged in the
wake of the Greek invasion of north India in 325 B.C.E. This dynasty reached its peak under
King Ashoka, who actively promoted Buddhism both within his realm and beyond it.
Not long after his reign, however, the empire broke up, and for several centuries India was
politically divided. Although India never had a single language and only periodically had a
centralized government, cultural elements dating back to the ancient period — the core
ideas of Brahmanism, the caste system, and the early epics — spread through trade and
other contact, even when the subcontinent was divided into hostile kingdoms.   •

**The Land and Its First Settlers,
ca. 3000–1500** B.C.E.

□ What does archaeology tell us about the Harappan civilization in India?

**The Aryans During the Vedic Age,
ca. 1500–500** B.C.E.

□ What kind of society and culture did the Indo-European Aryans create?

India's Great Religions

□ What ideas and practices were taught by the founders of Jainism, Buddhism, and Hinduism?

**Western Contact and the Mauryan Unification
of North India, ca. 513–185** B.C.E.

□ What was the result of Indian contact with the Persians and Greeks, and what were the consequences of unification under the Mauryan Empire?

**Small States and Trading Networks,
185** B.C.E.**–300** C.E.

□ How was India shaped by political disunity and contacts with other cultures during the five centuries from 185 B.C.E. to 300 C.E.?

The Land and Its First Settlers, ca. 3000–1500 B.C.E.

□ What does archaeology tell us about the Harappan civilization in India?

The subcontinent of India, a landmass as large as western Europe, juts southward into the warm waters of the Indian Ocean. Today this region is divided into the separate countries of Pakistan, Nepal, India, Bangladesh, and Sri Lanka, but these divisions are recent, and for premodern times the entire subcontinent will be called India here.

In India, as elsewhere, the possibilities for both agriculture and communication have always been strongly shaped by geography. Some regions of the subcontinent are among the wettest on earth; others are arid deserts and scrubland. Most areas in India are warm all year, with temperatures over 100°F common. Average temperatures range from 79°F in the north to 85°F in the south. Monsoon rains sweep northward from the Indian Ocean each summer. The lower reaches of the Himalaya Mountains in the northeast are covered by dense forests that are sustained by heavy rainfall. Immediately to the south are the fertile valleys of the Indus and Ganges Rivers. These lowland plains, which stretch all the way across the subcontinent, were tamed for agriculture over time, and India's great empires were centered there. To their west are the deserts of Rajasthan and southeastern Pakistan, historically important in part because their flat terrain enabled invaders to sweep into India from the northwest. South of the great river valleys rise the jungle-clad Vindhya Mountains and the dry, hilly Deccan Plateau. Only along the coasts of this part of India do the hills give way to narrow plains where crop agriculture flourished. India's long coastlines and predictable winds fostered maritime trade with other countries bordering the Indian Ocean.

Neolithic settlement of the Indian subcontinent occurred somewhat later than in the Near East, but agriculture followed a similar pattern of development and was well established by about 7000 B.C.E. Wheat and barley were the early crops, probably having spread in their domesticated form from the Middle East. Farmers also domesticated cattle, sheep, and goats and learned to make pottery.

The story of the first civilization in India is one of the most dramatic in the ancient world. From the Bible, people had known about ancient Egypt and Sumeria for centuries, but not until 1921 did anyone in Europe know that there was an ancient civilization in the Indus Valley. That was when archaeologists found astonishing evidence of a thriving and sophisticated Bronze Age urban culture dating to about 2500 B.C.E. at Mohenjo-daro in what is now Pakistan.

This civilization is known today as the Indus Valley or the **Harappan** civilization, from the modern names of the river and city near where the first ruins were discovered. Archaeologists have discovered some three hundred Harappan cities and many more towns and villages in both Pakistan and India, making it possible to see both the vast regional extent of the Harappan civilization and its evolution over a period of nearly a millennium (Map 3.1). It was a literate civilization, like those of Egypt and Mesopotamia, but no one has been able to decipher the more than four hundred symbols inscribed on stone seals and copper tablets. It is even possible that these symbols are not words but rather names or even nonlinguistic symbols. The civilization's most flourishing period was from 2500 to 2000 B.C.E.

• **Harappan** The first Indian civilization; also known as the Indus Valley civilization.

□ **CHRONOLOGY**

2800–1800 B.C.E. Height of Harappan civilization

ca. 1500–500 B.C.E. Vedic Age; flourishing of Aryan civilization; *Rigveda*

ca. 1000 B.C.E. Introduction of iron

750–500 B.C.E. *Upanishads*

ca. 513 B.C.E. Persians conquer the Indus Valley and Kashmir

ca. 500 B.C.E. Founding of Buddhism and Jainism

ca. 400 B.C.E.–**200** C.E. Gradual evolution of the Brahman religion into Hinduism

326 B.C.E. Alexander the Great enters Indus Valley

ca. 322–185 B.C.E. Mauryan Empire

ca. 300 B.C.E. Jain religion splits into two sects

ca. 269–232 B.C.E. Reign of Ashoka

ca. 200 B.C.E.–**200** C.E. Classical period of Tamil culture

ca. 100 C.E. More inclusive Mahayana form of Buddhism emerges

ca. 200 C.E. Code of Manu

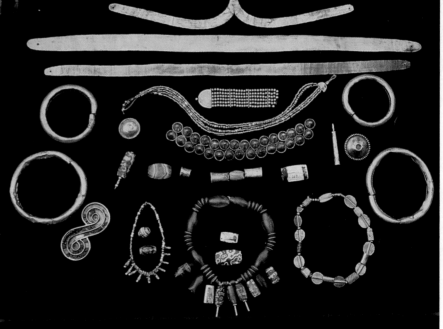

Harappan Artifacts Small objects like seals and jewelry found at Harappan sites provide glimpses of early Indian religious imagination and daily life. The molded tablet shown above depicts a female deity standing above an elephant battling two tigers. The jewelry found at these sites, such as the pieces shown on the right, makes much use of gold and precious stones. (both photos: J. M. Kenoyer/Harappa.com. Courtesy Department of Archaeology and Museums, Government of Pakistan)

The Harappan civilization extended over nearly five hundred thousand square miles in the Indus Valley, making it more than twice as large as ancient Egypt or Sumeria. Yet Harappan civilization was marked by a striking uniformity. Throughout the region, for instance, even in small villages, bricks were made to the same standard proportion (4:2:1). Figurines of preg-

nant women have been found throughout the area, suggesting common religious ideas and practices.

Like Mesopotamian cities, Harappan cities were centers for crafts and trade and were surrounded by extensive farmland. Craftsmen produced ceramics decorated with geometric designs. The Harappans were the earliest known manufacturers of cotton

MAP 3.1 Harappan Civilization, ca. 2500 B.C.E. The earliest civilization in India developed in the Indus River Valley in the west of the subcontinent.

cloth, and this cloth was so abundant that goods were wrapped in it for shipment. Trade was extensive. As early as the reign of Sargon of Akkad in the third millennium B.C.E. (see page 42), trade between India and Mesopotamia carried goods and ideas between the two cultures, probably by way of the Persian Gulf. The Harappan port of Lothal had a stone dock 700 feet long, next to which were massive granaries and bead-making factories. Hundreds of seals were found there, some of Persian Gulf origin, indicating that Lothal was a major port of exit and entry.

The cities of Mohenjo-daro in southern Pakistan, and Harappa, some 400 miles to the north, were huge for this period, more than 3 miles in circumference, with populations estimated at 35,000 to 40,000. Both were defended by great citadels that towered 40 to 50 feet above the surrounding plain. The cities had obviously been planned and built before being settled; they were not the outcomes of villages that grew and sprawled haphazardly. Large granaries stored food. Streets were straight and varied from 9 to 34 feet in width. The houses were substantial, many two stories tall, some perhaps three. The focal point of a house was a central courtyard onto which the rooms opened,

much like many houses today in both rural and urban India.

Perhaps the most surprising aspect of the elaborate planning of these cities was their complex system of drainage, which is well preserved at Mohenjo-daro. Each house had a bathroom with a drain connected to brick-lined sewers located under the major streets. Openings allowed the refuse to be collected, probably to be used as fertilizer on nearby fields. No other ancient city had such an advanced sanitation system.

Both cities also contained numerous large structures, which archaeologists think were public buildings. One of the most important was the large ventilated storehouse for the community's grain. Mohenjo-daro also had a marketplace or place of assembly, a palace, and a huge pool some 39 feet long by 23 feet wide by 8 feet deep. Like the later Roman baths, it had spacious dressing rooms for the bathers. Because the Great Bath at Mohenjo-daro resembles the ritual purification pools of later India, some scholars have speculated that power was in the hands of a priest-king and that the Great Bath played a role in the religious rituals of the city. In contrast to ancient Egypt and Mesopotamia, no great tombs have been discovered in Harappa, making it more difficult to envision the life of the elite.

The prosperity of the Indus civilization depended on constant and intensive cultivation of the rich river valley. Although rainfall seems to have been greater then than in recent times, the Indus, like the Nile, flowed through a relatively dry region made fertile by annual floods and irrigation. And as in Egypt, agriculture was aided by a long, hot growing season and near constant sunshine.

Because the written language of the Harappan people has not been deciphered, their political, intellectual, and religious life is largely unknown. There clearly was a political structure with the authority to organize city planning and facilitate trade, but we do not even know whether there were hereditary kings. There are clear connections between Harappan and Sumerian civilization, but just as clear differences. For instance, the Harappan script, like the Sumerian, was incised on clay tablets and seals, but it has no connection to Sumerian cuneiform, and the artistic style of the Harappan seals also is distinct.

Soon after 2000 B.C.E. the Harappan civilization mysteriously declined. The port of Lothal was abandoned by about 1900 B.C.E., and other major centers came to house only a fraction of their earlier populations. Scholars have offered many explanations for the mystery of the abandonment of these cities. The decline cannot be attributed to the arrival of powerful invaders, as was once thought. Rather it was internally generated. Environmental theories include an earthquake that led to a shift in the course of the river, or a

Aryans The dominant people in north India after the decline of the Indus Valley civilization; they spoke an early form of Sanskrit.

Mohenjo-daro Mohenjo-daro was a planned city built of fired mud brick. Its streets were straight, and covered drainpipes were installed to carry away waste. From sites like this, we know that the early Indian political elite had the power and technical expertise to organize large, coordinated building projects. Found in Mohenjo-daro, this small ceramic figurine (left) shows a woman adorned with six necklaces. (site: J. M. Kenoyer/Harrapan.com. Courtesy, Department of Archaeology and Museums, Government of Pakistan; figurine: Angelo Hornak/Alamy)

severe drought. Perhaps the long-term practice of irrigation led to the buildup of salt and alkaline in the soil until they reached levels toxic to plants, forcing the Harappan people to move in search of arable land. Some scholars speculate that long-distance commerce collapsed, leading to an economic depression. Others theorize that the population fell prey to diseases, such as malaria, that caused people to flee the cities.

Even though the Harappan people apparently lived on after scattering to villages, the large urban centers were abandoned, and key features of their high culture were lost. For the next thousand years, India had no large cities, no kiln-fired bricks, and no written language. There are, however, many signs of continuity with later Indian civilization, ranging from the sorts of pottery ovens used to some of the images of gods. Some scholars think that the people of Harappa were the ancestors of the Tamils and other Dravidian-speaking peoples of modern south India.

The Aryans During the Vedic Age, ca. 1500–500 B.C.E.

☐ What kind of society and culture did the Indo-European Aryans create?

After the decline of the Harappan civilization, a people who called themselves **Aryans** became dominant in north India. They were speakers of an early form of Sanskrit, an Indo-European language closely related to ancient Persian and more distantly related to Latin, Greek, Celtic, and their modern descendants, such as English. For example, the Sanskrit *nava,* "ship," is related to the English word *naval; deva,* "god," to *divine;* and *raja,* "ruler," to *regal.* The word *Aryan* itself comes from *Arya,* "noble" or "pure" in Sanskrit, and has the same linguistic root as *Iran* and *Ireland.* The Aryans flourished during the Vedic Age (ca. 1500–500 B.C.E.).

Named for the Vedas, a large and significant body of ancient sacred works written in Sanskrit, this period witnessed the Indo-Aryan development of the caste system and Brahman religion and the writing of the great epics that represent the earliest form of Indian literature.

Aryan Dominance in North India

Until relatively recently, the dominant theory was that the Aryans came into India from outside, perhaps as part of the same movements of people that led to the Hittites occupying parts of Anatolia, the Achaeans entering Greece, and the Kassites conquering Sumer — all in the period from about 1900 to 1750 B.C.E. Some scholars, however, have proposed that the Indo-European languages spread to this area much earlier; to them it seems possible that the Harappan people were speakers of an early Indo-European language. If that was the case, the Aryans would be one of the groups descended from this early population.

Modern politics complicates analysis of the appearance of the Aryans and their role in India's history. Europeans in the eighteenth and nineteenth centuries developed the concept of Indo-European languages, and they did so in an age both highly conscious of race and in the habit of identifying races with languages. The racist potential of the concept was exploited by the Nazis, who glorified the Aryans as a superior race. Even in less politicized contexts, the notion of a group of people who entered India from outside and made themselves its rulers is troubling to many. Does it mean that the non-Aryans are the true Indians? Does it add legitimacy to those who in later times conquered India from outside? Does it justify or undermine the caste system? One of the difficulties faced by scholars who wish to take a dispassionate view of these issues is that the evidence for the earlier Harappan culture is entirely archaeological, while the evidence for the Aryans is almost entirely based on linguistic analysis of modern languages and orally transmitted texts of uncertain date.

The central source of information on the early Aryans is the ***Rigveda***, the earliest of the Vedas, an originally oral collection of hymns, ritual texts, and philosophical treatises composed in Sanskrit between 1500 and 500 B.C.E. Like Homer's epics in Greece, written in this same period, these texts were transmitted orally and are in verse. The *Rigveda* portrays the Aryans as warrior tribes who glorified military skill and heroism; loved to drink, hunt, race, and dance; and counted their wealth in cattle. The Aryans did not sweep across India in a quick campaign, nor were they a disciplined army led by one conqueror. Rather they were a collection of tribes that frequently fought with each other and only over the course of several centuries came to dominate north India.

The key to the Aryans' success probably lay in their superior military technology. Those they fought often lived in fortified towns and put up a strong defense against them, but Aryan warriors had superior technology, including two-wheeled chariots, horses, and bronze swords and spears. Their epics present the struggle for north India in religious terms, describing their chiefs as godlike heroes and their opponents as irreligious savages who did not perform the proper sacrifices. In time, however, the Aryans clearly absorbed much from those they conquered, such as agricultural techniques and foods.

At the head of each Aryan tribe was a chief, or raja (RAH-juh), who led his followers in battle and ruled them in peacetime. The warriors in the tribe elected the chief for his military skills. Next in importance to the chief was the priest. In time, priests evolved into a distinct class possessing precise knowledge of the complex rituals and of the invocations and formulas that accompanied them, rather like the priest classes in ancient Egypt, Mesopotamia, and Persia. Below them in the pecking order was a warrior nobility who rode into battle in chariots and perhaps on horseback. The warrior class met at assemblies to reach decisions and advise the raja. The common tribesmen tended herds and worked the land. To the conquered non-Aryans fell the drudgery of menial tasks. It is difficult to define precisely their social status. Though probably not slaves, they were certainly subordinate to the Aryans and worked for them in return for protection.

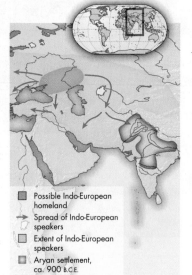

■ Possible Indo-European homeland
→ Spread of Indo-European speakers
☐ Extent of Indo-European speakers
■ Aryan settlement, ca. 900 B.C.E.

Indo-European Migrations and the Vedic Age

- ***Rigveda*** The earliest collection of Indian hymns, ritual texts, and philosophical treatises, it is the central source of information on early Aryans.
- **Brahmins** Priests of the Aryans; they supported the growth of royal power in return for royal confirmation of their own religious rights, power, and status.
- **caste system** The Indian system of dividing society into hereditary groups whose members interacted primarily within the group, and especially married within the group.

Bronze Sword This bronze sword, with a rib in the middle of the blade for strength, is a striking example of the quality of Aryan arms. Superior weapons gave the Aryans military advantage. (Courtesy of the Trustees of the British Museum)

Over the course of several centuries, the Aryans pushed farther east into the valley of the Ganges River, at that time a land of thick jungle populated by aboriginal forest peoples. The tremendous challenge of clearing the jungle was made somewhat easier by the introduction of iron around 1000 B.C.E., probably by diffusion from Mesopotamia. (See "Global Trade: Iron," page 54.) Iron made it possible to produce strong axes and knives relatively cheaply.

The Aryans did not gain dominance over the entire Indian subcontinent. South of the Vindhya range, people speaking Dravidian languages maintained their control. In the great Aryan epics the *Ramayana* and *Mahabharata*, the people of the south and Sri Lanka are spoken of as dark-skinned savages and demons who resisted the Aryans' conquests. Along with the *Rigveda*, these epics would become part of the common cultural heritage of all of India.

As Aryan rulers came to dominate large settled populations, the style of political organization changed from tribal chieftainship to territorial kingship. In other words, the ruler now controlled an area with people living in permanent settlements, not a nomadic tribe that moved as a group. Moreover, kings no longer needed to be elected by the tribe; it was enough to be invested by priests and to perform the splendid royal ceremonies they designed. The priests, or **Brahmins**, supported the growth of royal power in return for royal confirmation of their own power and status. The Brahmins also served as advisers to the kings. In the face of this royal-priestly alliance, the old tribal assemblies of warriors withered away. By the time Persian armies reached the Indus around 513 B.C.E., there were sixteen major Aryan kingdoms in north India.

Life in Early India

Caste was central to the social life of these north Indian kingdoms. Early Aryan society had distinguished among the warrior elite, the priests, ordinary tribes-

men, and conquered subjects. These distinctions gradually evolved into the **caste system**, which divided society into strictly defined hereditary groups. Society was conceived of as four hierarchical strata whose members did not eat with or marry each other. These strata, or varna, were Brahmin (priests), Kshatriya (warriors and officials), Vaishya (merchants), and Shudra (peasants and laborers). The Shudra stratum, which encompassed most of the conquered people, was the largest. By contrast, the three upper varnas probably accounted for no more than 30 percent of the population. The caste system thus allowed the numerically outnumbered Aryans to maintain dominance over their subjects and not be culturally absorbed by them.

Social and religious attitudes supported the caste system. Aryans considered the work of artisans impure. They left all such work to the local people, who were probably superior to them in these arts anyway. Trade, by contrast, was not viewed as demeaning. Brahmanic texts of the period refer to trade as equal in value to farming, serving the king, or being a priest.

In the *Rigveda*, the caste system is attributed to the gods:

> When they divided [the primeval man], into how
> 　many different portions did they arrange him?
> What became of his mouth, what of his two arms?
> What were his two thighs and his two feet called?
> His mouth became the brahman, his two arms was
> 　made into the [kshatriya]; his two thighs became
> 　the vaishyas, of his two feet the shudra was born.[1]

As priests the Brahmins were expected to memorize every syllable and tone of the Vedas so that their rituals would please the gods. Not only did they conduct the traditional ceremonies, but they also developed new ones for new circumstances. As agriculture became more important to the Aryans, for example, Brahmins acted as agents of Agni, the god of fire, to purify the land for crops. The Brahmins also knew the formulas and spells that were effective against diseases and calamities.

Those without places in the four varna—that is, newly conquered peoples and those who had lost their caste status through violations of ritual—were outcastes. That simply meant that they belonged to no caste. In time, some of them became "untouchables" because they were "impure." They were scorned because they earned their living by performing such "polluting" jobs as slaughtering animals and dressing skins.

Slavery was a feature of early social life in India, as it was in Egypt, Mesopotamia, and elsewhere in antiquity. People captured in battle often became slaves, but captives could also be ransomed by their families. Later, slavery was less connected with warfare and became

Listening to the Past

Conversations Between Rama and Sita from the *Ramayana*

The Ramayana, *an epic poem of about fifty thousand verses, is attributed to the third-century* B.C.E. *poet Valmiki. Its main character, Rama, the oldest son of a king, is an incarnation of the great god Vishnu. As a young man, he wins the princess Sita as his wife when he alone among her suitors proves strong enough to bend a huge bow. Rama and Sita love each other deeply, but court intrigue disturbs their happy life. After the king announces that he will retire and consecrate Rama as his heir, the king's beautiful junior wife, wishing to advance her own son, reminds the king that he has promised her a favor of her choice. She then asks to have him appoint her son heir and to have Rama sent into the wilderness for fourteen years. The king is forced to consent, and Rama obeys his father.*

The passage below gives the conversations between Rama and Sita after Rama learns he must leave. In subsequent parts of the very long epic, the lovers undergo many other tribulations, including Sita's abduction by the lord of the demons, the ten-headed Ravana, and her eventual recovery by Rama with the aid of monkeys.

The Ramayana *eventually appeared in numerous versions in all the major languages of India. Hearing it recited was said to bring religious merit. Sita, passionate in her devotion to her husband, has remained the favorite Indian heroine. Rama, Sita, and the monkey Hanuman are cult figures in Hinduism, with temples devoted to their worship.*

"For fourteen years I must live in Dandaka, while my father will appoint Bharata prince regent. I have come to see you before I leave for the desolate forest. You are never to boast of me in the presence of Bharata. Men in power cannot bear to hear others praised, and so you must never boast of my virtues in front of Bharata. . . . When I have gone to the forest where sages make their home, my precious, blameless wife, you must earnestly undertake vows and fasts. You must rise early and worship the gods according to custom and then pay homage to my father Dasaratha, lord of men. And my aged mother Kausalya, who is tormented by misery, deserves your respect as well, for she has subordinated all to righteousness. The rest of my mothers, too, must always receive your homage. . . . My beloved, I am going to the great forest, and you must stay here. You must do as I tell you, my lovely, and not give offense to anyone."

So Rama spoke, and Sita, who always spoke kindly to her husband and deserved kindness from him, grew angry just because she loved him, and said, "My lord, a man's father, his mother, brother, son, or daughter-in-law all experience the effects of their own past deeds and suffer an individual fate. But a wife, and she alone, bull among men, must share her husband's fate. Therefore I, too, have been ordered to live in the forest. It is not her father or mother, not her son or friends or herself, but her husband, and he alone, who gives a woman permanent refuge in this world and after death. If you must leave this very day for the trackless forest, Rama, I will go in front of you, softening the thorns and sharp *kusa* grass. Cast out your anger and resentment, like so much water left after drinking one's fill. Do not be reluctant to take me, my mighty husband. There is no evil in me. The shadow of a husband's feet in any circumstances surpasses the finest mansions, an aerial chariot, or even flying through the sky. . . . O Rama, bestower of honor, you have the power to protect any other person in the forest. Why then not me? . . .

"If I were to be offered a place to live in heaven itself, Rama, tiger among men, I would refuse it if you were not there. I will go to the trackless forest teeming with deer, monkeys, and elephants, and live there as in my father's house, clinging to your feet alone, in strict self-discipline. I love no one else; my heart is so attached to you that were we to be parted I am resolved to die. Take me, oh please grant my request. I shall not be a burden to you." . . .

more of an economic and social institution. As in ancient Mesopotamia, a free man might sell himself and his family into slavery because he could not pay his debts. And, as in Hammurabi's Mesopotamia, he could, if clever, hard-working, or fortunate, buy his and his family's way out of slavery. At birth, slave children automatically became the slaves of their parents' masters. Indian slaves could be bought, used as collateral, or given away.

Women's lives in early India varied according to their social status, much as men's did. Like most nomadic tribes, the Aryans were patrilineal and patriarchal (tracing descent through males and placing power in the senior men of the family). Thus the roles of women in Aryan society probably were more subordinate than were the roles of women in local Dravidian groups, many of which were matrilineal (tracing descent through females). But even in Aryan society women were treated somewhat more favorably than in later Indian society. They were not yet given in child-marriage, and widows had the right to remarry. In epics such as the *Ramayana*, women are often portrayed

When Sita finished speaking, the righteous prince, who knew what was right and cherished it, attempted to dissuade her. . . .

"Sita, give up this notion of living in the forest. The name 'forest' is given only to wild regions where hardships abound. . . . There are lions that live in mountain caves; their roars are redoubled by mountain torrents and are a painful thing to hear—the forest is a place of pain. At night worn with fatigue, one must sleep upon the ground on a bed of leaves, broken off of themselves—the forest is a place of utter pain. And one has to fast, Sita, to the limit of one's endurance, wear clothes of barkcloth and bear the burden of matted hair. . . . There are many creeping creatures, of every size and shape, my lovely, ranging aggressively over the ground. . . . Moths, scorpions, worms, gnats, and flies continually harass one, my frail Sita—the forest is wholly a place of pain. . . ."

Sita was overcome with sorrow when she heard what Rama said. With tears trickling down her face, she answered him in a faint voice. . . . "If from feelings of love I follow you, my pure-hearted husband, I shall have no sin to answer for, because my husband is my deity. My union with you is sacred and shall last even beyond death. . . . If you refuse to take me to the forest despite the sorrow that I feel, I shall have no recourse but to end my life by poison, fire, or water."

Though she pleaded with him in this and every other way to be allowed to go, great-armed Rama would not consent to taking her to the desolate forest. And when he told her as much, Sita fell to brooding, and drenched the ground, it seemed, with the hot tears that fell from her eyes. . . . She was nearly insensible with sorrow when Rama took her in his arms and comforted her. . . . "Without knowing your true feelings, my lovely, I could not consent to your living in the wilderness, though I am perfectly capable of protecting you. Since you are determined to live with me in the forest, Sita, I could no sooner abandon you than a self-respecting man his reputation. . . . My father keeps to the path of righteousness and truth, and I wish to act just as he instructs me. That is the eternal way of righteousness. Follow me, my timid one, be my companion in righteousness. Go now and bestow precious objects on the brahmins, give food to the mendicants and all who ask for it. Hurry, there is no time to waste."

Finding that her husband had acquiesced in her going, the lady was elated and set out at once to make the donations.

Source: *The Ramayana of Valmiki: An Epic of India*, vol. 2: *Ayodhyakanda*, trans. Sheldon I. Pollock, ed. Robert P. Goldman (Princeton, N.J.: Princeton University Press, 1986), pp. 134–142, modified slightly. Reprinted by permission of Princeton University Press.

Rama and Sita in the forest, from a set of miniature paintings done in about 1600. (National Museum, New Delhi)

QUESTIONS FOR ANALYSIS

1. What can you infer about early Indian family life and social relations from this story?
2. What do Sita's words and actions indicate about women's roles in Indian society of the time?
3. What do you think accounts for the continuing popularity of the story of Rama throughout Indian history?

as forceful personalities, able to achieve their goals both by using feminine ploys to cajole men and also by direct action. (See "Listening to the Past: Conversations Between Rama and Sita from the *Ramayana*," above.)

Brahmanism

The Aryans' religious beliefs recognized a multitude of gods. These gods shared some features with the gods of other early Indo-European societies such as the Per-sians and Greeks. Some of them were great brawling figures, such as Agni, the god of fire and, as in ancient Persia, a particularly important god; Indra, wielder of the thunderbolt and god of war, who each year slew a dragon to release the monsoon rains; and Rudra, the divine archer who spread disaster and disease by firing his arrows at people. Others were shadowy figures, such as Dyaus, the father of the gods, related to the Greek Zeus. Varuna, the god of order in the universe, was a hard god, quick to punish those who sinned and thus upset the balance of nature. Ushas, the goddess of dawn, was a gentle deity who welcomed the birds, gave delight to human beings, and warded off evil spirits.

Ordinary people dealt with these gods through priests who made animal sacrifices to them. By giving valued things to the gods, people strengthened both the power of the gods and their own relationships with them. Gradually, under the priestly monopoly of the Brahmins, correct sacrifice and proper ritual became so important that most Brahmins believed that a properly performed ritual would force a god to grant a worshipper's wish. Ordinary people could watch a ceremony, such as a fire ritual, which was often held outdoors, but could not perform the key steps in the ritual.

The *Upanishads* (oo-PAH-nih-shadz), composed between 750 and 500 B.C.E., record speculations about the mystical meaning of sacrificial rites and about cosmological questions of man's relationship to the universe. They document a gradual shift from the mythical worldview of the early Vedic age to a deeply philosophical one. Associated with this shift was a movement toward asceticism (uh-SEH-tuh-siz-uhm)—severe self-discipline and self-denial. In search of wisdom, some men (but not women) retreated to the forests. These ascetics concluded that disciplined meditation on the ritual sacrifice could produce the same results as the physical ritual itself. Thus they reinterpreted ritual sacrifices as symbolic gestures with mystical meanings.

Ancient Indian cosmology (theories of the universe) focused not on a creator who made the universe out of nothing, but rather on endlessly repeating cycles. Key ideas were **samsara**, the reincarnation of souls by a continual process of rebirth, and **karma**, the tally of good and bad deeds that determined the status of an individual's next life. Good deeds led to better future lives, evil deeds to worse future lives — even to reincarnation as an animal. Thus gradually arose the concept of a wheel of life that included human beings, animals, and gods. Reward and punishment worked automatically; there was no all-knowing god who judged people and could be petitioned to forgive a sin, and each individual was responsible for his or her own destiny in a just and impartial world.

To most people, especially those on the low end of the economic and social scale, these ideas were attractive. By living righteously and doing good deeds, people could improve their lot in the next life. Yet there was another side to these ideas: the wheel of life could be seen as a treadmill, giving rise to a yearning for release from the relentless cycle of birth and death. One solu-

tion offered in the *Upanishads* was moksha, or release from the wheel of life. Brahmanic mystics claimed that life in the world was actually an illusion and that the only way to escape the wheel of life was to realize that ultimate reality was unchanging.

The unchanging ultimate reality was called **brahman**. This important concept has been translated many ways. Scholars have offered both brief phrases — "the cosmic principle," "the principle of religious reality," "absolute reality," "eternal truth," and "universal soul"— and somewhat longer descriptions: "holy or sacred power that is the source and sustainer of the universe," "the ultimate unchanging reality, composed of pure being and consciousness," and "eternal, unchanging, infinite, and transcendent reality that is the divine ground of everything in this universe." Here *brahman* is defined simply as "ultimate reality."

Brahman was contrasted to the multitude of fleeting phenomena that people consider important in their daily lives. The individual soul or self was ultimately the same substance as the universal brahman, in the same way that each spark is in substance the same as a large fire.

The *Upanishads* gave the Brahmins a high status to which the poor and lowly could aspire in a future life. Consequently, the Brahmins greeted the concepts presented in these works and those who taught them with tolerance and understanding and made a place for them in traditional religious practice. The rulers of Indian society also encouraged the new trends, since the doctrines of samsara and karma encouraged the poor and oppressed to labor peacefully and dutifully. In other words, although the new doctrines were intellectually revolutionary, in social and political terms they supported the existing power structure.

India's Great Religions

☐ What ideas and practices were taught by the founders of Jainism, Buddhism, and Hinduism?

By the sixth and fifth centuries B.C.E., cities had reappeared in India, and merchants and trade were thriving. Bricks were again baked in kilns and used to build ramparts around cities. One particular kingdom, Magadha, had become much more powerful than any of the other states in the Ganges plain, defeating its enemies by using war elephants and catapults for hurling stones. Written language had reappeared.

This was a period of intellectual ferment throughout Eurasia—the period of the early Greek philosophers, the Hebrew prophets, Zoroaster in Persia, and Confucius and the early Daoists in China. In India it

- **samsara** The transmigration of souls by a continual process of rebirth.
- **karma** The tally of good and bad deeds that determines the status of an individual's next life.
- **brahman** The unchanging ultimate reality, according to the *Upanishads*.

led to numerous sects that rejected various elements of Brahmanic teachings. (See "Individuals in Society: Gosala," page 76.) The two most influential were Jainism and Buddhism. Their founders were contemporaries living in east India in minor states of the Ganges plain. Hinduism emerged in response to these new religions but at the same time was the most direct descendant of the old Brahmanic religion.

Jainism

The key figure of Jainism, Vardhamana Mahavira (fl. ca. 520 B.C.E.), was the son of the chief of a small state and a member of the warrior class. Like many ascetics of the period, he left home to become a wandering holy man. For twelve years, from ages thirty to forty-two, he traveled through the Ganges Valley until he found enlightenment and became a "completed soul." Mahavira taught his doctrines for about thirty years, founding a disciplined order of monks and gaining the support of many lay followers, male and female.

Mahavira accepted the Brahman doctrines of karma and rebirth but developed these ideas in new directions, founding a new religion referred to as Jainism. He argued that human beings, animals, plants, and even inanimate objects all have living souls enmeshed in matter, accumulated through the workings of karma. Even a rock has a soul locked inside it, enchained by matter but capable of suffering if someone kicks it. The souls conceived by the Jains have finite dimensions. They float or sink depending on the amount of matter with which they are enmeshed. The ascetic, who willingly undertakes suffering, can dissipate some of the accumulated karma and make progress toward liberation. If a soul at last escapes from all the matter weighing it down, it becomes lighter than ordinary objects and floats to the top of the universe, where it remains forever in inactive bliss.

Mahavira's followers pursued such liberation by living ascetic lives and avoiding evil thoughts and actions. The Jains considered all life sacred and tried to live without destroying other life. Some early Jains went to the extreme of starving themselves to death, since it is impossible to eat without destroying at least plants, but most took the less extreme step of distinguishing between different levels of life. The most sacred life-forms were human beings, followed by animals, plants, and inanimate objects. A Jain who wished to avoid vio-

Jain Ascetic The most extreme Jain ascetics not only endured the elements without the help of clothes, but they were also generally indifferent to bodily comfort. The Jain saint depicted in this eighth-century cave temple has maintained his posture for so long that vines have grown up around him. (Courtesy, Robert Fisher)

lence to life became a vegetarian and took pains not to kill any creature, even tiny insects in the air and soil. Farming was impossible for Jains, who tended instead to take up trade. Among the most conservative Jains, priests practiced nudity, for clinging to clothes, even a loincloth, was a form of attachment. Lay Jains could pursue Jain teachings by practicing nonviolence and not eating meat. The Jains' radical nonviolence was motivated by a desire to escape the karmic consequences of causing harm to a life. In other words, violence had to be avoided above all because it harms the person who commits it.

For the first century after Mahavira's death, the Jains were a comparatively small and unimportant sect. Jainism began to flourish under the Mauryan Dynasty (ca. 322–185 B.C.E.; see pages 82–84), and Jain tradition claims the Mauryan Empire's founder, Chandragupta, as a major patron. About 300 B.C.E. the Jain scriptures were recorded, and the religion split into two sects, one maintaining the tradition of total nudity, the other choosing to wear white robes on the grounds that clothes were an insignificant external sign, unrelated to true liberation. Over the next few centuries Jain monks were particularly important in spreading northern culture into the Deccan and Tamil regions of south India.

Individuals in Society

Gosala

TEXTS THAT SURVIVE FROM EARLY INDIA ARE rich in religious and philosophical speculation and in tales of gods and heroes, but not in history of the sort written by the early Chinese and Greeks. Because Indian writers and thinkers of antiquity had little interest in recording the actions of rulers or accounting for the rise and decline of different states, few people's lives are known in any detail.

Religious literature, however, does sometimes include details of the lives of followers and adversaries. The life of Gosala, for instance, is known primarily from early Buddhist and Jain scriptures. He was a contemporary of both Mahavira, the founder of the Jains, and Gautama, the Buddha, and both of them saw him as one of their most pernicious rivals.

According to the Jain account, Gosala was born in the north Indian kingdom of Magadha, the son of a professional beggar. The name Gosala, which means "cowshed," alluded to the fact that he was born in a cowshed where his parents had taken refuge during the rainy season. The Buddhist account adds that he became a naked wandering ascetic when he fled from his enraged master after breaking an oil jar. As a mendicant he soon fell in with Mahavira, who had recently commenced his

life as an ascetic. After accompanying Mahavira on his travels for at least six years, Gosala came to feel that he was spiritually more advanced than his master and left to undertake the practice of austerities on his own. According to the Jain account, after he gained magical powers, he challenged his master and gathered his own disciples.

Both Jain and Buddhist sources agree that Gosala taught a form of fatalism that they saw as dangerously wrong. A Buddhist source says that he taught that people are good or bad not because of their own efforts but because of fate. "Just as a ball of string when it is cast forth will spread out just as far and no farther than it can unwind so both fools and wise alike wandering in transmigration exactly for the allotted term shall then and only then make an end of pain."* Some people reach perfection not by their own efforts, but rather through the course of numerous rebirths over hundreds of thousands of years until they rid themselves of bad karma.

The Jains claimed that Gosala violated the celibacy expected of ascetics by living with a potter woman and, moreover, that he taught that sexual relations were not sinful. The followers of Gosala, a Buddhist source stated, wore no clothing and were particular about the food they accepted, refusing food specially prepared for them, food in a cooking pan, and food from couples or women with children. Like other ascetics, Gosala's followers owned no property, carrying the principle further than the Jains, who allowed the possession of a food bowl. They made a bowl from the palms of their hands, giving them the name "hand lickers."

Jain sources report that after sixteen years of separation, Mahavira happened to come to the town where Gosala lived. When Gosala heard that Mahavira spoke contemptuously of him, he and his followers went to Mahavira's lodgings, and the two sides came to blows. Soon thereafter, Gosala became unhinged, gave up all ascetic restraint, and, after six months of singing, dancing, drinking, and other riotous living, died, though not before telling his disciples, the Jains report, that Mahavira was right. Doubt is cast on this version of his end by the fact that for centuries to come, Gosala's followers, called the Ajivikas, were an important sect in several parts of India. The Mauryan ruler Ashoka honored them among other sects and dedicated some caves to them.

QUESTIONS FOR ANALYSIS

1. How would Gosala's own followers have described his life? What sorts of distortions are likely in a life known primarily from the writings of rivals?
2. How would the early Indian economy have been affected by the presence of ascetic beggars?

*A. F. R. Hoernle, "Ajivikas," in *Encyclopedia of Religion and Ethics*, vol. 1, ed. James Hastings (Edinburgh: T. & T. Clark, 1908), p. 262.

For several years before setting off on his own, Gosala followed Mahavira, depicted here at a Jain cave temple. (Dinodia Picture Agency)

Although Jainism never took hold as widely as Hinduism and Buddhism (discussed below), it has been an influential strand in Indian thought and has several million adherents in India today. Fasting and nonviolence as spiritual practices in India owe much to Jain teachings. In the twentieth century Mohandas Gandhi, leader of the Indian independence movement, was influenced by these ideas through his mother, and the American civil rights leader Dr. Martin Luther King, Jr., was influenced by Gandhi.

Siddhartha Gautama and Buddhism

Siddhartha Gautama (fl. ca. 500 B.C.E.), also called Shakyamuni ("sage of the Shakya tribe"), is best known as the Buddha ("enlightened one"). He was a contemporary of Mahavira and came from the same warrior social class. He was born the son of a chief of one of the tribes in the Himalayan foothills in what is now Nepal. At age twenty-nine, unsatisfied with his life of comfort and troubled by the suffering he saw around him, he left home to become a wandering ascetic. He traveled south to the kingdom of Magadha, where he studied with yoga masters, but later took up extreme asceticism. According to tradition, while meditating under a bo tree at Bodh Gaya, he reached enlightenment— that is, perfect insight into the processes of the universe. After several weeks of meditation, he preached his first sermon, urging a "middle way" between asceticism and worldly life. For the next forty-five years, the Buddha traveled through the Ganges Valley, propounding his ideas, refuting his adversaries, and attracting followers. To reach as wide an audience as possible, the Buddha preached in the local language, Magadhi, rather than in Sanskrit, which was already becoming a priestly language. Probably because he refused to recognize the divine authority of the Vedas and dismissed sacrifices, he attracted followers mostly from among merchants, artisans, and farmers, rather than Brahmins.

In his first sermon the Buddha outlined his main message, summed up in the **Four Noble Truths** and the **Eightfold Path**. The Four Noble Truths are as follows: (1) pain and suffering, frustration, and anxiety are ugly but inescapable parts of human life; (2) suffering and anxiety are caused by human desires and attachments; (3) people can understand these weaknesses and triumph over them; and (4) this triumph is made possible by following a simple code of conduct, the Eightfold Path. The basic insight of Buddhism is thus psychological. The deepest human longings can never be satisfied, and even those things that seem to give pleasure cause anxiety because we are afraid of losing them. Attachment to people and things causes sorrow at their loss.

The Buddha offered an optimistic message in that all people can set out on the Eightfold Path toward liberation. All they have to do is take a series of steps, beginning with recognizing the universality of suffering ("right knowledge"), deciding to free themselves from it ("right purpose"), and then choosing "right conduct" (including abstaining from taking life), "right speech," "right livelihood," and "right endeavor." The seventh step is "right awareness," constant contemplation of one's deeds and words, giving full thought to their importance and whether they lead to enlightenment. "Right contemplation," the last step, entails deep meditation on the impermanence of everything in the world. Those who achieve liberation are freed from the cycle of birth and death and enter the state called **nirvana**, a kind of blissful nothingness and freedom from reincarnation.

Although he accepted the Indian idea of reincarnation, the Buddha argued against belief in the integrity of the individual self or soul. He saw human beings as a collection of parts, physical and mental. As long as the parts remain combined, that combination can be called "I." When that combination changes, as at death, the various parts remain in existence, ready to become the building blocks of different combinations. According to Buddhist teaching, life is passed from person to person as a flame is passed from candle to candle.

Buddhism differed from Brahmanism and later Hinduism in that it ignored the caste system. Everyone, noble and peasant, educated and ignorant, male and female, could follow the Eightfold Path. Moreover, the Buddha was extraordinarily undogmatic. Convinced that each person must achieve enlightenment on his or her own, he emphasized that the path was important only because it led the traveler to enlightenment, not for its own sake. He compared it to a raft, essential to cross a river but useless once the traveler reaches the far shore. There was no harm in honoring local gods or observing traditional ceremonies, as long as one remembered the goal of enlightenment and did not let sacrifices become snares or attachments. The willingness of Buddhists to tolerate a wide variety of practices aided the spread of the religion.

Like Mahavira, the Buddha formed a circle of disciples, primarily men but including some women as well. He continually reminded them that each person must

• **Four Noble Truths** The Buddha's message that pain and suffering are inescapable parts of life; suffering and anxiety are caused by human desires and attachments; people can understand and triumph over these weaknesses; and the triumph is made possible by following a simple code of conduct.

• **Eightfold Path** The code of conduct set forth by the Buddha in his first sermon, beginning with "right conduct" and ending with "right contemplation."

• **nirvana** A state of blissful nothingness and freedom from reincarnation.

▫ Picturing the Past

Gandharan Frieze Depicting the Buddha This carved stone from ca. 200 C.E. is one in a series portraying scenes from the life of the Buddha. From the Gandharan kingdom (located in modern Pakistan), this frieze depicts the Buddha seated below the bo tree, where he was first enlightened.
(Freer Gallery of Art, Smithsonian Institution, Washington, D.C., Purchase. F1949.9b, F1954.20)

ANALYZING THE IMAGE What are the people around the Buddha doing? What animals are portrayed?

CONNECTIONS Does this frieze effectively convey any Buddhist principles? If so, which ones?

reach ultimate fulfillment by individual effort, but he also recognized the value of a group of people striving together for the same goal.

The Buddha's followers transmitted his teachings orally until they were written down in the second or first century B.C.E. These scriptures are called **sutras**. The form of monasticism that developed among the Buddhists was less strict than that of the Jains. Buddhist monks moved about for eight months of the year (except the rainy season), begging for their one meal a day, but they could bathe and wear clothes. Within a few centuries Buddhist monks began to overlook the rule that they should travel. They set up permanent monasteries, generally on land donated by kings or other patrons. Orders of nuns also appeared, giving

women the opportunity to seek truth in ways men had traditionally used. The main ritual that monks and nuns performed in their monastic establishments was the communal recitation of the sutras. Lay Buddhists could aid the spread of the Buddhist teachings by providing food for monks and support for their monasteries, and they could pursue their own spiritual progress by adopting practices such as abstaining from meat and alcohol.

Because Buddhism had no central ecclesiastical authority like the Christian papacy, early Buddhist communities developed several divergent traditions and came to stress different sutras. One of the most important of these, associated with the monk-philosopher Nagarjuna (fl. ca. 100 C.E.), is called **Mahayana**, or

"Great Vehicle," because it was a more inclusive form of the religion. It drew on a set of discourses allegedly given by the Buddha and kept hidden by his followers for centuries. One branch of Mahayana taught that reality is empty (that is, nothing exists independently of itself). Another branch held that ultimate reality is consciousness, that everything is produced by the mind.

Just as important as the metaphysical literature of Mahayana Buddhism was its devotional side, influenced by the religions then prevalent in Central Asia, such as Zoroastrianism (see page 61). The Buddha became deified and was placed at the head of an expanding pantheon of other Buddhas and **bodhisattvas** (boh-dih-SUHT-vuhz). Bodhisattvas were Buddhas-to-be who had stayed in the world after enlightenment to help others on the path to salvation. The Buddhas and bodhisattvas became objects of veneration, especially the Buddha of Infinite Light, Amitabha, and the bodhisattva of infinite compassion and mercy, Avalokitesvara (uh-vuh-lohk-ih-TEYSH-veh-ruh). With the growth of Mahayana, Buddhism attracted more and more laypeople.

Buddhism remained an important religion in India until about 1200 C.E. By that time it had spread widely through East, Central, and Southeast Asia. After 1200 Buddhism declined in India, losing out to both Hinduism and Islam, and the number of Buddhists in India today is small. Buddhism never lost its hold in Nepal and Sri Lanka, however, and today it is also a major religion in Southeast Asia, Tibet, China, Korea, and Japan.

Hinduism

Both Buddhism and Jainism were direct challenges to the old Brahmanic religion. Both rejected animal sacrifice, which by then was a central element in the rituals performed by Brahmin priests. Even more important, both religions tacitly rejected the caste system, accepting people of any caste into their ranks. Over the next several centuries (ca. 400 B.C.E.–200 C.E.), in response to this challenge, the Brahmanic religion evolved in a more devotional direction, developing into the religion commonly called Hinduism. In Hinduism Brahmins retained their high social status, but it became possible for individual worshippers to have more direct contact with the gods, showing their devotion without using priests as intermediaries.

The bedrock of Hinduism is the belief that the Vedas are sacred revelations and that a specific caste system is implicitly prescribed in them. Hinduism is a guide to life, the goal of which is to reach union with brahman, the unchanging ultimate reality. There are four steps in this search, progressing from study of the Vedas in youth to complete asceticism in old age. In their quest for brahman, people are to observe **dharma**

(DAHR-muh), the moral law. Dharma stipulates the legitimate pursuits of Hindus: material gain, as long as it is honestly and honorably achieved; pleasure and love for the perpetuation of the family; and moksha, release from the wheel of life and unity with brahman. Because it recognizes the need for material gain and pleasure, Hinduism allows a joyful embracing of life. This certainly was part of its appeal.

Hinduism assumes that there are innumerable legitimate ways of worshipping brahman, including devotion to personal gods. After the third century B.C.E. Hinduism began to emphasize the roles and personalities of thousands of powerful gods. Brahma, the creator, Shiva, the cosmic dancer who both creates and destroys, and Vishnu, the preserver and sustainer of creation, were three of the main male deities. Important female deities included Lakshmi, goddess of wealth, and Saraswati, goddess of learning and music. These gods were usually represented by images, either small ones in homes or larger ones in temples. People could show devotion to their personal gods by reciting hymns or scriptures and by making offerings of food or flowers before these images. A worshipper's devotion to one god did not entail denial of other deities; ultimately all were manifestations of brahman, the ultimate reality. Hinduism's embrace of a large pantheon of gods enabled it to incorporate new sects, doctrines, beliefs, rites, and deities.

A central ethical text of Hinduism is the *Bhagavad Gita* (BAH-guh-vahd GEE-tuh), a part of the world's longest ancient epic, the *Mahabharata*. The *Bhagavad Gita* offers guidance on the most serious problem facing a Hindu—how to live in the world and yet honor dharma and thus achieve release from the wheel of life. The heart of the *Bhagavad Gita* is the spiritual conflict confronting Arjuna, a human hero about to ride into battle against his kinsmen. As he surveys the battlefield, struggling with the grim notion of killing his relatives, Arjuna voices his doubts to his charioteer, none other than the god Krishna. When at last Arjuna refuses to spill his family's blood, Krishna instructs him on the true meaning of Hinduism:

> You grieve for those beyond grief,
> and you speak words of insight;
> but learned men do not grieve
> for the dead or the living.

- **sutras** The written teachings of the Buddha, first transcribed in the second or first century B.C.E.
- **Mahayana** The "Great Vehicle," a tradition of Buddhism that aspires to be more inclusive.
- **bodhisattvas** Buddhas-to-be who stayed in the world after enlightenment to help others on the path to salvation.
- **dharma** The Sanskrit word for moral law, central both to Buddhist and Hindu teachings.

> "Never have I not existed, nor you, nor these kings; and never in the future shall we cease to exist."
>
> **KRISHNA**, from the *Bhagavad Gita*

The God Vishnu Vishnu reclining on his protector, the serpent Shesha, is the subject of this stone relief from the Temple of Vishnu in central India at Deogarh, which dates from the Gupta period, ca. 500 C.E. (Deogarh, Uttar Pradesh, India/Giraudon/The Bridgeman Art Library)

Never have I not existed,
nor you, nor these kings;
and never in the future
shall we cease to exist.

Just as the embodied self
enters childhood, youth, and old age,
so does it enter another body;
this does not confound a steadfast man.

Contacts with matter make us feel
heat and cold, pleasure and pain.
Arjuna, you must learn to endure
fleeting things — they come and go!

When these cannot torment a man,
when suffering and joy are equal
for him and he has courage,
he is fit for immortality.

Nothing of nonbeing comes to be,
nor does being cease to exist;
the boundary between these two
is seen by men who see reality.

Indestructible is the presence
that pervades all this;
no one can destroy
this unchanging reality.

Our bodies are known to end,
but the embodied self is enduring,
indestructible, and immeasurable;
therefore, Arjuna, fight the battle!

He who thinks this self a killer
and he who thinks it killed,
both fail to understand;
it does not kill, nor is it killed.

It is not born,
it does not die;
having been,
it will never not be;
unborn, enduring,
constant, and primordial,
it is not killed
when the body is killed.[2]

Krishna then clarifies the relationship between human reality and the eternal spirit. He explains compassionately to Arjuna the duty to act — to live in the world and carry out his duties as a warrior. Indeed, the *Bhagavad Gita* emphasizes the necessity of action, which is essential for the welfare of the world. For Arjuna the warrior's duty is to wage war in compliance with his dharma. Only those who live within the divine law without complaint will be released from rebirth. One person's dharma may be different from another's, but both individuals must follow their own dharmas.

Hinduism provided a complex and sophisticated philosophy of life and a religion of enormous emotional appeal that was attractive to ordinary Indians. Over time it grew to be the most common religion in India. Hinduism also inspired the preservation of literary masterpieces in Sanskrit and the major regional languages of India. Among these are the *Puranas*, which are stories of the gods and great warrior clans, and the *Mahabharata* and *Ramayana*, which are verse epics of India's early kings. Hinduism validated the caste system, adding to the stability of everyday village life, since people all knew where they stood in society.

Western Contact and the Mauryan Unification of North India, ca. 513–185 B.C.E.

☐ What was the result of Indian contact with the Persians and Greeks, and what were the consequences of unification under the Mauryan Empire?

In the late sixth century B.C.E., with the creation of the Persian empire that stretched from the west coast of Anatolia to the Indus River (see pages 58–61), west India was swept up in events that were changing the face of the ancient Near East. A couple of centuries later, by 322 B.C.E., the Greeks had supplanted the Persians in northwest India. Chandragupta saw this as an opportunity to expand his territories, and he successfully unified all of north India. The Mauryan Empire that he founded flourished under the reign of his grandson, Ashoka, but after Ashoka's death the empire declined.

Encounters with the West

India became involved in the turmoil of the sixth century B.C.E. when the Persian emperor Darius conquered the Indus Valley and Kashmir about 513 B.C.E. Persian control did not reach eastward beyond the Punjab, but even so it fostered increased contact between India and the Near East and led to the introduction of new ideas, techniques, and materials into India. From Persian administrators Indians learned more about how to rule large tracts of land and huge numbers of people. They also learned the technique of minting silver coins, and they adopted the Persian monetary standard to facilitate trade with other parts of the empire. Even states in the Ganges Valley, which were never part of the Persian Empire, adopted the use of coinage.

Another result of contact with Persia was introduction of the Aramaic script, used to write the official language of the Persian Empire. To keep records and publish proclamations just as the Persians did, Indians in northwest India adapted the Aramaic script for writing several local languages (elsewhere, Indians developed the Brahmi script, the ancestor of the script used for modern Hindi). In time the sacred texts of the Buddhists and the Jains, as well as epics and other literary works, came to be recorded using Aramaic script to write down Indian languages.

The Persian Empire in turn succumbed to Alexander the Great, and in 326 B.C.E. Alexander led his Macedonian and Greek troops through the Khyber Pass into the Indus Valley (discussed in Chapter 5 on page 131). The India

Hellenistic Influences in Gandharan Art Because Alexander the Great's army had reached this region and Hellenistic states then controlled it for more than a century, the art of Gandhara was strongly influenced by Greek artistic styles. This stucco figure was excavated from a site in eastern Afghanistan where some 23,000 Greco-Buddhist sculptures were found. Hellenistic influence, as evidenced by the drape of the clothing and the modeling of the head, is particularly easy to recognize in this piece. (Erich Lessing/Art Resource, NY)

that Alexander encountered was composed of many rival states. He defeated some of these states in the northwest and heard reports of others. Porus, king of west Punjab, fought Alexander with a battalion of two thousand war elephants. After being defeated, he agreed to become a subordinate king under Alexander.

The Greeks were intrigued by the Indian culture they encountered. Alexander had heard of the sophistication of Indian philosophers and summoned some to instruct him or debate with him. The Greeks were also impressed with Indian cities, most notably Tax-

ila, a major center of trade in the Punjab. The Greeks described it as "a city great and prosperous, the biggest of those between the Indus River and the Hydaspes [the modern Jhelum River] — a region not inferior to Egypt in size, with especially good pastures and rich in fine fruits."[3] From Taxila, Alexander followed the Indus River south, hoping to find the end of the world. His men, however, mutinied and refused to continue. When Alexander turned back, he left his general Seleucus (suh-LOO-kuhs) in charge of his easternmost region.

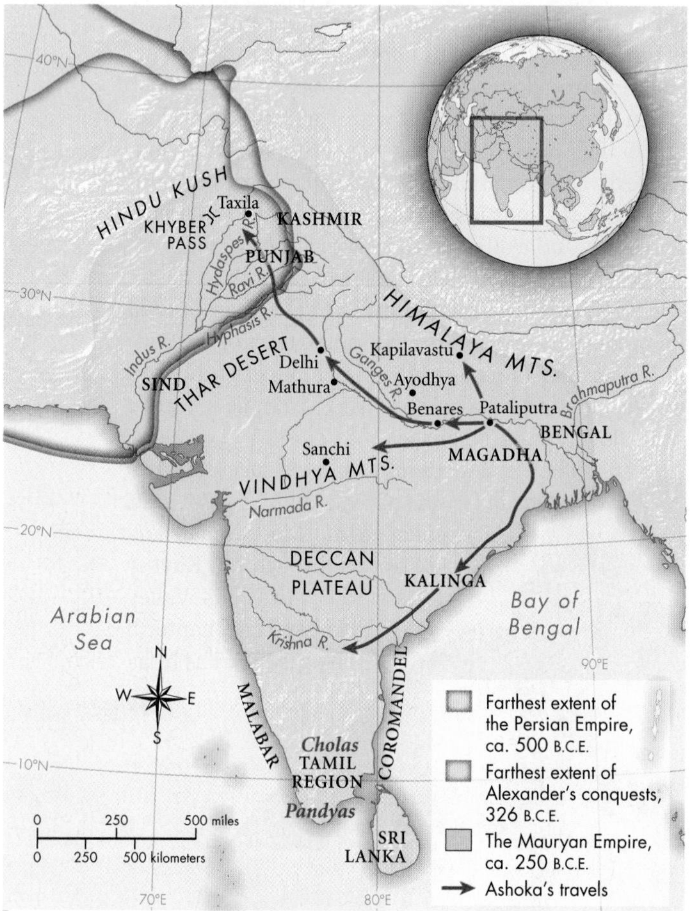

Chandragupta and the Founding of the Mauryan Empire

The one to benefit most from Alexander's invasion was Chandragupta, the ruler of a growing state in the Ganges Valley. He took advantage of the crisis caused by Alexander's invasion to expand his territories, and by 322 B.C.E. he had made himself sole master of north India (Map 3.2). In 304 B.C.E. he defeated the forces of Seleucus.

With stunning effectiveness, Chandragupta applied the lessons learned from Persian rule. He adopted the Persian practice of dividing the area into provinces. Each province was assigned a governor, usually drawn from Chandragupta's own family. He established a complex bureaucracy to see to the operation of the state and a bureaucratic taxation system that financed public services through taxes on agriculture. He also built a regular army, complete with departments for everything from naval matters to the collection of supplies.

For the first time in Indian history, one man governed most of the subcontinent, exercising control through delegated power. From his capital at Pataliputra in the Ganges Valley (now Patna in Bihar), Chandragupta sent agents to the provinces to oversee the workings of government and to keep him informed of conditions in his realm. In designing his bureaucratic system, Chandragupta enjoyed the able assistance of his great minister Kautilya, who wrote a treatise on how a king should seize, hold, and manipulate power, rather like the Legalist treatises produced in China later that century (discussed in Chapter 4 on page 110). Kautilya urged the king to use propaganda to gain support, for instance, to disguise secret agents to look like gods so that people would be awed when they saw him in their company. He stressed the importance of seeking the enemies of his enemies, who would make good allies. When a neighboring prince was in trouble, that was the perfect time to attack him. Interstate relations were likened to the law of the fish: the large swallow the small. (See "Viewpoints: On Enemies from *The Laws of Manu* and *The Arthashastra*," page 83.)

Megasthenes, a Greek ambassador sent by Seleucus, spent fourteen years in Chandragupta's court. He left

◻ Mapping the Past

MAP 3.2 The Mauryan Empire, ca. 250 B.C.E. The Ganges River Valley was the heart of the Mauryan Empire. Although India is protected from the cold by mountains in the north, mountain passes in the northwest allowed both migration and invasion.

ANALYZING THE MAP Where are the major rivers of India? How close are they to mountains?

CONNECTIONS Can you think of any reasons that the Persian Empire and Alexander's conquests both reached into the same region of northwest India?

Viewpoints

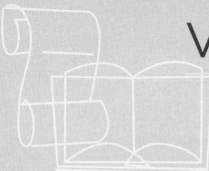

On Enemies from *The Laws of Manu* and *The Arthashastra*

> • *Advice on how to rule is found in two of the important books from early India,* The Laws of Manu, *dating perhaps to the second century C.E., and* The Arthashastra, *attributed to Kautilya, with material dating from the fourth century B.C.E. to the fourth century C.E. Both books cover many topics in addition to the advice on dealing with enemies excerpted below.*

"The Law for the King" from *The Laws of Manu*

[The King] should recognize that his immediate neighbor is his enemy, as also anyone rendering assistance to the enemy; that his enemy's immediate neighbor is an ally; and that the one beyond these two is neutral. He should prevail over them by conciliation and the other strategies, employed both separately and collectively, and by valor and policy. . . .

When he is convinced that his future dominance is certain and that any immediate disadvantage is slight, then he should resort to an alliance. When he believes that all his subjects are exceedingly content and that he himself is overwhelmingly powerful, then he should consider waging war. When he believes in his heart that his own army is in high spirit and prosperous and that the opposite is true of his adversary, then he should march into battle against his enemy. When he is weak in terms of mounted units and infantry, then he should diligently remain stationary, while gradually appeasing the enemy. When the king believes that the enemy is stronger in every respect, then he should divide his army in two and accomplish his objective. When he has become extremely vulnerable to his enemy's forces, then he should quickly seek asylum with a strong and righteous king. Should that king keep both his own subjects and the forces of his enemy in check, he should always serve him like a teacher with all his strength. Even in that case, however, if he notices a liability resulting from his asylum, he should, even in that condition, resort to the good war without hesitation. A politically astute king should employ all the strategies in such a way that his allies, neutrals, or enemies do not prevail over him.

"Capture of the Enemy by Means of Secret Contrivances" from *The Arthashastra*

Contrivances to kill the enemy may be formed in those places of worship and visit, which the enemy, under the influence of faith, frequents on occasions of worshipping gods and of pilgrimage. A wall or stone, kept by mechanical contrivance, may, by loosening the fastenings, be let to fall on the head of the enemy when he has entered into a temple; stones and weapons may be showered over his head from the topmost story; or a door-panel may be let to fall; or a huge rod kept over a wall or partly attached to a wall may be made to fall over him; or weapons kept inside the body of an idol may be thrown over his head; or the floor of those places where he usually stands, sits, or walks may be besprinkled with poison mixed with cowdung or with pure water; or, under the plea of giving him flowers, scented powders, or of causing scented smoke, he may be poisoned. . . .

Or having challenged the conqueror at night, he may successfully confront the attack; if he cannot do this, he may run away by a side path; or, disguised as a heretic, he may escape with a small retinue; or he may be carried off by spies as a corpse; or disguised as a woman, he may follow a corpse [as it were, of her husband to the cremation ground]; or on the occasion of feeding the people in honor of gods or of ancestors or in some festival, he may make use of poisoned rice and water, and having conspired with his enemy's traitors, he may strike the enemy with his concealed army; or, when he is surrounded in his fort, he may lie concealed in a hole bored into the body of an idol after eating sacramental food and setting up an altar; . . . and when he is forgotten, he may get out of his concealment through a tunnel, and, entering into the palace, slay his enemy while sleeping, or loosening the fastening of a machine he may let it fall on his enemy; or when his enemy is lying in a chamber which is besmeared with poisonous and explosive substances, or which is made of lac [varnish], he may set fire to it. . . .

Sources: Patrick Olivelle, trans., *Manu's Code of Law* (Oxford: Oxford University Press, 2005), 162–163. © 2004 by the University of Texas Center for Asian Studies. Used by permission of Oxford University Press, Inc.; Kautilya, *Kautilya's Arthashastra*, trans. R. Shamasastry (Bangalore: Government Press, 1915).

QUESTIONS FOR ANALYSIS

1. What can you infer about interstate relations in the period these texts were written?

2. How alike are these documents in their approach toward dealing with enemies?

3. How do these texts add to your understanding of early Indian religion?

a lively description of life there. He described the city as square and surrounded by wooden walls, twenty-two miles on each side, with 570 towers and 64 gates. It had a university, a library, and magnificent palaces, temples, gardens, and parks. The king personally presided over court sessions where legal cases were heard and petitions received. The king claimed for the state all mines and forests, and there were large state farms, granaries, shipyards, and spinning and weaving factories. Even prostitution was controlled by the state. Only a portion of the empire was ruled so directly, according to Megasthenes. In outlying areas, local kings were left in place if they pledged loyalty.

Megasthenes described Chandragupta as afraid of treachery and assassination attempts:

> Attendance on the king's person is the duty of women, who indeed are bought from their fathers. Outside the gates of the palace stand the bodyguards and the rest of the soldiers. . . . Nor does the king sleep during the day, and at night he is forced at various hours to change his bed because of those plotting against him. Of his non-military departures from the palace one is to the courts, in which he passes the day hearing cases to the end, even if the hour arrives for attendance on his person. . . . When he leaves to hunt, he is thickly surrounded by a circle of women, and on the outside by spear-carrying bodyguards. The road is fenced off with ropes, and to anyone who passes within the ropes as far as the women death is the penalty.[4]

> "Nor does the king sleep during the day, and at night he is forced at various hours to change his bed because of those plotting against him."
>
> MEGASTHENES

Those measures apparently worked, as Chandragupta lived a long life. According to Jain tradition, Chandragupta became a Jain ascetic and died a peaceful death in 298 B.C.E. Although he personally adopted a nonviolent philosophy, he left behind a kingdom with the military might to maintain order and defend India from invasion.

The Reign of Ashoka, ca. 269–232 B.C.E.

The years after Chandragupta's death were an epoch of political greatness, thanks largely to his grandson Ashoka, one of India's most remarkable figures. The era of Ashoka was enormously important in the religious history of the world, because Ashoka embraced Buddhism and promoted its spread beyond India.

As a young prince, Ashoka served as governor of two prosperous provinces where Buddhism flourished. At the death of his father about 274 B.C.E., Ashoka rebelled against his older brother, who had succeeded as king, and after four years of fighting won his bid for the throne. Crowned king, Ashoka ruled intelligently and energetically. He was equally serious about his pleasures, especially those of the banquet hall and harem.

In the ninth year of his reign, 261 B.C.E., Ashoka conquered Kalinga, on the east coast of India. In a grim and savage campaign, Ashoka reduced Kalinga by wholesale slaughter. As Ashoka himself admitted, "One hundred and fifty thousand were forcibly abducted from their homes, 100,000 were killed in battle, and many more died later on."[5] Instead of exulting like a conqueror, however, Ashoka was consumed with remorse and revulsion at the horror of war. He embraced Buddhism and used the machinery of his empire to spread Buddhist teachings throughout India. He supported the doctrine of not hurting humans or animals then spreading among religious people of all sects in India. He banned animal sacrifices, and in place of hunting expeditions he took pilgrimages. Two years after his conversion, he undertook a 256-day pilgrimage to all the holy sites of Buddhism, and on his return he sent missionaries to all known countries. Buddhist tradition also credits him with erecting 84,000 stupas (structures containing Buddhist relics) throughout India, among which the ashes or other bodily remains of the Buddha were distributed, beginning the association of Buddhism with monumental art and architecture.

Ashoka's remarkable crisis of conscience, like the later conversion to Christianity of the Roman emperor Constantine, affected the way he ruled. He emphasized compassion, nonviolence, and adherence to dharma. He appointed officials to oversee the moral welfare of the realm and required local officials to govern humanely. He may have perceived dharma as a kind of civic virtue, a universal ethical model capable of uniting the diverse peoples of his extensive empire. Ashoka erected stone pillars, on the Persian model, with inscriptions to inform the people of his policies. He also had long inscriptions carved into large rock surfaces near trade routes. In his last important inscription he spoke of his efforts to encourage his people toward the path of righteousness:

> I have had banyan trees planted on the roads to give shade to man and beast; I have planted mango groves, and I have had ponds dug and shelters erected along the roads at every eight kos. Everywhere I have had wells dug for the benefit of man and beast. But his benefit is but small, for in many ways the kings of olden time have worked for the welfare of the world; but what I have done has been done that men may conform to righteousness.[6]

The North Gate at Sanchi
This is one of four ornately carved gates guarding the stupa at Sanchi in the state of Madhya Pradesh in India. Containing the relics of the Buddha, this Buddhist memorial shrine from the second century B.C.E. was commissioned by Ashoka. (Jean-Louis Nou/akg-images)

These inscriptions are the earliest fully dated Indian texts. (Until the script in which they were written was deciphered in 1837, nothing was known of Ashoka's achievements.) The pillars on which they are inscribed are also the first examples of Indian art to survive since the end of the Indus civilization.

Ashoka felt the need to protect his new religion and to keep it pure. He warned Buddhist monks that he would not tolerate schism — divisions based on differences of opinion about doctrine or ritual. According to Buddhist tradition, a great council of Buddhist monks was held at Pataliputra, where the earliest canon of Buddhist texts was codified. At the same time, Ashoka honored India's other religions, even building shrines for Hindu and Jain worshippers. In one edict he banned rowdy popular fairs, allowing only religious gatherings.

Despite his devotion to Buddhism, Ashoka never neglected his duties as emperor. He tightened the central government of the empire and kept a close check on local officials. He built roads and rest spots to improve communication within the realm. These measures also facilitated the march of armies and the armed enforcement of Ashoka's authority. Ashoka described his work: "Whatever good I have done has indeed been accomplished for the progress and welfare of the world. By these shall grow virtues namely: proper support of mother and father, regard for preceptors and elders,

proper treatment of Brahmans and ascetics, of the poor and the destitute, slaves and servants."[7]

Ashoka's inscriptions indirectly tell us much about the Mauryan Empire. He directly administered the central part of the empire, focusing on Magadha. Beyond it were four large provinces under princes who served as viceroys, each with its own sets of smaller districts and officials. The interior of south India was described as inhabited by undefeated forest tribes. Farther south, along the coasts, were peoples that Ashoka maintained friendly relations with but did not rule, such as the Cholas and Pandyas. Relations with Sri Lanka were especially close under Ashoka, and the king sent a branch of the tree under which the Buddha gained enlightenment to the Sri Lankan king. According to Buddhist legend, Ashoka's son Mahinda traveled to Sri Lanka to convert the people there.

Ashoka ruled for thirty-seven years. After he died in about 232 B.C.E. the Mauryan Dynasty went into decline, and India broke up into smaller units, much like those in existence before Alexander's invasion. Even though Chandragupta had instituted bureaucratic methods of centralized political control and Ashoka had vigorously pursued the political and cultural integration of the empire, the institutions they created were not entrenched enough to survive periods with weaker kings.

Small States and Trading Networks, 185 B.C.E.–300 C.E.

☐ How was India shaped by political disunity and contacts with other cultures during the five centuries from 185 B.C.E. to 300 C.E.?

After the Mauryan Dynasty collapsed in 185 B.C.E., and for much of subsequent Indian history, political unity would be the exception rather than the rule. By this time, however, key elements of Indian culture — the caste system; the religious traditions of Hinduism, Buddhism, and Jainism; and the great epics and legends — had given India a cultural unity strong enough to endure even without political unity.

In the years after the fall of the Mauryan Dynasty, a series of foreign powers dominated the Indus Valley and adjoining regions. The first were hybrid Indo-Greek states ruled by the inheritors of Alexander's defunct empire stationed in what is now Afghanistan. The city of Taxila became a major center of trade, culture, and education, fusing elements of Greek and Indian culture.

The great, slow movement of nomadic peoples out of East Asia that brought the Scythians to the Near East brought the Shakas to northwest India. They controlled the region from about 94 to 20 B.C.E., when they were displaced by a new nomadic invader, the Kushans, who ruled the region of today's Afghanistan, Pakistan, and west India as far south as Gujarat. Buddhist sources refer to their king Kanishka (r. ca. 78–ca. 103 C.E.) as not only a powerful ruler but also a major patron of Buddhism. Some of the coins he issued had a picture of him on one side and of the Buddha on the other. The famous silk trade from China to Rome (see "Global Trade: Silk," page 184) passed through his territory.

During the Kushan period, Greek culture had a considerable impact on Indian art. Indo-Greek artists and sculptors working in India adorned Buddhist shrines, modeling the earliest representation of the Buddha on Hellenistic statues of Apollo. Another contribution from the Indo-Greek states was coin cast with images of the king, which came to be widely adopted by Indian rulers, aiding commerce and adding evidence of rulers' names and sequence to the historical record. Places where coins are found also show patterns of trade.

Cultural exchange also went in the other direction. Old Indian animal folktales were translated into Syriac and Greek and from that source eventually made their way to Europe. South India in this period was also the center of active seaborne trade, with networks reaching all the way to Rome. Indian sailing technology was highly advanced, and much of this trade was in the hands of Indian merchants. Roman traders based in Egypt followed the routes already used by Arab traders, sailing with the monsoon from the Red Sea to the west coast of India in about two weeks, returning about six months later when the direction of the winds reversed. In the first century C.E. a Greek merchant involved in this trade reported that the traders sold coins, topaz, coral, crude glass, copper, tin, and lead and bought pearls, ivory, silk (probably originally from China), jewels of many sorts (probably many from Southeast Asia), and above all cinnamon and pepper. More Roman gold coins of the first and second centuries C.E. have been found near the southern tip of India than in any other area. The local rulers had slits made across the image of the Roman emperor to show that his sovereignty was not recognized, but they had no objection to the coins' circulating. (By contrast, the Kushan rulers in the north had Roman coins melted down to make coins with their own images on them.)

Even after the fall of Rome, many of the traders on the southwest coast of India remained. These scattered communities of Christians and Jews lived in the coastal cities into modern times. When Vasco da Gama, the Portuguese explorer, reached Calicut in 1498, he found a local Jewish merchant who was able to interpret for him.

During these centuries there were significant advances in science, mathematics, and philosophy. Indian astronomers charted the movements of stars and planets and recognized that the earth was spherical. In the realm of physics, Indian scientists, like their Greek counterparts, conceived of matter in terms of five elements: earth, air, fire, water, and ether. This was also the period when Indian law was codified. The **Code of Manu**, which lays down family, caste, and commercial law, was compiled in the second or third century C.E., drawing on older texts.

Regional cultures tend to flourish when there is no dominant unifying state, and the Tamils of south India were one of the major beneficiaries of the collapse of the Mauryan Dynasty. The third century B.C.E.

The Kushan Empire, ca. 200 B.C.E.

- **Code of Manu** The codification of early Indian law that lays down family, caste, and commercial law.

Kushan Gold Coin Kanishka I had coins made depicting a standing Buddha with his left hand raised in a gesture of renunciation (left). The reverse side (below) shows the king performing a sacrifice, the legend reading "Kanishka the Kushan, king of kings." (Courtesy of the Trustees of the British Museum)

to the third century C.E. is considered the classical period of Tamil culture, when many great works of literature were written under the patronage of the regional kings. Some of the poems written then take a hard look at war:

"Harvest of War"

Great king
you shield your men from ruin,
so your victories, your greatness
are bywords.

Loose chariot wheels
lie about the battleground
with the long white tusks
of bull-elephants.

Flocks of male eagles
eat carrion
with their mates.

Headless bodies
dance about
before they fall
to the ground.

Blood glows,
like the sky before nightfall,
in the red center
of the battlefield.

Demons dance there.
And your kingdom
is an unfailing harvest
of victorious wars.[8]

Other poems provide evidence of lively commerce, mentioning bulging warehouses, ships from many lands, and complex import-export procedures. From contact of this sort, the south came to absorb many cultural elements from the north, but also retained differences. Castes were present in the south before contact with the Sanskrit north, but took distinct forms, as the Kshatriya (warrior) and Vaishya (merchant) varna were hardly known in the far south.

Ashokan Pillar The best preserved of the pillars that King Ashoka erected in about 240 B.C.E. is this one in the Bihar region, near Nepal. The solid shaft of polished sandstone rises 32 feet in the air. It weighs about 50 tons, making its erection a remarkable feat of engineering. Like other Ashokan pillars, it is inscribed with accounts of Ashoka's political achievements and instructions to his subjects on proper behavior. These pillars are the earliest examples of Indian writing still existing and a major historical source for the Mauryan period. (Borromeo/Art Resource, NY)

India was a very different place in the third century C.E. than it had been in the early phase of Harappan civilization more than two thousand years earlier. The region was still divided into many different polities, but people living there in 300 shared much more in the way of ideas and traditions. The great epics such as the *Mahabharata* and the *Ramayana* provided a cultural vocabulary for groups that spoke different languages and had rival rulers. New religions had emerged, notably Buddhism and Jainism, and Hinduism was much more a devotional religion. Contact with ancient Mesopotamia, Persia, Greece, and Rome had brought new ideas, practices, and products.

During this same time period, civilization in China underwent similar expansion and diversification. China was farther away than India from other Eurasian centers of civilization, and its developments were consequently not as closely linked. Logographic writing appeared with the Bronze-Age Shang civilization and was preserved into modern times, in striking contrast to India and lands to its west, which developed written languages that represented sounds. Still, some developments affected both India and China, such as the appearance of chariots and horseback riding. The next chapter takes up the story of these developments in early China. In Chapter 12, after considering early developments in Europe, Asia, Africa, and the Americas, we return to the story of India.

CHAPTER REVIEW

KEY TERMS

Harappan (p. 66)	Eightfold Path
Aryans (p. 69)	(p. 77)
Rigveda (p. 70)	nirvana (p. 77)
Brahmins (p. 71)	sutras (p. 78)
caste system (p. 71)	Mahayana (p. 78)
samsara (p. 74)	bodhisattvas (p. 79)
karma (p. 74)	dharma (p. 79)
brahman (p. 74)	Code of Manu
Four Noble Truths	(p. 86)
(p. 77)	

□ **What does archaeology tell us about the Harappan civilization in India? (p. 66)**

From archaeology we know that the Harappan civilization emerged in the Indus River Valley in the third millennium B.C.E. The archaeological record suggests a striking uniformity in architecture and religious ideas and practices throughout the region dominated by the Harappan culture. The large cities that have been excavated were made of kiln-dried brick and were carefully planned, with straight streets and sewers. Seals of Mesopotamian origin indicate trade between the Harappans and the Persian Gulf. Although many intriguing artifacts have been excavated, many questions remain about this civilization, and its script has not been deciphered. Scholars can only speculate why Harappan cities were largely abandoned by 1800 B.C.E.

□ **What kind of society and culture did the Indo-European Aryans create? (p. 69)**

From originally oral texts like the *Rigveda*, we know much about the values and social practices of the Aryans, speakers of an early form of the Indo-European language Sanskrit. During the Vedic Age Aryan warrior tribes fought using chariots and bronze swords and spears, gradually expanding into the Ganges River Valley. The first stages of the Indian caste system date to this period, when warriors and priests were ranked above merchants, artisans, and farmers. Key religious ideas were the notions of karma and rebirth and the importance of sacrifice.

□ **What ideas and practices were taught by the founders of Jainism, Buddhism, and Hinduism? (p. 74)**

Beginning around 500 B.C.E. three of India's major religions emerged. Mahavira was the founder of the Jain religion. He taught his followers to live ascetic lives, avoid doing harm to any living thing, and renounce evil thoughts and actions. The founder of Buddhism, Siddhartha Gautama or the Buddha, similarly taught his followers a path to liberation that involved avoiding violence and freeing themselves from desires. The Buddha, however, did not think extreme asceticism was the best path and put more emphasis on mental detachment. In response to the popularity of Jainism and Buddhism, both of which rejected animal sacrifice and ignored the caste system, the traditional Brahmanic religion evolved in a devotional direction that has been called Hinduism. Hindu traditions validated sacrifice and caste but stressed the individual's relationship to the gods he or she worshipped.

◻ **What was the result of Indian contact with the Persians and Greeks, and what were the consequences of unification under the Mauryan Empire? (p. 81)**

In the sixth century B.C.E. the Persian Empire expanded into the Indus River Valley, and in the fourth century Alexander the Great's troops took the same region. From contact with the Persians and Greeks, new political techniques, ideas, art styles, and the use of money entered the Indian repertoire. Shortly after the arrival of the Greeks, much of north India was politically unified by the Mauryan Empire under Chandragupta. His grandson Ashoka was the empire's greatest ruler. Ashoka converted to Buddhism and promoted its spread inside and outside of India. The inscriptions he had carved on stones and erected in many places in his empire provide some of the best-dated sources on early Indian history and show his efforts to centralize power.

◻ **How was India shaped by political disunity and contacts with other cultures during the five centuries from 185 B.C.E. to 300 C.E.? (p. 86)**

After the decline of the Mauryan Empire, India was politically fragmented. Indian cultural identity remained strong, however, because of shared religious ideas and shared literature, including the great early epics. A series of foreign powers came to dominate the Indus Valley and surrounding regions in this period. The Indo-Greek city of Taxila became a major center of trade, culture, and education. The movement of nomadic peoples out of East Asia brought the Shakas to northeast India, where they ruled until they were displaced by the Kushans, another nomadic group. Trade and other contact with the outside world brought new elements into Indian civilization, and Greek coinage was adopted widely by Indian rulers. Just as India came to absorb Persian and Greek bureaucratic techniques and artistic styles, cultures of western Eurasia were introduced to folktales, crops, textiles, inventions, and religious ideas from India. This cultural interchange was facilitated by the silk trade in northwest India and the maritime trade of southern India.

SUGGESTED READING

Basham, A. L. *The Wonder That Was India*, 3d rev. ed. 1968. Classic appreciative account of early Indian civilization by a scholar deeply immersed in Indian literature.

Embree, Ainslee, ed. *Sources of Indian Tradition*, 2d ed. 1988. An excellent introduction to Indian religion, philosophy, and intellectual history through translations of major sources.

Keay, John. *India: A History*. 2000. Wide-ranging history of India, with a strong narrative.

Koller, John M. *The Indian Way*, 2d ed. 2004. An accessible introduction to the variety of Indian religions and philosophies.

Kulke, Hermann, and Dietmar Rothermund. *A History of India*, 3d ed. 1998. A good balanced introduction to Indian history.

Lopez, Donald S., Jr. *The Story of the Buddha: A Concise Guide to Its History and Teachings*. 2001. Emphasizes Buddhist practice, drawing examples from many different countries and time periods.

Miller, Barbara, trans. *The Bhagavad-Gita: Krishna's Counsel in Time of War*. 1986. One of several excellent translations of India's classical literature.

Possehl, Gregory L. *The Indus Civilization*. 2002. Recent overview of Harappan civilization.

Renfew, Colin. *Archaeology and Language: The Puzzle of Indo-European Origins*. 1987. In-depth analysis of the question of the origins of the Aryans.

Scharff, Harmut. *The State in Indian Tradition*. 1989. Scholarly analysis of the period from the Aryans to the Muslims.

Thapar, Romilia. *Early India to 1300*. 2002. A freshly revised overview by a leading Indian historian.

Wright, Rita P. *The Ancient Indus: Urbanism, Economy, and Society*. 2010. Broad-ranging overview that brings in Mesopotamian sources.

NOTES

1. *Rigveda* 10.90, in Ainslie T. Embree, trans., *Sources of Indian Tradition*, 2d ed. Vol. 1: *From the Beginning to 1800*. Copyright © 1988 by Columbia University Press. Reprinted with permission of the publisher.

2. Excerpt from Barbara Stoler Miller, trans., *The Bhagavad-Gita: Krishna's Counsel in Time of War* (New York: Columbia University Press, 1986), pp. 31–32. Translation copyright © 1986 by Barbara Stoler Miller. Used by permission of Bantam Books, a division of Random House, Inc.

3. Arrian, *Anabasis* 5.8.2; Plutarch, *Alexander* 59.1. Translated by John Buckler.

4. *Strabo* 15.1.55. Translated by John Buckler.

5. Quoted in H. Kulke and D. Rothermund, *A History of India*, 3d ed. (London: Routledge, 1998), p. 62.

6. Embree, p. 148. Copyright © 1988 by Columbia University Press. Reprinted with permission of the publisher.

7. Quoted in B. G. Gokhale, *Asoka Maurya* (New York: Twayne Publishers, 1966), p. 169.

8. A. K. Ramanujan, ed. and trans., *Poems of Love and War: From the Eight Anthologies and the Ten Long Poems of Classical Tamil* (New York: Columbia University Press, 1985), p. 115. Copyright 1985 by Columbia University Press. Reproduced with permission of Columbia University Press in the format Textbook via Copyright Clearance Center.

For practice quizzes and other study tools, see the **Online Study Guide** at bedfordstmartins.com/mckayworld.

For primary sources from this period, see *Sources of World Societies*, **Second Edition**.

For Web sites, images, and documents related to topics in this chapter, visit **Make History** at bedfordstmartins.com/mckayworld.

• **Bronze Head from China** Archaeological discoveries continue to expand our knowledge of the cultures and civilizations of early China. This 20-inch-tall bronze head was found among a large set of sacrificial offerings in the modern province of Sichuan. These unusual objects, which were found only there, suggest a distinct culture. (Sanxingdui Museum, Guanghan, Sichuan Province, © Cultural Relics Press)

China's Classical Age
to 221 B.C.E.

In comparison to India and the ancient Middle East, China developed in relative isolation. Communication with West and South Asia was very difficult, impeded by high mountains and vast deserts. Though there was some trade, the distances were so great that it did not allow the kind of cross-fertilization that occurred in western Eurasia. Moreover, there were no cultural breaks comparable to the rise of the Aryans in India or the Assyrians in Mesopotamia to introduce new peoples and languages. The impact of early China's relative isolation is found in many distinctive features of its culture. Perhaps the most important is its writing system; unlike the other major societies of Eurasia, China retained a logographic writing system with a symbol for each word. This writing system shaped not only Chinese literature and thought but also key social and political processes, such as the nature of the ruling class and interactions with non-Chinese.

Chinese history is commonly discussed in terms of a succession of dynasties. The Shang Dynasty (ca. 1500–1050 B.C.E.) was the first to have writing, metalworking, cities, and chariots. The Shang kings played priestly roles, serving as intermediaries with both their royal ancestors and the high god Di. The Shang were overthrown by one of their vassal states, which founded the Zhou Dynasty (ca. 1050–256 B.C.E.). The Zhou rulers set up a decentralized feudal governmental structure that evolved over centuries into a multistate system. As warfare between the states intensified in the sixth century B.C.E., social and cultural change quickened. Aristocratic privileges declined, and China entered one of its most creative periods, when the philosophies of Confucianism, Daoism, and Legalism were developed. •

The Emergence of Civilization in China
□ What was the impact of China's geography on the development of Chinese societies?

The Shang Dynasty, ca. 1500–1050 B.C.E.
□ What was life like during the Shang Dynasty, and what effect did writing have on Chinese culture and government?

The Early Zhou Dynasty, ca. 1050–400 B.C.E.
□ How was China governed, and what was life like during the Zhou Dynasty?

The Warring States Period, 403–221 B.C.E.
□ How did advances in military technology contribute to the rise of independent states?

Confucius and His Followers
□ What ideas did Confucius teach, and how were they spread after his death?

Daoism, Legalism, and Other Schools of Thought
□ How did the teachings of Daoism, Legalism, and other schools of thought differ from Confucianism?

The Emergence of Civilization in China

□ What was the impact of China's geography on the development of Chinese societies?

The term *China*, like the term *India*, does not refer to the same geographical entity at all points in history. The historical China, also called China proper, was smaller than present-day China, not larger like the historical India. The contemporary People's Republic of China includes Tibet, Inner Mongolia, Turkestan, Manchuria, and other territories that in premodern times were neither inhabited by Chinese nor ruled directly by Chinese states. The geography of the region in which Chinese civilization developed has had an impact on its historical development to the present.

The Impact of Geography

China proper, about a thousand miles north to south and east to west, occupies much of the temperate zone of East Asia (Map 4.1). The northern part, drained by the Yellow River, is colder, flatter, and more arid than the south. Rainfall in many areas is less than twenty inches a year, making the land well suited to crops like wheat and millet. The dominant soil is **loess**—fine wind-driven earth that is fertile and easy to work even with simple tools. The soil gives the Yellow River its characteristic color, and because so much of the loess ends up as silt in the river, the riverbed rises and easily floods unless diked. Drought is another perennial problem for farmers in the north. The Yangzi (YANG-zuh) River is the dominant feature of the warmer, wetter, and more lush south, a region well suited to rice cultivation. Farmers in recent centuries have been able to get two rice crops a year from the land around the Yangzi River and farther south. The Yangzi and its many tributaries are navigable, so boats were traditionally the preferred means of transportation in the south.

Mountains, deserts, and grasslands separated China proper from other early civilizations. Between China and India lay Tibet, with its vast mountain ranges and high plateaus. North of Tibet are great expanses of desert where nothing grows except in rare oases, and north of the desert grasslands stretch from Ukraine to eastern Siberia. Chinese civilization did not spread into any of these Inner Asian regions, above all because they were not suited to growing crops. Inner Asia, where raising animals is a more productive use of land than planting crops, became the heartland of China's traditional enemies, such as the nomadic tribes of the Xiongnu (SHUHNG-noo) and Mongols.

Early Agricultural Societies of the Neolithic Age

From about 10,000 B.C.E. agriculture was practiced in China. It apparently originated independently of somewhat earlier developments in Egypt and Mesopotamia, but was perhaps influenced by developments in Southeast Asia, where rice was also cultivated very early. By 5000 B.C.E. there were Neolithic village settlements in several regions of China. The primary Neolithic crops were drought-resistant millet, grown in the loess soils of the north, and rice, grown in the wetlands of the lower reaches of the Yangzi River, where inhabitants supplemented their diet with fish. In both areas pigs, dogs, and cattle were domesticated, and by 3000 B.C.E. sheep had become important in the north and water buffalo in the south. Silk production can also be traced back to this period.

• **loess** Soil deposited by wind; it is fertile and easy to work.

Over the course of the fifth to third millennia B.C.E. many distinct regional Neolithic cultures emerged. One such culture emerged in the northwest during the fourth and third millennia B.C.E. These people are known for their fine red pottery vessels decorated in black pigment with bold designs, including spirals, sawtooth lines, and zoomorphic stick figures. At the same time in the east, a different culture made pottery that was rarely painted but had distinctive shapes, including three-legged, deep-bodied tripods. Jade ornaments, blades, and ritual objects, sometimes of extraordinary craftsmanship, have been found in several eastern sites but are rare in western ones.

These Neolithic societies left no written records, but we know from the material record that over time they came to share more and more social and cultural practices. Many practices related to treatment of the dead spread to other groups from their original area, including use of coffins, ramped chambers, large numbers of grave goods, and divination aimed at communicating with ancestors or gods based on interpreting cracks in cattle bones. Fortified walls made of rammed earth came to be built around settlements in many areas, suggesting not only increased contact between Neolithic societies but also increased conflict. (For more on life in Neolithic societies, see Chapter 1.)

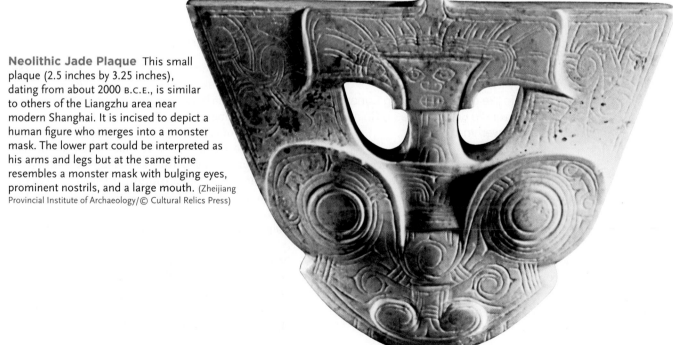

Neolithic Jade Plaque This small plaque (2.5 inches by 3.25 inches), dating from about 2000 B.C.E., is similar to others of the Liangzhu area near modern Shanghai. It is incised to depict a human figure who merges into a monster mask. The lower part could be interpreted as his arms and legs but at the same time resembles a monster mask with bulging eyes, prominent nostrils, and a large mouth. (Zheijiang Provincial Institute of Archaeology/© Cultural Relics Press)

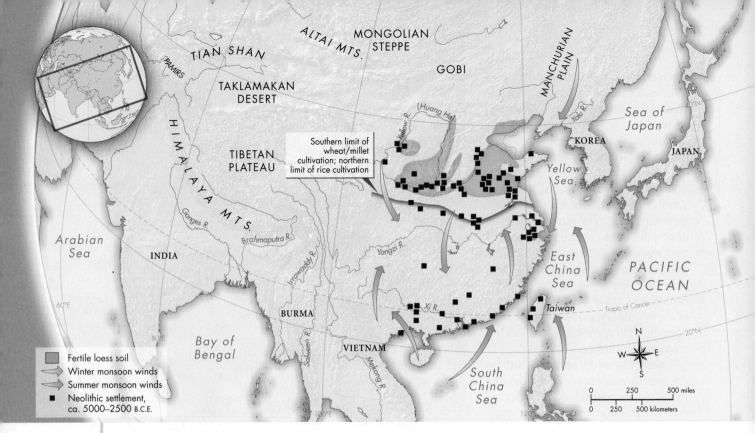

□ Mapping the Past

MAP 4.1 The Geography of Historical China Chinese civilization developed in the temperate regions drained by the Yellow and Yangzi Rivers.

ANALYZING THE MAP Trace the routes of the Yellow and Yangzi Rivers. Where are the areas of loess soil? Where are the Neolithic sites concentrated?

CONNECTIONS Does China's geography explain much about its history? (See also Map 4.2.) What geographical features had the greatest impact in the Neolithic Age? How might the fact that the Yellow and Yangzi Rivers flow west to east, rather than north to south, have influenced the development of Chinese society?

The Shang Dynasty, ca. 1500–1050 B.C.E.

□ What was life like during the Shang Dynasty, and what effect did writing have on Chinese culture and government?

After 2000 B.C.E. a Bronze Age civilization appeared in north China that shared traits with Bronze Age civilizations elsewhere in Eurasia, such as Mesopotamia, Egypt, and Greece. These traits included writing, metalworking, domestication of the horse, class stratification, and cult centers. These archaeological findings can be linked to the Shang Dynasty, long known from early texts.

• **Anyang** One of the Shang Dynasty capitals from which the Shang kings ruled for more than two centuries.

Shang Society

Shang civilization was not as densely urban as Mesopotamia, but Shang kings ruled from large settlements (Map 4.2). The best excavated is **Anyang**, from which the Shang kings ruled for more than two centuries. At the center of Anyang were large palaces, temples, and altars. These buildings were constructed on rammed-earth foundations (a feature of Chinese building practice that would last for centuries). Outside the central core were industrial areas where bronze workers, potters, stone carvers, and other artisans lived and worked. Many homes were built partly below ground level, probably as a way to conserve heat. Beyond these urban settlements were farming areas and large forests. Deer, bears, tigers, wild boars, elephants, and rhinoceros were still plentiful in north China in this era.

Texts found in the Shang royal tombs at Anyang show that Shang kings were military chieftains. The king regularly sent out armies of three thousand to five thousand men on campaigns, and when not at war they would go on hunts lasting for months. They fought rebellious vassals and foreign tribes, but the situation constantly changed as vassals became enemies and enemies accepted offers of alliance. War booty was an important source of the king's revenue, especially the war captives who could be made into slaves. Captives not needed as slaves might end up as sacrificial victims — or perhaps the demands of the gods and ancestors for sacrifices were a motive for going to war.

Bronze-tipped spears and halberds were widely used by Shang warriors, giving them an advantage over less technologically advanced groups. Bronze was also used for the fittings of the chariots that came into use around 1200 B.C.E. Chariot technology apparently spread by diffusion across Asia, passing from one society to the next. The chariot provided commanders with mobile stations from which they could supervise their troops; it also gave archers and soldiers armed with long halberds increased mobility.

Shang power did not rest solely on military supremacy. The Shang king was also the high priest, the one best qualified to offer sacrifices to the royal ancestors and the high god Di. Royal ancestors were viewed as able to intervene with Di, send curses, produce dreams,

MAP 4.2 The Shang and Early Zhou Dynasties, ca. 1500–400 B.C.E. The early Zhou government controlled larger areas than the Shang did, but the independent states of the Warring States Period were more aggressive about pushing out their frontiers, greatly extending the geographical boundaries of Chinese civilization.

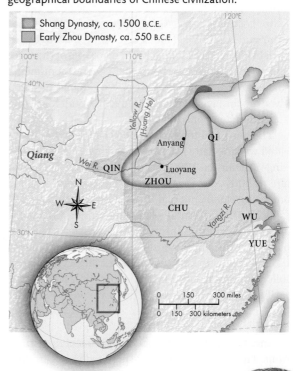

Royal Tomb at Anyang Eleven large tombs and more than a thousand small graves have been excavated at the royal burial ground at Anyang. This grave, about 60 feet deep and 300 feet long, would have taken thousands of laborers many months to complete. But even more wealth was expended to fill it with bronze, stone, pottery, textiles, and jade grave goods like this 2¾-inch-tall figure, one of seven hundred jade pieces in the tomb of Lady Hao, also in Anyang. (photo: Academia Sinica, Institute of History and Philology, Taiwan; figure: Institute of Archaeology, Beijing/© Cultural Relics Press)

assist the king in battle, and so on. The king divined his ancestors' wishes by interpreting the cracks made in heated cattle bones or tortoise shells prepared for him by professional diviners.

The Shang royal family and aristocracy lived in large houses built on huge platforms of rammed earth similar to those used in the Neolithic period. Shang palaces were undoubtedly splendid but were constructed of perishable material like wood, and nothing of them remains today, unlike the stone buildings and monuments so characteristic of the ancient West. What has survived are the lavish underground tombs built for Shang kings and their consorts.

The one royal tomb not robbed before it was excavated was for Lady Hao, one of the many wives of the king Wu Ding (ca. 1200 B.C.E.). The tomb was filled with almost 500 bronze vessels and weapons, over 700 jade and ivory ornaments, and 16 people who would tend to Lady Hao in the afterlife. Human sacrifice did not occur only at funerals. Inscribed bones report sacrifices of war captives in the dozens and hundreds. Some of those buried with kings were not sacrificial victims but followers or servants. The bodies of people who voluntarily followed their ruler to the grave were generally buried with their own ornaments and grave goods such as weapons.

Shang society was marked by sharp status distinctions. The king and other noble families had family and clan names transmitted along patrilineal lines, from father to son. Kingship similarly passed along patrilineal lines, from elder to younger brother and father to son, but never to or through sisters or daughters. The kings and the aristocrats owned slaves, many of whom had been captured in war. In the urban centers there were substantial numbers of craftsmen who worked in stone, bone, and bronze.

Shang farmers were essentially serfs of the aristocrats. Their lives were not that different from the lives of their Neolithic ancestors, and they worked the fields with similar stone tools. They usually lived in small, compact villages surrounded by fields. Some new crops became common in Shang times, most notably wheat, which had spread from West Asia. Farmers probably also raised silkworms, from whose cocoons fine silk garments could be made for the ruling elite.

Bronze Metalworking

As in Egypt, Mesopotamia, and India, the development of more complex forms of social organization in Shang China coincided with the mastery of metalworking, specifically bronze. The bronze industry required the coordination of a large labor force and skilled artisans. Bronze was used more for ritual than for war in Shang times. Most surviving Shang bronze objects are vessels such as cups, goblets, steamers, and cauldrons that would have originally been used during sacrificial ceremonies. They were beautifully formed in a great variety of shapes and sizes. Complex designs were achieved through mold casting and prefabrication of parts. For instance, legs, handles, and other protruding members were cast first, before the body was cast onto them.

The decoration on Shang bronzes seems to say something interesting about Shang culture, but scholars do not agree about what that is. In the art of ancient Egypt, Assyria, and Babylonia, representations of agriculture (domesticated plants and animals) and of social hierarchy (kings, priests, scribes, and slaves) are very common, matching our understandings of the social, political, and economic development of those societies. In Shang China, by contrast, images of wild

Bronze Vessels The Shang Dynasty bronze vessel on the left, dating to the twelfth century B.C.E. and about 10 inches tall, is covered with symmetrical animal imagery, including stylized taotie masks. The early Zhou Dynasty inscribed bronze pan (right), dating to before 900 B.C.E., was one of 103 vessels discovered in 1975 by farmers clearing a field. The inscription tells the story of the first six Zhou kings and of the family of scribes who served them. (pan: Zhou Yuan Administrative Office of Cultural Relics, Fufeng, Shaanxi Province, © Cultural Relics Press; taotie vessel: © Image Copyright Metropolitan Museum of Art/Art Resource, NY)

WORD	ox	goat, sheep	tree	moon	earth	water	to show, declare	then (men and bowl)	heaven	to pray
SHANG SYMBOL										
MODERN CHARACTER	牛	羊	木	月	土	水	示	就	天	祝

FIGURE 4.1 The Origins of Chinese Writing The modern Chinese writing system (bottom row) evolved from the script employed by diviners in the Shang period (upper row). (Source: Adapted from Patricia Buckley Ebrey, *The Cambridge Illustrated History of China* [Cambridge: Cambridge University Press, 1996], p. 26. Reprinted by permission of Cambridge University Press.)

animals predominate. Some animal images readily suggest possible meanings. Jade cicadas were sometimes found in the mouths of the dead, and images of cicadas on bronzes are easy to interpret as images evocative of rebirth in the realm of ancestral spirits, as cicadas spend years underground before emerging. Birds, similarly, suggest to many the idea of messengers that can communicate with other realms, especially realms in the sky. More problematic is the most common image, the stylized animal face called the **taotie** (taow-tyeh). To some it is a monster—a fearsome image that would scare away evil forces. Others imagine a dragon—an animal whose vast powers had more positive associations. Some hypothesize that it reflects masks used in rituals. Others associate it with animal sacrifices, totemism, or shamanism. Still others see these images as hardly more than designs. Without new evidence, scholars can only speculate.

Bronze technology spread beyond Shang territories into areas the Shang would have considered enemy lands. In 1986, in the western province of Sichuan, discovery was made of a bronze-producing culture contemporaneous with the late Shang but very different from it. This culture did not practice human sacrifice, but two sacrificial pits contained the burned remains of elephant tusks and a wide range of gold, bronze, jade, and stone objects. Among them were a life-size statue and many life-size bronze heads, all with angular facial features and enormous eyes. No human sacrifices were found, leading some scholars to speculate that the masks were used to top wood or clay statues buried in place of humans in a sacrificial ceremony. Archaeologists are continuing to excavate in this region, and new discoveries gradually are providing fuller understanding of the religion of the people who lived there.

The Development of Writing

The survival of divination texts inscribed on bones from Shang tombs demonstrates that writing was al-ready a major element in Chinese culture by 1200 B.C.E. Writing must have been developed earlier, but the early stages cannot be traced, probably because writing was done on wood, bamboo, silk, or other perishable materials. Once written texts survive, historians have much more material to draw on to reconstruct what life was like in a society.

The invention of writing had profound effects on China's culture and government. A written language made possible a bureaucracy capable of keeping records and corresponding with commanders and governors far from the palace. Hence literacy became the ally of royal rule, facilitating communication with and effective control over the realm. Literacy also preserved the learning, lore, and experience of early Chinese society and facilitated the development of abstract thought.

Like ancient Egyptian and Sumerian, the Chinese script was **logographic**: each word was represented by a single symbol. In the Chinese case, some of the symbols were pictures, but for the names of abstract concepts other methods were adopted. Sometimes the symbol for a different word was borrowed because the two words were pronounced alike. Sometimes two different symbols were combined; for instance, to represent different types of trees, the symbol for *tree* could be combined with another symbol borrowed for its pronunciation (Figure 4.1).

In western Eurasia logographic scripts were eventually modified or replaced by phonetic scripts, but that never happened in China (although, because of changes in the spoken language, today many words are represented by two or three characters rather than a single one). Because China retained its logographic writing system, many years were required to gain full mastery of reading and writing, which added to the prestige of education.

- **taotie** A stylized animal face commonly seen in Chinese bronzes.
- **logographic** A system of writing in which each word is represented by a single symbol, such as the Chinese script.

• **TABLE 4.1** Pronouncing Chinese Words

LETTER	PHONETIC EQUIVALENT IN CHINESE
Phonetic equivalents for the vowels and especially perplexing consonants are given here.	
a	ah
e	uh
i	ee; except after *z*, *c*, and *ch*, when the sound is closer to *i* in *it*
u	oo; as in English *food*
c	ts (*ch*, however, is like English *ch*)
q	ch
z	dz
zh	j
x	sh

Why did China retain a logographic writing system even after encounters with phonetic ones? Although phonetic systems have many real advantages, especially with respect to ease of learning to read, there are some costs to dropping a logographic system. People who learned to read Chinese could communicate with a wider range of people than can people who read scripts based on speech. Since characters did not change when the pronunciation changed, educated Chinese could read texts written centuries earlier without the need for them to be translated. Moreover, as the Chinese language developed regional variants, readers of Chinese could read books and letters by contemporaries whose oral language they could not comprehend. Thus the Chinese script played a large role in holding China together and fostering a sense of connection with the past. In addition, many of China's neighbors (Japan, Korea, and Vietnam, in particular) adopted the Chinese script, allowing communication through writing between people whose languages were totally unrelated. In this regard, the Chinese language was like Arabic numerals, which have the same meaning however they are pronounced (see Table 4.1).

The Early Zhou Dynasty, ca. 1050–400 B.C.E.

☐ How was China governed, and what was life like during the Zhou Dynasty?

The Shang campaigned constantly against enemies in all directions. To the west of the Shang were the fierce Qiang (chyang), considered barbarian tribesmen by the Shang and perhaps speaking an early form of Tibetan. Between the Shang capital and the Qiang were the Zhou

(joe), who seem to have both inherited cultural traditions from the Neolithic cultures of the northwest and absorbed most of the material culture of the Shang. In about 1050 B.C.E. the Zhou rose against the Shang and defeated them in battle. The cultural and political advances that the Shang rulers had introduced were maintained by their successors.

Zhou Politics

The early Zhou period is the first one for which transmitted texts exist in some abundance. The **Book of Documents** (ca. 900 B.C.E.) describes the Zhou conquest of the Shang as the victory of just and noble warriors over decadent courtiers led by an irresponsible and sadistic king. These documents also show that the Zhou recognized the Shang as occupying the center of the known world, were eager to succeed them in that role, and saw history as a major way to legitimate power. The three early Zhou rulers who are given the most praise are King Wen (the "cultured" or "literate" king), who expanded the Zhou domain; his son King Wu (the "martial" king), who conquered the Shang; and Wu's brother, the Duke of Zhou, who consolidated the conquest and served as loyal regent for Wu's heir.

Like the Shang kings, the Zhou kings sacrificed to their ancestors, but they also sacrificed to Heaven. The *Book of Documents* assumes a close relationship between Heaven and the king, who was called the Son of Heaven. According to the documents, Heaven gives the king a mandate to rule only as long as he rules in the interests of the people. Because the last king of the Shang had been decadent and cruel, Heaven took the mandate away from him and entrusted it to the virtuous Zhou kings. Because this theory of the **Mandate of Heaven** does not seem to have had any place in Shang cosmology, it may have been elaborated by the early Zhou rulers as a kind of propaganda to win over the conquered subjects of the Shang. Whatever its origins, it remained a central feature of Chinese political ideology from the early Zhou period on.

Rather than attempt to rule all their territories directly, the early Zhou rulers set up a decentralized feudal system. They sent relatives and trusted subordinates with troops to establish walled garrisons in the conquered territories. Such a vassal was generally able to pass his position on to a son, so that in time the domains became hereditary fiefs. By 800 B.C.E. there were about two hundred lords with domains large and small. Each lord appointed officers to serve him in ritual, administrative, or military capacities. These posts and their associated titles tended to become hereditary as well.

The decentralized rule of the early Zhou period had from the beginning carried within it the danger that the regional lords would become so powerful that they

Lacquer Cup This 6-inch-long lacquer cup, decorated with images of two intertwined birds, was one of many lacquered eating vessels found in a third-century B.C.E. Warring States Period tomb. Lacquer is made from the sap of a tree native to China. It is remarkably light, strong, smooth, and waterproof. Lacquered dishes, cups, boxes, musical instruments, and sculptures became highly sought-after luxury items. (Jingzhou Prefecture Museum, © Cultural Relics Press)

would no longer obey the commands of the king. As generations passed and ties of loyalty and kinship grew more distant, this happened. In 771 B.C.E. the Zhou king was killed by an alliance of non-Chinese tribesmen and Zhou vassals. One of his sons was put on the throne, and then for safety's sake the capital was moved east out of the Wei River Valley to modern Luoyang, just south of the Yellow River in the heart of the central plains (see Map 4.2).

The revived Zhou Dynasty never fully regained control over its vassals, and China entered a prolonged period without a strong central authority. For a couple of centuries a code of chivalrous or sportsmanlike conduct still regulated warfare between the states: one state would not attack another that was in mourning for its ruler; during battles one side would not attack before the other side had time to line up; ruling houses were not wiped out, so that successors could continue to sacrifice to their ancestors; and so on. Thereafter, however, such niceties were abandoned, and China entered a period of nearly constant conflict.

Life During the Zhou Dynasty

During the early Zhou period, aristocratic attitudes and privileges were strong. Inherited ranks placed people in a hierarchy ranging downward from the king to the rulers of states with titles like duke and marquis, the hereditary great officials of the states, the lower ranks of the aristocracy — men who could serve in either military or civil capacities, known as **shi** — and finally to the ordinary people (farmers, craftsmen, and traders). Patrilineal family ties were very important in this society, and at the upper reaches, at least, sacrifices to ancestors were one of the key rituals used to forge social ties.

Glimpses of what life was like at various social levels in the early Zhou Dynasty can be found in the ***Book of Songs*** (ca. 900 B.C.E.), which contains the earliest Chinese poetry. Some of the songs are hymns used

in court religious ceremonies, such as offerings to ancestors. Others clearly had their origins in folk songs. The seasons set the pace for rural life, and the songs contain many references to seasonal changes, such as the appearance of insects like grasshoppers and crickets. Some of these songs depict farmers at work clearing fields, plowing and planting, gathering mulberry leaves for silkworms, and spinning and weaving. Farming life involved not merely cultivating crops like millet, hemp (for cloth), beans, and vegetables, but also hunting small animals and collecting grasses and rushes to make rope and baskets.

Many of the folk songs are love songs that depict a more informal pattern of courtship than prevailed in later China. One stanza reads:

Please, Zhongzi,
Do not leap over our wall,
Do not break our mulberry trees.
It's not that I begrudge the mulberries,
But I fear my brothers.
You I would embrace,
But my brothers' words — those I dread.[1]

- • ***Book of Documents*** One of the earliest Chinese books, containing documents, speeches, and historical accounts about early Zhou rule.
- • **Mandate of Heaven** The theory that Heaven gives the king a mandate to rule only as long as he rules in the interests of the people.
- • **shi** The lower ranks of Chinese aristocracy; these men could serve in either military or civil capacities.
- • ***Book of Songs*** The earliest collection of Chinese poetry; it provides glimpses of what life was like in the early Zhou Dynasty.

There were also songs of complaint, such as this one in which the ancestors are rebuked for failing to aid their descendants:

> The drought has become so severe
> That it cannot be stopped.
> Glowing and burning, We have no place.
> The great mandate is about at an end.
> Nothing to look forward to or back upon.
> The host of dukes and past rulers
> Does not help us.
> As for father and mother and the ancestors,
> How can they bear to treat us so?[2]

Other songs in this collection are court odes that reveal attitudes of the aristocrats. One such ode expresses a deep distrust of women's involvement in politics:

> Clever men build cities,
> Clever women topple them.
> Beautiful, these clever women may be
> But they are owls and kites.
> Women have long tongues
> That lead to ruin.
> Disorder does not come down from heaven;
> It is produced by women.[3]

Part of the reason for distrust of women in politics was the practice of concubinage. Rulers regularly demonstrated their power and wealth by accumulating large numbers of concubines (legal spouses who ranked lower than the wife) and thus would have children by several women. In theory, succession went to the eldest son of the wife, then to younger sons by her, and only in their absence to sons of concubines; but in actual practice, the ruler of a state or the head of a powerful ministerial family could select a son of a concubine to be his heir if he wished. This led to much scheming for favor among the various sons and their mothers and the common perception that women were incapable of taking a disinterested view of the larger good.

Social and economic change quickened after 500 B.C.E. Cities began appearing all over north China. Thick earthen walls were built around the palaces and ancestral temples of the ruler and other aristocrats, and often an outer wall was added to protect the artisans, merchants, and farmers who lived outside the inner wall. Accounts of sieges launched against these walled citadels, with scenes of the scaling of walls and the storming of gates, are central to descriptions of military confrontations in this period.

The development of iron technology in the early Zhou Dynasty promoted economic expansion and allowed some people to become very rich. By the fifth century B.C.E. iron was being widely used for both farm tools and weapons. In the early Zhou, inherited status and political favor had been the main reasons some people had more power than others. Beginning in the fifth century wealth alone also was an important basis for social inequality. Late Zhou texts frequently mention trade across state borders in goods such as furs, copper, dyes, hemp, salt, and horses. People who grew wealthy from trade or industry began to rival rulers for influence. Rulers who wanted trade to bring prosperity to their states welcomed traders and began casting coins to facilitate trade.

Social mobility increased over the course of the Zhou period. Rulers often sent out their own officials rather than delegate authority to hereditary lesser lords. This trend toward centralized bureaucratic control created opportunities for social advancement for the shi on the lower end of the old aristocracy. Competition among such men guaranteed rulers a ready supply of able and willing subordinates, and competition among rulers for talent meant that ambitious men could be selective in deciding where to offer their services. (See "Individuals in Society: Lord Mengchang," page 101.)

Bells of the Marquis of Zeng Music played a central role in court life in ancient China, and bells are among the most impressive bronze objects of the period. The tomb of a minor ruler who died about 400 B.C.E. contained 124 musical instruments, including drums, flutes, mouth organs, pan pipes, zithers, a set of 32 chime stones, and this 64-piece bell set. The bells bear inscriptions that name the two tones each bell could make, depending on where it was struck. Five men, using poles and mallets and standing on either side of the set of bells, would have played the bells by hitting them from outside. (© Cultural Relics Press)

Individuals in Society

Lord Mengchang

DURING THE WARRING STATES PERIOD, MEN often rose to high rank on the basis of political talent. Lord Mengchang rose on the basis of his people skills: he treated his retainers so well that he attracted thousands of talented men to his service, enabling him to rise to prime minister of his native state of Qi (chee) in the early third century B.C.E.

Lord Mengchang's beginnings were not promising. His father, a member of the Qi royal family, already had more than forty sons when Mengchang was born, and he ordered the mother, one of his many concubines, to leave the baby to die. However, she secretly reared him, and while still a child he was able to win his father's approval through his cleverness.

At his father's death Mengchang succeeded him. Because Mengchang would provide room and board to men who sought to serve him, he soon attracted a few thousand retainers, many of humble background, some fleeing justice. Every night, we are told, he ate with them all in his hall, treating them equally no matter what their social origins.

Most of the stories about Mengchang revolve around retainers who solved his problems in clever ways. Once, when Mengchang had been sent as an envoy to Qin, the king of Qin was persuaded not to let so talented a minister return to help Qi. Under house arrest, Mengchang was able to ask one of the king's consorts to help him, but in exchange she wanted a fur coat kept in the king's treasury. A former thief among Mengchang's retainers stole it for him, and Mengchang was soon on his way. By the time he reached the barrier gate, Qin soldiers were pursuing him, and he knew that he had to get through quickly. One of his retainers imitated the crowing of a cock, which got the other cocks to crow, making the guards think it was dawn, so they opened the gates and let his party through.

When Mengchang served as prime minister of Qi, his retainers came up with many clever stratagems that convinced the nearby states of Wei and Han to join Qi in resisting Qin. Several times, one of his retainers of modest origins, Feng Xuan (schwan), helped Mengchang withstand the political vicissitudes of the day. When sent to collect debts owed to Mengchang in his fief of Xue, Feng Xuan instead forgave all the debts of those too poor to repay their loans. Later, when Lord Mengchang lost his post at court and returned to his fief, most of his retainers deserted him, but he found himself well loved by the local residents, all because of Feng Xuan's generosity in his name. After Mengchang reattained his court post and was traveling back to Qi, he complained to Feng Xuan about those who had deserted him. Feng Xuan, we are told, got down from the carriage and bowed to Lord Mengchang, and when pressed said that the lord should accept the retainers' departures as part of the natural order of things:

Wealth and honor attract while poverty and lowliness repel; such is the nature of things. Think of it like the market. In the morning it is crowded and in the evening it is deserted. This is not because people prefer the morning to the evening, but rather because what they want can not be found there [in the evening]. Do not let the fact that your retainers left when you lost your position lead you to bar them from returning. I hope that you will treat them just the way you did before.*

QUESTIONS FOR ANALYSIS

1. How did Mengchang attract his many retainers, and how did their service benefit him?
2. Who in this story benefited from hereditary privilege and who advanced because of ability? What does this suggest about social mobility during the Warring States Period?
3. Many of the stories about Mengchang are included in *Intrigues of the Warring States*, a book that Confucians disapproved of. What do you think they found objectionable?

*Shi ji 75.2362. Translated by Patricia Ebrey.

● Mengchang promoted trade by issuing coins. Some Zhou coins, like this one, were shaped like miniature knives. (Courtesy of the Trustees of the British Museum)

Religion in Zhou times was not simply a continuation of Shang practices. The practice of burying the living with the dead — so prominent in the royal tombs of the Shang — steadily declined in the middle Zhou period. Still, a ruler who died in 433 B.C.E. had his female musicians buried with him, evidence that some rulers still had their servants buried with them. The musicians and their instruments also testify to the role that music played in court entertainment. New deities and cults also appeared, especially in the southern state of Chu, where areas that had earlier been considered barbarian were being incorporated into the cultural sphere of the Central States, as the core region of China was called. The state of Chu expanded rapidly in the Yangzi Valley, defeating and absorbing fifty or more small states as it extended its reach north to the heartland of Zhou and east to absorb the old states of Wu and Yue. By the late Zhou period Chu was on the forefront of cultural innovation and produced the greatest literary masterpiece of the era, the *Songs of Chu*, a collection of fantastical poems full of images of elusive deities and shamans who can fly through the spirit world. Images found in Chu tombs, painted on coffins or pieces of silk, show both fearsome deities and spirit journeys.

The Warring States, 403–221 B.C.E.

☐ Qin Empire, 221 B.C.E.

YAN
ZHAO
Yellow R.
Huang He)
WEI
QI
QIN
HAN
Yangzi R.
CHU

The Warring States Period, 403–221 B.C.E.

☐ How did advances in military technology contribute to the rise of independent states?

By 400 B.C.E. advances in military technology were undermining the old aristocratic social structure of the Zhou. Large, well-drilled infantry armies able to withstand and defeat chariot-led forces became potent military forces in the **Warring States Period**, which lasted from 403 to 221 B.C.E. Fueled by the development of new weaponry and war tactics, the Chinese states destroyed each other one by one until only one state was left standing — the state of Qin (chin). In response to the human and economic costs of war, rulers sought ways to increase population and expand trade even while they destroyed one another.

New Technologies for War

By 300 B.C.E. states were sending out armies of a few hundred thousand drafted foot soldiers, usually accompanied by horsemen. Adding to their effectiveness was the development of the **crossbow** around 350 B.C.E. The intricate bronze trigger of the crossbow allowed a foot soldier to shoot farther than could a horseman carrying a light bow. One text of the period reports that a skilled soldier with a powerful crossbow and a sharp sword was the match of a hundred ordinary men. To defend against crossbows soldiers began wearing armor and helmets. Most of the armor was made of leader strips tied with cords. Helmets were sometimes made of iron.

The introduction of cavalry in this period further reduced the need for a chariot-riding aristocracy. Shooting bows and arrows from horseback was first perfected by non-Chinese peoples to the north of China proper who at that time were making the transition to a nomadic pastoral economy. The northern state of Jin developed its own cavalry armies to defend itself from the attacks of these horsemen. Once it started using cavalry against other Chinese states, they too had to

Mounted Swordsman This depiction of a warrior fighting a leopard decorates a bronze mirror inlaid with gold and silver dating from the Warring States Period. (From *Gugong wenwu yuekan*, 91 [1990])

> **"**Attack where he does not expect it and go where he has not imagined. This is how military experts are victorious.**"**
>
> **SUN WU**

master the new technology. From this time on, acquiring and pasturing horses was a key component of military preparedness.

Because these developments made commoners and craftsmen central to military success, rulers tried to find ways to increase their populations. To increase agricultural output, they brought new land into cultivation, drained marshes, and dug irrigation channels. Rulers began surveying their land and taxing farmers. They wanted to undermine the power of lords over their subjects in order to get direct access to the peasants' labor power. Serfdom thus gradually declined. Registering populations led to the extension of family names to commoners at an earlier date than anywhere else in the world.

The development of infantry armies also created the need for a new type of general, and rulers became less willing to let men lead troops merely because of aristocratic birth. Treatises on the art of war described the ideal general as a master of maneuver, illusion, and deception. In *The Art of War* (453–403 B.C.E.) Sun Wu argued that heroism is a useless virtue that leads to needless deaths. But discipline is essential, and he insisted that the entire army had to be trained to follow the orders of its commanders without questioning them. He also explicitly called for use of deceit:

> War is the Way of deceit. Thus one who is competent pretends to be incompetent; one who uses [his army] pretends not to use it; one who draws near pretends to be distant; one who is distant pretends to draw near. If [the enemy desires] some advantage, entice him [with it]. If he is in disorder, seize him. If he is substantial, be prepared for him. If he is strong, evade him. If he is enraged, irritate him [further]. If he is humble, make him haughty. If he is rested, make him toil. If he is intimate [with his ranks], separate them. Attack where he does not expect it and go where he has not imagined. This is how military experts are victorious.[4]

The Victorious States

During the Warring States Period states on the periphery of the Zhou realm had more room to expand than states in the center. With access to more resources, they were able to pick off their neighbors, one after the other. Still, for a couple of centuries the final outcome

was far from clear, as alliances among states were regularly made and nearly as regularly broken.

By the third century B.C.E. there were only seven important states remaining. These states were much more centralized than their early Zhou predecessors. Their kings had eliminated indirect control through vassals and in its place dispatched royal officials to remote cities, controlling them from a distance through the transmission of documents and dismissing them at will. By the end of the third century one state, Qin, would have conquered all of the others, a development discussed in Chapter 7.

Confucius and His Followers

☐ *What ideas did Confucius teach, and how were they spread after his death?*

The Warring States Period was the golden age of Chinese philosophy, the era when the "Hundred Schools of Thought" contended. During the same period in which Indian sages and mystics were developing religious speculation about karma, souls, and eons of time (see Chapter 3), Chinese thinkers were arguing about the ideal forms of social and political organization and man's connections to nature.

Confucius

Confucius (traditional dates: 551–479 B.C.E.) was one of the first men of ideas. As a young man, he had served in the court of his home state of Lu without gaining much influence. After leaving Lu, he set out with a small band of students and wandered through neighboring states in search of a ruler who would take his advice.

Confucius's ideas are known to us primarily through the sayings recorded by his disciples in the *Analects*. The thrust of his thought was ethical rather than theoretical or metaphysical. He talked repeatedly of an ideal age in the early Zhou Dynasty when everyone was devoted to fulfilling his or her role: superiors looked after those dependent on them; inferiors devoted themselves to the service of their superiors; parents and children, husbands and wives all wholeheartedly embraced what was expected of them.

- **Warring States Period** The period of Chinese history between 403 and 221 B.C.E. when states fought each other and one state after another was destroyed.
- **crossbow** A powerful mechanical bow developed during the Warring States Period.

Listening to the Past

The Book of Mencius

The book that records the teachings of Mencius (ca. 370–300 B.C.E.) was modeled on the Analects of Confucius. *It presents, in no particular order, conversations between Mencius and several rulers, philosophers, and disciples. Unlike the* Analects, *however, the* Book of Mencius *includes extended discussions of particular points, suggesting that Mencius had a hand in recording the conversations.*

"Mencius had an audience with King Hui of Liang. The king said, "Sir, you did not consider a thousand *li* too far to come. You must have some ideas about how to benefit my state."

Mencius replied, "Why must Your Majesty use the word 'benefit'? All I am concerned with are the benevolent and the right. If Your Majesty says, 'How can I benefit my state?' your officials will say, 'How can I benefit my family,' and officers and common people will say, 'How can I benefit myself?' Once superiors and inferiors are competing for benefit, the state will be in danger.

"When the head of a state of ten thousand chariots is murdered, the assassin is invariably a noble with a fief of a thousand chariots. When the head of a fief of a thousand chariots is murdered, the assassin is invariably head of a subfief of a hundred chariots. Those with a thousand out of ten thousand, or a hundred out of a thousand, had quite a bit. But when benefit is put before what is right, they are not satisfied without snatching it all. By contrast, there has never been a benevolent person who neglected his parents or a righteous person who put his lord last. Your Majesty perhaps will now also say, 'All I am concerned with are the benevolent and the right.' Why mention 'benefit'?"

After seeing King Xiang (SHEE-ang) of Liang, Mencius said to someone, "When I saw him from a distance, he did not look like a ruler, and when I got closer, I saw nothing to command respect. But he asked, 'How can the realm be settled?'

"I answered, 'It can be settled through unity.'

"'Who can unify it?' he asked.

"I answered, 'Someone not fond of killing people.'

"'Who could give it to him?'

"I answered, 'Everyone in the world will give it to him. Your Majesty knows what rice plants are? If there is a drought in the seventh and eighth months, the plants wither, but if moisture collects in the sky and forms clouds and rain falls in torrents, the plants suddenly revive. This is the way it is; no one can stop the process. In the world today there are no rulers disinclined toward killing. If there were a ruler who did not like to kill people, everyone in the world would crane their necks to catch sight of him. This is really true. The people would flow toward him the way water flows down. No one would be able to repress them.'"

After an incident between Zou and Lu, Duke Mu asked, "Thirty-three of my officials died but no common people died. I could punish them, but I could not punish them all. I could refrain from punishing them, but they did angrily watch their superiors die without saving them. What would be the best course for me to follow?"

Mencius answered, "When the harvest failed, even though your granaries were full, nearly a thousand of your subjects were lost—the old and weak among them dying in the gutters, the able-bodied scattering in all directions. Your officials never reported the situation, a case of superiors callously inflicting suffering on their subordinates. Zengzi said, 'Watch out, watch out! What you do will be done to you.' This was the first chance the people had to pay them back. You should not resent them. If Your Highness practices benevolent government, the common people will love their superiors and die for those in charge of them."

King Xuan of Qi asked, "Is it true that Tang banished Jie and King Wu took up arms against Zhou?"

Mencius replied, "That is what the records say."

"Then is it permissible for a subject to assassinate his lord?"

Confucius considered the family the basic unit of society. He extolled **filial piety**, which to him meant more than just reverent obedience of children to their parents:

The Master said, "You can be of service to your father and mother by remonstrating with them tactfully. If you perceive that they do not wish to follow your advice, then continue to be reverent toward them without offending or disobeying them; work hard and do not murmur against them."[5]

The relationship between father and son was one of the five cardinal relationships stressed by Confucius. The others were between ruler and subject, husband

• filial piety Reverent attitude of children to their parents extolled by Confucius.

Mencius said, "Someone who does violence to the good we call a villain; someone who does violence to the right we call a criminal. A person who is both a villain and a criminal we call a scoundrel. I have heard that the scoundrel Zhou was killed, but have not heard that a lord was killed."

King Xuan of Qi asked about ministers.

Mencius said, "What sort of ministers does Your Majesty mean?"

The king said, "Are there different kinds of ministers?"

"There are. There are noble ministers related to the ruler and ministers of other surnames."

The king said, "I'd like to hear about noble ministers."

Mencius replied, "When the ruler makes a major error, they point it out. If he does not listen to their repeated remonstrations, then they put someone else on the throne."

The king blanched. Mencius continued, "Your Majesty should not be surprised at this. Since you asked me, I had to tell you truthfully."

After the king regained his composure, he asked about unrelated ministers. Mencius said, "When the king makes an error, they point it out. If he does not heed their repeated remonstrations, they quit their posts."

Bo Gui said, "I'd like a tax of one part in twenty. What do you think?"

Mencius said, "Your way is that of the northern tribes. Is one potter enough for a state with ten thousand households?"

"No, there would not be enough wares."

"The northern tribes do not grow all the five grains, only millet. They have no cities or houses, no ritual sacrifices. They do not provide gifts or banquets for feudal lords, and do not have a full array of officials. Therefore, for them, one part in twenty is enough. But we live in the central states. How could we abolish social roles and do without gentlemen? If a state cannot do without potters, how much less can it do without gentlemen.

"Those who want to make government lighter than it was under Yao and Shun are to some degree barbarians. Those who wish to make government heavier than it was under Yao and Shun are to some degree [tyrants like] Jie."

Gaozi said, "Human nature is like whirling water. When an outlet is opened to the east, it flows east; when an outlet is opened to the west, it flows west. Human nature is no more inclined to good or bad than water is inclined to east or west."

Mencius responded, "Water, it is true, is not inclined to either east or west, but does it have no preference for high or low?

Opening page of a 1617 edition of the **Book of Mencius.** (Rare Books Collections, Harvard-Yenching Library, Harvard University)

Goodness is to human nature like flowing downward is to water. There are no people who are not good and no water that does not flow down. Still, water, if splashed, can go higher than your head; if forced, it can be brought up a hill. This isn't the nature of water; it is the specific circumstances. Although people can be made to be bad, their natures are not changed."

Source: Reprinted and edited with the permission of The Free Press, a Division of Simon & Schuster Adult Publishing Group, from *Chinese Civilization: A Sourcebook*, Second Edition, revised and expanded by Patricia Buckley Ebrey. Copyright © 1993 by Patricia Buckley Ebrey. All rights reserved.

QUESTIONS FOR ANALYSIS

1. Does Mencius give consistent advice to the kings he talks to?
2. Do you see a link between Mencius's views on human nature and his views on the true king?
3. What role does Mencius see for ministers?

and wife, elder and younger brother, and friend and friend. Mutual obligations of a hierarchical sort underlay the first four of these relationships: the senior leads and protects; the junior supports and obeys. The exception was the relationship between friends, which was conceived in terms of mutual obligations between equals.

A man of moderation, Confucius was an earnest advocate of gentlemanly conduct. He redefined the term *gentleman (junzi)* to mean a man of moral cultivation rather than a man of noble birth. He repeatedly urged his followers to aspire to be gentlemen rather than petty men intent on personal gain. The gentleman, he said, "feels bad when his capabilities fall short of the task. He does not feel bad when people fail to recognize him."[6] Confucius did not advocate social equality, but his teachings minimized the importance of class distinctions and opened the way for intelligent and talented people to rise in the social scale. The Confucian gentleman found his calling in service to the ruler.

> "When you go out, treat everyone as if you were welcoming a great guest. . . . Do not do unto others what you would not have them do unto you."
>
> **CONFUCIUS**

Loyal advisers should encourage their rulers to govern through ritual, virtue, and concern for the welfare of their subjects, and much of the *Analects* concerns the way to govern well.

To Confucius the ultimate virtue was **ren** (humanity). A person of humanity cares about others and acts accordingly:

[The disciple] Zhonggong asked about humanity. The Master said, "When you go out, treat everyone as if you were welcoming a great guest. Employ people as though you were conducting a great sacrifice. Do not do unto others what you would not have them do unto you. Then neither in your country nor in your family will there be complaints against you."[7]

In the Confucian tradition, studying texts came to be valued over speculation, meditation, and mystical identification with deities. Confucius encouraged the men who came to study with him to master the poetry, rituals, and historical traditions that we know today as Confucian classics. Many passages in the *Analects* reveal Confucius's confidence in the power of study:

The Master said, "I am not someone who was born wise. I am someone who loves the ancients and tries to learn from them."

The Master said, "I once spent a whole day without eating and a whole night without sleeping in order to think. It was of no use. It is better to study."[8]

The Spread of Confucian Ideas

The eventual success of Confucian ideas owes much to Confucius's followers in the three centuries following his death. The most important of them were Mencius (ca. 370–300 B.C.E.) and Xunzi (ca. 310–215 B.C.E.).

Mencius, like Confucius, traveled around offering advice to rulers of various states. (See "Listening to the Past: The Book of Mencius," page 104.) Over and over he tried to convert them to the view that the ruler able to win over the people through benevolent government would succeed in unifying "all under Heaven." Mencius proposed concrete political and financial measures to ease tax burdens and otherwise improve the people's lot. Men willing to serve an unworthy ruler earned his contempt, especially when they worked hard to fill the ruler's coffers or expand his territory. With his disciples

Serving Parents with Filial Piety This twelfth-century C.E. illustration of a passage in the *Classic of Filial Piety* shows how commoners should serve their parents: by working hard at productive jobs such as farming and tending to their parents' daily needs. The married son and daughter-in-law offer food or drink to the older couple as their own children look on, thus learning how they should treat their own parents after they become aged. (National Palace Museum, Taipei, Taiwan)

and fellow philosophers, Mencius also discussed other issues in moral philosophy, arguing strongly, for instance, that human nature is fundamentally good, as everyone is born with the capacity to recognize what is right and act on it.

Xunzi, a half century later, took the opposite view of human nature, arguing that people are born selfish and that only through education and ritual do they learn to put moral principle above their own interest. Much of what is desirable is not inborn but must be taught:

> When a son yields to his father, or a younger brother yields to his elder brother, or when a son takes on the work for his father or a younger brother for his elder brother, their actions go against their natures and run counter to their feelings. And yet these are the way of the filial son and the principles of ritual and morality.[9]

Neither Confucius nor Mencius had had much actual political or administrative experience, but Xunzi had worked for many years in the court of his home state. Not surprisingly, he showed more consideration than either Confucius or Mencius for the difficulties a ruler might face in trying to rule through ritual and virtue. Xunzi was also a more rigorous thinker than his predecessors and developed the philosophical foundations of many ideas merely outlined by Confucius and Mencius. Confucius, for instance, had declined to discuss gods, portents, and anomalies and had spoken of sacrificing as if the spirits were present. Xunzi went further and explicitly argued that Heaven does not intervene in human affairs. (See "Viewpoints: Mozi and Xunzi on Divine Response," page 108.)

Still, Xunzi did not propose abandoning traditional rituals. In contrast to Daoists (discussed below), who saw rituals as unnatural or extravagant, Xunzi saw them as an efficient way to attain order in society. Rulers and educated men should continue traditional ritual practices such as complex funeral protocols because the rites themselves have positive effects on performers and observers. Not only do they let people express feelings and satisfy desires in an orderly way, but because they specify graduated ways to perform the rites according to social rank, ritual traditions sustain the social hierarchy. Xunzi compared and contrasted ritual and music: music shapes people's emotions and creates feelings of solidarity, while ritual shapes people's sense of duty and creates social differentiation.

The Confucian vision of personal ethics and public service found a small but ardent following in the Warring States Period. In later centuries rulers came to see men educated in Confucian virtues as ideal advisers and officials. Neither revolutionaries nor flatterers, Confucian scholar-officials opposed bad government

and upheld the best ideals of statecraft. Confucian political ideals shaped Chinese society into the twentieth century.

The Confucian vision also provided the moral basis for the Chinese family into modern times. Repaying parents and ancestors came to be seen as a sacred duty. Because people owe their very existence to their parents, they should reciprocate by respecting their parents, making efforts to please them, honoring their memories, and placing the interests of the family line above personal preferences. Since the family line is a patrilineal line from father to son to grandson, placing great importance on it has had the effect of devaluing women.

Daoism, Legalism, and Other Schools of Thought

☐ How did the teachings of Daoism, Legalism, and other schools of thought differ from Confucianism?

During the Warring States Period, rulers took advantage of the destruction of states to recruit newly unemployed men to serve as their advisers and court assistants. Lively debate often resulted as these strategists proposed policies and defended their ideas against challengers. Followers took to recording their teachers' ideas, and the circulation of these "books" (rolls of silk, or strips of wood or bamboo tied together) served further to stimulate debate.

Many of these schools of thought directly opposed the ideas of Confucius and his followers. Most notable were the Daoists, who believed that the act of striving to improve something only made it worse, and the Legalists, who argued that a strong government rested not just on moral leadership but also on effective laws and procedures.

Daoism

Confucius and his followers believed in moral effort and statecraft. They thought men of virtue should devote themselves to making the government work to the benefit of the people. Those who came to be labeled Daoists disagreed. They thought striving to make things better generally made them worse. Daoists defended

---

• **ren** The ultimate Confucian virtue; it is translated as perfect goodness, benevolence, humanity, human-heartedness, and nobility.

Viewpoints

Mozi and Xunzi on Divine Response

> Understandings of the nature of gods, ghosts, ancestors, and the deity Heaven varied a lot in early China. Confucius strongly supported the practice of ritual, especially sacrifices to ancestors, but he avoided talk about gods or ghosts, preferring to focus on the human world. Mozi, in the next century, was concerned that skepticism about the gods would lead people to act in undesirable ways because they would not fear divine punishment. Xunzi, later still, approved of rituals for their social effects and drew a distinction between what the educated and the uneducated thought.

Mozi, from *The Mozi*

Long ago, in the time of Lord Zhuang of Qi [794–731 B.C.E.], there were two ministers named Wangli Guo and Zhongli Jiao. These two men had been engaged in a lawsuit for three years, but no judgment had been handed down. Lord Zhuang thought of executing them both, but he was afraid of killing an innocent man. He also thought of acquitting them both, but he was afraid of setting free one who was guilty. He therefore ordered the two men to bring a lamb and take an oath on the Qi altar of the soil. The two men agreed to take the oath of blood. The throat of the lamb was cut, its blood sprinkled on the altar, and Wangli Guo's version of the case read through to the end. Zhongli Jiao's version was read, but before it had been read half through, the lamb rose up, butted Zhongli Jiao, broke his leg, and then struck him down on the altar. At that time there were none of the attendants of Qi who did not see what happened, and no one in distant regions who did not hear about it. It was recorded in the spring and autumn annals of Qi, and the feudal lords handed down the story, saying, "All those who take oaths in insincerity will incur the punishment of the ghosts and spirits with just such rapidity!" If we examine what is written in the book, how can we doubt that ghosts and spirits exist?

Therefore Mozi said: Even in the deep valleys, the broad forests, the dark and distant places where no one lives, you must not fail to act with sincerity, for the ghosts and spirits will see you even there!

Xunzi, from *The Xunzi*

You pray for rain and it rains. Why? For no particular reason, I say. It is just as though you had not prayed for rain and it rained anyway. The sun and moon undergo an eclipse and you try to save them; a drought occurs and you pray for rain; you consult the arts of divination before making a decision on some important matter. But it is not as though you could hope to accomplish anything by such ceremonies. They are done merely for ornament. Hence the gentleman regards them as ornaments, but the common people regard them as supernatural. He who considers them ornaments is fortunate; he who considers them supernatural is unfortunate.

Source: Burton Watson, trans., *The Basic Writings of Mo Tzu, Hsün Tzu, and Han Fei Tzu* (Columbia University Press, 1967), 98–99, 85. Copyright © 1967 by Columbia University Press. Reprinted with permission of the publisher.

QUESTIONS FOR ANALYSIS

1. What can we infer about ordinary people's ideas about religion from these passages? How complete of a view of the religious attitudes of the time do you think these passages give us?
2. Do you find one of these thinkers more persuasive than the other, and why? How would people of the time have read these arguments?

---

private life and wanted the rulers to leave the people alone. They sought to go beyond everyday concerns and to let their minds wander freely. Rather than making human beings and human actions the center of concern, they focused on the larger scheme of things, the whole natural order identified as the Way, or **Dao**.

Early Daoist teachings are known from two surviving books, the *Laozi* and the *Zhuangzi*, both dating to the third century B.C.E. Laozi, the putative author of the *Laozi*, may not be a historical figure, but the text as-cribed to him has been of enduring importance. A recurrent theme in this brief, aphoristic text is the mystical superiority of yielding over assertion and silence over words: "The Way that can be discussed is not the constant Way."[10] The highest good is like water: "Water benefits all creatures but does not compete. It occupies the places people disdain and thus comes near to the Way."[11]

Because purposeful action is counterproductive, the ruler should let people return to a natural state of ignorance and contentment:

> Do not honor the worthy,
> And the people will not compete.

Dao The Way, the whole natural order in Daoist philosophy. In Confucianism it means the moral order.

Do not value rare treasures,
And the people will not steal.
Do not display what others want,
And the people will not have their hearts confused.
A sage governs this way:
He empties people's minds and fills their bellies.
He weakens their wills and strengthens their bones.
Keep the people always without knowledge and
  without desires,
For then the clever will not dare act.
Engage in no action and order will prevail.[12]

In the philosophy of the *Laozi*, the people would be better off if they knew less, gave up tools, renounced writing, stopped envying their neighbors, and lost their desire to travel or engage in war.

Zhuangzi (369–286 B.C.E.), the author of the book of the same name, shared many of the central ideas of the *Laozi*. He was proud of his disinterest in politics. In one of his many anecdotes, he reported that the king of Chu once sent an envoy to invite him to take over the government of his realm. In response Zhuangzi asked the envoy whether a tortoise that had been held as sacred for three thousand years would prefer to be dead with its bones venerated or alive with its tail dragging in the mud. When the envoy agreed that life was preferable, Zhuangzi told the envoy to leave. He preferred to drag his tail in the mud.

The *Zhuangzi* is filled with parables, flights of fancy, and fictional encounters between historical figures, including Confucius and his disciples. A more serious strain of Zhuangzi's thought concerned death. He questioned whether we can be sure life is better than death. People fear what they do not know, the same way a captive girl will be terrified when she learns she is to become the king's concubine. Perhaps people will discover that death has as many delights as life in the palace.

When a friend expressed shock that Zhuangzi was not weeping at his wife's death but rather singing, Zhuangzi explained:

When she first died, how could I have escaped feeling the loss? Then I looked back to the beginning before she had life. Not only before she had life, but before she had form. Not only before she had form, but before she had vital energy. In this confused amorphous realm, something changed and vital energy appeared; when the vital energy was changed, form appeared; with changes in form, life began. Now there is another change bringing death. This is like the progression of the four seasons of spring and fall, winter and summer. Here she was lying down to sleep in a huge room and I followed her, sobbing and wailing. When I realized my actions showed I hadn't understood destiny, I stopped.[13]

Zhuangzi was similarly iconoclastic in his political ideas. In one parable a wheelwright insolently tells a duke that books are useless because all they contain are the dregs of men long dead. The duke, insulted, threatens to execute the wheelwright if he cannot give an adequate explanation of his remark. The wheelwright replies:

I see things in terms of my own work. When I chisel at a wheel, if I go slow, the chisel slides and does not stay put; if I hurry, it jams and doesn't move properly. When it is neither too slow nor too fast, I can feel it in my hand and respond to it from my heart. My mouth cannot describe it in words, but there is something there. I cannot teach it to my son, and my son cannot learn it from me. So I have gone on for seventy years, growing old chiseling wheels. The men of old died in possession of what they could not transmit. So it follows that what you are reading are their dregs.[14]

To put this another way, truly skilled craftsmen respond to situations spontaneously; they do not analyze or

◻ Picturing the Past

Inscribed Bamboo Slips In 1993 Chinese archaeologists discovered a late-fourth-century B.C.E. tomb in Hubei province that contained 804 bamboo slips bearing some 12,000 Chinese characters. Scholars have been able to reconstruct more than a dozen books from them, many of them previously unknown. (Jingmen City Museum, © Cultural Relics Press)

ANALYZING THE IMAGE Can you spot any repeated characters? Can you see any very simple characters? Look in particular at the strip that is at far right. Do you see the name of the deity Taiyi (Great One) twice? Hint: *One* is a single horizontal line.

CONNECTIONS What were the consequences of recording texts on bamboo or wooden strips? How might doing so have shaped reading and writing in Zhou times? For modern archaeologists who discover these texts in tombs, would the medium used pose any challenges?

reason or even keep in mind the rules they have mastered. This strain of Daoist thought denies the validity of verbal reasoning and the sorts of knowledge conveyed through words.

Daoism can be seen as a response to Confucianism, a rejection of many of its basic premises. Nevertheless, over the course of Chinese history, many people felt the pull of both Confucian and Daoist ideas and studied the writings of both schools. Even Confucian scholars who had devoted much of their lives to public service might find that the teachings of the *Laozi* or *Zhuangzi* helped to put their frustrations in perspective. Whereas Confucianism often seems sternly masculine, Daoism is more accepting of feminine principles and even celebrates passivity and yielding. Those drawn to the arts were also often drawn to Daoism, with its validation of spontaneity and freedom. Rulers, too, were drawn to the Daoist notion of the ruler who can have great power simply by being himself without instituting anything.

Legalism

Over the course of the fourth and third centuries B.C.E. one small state after another was conquered, and the number of surviving states dwindled. Rulers fearful that their states might be next were ready to listen to political theorists who claimed expertise in the accumulation of power. These theorists, labeled **Legalists** because of their emphasis on the need for rigorous laws, argued that strong government depended not on the moral qualities of the ruler and his officials, as Confucians claimed, but on establishing effective laws and procedures. Legalism, though eventually discredited, laid the basis for China's later bureaucratic government.

In the fourth century B.C.E. the state of Qin radically reformed itself. The king of Qin, under the guidance of Lord Shang (d. 338 B.C.E.), his chief minister, adopted many Legalist policies. He abolished the aristocracy. Social distinctions were to be based on military ranks determined by the objective criterion of the number of enemy heads cut off in battle. In place of the old fiefs, the Qin king created counties and appointed officials to govern them according to the laws he decreed at court. To increase the population, Qin recruited migrants from other states with offers of land and houses. To encourage farmers to work hard and improve their land, they were allowed to buy and sell it. Ordinary farmers were thus freed from serf-like obli-

gations to the local nobility, but direct control by the state could be even more onerous. Taxes and labor service obligations were heavy. Travel required a permit, and vagrants could be forced into penal labor service. All families were grouped into mutual responsibility groups of five and ten families; whenever anyone in the group committed a crime, all the others were equally liable unless they reported it.

In the century after Lord Shang, Legalism found its greatest exponent in Han Feizi (ca. 280?–233 B.C.E.). Han Feizi had studied with the Confucian master Xunzi but had little interest in Confucian values of goodness or ritual. In his writings he warned rulers of the political pitfalls awaiting them. They had to be careful where they placed their trust, for "when the ruler trusts someone, he falls under that person's control."[15] This is true even of wives and concubines, who think of the interests of their sons. Given subordinates' propensities to pursue their own selfish interests, the ruler should keep them ignorant of his intentions and control them by manipulating competition among them. Warmth, affection, or candor should have no place in his relationships with others.

Han Feizi saw the Confucian notion that government could be based on virtue as naive:

> Think of parents' relations to their children. They congratulate each other when a son is born, but complain to each other when a daughter is born. Why do parents have these divergent responses when both are equally their offspring? It is because they calculate their long-term advantage. Since even parents deal with their children in this calculating way, what can one expect where there is no parent-child bond? When present-day scholars counsel rulers, they all tell them to rid themselves of thoughts of profit and follow the path of mutual love. This is expecting rulers to go further than parents.[16]

If rulers would make the laws and prohibitions clear and the rewards and punishments automatic, then the officials and common people would be easy to govern. Uniform laws get people to do things they would not otherwise be inclined to do, such as work hard and fight wars, essential to the goal of establishing hegemony over all the other states.

The laws of the Legalists were designed as much to constrain officials as to regulate the common people. The third-century B.C.E. tomb of a Qin official has yielded statutes detailing the rules for keeping accounts, supervising subordinates, managing penal labor, conducting investigations, and many other responsibilities of officials. Infractions were generally punishable through the imposition of fines.

Legalism saw no value in intellectual debate or private opinion. Divergent views of right and wrong lead

• **Legalists** Political theorists who emphasized the need for rigorous laws and laid the basis for China's later bureaucratic government.

• **yin and yang** A concept of complementary poles, one of which represents the feminine, dark, and receptive, and the other the masculine, bright, and assertive.

to weakness and disorder. The ruler should not allow others to undermine his laws by questioning them. In Legalism, there were no laws above or independent of the wishes of the rulers, no laws that might set limits on rulers' actions in the way that natural or divine laws did in Greek thought. Indeed, a ruler's right to exercise the law as he saw fit was demonstrated by the violent deaths of the two leading Legalist thinkers: Lord Shang was drawn and quartered by chariots in 338 B.C.E., and Han Feizi was imprisoned and forced to drink poison in 233 B.C.E.

Rulers of several states adopted some Legalist ideas, but only the state of Qin systematically followed them. The extraordinary but brief success Qin had with these policies is discussed in Chapter 7.

Yin and Yang

Confucians, Daoists, and Legalists had the greatest long-term impact on Chinese civilization, but the Hundred Schools of Thought also included everyone from logicians, hedonists, and utopians to agriculturalists who argued that no one should eat who does not farm, and hermits who justified withdrawal from social life. Natural philosophy was one of the most important of these alternative schools of early Chinese thought.

One such philosophy was the cosmological concept of **yin and yang**, first described in the divination manual called the *Book of Changes* (ca. 900 B.C.E.), and developed into much more elaborate theories by late Zhou theorists. Yin is the feminine, dark, receptive, yielding, negative, and weak; yang is the masculine, bright, assertive, creative, positive, and strong. Yin and yang are complementary poles rather than distinct entities or opposing forces. The movement of yin and yang accounts for the transition from day to night and from summer to winter. These models based on observation of nature were extended to explain not only

phenomena we might classify as natural, such as illness, storms, and earthquakes, but also social phenomena, such as the rise and fall of states and conflict in families. In all these realms, unwanted things happen when the balance between yin and yang gets disturbed.

In recent decades archaeologists have further complicated our understanding of early Chinese thought by unearthing records of the popular religion of the time—astrological manuals, handbooks of lucky and unlucky days, medical prescriptions, exercises, and ghost stories. The tomb of an official who died in 316 B.C.E., for example, has records of divinations showing that illness was seen as the result of unsatisfied spirits or malevolent demons, best dealt with through exorcisms or offering sacrifices to the astral god Taiyi (Grand One).

Dagger Depicting Taiyi
Recent archaeological excavations of manuscripts from the Warring States Period have given us a much clearer understanding of religious beliefs and practices in early China. The deity Taiyi, depicted on this late-fourth-century B.C.E. drawing of a dagger, was the god of the pole star. Sacrifices were made to Taiyi to avert evil or gain his protection in battle. (Jingzhou Museum, © Cultural Relics Press)

CONNECTIONS

China's transition from Neolithic farming villages to a much more advanced civilization with writing, metalworking, iron coinage, crossbows, philosophical speculation, and competing states occurred centuries later than in Mesopotamia or India, but by the Warring States Period China was at much the same stage of development as other advanced societies in Eurasia. Although many elements of China's civilization were clearly invented in China—such as its writing system, its method of casting bronze, and its Confucian philosophy—it also adopted elements that diffused across Asia, such as the cultivation of wheat, the horse-driven chariot, and riding horseback.

Greece, the subject of the next chapter, is located very close to the ancient Near Eastern civilizations, so its trajectory was quite different from China's. It was also much smaller than China, yet in time had enormous impact on the wider world. With India and China in mind, the originality of the political forms and ideas of early Greece will stand out more clearly. We return to China's history in Chapter 7, after looking at Greece and Rome.

□ CHAPTER REVIEW

KEY TERMS

loess (p. 92)
Anyang (p. 94)
taotie (p. 97)
logographic (p. 97)
Book of Documents
   (p. 98)
Mandate of Heaven
   (p. 98)
shi (p. 99)

Book of Songs (p. 99)
Warring States Period
   (p. 102)
crossbow (p. 102)
filial piety (p. 104)
ren (p. 106)
Dao (p. 108)
Legalists (p. 110)
yin and yang (p. 111)

□ **What was the impact of China's geography on the development of Chinese societies? (p. 92)**

Chinese civilization did not spread into the Inner Asian region primarily because the mountains, deserts, and grasslands of these areas were not suited for agriculture. Instead Chinese civilizations arose in the fertile lands of the temperate zone of East Asia. The fertile loess soil of northern China was ideally suited for growing wheat and millet. Dry and cold, this region was prone to droughts and flooding from the Yellow River. Southern China was warmer and wetter, and the region around the Yangzi River was well suited for growing rice. It was in these regions of historical China that early Neolithic societies arose. By around 5000 B.C.E. many distinct regional Neolithic cultures had emerged. Over time these cultures came to share social and cultural practices, such as burial traditions, divination based on reading the cracks in bones, and fortified settlements, suggesting that there was contact and conflict between Neolithic societies.

□ **What was life like during the Shang Dynasty, and what effect did writing have on Chinese culture and government? (p. 94)**

After a long Neolithic period, China entered the Bronze Age with the Shang Dynasty. Shang kings ruled over large settlements that contained palaces, temples, and altars built on rammed-earth foundations and ringed by industrial areas where artisans and craftsmen lived. War booty, including slaves who were often sacrificed to the gods, provided the king with revenue. Large armies were routinely sent out on military campaigns, and their bronze-tipped weapons and chariots gave them technological superiority over their neighbors. Shang kings served also as priests, and great wealth was invested in extraordinarily complex bronze ritual vessels. Society was sharply defined by status distinctions that were carried along patrilineal lines. From Shang times on, the Chinese language has been written in a logographic script. Written language allowed for the development of a government bureaucracy capable of ruling over a large realm. Logographic script shaped the ways people became educated and the value assigned to education.

□ **How was China governed, and what was life like during the Zhou Dynasty? (p. 98)**

The Zhou Dynasty, which overthrew the Shang in about 1050 B.C.E., parceled out its territory to lords, whose titles gradually became hereditary. The *Book of*

Documents described Zhou rule and the close relationship between Heaven and the king, the Son of Heaven. The Mandate of Heaven justified Zhou rule. If kings did not rule in the interests of the people, Heaven could take the Mandate away from them and confer it on a worthier person. The hereditary nature of Zhou society contributed to aristocratic attitudes and privileges. The *Book of Songs* offers glimpses into what life was like for elites and ordinary people alike. The practice of concubinage led to a distrust of women in politics. By the fifth century B.C.E. societal changes quickened as cities were built across China and iron technology promoted economic expansion. As a result, social mobility increased.

□ **How did advances in military technology contribute to the rise of independent states? (p. 102)**

The ties between the Zhou king and his lords gradually weakened, and over time the domains came to act like independent states. After 500 B.C.E. China is best thought of as a multistate realm. The Warring States Period witnessed many advances in military technology. The introduction of cavalry, infantry armies, and the crossbow made warfare more deadly. The stakes rose as the independent states destroyed one another in a battle for supremacy. The warfare of this period undermined the old aristocratic social structure of Zhou society. To increase population and fund their armies, vassal lords increased agricultural output and taxed farmers. As a result, serfdom declined.

□ **What ideas did Confucius teach, and how were they spread after his death? (p. 103)**

The Warring States Period was the golden age of Chinese philosophy. Confucius and his followers advocated a deeply moral view of the way to achieve order through the cultivation of virtues by everyone from the ruler on down. Key virtues were sincerity, loyalty, benevolence, and filial piety. Over the next two centuries Confucius's message was elaborated by important followers, including Mencius, who urged rulers to rule through goodness and argued that human nature is good, and Xunzi, who stressed the power of ritual and argued that human nature is selfish and must be curbed through education.

□ **How did the teachings of Daoism, Legalism, and other schools of thought differ from Confucianism? (p. 107)**

In the contentious spirit of the age, many thinkers countered Confucian principles. Daoists like Laozi and Zhuangzi looked beyond the human realm to the entire cosmos and spoke of the relativity of concepts such as good and bad and life and death. Opposed to the Confucian emphasis on moral effort and statecraft, Daoists believed that striving to make something better could in fact make it worse. They defended the right to private life and opposed government interference. Legalists heaped ridicule on the Confucian idea that a ruler could get his people to be good by being good himself and proposed instead a strong government and rigorous laws with strict rewards and punishments. Natural philosophers explored issues that Confucius had neglected, such as the yin and yang forces that bring about the changes in the seasons, the transition from day to night, and cycles of health and illness.

SUGGESTED READING

Blunden, Caroline, and Mark Elvin. *Cultural Atlas of China.* 1983. Valuable both for its historical maps and its well-illustrated topical essays.

Chang, Kwang-chih, and Xu Pingfang. *The Formation of Chinese Civilization: An Archaeological Perspective.* 2005. Essays by leading archaeologists in China.

de Bary, William Theodore, and Irene Bloom. *Sources of Chinese Tradition.* 1999. Large collection of primary sources for Chinese intellectual history, with lengthy introductions.

Ebrey, Patricia Buckley. *Cambridge Illustrated History of China.* 2d ed. 2010. Well-illustrated brief overview of Chinese history.

Graham, A. C. *Disputers of the Tao: Philosophical Argument in Ancient China.* 1989. A philosophically rich overview of the intellectual flowering of the Warring States Period.

Ledderose, Lothar. *Ten Thousand Things: Module and Mass Production in Chinese Art.* 2000. A new interpretation of Chinese culture in terms of modules; offers fresh perspectives on the Chinese script and the production of bronzes.

Lewis, Mark. *Writing and Authority in Early China.* 1999. An examination of early Chinese thought in terms of the ways that texts create authority.

Loewe, Michael, and Edward Shaughnessy, eds. *The Cambridge History of Ancient China: From the Origins of Civilization to 221 B.C.* 1999. An authoritative collection of chapters, half by historians, half by archaeologists.

Mote, F. W. *Intellectual Foundations of China.* 1989. Brief but stimulating introduction to early Chinese thought.

Sterckx, Roel, ed. *Of Tripod and Palate: Food, Politics, and Religion in Traditional China.* 2005. Provides a fresh look at many elements in early Chinese culture.

Thorp, Robert. *China in the Early Bronze Age: Shang Civilization.* 2005. Clear synthesis based on recent research.

Thorp, Robert, and Richard Vinograd. *Chinese Art and Culture.* 2001. Broad coverage of all of China's visual arts.

Yang, Xin, ed. *The Golden Age of Chinese Archaeology.* 1999. The well-illustrated catalogue of a major show of Chinese archaeological finds.

NOTES

1. Patricia Buckley Ebrey, *Chinese Civilization: A Sourcebook*, 2d ed., revised and expanded (New York: Free Press/Macmillan, 1993), p. 11. All quotations from this work reprinted and edited with the permission of The Free Press, a Division of Simon & Schuster, Inc. Copyright © 1993 by Patricia Buckley Ebrey. Copyright © 1981 by The Free Press. All rights reserved.
2. Edward Shaughnessy, "Western Zhou History," in *The Cambridge History of Ancient China*, ed. M. Loewe and E. Shaughnessy (New York: Cambridge University Press, 1999), p. 336. Reprinted with the permission of Cambridge University Press.
3. Patricia Buckley Ebrey, *The Cambridge Illustrated History of China* (Cambridge: Cambridge University Press, 1996), p. 34.
4. Victor H. Mair, Nancy S. Steinhardt, and Paul Goldin, ed., *Hawai'i Reader in Traditional Chinese Culture* (Honolulu: University of Hawai'i Press, 2005), p. 117. Copyright © 2005 by University of Hawaii Press. Reprinted with permission of the publisher.
5. Ebrey, *Chinese Civilization*, p. 21.
6. Ibid., p. 19.
7. Ibid.
8. *Analects* 7.19, 15.30. Translated by Patricia Ebrey.
9. Ebrey, *Chinese Civilization*, p. 26.
10. Ibid., p. 27.
11. Ibid., p. 28, modified.
12. Ibid., p. 28.
13. Ibid., p. 31.
14. Ibid.
15. Ibid., p. 33.
16. Ibid., p. 35.

For practice quizzes and other study tools, see the **Online Study Guide** at bedfordstmartins.com/mckayworld.

For primary sources from this period, see *Sources of World Societies*, **Second Edition**.

For Web sites, images, and documents related to topics in this chapter, visit **Make History** at bedfordstmartins.com/mckayworld.

• **Greek Boy with Goose** In the Hellenistic culture that developed across a huge area after Alexander the Great's conquests, wealthy urban residents wanted art that showed real people rather than gods. This statue of a little boy wrestling a goose, originally carved about 200 B.C.E., no doubt found an eager buyer. (Vanni/Art Resource, NY)

5

The people of ancient Greece developed a culture that fundamentally shaped the civilization of the western part of Eurasia much as the Chinese culture shaped the civilization of the eastern part. The Greeks were the first in the Mediterranean and neighboring areas to explore most of the philosophical questions that still concern thinkers today. Going beyond mythmaking, the Greeks strove to understand the world in logical, rational terms. The result was the birth of philosophy and science, subjects as important to many Greeks as religion. Drawing on their day-by-day experiences, the Greeks also developed the concept of politics, and their contributions to literature still fertilize intellectual life today.

The history of the Greeks is divided into two broad periods: the Hellenic, roughly the time between the founding of the first complex societies in the area that is now the Greek islands and mainland, about 3500 B.C.E., and the rise of the kingdom of Macedonia in the north of Greece in 338 B.C.E.; and the Hellenistic, the years from the reign of Alexander the Great (336–323 B.C.E.) through the spread of Greek culture from Spain to India (ca. 100 B.C.E.; see Chapter 3). During the Hellenic period Greeks developed a distinctive form of city-state known as the polis and made lasting cultural and intellectual achievements. During the Hellenistic period Macedonian and Greek armies defeated the Persian Empire and built new cities and kingdoms. During their conquests they blended their ideas and traditions with those of the societies they encountered, creating a vibrant culture. •

The Greek Experience

3500–100 B.C.E.

**Hellas: The Land and the Polis,
ca. 3500–800** B.C.E.

☐ How did the geography of Greece shape its earliest history and lead to the growth of the polis?

**Population and Politics in the Archaic Age,
ca. 800–500** B.C.E.

☐ What were the major developments of the Archaic age, and how did Sparta and Athens create new forms of government?

**Thought and Culture in the Classical Period,
500–338** B.C.E.

☐ What were the lasting cultural and intellectual achievements of the classical period?

Hellenistic Society, 336–100 B.C.E.

☐ How did Alexander the Great's conquests shape society in the Hellenistic period?

Hellenistic Religion, Philosophy, and Science

☐ How did the meeting of cultures in the Hellenistic world shape religion, philosophy, and science?

Hellas: The Land and the Polis, ca. 3500–800 B.C.E.

☐ How did the geography of Greece shape its earliest history and lead to the growth of the polis?

Hellas, as the Greeks call their land, encompasses the Greek peninsula with its southern peninsular extension, known as the Peloponnesus (peh-luh-puh-NEE-suhs), and the islands surrounding it, an area known as the Aegean basin (Map 5.1). In ancient times this basin included the Greek settlements in Ionia, the western coast of the area known as Anatolia in modern western Turkey. Geography acts as an enormously divisive force in Greek life; mountains divide the land, and, although there are good harbors on the sea, there are no navigable rivers. The geographical fragmentation of Greece encouraged political fragmentation. Communications were poor, with rocky tracks far more common than

MAP 5.1 Classical Greece, ca. 450 B.C.E. In antiquity the home of the Greeks included the islands of the Aegean and the western shore of Turkey as well as the Greek peninsula itself. Crete, the home of Minoan civilization, is the large island at the bottom of the map. The Peloponnesian peninsula, where Sparta is located, is connected to the rest of mainland Greece by a very narrow isthmus at Corinth.

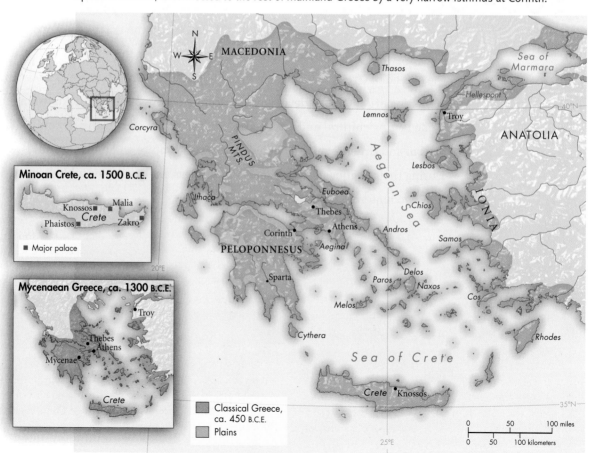

roads. Early in Greek history several kingdoms did emerge, which later became known as the Minoan (muh-NOH-uhn) and Mycenaean (migh-suh-NEE-uhn), but the rugged terrain prohibited the growth of a great empire like those of Mesopotamia or Egypt. Instead the independent city-state, known as the polis, became the most common form of government.

The Minoans and Mycenaeans

Humans came into Greece over many thousands of years, in waves of immigration whose place of origin and cultural characteristics have been the source of much scholarly debate. The first to arrive were hunter-gatherers, but techniques of agriculture and animal domestication had spread into Greece from Turkey by about 6500 B.C.E., after which small farming communities worked much of the land. Early Greek settlers brought skills in making bronze weapons and tools, which had became more common about 3500 B.C.E.

On the large island of Crete, farmers and fishermen began to trade their surpluses with their neighbors, and cities grew, housing artisans and merchants. Beginning about 2000 B.C.E. Cretans voyaged throughout the eastern Mediterranean and the Aegean, carrying the copper and tin needed for bronze and many other goods. Social hierarchies developed, and in many cities certain individuals came to hold power, although exactly how this happened is not clear. The Cretans began to use writing about 1900 B.C.E., in a form later scholars called Linear A, but this has not been deciphered. What we can know about the culture of Crete thus depends on archaeological and artistic evidence, and of this there is a great deal. At about the same time that writing began, rulers in several cities of Crete began to build large structures with hundreds of interconnected rooms. The largest of these, at Knossos (NO-suhs), has over a thousand rooms along with pipes for bringing in drinking water and sewers to get rid of waste. The archaeologists who discovered these huge structures called them palaces, and they named the flourishing and vibrant culture of this era Minoan, after the mythical king of Crete, Minos.

Minoan society was wealthy and, to judge by the absence of fortifications on the island, relatively peaceful. Few specifics are known about Minoan political life except that a king and a group of nobles stood at its head. In terms of their religious life, Minoans ap-

□ **CHRONOLOGY**

ca. 3500–338 B.C.E. Hellenic period

ca. 2000–1000 B.C.E. Minoan and Mycenaean civilizations

ca. 1100–800 B.C.E. Greece's Dark Age; evolution of the polis

ca. 800–500 B.C.E. Archaic age; rise of Sparta and Athens

776 B.C.E. Founding of the ancient Olympic games

ca. 750–550 B.C.E. Spread of Greek population in the Mediterranean

ca. 525–322 B.C.E. Birth and development of tragic drama, historical writing, and philosophy

499–404 B.C.E. Persian and Peloponnesian wars

ca. 470–322 B.C.E. Rise of the philosophies of Socrates, Plato, and Aristotle

340–250 B.C.E. Rise of Epicurean and Stoic philosophies

336–323 B.C.E. Reign of Alexander the Great

336–100 B.C.E. Hellenistic period

pear to have worshipped goddesses far more than gods. Whether this translated into more egalitarian gender roles for real people is unclear, but surviving Minoan art, including frescoes and figurines, shows women as well as men leading religious activities, watching entertainment, and engaging in athletic competitions, such as leaping over bulls. Beginning about 1700 B.C.E. Minoan society was disrupted by a series of earthquakes and volcanic eruptions on nearby islands, some of which resulted in large tsunamis. But new settlements and palaces were often built following these disasters.

As Minoan culture was flourishing on Crete, a different type of society developed on the mainland. This society was founded by groups who had migrated in during the period after 2000 B.C.E., and its members spoke an early form of Greek. By about 1650 B.C.E. one group of these immigrants had founded a powerful kingdom at Mycenae in the Peloponnesus, from which later scholars gave the culture its name, Mycenaean. Early Mycenaean Greeks raised palaces and established cities at Thebes, Athens, and elsewhere. As in Crete, the political unit was the kingdom, and the king and his warrior aristocracy stood at the top of society. The seat and symbol of the king's power was his palace, which was also the economic center of the kingdom. Within its walls royal artisans fashioned gold jewelry and rich ornaments, made and decorated fine pottery, forged weapons, prepared hides and wool for clothing, and manufactured the other goods needed by the king and his supporters.

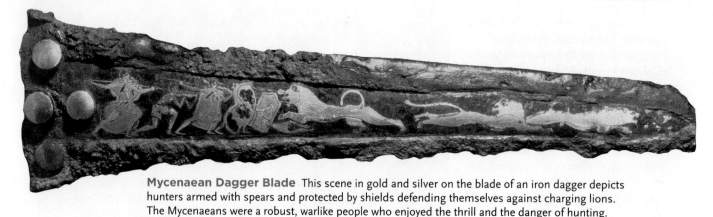

Mycenaean Dagger Blade This scene in gold and silver on the blade of an iron dagger depicts hunters armed with spears and protected by shields defending themselves against charging lions. The Mycenaeans were a robust, warlike people who enjoyed the thrill and the danger of hunting. (National Archaeological Museum, Athens/Ancient Art & Architecture Collection/The Bridgeman Art Library)

Palace scribes kept records with a script known as Linear B, which has been deciphered so that information on Mycenaean culture comes through inscriptions and other forms of written records as well as buildings and other objects. All of these point to a society in which war was common. Mycenaean cities were all fortified by thick stone walls, and graves contain spears, javelins, swords, helmets, and the first examples of metal armor known in the world.

Contacts between the Minoans and Mycenaeans were originally peaceful, and Minoan culture and trade goods flooded the Greek mainland. But around 1450 B.C.E., possibly in the wake of an earthquake that left Crete vulnerable, the Mycenaeans attacked Crete, destroying many towns and occupying Knossos. For about the next fifty years, the Mycenaeans ruled much of the island. The palaces at Knossos and other cities of the Aegean became grander as wealth gained through trade and tribute flowed into the treasuries of various Mycenaean kings. Prosperity, however, did not bring peace, and between 1300 and 1000 B.C.E. various kingdoms in and beyond Greece ravaged one another in a savage series of wars that destroyed both the Minoan and Mycenaean civilizations.

The fall of the Minoans and Mycenaeans was part of what some scholars see as a general collapse of Bronze Age civilizations in the eastern Mediterranean, including the end of the Egyptian New Kingdom and the fall of the Hittite Empire (see Chapter 2). This collapse appears to have had a number of causes: invasions and migrations by outsiders, including groups the Egyptians called the Sea Peoples and later Greeks called the Dorians, who destroyed cities and disrupted trade and production; changes in warfare and weaponry, which made foot soldiers the most important factor in battles and reduced the power of kings and wealthy nobles fighting from chariots; and natural disasters such as volcanic eruptions, earthquakes, and droughts, which reduced the amount of food and contributed to famines.

In Greece these factors worked together to usher in a period of poverty and disruption that historians have traditionally called the "Dark Age" of Greece (ca. 1100–800 B.C.E.). Even writing, which was not widespread in any case, was a casualty of the chaos. Traditions and stories continued to circulate orally, however. These included tales of the heroic deeds of legendary heroes similar to the epic poems of Mesopotamia. Sometime in the eighth or seventh century many of these were gathered together in two long epic poems, the *Iliad*, which tells of a war similar to those fought by Mycenaean kings, and the *Odyssey*, which records the adventures of one of the heroes of that war. These poems were recited orally, and once writing was reintroduced to Greece, they were written down and attributed to an author named Homer, about whom there are many legends but no historical sources. The two poems present human and divine characters who are larger than life but also petty, vindictive, pouting, and deceitful, flaws that drive the action forward, usually with tragic results. The first lines of the *Iliad*, which speak of the actions of the war hero Achilles against the Achaeans (uh-KEE-uhnz), capture such results well:

> Sing, O goddess, the anger of Achilles son of Peleus, that brought countless ills upon the Achaeans. Many a brave soul did it send hurrying down to Hades [hell], and many a hero did it yield as prey to dogs and vultures.[1]

The Development of the Polis

Greece's Dark Age actually saw two developments that would be central to later Greek history and to Greek influence on the world. The first of these was the migration of Greek-speaking peoples around the Aegean, spreading their culture to the islands and to the shores of Anatolia. The second, and more important, development was the **polis** (plural *poleis*), which is generally translated as "city-state." The earliest states in Sumeria were also city-states, as were many of the small Mycenaean kingdoms. What differentiated this new Greek form from the older models is the fact that the polis was more than a political institution; it was a community of citizens with their own customs and laws. The physical, religious, and political form of the polis varied from place to place, but everywhere it was relatively small, reflecting the fragmented geography of Greece. The very smallness of the polis enabled Greeks to see how they fit individually into the overall system—and in this way, how the individual parts made up the social whole. This notion of community was fundamental to the polis and was the very badge of Greekness.

The polis included a city and its surrounding countryside. The people of the polis typically lived in a compact group of houses within the city, which by the fifth century B.C.E. was generally surrounded by a wall. Another feature was a usually elevated area called the acropolis, where the people erected temples, altars, public monuments, and various dedications to the gods of the polis. The polis also contained a public square or marketplace, the agora, where there were porticoes, shops, public buildings, and courts. Originally the place where the warrior assembly met, the agora became the political center of the polis.

The *chora* (KOHR-uh), which included the surrounding countryside of the polis, was typically the community's source of wealth. Farmers left the city each morning to work their fields or tend their flocks of sheep and goats, and they returned at night. On the lands not suitable for farming or grazing, people often quarried stone or mined for precious metals. Thus the polis was the scene of both urban and agrarian life.

The average polis did not have a standing army. For protection it instead relied on its citizens, who met, when necessary, as a warrior assembly. Very rich citizens often served as cavalry, which was, however, never as important as the heavily armed infantrymen known as **hoplites**, who were the backbone of the army. Hoplites wore metal helmets and body armor, carried heavy, round shields, and armed themselves with spears and swords.

Greek poleis had several different types of government, of which the most common were democracy and oligarchy. In principle, **democracy**, which translates as "the power of the people," meant that all people, without respect to birth or wealth, had a say in how the government was run. In reality, however, Greek democracy meant the rule of citizens, not the people as a whole, and citizenship was limited to free adult men who had lived in the polis a long time. The remaining free men, resident foreigners, slaves, and all women were not citizens and had no political voice. In other words, none of the Greek democracies reflected the modern concept that all people are created equal. Still, democracy was attractive because it permitted male citizens to share equally in determining the diplomatic and military policies of the polis.

Spartan Hoplite This bronze figurine portrays an armed foot soldier about to strike an enemy. His massive helmet with its full crest gives his head nearly complete protection, while a metal corselet covers his chest and back, and greaves (similar to today's shin guards) protect his shins. In his right hand he carries a thrusting spear (now broken off), and in his left a large round shield. (Bildarchiv Preussischer Kulturbesitz/Art Resource, NY)

- **polis** Generally translated as "city-state," it was the basic political and institutional unit of ancient Greece.
- **hoplites** Heavily armed citizens who served as infantrymen and fought to defend the polis.
- **democracy** A type of Greek government in which all citizens administered the workings of government.

Oligarchy, which literally means "the rule of the few," was government by a small group of wealthy citizens. Many Greeks preferred oligarchy because it provided more political stability than did democracy. Although oligarchy was the government of the prosperous, it left the door open to political and social advancement. If members of the polis could meet property or money qualifications, they could enter the governing circle. Moreover, oligarchs generally listened to the concerns of the people, a major factor in the long success of this form of government.

Sporadic periods of violent political and social upheaval often led to a third type of government — tyranny. **Tyranny** was rule by one man who had seized power by unconstitutional means, generally by using his wealth to win a political following that toppled the existing legal government. Tyrants were not always oppressive rulers, however, and sometimes used their power to benefit average citizens.

Population and Politics in the Archaic Age, ca. 800–500 B.C.E.

☐ What were the major developments of the Archaic age, and how did Sparta and Athens create new forms of government?

The maturation of the polis coincided with an era, later termed the Archaic age, that saw two developments of lasting importance. The first was the even wider geographical reach of the Greeks, who now ventured as far east as the Black Sea and as far west as the Atlantic Ocean. The next was the rise to prominence of two particular poleis, Sparta and Athens, each with a distinctive system of government.

Greece's Overseas Expansion

With stability and prosperity, the Greek world grew in wealth and numbers, which brought new problems. The increase in population created more demand for food than the land could supply. The resulting social and political tensions drove many people to seek new homes outside of Greece (Map 5.2).

From about 750 to 550 B.C.E. Greeks poured onto the coasts of the northern Aegean and the Black Sea,

southward along the North Africa coast, and then westward to Sicily, southern Italy, and beyond to Spain and the Atlantic. In contrast to earlier military invasions and migrations of peoples, these were very often intentional colonizing ventures, organized and planned by a specific polis seeking new land for its residents. In all these places the Greeks established flourishing cities that created a much larger market for agricultural and manufactured goods. A later wave of colonization from 500 to 400 B.C.E. spread Greeks throughout the northern coast of the Black Sea as far east as southern Russia. Colonization on this scale meant that the future culture of this entire area would be Greek, a heritage that Rome would later share.

Around the time of these territorial expansions, important changes were taking place within Greece, in Sparta and Athens. These included the formation of new social and political structures.

The Growth of Sparta

During the Archaic period, one of the poleis on the Peloponnesian peninsula, Sparta, also faced problems of overpopulation and shortages of fertile land. The Spartans solved both by conquering the agriculturally rich region of Messenia to the west of Sparta in 715 B.C.E. (see Map 5.1), making the Messenians helots, state slaves. The helots soon rose in a revolt that took the Spartans thirty years to crush. Afterward, non-nobles who had shared in the fighting as foot soldiers appear to have demanded rights equal to those of the nobility and a voice in the government. (In more recent history, similar demands in the United States during the Vietnam War led to a lowering of the voting age to eighteen, to match the age at which soldiers were drafted.)

Under intense pressure the aristocrats agreed to remodel the state into a new system, called the Lycurgan regimen after Lycurgus (ligh-KUHR-guhs), a legendary lawgiver. Under this system all Spartan citizens were given equal political rights. Two kings, who were primarily military leaders, and a council of nobles shared executive power with five ephors (EH-fuhrs), overseers elected by the citizens. Economically, the helots did all the work, while Spartan citizens devoted their time to military training, and Sparta became extremely powerful.

In the Lycurgan system every citizen owed primary allegiance to Sparta, and individuals placed the defense of Sparta over their own needs. Even family life was sacrificed to the polis. After long, hard military training that began at age seven, citizens became lifelong soldiers, the best in Greece. In battle Spartans were supposed to stand and die rather than retreat. An anecdote frequently repeated about one Spartan mother sums up Spartan military values. As her son

---

• **oligarchy** A type of Greek government in which a small group of wealthy citizens, not necessarily of aristocratic birth, ruled.

• **tyranny** Rule by one man who took over an existing government, generally by using his wealth to gain a political following.

was setting off to battle, the mother handed him his shield and advised him to come back either victorious, carrying the shield, or dead, being carried on it. Spartan men were expected to train vigorously, do with little, and like it, qualities reflected even today in the word *spartan*.

Similar rigorous requirements applied to Spartan women, who were unique in all Greek society. Xenophon, a later Athenian admirer of the Spartans, commented that Lycurgus had:

> insisted on the training of the body as incumbent no less on the female than the male; and in pursuit of the same idea instituted rival contests in running and feats of strength for women as for men. His belief was that where both parents were strong their progeny would be found to be more vigorous.[2]

With men in military service much of their lives, women in citizen families ran the estates and owned land in their own right, and they were not physically restricted or secluded. But Spartans expected them to be good wives and strict mothers of future soldiers. Because men often did not see their wives or other women for long periods not only in times of war but also in peace, their most meaningful relations were same-sex ones. The Spartan military leaders viewed such relationships as militarily advantageous because they believed that men would fight even more fiercely for lovers and comrades. Close links among men thus contributed to Spartan civic life, which was admired throughout the Greek world.

Golden Comb This golden comb, made about 400 B.C.E. in Scythia (now part of Ukraine), shows a battle between three warriors, perhaps the three brothers who are the legendary founders of Scythia. Their dress shows a combination of Greek and Eastern details; the mounted horseman is clothed with largely Greek armor, while the warriors on foot are wearing Eastern dress. The comb may have been made by a Greek craftsman who had migrated to the Black Sea area as the Greeks established colonies there, but it was buried in a Scythian burial mound. (© Boltin Picture Library/The Bridgeman Art Library)

MAP 5.2 Greek Colonization, ca. 750–550 B.C.E. The Greeks established colonies along the shores of the Mediterranean and the Black Seas, spreading Greek culture and creating a large trading network.

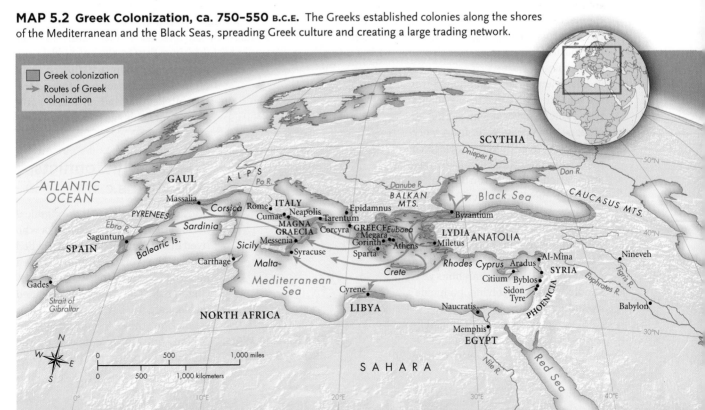

The Evolution of Athens

Like Sparta, Athens faced pressing social and economic problems during the Archaic period. The late seventh century B.C.E. was for Athens a time of turmoil because aristocrats, many of them wealthy from trade, had begun to seize the holdings of smaller landowners. In 621 B.C.E. the aristocrat Draco (DRAY-koh), under pressure from small landholders and with the consent of the nobles, published the first law code of the Athenian polis. His code was harsh—and for this reason was the origin of the word *draconian*—but it embodied the ideal that the law belonged to all citizens. Yet the aristocracy still governed Athens oppressively, and the social and economic situation remained dire. Despite Draco's code, noble landholders continued to force small farmers and artisans into economic dependence. Many families were sold into slavery as settlement for debts, while others were exiled and their land mortgaged to the rich. Solon (SOH-luhn), an aristocrat and a poet, railed against these injustices in his poems, which he recited in the agora for all to hear. Solon's sincerity and good sense convinced other aristocrats that he was no crazed revolutionary. Moreover, he gained the trust of the common people, whose problems provoked them to demand access to political life, much as commoners in Sparta had. Around 594 B.C.E. the nobles elected him *archon* (AHR-kahn), chief magistrate of the polis, and gave him extraordinary power to reform the state.

Solon allowed nobles to keep their land, but he immediately freed all people enslaved for debt, recalled all exiles, canceled all debts on land, and made enslavement for debt illegal. Also, he allowed commoners into the old aristocratic assembly, where they could vote in the election of magistrates. Later sixth-century leaders further broadened the opportunities for commoners to take part in government, transforming Athens into a democracy.

The democracy functioned on the ideal that all full citizens should play a role in government, yet not all citizens could take time from work to do this. They therefore delegated their power to other citizens by creating various offices to run the democracy. The most prestigious of these offices was the board of ten archons, whose members, elected for one year, handled legal and military affairs. After leaving office, they entered a select council of former archons who handled cases involving homicide, wounding, and arson.

Making laws was the responsibility of two bodies, the boule (BOO-lee), or council, composed of five hundred members, and the ecclesia (ee-KLEE-zhee-uh), the assembly of all citizens. The boule was perhaps the major institution of the democracy. By supervising the various committees of government and proposing bills to the assembly, it guided Athenian political life. It received foreign envoys and forwarded treaties to the assembly for ratification. However, the ecclesia, by a simple majority vote, had the final word.

Athenian democracy demonstrated that a large group of people, not just a few, could run the affairs of state. Because citizens could speak their minds, they were not forced into rebellion or conspiracy to express their views. Like all democracies in ancient Greece, however, the one in Athens was limited. Women, slaves, and outsiders could not be citizens, and their opinions were neither recorded nor legally binding.

Thought and Culture in the Classical Period, 500–338 B.C.E.

☐ What were the lasting cultural and intellectual achievements of the classical period?

Between 500 and 338 B.C.E. Greek civilization reached its highest peak in politics, thought, and art, even as it engaged in violent conflicts. First, the Greeks beat back the armies of the Persian Empire. Then, turning their spears against one another, they destroyed their own political system in a century of warfare that began with the Peloponnesian War. Some thoughtful Greek historians recorded these momentous events. This era also saw the flowering of philosophy as thinkers pondered the meaning of the universe and human nature. In other achievements of this time, the Greeks invented drama and reached their artistic zenith in architecture. Because of these various intellectual and artistic accomplishments, this age is called the classical period.

The Deadly Conflicts, 499–404 B.C.E.

Warfare marked most of the classical period. In 499 B.C.E. the Greeks who lived in Ionia unsuccessfully rebelled against the Persian Empire, which had ruled the area for fifty years (see Chapter 2). The Athenians provided feeble help to the Ionians, and in retaliation the Persians struck at Athens, only to be defeated by the Athenian hoplites at the battle of

Areas of Persian control
Greek states at war with Persia
Neutral Greek states

Thermopylae 480 B.C.E.
Artemisium 480 B.C.E.
Plataea 479 B.C.E.
Marathon 490 B.C.E.
Salamis 480 B.C.E.

Crete

The Persian Wars, 499–479 B.C.E.

Marathon. (According to legend, a Greek runner carried the news of the victory to Athens and then died from the exertion. When the modern Olympics were founded in 1896, they included a long-distance running race between Marathon and Athens, a distance of about twenty-six miles, designed to honor the ancient Greeks.) In 480 B.C.E. the Persian king Xerxes (ZUHRK-seez) personally led a massive invasion of Greece. Under the leadership of Sparta by land and Athens by sea, many Greeks united to fight the Persians, and they engaged in major battles at the pass of Thermopylae and in the waters off Artemisium. The larger Persian army was victorious and occupied Athens, but only a month or so later the Greeks defeated the Persian navy in the decisive battle of Salamis, and in 479 B.C.E. they overwhelmed the Persian army at Plataea.

The victorious Athenians and their allies then formed the **Delian League**, a grand naval alliance intended to liberate Ionia from Persian rule. While driving the Persians out of Asia Minor, the Athenians also turned the league into an Athenian empire. They often collected tribute from other cities by force and took control of their economic resources. Athenian ideas of freedom and democracy did not extend to conquered peoples, and cities that objected to or revolted over Athenian actions were put down. (See "Viewpoints:

> **"This day will be the beginning of great evils for the Greeks."**
>
> **SPARTAN AMBASSADOR**

Two Opinions About Athenian Democracy," page 124.) Under their great leader Pericles (PEHR-uh-kleez; ca. 494–429 B.C.E.) the Athenians grew so powerful and aggressive that they alarmed Sparta and its allies. In 431 B.C.E. Athenian imperialism finally drove Sparta into the conflict known as the Peloponnesian War. The Peloponnesian War lasted a generation (431–404 B.C.E.) and brought widespread civil wars, destruction, famine, and huge loss of life. With thousands of soldiers, Athens launched an attack on the island of Sicily, which ended in disaster. The Spartans encouraged revolts in cities that were subject to Athens and defeated the once-mighty Athenian fleet in naval battles. In 404 B.C.E. the Athenians finally surrendered; Sparta stripped it of its empire, but did not destroy the city itself.

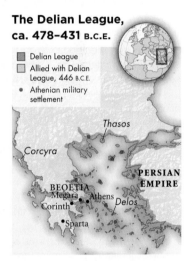

The Delian League, ca. 478–431 B.C.E.

- ■ Delian League
- □ Allied with Delian League, 446 B.C.E.
- ● Athenian military settlement

Writers at the time described and analyzed these wars, seeking to understand their causes and consequences. Herodotus (ca. 484–425 B.C.E.) traveled the Greek world to piece together the course of the Persian wars. Although he consulted documents when he could find them, he relied largely on the memories of the participants, and he presented all sides if there were conflicting views. Thucydides (ca. 460–ca. 399 B.C.E.) was an Athenian general in the Peloponnesian War but was banished early in the conflict because of a defeat; he traveled throughout Greece seeking information about the war from all sides. His account of the war saw human greed and desire for power as the root of the conflict, and he viewed the war itself as a disaster. As he told it, at the outbreak a Spartan ambassador warned the Athenians: "This day will be the beginning of great evils for the Greeks."[3] Thucydides agreed.

The Discus Thrower This marble statue shows an athlete in mid-throw, capturing the tension in the muscles and tendons. The original was made about 450 B.C.E., perhaps by the sculptor Myron of Athens. As is true of so much Greek statuary, the original is lost, and this is a Roman copy. (Scala/Art Resource, NY)

• **Delian League** A grand naval alliance created by the Athenians aimed at liberating Ionia from Persian rule.

Viewpoints

Two Opinions About Athenian Democracy

• *Modern scholars often debate the extent and character of Athenian democracy, but such debates actually started in ancient Athens itself. Pericles, the leader of Athens, portrayed Athenian democracy very positively in a public funeral speech given, according to the historian Thucydides, in 430 B.C.E. to honor those who had died in the first year of the Peloponnesian War against Sparta. By contrast, five years later an unknown author highlighted a more negative view of Athenian democracy.*

Pericles's Funeral Speech

"Our constitution does not copy the laws of neighbouring states; we are rather a pattern to others than imitators ourselves. Its administration favours the many instead of the few; this is why it is called a democracy. If we look to the laws, they afford equal justice to all in their private differences; if no social standing, advancement in public life falls to reputation for capacity, class considerations not being allowed to interfere with merit; nor again does poverty bar the way, if a man is able to serve the state, he is not hindered by the obscurity of his condition. . . .

The magnitude of our city draws the produce of the world into our harbour, so that to the Athenian the fruits of other countries are as familiar a luxury as those of his own. . . .

Nor are these the only points in which our city is worthy of admiration. We cultivate refinement without extravagance and knowledge without effeminacy; wealth we employ more for use than for show, and place the real disgrace of poverty not in owning to the fact but in declining the struggle against it. Our public men have, besides politics, their private affairs to attend to, and our ordinary citizens, though occupied with the pursuits of industry, are still fair judges of public matters. . . .

In short, I say that as a city we are the school of Hellas, while I doubt if the world can produce a man who, where he has only himself to depend upon, is equal to so many emergencies, and graced by so happy a versatility, as the Athenian."

Unknown Author on the Athenian Constitution

"As for the constitution of the Athenians, their choice of this type of constitution I do not approve, for in choosing thus they choose that thieves should fare better than the elite. . . . I shall say that at Athens the poor and the commons seem justly to have the advantage over the well-born and the wealthy; for it is the poor which mans the fleet and has brought the state her power. . . . [However] in those offices which bring security to the whole people if they are in the hands of good citizens, but, if not, ruin, the poor desires to have no share. . . . All those offices, however, whose end is pay and family benefits the poor do seek to hold. . . .

Secondly, some people are surprised that everywhere they give the advantage to thieves, the poor, and the radical elements rather than to the elite. This is just where they will be seen to be preserving democracy. For if the poor and the common people and the worse elements are treated well, the growth of these classes will exalt the democracy; whereas if the rich and the elite are treated well the democrats strengthen their own opponents. In every land the elite are opposed to democracy. Among the elite there is very little license and injustice, very great discrimination as to what is worthy, while among the poor there is very great ignorance, disorderliness, and thievery. . . .

Of such mainland states as are subject to Athenian rule the large are in subjection because of fear, the small simply because of need; there is not a city which does not require both import and export trade, and it will not have that unless it is subject to Athens—the rulers of the seas. . . . The Athenians alone possess the wealth of the Hellenes and the foreigners."

Sources: Thucydides, *History of the Peloponnesian War*, translated by Richard Crawley (New York: Modern Library, 1951), pp. 103–106; unknown author from Fred Fling, ed., *A Source Book of Greek History*, (Boston: D. C. Heath, 1907), pp. 155–158.

QUESTIONS FOR ANALYSIS

1. What differences do you see between the views of Pericles and the unknown author about whether democracy promotes merit and good government, and about whether the poor should have a voice in government?
2. How do the two authors differ about the reasons that Athens dominated trade?

Athenian Arts in the Age of Pericles

Although Athens eventually lost to Sparta on the battlefield, in terms of cultural and intellectual legacy Athens has been long viewed as the most important polis. Some contemporary historians, noting that this Athenocentrism fails to do justice to the other Greeks who also shaped society, culture, and history, are increasingly focusing on areas other than Athens. But Athens remains the best-studied city.

In the last half of the fifth century B.C.E. Pericles turned Athens into the showplace of Greece by making the Acropolis a wonder for all time. He appropriated

Delian League money to fund a huge building program for the Acropolis, and he gained support for the program by pointing out that it would employ many Athenians and bring economic prosperity to the city. Workers erected temples and other buildings housing statues and carvings, often painted in bright colors, showing the gods in human form and celebrating the Athenian victory over the Persians. (The paint later washed away, leaving the generally white sculpture that we think of as "classical.") The Acropolis was crowned by the Parthenon, a temple that celebrated the greatness of Athens and its patron goddess, Athena, who was represented by a huge ivory and gold statue. Even though the pollution of modern Athens is destroying these ancient buildings, it cannot rob them of their nobility and charm.

Other aspects of Athenian culture, including the development of drama, were also rooted in the life of the polis. The polis sponsored plays as part of the city's religious festivals and required wealthy citizens to pay the expenses of their production. Although many plays were highly controversial, they were neither suppressed nor censored. Not surprisingly, given the incessant warfare, conflict was a constant element in Athenian drama, and playwrights used their art in attempts to portray, understand, and resolve life's basic conflicts.

Aeschylus (EHS-kuh-luhs; 525–456 B.C.E.) was the first dramatist to explore such basic questions as the rights of the individual, the conflict between the individual and society, and the nature of good and evil. In his trilogy of plays, *The Oresteia*, he treats the themes of betrayal, murder, and reconciliation, urging the use

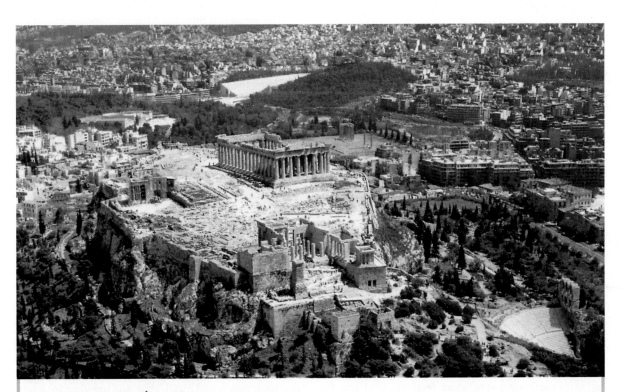

□ Picturing the Past

The Acropolis of Athens The natural rock formation of the Acropolis probably had a palace on top as early as the Mycenaean period, when it was also surrounded by a defensive wall. Temples were constructed beginning in the sixth century B.C.E., and after the Persian War Pericles ordered the reconstruction and expansion of many of these, as well as the building of new and more magnificent temples and an extension of the defensive walls. The largest building is the Parthenon, a temple dedicated to the goddess Athena, which originally housed a 40-foot-tall statue of Athena made of ivory and gold sheets attached to a wooden frame. Much of the Parthenon was damaged when it was shelled during a war between Venice and the Ottoman Empire in the seventeenth century, and air pollution continues to eat away at the marble. (Courtesy, Sotiris Toumbis Editions)

ANALYZING THE IMAGE Imagine yourself as an Athenian walking up the hill toward the Parthenon. What impression would the setting and the building itself convey?

CONNECTIONS What were the various functions of the Acropolis?

of reason and justice to reconcile fundamental conflicts. The final play concludes with a prayer that civil dissension never be allowed to destroy Athens.

The plays of Sophocles (SAH-fuh-kleez; 496–406 B.C.E.) also deal with matters personal, political, and divine. In *Antigone*—which tells of how a king's mistakes in judgment lead to the suicides of his son, his son's fiancée, and his wife—Sophocles emphasizes the precedence of divine law over political law and family custom. In the closing lines he writes:

> Good sense is by far the chief part of happiness; and we must not be impious towards the gods. The great words of boasters are always punished with great blows, and as they grow old teach them wisdom.[4]

In *Oedipus the King* Sophocles tells the story of a good man doomed by the gods to kill his father and marry his mother. When Oedipus fails to avoid his fate, he blinds himself in despair and flees into exile. In *Oedipus at Colonus* Sophocles treats the last days of the broken man, whose patient suffering and uncomplaining piety ultimately win the blessings and honor of the gods.

Euripides (you-RIH-puh-deez; ca. 480–406 B.C.E.) likewise explored the theme of personal conflict within the polis and sounded the depths of the individual. With Euripides drama entered a new and more personal phase. To him the gods mattered far less than people.

Aeschylus, Sophocles, and Euripides are considered writers of tragedies: the stories of flawed people who bring disaster on themselves because their passions overwhelm reason. Athens also produced writers of comic dramas, which used humor as political commentary in an effort to suggest and support the best policies for the polis. Although comedies treated the affairs of the polis bawdily and often coarsely, they too were performed at religious festivals. Best known of the comedians is Aristophanes (eh-ruh-STAH-fuh-neez; ca. 445–386 B.C.E.), a merciless critic of cranks, quacks, and fools. He used his art of sarcasm to dramatize his ideas on the right conduct of the citizen and his leaders for the good of the polis.

Daily Life and Social Conditions in Athens

The Athenians, like other Greeks, lived with comparatively few material possessions in houses that were rather simple. A typical Athenian house consisted of a series of rooms opening onto a central courtyard that contained a well, an altar, and a washbasin. Larger houses often had a front room where the men of the family ate and entertained guests, as well as women's quarters at the back. Meals consisted primarily of various grains, especially wheat and barley, as well as lentils, olives, figs, grapes, fish, and a little meat, foods that are now part of the highly touted "Mediterranean diet."

> "Good sense is by far the chief part of happiness; and we must not be impious towards the gods."
>
> **SOPHOCLES**

In the city a man might support himself as a craftsman, potter, bronze smith, or tanner, or he could contract with the polis to work on public buildings. Certain crafts, including spinning and weaving, were generally done by women. Men and women without skills worked as paid laborers. Slavery was commonplace in Greece, as it was throughout the ancient world. Slaves, who were paid for their work, were usually foreigners and often "barbarians," people whose native language was not Greek.

The social conditions of Athenian women have been the subject of much debate, in part because the sources are fragmentary. The available sources suggest that women rarely played notable roles in public affairs, and we know the names of no female poets, artists, or philosophers from classical Athens. The status of a free woman was strictly protected by law. Only her sons could be citizens. Only she was in charge of the household and the family's possessions, yet the law gave her these rights primarily to protect her husband's interests. Women in Athens and elsewhere in Greece, like those in Mesopotamia, brought dowries to their husbands upon marriage, which went back to their fathers in cases of divorce.

In ancient Athens the main function of women from citizen families was to bear and raise children. They ideally lived secluded lives in which the only men they usually saw were relatives and tradesmen. How far this ideal was actually a reality is impossible to say, but women in citizen families probably spent most of their time at home, leaving the house only to attend religious festivals, and perhaps occasionally plays, although this is debated. In their quarters of the house they oversaw domestic slaves and hired labor, and together with servants and friends worked wool into cloth. Women from noncitizen families lived freer lives, although they worked harder and had fewer material comforts. They performed manual labor in the fields or sold goods in the agora, going about their affairs much as men did. Prostitution was legal in Athens, and sophisticated courtesans known as hetaerae added intellectual accomplishments to physical beauty. Hetaerae accompanied men in public settings where their wives would not have been welcome, serving men as social as well as sexual partners.

Same-sex relations were generally accepted in all of ancient Greece, not simply in Sparta. In classical Athens part of a male adolescent citizen's training was supposed to entail a hierarchical sexual and tutorial relationship with an older man, who most likely was married and may have had female sexual partners as well. These relationships between adolescents and men were often celebrated in literature and art, in part because Athenians regarded perfection as possible only in the male. Women were generally seen as inferior to men, dominated by their bodies rather than their minds.

How often actual sexual relations between men or between men and women approached the ideal in Athens is very difficult to say, as most of our sources are prescriptive, idealized, or fictional. A small number of sources refer to female-female sexual desire, the most famous of which are the poems of Sappho (SA-foh), a female poet of the sixth century B.C.E. Today the English word *lesbian* is derived from Sappho's home island of Lesbos in the northern Aegean Sea.

Same-sex relations did not mean that people did not marry, for Athenians saw the continuation of the family line as essential. Sappho herself, for example, appears to have had a daughter. Sexual desire and procreation were both important aspects of life, but ancient Greeks did not necessarily link them.

Greek Religion in the Classical Period

Like most peoples of the ancient world, the Greeks were polytheists, worshipping a variety of gods and goddesses who were immortal but otherwise acted just like people. Migration, invasion, and colonization brought the Greeks into contact with other peoples and caused their religious beliefs to evolve. But by the classical era these beliefs centered on a group of gods understood to live on Mount Olympus, the highest mountain in Greece. Zeus was the king of the gods and the most powerful of them, and he was married to Hera, who was also his sister (just as, in Egypt, Isis was Osiris's wife and sister; see Chapter 2). Zeus and Hera had several children, including Ares, the god of war, and Zeus's children with other women included gods such as Apollo and Athena and heroes such as Hercules and Perseus. Apollo represented the epitome of youth, beauty, and athletic skill, and he served as the patron god of music and poetry. His half-sister Athena was a warrior-goddess who had been born from the head of Zeus. Best known for her cult at Athens, to which she gave her name, she was highly revered throughout Greece.

Besides these Olympian gods, each polis had its own minor deities, each with his or her own local group of worshippers. The polis administered the cults and religious festivals, and everyone was expected to participate in these civic rituals, which were more like today's patriotic parades or ceremonies than expressions of

belief. Individual families also honored various deities in their homes, and some people turned to what later became known as "mystery religions" (see page 136).

The Greeks had no sacred books such as the Bible, nor did religion impose an ethical code of conduct. In contrast to Mesopotamia, Egypt, and Vedic India, priests held little power in Greece; their purpose was to care for temples and sacred property and to conduct the proper rituals, but not to make religious or political rules or doctrines, much less to enforce them.

Though much of Greek religion was local and domestic, the Greeks also shared some Pan-Hellenic festivals, the chief of which were held at Olympia to honor Zeus and at Delphi to honor Apollo. The festivities at Olympia included the famous athletic contests that inspired the modern Olympic games. Held every four years after they started in 776 B.C.E., the contests attracted visitors from all over the Greek world and lasted well into Christian times. The Pythian games at Delphi were also held every four years, but these contests included musical and literary competitions. Both the Olympic and Pythian games were unifying factors in Greek life.

Hetaera and Young Man In this scene painted on the inside of a drinking cup, a hetaera holds the head of a young man who has clearly had too much to drink. Sexual and comic scenes were common on Greek pottery, particularly on objects that would have been used at a private dinner party hosted by a citizen, known as a symposium. Wives did not attend symposia, but hetaerae and entertainers were often hired to perform for the male guests. (Martin von Wagner Museum der Universität Würzburg. Photo: Karl Oehrlein)

Aristotle, On the Family and On Slavery, from *The Politics*

The Athenian philosopher Aristotle sought to understand everything in the world around him, including human society as well as the physical world. In The Politics, *one of his most important works, he examines the development of government, which he sees as originating in the family. Thus before discussing relations of power within the city, he discusses them within the household, which requires him to confront the issue of slavery and the very unequal relations between men and women.*

The city belongs among the things that exist by nature, and man is by nature a political animal. . . .

He who thus considers things in their first growth and origin, whether a state or anything else, will obtain the clearest view of them. . . . Out of these two relationships between man and woman, master and slave, the first thing to arise is the family, and Hesiod is right when he says,

First house and wife and an ox for the plough,

for the ox is the poor man's slave. The family is the association established by nature for the supply of men's everyday wants.

Seeing then that the state is made up of households, before speaking of the state we must speak of the management of the household. The parts of household management correspond to the persons who compose the household, and a complete household consists of slaves and freemen. . . .

Property is a part of the household, and the art of acquiring property is a part of the art of managing the household; for no man can live well, or indeed live at all, unless he be provided with necessaries. And as in the arts which have a definite sphere the workers must have their own proper instruments for the accomplishment of their work, so it is in the management of a household. Now instruments are of various sorts; some are living, others lifeless; in the rudder, the pilot of a ship has a lifeless, in the look-out man, a living instrument; for in the arts

the servant is a kind of instrument. Thus, too, a possession is an instrument for maintaining life. And so, in the arrangement of the family, a slave is a living possession. . . .

It is clear that the rule of the soul over the body, and of the mind and the rational element over the passionate, is natural and expedient; whereas the equality of the two or the rule of the inferior is always hurtful. The same holds good of animals in relation to men; for tame animals have a better nature than wild, and all tame animals are better off when they are ruled by man; for then they are preserved. Again, the male is by nature superior, and the female inferior; and the one rules, and the other is ruled; this principle, of necessity, extends to all mankind.

Where then there is such a difference as that between soul and body, or between men and animals (as in the case of those whose business is to use their body, and who can do nothing better), the lower sort are by nature slaves, and it is better for them as for all inferiors that they should be under the rule of a master. For he who can be, and therefore is, another's and he who participates in the rational principle enough to apprehend, but not to have, such a principle, is a slave by nature. Whereas the lower animals cannot even apprehend a principle; they obey their instincts. And indeed the use made of slaves and of tame animals is not very different; for both with their bodies minister to the needs of life. . . .

A question may indeed be raised, whether there is any excellence at all in a slave beyond and higher than merely instrumental and ministerial qualities—whether he can have the virtues of temperance, courage, justice, and the like; or whether slaves possess only bodily and ministerial qualities. And, whichever way we answer the question, a difficulty arises; for, if they have virtue, in what will they differ from freemen? On the other hand, since they are men and share in rational principle, it seems absurd to say that they have no virtue. A similar question may be raised about women and children, whether they too have virtues: ought a woman to be temperate

The Flowering of Philosophy

Just as the Greeks developed rituals to honor gods, they spun myths and epics to explain the origin of the universe. Over time, however, as Greeks encountered other peoples with different beliefs, some of them began to question their old gods and myths, and they sought rational rather than supernatural explanations for natural phenomena. These Greek thinkers, based in Ionia, are called the Pre-Socratics because their rational efforts preceded those of Socrates. Taking indi-

vidual facts, they wove them into general theories that led them to conclude that, despite appearances, the universe is actually simple and subject to natural laws. The Pre-Socratics began an intellectual revolution that still flourishes today, creating what we now call philosophy and science.

Drawing on their observations, the Pre-Socratics speculated about the basic building blocks of the universe, and most decided that all things were made of four simple substances: fire, air, earth, and water. Democritus (dih-MAH-kruh-tuhs; ca. 460 B.C.E.) broke

In this painting from the side of a vase made in the fifth century B.C.E., a well-to-do young woman sits on an elegant chair inside a house, spinning and weaving. The bed piled high with coverlets on the left was a symbol of marriage in Greek art. The young woman's body language and facial expression suggest that she was not particularly happy with her situation. (Erich Lessing/Art Resource, NY)

and brave and just, and is a child to be called temperate, and intemperate, or not. . . . Here the very constitution of the soul has shown us the way; in it one part naturally rules, and the other is subject, and the virtue of the ruler we maintain to be different from that of the subject; the one being the virtue of the rational, and the other of the irrational part. Now, it is obvious that the same principle applies generally, and therefore almost all things rule and are ruled according to nature. But the kind of rule differs; the freeman rules over the slave after another manner from that in which the male rules over the female, or the man over the child; although the parts of the soul are present in any of them, they are present in different degrees. For the slave has no deliberative faculty at all; the woman has, but it is without authority, and the child has, but it is immature. So it must necessarily be supposed to be with the moral virtues also; all should partake of them, but only in such manner and degree as is required by each for the fulfillment of his duty. . . . Clearly, then, moral virtue belongs to all of them; but the temperance of a man and of a woman, or the courage and justice of a man and of a woman, are not, as Socrates maintained, the same; the courage of a man is shown in commanding, of a woman in obeying. . . .

All classes must be deemed to have their special attributes; as the poet says of women,

Silence is a woman's glory,

but this is not equally the glory of man. The child is imperfect, and therefore obviously his virtue is not relative to himself alone, but to the perfect man and to his teacher, and in like manner the virtue of the slave is relative to a master. Now we determined that a slave is useful for the wants of life, and therefore he will obviously require only so much virtue as will prevent him from failing in his duty through cowardice or lack of self-control. "

Source: Aristotle, *Politics*, Book One, translated by Benjamin Jowett, at: http://classics.mit.edu/Aristotle/politics.1.one.html.

QUESTIONS FOR ANALYSIS

1. What does Aristotle see as the purpose of the family, and why does he begin his discussion of politics with relations within the family?
2. How does Aristotle explain and justify slavery? Given what you have read about Athenian slavery, does this argument make sense to you?
3. How does Aristotle explain and justify the differences between men and women?

this down further and created the atomic theory that the universe is made up of invisible, indestructible particles. The stream of thought started by the Pre-Socratics branched into several directions. Hippocrates (hih-PAH-kruh-teez; ca. 470–400 B.C.E.), often called the father of Western medicine, sought natural explanations for diseases and natural means to treat them. Illness was not caused by evil spirits, he asserted, but by physical problems in the body, particularly by imbalances in what he saw as four basic bodily fluids: blood, phlegm, black bile, and yellow bile. In a healthy

body these fluids, called humors, were in perfect balance, and medical treatment of the ill sought to help the body bring them back into balance. Hippocrates seems to have advocated letting nature take its course and not intervening too much, though later medicine based on the humoral theory would be much more interventionist, with bloodletting emerging as the central treatment for any illness.

The Sophists (SOF-ists), a group of thinkers in fifth century B.C.E. Athens, applied philosophical speculation to politics and language, questioning the beliefs

Procession to a Temple This detail from a vase shows Greek men and women approaching a temple, where a priestess, bough in hand, greets them. In this type of Greek pottery, men are shown with dark skin and women with white, reflecting the ideal that men's lives took place largely outside in the sun-filled public squares, and women's in the shaded interiors of homes. (Image copyright © The Metropolitan Museum of Art/Art Resource, NY)

and laws of the polis to understand their origin. They believed that excellence in both politics and language could be taught, and they provided lessons for the young men of Athens who wished to learn how to persuade others in the often tumultuous Athenian democracy. Their later opponents criticized them for charging fees and also accused them of using rhetoric to deceive people instead of presenting the truth. (Today the word *sophist* is usually used in this sense, describing someone who deceives people with clever-sounding but false arguments.)

Socrates (ca. 470–399 B.C.E.), whose ideas are known only through the works of others, also applied philosophy to politics and to people. He seemed to many Athenians to be a Sophist because he also questioned Athenian traditions, although he never charged fees. His approach when exploring ethical issues and defining concepts was to start with a general topic or problem and to narrow the matter to its essentials. He did so by continuously questioning participants in a discussion or argument rather than lecturing, a process known as the Socratic dialogue. Because he posed questions rather than giving answers, it is difficult to say exactly what Socrates thought about many things, although he does seem to have felt that through knowledge people could approach the supreme good and thus find happiness. He clearly thought that Athenian leaders were motivated more by greed and opportunism than by a desire for justice in the war with Sparta, and he criticized Athenian democracy openly. His views brought him into conflict with the government. The leaders of Athens tried him for corrupting the youth of the city, and in 399 B.C.E. they executed him.

Most of what we know about Socrates comes from his student Plato (427–347 B.C.E.), who wrote dialogues in which Socrates asks questions and who also founded the Academy, a school dedicated to philosophy. Plato developed the theory that there are two worlds: the impermanent, changing world that we know through our senses, and the eternal, unchanging realm of "forms" that constitute the essence of true reality. According to Plato, true knowledge and the possibility of living a virtuous life come from contemplating ideal forms, not from observing the visible world. Thus if you want to understand justice, asserted Plato, you should think about what would make perfect justice, not study the imperfect examples of justice around you.

Plato's student Aristotle (384–322 B.C.E.) also thought that true knowledge was possible, but he believed that such knowledge came from observation of the world, analysis of natural phenomena, and logical reasoning, not contemplation. Aristotle thought that everything had a purpose, so that to know something, one also had to know its function. (See "Listening to the Past: Aristotle, On the Family and On Slavery, from *The Politics*," page 128.) The range of Aristotle's thought is staggering. His interests embraced logic, ethics, natural science, physics, politics, poetry, and art. He studied the heavens as well as earth and judged the earth to be the center of the universe, with the stars and planets revolving around it.

Plato's idealism profoundly shaped Western philosophy, but Aristotle came to have an even wider influence; for many centuries in Europe, the authority of his ideas was second only to the Bible's. His works— which are actually a combination of his lecture notes and those of his students, copied and recopied many times — were used as the ultimate proof that something was true, even if closer observation of the phenomenon indicated that it was not. Thus, ironically, Aristotle's authority was sometimes invoked in a way that contradicted his own ideas. Despite these limitations, the broader examination of the universe and the place of humans in it that Socrates, Plato, and Aristotle engaged in is widely regarded as Greece's most important intellectual legacy.

Hellenistic Society, 336–100 B.C.E.

☐ How did Alexander the Great's conquests shape society in the Hellenistic period?

The Greek city-states wore themselves out fighting one another, and Philip II, the ruler of Macedonia, a kingdom in the north of Greece, gradually conquered one after another and took over their lands. He then turned against the Persian Empire but was killed by an assassin, and his son Alexander continued the fight. A brilliant military leader, Alexander conquered the entire Persian Empire, along with many territories to the east of Persia. He also founded new cities in which Greek and local populations mixed. Although he, too, died prematurely, his successors continued to build cities and colonies, which became powerful instruments in the spread of Greek culture and in the blending of Greek traditions and ideas with those of other peoples.

Because they understood themselves to be part of "the West," Greeks generally referred to Egypt and what we now call the Near East and western Asia collectively as "the East." Many historians have continued that usage. Despite distinctions between East and West, however, they see this period as a time when Greek and "Eastern" ways of doing things blended to some degree to create a culture that is now called "Hellenistic." During the Hellenistic period, marked by the start of Alexander's reign in 336 B.C.E., Greek became the common language of learning and business, which made trade easier and contributed to the prosperity of this era.

From Polis to Monarchy, 404–200 B.C.E.

Immediately after the Peloponnesian War, Sparta began striving for empire over all of the Greeks, but could not maintain its hold. In 371 B.C.E. an army from the polis of Thebes destroyed the Spartan army, but the The-

bans were unable to bring peace to Greece. Philip II, ruler of the kingdom of Macedonia on the northern border of Greece (r. 359–336 B.C.E.), turned the situation to his advantage. By clever use of his wealth and superb army, Philip won control of the northern Aegean, and in 338 B.C.E. he defeated a combined Theban-Athenian army, conquering Greece. Because the Greek city-states could not put aside their quarrels with one another, they fell to an invader.

After his victory, Philip united the Greek states with his Macedonian kingdom and got the states to cooperate in a crusade to liberate the Ionian Greeks from Persian rule. Before he could launch his crusade, Philip fell to an assassin's dagger in 336 B.C.E. His young son Alexander, who had been tutored by Aristotle, vowed to carry on Philip's mission and led an army of Macedonians and Greeks into western Asia. He won major battles against the Persians and seized Egypt from them without a fight. He ordered the building of a new city where the Nile meets the Mediterranean, a city that would soon be called Alexandria and that within a century would be the largest city in the world. After honoring the priestly class, Alexander was proclaimed pharaoh, the legitimate ruler of Egypt. He also took the principal Persian capital of Persepolis and performed a symbolic act of retribution by burning the buildings of Xerxes, the invader of Greece during the Persian War 150 years earlier.

By 330 B.C.E. the Persian Empire had fallen, but Alexander had no intention of stopping, and he set out to conquer the rest of Asia. He plunged deeper into the East, into lands completely unknown to the Greek world. After four years of fighting his soldiers crossed the Indus River into India, but, finally, at the Hyphasis River the exhausted troops refused to go farther. Alexander reluctantly turned south to the Arabian Sea and then back west (Map 5.3). He never saw Macedonia again, however, as he died in Babylon in 323 B.C.E. from fever, wounds, and excessive drinking. He was only thirty-two, but in just thirteen years he had created an empire that stretched from his homeland of Macedonia to India, gaining the title "the Great" along the way. Alexander was instrumental in changing the face of politics in the eastern Mediterranean. His campaign swept away the Persian Empire, which had ruled the East for over two hundred years. In its place he established a Macedonian monarchy, although this fell apart with his death.

Several of the chief Macedonian generals aspired to become sole ruler, which led to a civil war lasting forty-three years that tore Alexander's empire apart. By the end of this conflict, the most successful generals had carved out their own smaller monarchies. Ptolemy (TAH-luh-mee) seized Egypt, and his descendants, the Ptolemies, assumed the powers and position of pharaohs. Antigonus (an-TIH-guh-nuhs) and his descendants, the Antigonids, maintained control of the Macedonian kingdom in Europe. Seleucus (suh-LOO-kuhs) won the bulk of Alexander's empire, his monarchy extending from western Asia to India (see page 133), but this Seleucid kingdom gradually broke into smaller states. Until the arrival of the Romans in the eastern Mediterranean in the second century B.C.E., the Hellenistic monarchies waged frequent wars that brought no lasting results. In terms of political stability and peace, these monarchies were no improvement on the Greek polis.

To encourage obedience Hellenistic kings often created ruler cults that linked the king's authority with that of the gods, or they adopted ruler cults that already existed, as Alexander did in Egypt. This created a symbol of unity within kingdoms ruling different peoples who at first had little in common; however, kingdoms never won the deep emotional loyalty that Greeks had once felt for the polis. Kings sometimes gave the cities in their territory all the external trappings of a polis, such as a council or an assembly of citizens, but these had no power. The city was not autonomous, as the polis had been, but had to follow royal orders. Hellenistic rulers generally relied on paid professionals to staff their bureaucracies and on trained, paid, full-time soldiers rather than citizen hoplites to fight their wars.

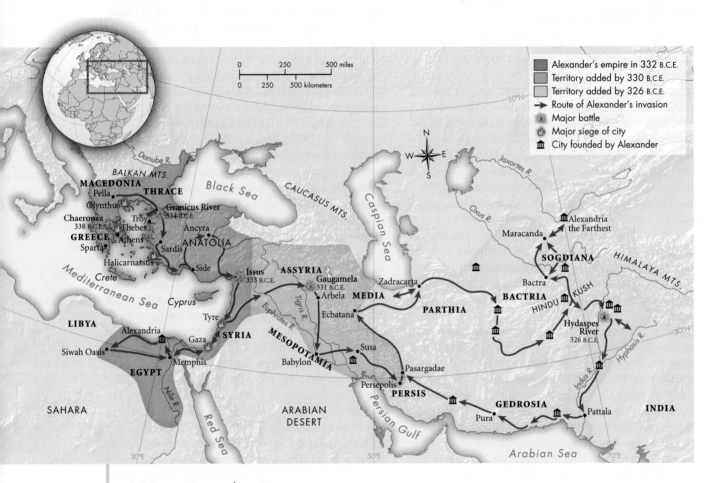

□ Mapping the Past

MAP 5.3 Alexander's Conquests, 336–324 B.C.E. Alexander's campaign of conquest was extensive and speedy. More important than the great success of his military campaigns was his founding of Hellenistic cities.

ANALYZING THE MAP Where are most of the cities founded by Alexander located in relation to Greece? What does this suggest about his aims?

CONNECTIONS Compare this map with Map 5.2, which shows Greek colonization in the Hellenic period (page 121). What are the major differences between the two processes of expansion?

Building a Shared Society

Alexander's most important legacy was clearly not political unity. Instead it was the spread of Greek ideas and traditions across a wide area. To maintain contact with the Greek world as he moved farther eastward, he founded new cities and military colonies and settled Greek and Macedonian troops and veterans in them. This practice continued after his death, with more than 250 new cities founded in North Africa, West and Central Asia, and southeastern Europe. These cities and colonies became powerful instruments in the spread of Hellenism and in the blending of Greek and other cultures. No comparable spread and sharing of cultures had occurred in this area since the days of the Mesopotamians.

Wherever it was established, the Hellenistic city resembled a modern city. It was a cultural center with theaters, temples, and libraries — a seat of learning and a place for amusement. The Hellenistic city was also an economic center — a marketplace and a scene of trade and manufacturing.

The ruling dynasties of the Hellenistic world were Macedonian in origin, and Greeks and Macedonians initially filled all important political, military, and diplomatic positions. The prevailing institutions and laws were Greek, and Greek became the common spoken language of the entire eastern Mediterranean. Also, a new Greek dialect called the koine (kaw-NAY), which means common, became the spoken language of the royal court, bureaucracy, and army. Everyone, Greek or easterner, who wanted to find an official position or compete in business had to learn it. Those who did gained an avenue of social mobility, and as early as the third century B.C.E. local people in some Greek cities began to rise in power and prominence. Cities granted citizenship to Hellenized natives, although because real power was held by monarchs, not citizens, the political benefits of citizenship were less than they had been in the classical period. The benefits natives gave to Hellenistic society were considerable, however. Their traditions mingled with Greek traditions to create an energetic and dynamic culture.

Although cultures blended in the Hellenistic world, the kingdoms were never entirely unified in language, customs, and thought. Greek culture generally did not extend far beyond the reaches of the cities. Many urban residents adopted the aspects of Hellenism that they found useful, but people in the countryside generally did not embrace it wholly. This meant that the spread of Greek culture was wider than it was deep, a very common pattern all over the world in eras of cultural change.

The spread of Greek culture was also shaped by the actions of rulers. The Seleucid kings built a shared society through extensive colonization. Their military settlements and cities spread from western Asia Minor along the banks of the Tigris and Euphrates Rivers and father east to India. Although the Seleucids had no elaborate plan for Hellenizing the native population, they nevertheless introduced a large and vigorous Greek population to these lands. Their presence alone had an impact. Seleucid military colonies were generally founded near native villages, thus exposing one culture to the other.

In the eastern part of the large Seleucid kingdom, several Greek leaders defeated the Seleucids and established the independent kingdoms of Parthia and Bactria in today's Afghanistan and Turkmenistan (see Map 5.3). Bactria became an outpost of Hellenism, from which the Han Dynasty of China (Chapter 7) and the Mauryan Empire of India (Chapter 3) learned of sophisticated societies other than their own. The Bactrian city of Ay Khanoum on the Oxus River, on the modern border of Russia and Afghanistan not far from China, is a good example of a far-flung city where cultures met. It had Greek temples and administration

Metal Plate from Ay Khanoum This spectacular metal plate, made in the Bactrian city of Ay Khanoum in the second century B.C.E., probably depicts the goddess Cybele being pulled in a chariot by lions with the sun god above. Worship of Cybele, an earth-mother goddess, spread into Greece from Turkey and was then spread by Greek followers as they traveled and migrated. (Courtesy, National Museum, Kabul)

> **"**In youth, control your passions; in middle age, practice justice; in old age, be of good counsel; in death, have no regrets.**"**
>
> **GREEK INSCRIPTION**

buildings, and on a public square was a long inscription carved in stone in Greek verse relating Greek ideals:

> In childhood, learn good manners
> In youth, control your passions
> In middle age, practice justice
> In old age, be of good counsel
> In death, have no regrets.[5]

The city also had temples to local deities and artwork that blended Greek and local styles (for an example, see page 133). Also, some Greeks in Bactria, including several rulers, converted to Buddhism. In the second century B.C.E., after the collapse of the Mauryan Empire, Bactrian armies conquered part of northern India, establishing several small Indo-Greek states where the mixing of religious and artistic traditions was particularly pronounced (see pages 81–82).

In the booming city of Alexandria the Ptolemies generally promoted Greek culture over that of the local Egyptians. This favoritism eventually led to civil unrest, but it also led the Ptolemies to support anything that enhanced Greek learning or traditions. Ptolemaic kings established what became the largest library in the ancient world, where scholars copied works loaned from many places onto papyrus scrolls, translating them into Greek if they were in other languages. They also studied the newest discoveries in science and mathematics. Alexandria was home to the largest Jewish community in the ancient world, and here Jewish scholars translated the Hebrew Bible into Greek for the first time.

The Growth of Trade and Commerce

Alexander's conquests not only changed the political face of the ancient world but also merged it into one broad economic sphere. The period did not see a dramatic change in the way most people lived and worked; they continued to raise crops and animals, paying rents to their landlords and taxes to the state. All Hellenistic kings paid attention to agriculture, for much of their revenue came from the produce of royal lands and the rents and taxes paid by their tenants, but farming methods changed little. By contrast, trade grew significantly as the spread of Greeks eastward created new markets. The economic unity of the Hellenistic world, like its cultural bonds, later proved valuable to the Romans, allowing them to trade products and ideas more easily over a broad area.

When Alexander conquered the Persian Empire, he found the royal treasury filled with vast sums of gold, silver, and other treasure. The victors used this wealth to finance the building of roads, the development of harbors, and, as noted earlier, especially the founding of new cities. These cities opened whole new markets to all merchants, who eagerly took advantage of the unforeseen opportunities. Whenever possible, merchants sent their goods by water, but overland trade also became more prominent in the Hellenistic era. Overland trade with India was conducted by caravans that were largely in the hands of easterners, who led camels through the harsh terrain of western Asia. Once goods reached the Hellenistic monarchies, Greek merchants took a hand in the trade. Commerce from the east arrived at Egypt and the harbors of Palestine, Phoenicia, and Syria. From these ports goods flowed to Greece, Italy, and Spain. This period also saw the development of standardized business customs, so that merchants of different nationalities, aided especially by the koine, communicated in a way understandable to them all. Trade was further facilitated by the coining of money, which provided merchants with a standard way to value goods as well as a convenient method of payment.

The increased volume of trade helped create prosperity that made luxury goods affordable to more people. As a result, overland traders brought easily transportable luxuries such as gold, silver, and precious stones to market. They extended their networks into China in order to obtain silk, which became the most valuable overland commodity and gave the major route the name the Silk Road. (See "Global Trade: Silk," page 184.) In return the peoples of the eastern Mediterranean sent east manufactured or extracted goods, especially metal weapons, cloth, wine, and olive oil. (For more on the Silk Road in East Asia, see Chapter 7.)

More economically important than trade in exotic goods were commercial dealings in essential commodities like raw materials (such as wood), grain, and industrial products. The Hellenistic monarchies usually raised enough grain for their own needs as well as a surplus for export. For the cities of the Aegean the trade in grain was essential, because many of them could not grow enough in their mountainous terrain. Fortunately for them, abundant wheat supplies were available nearby in Egypt and in the Crimea in southern Russia.

The Greek cities paid for their grain by exporting olive oil, wine, honey, dried fruit, nuts, and vegetables. Another significant commodity supplied by the Greeks was fish, which for export was salted, pickled, or dried. This trade was doubly important because fish provided poor people with an essential element of their diet.

Harbor and Marketplace at Delos During the Hellenistic period the tiny island of Delos in the Aegean became a thriving trading center, with a paved marketplace filled with shops and stands, as well as temples paid for by merchants and ship captains. From Delos cargoes were shipped to virtually every part of the Mediterranean. Liquids such as wine and oil were generally shipped in amphora (inset) made of baked clay. Amphora were easy and cheap to make and surprisingly durable. (harbor: Rolf Richardson/age footstock/superstock; amphora: Alexis Rosenfeld/Photo Researchers)

Throughout the Hellenistic world slave traders almost always found a ready market. Only the Ptolemies discouraged both the trade and slavery itself, but they did so for purely economic reasons. Their system had no room for slaves, who only would have competed with inexpensive labor provided by free people. Otherwise slave laborers could be found in cities and temples, in factories and fields, and in the homes of wealthier people.

Most trade in bulk commodities like grain and wood was seaborne, and Hellenistic merchant ships were the workhorses of the day. A merchant ship had a broad beam, which made it more stable and allowed large cargoes, and it relied on sails for propulsion. Such ships were far more seaworthy than Hellenistic warships, which were long, narrow, and built for speed. A small crew of experienced sailors easily handled the merchant vessels. Aside from providing work for sailors, maritime trade also presented opportunities for shipbuilders, dockworkers, teamsters, and pirates. Piracy was a constant factor in the Hellenistic world and remained so until Rome cleared it from the seas.

While demand for goods increased during the Hellenistic period, few new techniques of production appeared. Manual labor far more than machinery continued to turn out agricultural produce, raw materials, and the few manufactured goods the Hellenistic world used. A typical form of manual labor was mining, in which slaves, criminals, or forced laborers dug the ore under frightful conditions. The Ptolemies ran their gold mines along harsh lines, as evident from one ancient Greek historian's description of the miners' lives:

The kings of Egypt condemn [to the mines] those found guilty of wrong-doing and those taken prisoner in war, those who were victims of false accusations and were put into jail because of royal anger.... The condemned — and they are very many — all of them are put in chains, and they work persistently and continually, both by day and throughout the night, getting no rest and carefully cut off from escape.[6]

The Ptolemies even condemned women and children to work in the mines. Besides gold and silver, used primarily for coins and jewelry, iron was the most important metal and saw the most varied use.

Hellenistic Religion, Philosophy, and Science

☐ How did the meeting of cultures in the Hellenistic world shape religion, philosophy, and science?

The mixing of peoples in the Hellenistic era influenced religion, philosophy, and science. The Hellenistic kings built temples to the old Olympian gods and promoted rituals and ceremonies like those in earlier Greek

Hellenistic Magical Text This text, written in Greek and Egyptian on papyrus, presents a magical incantation surrounded by a lion-headed snake. Both Hellenic and Hellenistic Greeks sought to know the future through various means of divination and to control the future through rituals and formulas that called on spirits and gods. (© British Library Board, PAP. 121 fr 3)

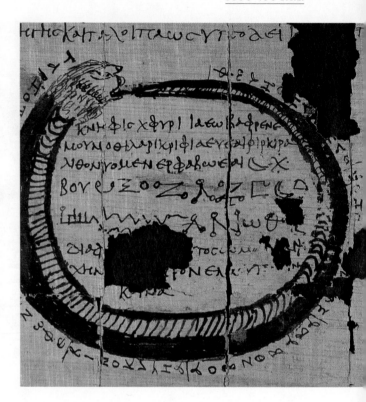

cities. But because many people found the rituals and ceremonies spiritually unsatisfying, they turned instead to mystery religions. In these religions, which blended Greek and non-Greek elements, followers gained secret knowledge in initiation rituals and were promised eternal life. Others turned away from religion to practical philosophies that provided advice on how to live a good life. In the scholarly realm, Hellenistic thinkers made advances in mathematics, astronomy, and mechanical design. Additionally, physicians used observation and dissection to better understand the way the human body works and to develop treatments for disease.

Religion in the Hellenistic World

When Hellenistic kings founded cities, they also built temples, staffed by priests, for the old Olympian gods. In this way they spread Greek religious beliefs throughout the Near East. The transplanted religions, like those in Greece itself, sponsored literary, musical, and athletic contests, which were staged in beautiful surroundings among splendid Greek-style buildings. On the whole, however, the civic religions were primarily concerned with ritual and did not embrace such matters as morality and redemption. While lavish in pomp and display, they did not inspire deep religious feelings or satisfy spiritual yearnings.

Consequently, people increasingly sought solace from other sources. Some relied on philosophy as a guide to life, while others turned to religion, magic, or astrology. Still others shrugged and spoke of Tyche (TIE-kee), which means "fate," "chance," or "doom" — a capricious and sometimes malevolent force.

Increasingly, many people were attracted to **mystery religions**, so called because they featured a body of rituals and beliefs not divulged to anyone not initi-

- **mystery religions** Religious systems in the Hellenistic world that incorporated aspects of both Greek and Eastern religions; they were characterized by secret doctrines, rituals of initiation, and the promise of an afterlife.
- **Epicureanism** A Greek system of philosophy founded on the teachings of Epicurus that viewed a life of contentment, free from fear and suffering, as the greatest good.
- **Stoicism** The most popular of Hellenistic philosophies, it considered nature an expression of divine will and held that people can be happy only when living in accordance with nature.

ated into them. Early mystery religions in the Hellenic period were linked to specific gods in particular places, so that people who wished to become members had to travel; therefore, these religions never became very popular. But new mystery religions, like Hellenistic culture in general, were not tied to a particular place; instead they were spread throughout the Hellenistic world. People did not have to undertake long and expensive pilgrimages just to become members. In that sense the mystery religions came to the people, for temples of the new deities sprang up wherever Greeks lived.

Mystery religions, which incorporated aspects of both Greek and Eastern religions, all claimed to save their adherents from the worst that fate could do and promised life for the soul after death. Most had a single concept in common: the belief that by the rites of initiation, in which the secrets of the religion were shared, devotees became united with a deity who had also died and risen from the dead. The sacrifice of the god and his victory over death saved the devotee from eternal death. Similarly, mystery religions demanded a period of preparation in which the converts strove to become holy, that is, to live by the religion's precepts. Once aspirants had prepared themselves, they went through the initiation, usually a ritual of great emotional intensity symbolizing the entry into a new life.

Among the mystery religions the Egyptian cult of Isis took the Hellenistic world by storm. In Egyptian mythology, Isis brought her husband Osiris back to life (see page 46), and during the Hellenistic era this power came to be understood by her followers as extending to them as well. She promised to save any mortal who came to her, and her priests asserted that she had bestowed on humanity the gift of civilization and founded law and literature. Isis was understood to be a devoted mother as well as wife, and she became the goddess of marriage, conception, and childbirth. She became the most important goddess of the Hellenistic world. Devotion to Isis, and to many other mystery religions, spread to the Romans as well as the Greeks when the two civilizations came into greater contact.

Philosophy and Its Guidance for Life

While some people turned to mystery religions to overcome Tyche and provide something permanent in a world that seemed unstable, others turned to philosophy. Several new schools of philosophical thought emerged, all of them teaching that people could be truly happy only when they had turned their backs on the world and focused full attention on one enduring thing. They differed chiefly on what that enduring thing was.

Two significant philosophies caught the minds and hearts of many Greeks and easterners, as well as many later Romans. The first was **Epicureanism**, a practical philosophy that sought serenity in an often tumultuous world. Epicurus (340–270 B.C.E.) taught that the principal good of life is pleasure, which he defined as the absence of pain. He concluded that any violent emotion is undesirable. He advocated instead mild self-discipline and even considered poverty good so long as people had enough food, clothing, and shelter. Epicurus also taught that people can most easily attain peace and serenity by ignoring the outside world and looking instead into their personal feelings. His followers ignored politics because it led to tumult, which would disturb the soul.

Isis and Horus In this small statue from Egypt, the goddess Isis is shown suckling her son Horus. Worship of Isis spread throughout the Hellenistic world; her followers believed that Isis offered them life after death, just as she had brought Horus's father Osiris back to life. (Scala/Art Resource, NY)

Opposed to the passivity of the Epicureans, Zeno (335–262 B.C.E.) formed his own school of philosophy, **Stoicism**, named after the Stoa, the building where he taught. To the Stoics the important matter was not whether they achieved anything but whether they lived virtuous lives. In that way they could triumph over Tyche, which could destroy their achievements but not the nobility of their lives. Stoicism became the most popular Hellenistic philosophy and later gained many followers among the Romans.

Zeno and his fellow Stoics considered nature an expression of divine will, and they believed that people could be happy only when living in accordance with nature. They also stressed the brotherhood of man, the concept that all people were kindred who were obliged to help one another. The Stoics' most lasting practical achievement was the creation of the concept of natural law. They concluded that as all people were brothers, partook of divine reason, and were in harmony with the universe, one natural law governed them all.

Hellenistic Science and Medicine

Hellenistic culture achieved its greatest triumphs in science and medicine. In astronomy the most notable of the Hellenistic contributors to the field was Aristarchus of Samos (ca. 310–230 B.C.E.), who was educated at Aristotle's school. Aristarchus rightly concluded that the sun is far larger than the earth and that the stars are enormously distant from the earth. He also argued against Aristotle's view that the earth is the center of the universe, instead propounding the heliocentric theory—that the earth and planets revolve around the sun. His work is all the more impressive because he lacked even a rudimentary telescope. Aristarchus's theories did not persuade the ancient world, and his heliocentric theory lay dormant until resurrected in the sixteenth century by the brilliant astronomer Nicolaus Copernicus.

In geometry Euclid (YOO-kluhd; ca. 300 B.C.E.), a mathematician living in Alexandria, compiled a valuable textbook of existing knowledge. His *The Elements of Geometry* became the standard introduction to

Individuals in Society

Archimedes, Scientist and Inventor

ARCHIMEDES (CA. 287–212 B.C.E.) **WAS BORN IN** the Greek city of Syracuse in Sicily, an intellectual center in which he pursued scientific interests. He was the most original thinker of his time and a practical inventor. In his book *On Plane Equilibriums* he dealt for the first time with the basic principles of mathematics, including the principle of the lever. He once said that if he were given a lever and a suitable place to stand, he could move the world. He also demonstrated how easily his compound pulley could move huge weights with little effort:

> A three-masted merchant ship of the royal fleet had been hauled on land by hard work and many hands. Archimedes put aboard her many men and the usual freight. He sat far away from her; and without haste, but gently working a compound pulley with his hand, he drew her towards him smoothly and without faltering, just as though she were running on the surface.*

He likewise invented the Archimedian screw, a pump to bring subterranean water up to irrigate fields, which quickly came into common use. In his treatise *On Floating Bodies* Archimedes founded the science of hydrostatics. He concluded that whenever a solid floats in a liquid, the weight of the solid equals the weight of the liquid displaced. This discovery and his reaction to it has become famous:

> When he was devoting his attention to this problem, he happened to go to a public bath. When he climbed down into the bathtub there, he noticed that water in the tub equal to the bulk of his body flowed out. Thus, when he observed this method of solving the problem, he did not wait. Instead, moved with joy, he sprang out of the tub, and rushing home naked he kept indicating in a loud voice that he had indeed discovered what he was seeking. For while running he was shouting repeatedly in Greek, "Eureka, eureka" ("I have found it, I have found it").†

War between Rome and Syracuse unfortunately interrupted Archimedes's scientific life. In 213 B.C.E. during the Second Punic War, the Romans besieged the city. Hiero, its king and Archimedes's friend, asked the scientist for help in repulsing Roman attacks. Archimedes began to build remarkable devices that served as artillery. One shot missiles to break up infantry attacks. Others threw huge masses of stones that fell on the enemy with incredible speed and noise. They tore gaping holes in the Roman lines and broke up attacks. Against Roman warships he built a machine consisting of huge beams that projected over the targets. Then the artillerymen dropped great weights onto the ships, like bombs. Even more complicated was an apparatus with beams from which large claws dropped onto the hulls of enemy warships, hoisted them into the air, and dropped them back into the sea. In response, the Romans brought up an exceptionally large scaling ladder carried on ships. While the ships approached, Archimedes's artillery disabled the ladders by hitting them repeatedly with stones weighing

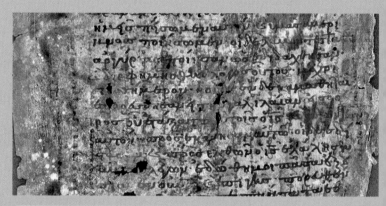

● **Archimedes's treatises were found on a palimpsest, a manuscript that was scraped and washed so that another text could be written over it, thus reusing the expensive parchment. In the thirteenth century Christian monks used tenth-century manuscripts of several ancient works in this way, writing over them and rebinding them into a prayer book. Scientists were able to read the original texts, which included seven works by Archimedes, using digital processing of various types of light and X-rays.** (Image by the Rochester Institute of Technology. Copyright resides with the owner of the Archimedes Palimpsest, but digital images of the entire manuscript can be found at: www.archimedespalimpsest.org)

500 pounds. At last the Romans became so fearful that whenever they saw a bit of rope or a stick of timber projecting over one of the walls protecting Syracuse, they shouted, "There it is. Archimedes is trying some engine on us" and fled. When the Romans finally breached the walls of Syracuse in 212 B.C.E., a Roman soldier came upon Archimedes in his study and killed him.

Much but not all of Archimedes's work survived him. In the early twentieth century a scholar examining a thirteenth-century parchment manuscript realized that underneath the top text was another, partially scraped-off text, and that this was several works of Archimedes. He used a camera to help read the underlying text, but then the manuscript vanished. It turned up again in 1998 at a Christie's auction in New York, where it was purchased by an anonymous buyer and generously deposited at the Walters Art Museum in Baltimore. For ten years the manuscript was studied using ultraviolet and visible light and X-rays, which made the entire text visible. Contemporary science is enabling scholars of the classical world to read some of Archimedes's lost works.

QUESTIONS FOR ANALYSIS

1. What applications do you see in the world around you of the devices Archimedes improved or invented: the lever, the pulley, and artillery?
2. What effect did his weapons have on the Roman soldiers and their willingness to attack Syracuse?

*Plutarch, *Life of Marcellus*.

†Vitruvius, *On Architecture*, 9 Preface, 10.

138 ●

the subject. Generations of students from antiquity to the present have learned the essentials of geometry from it.

The greatest thinker of the period was Archimedes (ah-kuh-MEE-deez; ca. 287–212 B.C.E.). A clever inventor, he devised new artillery for military purposes. In peacetime he created the Archimedian screw to draw water from a lower to a higher level. (See "Individuals in Society: Archimedes: Scientist and Inventor," page 138.) He also invented the compound pulley to lift heavy weights. His chief interest, however, lay in pure mathematics. He founded the science of hydrostatics (the study of fluids at rest) and discovered the principle that the weight of a solid floating in a liquid is equal to the weight of the liquid displaced by the solid.

Archimedes willingly shared his work with others, among them Eratosthenes (ehr-uh-TAHS-thuh-neez; 285–ca. 204 B.C.E.), who was the librarian of the vast Ptolemaic royal library in Alexandria. Eratosthenes used mathematics to further the geographical studies for which he is most famous. He calculated the circumference of the earth geometrically, estimating it at about 24,675 miles. He was not wrong by much: the earth is actually 24,860 miles in circumference. Eratosthenes further concluded that the earth is a spherical globe and that the ocean surrounds the landmass.

As the new artillery devised by Archimedes indicates, Hellenic science was used for purposes of war as well as peace. Theories of mechanics were applied to build machines that revolutionized warfare. The catapult shot large arrows and small stones against enemy targets. Engineers built wooden siege towers as artillery platforms. Generals added battering rams to bring down large portions of walls. If these new engines made warfare more efficient, they also added to the misery of the people. War came to embrace the whole population.

Physician with Young Patient This plaster cast from ca. 350 B.C.E. shows a physician examining a child, while Asclepius, the god of healing, observes. Asclepius holds a staff with a snake coiled around it, which remains the symbol of medicine today. This cast was made through a process known as intaglio in which the picture was carved onto a cylinder-shaped gemstone, then rolled across wet clay to produce the image. (Hulton Archive/Getty Images)

War and illness fed the need for medical advances, and the study of medicine flourished during the Hellenistic period, when physicians carried the work of Hippocrates into new areas. Herophilus, who lived in the first half of the third century B.C.E., approached the study of medicine in a systematic, scientific fashion. He dissected corpses and measured what he observed. He discovered the nervous system and concluded that two types of nerves, motor and sensory, existed. Herophilus also studied the brain, which he considered the center of intelligence. In the process he distinguished the cerebrum from the cerebellum. His other work dealt with the liver, lungs, and uterus. His students carried on his work, and they also discovered new means of treating disease and relieving pain, including opium.

CONNECTIONS

The ancient Greeks built on the achievements of earlier societies in the eastern Mediterranean, but they also added new elements, including history, drama, philosophy, science, and realistic art. The Greek world was largely conquered by the Romans, as you will learn in the following chapter, and the various Hellenistic monarchies became part of the Roman Empire. In cultural terms the lines of conquest were reversed: the Romans derived their alphabet from the Greek alphabet, though they changed the letters somewhat. Roman statuary was modeled on Greek and was often, in fact, made by Greek sculptors, who found ready customers among wealthy Romans. Furthermore, the major Roman gods and goddesses were largely the same as Greek ones, though they had different names. Although the Romans did not seem to have been particularly interested in the speculative philosophy of Socrates and Plato, they were drawn to the more practical philosophies of the Epicureans and Stoics. And like the Hellenistic Greeks, many Romans became dissatisfied with traditional religions, turning instead to mystery religions that offered secret knowledge and promised eternal life.

The influence of the ancient Greeks was not limited to the Romans, of course. As discussed in Chapter 3, art and thought in northern India was shaped by the blending of Greek and Buddhist traditions. And as you will see in Chapter 15, European thinkers and writers made conscious attempts to return to classical ideals in art, literature, and philosophy during the Renaissance. In America political leaders from the Revolutionary era on decided that important government buildings should be modeled on the Parthenon or other temples, complete with marble statuary of their own heroes. In some ways, capitol buildings in the United States are good symbols of the legacy of Greece — gleaming ideals of harmony, freedom, democracy, and beauty that (as with all ideals) do not always correspond with realities.

☐ CHAPTER REVIEW

KEY TERMS

polis (p. 118)
hoplites (p. 119)
democracy (p. 119)
oligarchy (p. 120)
tyranny (p. 120)

Delian League (p. 123)
mystery religions (p. 136)
Epicureanism (p. 137)
Stoicism (p. 137)

☐ How did the geography of Greece shape its earliest history and lead to the growth of the polis? (p. 116)

Greece's mountainous terrain and lack of navigable rivers led to the development of small, independent communities and political fragmentation. Some groups of people joined together in kingdoms, notably those of the Minoans on Crete and the Mycenaeans on the mainland, but the rugged terrain prohibited the growth of a great empire like those of Mesopotamia and Egypt. The fall of these kingdoms led to a period known as the Greek Dark Age (ca. 1100–ca. 800 B.C.E.). However, Greek culture survived, and Greeks developed the independent city-state, known as the polis, in which individuals governed themselves without elaborate political machinery. The physical, religious, and political form of the polis varied from place to place, but everywhere it was relatively small, reflecting the fragmented geography of Greece.

☐ What were the major developments of the Archaic age, and how did Sparta and Athens create new forms of government? (p. 120)

The maturation of the polis coincided with an era, later termed the Archaic age, that gave rise to two developments of lasting importance. The first was the spread of the Greek people, who now ventured as far east as the Black Sea and as far west as the Atlantic Ocean. The second development was the rise of Sparta and Athens, which formed new social and political structures. Sparta created a military state in which men remained in the army most of their lives and women concentrated on raising healthy soldiers. After much social conflict, Athens created a democracy in which male citizens both voted for their leaders and had a direct voice in an assembly. As was the case in all democracies in ancient Greece, women, slaves, and outsiders could not be citizens.

☐ What were the lasting cultural and intellectual achievements of the classical period? (p. 122)

In the classical period, between 500 and 336 B.C.E., Greek civilization reached its highest peak in politics, thought, and art, even as it engaged in violent conflicts. The Greeks successfully defended themselves from Persian invasions but nearly destroyed themselves in the Peloponnesian War, which pitted Sparta and its allies against Athens and its allies. In the last half of the fifth century B.C.E. the brilliant Athenian leader Pericles turned Athens into the showplace of Greece by sponsoring the building of temples and other buildings. He also oversaw the creation of statues and carvings that showed the gods in human form and highlighted Athenian victories. In other artistic developments, wealthy Athenians paid for theater performances in which dramatists used their art in attempts to portray, understand, and resolve life's basic conflicts. During the classical period the Greeks honored a variety of gods and goddesses with rituals and festivals, but they did not look to religion for moral guidance. This period also saw the rise of philosophy; and Socrates, Plato, and Aristotle began a broad examination of the universe and the place of humans in it.

☐ **How did Alexander the Great's conquests shape society in the Hellenistic period? (p. 131)**

In the middle of the fourth century B.C.E. the Greek city-states were conquered by the Macedonians under King Philip II and his son Alexander. A brilliant military leader, Alexander conquered the entire Persian Empire, along with many territories to the east of Persia. He also founded new cities in which Greek and local populations mixed. His successors continued to build cities and colonies, which became powerful instruments in the spread of Greek culture and in the blending of Greek traditions and ideas with those of other peoples. Greek became the common language of learning and business, which made trade easier and contributed to the prosperity of this era.

☐ **How did the meeting of cultures in the Hellenistic world shape religion, philosophy, and science? (p. 135)**

The mixing of peoples in the Hellenistic era influenced religion, philosophy, and science. The Hellenistic kings built temples to the old Olympian gods and established cults like those in earlier Greek cities. But because many people found these spiritually unsatisfying, they turned instead to mystery religions. In these religions, which blended Greek and non-Greek elements, followers gained secret knowledge in initiation rituals and were promised eternal life. Others turned to practical philosophies instead of religion; these provided advice on how to live a good life. In the scholarly realm, advances were made in mathematics, astronomy, and mechanical design. The greatest thinker of the Hellenistic period was Archimedes, who devised new artillery for military purposes and created a screw to draw water from a lower to a higher level, among other inventions. Also during this period, physicians used observation and dissection to better understand the way the human body works and to develop treatments for disease.

SUGGESTED READING

Bosworth, A. B. *Conquest and Empire: The Reign of Alexander the Great.* 1988. Still the best one-volume treatment of Alexander that sets his career in a broad context.

Buckler, John. *Aegean Greece in the Fourth Century B.C.E.* 2003. Treats the history of this very influential century in detail.

Burkert, Walter. *Greek Religion.* 1987. The authoritative study of ancient religious beliefs, with much material from the sources.

Cartledge, Paul. *The Spartans: The World of the Warrior Heroes of Ancient Greece.* 2002. A readable general book on the history and legacy of Sparta.

Errington, R. Malcom. *A History of the Hellenistic World, 323–30 B.C.* 2008. Easily the best coverage of the period: full, scholarly, and readable.

Frazer, Peter M. *Cities of Alexander the Great.* 1996. Treats the impact of Greek urbanism in its eastern setting.

Hansen, Mogens Herman. *Polis: An Introduction to the Ancient Greek City-State.* 2006. The authoritative study of the polis.

Kagan, Donald. *Pericles of Athens and the Birth of Democracy.* 1991. A readable account of political changes in the era of Pericles.

Osborne, Robin. *Greece in the Making, 1200–479 B.C.* 2003. Traces the evolution of Greek communities from villages to cities and the development of their civic institutions.

Patterson, Cynthia B. *The Family in Greek History.* 2001. Treats public and private family relations.

Roochnik, David. *Retrieving the Ancients: An Introduction to Greek Philosophy.* 2004. A sophisticated and well-written narrative of ancient Greek thought designed for students.

Tsetskhladze, Gocha R., ed. *Greek Colonization: An Account of Greek Colonies and Other Settlements Overseas,* vol. 1, 2006; vol. 2, 2008. The definitive work on the entire span of Greek colonization.

NOTES

1. Homer, *Iliad,* translated by Samuel Butler, Book 1, lines 1–5.
2. In *The Works of Xenophon,* translated by Henry G. Dakyns (London: Macmillan and Co., 1892), p. 296.
3. Thucydides 2.12, translated by J. Buckler.
4. Sophocles, *Antigone,* edited and translated by Hugh Lloyd-Jones (Cambridge, Mass.: Harvard University Press, 1994), p. 127.
5. Ahmad Hasan Dani et al., *History of Civilizations of Central Asia* (Paris: UNESCO, 1992), p. 107.
6. Diodoros 3.12.2–3, translated by J. Buckler.

For practice quizzes and other study tools, visit the **Online Study Guide** at bedfordstmartins.com/mckayworld.

For primary sources from this period, see *Sources of World Societies*, **Second Edition**.

For Web sites, images, and documents related to topics in this chapter, visit **Make History** at bedfordstmartins.com/mckayworld.

● **Woman from Pompeii** This brightly painted fresco from a villa in Pompeii shows a young woman carrying a tray in a religious ritual. Pompeii was completely buried in ash in a volcanic explosion in 79 C.E., and excavations have revealed life in what was a vacation spot for wealthy Romans. (Villa dei Misteri, Pompeii/The Bridgeman Art Library)

6

Like the Persians under Cyrus, the Mauryans under Chandragupta, and the Macedonians
under Alexander, the Romans conquered vast territories. Their singular achievement lay in their
ability to incorporate conquered peoples into the
Roman system. Unlike the Greeks, who mostly refused to share citizenship, the Romans extended
citizenship first to other peoples in Italy and later to inhabitants of Roman provinces.
After a grim period of civil war that ended in 31 B.C.E., the emperor Augustus restored peace
and expanded Roman power and law as far east as the Euphrates River, creating the institu-

The World
of Rome
750 B.C.E.–400 C.E.

tion that the modern world calls the "Roman
Empire." Later emperors extended Roman
authority farther still, so that at its largest the
Roman Empire stretched from England to
Egypt and from Portugal to Persia.

Roman history is usually divided into
two periods. The first is the republic (509–
27 B.C.E.), the age in which Rome grew through
military conquest from a small group of cities
in the middle of the Italian peninsula to a
state that ruled much of the Mediterranean. To administer their growing territory, Romans
established a republican form of government in which power was held by the senate whose
members were primarily wealthy landowners. Social conflicts and wars of conquest led to
serious political problems, and the republican constitution gave way to rule by a single individual, who took the title "emperor." Thus the second period in Roman history is the empire
(27 B.C.E.–476 C.E.), which saw further expansion, enormous building projects, and cultural
flowering but also social upheavals and economic hardship. Rome's large territory eventually was split into eastern and western halves.   •

The Romans in Italy
☐ How did the Romans come to dominate Italy, and what political institutions and changes did they bring about?

Roman Expansion and Its Repercussions
☐ How did Rome expand its power beyond Italy, and what were the effects of this success?

The Pax Romana
☐ How did efficient Roman rule lead to a period of prosperity and relative peace?

The Coming of Christianity
☐ What was Christianity, and how did it affect life in the Roman Empire?

Turmoil and Reform
☐ How did the emperors Diocletian and Constantine respond to the problems created by barbarian invasions and political turmoil in the third and fourth centuries?

The Romans in Italy

☐ How did the Romans come to dominate Italy, and what political institutions and changes did they bring about?

The colonies established by Greek poleis (city-states) in the Hellenic era included a number along the coast of southern Italy and Sicily, an area already populated by a variety of different groups that farmed, fished, and traded. So many Greek settlers came to this area that it later became known as Magna Graecia—Greater Greece. Although Alexander the Great created an empire that stretched from his homeland of Macedonia to India, his conquests did not reach as far as southern Italy and Sicily. Thus the Greek colonies there remained independent, and they transmitted much of their culture to people who lived farther north in the Italian peninsula. These included the Etruscans (ih-TRUHS-kuhns), who built the first cities north of Magna Graecia, and then the Romans, who eventually came to dominate the peninsula. In addition to allying with conquered peoples and granting them citizenship, the Romans established a republic ruled by a senate. However, class conflicts over the rights to power eventually erupted and had to be resolved.

The Etruscans and Rome

The culture that is now called Etruscan developed from that of peoples who either were already living in north-central Italy or who spread into this area from unknown locations about 750 B.C.E. The Etruscans

The Etruscans, ca. 500 B.C.E.

spoke a language that was not in the Indo-European language family (see page 49), so it is very different from Greek and Latin; however, they adopted the Greek alphabet to write their language. Though we know they wrote letters, records, and literary works, once the Romans conquered them knowledge of how to read and write Etruscan died out. Also, the writings themselves largely disappeared, other than inscriptions on stone or engravings in metal. Modern scholars have learned to read Etruscan again to some degree, but most of what we know about their civilization comes from archaeological evidence and from the writings of other peoples who lived around them at the same time.

The Etruscans established permanent settlements that evolved into cities resembling the Greek city-states in political organization (see page 118). They spread their influence over the surrounding countryside, which they farmed and mined for its rich mineral resources. From an early period the Etruscans began to trade natural products, especially iron, with their Greek neighbors to the south and with other peoples throughout the Mediterranean in exchange for luxury goods. The Etruscans thereby built a rich cultural life, full of art and music, that became the foundation of civilization throughout Italy, and they began to take political control of a larger area.

In the process they encountered a small collection of villages subsequently called Rome. Located at an easy crossing point on the Tiber River, Rome stood astride the main avenue of communication between northern and southern Italy. Its seven hills provided safety from attackers and from the floods of the Tiber (Map 6.1).

Under Etruscan influence the Romans occupied all of Rome's seven hills and prospered. During the rule of Etruscan kings (ca. 750–509 B.C.E.) Rome enjoyed contacts with the larger Mediterranean world, while the city continued to grow. Temples and public buildings began to grace Rome, and the Forum (see Map 6.1), originally a cemetery, became a public meeting place similar to the Greek agora. In addition, trade in metalwork became common, and wealthier Romans began to import fine Greek vases. In cultural developments, the Romans adopted the Etruscan alphabet and even the Etruscan toga, the white woolen robe worn by citizens. Another custom the Romans adopted from the Etruscans was the use of a certain image, a bundle of rods tied together with an ax emerging from the center, to symbolize the Etruscan king's power. This symbol was called the fasces (FAS-eez), and it was carried by an official on ceremonial occasions. When the Romans expelled the Etruscan kings (see below), they continued using the fasces in this manner. (In the twentieth century Mussolini would use the fasces as the symbol of his political party, the Fascists, and it is also used by many other governmental groups, including some in the United States.)

The Roman Conquest of Italy

Although it is certain that the Etruscans once ruled Rome, much else about early Roman history is an uneven mixture of fact and legend. Stories about early Rome often contain an important kernel of truth, but that does not make them history. Nevertheless, legends can illustrate the ethics, morals, and ideals that Roman society considered valuable.

The Romans have several different foundation myths, which themselves were told in a number of different versions. In the most common of these, Romulus and Remus founded the city, an event later Roman authors dated precisely to 753 B.C.E. These twin brothers were descendants of a god on their father's side, and descendants on their mother's

□ CHRONOLOGY

753 B.C.E.	Traditional founding of Rome
ca. 750–509 B.C.E.	Etruscan rule of an evolving Rome
ca. 500–265 B.C.E.	Roman conquest of Italy
509–27 B.C.E.	Roman republic
494–287 B.C.E.	Struggle of the Orders
264–146 B.C.E.	Punic Wars
53–31 B.C.E.	Civil wars among rival claimants to power
44 B.C.E.	Assassination of Julius Caesar
31 B.C.E.	Triumph of Augustus
27 B.C.E.–**476** C.E.	Roman Empire
27 B.C.E.–**68** C.E.	Rule of Julio-Claudian emperors
ca. 3 B.C.E.–**29** C.E.	Life of Jesus
284–337 C.E.	Diocletian and Constantine reconstruct the empire, dividing it into western and eastern halves; construction of Constantinople
312 C.E.	Constantine legalizes Christianity
380 C.E.	Christianity made the official religion of the empire

Sarcophagus of Lartie Seianti The woman portrayed on this lavish sarcophagus is the noble Etruscan Lartie Seianti. Although the sarcophagus is her place of burial, she is portrayed as in life, comfortable and at rest. The influence of Greek art on Etruscan is apparent in almost every feature of the sarcophagus. (Archaeological Museum, Florence/Nimatallah/Art Resource, NY)

side of Aeneas (ih-NEE-uhs), a brave and pious Trojan who left Troy (in Anatolia, now Turkey) after it was destroyed by the Greeks. The brothers, who were left to die by a jealous uncle, were raised by a female wolf. When they were grown they decided to build a city in the hills that became part of Rome, but they quarreled over which hill should be the site of the city. Romulus chose one hill and started to build a wall around it, and Remus chose another. After Remus jumped mockingly over Romulus's wall, Romulus killed him and named the city after himself. He also established a council of advisers later called the senate, which means council of old men. He and his mostly male followers expanded

their power over neighboring peoples, in part by abducting and marrying their women. The women then arranged a peace by throwing themselves between their brothers and their husbands, convincing them that killing kin would make the men cursed. The Romans, favored by the gods, continued their rise to power. Despite its tales of murder and kidnapping, this founding myth ascribes positive traits to the Romans: they are descended from gods and heroes, can thrive in wild and tough settings, will defend their boundaries at all costs, and mix with other peoples rather than simply conquering them. Also, the story portrays the mothers of Rome as virtuous and brave.

MAP 6.1 Roman Italy, ca. 265 B.C.E. As Rome expanded, it built roads linking major cities and offered various degrees of citizenship to the territories it conquered or with which it made alliances. The territories outlined in green were added by 218 B.C.E., largely as a result of the Punic Wars.

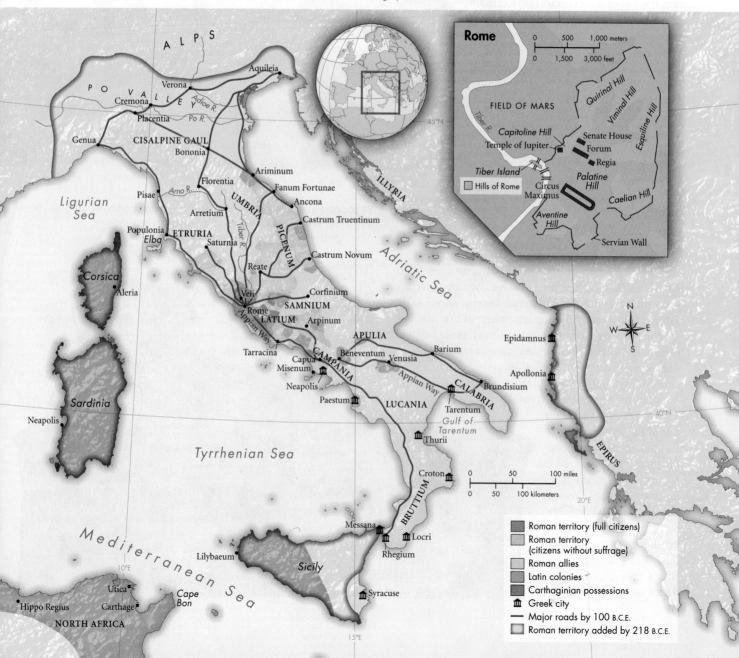

Later Roman historians continued the story by describing a series of kings after Romulus — the traditional number is seven — each elected by the senate. Because they had to fit this succession with the reality that, starting around 750 B.C.E., Rome was ruled by Etruscans, the historians described the last few of these kings as Etruscans. The kings apparently became more authoritarian, one possible reason they were overthrown. An additional reason was described in another story involving female virtue. In this story the son of the Etruscan king Tarquin raped Lucretia, a virtuous Roman wife, who committed suicide out of shame, causing the people to rise up in anger and avenge her death. Whether the rape happened can never be known, but the Romans threw out the last Etruscan king in 509 B.C.E. and established a republic, led by the senate and two **consuls** elected for one-year terms.

In the following years the Romans fought numerous wars with their Italian neighbors, including the Etruscans. They became soldiers, and the grim fighting bred tenacity, a prominent Roman trait. War also involved diplomacy, at which the Romans became masters. They very early learned the value of alliances with the towns in the province of Latium that surrounded Rome, which provided them all with security and the Romans with a large reservoir of manpower. These alliances involved the Romans in still other wars that took them farther afield in the Italian peninsula.

Around 390 B.C.E. the Romans suffered a major setback when a people new to the Italian peninsula, the Celts — or Gauls, as the Romans called them — moved down from the north, swept aside a Roman army, and sacked Rome. More intent on loot than land, they agreed to abandon Rome in return for a thousand pounds of gold. In the century that followed the Romans rebuilt their city and recouped their losses. They brought Latium and their Latin allies fully under their control and conquered the Etruscans. In a series of bitter wars the Romans also subdued southern Italy, including much of Magna Graecia, and then turned north. Their superior military institutions, organization, and manpower allowed them to conquer most of Italy by about 265 B.C.E. (see Map 6.1).

As they expanded their territory, the Romans spread their religious traditions throughout Italy, blending them with local beliefs and practices. Victorious generals made sure to honor the gods of people they had conquered, and by doing so transformed them into gods they could also call on for assistance in their future campaigns. As the Romans conquered the cities of Magna Graecia, the Greek deities were absorbed into the Roman pantheon. Their names were changed to Roman names, so that Zeus (the king of the gods), for example, became Jupiter, and Ares (the god of war) became Mars, but their personal qualities and powers were largely the same. As it was in Greece, religion was largely a matter of rites and ceremonies, not inner piety. Such rituals were an important way to express common values, however, which for Romans meant those evident in their foundation myths: bravery, morality, family, and home.

Once they had conquered an area, the Romans did what the Persians had earlier done to help cement their new territory: they built roads. Roman roads facilitated the flow of communication, trade, and armies from the capital to outlying areas. They were the tangible sinews of unity, and many were marvels of engineering, as were the stone bridges the Romans built over Italy's many rivers.

In politics the Romans shared full Roman citizenship with many of their oldest allies, particularly the inhabitants of the cities of Latium. In other instances they granted citizenship without the franchise, that is, without the right to vote or hold Roman office. These allies were subject to Roman taxes and calls for military service but ran their own local affairs.

The Distribution of Power in the Roman Republic

Along with citizenship, the republican government was another important institution of Roman political life. The Romans summed up their political existence in a single phrase: *senatus populusque Romanus*, "the Roman senate and the people," which they abbreviated "SPQR." This sentiment reflects the republican ideal of shared government rather than power concentrated in a monarchy. It stands for the beliefs, customs, and laws of the republic — its unwritten constitution that evolved over two centuries to meet the demands of the governed.

In the early republic social divisions determined the shape of politics. Political power was in the hands of the aristocracy — the **patricians**, who were wealthy landowners. Patrician men dominated the affairs of state, provided military leadership in time of war, and monopolized knowledge of law and legal procedure. The common people of Rome, the **plebeians** (plih-BEE-uhns), were free citizens with a voice in politics, but they had few of the patricians' political and social advantages. They could not hold high office or marry into patrician families. While some plebeian

- **consuls** Primary executives in the Roman republic, elected for one-year terms, who commanded the army in battle, administered state business, and supervised financial affairs; originally the office was limited to patricians.
- **patricians** The Roman aristocracy; wealthy landowners who held political power.
- **plebeians** The common people of Rome, who had few of the patricians' advantages.

◻ Picturing the Past

Battle Between the Romans and the Germans Rome's wars with the barbarians of western Europe come to life in this relief from a Roman sarcophagus of 225 C.E. The Romans are wearing helmets, with the soldier at the right even wearing iron or bronze chain mail, a technology they had most likely only recently picked up from the Germans. (Vanni/Art Resource, NY)

ANALYZING THE IMAGE How would you describe this depiction of war? How does the artist show Roman superiority over the barbarians through the placement, dress, and facial features of the soldiers?

CONNECTIONS How does this funeral sculpture reinforce or challenge what you have learned about Roman expansion and the Romans' treatment of the peoples they conquered?

merchants rivaled the patricians in wealth, most plebeians were poor artisans, small farmers, and landless urban dwellers.

The most important institution in the Roman government was the **senate**, which had originated under the Etruscans as a council of noble elders who advised the king. During the republic the senate advised the consuls and other officials about military and political matters and handled government finances. Because the same senators sat year after year, while the consuls changed annually, the senate also provided stability. The senate could not technically pass legislation; it could only offer its advice. Yet increasingly, because

of the senate's prestige, its advice came to have the force of law. Another responsibility of the senate was to handle relations between Rome and other powers, as Polybius, a Greek politician and historian writing in the middle of the second century B.C.E., reported:

> If it is necessary to send an embassy to reconcile warring communities, or to remind them of their duty, or sometimes to impose requisitions upon them, or to receive their submission, or finally to proclaim war against them — this too is the business of the Senate.[1]

The primary executives in the republic were the two consuls, positions initially open only to patrician men. The consuls commanded the army in battle, administered state business, and supervised financial

---

• **senate** The assembly that was the main institution of government in the Roman republic. It grew out of an earlier council of advisers to the king.

affairs. When the consuls were away from Rome, praetors (PREE-tuhrz) acted in their place. Otherwise, the praetors dealt primarily with the administration of justice. After the age of overseas conquest (see below), the Romans divided their lands in the Mediterranean into provinces governed by ex-consuls and ex-praetors. Because of these officials' experience in Roman politics, they were all suited to administer the affairs of the provinces and to adapt Roman law and customs to new contexts. Other officials worked with the senate to oversee the public treasury, register citizens, and supervise the city of Rome.

A lasting achievement of the Romans was their development of law. Roman civil law, the *ius civile*, consisted of statutes, customs, and forms of procedure that regulated the lives of citizens. As the Romans came into more frequent contact with foreigners, the praetors applied a broader *ius gentium*, the "law of the peoples," to such matters as peace treaties, the treatment of prisoners of war, and the exchange of diplomats. In the ius gentium, all sides were to be treated the same regardless of their nationality. By the late republic Roman jurists had widened this still further into the concept of *ius naturale*, "natural law" based in part on Stoic beliefs (see page 137). Natural law, according to these thinkers, is made up of rules that govern human behavior that come from applying reason rather than customs or traditions, and so apply to all societies.

Social Conflict in Rome

Inequality between plebeians and patricians led to a conflict known as the Struggle of the Orders. In this conflict the plebeians sought to increase their power by taking advantage of the fact that Rome's survival depended on its army, which needed plebeians to fill the ranks of the infantry. According to tradition, in 494 B.C.E. the plebeians literally walked out of Rome and refused to serve in the army. Their general strike worked, and the patricians made important concessions. For one thing they allowed patricians and plebeians to marry one another. They also recognized the right of plebeians to elect their own officials, the tribunes, who could bring plebeian grievances to the senate for resolution and could also veto the decisions of the consuls. Thus, as in Archaic age Greece (see page 120), political rights were broadened because of military needs for foot soldiers.

The law itself was the plebeians' primary target. As noted above, only the patricians knew what the law was, and only they could argue cases in court. All too often they used the law for their own benefit. The plebeians wanted the law codified and published. In response, the patricians surrendered their legal monopoly and codified and published the Laws of the

Twelve Tables, so called because they were inscribed on twelve bronze plaques. The patricians also made legal procedures public so that plebeians could argue cases in court.

After a ten-year battle, the Licinian-Sextian laws passed, giving wealthy plebeians access to all the offices of Rome, including the right to hold one of the two consulships. Once plebeians could hold the consulship, they could also sit in the senate and advise on policy. Though decisive, this victory did not automatically end the Struggle of the Orders. That happened only in 287 B.C.E. with the passage of the *lex Hortensia*, which gave the resolutions of the *concilium plebis*, the plebeian assembly, the force of law for patricians and plebeians alike. This compromise established a new elite of wealthy plebeians and patricians. Yet the Struggle of the Orders had made all citizens equal before the law, resulting in a Rome stronger and more united than before.

Roman Expansion and Its Repercussions

☐ How did Rome expand its power beyond Italy, and what were the effects of this success?

With their internal affairs settled, the Romans turned their attention abroad. In a series of wars they conquered lands all around the Mediterranean, creating an overseas empire that brought them unheard of power and wealth. As a result many Romans became more cosmopolitan and comfortable, and they were especially influenced by the culture of one conquered land: Greece. Yet social unrest also came in the wake of the wars, opening unprecedented opportunities for ambitious generals who wanted to rule Rome like an empire. Civil war ensued, which was quelled briefly by the great politician and general Julius Caesar. Only his grandnephew Octavian, better known to history as Augustus, finally restored peace and order to Rome.

Overseas Conquests and the Punic Wars, 264–133 B.C.E.

In 282 B.C.E., when the Romans reached southern Italy, they embarked upon a series of wars that left them the rulers of the Mediterranean world. Although they sometimes declared war reluctantly, they nonetheless felt the need to dominate, to eliminate any state that could endanger them. Yet they did not map out grandiose strategies to conquer the world, as had Alexander the Great. Rather they responded to situations as they arose.

Two Triremes Race In this fresco painting from the temple of Isis in Pompeii, two triremes — narrow warships powered by several banks of long oars — race in what was most likely a festival celebrating the goddess. Greeks, Carthaginians, and Romans all used triremes, which had bronze front pieces designed to smash into enemy ships. The 100 to 200 oarsmen had to row in time to achieve the necessary speed, which took long practice, so this religious celebration also served a military purpose. The ruins of Pompeii provide an extremely rich source for all aspects of Roman life. (© Ministero per I Beni e le Attivita Culturali — Soprintendenza archeologia de Napoli)

Their presence in southern Italy brought the Romans to the island of Sicily, where they confronted another great power in the western Mediterranean, Carthage (CAHR-thij). The city of Carthage had been founded by Phoenicians as a trading colony in the eighth century B.C.E. (see page 51). It commanded one of the best harbors on the northern African coast and was supported by a fertile inland. By the fourth century B.C.E. the Carthaginians began to expand their holdings, and they engaged in war with the Etruscans and Greeks. At the end of a long string of wars, the Carthaginians had created and defended a mercantile empire that stretched from western Sicily to beyond Gibraltar.

The Carthaginian Empire and Roman Republic, 264 B.C.E.

The conflicting ambitions of the Romans and Carthaginians led to the First Punic (PYOO-nik) War, which lasted from 264 to 241 B.C.E. During the course of the war, Rome built a navy and defeated Carthage in a series of sea battles. Sicily became Rome's first province, but despite a peace treaty the conflict was not over.

Carthaginian armies moved into Spain, where Rome was also claiming territory. The brilliant general Hannibal (ca. 247–183 B.C.E.) marched an army of tens of thousands of troops — and, more famously, several dozen war elephants — from Spain across what is now France and over the Alps into Italy, beginning the Second Punic War (218–201 B.C.E.). Hannibal won three major victories, including a devastating blow at Cannae in southeastern Italy in 216 B.C.E. There, he inflicted some forty thousand casualties on the Romans. He then spread devastation throughout Italy, and a number of cities in central and southern Italy rebelled against Rome because it appeared to them that Hannibal would be victorious. Yet Hannibal was not able to win areas near Rome in central Italy. His allies, who included Philip V, the Antigonid king of Macedonia (see page 131), did not supply him with enough food and supplies to sustain his troops, and Rome fought back.

The Roman general Scipio Africanus (ca. 236–ca. 183 B.C.E.) copied Hannibal's methods of mobile warfare, streamlining the legions (army divisions) by making their components capable of independent action and using guerrilla tactics. He took Spain from the Carthaginians and then struck directly at Carthage itself, prompting the Carthaginians to recall Hannibal from Italy to defend the homeland. In 202 B.C.E., near the town of Zama, Scipio defeated Hannibal in one of the world's truly decisive battles. Scipio's victory meant that the world of the western Mediterranean would henceforth be Roman. Roman language, law, and culture, fertilized by Greek influences, would in time permeate this entire region.

The Second Punic War contained the seeds of still other wars. Unabated fear of Carthage led to the Third Punic War, a needless, unjust, and savage conflict that ended in 146 B.C.E. when Scipio Aemilianus, grandson of Scipio Africanus, destroyed the hated rival and burned Carthage to the ground.

After the final defeat of Carthage, the Romans turned east. They remembered the alliance between Philip of Macedonia and Hannibal, and after provocation from the current king of Macedonia, Roman legions quickly conquered Macedonia and Greece. Then they moved farther east and defeated the Seleucid monarchy. In 133 B.C.E. the king of Pergamum in Asia Minor willed his kingdom to Rome when he died. The Ptolemies of Egypt retained formal control of their kingdom, but they meekly obeyed Roman wishes in terms of trade policy. Declaring the Mediterranean *mare nostrum*, "our sea," the Romans began to create a political and administrative machinery to hold the Mediterranean together under a mutually shared cultural and political system of provinces ruled by governors sent from Rome.

Not all Romans were joyful over Rome's conquest of the Mediterranean world; some considered that victory a misfortune. The historian Sallust (86–34 B.C.E.), writing from hindsight, complained that the acquisition of an empire was the beginning of Rome's troubles:

> But when through labor and justice our Republic grew powerful . . . then fortune began to be harsh and to throw everything into confusion. The Romans had easily borne labor, danger, and hardship. To them leisure, riches — otherwise desirable — proved to be burdens and torments. So at first money, then desire for power, grew great. These things were a sort of cause of all evils.[2]

New Influences and Old Values in Roman Culture

With the conquest of the Mediterranean world, Rome became a great city. The spoils of war went to build baths, theaters, and other places of amusement, and Romans and Italian townspeople began to spend more

> " The Romans had easily borne labor, danger, and hardship. To them leisure, riches — otherwise desirable — proved to be burdens and torments. "
>
> **SALLUST**

of their time in leisure pursuits. This new urban culture reflected Hellenistic influences. Romans developed a liking for Greek literature, and it became common for an educated Roman to speak both Latin and Greek. Furthermore, the Roman conquest of the Hellenistic East resulted in wholesale confiscation of Greek paintings and sculpture to grace Roman temples, public buildings, and private homes.

The baths were built in response to another Greek influence: a passion for bathing, which Romans came to share. The large buildings containing pools supplied by intricate systems of aqueducts became essential parts of the Roman city. They were more than just places to bathe. Baths included gymnasia where men exercised, snack bars and halls where people chatted and read, and even libraries and lecture halls. Women had opportunities to bathe, generally in separate facilities or at separate times, and both women and men went to the baths to see and be seen. Conservative commentators objected to these new pastimes as a corruption of traditional Roman values, but they were widely adopted in the cities, and they do not seem to have interfered with Romans' abilities to rule their huge territory.

New customs did not change the core Roman social structures. The head of the family remained the **paterfamilias**, the oldest dominant male of the family. He held nearly absolute power over his wife and children as long as he lived. Until he died, his sons could not legally own property. To deal with important matters, he usually called a council of the family's adult males. The women of the family had no formal part in these councils, but they could inherit and own property. The Romans praised women, like Lucretia of old, who were virtuous and loyal to their husbands. (See "Viewpoints: On Roman Wives from a Tombstone Inscription and Juvenal's Sixth Satire," page 152.) They also accorded respect to women as mothers and thought that children should be raised by their mothers. Though women handled the early education of their children, after the age of seven, sons and occasionally daughters in wealthy families began a formal

---

• **paterfamilias** The oldest dominant male of the family, who held nearly absolute power over the lives of family members as long as he lived.

Viewpoints

On Roman Wives from a Tombstone Inscription and Juvenal's Sixth Satire

> • *Most Romans married, and a great variety of sources portray husbands and wives visually and in words. These include idealizations, such as those found on tombstones, and biting critiques, including those by satirists such as the poet Juvenal.*

Epitaph on a Roman Tombstone from Around 130 B.C.E.

"Stranger, my message is short. Stand by and read it through. Here is the unlovely tomb of a lovely woman. Her parents called her Claudia by name. She loved her husband with all her heart. She bore two sons; of these she leaves one on earth; under the earth she has placed the other. She was charming in converse, yet gentle in bearing. She kept house, she made wool. That's my last word. Go your way."

Juvenal's Sixth Satire, Written Sometime in the Early Second Century C.E.

"[Y]ou are preparing for a covenant, a marriage-contract and a betrothal; you are by now getting your hair combed by a master barber; you have also perhaps given a pledge to her finger. What! Postumus, are you, you who once had your wits, taking to yourself a wife? Tell me . . . what snakes are driving you mad? Can you submit to a she-tyrant when there is so much rope to be had, so many dizzy heights of windows standing open? . . . If you are honestly uxorious, and devoted to one woman, then bow your head and submit your neck ready to bear the yoke. Never will you find a woman who spares the man who loves her; for though she be herself aflame, she delights to torment and plunder him. So the better the man, the more desirable he be as a husband, the less good by far will he get out of his wife. No present will you ever make if your wife forbids; nothing will you ever sell if she objects; nothing will you buy without her consent. She will arrange your friend-ships for you; she will turn your now-aged friend from the door which saw the beginnings of his beard. . . . Give up all hope of peace so long as your mother-in-law is alive. It is she that teaches her daughter to revel in stripping and despoiling her husband; it is she that teaches her to reply to a seducer's love-letters in no unskilled and innocent fashion; she eludes or bribes your guards. . . . The bed that holds a wife is never free from wrangling and mutual bickerings; no sleep is to be got there! It is there that she sets upon her husband, more savage than a tigress that has lost her cubs; conscious of her own secret slips, she affects a grievance, abusing his boys, or weeping over some imagined mistress. She has an abundant supply of tears always ready in their place, awaiting her com-mand in which fashion they should flow. . . . But whence come these monstrosities? you ask; from what fountain do they flow? In days of old, the wives of Latium were kept chaste by their humble fortunes. It was toil and brief slumbers that kept vice from polluting their modest homes; hands chafed and hardened by Tuscan fleeces, Hannibal nearing the city, and husbands standing to arms. . . . We are now suffering the calamities of long peace. Luxury, more deadly than any foe, has laid her hand upon us, and avenges a conquered world."

QUESTIONS FOR ANALYSIS

1. How does the wife in Juvenal's satire compare to the wife in the epitaph?

2. How does the type of sources that these are—one a tombstone inscription and one a satire—shape their portrayals of Roman wives?

3. Juvenal wrote more than two centuries after the tombstone was erected. In his opinion, how had Roman history in the intervening centuries shaped the behavior of Roman wives?

Sources: Tombstone: Naphtali Lewis and Meyer Reinhold, *Roman Civilization*, vol. 1 (New York: Columbia University Press, 1990), p. 524; Juvenal: *Juvenal*, translated by G. G. Ramsay, Loeb Classical Library (Cambridge, Mass.: Harvard University Press, 1918), pp. 85, 99, 101, 103, 105, 107.

Roman Bath This Roman bath in Bath, England (a city to which it gave its name), was built around a natural hot spring beginning in the first century C.E. The Romans spread the custom of bathing, which they had adopted from the Greeks, to the outer reaches of their empire. In addition to hot water, bathers used oil for massage and metal scrapers (inset) to clean and exfoliate their skin. Many Roman artifacts have been unearthed at Bath, including a number of curse tablets, small tablets made of lead calling on the gods to harm someone, which were common in the Greco-Roman world. Not surprisingly, many of the curse tablets found at Bath relate to the theft of clothing while people were bathing. (baths: Horst Schafer/Photolibrary/Peter Arnold Inc.; artifact: Courtesy of the Trustees of the British Museum)

education under Greek tutors. Most children learned what they needed from their parents or through apprenticeships with artisans.

Most Romans continued to work long days, but an influx of slaves from Rome's conquests provided labor for the fields and cities. To the Romans slavery was a misfortune that befell some people, but it was not based on racial theories. For loyal slaves the Romans always held out the possibility of freedom, and **manumission**, the freeing of individual slaves by their masters, became common. Nonetheless, slaves rebelled from time to time.

Religion played an important role in the lives of most Romans before and after the conquests. They honored Jupiter (Zeus's counterpart) and his wife Juno, as well as Mars, the god of war who also guaranteed the welfare of the farm. The Romans honored the cults of their gods, hoping for divine favor. For example, in the city of Rome the shrine of Vesta, the goddess of hearth and home, was tended by six "vestal virgins" chosen from patrician families. Roman military losses were sometimes blamed on inattention by the vestal virgins, another link between female honor and the Roman state. In addition to the great gods, the Romans believed in spirits who haunted fields and even homes. Some of the deities were hostile, and only magic could ward them off. Some spirits were ghosts who haunted places where they had lived.

The Late Republic and the Rise of Augustus, 133–27 B.C.E.

The wars of conquest eventually created serious political problems for the Romans. When the legionaries (soldiers) returned home, they found their farms practically in ruins. Many were forced to sell their land to ready buyers who had grown rich from the wars. These wealthy men created huge estates called latifundia. Now landless, veterans moved to the cities, especially

• **manumission** The freeing of individual slaves by their masters.

Rome, but could not find work. These developments not only created unrest in the city but also threatened Rome's army by reducing its ranks. The Romans had always believed that only landowners should serve in the army, for only they had something to fight for. Landless men, even if they were Romans and lived in Rome, were forbidden to serve. The landless veterans were willing to follow any leader who promised help. The leader who answered their call was Tiberius Gracchus (163–133 B.C.E.), an aristocrat who was appalled by the situation. Elected tribune in 133 B.C.E., he proposed dividing public land among the poor. But a group of wealthy senators murdered him, launching a long era of political violence that would destroy the republic. Still, Tiberius's brother Gaius Gracchus (153–121 B.C.E.) passed a law providing the urban poor with cheap grain and urged practical reforms. Once again senators tried to stem the tide of reform by murdering him.

The next reformer, Gaius Marius (ca. 157–86 B.C.E.), recruited landless men into the army to put down a rebel king in Africa. He promised them land for their service. But after his victory, the senate refused to honor his promise. From then on, Roman soldiers looked to their commanders, not to the senate or the state, to protect their interests. The turmoil continued until 88 B.C.E., when the Roman general Sulla made himself dictator, an official office in the Roman republic given to a man who was granted absolute power temporarily to handle an emergency such as a war. Dictators were supposed to step down after six months — and more than eighty dictators had done so in Roman history — but Sulla held this position for nine years, and after that it was too late to restore the republican constitution. The senate and other institutions of the Roman state had failed to meet the needs of the people, and they had lost control of their generals and army. The soldiers put their faith in generals rather than the state, and that doomed the republic.

The history of the late republic is the story of power struggles among many famous Roman figures, which led to a series of civil wars. Pompey (PAHM-pee), who had been one of Sulla's officers, used military success in Spain to force the senate to allow him to run for consul. In 59 B.C.E. he was joined in a political alliance called the First Triumvirate by Crassus, another ambitious politician, and by Julius Caesar (100–44 B.C.E.). Born of a noble family, Caesar, an able general, was also a brilliant politician with unbridled ambition and a superb orator with immense literary ability. Recognizing that military success led to power, he led his troops to victory in Spain and Gaul, modern France. The First Triumvirate fell apart after Crassus was killed in battle in 53 B.C.E., leaving Caesar and Pompey in competition with each other for power. The result was civil war. The

Ptolemaic rulers of Egypt became mixed up in this war, particularly Cleopatra VII, who allied herself with Caesar and had a son by him. (See "Individuals in Society: Queen Cleopatra," page 155.) Although the senate backed Pompey, Caesar was victorious. The senate then began appointing Caesar to various offices, including that of consul, dictator, and imperator (ihm-puh-RAH-tuhr), a title given to victorious commanders.

Using his victory wisely, Caesar enacted basic reforms. He extended citizenship to many provincials outside Italy who had supported him. To relieve the pressure of Rome's huge population, he sent eighty thousand poor people to establish colonies in Gaul, Spain, and North Africa. These new communities — formed of Roman citizens, not subjects — helped spread Roman culture.

In 44 B.C.E. a group of conspirators assassinated Caesar and set off another round of civil war. (See "Listening to the Past: Cicero and the Plot to Kill Caesar," page 156.) His grandnephew and heir, the eighteen-year-old Octavian (63 B.C.E.–14 B.C.E.), joined with two of Caesar's followers, Marc Antony and Lepidus, in the Second Triumvirate. After defeating Caesar's murderers, they had a falling-out. Octavian forced Lepidus out of office and waged war against Antony, who had now also become allied with Cleopatra. In 31 B.C.E., with the might of Rome at his back, Octavian defeated the combined forces of Antony and Cleopatra at the Battle of Actium in Greece. His victory ended the age of civil war. For his success, the senate in 27 B.C.E. gave Octavian the name Augustus, meaning "revered one." Tradition recognizes this date and Augustus's leadership as the start of the Roman Empire.

The Successes of Augustus

After Augustus ended the civil wars, he faced the monumental problems of reconstruction, and from 29–23 B.C.E. he toiled to heal Rome's wounds. He first had to rebuild the constitution and the organs of government. Next he had to demobilize much of the army and care for the welfare of the provinces. Then he had to address the danger of various groups on Rome's European frontiers. Augustus was highly successful in meeting these challenges.

Augustus claimed that in restoring the constitutional government he was also restoring the republic. Yet he had to modify republican forms and offices to meet the new circumstances. While expecting the senate to shoulder heavy administrative burdens, he failed to give it enough actual power to do the job. Many of the senate's prerogatives thus shifted to Augustus and his successors.

Augustus also had to fit his own position into the republican constitution. He did this not by creating a new

Queen Cleopatra

CLEOPATRA VII (69–30 B.C.E.) WAS A MEMBER OF the Ptolemy Dynasty, the Hellenistic rulers of Egypt who had established power in the third century B.C.E. Although she was a Greek, she was passionately devoted to her Egyptian subjects and was the first in her dynasty who could speak Egyptian in addition to Greek. Just as ancient pharaohs had linked themselves with the gods, she had herself portrayed as the goddess Isis and may have seen herself as a reincarnation of Isis (see page 45).

At the time civil war was raging in the late Roman republic, Cleopatra and her brother Ptolemy XIII were in a dispute over who would be supreme ruler in Egypt. Julius Caesar captured the Egyptian capital of Alexandria, Cleopatra arranged to meet him, and the two became lovers, although Cleopatra was much younger and Caesar was married. The two apparently had a son, Caesarion, and Caesar's army defeated Ptolemy's army, ending the power struggle. Cleopatra came to Rome in 46 B.C.E., where Caesar put up a statue of her as Isis in one of the city's temples. The Romans hated her because they saw her as a decadent Eastern queen and a threat to what were considered traditional Roman values.

After Caesar's assassination, Cleopatra returned to Alexandria. There she witnessed the outbreak of another Roman civil war that pitted Octavian, Caesar's heir, against Marc Antony, who commanded the Roman army in the East. When Antony visited Alexandria in 41 B.C.E. he met Cleopatra, and though he was already married to Octavian's sister, he became her lover. He abandoned (and later divorced) his Roman wife, married Cleopatra in 37 B.C.E., and changed his will to favor his children by Cleopatra. Antony's wedding present to Cleopatra was a huge grant of territory, much of it Roman, that greatly increased her power and that of all her children, including Caesarion. Antony also declared Caesarion to be Julius Caesar's rightful heir.

Octavian used the wedding gift as the reason to declare Antony a traitor. He and other Roman leaders described Antony as a romantic fool captivated by the seductive Cleopatra. Roman troops turned against Antony and joined with

Octavian, and at the battle of Actium in 31 B.C.E. Octavian defeated the army and navy of Antony and Cleopatra. Antony committed suicide, as did Cleopatra shortly afterward. Octavian ordered the teenage Caesarion killed, but the young children of Antony and Cleopatra were allowed to go back to Rome, where they were raised by Antony's widow. In another consequence of Octavian's victory, Egypt became a Roman province.

Roman sources are viciously hostile to Cleopatra, and she became the model of the femme fatale whose sexual attraction led men to their doom. Stories about her beauty, sophistication, allure, lavish spending, desire for power, and ruthlessness abounded and were retold for centuries. The most dramatic story was that she committed suicide through the bite of a poisonous snake, which may have been true and which has been the subject of countless paintings. Her tumultuous relationships with Caesar and Antony have been portrayed in plays, novels, movies, and television programs.

QUESTIONS FOR ANALYSIS

1. How did Cleopatra benefit from her relationships with Caesar and Antony? How did they benefit from their relationships with her?

2. How did ideas about gender and Roman suspicion of the more sophisticated Greek culture combine to shape Cleopatra's fate and the way she is remembered?

3. The "Individuals in Society" in Chapter 2 also focuses on leading female figures in Egypt, but they lived more than a thousand years before Cleopatra. How would you compare their situation with hers?

Bust of Cleopatra, probably from Alexandria.
(Bildarchiv Preussischer Kulturbesitz/Art Resource, NY)

Listening to the Past

Cicero and the Plot to Kill Caesar

Marcus Tullius Cicero was born in January 106 B.C.E. After an excellent education, he settled in Rome to practice law. His meteoric career took him to the consulship in 63 B.C.E. By the time of Caesar's death in 44 B.C.E., Cicero was sixty-two years old and a senior statesman. Like many others, he was fully caught up in the events leading to Caesar's assassination and the resulting revolution. Shortly before the plot was carried out on March 15, 44 B.C.E. — the Ides of March — Caesar wrote Cicero a flattering letter telling him that "your approval of my actions elates me beyond words. . . . As for yourself, I hope I shall see you at Rome so that I can avail myself as usual of your advice and resources in all things."[1] By then, however, Cicero knew of and supported the plot to assassinate Caesar and prudently decided not to meet him. The following letters and speeches offer a personal account of Cicero's involvement in the plot and its aftermath.

Trebonius, one of the assassins, wrote to Cicero describing the murder, and on February 2, 43 B.C.E., Cicero gave this frank opinion of the events:

> Would to heaven you had invited me to that noble feast that you made on the Ides of March: no remnants, most assuredly, should have been left behind. Whereas the part you unluckily spared gives us so much perplexity that we find something to regret, even in the godlike service that you and your illustrious associates have lately rendered to the republic. To say the truth, when I reflect that it was owing to the favor of so worthy a man as yourself that Antony now lives to be our general bane, I am sometimes inclined to be a little angry with you for taking him aside when Caesar fell as by this means you have occasioned more trouble to myself in particular than to all the rest of the whole community.[2]

By the "part [of the feast] you unluckily spared" he meant Marc Antony, Caesar's firm supporter and a fierce enemy of the assassins. Another reason that Cicero was not entirely pleased with the results of the assassination was that it led to civil war. Two men led the cause for restoring the republic: Brutus, an aristocrat who favored traditional Roman values,

and Cassius, an unpopular but influential senator. Still undecided about what to do after the assassination, Cassius wrote to Cicero asking for advice. Cicero responded:

> Where to advise you to begin to restore order I must acknowledge myself at a loss. To say the truth, it is the tyrant alone, and not the tyranny, from which we seem to be delivered: for although the man [Caesar] is destroyed, we still servilely maintain all his despotic ordinances. We do more: and under the pretence of carrying his designs into execution, we approve of measures which even he himself would never have pursued. . . . This outrageous man [Antony] represents me as the principal advisor and promoter of your glorious efforts. Would to heaven the charge were true! For had I been a party in your councils, I should have put it out of his power thus to bother and embarrass our plans. But this was a point that depended on yourselves to decide; and since the opportunity is now over, I can only wish that I were capable of giving you any effective advice. But the truth is that I am utterly at a loss in how to act myself. For what is the purpose of resisting where one cannot oppose force by force?[3]

At this stage the young Octavian, the future Augustus and Caesar's heir, appeared to claim his inheritance. He too sought Cicero's advice, and in a series of letters to his close friend Atticus, Cicero discussed the situation:

> On the second or third of November 44 B.C.E. a letter arrived from Octavian. He has great schemes afoot. He has won the veterans at Casilinum and Calatia over to his views, and no wonder since he gives them 500 denarii apiece. He plans to make a round of the other colonies. His object is plain: war with Antony and himself as commander-in-chief. So it looks to me as though in a few days' time we shall be in arms. But whom are we to follow? Consider his name; consider his age. . . . In short, he proffers himself as our leader and expects me to back him up. For my part I have recommended him to go to Rome. I imagine he will have the city rabble behind him, and the honest men too if he convinces them of his sincerity. Ah Brutus, where are you? What a golden opportunity you are losing! I could not foretell *this*, but I thought something of the kind would happen.[4]

office for himself but by gradually taking over many of the offices that traditionally had been held by separate people. The senate named him as a consul every year and also as a tribune, though the former office was normally held by a patrician and the latter by a plebeian. He was also named imperator and held control of the

army, which he made a permanent standing organization. Furthermore, recognizing the importance of religion, he had himself named pontifex maximus, or chief priest. The senate also gave him the honorary title princeps civitatis, "first citizen of the state." That title had no official powers attached to it, but the fact that it

Four days later Cicero records news of the following developments:

"Two letters for me from Octavian in one day! Now he wants me to return to Rome at once, says he wants to work through the senate. . . . In short, he presses and I play for time. I don't trust his age and I don't know what he's after. . . . I'm nervous of Antony's power and don't want to leave the coast. But I'm afraid of some star performance during my absence. Varro [an enemy of Antony] doesn't think much of the boy's [Octavian's, who was only eighteen] plan; I take a different view. He has a strong force at his back and *can* have Brutus. And he's going to work quite openly, forming companies at Capua and paying out bounties. War is evidently coming any minute now."[5]

At last Cicero openly sided with Octavian. On April 21, 43 B.C.E., he denounced Antony in a speech to the senate. He reminded his fellow senators how they had earlier opposed Antony:

"Do you not remember, in the name of the immortal gods, what resolutions you have made against these men [Antony and his supporters]? You have repealed the acts of Antony. You have taken down his law. You have voted that they were carried by violence and with a disregard of the auspices. You have called out the troops throughout all Italy. You have pronounced that colleague and ally of all wickedness a public enemy. What peace can there be with this man? Even if he were a foreign enemy, still, after such actions as have taken place, it would be scarcely possible by any means whatever to have peace. Though seas and mountains and vast regions lay between you, still you would hate such a man without seeing him. But these men will stick to your eyes, and when they can to your very throats; for what fences will be strong enough for us to restrain savage beasts? Oh, but the result of war is uncertain. It is at all events in the power of brave men such as you ought to be to display your valor, for certainly brave men can do that, and not to fear the caprice of fortune."[6]

When war broke out Cicero continued to speak out in the senate against Antony. Yet Cicero commanded no legions, and only legions commanded respect. At last Antony got his revenge when he had Cicero prosecuted as a public enemy. An ill and aging Cicero fled to the sea in a litter but was intercepted by Antony's men. With dignity Cicero stretched his head out of the window of the litter, and a centurion cut it off together, along with the hand that had written the speeches against Antony. Cicero's hands and head were displayed in the Roman Forum, showing the revenge taken on an enemy of the state. But years later Octavian, then the Roman emperor Augustus, said of Cicero: "A learned man, learned and a lover of his country."[7]

● **Bust of Cicero.**
(Alinari/Art Resource, NY)

QUESTIONS FOR ANALYSIS

1. What can you infer from these letters about how well prepared Brutus and Cassius were to take control of the government after Caesar's death?

2. What do these sources suggest about Cicero's importance?

3. What was Cicero's view of Octavian? Of Antony?

1. *To Atticus* 9.16.2 in D. R. Shackleton-Bailey, *Cicero's Letters to Atticus*, vol. IV (Cambridge, U.K.: Cambridge University Press, 1968), pp. 203–205.

2. *To Trebonius* in T. de Quincy, *Cicero: Offices, Essays, and Letters* (New York: E. P. Dutton, 1942), pp. 328–329.

3. *To Cassius*, ibid., pp. 324–325.

4. *To Atticus* 16.8.1–2 in D. R. Shackleton-Bailey, *Cicero's Letters to Atticus*, vol. VI (Cambridge, U.K.: Cambridge University Press, 1967), pp. 185–187.

5. *To Atticus* 16.9, ibid., p. 189.

6. *The Fourteenth Phillipic* in C. D. Yonge, *Cicero, Select Orations* (New York: Harper and Brothers, 1889), p. 499.

7. Plutarch, *Cicero* 49.15.

is the origin of the word *prince*, meaning sovereign ruler, is an indication of what Augustus actually did.

Considering what had happened to Julius Caesar, Augustus wisely kept all this power in the background, and his period of rule is officially called the "principate." Although principate leaders were said to be "first among equals," Augustus's tenure clearly marked the end of the republic, and without specifically saying so, Augustus created the office of emperor. That word is derived from *imperator*, commander of the army, a link that reflects the fact that the main source of Augustus's power was his position as commander of the Roman army. The changes that Augustus made created a stable government, although the fact that the army was loyal to him as a person, not as the head of the Roman state, would lead to trouble later.

In other political reforms, Augustus made provincial administration more orderly and improved its functioning. He encouraged local self-government and the development of cities. As a spiritual bond between the provinces and Rome, Augustus encouraged the cult of *Roma et Augustus* (Rome and Augustus) as the guardian of the state. The cult spread rapidly and became a symbol of Roman unity. Augustus had himself portrayed on coins standing alongside the goddess Victory and on celebratory stone arches built to commemorate military victories. In addition, he had temples, stadiums, marketplaces, and public buildings constructed in Rome and other cities.

In the social realm, Augustus promoted marriage and childbearing through legal changes that released free women and freedwomen (female slaves who had been freed) from male guardianship if they had given birth to a certain number of children. Men and women who were unmarried or had no children were restricted in the inheritance of property. Same-sex relationships were denounced as immoral for not producing children, although no laws were passed against them.

Aside from addressing legal issues and matters of state, Augustus actively encouraged poets and writers. For this reason the period of his rule is known as the golden age of Latin literature. Roman poets and prose writers celebrated human accomplishments in works that were highly polished, elegant in style, and intellectual in conception.

Rome's greatest poet was Virgil (70–19 B.C.E.), whose masterpiece is the *Aeneid* (uh-NEE-id), an epic poem that is the Latin equivalent of the Greek *Iliad* and *Odyssey* (see page 118). Virgil's account of the founding of Rome and the early years of the city gave final form to the legend of Aeneas, the Trojan hero (and ancestor of Romulus and Remus; see page 145) who escaped to Italy at the fall of Troy:

> Arms and the man I sing, who first made way,
> predestined exile, from the Trojan shore
> to Italy, the blest Lavinian strand.
> Smitten of storms he was on land and sea
> by violence of Heaven, to satisfy
> stern Juno's sleepless wrath; and much in war
> he suffered, seeking at the last to found
> the city, and bring o'er his fathers' gods
> to safe abode in Latium; whence arose
> the Latin race, old Alba's reverend lords,
> and from her hills wide-walled, imperial Rome.[3]

As Virgil told it, Aeneas became the lover of Dido (DIE-doh), the widowed queen of Carthage, but left her because his destiny called him to found Rome. Dido committed suicide, and, according to Virgil, distress over the end of their relationship helped cause the Punic Wars. In leaving Dido, an "Eastern" queen, Aeneas put the good of the state ahead of marriage or

Augustus as Imperator In this marble statue, found in the villa of Augustus's widow, Augustus is dressed in a military uniform and in a pose usually used to show leaders addressing their troops. This emphasizes his role as imperator, the head of the army. The figures on his breastplate show various peoples the Romans had defeated or with whom they had made treaties, along with assorted deities. Although Augustus did not declare himself a god—as later Roman emperors would—this statue shows him barefoot, just as gods and heroes were in classical Greek statuary, and accompanied by Cupid riding a dolphin, both symbols of the goddess Venus, whom he claimed as an ancestor. (Scala /Art Resource, NY)

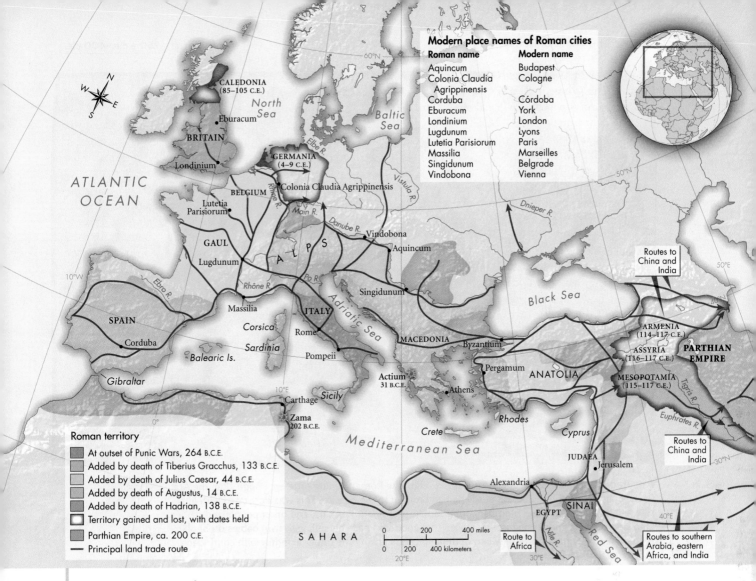

Modern place names of Roman cities

Roman name	Modern name
Aquincum	Budapest
Colonia Claudia Agrippinensis	Cologne
Corduba	Córdoba
Eburacum	York
Londinium	London
Lugdunum	Lyons
Lutetia Parisiorum	Paris
Massilia	Marseilles
Singidunum	Belgrade
Vindobona	Vienna

Roman territory

- At outset of Punic Wars, 264 B.C.E.
- Added by death of Tiberius Gracchus, 133 B.C.E.
- Added by death of Julius Caesar, 44 B.C.E.
- Added by death of Augustus, 14 B.C.E.
- Added by death of Hadrian, 138 B.C.E.
- Territory gained and lost, with dates held
- Parthian Empire, ca. 200 C.E.
- Principal land trade route

◻ Mapping the Past

MAP 6.2 Roman Expansion, 282 B.C.E.–138 B.C.E. Rome expanded in all directions, eventually controlling every shore of the Mediterranean and vast amounts of land.

ANALYZING THE MAP How would you summarize the pattern of Roman expansion—that is, which areas were conquered first and which later? How long was Rome able to hold on to territories at the outermost boundaries of its empire?

CONNECTIONS Many of today's major cities in these areas were founded as Roman colonies. Why do you think so many of these cities were founded along the northern border of Roman territory?

pleasure. The parallels between this story and the real events involving Antony and Cleopatra were not lost on Virgil's audience. Making the public aware of these parallels, and of Virgil's description of Aeneas as an ancestor of Julius Caesar, fit well with Augustus's aims. Therefore, he encouraged Virgil to write the *Aeneid* and made sure it was circulated widely immediately after Virgil died.

One of the most momentous aspects of Augustus's reign was Roman expansion into northern and west-

ern Europe (Map 6.2). Augustus completed the conquest of Spain, founded twelve new towns in Gaul, and saw that the Roman road system linked new settlements with one another and with Italy. After hard fighting, he made the Rhine River the Roman frontier in Germania (Germany). Meanwhile, generals conquered areas as far as the Danube River, and Roman legions penetrated the areas of modern Austria, southern Bavaria, and western Hungary. The regions of modern Serbia, Bulgaria, and Romania also fell. Within this

Ara Pacis In the middle years of Augustus's reign, the Roman senate ordered a huge altar, the Ara Pacis, built to honor him and the peace he had brought to the empire. This was decorated with life-size reliefs of Augustus and members of his family, prominent Romans, and other people and deities. One side shows a goddess figure, most likely the goddess Peace herself, with twin babies on her lap, surrounded by symbols of fertility and dominance, thus linking the imperial family with continued prosperity. (Scala/Art Resource, NY)

area the legionaries built fortified camps. Roads linked these camps with one another, and settlements grew up around the camps, eventually becoming towns. Traders began to frequent the frontier and to do business with the native people who lived there; as a result, for the first time, central and northern Europe came into direct and continuous contact with Mediterranean culture. Romans generally referred to these native people as barbarians, a word derived from a Greek word for people who did not speak Greek. The Romans maintained peaceful relations with the barbarians whenever possible, but Roman legions remained on the frontier to repel hostile barbarians.

Romans did not force their culture on native people in Roman territories. However, just as earlier ambitious people in the Hellenistic world knew that the surest path to political and social advancement lay in embracing Greek culture and learning to speak Greek (see page 133), those determined to get ahead now learned Latin and adopted aspects of Roman culture.

The Pax Romana

☐ How did efficient Roman rule lead to a period of prosperity and relative peace?

Augustus's success in creating solid political institutions was tested by the ineptness of some leaders who followed him, but later in the first century C.E. Rome entered a period of political stability, prosperity, and relative peace that lasted until the end of the second century. In the eighteenth century historians dubbed this period the **pax Romana**, the Roman peace. During this time the growing city of Rome saw great improvements, and trade and production flourished in the provinces. Rome also expanded eastward and came into indirect contact with China.

Political and Military Changes in the Empire

For fifty years after Augustus's death in 14 C.E. the dynasty that he established—known as the Julio-Claudians because all were members of the Julian and

Claudian clans — provided the emperors of Rome. Some of the Julio-Claudians, such as Tiberius and Claudius, were sound rulers and created a bureaucracy of able administrators to help them govern. Others, including Caligula and Nero, were weak and frivolous.

In 68 C.E. Nero's inept rule led to military rebellion and widespread disruption. Yet only two years later Vespasian (r. 69–79 C.E.), who established the Flavian dynasty, restored order. He also turned Augustus's principate into a hereditary monarchy and expanded the emperor's powers. The Flavians (69–96 C.E.) repaired the damage of civil war to give the Roman world peace and paved the way for the Antonines (96–192 C.E.), a dynasty of emperors under whose leadership the Roman Empire experienced a long period of prosperity. Wars generally ended victoriously and were confined to the frontiers. In addition to the full-blown monarchy of the Flavians, other significant changes had occurred in Roman government since Augustus's day. Hadrian (HAY-dree-uhn), who became emperor in 117 C.E., made the imperial bureaucracy created by Claudius more organized. He established imperial administrative departments and separated civil from military service. In addition, he demanded professionalism from members of the bureaucracy. These innovations helped the empire run more efficiently while increasing the authority of the emperor, who was now the ruling power of the bureaucracy.

The Roman army also saw changes, transforming from a mobile unit to a defensive force. The frontiers became firmly fixed and defended by a system of forts and walls, some of which, such as sections of Hadrian's Wall in England, are still standing today. Behind them the network of roads was expanded and improved both to supply the forts and to reinforce them in times of trouble. The Roman road system eventually grew to over fifty thousand miles, longer than the current interstate highway system in the United States; some of those roads are still usable today.

The personnel of the legions were changing, too. Because Italy could no longer supply all the recruits needed for the army, increasingly only the officers came from Italy, while the soldiers were mostly drawn from the provinces. Among the provincial soldiers were barbarians who joined the army to gain Roman citizenship.

Life in Rome

The era of peace created great wealth, much of which flowed into Rome. The city, with a population of somewhere between 500,000 and 750,000, became the largest in the world at that time. Although Rome could boast of stately palaces, noble buildings, and beautiful residential areas, most people lived in shoddily constructed houses. They took whatever work was available, making food, clothing, construction materials, and the many other things needed by the city's residents, or selling these products from small shops or at the city's many marketplaces.

Fire and crime were perennial problems even in Augustus's day, and sanitation was poor. In the second century urban planning and new construction greatly improved the situation. For example, engineers built an elaborate system that collected sewage from public baths, the ground floors of buildings, and public latrines. They also built hundreds of miles of aqueducts, most of them underground, to bring fresh water into the city from the surrounding hills. The aqueducts, powered entirely by gravity, were a sophisticated system that required regular maintenance. But they were a great improvement and helped make Rome a very attractive place to live. Building aqueducts required thousands and sometimes tens of thousands of workers, who were generally paid out of the imperial treasury.

Rome grew so large that it became ever more difficult to feed. Emperors solved the problem by providing citizens with free bread, oil, and wine. By doing so, they also stayed in favor. They likewise entertained the people with gladiatorial contests in which participants fought to the death using swords and other weapons. Many gladiators were criminals, some the slaves of gladiatorial schools, and others prisoners of war. A few free people, men and very occasionally women, volunteered for the arena. The Romans actually preferred chariot racing to gladiatorial contests. In these races two-horse and four-horse chariots ran a course of seven laps, about five miles. Four permanent teams, each with its own color, competed against one other. Winning charioteers were idolized just as sports stars are today.

Prosperity in the Roman Provinces

Like Rome, the Roman provinces and frontiers saw extensive prosperity in the second century C.E. through the growth of agriculture, trade, and industry, among other factors. Peace and security opened Britain, Gaul, Germany, and the lands of the Danube to settlers from other parts of the Roman Empire. Many of these settlers became tenant farmers on small parcels of land, and eventually these farmers became the backbone of Roman agriculture.

In continental Europe the army was largely responsible for the new burst of expansion. The areas where legions were stationed became Romanized because legionaries, upon retirement, often settled where they had served, frequently marrying local women. Having learned a trade, such as carpentry or metalworking, in

• **pax Romana** A period of Roman security, order, harmony, flourishing culture, and expanding economy during the first and second centuries C.E.

Roman Architecture These three structures demonstrate the beauty and utility of Roman architecture. The Coliseum in Rome (below),a sports arena that could seat 50,000 spectators built between 70 and 80 C.E., was the site of gladiatorial games, animal spectacles, executions, and mock naval battles. The Pantheon in Rome (right) is a temple dedicated to all the gods, built in its present form about 130 C.E. after earlier temples on this site burned down. Its dome, 140 feet in diameter, remains the largest unreinforced concrete dome in the world. Romans also used concrete for more everyday purposes. The Pont du Gard at Nîmes in France (above), is a bridge over a river carrying an aqueduct that supplied millions of gallons of water per day to the Roman city of Nîmes in Gaul; the water flowed in a channel at the very top. Although this bridge was built largely without mortar or concrete, many Roman aqueducts and bridges relied on concrete for their strength. (Pont du Gard: Vanni/Art Resource, NY; Pantheon: Gianni Dagli Orti/The Art Archive; Coliseum: Scala/Art Resource, NY)

the army, they brought essential skills to areas that badly needed trained men. These veterans also used their retirement pay to set themselves up in business.

The eastern part of the empire, including Greece, Anatolia, and Syria, shared in the boom in part by trading with other areas and in part because of local industries. The cities of the East built extensively, beautifying themselves with new amphitheaters, temples, and other public buildings.

The expansion of trade during the pax Romana made the Roman Empire an economic as well as a political force. Britain and Belgium became prime grain producers, with much of their harvests going to the armies of the Rhine, and Britain's wool industry probably got its start under the Romans. Italy and southern Gaul produced huge quantities of wine, which was shipped in large pottery jugs wherever merchant vessels could carry it. Roman colonists introduced the olive to southern Spain and northern Africa, which soon produced most of the oil consumed in the western part of the empire. In the East the olive oil production of Syrian farmers reached an all-time high, and Egypt produced tons of wheat that fed the Roman populace. Additionally, the Roman army in Mesopotamia consumed a high percentage of the raw materials and manufactured products from Syria and Asia Minor.

The growth of industry in the provinces was another striking development of this period. Cities in Gaul and Germany eclipsed the old Mediterranean manufacturing centers, and in the second century C.E. Gaul and Germany took over the pottery market. Lyons in Gaul and later Cologne in Germany became the new centers of the glassmaking industry, and the cities of Gaul were nearly unrivaled in the manufacture of bronze and brass. Aided by all this growth in trade and industry, Europe and western Asia were linked in ways they had not been before.

Eastward Expansion and Contacts Between Rome and China

The expansion of their empire took the Romans into West and Central Asia, which had two immediate effects. The first was a long military confrontation between the Romans and several western Asian empires. The second was a period of contact (often indirect) between the major ancient civilizations of the world, as Roman movement eastward coincided with Chinese expansion into the West (see page 183).

As the Romans drove farther eastward, they encountered the Parthians, who had established a kingdom in what is now Afghanistan and Iran in the Helle-

nistic period (see page 133). In the second century the Romans tried unsuccessfully to drive the Parthians out of Armenia and the Tigris and Euphrates Valleys. In 226 C.E. the Parthians were defeated by the Sassanids, a new dynasty in the area (see page 208). When the Romans continued their attacks against this new enemy, the Sassanid king Shapur conquered the Roman legions of the emperor Valerian, whom he took prisoner.

Although warfare disrupted parts of Asia, it did not stop trade that had prospered from Hellenistic times (see pages 134–135). Rarely did a merchant travel the entire distance from China to Mesopotamia. The Chinese and Romans were prevented from making direct contact because Parthians acted as middlemen between them. Chinese merchants sold their wares to the Parthians at the Stone Tower, located in modern Tashkurghan in Afghanistan. The Parthians then carried the goods overland to Mesopotamia or Egypt, from where they were shipped throughout the Roman Empire. Silk was still a major commodity from east to west, along with other luxury goods. In return the Romans traded glassware, precious gems, and slaves. The Parthians added exotic fruits, rare birds, and other products desired by the Chinese. (See "Global Trade: Pottery," page 164.)

The pax Romana was also an era of maritime trade, and Roman ships sailed from Egyptian ports to the mouth of the Indus River, where they traded local merchandise and wares imported by the Parthians. Merchants who made the voyage contended with wind, shoal waters, and pirates. Despite the dangers and discomforts, hardy mariners pushed into the Indian Ocean and beyond, reaching Malaya, Sumatra, and Java in Southeast Asia, where they traded with equally hardy local sailors.

Maritime trade between Chinese and Roman ports began in the second century C.E., though no merchant traveled the entire distance. The period of this contact coincided with the era of Han greatness in China (see pages 178–183). The Han emperor Wu encouraged trade by sea as well as by land, and during the reign of the Roman emperor Nerva (r. 96–98 C.E.), a later Han emperor sent an ambassador, Gan Ying, to make contact with the Roman Empire. Gan Ying made it as far as the Persian Gulf ports, where he heard about the Romans from Parthian sailors and reported back to his emperor that the Romans were wealthy, tall, and strikingly similar to the Chinese. His report became part of a group of accounts about the Romans and other "western" peoples that circulated widely among scholars and officials in Han China. Educated Romans did not have a corresponding interest in China. For them, China remained more of a mythical than a real place, and they never bothered to learn more about it.

Global Trade

Pottery

is used primarily for dishes today, but it served a surprisingly large number of purposes in the ancient world. Families used earthen pottery for cooking and tableware, for storing grains and liquids, and for lamps. On a larger scale pottery was used for the transportation and protection of goods traded overseas, much as today's metal storage containers are used.

The creation of pottery dates back to the Neolithic period. Few resources were required to make it, only abundant sources of good clay and wheels upon which potters could throw their vessels. Once made, the pots were baked in specially constructed kilns. Although the whole process was relatively simple, skilled potters formed groups that made utensils for entire communities. Later innovations occurred when the artisans learned to glaze their pots by applying a varnish before baking them in a kiln.

The earliest potters focused on coarse ware: plain plates, cups, and cooking pots that remained virtually unchanged throughout antiquity. Increasingly, however, potters began to decorate these pieces with simple designs. In this way pottery became both functional and decorative. One of the most popular pieces was the amphora, a large two-handled jar with a wide mouth, a round belly, and a base. It became the workhorse of maritime shipping because it protected contents from water and rodents, was easy and cheap to produce, and could be

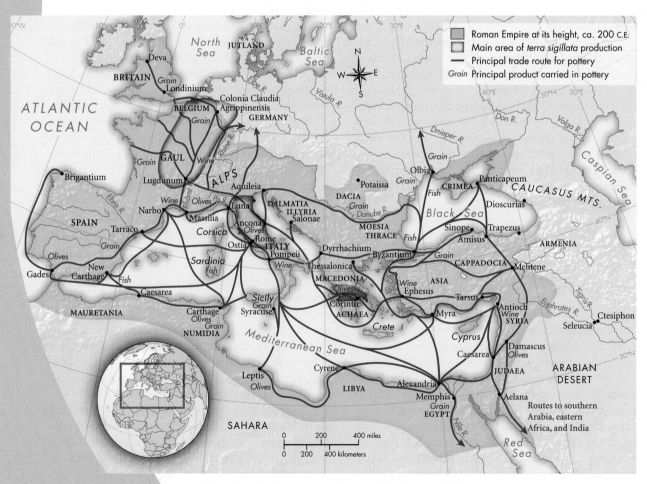

MAP 6.3 The Roman Pottery Trade, ca. 200 C.E.

reused. Amphorae contained goods as varied as wine and oil, spices and unguents, dried fish and pitch. The amphora's dependability and versatility kept it in use from the fourth century B.C.E. to the beginning of the Middle Ages.

In the Hellenistic and Roman periods amphorae became common throughout the Mediterranean and carried goods eastward to the Black Sea, Persian Gulf, and Red Sea. The Ptolemies of Egypt sent amphorae and their contents even farther, to Arabia, eastern Africa, and India. Thus merchants and mariners who had never seen the Mediterranean depended on these containers.

Other pots proved as useful as the amphora, and all became a medium of decorative art. By the eighth century B.C.E. Greek potters and artists began to decorate their wares by painting them with patterns and scenes from mythology, legend, and daily life. They portrayed episodes such as famous chariot races or battles from the *Iliad*. Some portrayed the gods, such as

Wrecks of Roman ships in the Mediterranean often contain amphorae. This merchant ship from the first century C.E., discovered off the island of Sicily, contained 500 amphorae originally filled with oil, fruits, and vegetables. (Corrado Giavara/StockphotoPro)

Dionysus at sea. These images widely spread knowledge of Greek religion and culture. In the West, especially, the Etruscans in Italy and the Carthaginians in North Africa eagerly welcomed the pots, their decoration, and their ideas. The Hellenistic kings shipped these pots as far east as China. Pottery thus served as a means of cultural exchange among people scattered across huge portions of the globe.

The Romans took the manufacture of pottery to an advanced stage by introducing a wider range of vessels and by making some in industrial-scale kilns that were large enough to fire tens of thousands of pots at once. The most prized pottery was *terra sigillata*, reddish decorated tableware with a glossy surface. Methods for making *terra sigillata* spread from Italy northward into Europe, often brought by soldiers in the Roman army who had been trained in pottery making in Italy. They set up facilities to make roof tiles, amphorae, and dishes for their units, and local potters began to copy their styles and methods of manufacturing. *Terra sigillata* often portrayed Greco-Roman gods and heroes, and so the pottery spread Mediterranean myths and stories. Local artisans added their own distinctive flourishes and sometimes stamped their names on the pots; these individual touches have allowed archaeologists to trace the pottery trade throughout the Roman Empire in great detail.

The Coming of Christianity

☐ What was Christianity, and how did it affect life in the Roman Empire?

During the reign of the emperor Tiberius (r. 14–37 C.E.), in the Roman province of Judaea, which had been created out of the Jewish kingdom of Judah, a Jewish man named Jesus of Nazareth preached, attracted a following, and was executed on the order of the Roman prefect Pontius Pilate. At the time this was a minor event, but Christianity, the religion created by Jesus's followers, came to have an enormous impact first in the Roman Empire and later throughout the world.

Factors Behind the Rise of Christianity

The civil wars that destroyed the Roman republic left their mark on Judaea, where Jewish leaders had taken sides in the conflict. The turmoil created a climate of violence throughout the area, and among the Jews two movements in opposition to the Romans spread. First were the Zealots (ZEH-luhts), who fought to rid Judaea of the Romans. The second movement was the growth of militant apocalypticism — the belief that the end of the world was near and that it would happen with the coming of a savior, or Messiah, who would destroy the Roman legions and inaugurate a period of happiness and plenty for Jews. This belief was an old one among Jews, but by the first century C.E. it had become more widespread than ever.

The pagan world also played its part in the story of early Christianity. The term **pagan** refers to all those who believed in the Greco-Roman gods. Paganism at the time of Jesus's birth can be broadly divided into three spheres: the official state religion of Rome; the traditional Roman veneration of hearth, home, and countryside; and the new mystery religions that arose in the Hellenistic world (see pages 136–137). The mystery religions gave their adherents what neither the official religion nor traditional practices could — spiritual satisfaction and the promise of eternal life — but they were exclusive. Therefore, many people's spiritual needs were unmet by these religious traditions, further paving the way for the rise of Christianity.

The Life and Teachings of Jesus

Into this climate of Messianic hope and Roman religious yearning came Jesus of Nazareth (ca. 3 B.C.E.–29 C.E.). According to Christian scripture, he was born to deeply religious Jewish parents and raised in Galilee, stronghold of the Zealots and a trading center where Greeks and Romans interacted with Jews. His ministry began when he was about thirty, and he taught by preaching and telling stories.

Like Socrates and the Buddha, Jesus left no writings. Accounts of his sayings and teachings first circulated orally among his followers and were later written down. The principal evidence for his life and deeds are the four Gospels of the Bible, books that are part of what Christians later termed the New Testament. These Gospels — the name means "good news" — are records of Jesus's teachings, written to build a community of faith sometime in the late first century. The Gospels include certain details of Jesus's life, but they were not meant to be biographies. Their authors had probably heard many different people talk about what

Depiction of Jesus This mural, from a Roman camp at Dura-Europos on the Euphrates River, may be the earliest known depiction of Jesus. Dating to 235 C.E., it depicts Jesus healing a paralytic man, an incident described in the New Testament. Early Christians used art to spread their message. (Yale University Art Gallery, Dura-Europos Collection)

Catacombs of Rome Christians favored burial of the dead rather than the more common Roman practice of cremation, and in the second century they began to dig tunnels in the soft rock around Rome for burials. The bodies were placed in niches along the walls of these passageways and then sealed up. Memorial services for martyrs were sometimes held in or near catacombs, but they were not regular places of worship. Many catacombs contain some of the earliest examples of Christian art, and others, dug by Jews for their own dead, contain examples of Jewish art from this period. (Catacombe di Priscilla, Rome/Scala/Art Resource, NY)

Jesus said and did, and there are discrepancies among the four accounts. These differences indicate that early followers had a diversity of beliefs about Jesus's nature and purpose. This diversity of beliefs about Jesus continues today. Some see him as a moral teacher, some as a prophet, and many as the son of God who rose from the dead and is himself divine.

However, almost all the early sources agree on certain aspects of Jesus's teachings: he preached of a heavenly kingdom of eternal happiness in a life after death and of the importance of devotion to God and love of others. His teachings were essentially Jewish, based on a group of Jewish books and with a conception of God and morality that came from Jewish tradition. Jesus's orthodoxy enabled him to preach in the synagogue and the temple, but he deviated from orthodoxy in insisting that he taught in his own name, not in the name of Yahweh (the Hebrew name for God). Was he the Messiah — in the Greek translation of the Hebrew word *Messiah*, the Christ? A small band of followers thought so, and Jesus claimed that he was. Yet Jesus had his own conception of the Messiah. He would establish a spiritual kingdom, not an earthly one. As recounted in one of the Gospels, he commented:

> Do not lay up for yourselves treasures on earth, where moth and rust consume and where thieves break in and steal, but lay up for yourselves treasures in heaven, where neither moth nor rust consumes and where thieves do not break in and steal. For where your treasure is, there will your heart be also.[4]

The prefect Pontius Pilate knew little about Jesus's teachings. He was concerned with maintaining peace and order. Crowds followed Jesus at the time of Passover, a highly emotional time in the Jewish year that marked the Jewish people's departure from Egypt under the leadership of Moses (see page 53). The prospect that these crowds would spark violence alarmed Pilate. Some Jews believed that Jesus was the long-awaited Messiah. Others hated and feared him because they thought him religiously dangerous. To avert riot and bloodshed, Pilate condemned Jesus to death, and his soldiers carried out the sentence. On the third day after Jesus's crucifixion, some of his followers claimed that he had risen from the dead. For his earliest followers and for generations to come, the resurrection of Jesus became a central element of faith.

The Spread of Christianity

The memory of Jesus and his teachings survived and flourished. Believers in his divinity met in small assemblies or congregations, often in one another's homes, to discuss the meaning of Jesus's message and to celebrate a ritual (later called the Eucharist or Lord's Supper) commemorating his last meal with his disciples before his arrest. Because they expected Jesus to return to the world very soon, they regarded

• **pagan** From a Latin term meaning "of the country," used to describe non-Christian followers of Greco-Roman gods.

earthly life and institutions as unimportant. Only later did these congregations evolve into what came to be called the religion of Christianity, with a formal organization and set of beliefs.

The catalyst in the spread of Jesus's teachings and the formation of the Christian Church was Paul of Tarsus, a well-educated Hellenized Jew who was comfortable in both the Roman and the Jewish worlds. At first he persecuted members of the new sect, but on the road to the city of Damascus in Syria he was converted to belief in Jesus and became a vigorous promoter of Jesus's ideas. Paul traveled all over the Roman Empire and wrote letters of advice to many groups. These letters were copied and widely circulated, transforming Jesus's ideas into more specific moral teachings. As a result of his efforts Paul became the most important figure in changing Christianity from a Jewish sect into a separate religion, and many of his letters became part of Christian scripture.

The breadth of the Roman Empire was another factor behind the spread of Christianity. If all roads led to Rome, they also led outward to the provinces. This enabled early Christians to spread their faith easily throughout the known world, as Jesus had told his followers to do, thus making his teachings universal. The pagan Romans also considered their secular empire universal, and the early Christians combined the two concepts of universalism.

Though most of the earliest converts seem to have been Jews, or Greeks and Romans who were already interested in Jewish moral teachings, Paul urged that Gentiles, or non-Jews, be accepted on an equal basis. The earliest Christian converts included people from all social classes. These people were reached by missionaries and others who spread the Christian message through family contacts, friendships, and business networks. Many women were active in spreading Christianity. Paul greeted male and female converts by name in his letters and noted that women often provided financial support for his activities. The growing Christian communities differed about the extent to which women should participate in the workings of the religion; some favored giving women a larger role in church affairs, while others were more restrictive.

People were attracted to Christian teachings for a variety of reasons. It was in many ways a mystery religion, offering its adherents special teachings that would give them immortality. But in contrast to traditional mystery religions, Christianity promised this immortality widely, not only to a select few. Christianity also offered the possibility of forgiveness, for believers accepted that human nature is weak and that even the best Christians could fall into sin. But Jesus loved sinners and forgave those who repented. Christianity was also attractive to many because it gave the Roman world a cause. Instead of passivity, Christians stressed the ideal of striving for a goal. By spreading the word of Christ, Christians played their part in God's plan for the triumph of Christianity on earth. They were not discouraged by temporary setbacks, believing Christianity to be invincible. Christianity likewise gave its devotees a sense of community, which was very welcome in the often highly mobile world of the Roman Empire. To stress the spiritual kinship of this new type of community, Christians often called one another brother and sister. Also, many Christians took Jesus's commandment to love one another as a guide and provided support for widows, orphans, and the poor, just as they would for family members.

The Growing Acceptance and Evolution of Christianity

At first many pagans in the Roman Empire misunderstood Christian practices and beliefs. Pagans thought that Christianity was one of the worst of the mystery cults, with immoral and indecent rituals. For instance, they thought that the ritual of the Lord's Supper, at which Christians said that they ate and drank the body and blood of Jesus, was an act of cannibalism. Pagans also feared that the Greco-Roman gods would withdraw their favor from the Roman Empire because of the Christian insistence that the pagan gods either did not exist or were evil spirits. And many worried that Christians were trying to destroy the Roman family with their insistence on a new type of kinship.

Christians themselves were partly responsible for the religious misunderstandings. They exaggerated the degree of pagan hostility to them, and most of the gory stories about the martyrs (Christians who were tortured and executed because of their beliefs) are fictitious. Although there were some cases of pagan persecution of the Christians, with few exceptions they were local and sporadic in nature. Even Emperor Nero's notorious persecution of Christians was temporary and limited to Rome. As time went on, pagan hostility and suspicion decreased. Pagans realized that Christians were not working to overthrow the state and that Jesus was no rival of Caesar. The emperor Trajan (r. 98–117 C.E.) forbade his governors to hunt down Christians. Though admitting that he considered Christianity an abomination, he preferred to leave Christians in peace.

By the second century C.E. Christianity was also changing. The belief that Jesus was soon coming again gradually waned, and as the number of converts in-

• **bishop** A Christian Church official with jurisdiction over a certain area and the power to determine the correct interpretation of Christian teachings.

• **heresy** A religious practice or belief judged unacceptable by church officials.

creased, permanent institutions were established instead of simple house churches. These included buildings and a hierarchy of officials often modeled on those of the Roman Empire. **Bishops**, officials with jurisdiction over a certain area, became especially important. They began to assert that they had the right to determine the correct interpretation of Christian teachings and to choose their successors. As the rise of the bishops shows, lines began to be drawn between what was considered correct teaching and what was considered incorrect, or **heresy**.

Christianity also began to attract more highly educated individuals who developed complex theological interpretations of issues that were not clear in scripture. Often drawing on Greek philosophy and Roman legal traditions, they worked out understandings of such issues as how Jesus could be both divine and human and how God could be both a father and a son (and later a spirit as well, a Christian doctrine known as the Trinity). Bishops and theologians often modified teachings that seemed upsetting to Romans, such as Jesus's harsh words about wealth. Given all these changes, Christianity became more formal in the second century, with power more centralized.

Turmoil and Reform

☐ How did the emperors Diocletian and Constantine respond to the problems created by barbarian invasions and political turmoil in the third and fourth centuries?

The prosperity of the second century gave way to a period of chaos and stress in the Roman Empire. Trying to repair the damage was the major work of the emperors Diocletian and Constantine (r. 306–337 C.E.), both of whom rose to leadership through the ranks of the military. They enacted political and religious reforms that dramatically changed the empire.

Diocletian's Reforms

During the third century C.E. the Roman Empire was stunned by civil war, as different individuals claimed rights to leadership of the empire. Emperors often ruled for only a few years or even months. Army leaders in the provinces declared their loyalty to one faction or another, or they broke from the empire entirely, thus ceasing to supply troops or taxes. Barbarian groups invaded Roman-held territory along the Rhine and Danube, occasionally even crossing the Alps to maraud in Italy. In the East, Sassanid armies advanced all the way to the Mediterranean. By the time peace was restored, the empire's economy was shattered, cities had shrunk

in size, and many farmers had left their lands.

At the close of the third century C.E. the emperor Diocletian ended the period of chaos. Under Diocletian the princeps became *dominus*, "lord," reflecting the emperor's claim that he was "the elect of god," ruling because of divine favor. To underscore the emperor's exalted position, Diocletian and his successor, Constantine, adopted the court ceremonies and trappings of the Persian Empire.

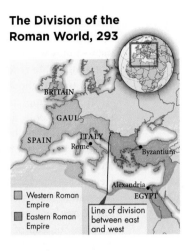

The Division of the Roman World, 293

Diocletian recognized that the empire had become too great for one man to handle and so divided it into a western and an eastern half. He assumed direct control of the eastern part, giving a colleague the rule of the western part along with the title *augustus*, which had become synonymous with *emperor*. Diocletian and his fellow augustus further delegated power by appointing two men to assist them. Each man was given the title *caesar* to indicate his exalted rank. Although this system is known as the Tetrarchy (TEH-trahr-kee) because four men ruled the empire, Diocletian was clearly the senior partner and final source of authority.

Although the Tetrarchy soon failed, Diocletian's division of the empire into two parts became permanent. Throughout the fourth century C.E. the eastern and western sections drifted apart. In later centuries the western part witnessed the decline of Roman government and the rise of barbarian kingdoms, while the eastern half evolved into the Byzantine Empire.

Economic Hardship and Its Consequences

Major economic problems also confronted Diocletian and Constantine at a time when the empire was less capable of recovery than in previous eras. The emperors needed additional revenues to support the army and the imperial court, but the wars and invasions had harmed Roman agriculture, the primary source of tax revenues. The wars and invasions had also disrupted normal commerce and the means of production. Mines were exhausted by the attempt to supply much-needed ores, especially gold and silver. In the cities, markets, trade, and industry were disrupted, and travel between cities became dangerous, with pirates attacking ships at sea and robber bands capturing merchant caravans. The devastation of the countryside increased the difficulty of feeding and supplying the cities, and merchant and artisan families rapidly left devastated regions.

Economic hardship had been met by cutting the silver content of coins until money was virtually worthless. The immediate result was crippling inflation throughout the empire.

In an attempt to curb inflation, Diocletian took a step unprecedented in Roman history: he issued an edict that fixed maximum prices and wages throughout the empire. He and his successors dealt with the tax system just as strictly and inflexibly. Taxes became payable in kind, that is, in goods and services instead of money. All those involved in the growing, preparation, and transportation of food and other essentials were locked into their professions, as the emperors tried desperately to assure a steady supply of these goods. A baker, for example, could not go into any other business, and his son was required to take up the trade at his death. In this period of severe depression, many localities could not pay their taxes. In such cases local tax collectors, who were themselves locked into service, had to make up the difference from their own funds. This system soon wiped out a whole class of moderately wealthy people.

During the third century C.E. many free tenant farmers and their families were killed in barbarian invasions. Others fled in advance of the invasions or after devastation from the fighting. Large tracts of land consequently lay deserted. Great landlords with ample resources began at once to claim as much of this land as they could. The huge estates that resulted, called villas, were self-sufficient. Because they often produced more than they consumed, they successfully competed with the declining cities by selling their surpluses in the countryside. They became islands of stability in an

> "Every man, when dying, shall have the right to bequeath as much of his property as he desires to the holy and venerable Catholic Church. And such wills are not to be broken."
>
> **MEGASTHENES**

unsettled world, and in return for the protection and security landlords could offer, many small landholders who remained in the countryside gave over their lands and their freedom. They continued to work the land, but it was no longer their own, and they could no longer decide to move elsewhere. In this way, free people become what would later be called serfs.

Constantine, Christianity, and the Rise of Constantinople

The stress of the third century C.E. seemed to some emperors the punishment of the gods. Diocletian increased persecution of Christians, hoping that the gods would restore their blessing on Rome. Yet his persecutions were never very widespread or long-lived, and by the late third century most pagans accepted Christianity, even if they did not practice it. Constantine made this toleration official, legalizing the practice of Christianity throughout the empire in 312 and later being baptized as a Christian. He supported the church throughout his reign, expecting in return the support of church officials in maintaining order. Constantine also freed the clergy from imperial taxation and endowed the building of Christian churches. He allowed others to make gifts to the church as well, decreeing in 321 that "Every man, when dying, shall have the right to bequeath as much of his property as he desires to the holy and venerable Catholic Church. And such wills are not to be broken."[5] Constantine also declared Sunday a public holiday, choosing it over the Jewish holy

Gold Solidi of Constantine and Helena
These gold coins, issued in the fourth century by the emperor Constantine and his mother Helena, show the imperial figures in profile, surrounded by their names and shortened versions of their titles. Every Roman emperor issued coins, which served as means of exchange and also as transmitters of political propaganda. The front showed a carefully chosen portrait, and the reverse often depicted a recent victory or an abstract quality such as health or peace. Helena's ability to issue her own coins indicates her status in the imperial household. (Constantine: Yale University Art Gallery/ Art Resource, NY; Helena: Morelli Collection, Lugano, Switzerland/Visual Connection Archive)

day of Saturday because it fit with his own worship of the sun god, a practice shared by many Romans. Christians altered their practices to follow the emperor's decrees, and because of its favored position in the empire, Christianity slowly became the leading religion.

In time the Christian triumph would be complete. In 380 C.E. the emperor Theodosius (r. 379–395 C.E.) made Christianity the official religion of the Roman Empire. He allowed the church to establish its own courts and to use its own body of law, called "canon law." At that point Christians began to persecute the pagans for their religion. History had come full circle.

The acceptance of Christianity was not the only event that made Constantine's reign a turning point in Roman history. Constantine took the bold step of building a new capital for the empire. Constantinople, the New Rome, was constructed on the site of Byzantium, an old Greek city on the Bosporus, a strait on the boundary between Europe and Asia. Byzantium was chosen as the site of Constantinople for several reasons. First, it was in the eastern part of the empire, which was easier to defend than the western part and thus had escaped the worst of the barbarian devastation. Also, it was wealthy and its urban life still vibrant. Moreover, Christianity was more widespread in the East than in the West, and the city of Constantinople was intended to be a Christian center.

In his new capital Constantine built palaces, warehouses, public buildings, and even a hippodrome for horse racing, modeling them on Roman buildings. In addition, he built defensive works along the borders of the empire, trying hard to keep it together, as did his successors. Despite their efforts, the eastern and the western halves drifted apart throughout the fourth century.

CONNECTIONS

The Roman Empire, with its powerful—and sometimes bizarre—leaders, magnificent buildings, luxurious clothing, and bloody amusements, has long fascinated people. Politicians and historians have closely studied the reasons for its successes and have even more closely analyzed the weaknesses that led to its eventual collapse. Despite the efforts of emperors and other leaders, the Western Roman Empire slowly broke apart and by the fifth century no longer existed. By the fourteenth century European scholars were beginning to see the fall of the Roman Empire as one of the great turning points in Western history, the end of the classical era. That began the practice of dividing Western history into different periods—eventually, the ancient, medieval, and modern eras. Those categories still shape the way that Western history is taught and learned.

This three-part conceptualization also shapes the periodization of world history. As you saw in Chapter 4 and will see in Chapter 7, China is also understood to have had a classical age, and, as you will read in Chapter 11, the Maya of Mesoamerica did as well. The dates of these ages are different from those of the classical period in the Mediterranean, but there are striking similarities among all three places: successful large-scale administrative bureaucracies were established, trade flourished, cities grew, roads were built, and new cultural forms developed. In all three places—and in other countries described as having a classical era—this period was followed by an era of less prosperity and more warfare and destruction.

No large-scale story of rise and fall captures the experience of everyone, of course. For many people in the Roman world, neither the change from republic to empire nor the end of the empire altered their lives very much. They farmed or worked in cities, and hoped for the best for their families. They took in new ideas but blended them with old traditions. And for some, the judgment of later scholars that there was a pax Romana would have seemed a cruel joke. In a speech the Roman historian Tacitus put in the mouth of Calgacus, a leader of the Britons, right before a battle with Roman invaders of his homeland, "They make a desert and call it 'peace.'"[6]

□ CHAPTER REVIEW

□ How did the Romans come to dominate Italy, and what political institutions and changes did they bring about? (p. 144)

The Etruscans and Romans both settled in Italy, with the Etruscans establishing permanent settlements that evolved into cities resembling the Greek city-states. The Etruscans introduced Romans to urbanism, industry, trade, and the alphabet. Under Etruscan rule, the Romans prospered, making contact with the larger Mediterranean world, while the city of Rome continued to grow. In 509 B.C.E. the Romans won independence from Etruscan rule and continued to expand their territories. They also established a republic, which functioned through a shared government of the people directed by the senate, summarized by the expression SPQR — *senatus populusque Romanus*, meaning "the Roman senate and people." In the resolution to a social conflict known as the Struggle of the Orders, nobles and ordinary people created a state administered by magistrates elected from the entire population and established a uniform legal code.

□ How did Rome expand its power beyond Italy, and what were the effects of this success? (p. 149)

In a series of wars (most significantly, the Punic Wars) the Romans conquered the Mediterranean, creating an overseas empire that brought them unheard of power and wealth. Yet social unrest came in the wake of the war, opening unprecedented opportunities for ambitious generals who wanted to rule Rome like an empire. Civil war ensued, and it appeared as if the great politician and general Julius Caesar would emerge victorious, but he was assassinated by a group of senators. After his assassination and another period of civil war, his grandnephew Augustus finally restored peace and order to Rome. Augustus did not create a new office for himself but instead assumed control over many of the offices that traditionally had been held by separate people. His tenure clearly marked the end of the republic, and without specifically saying so, Augustus created the office of emperor. One of the most momentous aspects of his reign was the further expansion of Roman territories.

KEY TERMS

consuls (p. 147)
patricians (p. 147)
plebeians (p. 147)
senate (p. 148)
paterfamilias (p. 151)
manumission (p. 153)
pax Romana (p. 160)
pagan (p. 166)
bishop (p. 169)
heresy (p. 169)

□ How did efficient Roman rule lead to a period of prosperity and relative peace? (p. 160)

Augustus's success in creating solid political institutions was tested by the ineptness of some leaders who followed him, but later in the first century C.E. Rome entered a period of political stability, prosperity, and relative peace that lasted until the end of the second century C.E. During this period, later dubbed the pax Romana, the city of Rome became the magnificent capital of the empire, increasingly adorned with beautiful buildings and improved urban housing, and harboring a well-fed populace. To entertain the public, Roman rulers presented gladiatorial games and chariot racing. The Roman provinces and frontiers also saw extensive prosperity in the second century through the growth of agriculture, trade, and industry, among other factors. As the Roman Empire expanded eastward from Europe, it met opposition; yet even during the fighting, commerce among the Romans, the Parthians, and the Chinese empire thrived along a series of trade routes.

□ What was Christianity, and how did it affect life in the Roman Empire? (p. 166)

Christianity was a religion created by the followers of Jesus of Nazareth, a Jewish man who taught that belief in his divinity led to eternal life. His followers spread their belief across the empire, transforming Christianity from a Jewish sect into a new religion. Christian groups were informal at first, but by the second century they began to develop hierarchical institutions modeled on those of the Roman Empire. At first many pagans in the Roman Empire misunderstood Christian practices and rites, and they feared that the gods would withdraw their favor from the Roman Empire because of the Christian insistence that the pagan gods either did not exist or were evil spirits. As a result, Christians suffered sporadic persecution under certain Roman emperors. Gradually, however, tensions between pagans and Christians lessened, particularly as Christianity modified its teachings to make them more acceptable to wealthy and educated Romans.

◻ How did the emperors Diocletian and Constantine respond to the problems created by barbarian invasions and political turmoil in the third and fourth centuries? (p. 169)

The prosperity of the second century C.E. gave way in the third century to a period of civil war, barbarian invasions, and conflict with foreign armies. These disrupted agriculture, trade, and production and damaged the flow of taxes and troops. At the close of the third century the emperor Diocletian ended the period of chaos, in part because he recognized that the empire had become too great for one man to handle. He therefore divided it into a western and an eastern half, assuming direct control of the eastern part and giving a colleague the rule of the western part. Diocletian and his successor, Constantine, also took rigid control of the struggling economy, but their efforts were not successful. Free tenant farmers lost control of their lands, exchanging them for security that landlords offered against barbarians and other threats. Meanwhile, tolerance of Christianity grew, and Constantine legalized the practice of this religion throughout the empire. The symbol of all the changes in the empire became the establishment of its new capital, Constantinople, the new Rome.

SUGGESTED READING

Aldrete, Gregory S. *Daily Life in the Roman City*. 2004. Reveals the significance of ordinary Roman life in the city of Rome, its port Ostia, and Pompeii.

Canfora, Luciano. *Julius Caesar: The Life and Times of the People's Dictator*. 2007. Provides a new interpretation of Caesar that puts him fully in the context of his times.

Clark, Gillian. *Christianity and Roman Society*. 2004. Surveys the evolution of Christian life among Christians and with their pagan neighbors.

Evans, J. K. *War, Women, and Children in Ancient Rome*. 2000. Provides a concise survey of how war affected the home front in wartime.

Forsythe, Gary A. *A Critical History of Early Rome from Prehistory to the First Punic War*. 2005. Uses archaeological findings as well as written sources to examine the political, social, and religious developments of early Rome.

Goldsworthy, Adrian. *Roman Warfare*. 2000. A concise treatment of warfare from republican to imperial times.

Haynes, Sybille. *Etruscan Civilization: A Cultural History*. 2000. Deals with cultural history, with special emphasis on Etruscan women.

Holland, Tom. *Rubicon, the Triumph and Tragedy of the Roman Republic*. 2003. Gives a lively account of the disintegration of the republic from the Gracchi to Caesar's death.

Kyle, Donald G. *Sport and Spectacle in the Ancient World*. 2007. Deals in grim detail with the ritualized violence of the gladiatorial games.

MacMullen, R. *Roman Social Relations, 50 B.C.–A.D. 284*. 1981. Still an excellent discussion of the topic by a leading scholar.

Matz, David. *Daily Life of the Ancient Romans*. 2008. A brief but valuable account of the ordinary things in Roman life.

Scullard, H. H. *A History of the Roman World*. 4th ed. 1993. Still the best single account of Roman history.

Turcam, R. *The Gods of Ancient Rome*. 2000. Provides a concise survey of the Roman pantheon.

NOTES

1. Polybius, *Histories*, vol. 1, translated by Evelyn Shuckburgh (New York: Macmillan and Co., 1889), p. 469.
2. Sallust, *War with Cataline* 10.1–3, translated by John Buckler.
3. Virgil, *Aeneid*, translated by Theodore C. Williams (Boston: Houghton Mifflin, 1910).
4. Matthew 6: 19-21.
5. Maude Aline Huttman, ed. and trans., *The Establishment of Christianity and the Proscription of Paganism* (New York: AMS Press, 1967), p. 164.
6. Tacitus, *Agricola*, translated by A.R. Birley (Oxford: Oxford University Press, 1999), p. 22.

For practice quizzes and other study tools, visit the **Online Study Guide** at bedfordstmartins.com/mckayworld.

For primary sources from this period, see *Sources of World Societies*, **Second Edition**.

For Web sites, images, and documents related to topics in this chapter, visit **Make History** at bedfordstmartins.com/mckayworld.

• **Buddhist Monk** Buddhism became the religion of much of Asia in the period from 200 to 800 C.E. Art styles spread as well, with Buddhas, bodhisattvas, and monks depicted in both sculpture and painting. This statue of a monk is among the many that have survived in the cave temples of Dunhuang in northwest China. (Wang Lu/ChinaStock)

East Asia was transformed over the millennium from 221 B.C.E. to 800 C.E. At the beginning of this era, China had just been unified into a single state upon the Qin defeat of all the rival states of the Warring States Period, but it still faced major military challenges with the confederation of the nomadic Xiongnu to its north. At the time China was the only place in East Asia with writing, iron technology, large cities, and complex state organizations. Over the next several centuries East Asia changed dramatically as new states emerged. To protect an emerging trade in silk and other valuables, Han China sent armies far into Central Asia. War, trade, diplomacy, missionary activity, and the pursuit of learning led the Chinese to travel to distant lands and people from distant lands to go to China. Among the results were the spread of Buddhism from India and Central Asia to China and the adaptation of many elements of Chinese culture by near neighbors, especially Korea and Japan. Buddhism came to provide a common set of ideas and visual images to all of the cultures of East Asia, much the way Christianity linked societies in Europe.

Increased communication stimulated state formation among China's neighbors: Tibet, Korea, Manchuria, Vietnam, and Japan. Written Chinese was increasingly used as an international language by the ruling elites of these countries, and the new states usually adopted political models from China as well. By 800 C.E. each of these regions was well on its way to developing a distinct political and cultural identity. •

East Asia and the Spread of Buddhism

221 B.C.E.–800 C.E.

The Age of Empire in China: The Qin and Han Dynasties

□ What were the social, cultural, and political consequences of the unification of China under the strong centralized governments of the Qin and Han empires?

In much the same period in which Rome created a huge empire, the Qin and Han rulers in China created an empire on a similar scale. Like the Roman Empire (see Chapter 6), the Chinese empire was put together through force of arms and held in place by sophisticated centralized administrative machinery. The bureaucracies created by the Qin and Han empires affected many facets of Chinese social, cultural, and intellectual life.

The Qin Unification, 221–206 B.C.E.

In 221 B.C.E., after decades of constant warfare, Qin (chin), the state that had adopted Legalist policies during the Warring States Period (see page 110), succeeded in defeating the last of its rivals, and China was unified for the first time in many centuries. Deciding that the title *king* was not grand enough, the king of Qin invented the title emperor (*huangdi*). He called himself the First Emperor (*Shihuangdi*) in anticipation of a long line of successors. His state, however, did not long outlast him.

Once Qin ruled all of China, the First Emperor and his shrewd Legalist minister Li Si embarked on a sweeping program of centralization that touched the lives of nearly everyone in China. To cripple the nobility of the defunct states, who could have posed serious threats, the First Emperor ordered the nobles to leave their lands and move to the capital. The private possession of arms was outlawed to make it more difficult for subjects to rebel. The First Emperor dispatched officials to administer the territory that had been conquered and controlled the officials through a long list of regulations, reporting requirements, and penalties for inadequate performance. These officials owed their power and positions entirely to the favor of the em-

Army of the First Emperor The thousands of life-size ceramic soldiers buried in pits about a half mile from the First Emperor's tomb help us imagine the Qin military machine. It was the Qin emperor's concern with the afterlife that led him to construct such a lifelike guard. The soldiers were originally painted in bright colors, and they held real bronze weapons. (Robert Harding World Imagery)

peror and had no hereditary rights to their offices.

To harness the enormous human resources of his people, the First Emperor ordered a census of the population. Census information helped the imperial bureaucracy to plan its activities: to estimate the cost of public works, the tax revenues needed to pay for them, and the labor force available for military service and building projects. To make it easier to administer all regions uniformly, Chinese script was standardized, outlawing regional variations in the ways words were written. This standardization would prove to be one of the most significant contributions of the Qin Dynasty. The First Emperor also standardized weights, measures, coinage, and even the axle lengths of carts (important because roads became deeply rutted from carts' wheels). To make it easier for Qin armies to move rapidly, thousands of miles of roads were built. These achievements indirectly facilitated trade. Most of the labor on the projects came from drafted farmers or convicts working out their sentences.

Some twentieth-century Chinese historians have glorified the First Emperor as a bold conqueror who let no obstacle stop him, but the traditional evaluation was almost entirely negative. For centuries Chinese historians castigated him as a cruel, arbitrary, impetuous, suspicious, and superstitious megalomaniac. Hundreds of thousands of subjects were drafted to build the **Great Wall** (ca. 230–208 B.C.E.), a rammed-earth fortification along the northern border between the Qin realm and the land controlled by the nomadic Xiongnu. After Li Si complained that scholars (especially Confucians) used records of the past to denigrate the emperor's achievements and undermine popular support, the emperor had all writings other than useful manuals on topics such as agriculture, medicine, and divination collected and burned. As a result of this massive book burning, many ancient texts were lost.

Assassins tried to kill the First Emperor three times, and perhaps as a consequence he became obsessed with discovering the secrets of immortality. He spent lavishly on a tomb designed to protect him in the

□ CHRONOLOGY

ca. 230–208 B.C.E. Construction of Great Wall

221 B.C.E. China unified under Qin Dynasty

206 B.C.E.–220 C.E. Han Dynasty

145–ca. 85 B.C.E. Sima Qian, Chinese historian

114 B.C.E. Han government gains control over Silk Road trade routes across Central Asia

111 B.C.E. Emperor Wu conquers Nam Viet

108 B.C.E. Han government establishes colonies in Korea

105 C.E. Chinese invention of paper

ca. 200 C.E. Buddhism begins rapid growth in China

220–589 C.E. Age of Division in China

313–668 C.E. Three Kingdoms Period in Korea

372 C.E. Buddhism introduced in Korea

538 C.E. Buddhism introduced in Japan

581–618 C.E. Sui Dynasty

604 C.E. Prince Shōtoku introduces Chinese-style government in Japan

605 C.E. Introduction of merit-based examination system for the selection of officials in China

618–907 C.E. Tang Dynasty; great age of Chinese poetry

668 C.E. First political unification of Korea under Silla

690 C.E. Empress Wu declares herself emperor, becoming the only Chinese woman emperor

710 C.E. Nara made the capital of Japan

735–737 C.E. Smallpox epidemic in Japan

845 C.E. Tang emperor begins persecution of Buddhism

afterlife. Although the central chambers have not yet been excavated, in nearby pits archaeologists have unearthed thousands of life-size terra-cotta figures of armed soldiers and horses lined up to protect him.

Like Ashoka in India a few decades earlier (see page 84), the First Emperor erected many stone inscriptions to inform his subjects of his goals and accomplishments. He had none of Ashoka's modesty,

• **Great Wall** A rammed-earth fortification built along the northern border of China during the reign of the First Emperor.

however. On one stone he described the conquest of the other states this way:

> The six states, insatiable and perverse, would not make an end of slaughter, until, pitying the people, the emperor sent troops to punish the wicked and display his might. His penalties were just, his actions true, his power spread far, all submitted to his rule. He wiped out tyrants, rescued the common people, brought peace to the four corners of the earth. His enlightened laws spread far and wide as examples to All Under Heaven until the end of time. Great is he indeed! The whole universe obeys his sagacious will; his subjects praise his achievements and have asked to inscribe them on stone for posterity.[1]

After the First Emperor died in 210 B.C.E., the Qin state unraveled. The Legalist institutions designed to concentrate power in the hands of the ruler made the stability of the government dependent on his strength and character, and his heir proved ineffective. The heir was murdered by his younger brother, and uprisings soon followed.

The Han Dynasty, 206 B.C.E.–220 C.E.

The eventual victor in the struggle for power that ensued in the wake of the collapse of the Qin Dynasty was Liu Bang, known in history as Emperor Gaozu (r. 202–195 B.C.E.). The First Emperor of Qin was from the Zhou aristocracy. Gaozu was, by contrast, from a modest family of commoners, so his elevation to emperor is evidence of how thoroughly the Qin Dynasty had destroyed the old order.

Gaozu did not disband the centralized government created by the Qin, but he did remove its most unpopular features. Harsh laws were canceled, taxes were sharply reduced, and a policy of noninterference was adopted in an effort to promote economic recovery. With policies of this sort, relative peace, and the extension of China's frontiers, the Chinese population grew rapidly in the first two centuries of the Han Dynasty (Map 7.1). The census of 2 C.E. recorded a population of 58 million, the earliest indication of the large size of China's population. Few other societies kept as good records, making comparisons difficult, but high-end estimates for the Roman Empire are in a similar range (50–70 million).

The Han government was largely supported by the taxes and forced labor demanded of farmers, but this revenue regularly fell short of the government's needs. To pay for his military campaigns, Emperor Wu, the

"Martial Emperor" (r. 141–87 B.C.E.), took over the minting of coins, confiscated the land of nobles, sold offices and titles, and increased taxes on private businesses. A widespread suspicion of commerce as an unproductive exploitation of the true producers made it easy to levy especially heavy assessments on merchants. The worst blow to businessmen, however, was the government's decision to enter into market competition with them by selling the commodities that had been collected as taxes. In 119 B.C.E. government monopolies were established in the production of iron, salt, and liquor. These enterprises had previously been sources of great profit for private entrepreneurs. Large-scale grain dealing also had been a profitable business, and the government now took that over as well. Grain was to be bought where it was plentiful and its price low and to be either stored in granaries or transported to areas of scarcity. This procedure was supposed to eliminate speculation in grain, provide more constant prices, and bring profit to the government.

Han Intellectual and Cultural Life

In contrast to the Qin Dynasty, which favored Legalism, the Han came to promote Confucianism and recruit officials on the basis of their Confucian learning or Confucian moral qualities. The Han government's efforts to recruit men trained in the Confucian classics marked the beginning of the Confucian scholar-official system, one of the most distinctive features of imperial China.

Under the most activist of the Han emperors, Emperor Wu, Confucian scholars were given a privileged position. Confucian officials did not always please Emperor Wu and other emperors. Seeing criticism of the government as one of their duties, the officials tried to check abuse of power. Their willingness to stand up to the ruler also reflected the fact that most of the Confucian scholars selected to serve as officials came from landholding families, much like those who staffed the Roman government, which gave them some economic independence.

The Confucianism that made a comeback during the Han Dynasty was a changed Confucianism. Although Confucian texts had fed the First Emperor's bonfires, some dedicated scholars had hidden their books, and others had memorized whole works: one ninety-year-old man was able to recite two long books almost in their entirety. The ancient books recovered in this way—called the **Confucian classics**—were revered as repositories of the wisdom of the past. Confucian scholars treated these classics with piety and attempted to make them more useful as sources of moral guidance by writing commentaries on them. Many Confucian scholars specialized in a single classic, and teachers passed on to their disciples their understanding of

• **Confucian classics** The ancient texts recovered during the Han Dynasty that Confucian scholars treated as sacred scriptures.

each sentence in the work. Other Han Confucians went to the opposite extreme, developing comprehensive cosmological theories that explained the world in terms of cyclical flows of yin and yang (see page 111) and the five phases (fire, water, earth, metal, and wood). Some used these theories to elevate the role of the emperor, who alone had the capacity to link the realms of Heaven, earth, and man. Natural disasters such as floods or earthquakes were viewed as portents that the emperor had failed in his role of maintaining the proper balance among the forces of Heaven and earth.

Han art and literature reveal a fascination with omens, portents, spirits, immortals, and occult forces. Emperor Wu tried to make contact with the world of

gods and immortals through elaborate sacrificial offerings of food and wine, and he welcomed astrologers, alchemists, seers, and shamans to his court. He marveled at stories of deities such as the Queen Mother of the West and the Yellow Emperor, who had taken his entire court with him when he ascended to the realm of the immortals. Much of this interest in immortality and communicating with the spirit world was absorbed into the emerging religion of Daoism, which also drew on the philosophical ideas of Laozi and Zhuangzi (see pages 107–110).

A major intellectual accomplishment of the Han Dynasty was history writing. Sima Qian (145–ca. 85 B.C.E.) wrote a comprehensive history of China from the time

MAP 7.1 The Han Empire, 206 B.C.E.–270 C.E. The Han Dynasty asserted sovereignty over vast regions from Korea in the east to Central Asia in the west and Vietnam in the south. Once garrisons were established, traders were quick to follow, leading to considerable spread of Chinese material culture in East Asia. Chinese goods, especially silk, were in demand far beyond East Asia, promoting long-distance trade across Eurasia.

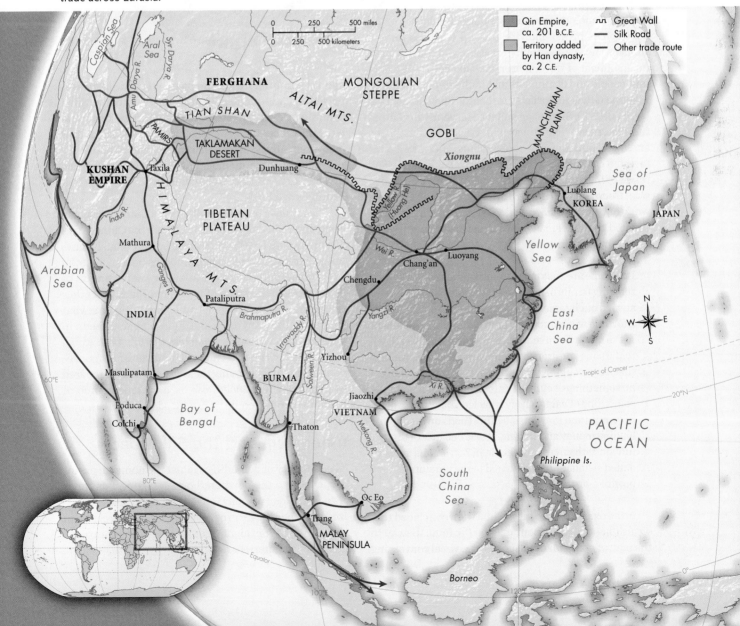

Bronze Mirror The back side of a bronze mirror was frequently decorated with images of deities and animals and with auspicious words. As the viewer turned the mirror, he saw different scenes. This Han mirror features an outer border with semicircles decorated with cloud patterns and squares with words written on them. In the center are deities. (Mirror Featuring Deities and Kings in Three Sections Surrounded by Rings of Squares and Semicircles. China, Eastern Han dynasty [25–220], late 2nd–early 3rd century. Bronze; diameter 13.9 cm. The Cleveland Museum of Art. Gift of Drs. Thomas and Martha Carter in Honor of Sherman E. Lee 1995.328)

of the mythical sage-kings of high antiquity to his own day, dividing his account into a chronology recounting political events, biographies of key individuals, and treatises on subjects such as geography, taxation, and court rituals. As an official of the emperor, he had access to important people and documents and to the imperial library. Like the Greek historians Herodotus and Thucydides (see page 123), Sima Qian believed fervently in visiting the sites where history was made, examining artifacts, and questioning people about events. He was also interested in China's geography and local history. The result of his research, ten years or more in the making, was **Records of the Grand Historian**, a massive work of literary and historical genius. In the chapter devoted to moneymakers, he described how the Ping family made its fortune:

> Lu people are customarily cautious and miserly, but the Ping family of Cao were particularly so. They started out by smelting iron and in time accumulated a fortune of a hundred million cash. All the members of the family from the father and elder brothers down to the sons and grandsons, however, made a promise that they would "Never look down without picking up something useful; never look up without grabbing something of value." They traveled about to all the provinces and kingdoms, selling goods on credit, lending money and trading. It was because of their influence that so many people in Zou and Lu abandoned scholarship and turned to the pursuit of profit.[2]

From examples like these Sima Qian concluded that wealth has no permanent master: "It finds its way to the man of ability like the spokes of a wheel converging upon the hub, and from the hands of the worthless it falls like shattered tiles."[3] For centuries to come, Sima Qian's work set the standard for Chinese historical writing, although most of the histories modeled after it covered only a single dynasty. The first of these was the work of three members of the Ban family in the first century C.E. (See "Individuals in Society: The Ban Family," page 186.)

The circulation of books like Sima Qian's was made easier by the invention of paper, which the Chinese traditionally date to 105 C.E. Scribes had previously written on strips of bamboo and wood or rolls of silk. Cai Lun, to whom the Chinese attribute the invention of paper, worked the fibers of rags, hemp, bark, and other scraps into sheets of paper. Paper, thus, was somewhat similar to the papyrus made from pounded reeds in ancient Egypt. Though much less durable than wood, paper was far cheaper than silk and became a convenient means of conveying the written word. Compared to papyrus, it depended less on a specific source of plant fiber and so could be produced many places.

Inner Asia and the Silk Road

The difficulty of defending against the nomadic pastoral peoples to the north in the region known as Inner Asia is a major reason China came to favor a centralized bureaucratic form of government. Resources from the entire subcontinent were needed to maintain control of the northern border.

Beginning long before the Han Dynasty, China's contacts with its northern neighbors had involved both trade and military conflict. China's neighbors sought Chinese products such as silk and lacquer ware. When they did not have goods to trade or when trading relations were disrupted, raiding was considered an acceptable alternative in the tribal cultures of the region. Chinese sources speak of defending against raids of "barbarians" from Shang times (ca. 1500–ca. 1050 B.C.E.) on, but not until the rise of nomadism in the mid-Zhou period (fifth to fourth centuries B.C.E.) did the horsemen of the north become China's main threat.

The economy of these nomads was based on raising sheep, goats, camels, and horses. Families lived in tents that could be taken down and moved north in summer and south in winter when groups of families moved in search of pasture. Herds were tended on horseback, and everyone learned to ride from a young age. Especially awesome from the Chinese perspective was the ability of nomad horsemen to shoot arrows while riding horseback. The typical social structure of the steppe nomads was fluid, with family and clan units linked through loyalty to tribal chiefs selected for their military prowess. Charismatic tribal leaders could form large coalitions and mobilize the entire society for war.

Chinese farmers and Inner Asian herders had such different modes of life that it is not surprising that they had little respect for each other. For most of the imperial period, Chinese farmers looked on the northern non-Chinese horsemen as gangs of bullies who thought robbing was easier than working for a living. The nomads identified glory with military might and viewed farmers as contemptible weaklings.

In the late third century B.C.E. the Xiongnu (known in the West as the Huns) formed the first great confederation of nomadic tribes (see Map 7.1). The Qin's Great Wall was built to defend against them, and the Qin sent out huge armies in pursuit of them. The early Han emperors tried to make peace with them, offering generous gifts of silk, rice, cash, and even imperial princesses as brides. But these policies were controversial, since critics thought they merely strengthened the enemy. Xiongnu power did not decline, and in 166 B.C.E. 140,000 Xiongnu raided to within a hundred miles of the Chinese capital.

Emperor Wu decided that China had to push the Xiongnu back. He sent several armies of 100,000 to 300,000 troops deep into Xiongnu territory. These costly campaigns were of limited value because the Xiongnu were a moving target: fighting nomads was not like attacking walled cities. If the Xiongnu did not want to fight the Chinese troops, they simply moved their camps. To try to find allies and horses, Emperor Wu turned his attention west, toward Central Asia. From the envoy he sent into Bactria, Parthia, and Ferghana in 139 B.C.E., the Chinese learned for the first time of other civilized states comparable to China (see Map 7.1). The envoy described Ferghana as an urban society 10,000 *li* (about 3,000 miles) west of China, where grapes were grown for wine and the horses were particularly fine. In Parthia he was impressed by the use of silver coins stamped with the image of the king's face. These regions, he reported, were familiar with Chinese products, especially silk, and did a brisk trade in them.

In 114 B.C.E. Emperor Wu sent an army into Ferghana and gained recognition of Chinese overlordship in the area, thus obtaining control over the trade routes across Central Asia commonly called the **Silk Road** (see Map 7.1). The city-states along this route did not resist the Chinese presence. They could carry out the trade on which they depended more conveniently with Chinese garrisons to protect them than with rival tribes raiding them.

Xiongnu Metalwork The metal ornaments of the Xiongnu provide convincing evidence that they were in contact with nomadic pastoralists farther west in Asia, such as the Scythians, who also fashioned metal plaques and buckles in animal designs. This buckle or ornament is made of gold and is about 3 inches tall. (Image copyright © The Metropolitan Museum of Art/Art Resource, NY)

- **Records of the Grand Historian** A comprehensive history of China written by Sima Qian.
- **Silk Road** The trade routes across Central Asia through which Chinese silk and other items were traded.

> "If a country possesses a wealth of fertile land and yet its people are underfed, the reason is that merchants and workers have prospered while agriculture has been neglected."

CONFUCIAN SCHOLAR, 81 B.C.E.

At the same time, Emperor Wu sent troops into northern Korea to establish military districts that would flank the Xiongnu on their eastern border. By 111 B.C.E. the Han government also had extended its rule south into Nam Viet, which extended from south China into what is now northern Vietnam. Thus during Emperor Wu's reign, the territorial reach of the Han state was vastly extended.

During the Han Dynasty China developed a **tributary system** to regulate contact with foreign powers. States and tribes beyond its borders sent envoys bearing gifts and received gifts in return. Over the course of the dynasty the Han government's outlay on these gifts was huge, perhaps as much as 10 percent of state revenue. In 25 B.C.E., for instance, the government gave tributary states twenty thousand rolls of silk cloth and about twenty thousand pounds of silk floss. Although the tributary system was a financial burden to the Chinese, it reduced the cost of defense and offered China confirmation that it was the center of the civilized world.

The silk given to the Xiongnu and other northern tributaries often entered the trading networks of Sogdian, Parthian, and Indian merchants, who carried it by caravans across Asia. There was a market both for skeins of silk thread and for silk cloth woven in Chinese or Syrian workshops. Caravans returning to China carried gold, horses, and occasionally handicrafts of West Asian origin, such as glass beads and cups. Through the trade along the Silk Road, the Chinese learned of new foodstuffs, including walnuts, pomegranates, sesame, and coriander, all of which came

to be grown in China. This trade was largely carried by the two-humped Bactrian camel, which had been bred in Central Asia since the first century B.C.E. With a heavy coat of hair to withstand the bitter cold of winter, each camel could carry about five hundred pounds of cargo. (See "Global Trade: Silk," page 184.)

Maintaining a military presence so far from the center of China was expensive. To cut costs, the government set up self-supporting military colonies, recruited Xiongnu tribes to serve as auxiliary forces, and established vast government horse farms. Still, military expenses threatened to bankrupt the Han government.

Life in Han China

How were ordinary people's lives affected by the creation of a huge Han bureaucratic empire? The lucky ones who lived in Chang'an or Luoyang, the great cities of the empire, got to enjoy the material benefits of increased long-distance trade and a boom in the production of luxury goods.

The government did not promote trade per se. The Confucian elite, like ancient Hebrew wise men, considered trade necessary but lowly. Agriculture and crafts were more honorable because they produced something, but merchants merely took advantage of others' shortages to make profits as middlemen. In a debate conducted in 81 B.C.E., the Confucian scholars argued that "If a country possesses a wealth of fertile land and yet its people are underfed, the reason is that merchants and workers have prospered while agriculture has been neglected."[4] This attitude justified the government's takeover of the grain,

Ceramic Model of a Pigsty Chinese farmers regularly raised pigs, keeping them in walled-off pens and feeding them scraps. This Han Dynasty model of such a pigsty was placed in a tomb to represent the material goods one hoped the deceased would enjoy in the afterlife. (The Minneapolis Institute of Arts, Gift of Alan and Dena Naylor in memory of Thomas E. Leary)

iron, and salt businesses. Still, the government indirectly promoted commerce by building cities and roads.

Markets were the liveliest places in the cities. Besides stalls selling goods of all kinds, markets offered fortune-tellers and entertainers. People flocked to puppet shows and performances of jugglers and acrobats. The markets also were used for the execution of criminals, to serve as a warning to onlookers.

Government patronage helped maintain the quality of craftsmanship in the cities. By the beginning of the first century C.E. China also had about fifty state-run ironworking factories. Chinese metalworking was the most advanced in the world at the time. In contrast to Roman blacksmiths, who hammered heated iron to make wrought iron tools, the Chinese knew how to liquefy iron and pour it into molds, producing tools with a higher carbon content that were harder and more durable. Han workmen turned out iron plowshares, agricultural tools with wooden handles, and weapons and armor.

Iron was replacing bronze in tools, but bronzeworkers still turned out a host of goods. Bronze was prized for jewelry, mirrors, and dishes. Bronze was also used for minting coins and for precision tools such as carpenters' rules and adjustable wrenches. Surviving bronze gear-and-cog wheels bear eloquent testimony to the sophistication of Han machinery. Han metalsmiths were mass-producing superb crossbows long before the crossbow was dreamed of in Europe.

The bulk of the population in Han times and even into the twentieth century consisted of peasants living in villages of a few hundred households. Because the Han empire, much like the contemporaneous Roman Empire, drew its strength from a large population of free peasants who contributed both taxes and labor services to the state, the government had to try to keep peasants independent and productive. The economic insecurity of smallholders was described by one official in 178 B.C.E. in terms that could well have been repeated in most later dynasties:

> They labour at plowing in the spring and hoeing in the summer, harvesting in the autumn and storing foodstuff in winter, cutting wood, performing labour service for the local government, all the while exposed to the dust of spring, the heat of summer, the storms of autumn, and the chill of winter. Through all four seasons they never get a day off. They need funds to cover such obligations as entertaining guests, burying the dead, visiting the sick, caring for orphans, and bringing up the young. No matter how hard they work they can be ruined by floods or droughts, or cruel and arbitrary officials who impose taxes at the wrong times or keep changing their orders. When taxes fall due, those with produce have to sell it at half price [to raise the needed cash], and those without [anything to sell] have to borrow [at such high rates] they will have to pay back twice what they borrowed. Some as a consequence sell their lands and houses, even their children and grandchildren.[5]

To fight peasant poverty, the government kept land taxes low (one-thirtieth of the harvest), provided relief in time of famine, and promoted up-to-date agricultural methods. Still, many hard-pressed peasants were left to choose between migration to areas where new lands could be opened and quasi-servile status as the dependents of a magnate. Throughout the Han period Chinese farmers in search of land to till pushed into frontier areas, expanding Chinese domination at the expense of other ethnic groups, especially in central and south China.

The Chinese family in Han times was much like the Roman (see page 151) and the Indian (see page 72) families. In all three societies senior males had great authority, marriages were arranged by parents, and brides normally joined their husbands' families. Other practices were more distinctive to China, such as the universality of patrilineal family names, the practice of dividing land equally among the sons in a family, and the great emphasis placed on the virtue of filial piety. The brief *Classic of Filial Piety*, which claimed that filial piety was the root of all virtue, gained wide circulation in Han times. The virtues of loyal wives and devoted mothers were extolled in the *Biographies of Exemplary Women*, which told the stories of women from China's past who were notable for giving their husbands good advice, knowing how to educate their sons, and sacrificing themselves when forced to choose between their fathers and husbands. The book also contained a few cautionary tales of scheming, jealous, manipulative women who brought destruction to all around them. One of the most commonly used texts for the education of women is Ban Zhao's *Admonitions for Women*, in which she extols the feminine virtues, such as humility. (See "Individuals in Society: The Ban Family," page 186.)

China and Rome

The empires of China and Rome (discussed in Chapter 6) were large, complex states governed by monarchs, bureaucracies, and standing armies. Both reached

---

• **tributary system** A system first established during the Han Dynasty to regulate contact with foreign powers. States and tribes beyond its borders sent envoys bearing gifts and received gifts in return.

Global Trade

Silk was one of the earliest commodities to stimulate international trade. By 2500 B.C.E. Chinese farmers had domesticated *Bombyx mori*, the Chinese silkworm, and by 1000 B.C.E. they were making fine fabrics with complex designs. Sericulture (silk making) is labor-intensive. In order for silkworms to spin their cocoons, they have to be fed chopped leaves from mulberry trees every few hours, day and night, during the month between hatching and spinning. The cocoons consist of a single filament several thousand feet long but a minuscule 0.025 millimeter thick. More than two thousand cocoons are needed to make a pound of silk. After the cocoons are boiled to loosen the natural gum that binds the filament, several strands of filament are twisted together to make yarns.

What made silk the most valued of all textiles was its beauty and versatility. It could be made into sheer gauzes, shiny satins, multicolored brocades, and plush velvets. Fine Han silks have been found in Xiongnu tombs in northern Mongolia. Korea and Japan not only imported silk but also began silk production themselves, and silk came to be used in both places in much the way it was used in China—for the clothes of the elite, for temple banners, and as a surface for writing and painting. Central Asia, Persia, India, and Southeast Asia also became producers of silk in distinctive local styles. Lacking suitable climates to produce silk, Mongolia and Tibet remained major importers of Chinese silks into modern times.

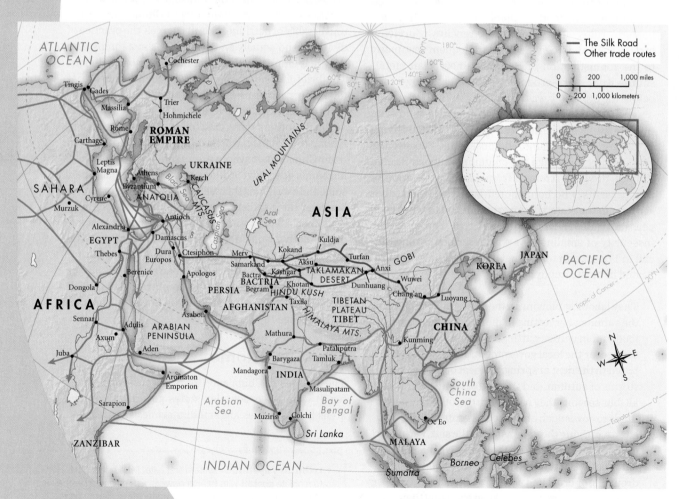

MAP 7.2 The Silk Trade in the Seventh Century C.E.

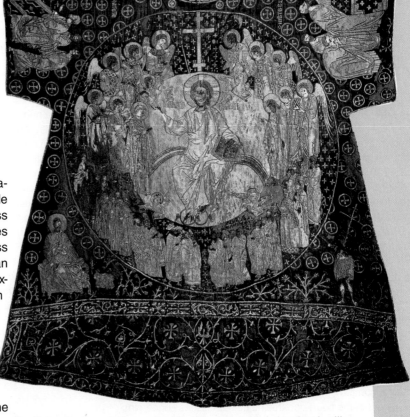

Designed to be worn by a priest in the Eastern Orthodox Church, this fourteenth-century silk garment is embellished with silver- and silver-gilt-covered threads. It was probably made in Constantinople, though the silk floss may well have been imported, perhaps from Syria or Persia. (Courtesy, Library of the Chapter of St. Peter and the Museum of the Treasury, Vatican City)

What makes the silk trade famous, however, is not the trade within Asia but the trade across Asia to Europe. In Roman times silk carried by caravans across Asia or by ships across the Indian Ocean became a high-status luxury item, said to cost its weight in gold. To satisfy Roman taste, imported silk fabrics were unraveled and rewoven in Syrian workshops. Although the techniques of sericulture gradually spread through Asia, they remained a mystery in the West until the Byzantine emperor Justinian in the sixth century had two monks bring back silkworms from China along with knowledge of how to care for them and process their cocoons.

In medieval times most of the silk imported into Europe came from Persia, the Byzantine Empire, or the Arab world. Venetian merchants handled much of the trade. Some of this fabric still survives in ancient churches, where it was used for vestments and altar clothes and to wrap relics. In the eleventh century Roger I, king of Sicily, captured groups of silk-workers from Athens and Corinth and moved them to Sicily, initiating the production of silk in western Europe. Over the next couple of centuries, Italy became a major silk producer, joined by France in the fifteenth century.

When the Venetian merchant Marco Polo traveled across Asia in the late thirteenth century, he found local silk for sale in Baghdad, Georgia, Persia, and elsewhere, but China remained the largest producer. He claimed that more than a thousand cartloads of silk were brought into the capital of China every day.

With the development of the sea route between western Europe and China from the sixteenth century on, Europe began importing large quantities of Chinese silk, much of it as silk floss—raw silk—to supply Italian, French, and English silk weavers. In 1750 almost 77.2 tons of raw silk and nearly 20,000 bolts of silk cloth were carried from China to Europe. By this period the aristocracy of Europe regularly wore silk clothes, including silk stockings.

Mechanization of silkmaking began in Europe in the seventeenth century. The Italians developed machines to "throw" the silk—doubling and twisting raw silk into threads suitable for weaving. In the early nineteenth century the introduction of Jacquard looms using punched cards made complex patterns easier to weave.

In the 1920s the silk industry was hit hard by the introduction of synthetic fibers, especially rayon and nylon. In the 1940s women in the United States and Europe switched from silk stockings to the much less expensive nylon stockings. European production of silk almost entirely collapsed. After China reentered world trade in the early 1980s China rapidly expanded its silk production for export. By 2003 there were more than two thousand silk enterprises in China, employing a million workers and supplying 80 percent of the total world trade in silk.

Individuals in Society

The Ban Family

BAN BIAO (3–54 c.e.), A SUCCESSFUL OFFICIAL from a family with an envied library, had three highly accomplished children: his twin sons, the general Ban Chao (32–102) and the historian Ban Gu (32–92), and his daughter, Ban Zhao (ca. 45–120). After distinguishing himself as a junior officer in campaigns against the Xiongnu, Ban Chao was sent in 73 c.e. to the Western Regions to see about the possibility of restoring Chinese overlordship there, lost several decades earlier. Ban Chao spent most of the next three decades in Central Asia. Through patient diplomacy and a show of force, he re-established Chinese control over the oasis cities of Central Asia, and in 92 he was appointed protector general of the area.

His twin brother Ban Gu was one of the most accomplished writers of his age, excelling in a distinctive literary form known as the rhapsody *(fu)*. His "Rhapsody on the Two Capitals" is in the form of a dialogue between a guest from Chang'an and his host in Luoyang. It describes the palaces, spectacles, scenic spots, local products, and customs of the two great cities. Emperor Zhang (r. 76–88) was fond of literature and often had Ban Gu accompany him on hunts or travels. He also had him edit a record of the court debates he held on issues concerning the Confucian classics.

Ban Biao was working on the *History of the Western Former Han Dynasty*, when he died in 54. Ban Gu took over this project, modeling it on Sima Qian's *Records of the Grand Historian*. He added treatises on law, geography, and bibliography, the last a classified list of books in the imperial library.

Because of his connection to a general out of favor, Ban Gu was sent to prison in 92, where he soon died. At that time the *History of the Former Han Dynasty* was still incomplete. The emperor called on Ban Gu's widowed sister, Ban Zhao, to finish it. She came to the palace, where she not only worked on the history but also became a teacher of the women of the palace. According to the *History of the Later Han*, she taught them the classics, history, astronomy, and mathematics. In 106 an infant succeeded to the throne, and the widow of an earlier emperor became regent. This empress frequently turned to Ban Zhao for advice on government policies.

Ban Zhao credited her own education to her learned father and cultured mother and became an advocate of the education of girls. In her *Admonitions for Women* Ban Zhao objected that many families taught their sons to read but not their daughters. She did not claim girls should have the same education as boys; after all, "just as yin and yang differ, men and women have different characteristics." Women, she wrote, will do well if they cultivate the womanly virtues such as humility. "Humility means yielding and acting respectful, putting others first and oneself last, never mentioning one's own good deeds or denying one's own faults, enduring insults and bearing with mistreatment, all with due trepidation."* In subsequent centuries Ban Zhao's *Admonitions* became one of the most commonly used texts for the education of Chinese girls.

QUESTIONS FOR ANALYSIS

1. What inferences can you draw from the fact that a leading general had a brother who was a literary man?
2. What does Ban Zhao's life tell us about women in her society? How do you reconcile her personal accomplishments with the advice she gave for women's education?

*Patricia Buckley Ebrey, ed., *Chinese Civilization: A Sourcebook*, rev. ed. (New York: Free Press, 1993), p. 75.

• **Ban Zhao continued to be considered the ideal woman teacher into the eighteenth century, when this imaginary portrait depicted her taking up her brush among women and children.** (National Palace Museum, Taipei, Taiwan)

directly to the people through taxation and conscription policies, and both invested in infrastructure such as roads and waterworks. The empires faced the similar challenge of having to work hard to keep land from becoming too concentrated in the hands of hard-to-tax wealthy magnates. In both empires people in neighboring areas that came under political domination were attracted to the conquerors' material goods, productive techniques, and other cultural products, resulting in gradual cultural assimilation. China and Rome also had similar frontier problems and tried similar solutions, such as recruiting "barbarian" soldiers and settling soldier-colonists.

Nevertheless, the differences between Rome and Han China are worth as much notice as the similarities. The Roman Empire was linguistically and culturally more diverse than China. In China there was only one written language; people in the Roman Empire still wrote in Greek and several other languages, and people in the eastern Mediterranean could claim more ancient civilizations. China did not have comparable cultural rivals. Politically the dynastic principle was stronger in China than in Rome. Han emperors were never chosen by the army or by any institution comparable to the Roman senate, nor were there republican ideals in China. In contrast to the graduated forms of citizenship in Rome, Han China drew no distinctions between original and added territories. The social and economic structures also differed in the two empires. Slavery was much more important in Rome than in China, and merchants were more favored. Over time these differences put Chinese and Roman social and political development on different trajectories.

The Fall of the Han and the Age of Division

In the second century C.E. the Han government suffered a series of blows. A succession of child emperors required regents to rule in their place until they reached maturity, allowing the families of empresses to dominate the court. Emperors, once grown, turned to **eunuchs** (castrated palace servants) for help in ousting the empresses' families, only to find that the eunuchs were just as difficult to control. In 166 and 169 scholars who had denounced the eunuchs were arrested, killed, or banished from the capital and official life. Then in 184 a millenarian religious sect rose in massive revolt. The armies raised to suppress the rebels soon took to fighting among themselves. In 189 one general slaughtered two thousand eunuchs in the palace and took the Han emperor captive. After years of fighting, a stalemate was reached, with three warlords each controlling distinct territories in the north, the southeast, and the southwest. In 220 one of them

forced the last of the Han emperors to abdicate, formally ending the Han Dynasty.

The period after the fall of the Han Dynasty is often referred to as the **Age of Division** (220–589). A brief reunification from 280 to 316 came to an end when non-Chinese who had been settling in north China since Han times seized the opportunity afforded by the political turmoil to take power. For the next two and a half centuries north China was ruled by one or more non-Chinese dynasties (the Northern Dynasties), and the south was ruled by a sequence of four short-lived Chinese dynasties (the Southern Dynasties) centered in the area of the present-day city of Nanjing.

In the south a hereditary aristocracy entrenched itself in the higher reaches of officialdom. These families intermarried only with families of equivalent pedigree and compiled lists and genealogies of the most eminent families. They saw themselves as maintaining the high culture of the Han and looked on the emperors of the successive dynasties as upstarts — as military men rather than men of culture. In this aristocratic culture, the arts of poetry and calligraphy flourished, and people began collecting writings by famous calligraphers.

Establishing the capital at Nanjing, south of the Yangzi River, had a beneficial effect on the economic development of the south. To pay for an army and to support the imperial court and aristocracy in a style that matched their pretensions, the government had to expand the area of taxable agricultural land, whether by settling migrants or converting the local inhabitants into taxpayers. The south, with its temperate climate and ample supply of water, offered nearly unlimited possibilities for such development.

The Northern Dynasties are interesting as the first case of alien rule in China. Ethnic tensions flared from time to time. In the late fifth century the Northern Wei (way) Dynasty (386–534) moved the capital from near the Great Wall to the ancient city of Luoyang, adopted Chinese-style clothing, and made Chinese the official language. But the armies remained in the hands of the Xianbei tribesmen. Soldiers who saw themselves as marginalized by the pro-Chinese reforms rebelled in 524. For the next fifty years north China was torn apart by struggles for power. It had long been the custom of the northern pastoral tribes to enslave those they captured; sometimes the residents of entire cities were enslaved. In 554, when the city of Jiangling was taken, a hundred thousand civilians were enslaved and distributed to generals and officials.

- **eunuchs** Castrated males who played an important role as palace servants.
- **Age of Division** The period after the fall of the Han Dynasty, when China was politically divided.

The Spread of Buddhism Out of India

☐ How did Buddhism find its way into East Asia, and what was its appeal and impact?

In much the same period that Christianity was spreading out of its original home in ancient Israel, Buddhism was spreading beyond India. Buddhism came to Central, East, and Southeast Asia with merchants and missionaries along the overland Silk Road, by sea from India and Sri Lanka, and also through Tibet. Like Christianity, Buddhism was shaped by its contact with cultures in the different areas into which it spread, leading to several distinct forms.

Buddhism's Path Through Central Asia

Central Asia is a loose term used to refer to the vast area between the ancient civilizations of Persia, India, and China. Modern political borders are a product of competition for empire among the British, Russians, and Chinese in the mid-nineteenth century and have relatively little to do with the earlier history of the region. Through most of recorded history, the region was ethnically and culturally diverse; it was home to urban centers, especially at the oases along the Silk Road, and to animal herders in the mountains and grasslands.

Under Ashoka in India (see pages 84–85) Buddhism began to spread to Central Asia. This continued under the Kushan empire (ca. 50–250 C.E.), especially under the greatest Kushan king Kanishka I (ca. 100 C.E.). In this region, where the influence of Greek art was strong, artists began to depict the Buddha in human form. Over the next several centuries most of the city-states of Central Asia became centers of Buddhism, from Bamiyan northwest of Kabul, to Kucha, Khotan, Loulan, Turfan, and Dunhuang (Map 7.3). Because the remarkable Buddhist civilization of Central Asia was later supplanted by Islam, it was not until early in the twentieth century that European archaeologists discovered its traces. The main sites yielded not only numerous Buddhist paintings but also thousands of texts in a variety of languages. In Khotan, for instance, an Indian language was used for administrative purposes long after the fall of the Kushan empire. Other texts were in various Persian languages, showing the cultural mix of the region.

The form of Buddhism that spread from Central Asia to China, Japan, and Korea was called Mahayana, which means "Great Vehicle" (see page 78), reflecting the claims of its adherents to a more inclusive form of the religion. Influenced by the Iranian religions then prevalent in Central Asia, Buddhism became more devotional. The Buddha came to be treated as a god, the head of an expanding pantheon of other Buddhas and bodhisattvas (Buddhas-to-be). With the growth of this pantheon, Buddhism became as much a religion for laypeople as for monks and nuns.

The first translators of Buddhist texts into Chinese were not Indians but Parthians, Sogdians, and Kushans from Central Asia. One of the most important interpreters of Buddhism in China was the eminent Central

Meditating Monk This monk, wearing the traditional patchwork robe, sits in the crossed-legged meditation position. His small niche is to the left of the main image of the Buddha in cave 285 at Dunhuang, a cave completed in 539 under the patronage of a prince of the Northern Wei imperial house who was then the local governor. (Photo: Lois Conner. Courtesy, Dunhuang Academy)

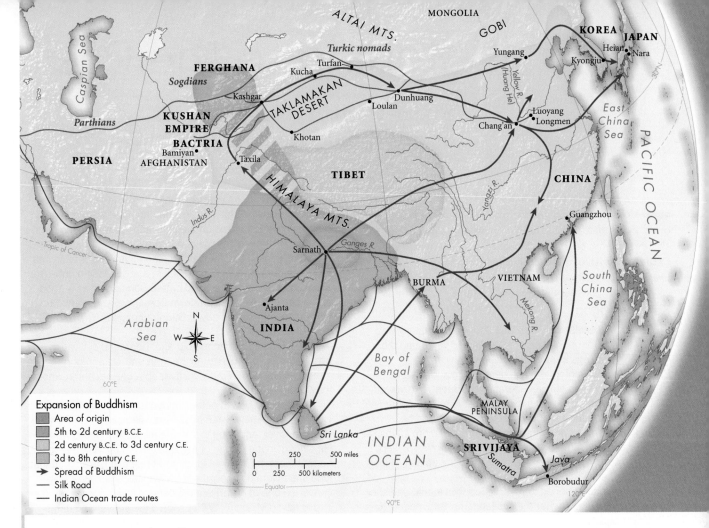

□ Mapping the Past

MAP 7.3 The Spread of Buddhism, ca. 500 B.C.E.–800 C.E. Buddhism spread throughout India in Ashoka's time and beyond India in later centuries. The different forms of Buddhism found in Asia today reflect this history. The Mahayana Buddhism of Japan came via Central Asia, China, and Korea, with a secondary later route through Tibet. The Theravada Buddhism of Southeast Asia came directly from India and indirectly through Sri Lanka.

ANALYZING THE MAP Trace the routes of the spread of Buddhism by time period. How fast did Buddhism spread?

CONNECTIONS Why do you think Buddhism spread more to the east of India than to the west?

Asian monk Kumarajiva (350–413) from Kucha, who settled in Chang'an and directed several thousand monks in the translation of Buddhist texts.

The Appeal and Impact of Buddhism in China

Why did Buddhism find so many adherents in China during the three centuries after the fall of the Han Dynasty in 220? There were no forced conversions, but still the religion spread rapidly. In the unstable political environment, many people were open to new ideas. To Chinese scholars the Buddhist concepts of the rein-

carnation of souls, karma, and nirvana posed a stimulating intellectual challenge. To rulers the Buddhist religion offered a source of magical power and a political tool to unite Chinese and non-Chinese. In a rough and tumultuous age Buddhism's emphasis on kindness, charity, and eternal bliss was deeply comforting. As in India, Buddhism posed no threat to the social order, and the elite who were drawn to Buddhism encouraged its spread to people of all classes.

The monastic establishment grew rapidly in China. Like their Christian counterparts in medieval Europe, Buddhist monasteries played an active role in social, economic, and political life. By 477 there were said to

Listening to the Past

Sixth-Century Biographies of Buddhist Nuns

Women drawn to Buddhism could leave secular life to become nuns. Most nuns lived with other nuns in convents, but they could also work to spread Buddhist teachings outside the cloister. The first collection of biographies of eminent nuns in China was written in 516. Among the sixty-five nuns whose lives it recounted are these three.

Kang Minggan

"Minggan's secular surname was Zhu, and her family was from Kaoping. For generations the family had venerated the [Buddhist] teachings known as the Great Vehicle.

A bandit who wanted to make her his wife abducted her, but, even though she suffered increasing torment, she vowed not to give in to him. She was forced to serve as a shepherdess far from her native home. Ten years went by and her longing for her home and family grew more and more intense, but there seemed to be no way back. During all this she kept her mind fixed on the Three Treasures, and she herself wished to become a nun.

One day she happened to meet a Buddhist monk, and she asked him to bestow on her the five fundamental precepts [of a Buddhist householder]. He granted her request and also presented her with a copy of the Bodhisattva Guanshiyin Scripture, which she then practiced chanting day and night without pause.

Deciding to return home to build a five-story pagoda, she fled to the east in great anxiety and distress. At first she did not know the road but kept traveling both day and night. When crossing over a mountain she saw a tiger lying only a few steps away from her. After momentary terror she composed her mind, and her hopes were more than met, for the tiger led the way for her, and, after the days had grown into weeks, she finally arrived in her home territory of Qing Province. As she was about to enter the village, the tiger disappeared, but at that moment, having arrived in the province, Minggan was again abducted, this time by Ming Bolian. When word reached her family, her husband and son ransomed her, but the family did not let her carry out her wishes [to enter the life of a Buddhist nun]. Only after three years of cultivating stringent religious practices was she able to follow her intention. As a nun, she especially concentrated on the cultivation of meditation, and she kept all the regulations of a monastic life without any transgressions. If she happened to commit a minor fault, she would confess it several mornings in a row, ceasing only after she received a sign or a good omen. Sometimes as a good omen she saw flowers rain down from the sky or she heard a voice in the sky or she saw a Buddha image or she had auspicious dreams.

As Minggan approached old age, her moral cultivation was even more strict and lofty. All the men and women north of the Yangtze River honored her as their spiritual teacher in whom they could take refuge.

In the spring of 348 of the Jin dynasty, she, together with Huichan and others—ten in all—traveled south, crossed the Yangtze River, and went to see the minister of public works, He Chong, in the capital of the Eastern Jin dynasty. As soon as he met them, he showed them great respect. Because at that time there were no convents in the capital region He Chong converted one of his private residences into a convent for them.

He asked Minggan, "What should the convent be named?"

She replied, "In the great realm of the Jin dynasty all the four Buddhist assemblies of monks, nuns, and male and female householders are now established for the first time. Furthermore, that which you as donor have established will bestow blessings and merit. Therefore, let us call the convent 'Establishing Blessings Convent.'" He Chong agreed to her suggestion. Not long afterward Minggan took sick and died."

Daoqiong

"Daoqiong's secular surname was Jiang. Her family was from Danyang. When she was a little more than ten years old, she was already well educated in the classics and history, and after her full admission to the monastic assembly she became learned in the Buddhist writings as well and also diligently cultivated a life of asceticism. In the Taiyuan reign period [376–396] of the Eastern Jin dynasty, the empress admired her exalted

be 6,478 Buddhist temples and 77,258 monks and nuns in the north. Some decades later south China had 2,846 temples and 82,700 clerics. Given the importance of family lines in China, becoming a monk was a major decision, since a man had to give up his surname and take a vow of celibacy, thus cutting himself off from the ancestral cult. Those not ready to become monks or nuns could pursue Buddhist goals as pious laypeople by per-forming devotional acts and making contributions to monasteries. Among the most generous patrons were rulers in both the north and south.

In China women turned to Buddhism as readily as men. Although birth as a female was considered lower than birth as a male, it was also viewed as temporary, and women were encouraged to pursue salvation on terms nearly equal to men. Joining a nunnery became conduct, and, whenever she wished to gain merit by giving gifts or by listening to religious exhortations, she most often depended on the convent where Daoqiong lived for such opportunities. Ladies of noble family vied with one another to associate with Daoqiong.

In 431 she had many Buddhist images made and placed them everywhere: in Pengcheng Monastery, two gold Buddha images with a curtained dais and all accessories; in Pottery Office Monastery, a processional image of Maitreya, the future Buddha, with a jeweled umbrella and pendants; in Southern Establishing Joy Monastery, two gold images with various articles, banners, and canopies. In Establishing Blessings Convent, she had an image of the reclining Buddha made, as well as a hall to house it. She also had a processional image of the bodhisattva, Puxian [or Samantabhadra], made. Of all these items, there was none that was not extremely beautiful. Again, in 438, Daoqiong commissioned a gold Amitayus [or Infinite Life] Buddha, and in the fourth month and tenth day of that same year a golden light shone forth from the mark between the eyebrows of the image and filled the entire convent. The news of this event spread among religious and worldly alike, and all came to pay honor, and, gazing at the unearthly brilliance, there was none who was not filled with great happiness. Further, using the materials bequeathed to her by the Yuan empress consort, she extended the convent to the south to build another meditation hall. 99

Daozong

66 Daozong, whose family origins are unknown, lived in Three-Story Convent in Jiangling. As a child she had no intention of setting herself apart; as an adult she did not consider associating with others a defilement. She merely followed a course along the boundary between the wise and the foolish, and, although outwardly she seemed muddled, yet within she traversed hidden profundities.

On the full-moon night of the fifteenth day of the third month, in 463 . . . , Daozong, as an offering to the Buddha, purified herself in a fire fed by oil. Even though she was engulfed by flames up to her forehead, and her eyes and ears were nearly consumed, her chanting of the scriptures did not falter. Monastics and householders sighed in wonder; the demonic and upright were alike startled. When the country heard this news, everyone aspired to attain enlightenment. The appointed court scholar . . . , Liu Qiu, especially revered her and composed a Buddhist-style poetic verse to praise her. 99

Source: Kathryn Ann Tsai, trans., *Lives of the Nuns: Biographies of Chinese Buddhist Nuns from the Fourth to Sixth Centuries.* Copyright © 1994 University of Hawai'i Press. Reprinted with permission.

QUESTIONS FOR ANALYSIS

1. Why were the lives of these three particular nuns considered worth recording? What was admirable or inspiring about their examples?

2. What do the nuns' spiritual journeys reveal about the virtues associated with Buddhist monastic life?

3. Do you see a gender element in these accounts? Were the traits that made a nun admirable also appropriate for monks?

an alternative for a woman who did not want to marry or did not want to stay with her husband's family in widowhood. (See "Listening to the Past: Sixth-Century Biographies of Buddhist Nuns," above.) Later, the only woman ruler of China, Empress Wu, invoked Buddhist principles to justify her role (see page 194), which reveals how significant a break with Confucianism Buddhism was for women.

Buddhism had an enormous impact on the visual arts in China, especially sculpture and painting. Before Buddhism, Chinese had not set up statues of gods in temples, but now they decorated temples with a profusion of images. Inspired by the cave-temples of India and Central Asia, in China, too, caves were carved into rock faces to make temples.

Yungang Colossal Buddha Beginning about 460 C.E. the Northern Wei rulers constructed a series of caves at Yungang, not far from their capital. The large Buddha shown here in a lotus meditation posture is 45 feet (13.7 meters) tall. Notice the long ears and the robe across the Buddha's shoulders, both features associated with the Buddha. (Dean Conger/Corbis)

Urban temples could be just as splendid. One author described the ceremony held each year on the seventh day of the fourth month at the largest monastery in the northern capital, Luoyang. All the Buddhist statues in the city, more than a thousand altogether, would be brought to the monastery, and the emperor would come in person to scatter flowers as part of the Great Blessing ceremony:

> The gold and the flowers dazzled in the sun, and the jewelled canopies floated like clouds; there were forests of banners and a fog of incense, and the Buddhist music of India shook heaven and earth. All kinds of entertainers and trick riders performed shoulder to shoulder. Virtuous hosts of famous monks came, carrying their staves; there were crowds of the Buddhist faithful, holding flowers; horsemen and carriages were packed beside each other in an endless mass.[6]

Not everyone was won over by Buddhist teachings. Critics of Buddhism labeled it immoral, unsuited to China, and a threat to the state since monastery land was not taxed and monks did not perform labor service. Twice in the north orders were issued to close monasteries and force monks and nuns to return to lay life, but these suppressions did not last long. No at-

tempt was made to suppress belief in Buddhism, and the religion continued to thrive in the subsequent Sui and Tang periods.

The Chinese Empire Re-created: Sui (581–618) and Tang (618–907)

☐ What were the lasting accomplishments of the Sui and Tang Dynasties?

Political division was finally overcome when the Sui Dynasty conquered its rivals to reunify China in 581. Although the dynasty lasted only thirty-seven years, it left a lasting legacy in the form of political reform, the construction of roads and canals, and the institution of merit-based exams for the appointment of officials. The Tang Dynasty that followed would last for centuries and would build upon the Sui's accomplishments to create an era of impressive cultural creativity and political power.

The Sui Dynasty, 581-618

In the 570s and 580s, the long period of division in China was brought to an end under the leadership of the Sui (sway) Dynasty. Yang Jian, who both founded

---

• **Grand Canal** A canal, built during the Sui Dynasty, that connected the Yellow and Yangzi Rivers, notable for strengthening China's internal cohesion and economic development.

the Sui Dynasty and oversaw the reunification of China, was from a Chinese family that had intermarried with the non-Chinese elite of the north. His conquest of the south involved naval as well as land battles, with thousands of ships on both sides contending for control of the Yangzi River. The Sui reasserted Chinese control over northern Vietnam and campaigned into Korea and against the new force on the steppe, the Turks. The Sui strengthened central control of the government by curtailing the power of local officials to appoint their own subordinates and by instituting in 605 C.E. competitive written examinations for the selection of officials, a practice that would come to dominate the lives of educated men in later centuries.

The crowning achievement of the Sui Dynasty was the construction of the **Grand Canal**, which connected the Yellow and Yangzi River regions. The canal facilitated the shipping of tax grain from the prosperous Yangzi Valley to the centers of political and military power in north China. Henceforth the rice-growing Yangzi Valley and south China played an ever more influential role in the country's economic and political life, strengthening China's internal cohesion and facilitating maritime trade with Southeast Asia, India, and areas farther west.

Despite these accomplishments, the Sui Dynasty lasted for only two reigns. The ambitious projects of the two Sui emperors led to exhaustion and unrest, and in the ensuing warfare Li Yuan, a Chinese from the same northwest aristocratic circles as the founder of the Sui, seized the throne.

The Tang Dynasty, 618–907

The dynasty founded by Li Yuan, the Tang, was one of the high points of traditional Chinese civilization. Especially during this dynasty's first century, its capital, Chang'an, was the cultural center of East Asia, drawing in merchants, pilgrims, missionaries, and students to a degree never matched before or after. This position of strength gave the Chinese the confidence to be open to learning from the outside world, leading to a more cosmopolitan culture than in any other period before the twentieth century.

The first two Tang rulers, Gaozu (r. 618–626) and Taizong (r. 626–649), were able monarchs. Adding auxiliary troops composed of Turks, Tanguts, Khitans, and other non-Chinese led by their own chieftains to their

Tang China, ca. 750 C.E.

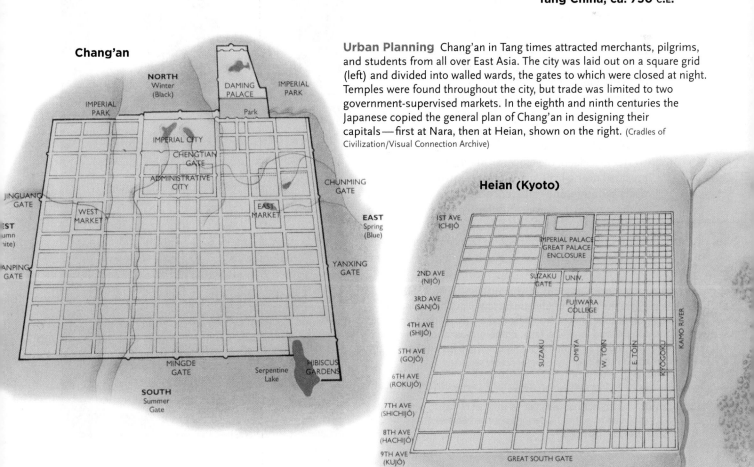

Chang'an

Urban Planning Chang'an in Tang times attracted merchants, pilgrims, and students from all over East Asia. The city was laid out on a square grid (left) and divided into walled wards, the gates to which were closed at night. Temples were found throughout the city, but trade was limited to two government-supervised markets. In the eighth and ninth centuries the Japanese copied the general plan of Chang'an in designing their capitals—first at Nara, then at Heian, shown on the right. (Cradles of Civilization/Visual Connection Archive)

Heian (Kyoto)

armies, they campaigned into Korea, Vietnam, and Central Asia. In 630 the Chinese turned against their former allies, the Turks, gaining territory from them and winning for Taizong the title of Great Khan, so that for a short period he was simultaneously head of both the Chinese and the Turkish empires.

In the civil sphere Tang accomplishments far outstripped anything known in Europe until the growth of national states in the seventeenth century. Tang emperors subdivided the administration of the empire into departments, much like the numerous agencies of modern governments. They built on the Sui precedent of using written examinations to select officials. Although only about thirty men were recruited this way each year, the prestige of passing the examinations became so great that more and more men attempted them. Candidates had to master the Confucian classics and the rules of poetry, and they had to be able to analyze practical administrative and political matters. Government schools were founded to prepare the sons of officials and other young men for service as officials.

The mid-Tang Dynasty saw two women — Empress Wu and Consort Yang Guifei — rise to positions of great political power. Empress Wu was the consort of the weak and sickly Emperor Gaozong. After Gaozong suffered a stroke in 660, she took full charge. She continued to rule after Gaozong's death, summarily deposing her own two sons and dealing harshly with all opponents. In 690 she proclaimed herself emperor, the only woman who took that title in Chinese history. To gain support, she circulated a Buddhist sutra that predicted the imminent reincarnation of the Buddha Maitreya as a female monarch, during whose reign the world would be free of illness, worry, and disaster. Although despised by later Chinese historians as an evil usurper, Empress Wu was an effective leader. It was not until she was over eighty that members of the court were able to force her out in favor of her son.

Her grandson, the emperor Xuanzong (r. 713–756), presided over a brilliant court and patronized leading poets, painters, and calligraphers in his early years. In his later years, however, after he became enamored of his consort Yang Guifei, he did not want to be bothered by the details of government. In this period ample and rounded proportions were much admired in women,

and Yang was said to be such a full-figured beauty. The emperor allowed her to place friends and relatives in important positions in the government. One of her favorites was the general An Lushan, who, after getting into a quarrel with Yang's brother over control of the government, rebelled in 755. Xuanzong had to flee the capital, and the troops that accompanied him forced him to have Yang Guifei executed.

The rebellion of An Lushan was devastating to the Tang Dynasty. Peace was restored only by calling on the Uighurs (WEE-grz), a Turkish people allied with the Tang, who looted the capital after taking it from the rebels. After the rebellion was finally suppressed in

Figurine of a Woman Notions of what makes women attractive have changed over the course of Chinese history. Figurines found in Tang tombs like this one show that full-figured women with plump faces were admired in the mid- and late Tang. Emperor Xuanzong's favorite, Yang Guifei, was said to be a plump woman, and the fashion is thought to have spread from the court. (Werner Forman/Art Resource, NY)

• **Pure Land** A school of Buddhism that taught that by calling on the Buddha Amitabha and his chief helper, one could achieve rebirth in Amitabha's Pure Land paradise.

763, the central government had to keep meeting the extortionate demands of the Uighurs. Many military governors came to treat their provinces as hereditary kingdoms and withheld tax returns from the central government. In addition, eunuchs gained increasing power at court and were able to prevent both the emperors and the Confucian officials from doing much about them.

Tang Culture

The reunification of north and south led to cultural flowering. The Tang capital cities of Chang'an and Luoyang became great metropolises; Chang'an and its suburbs grew to more than 2 million inhabitants (probably making it the largest city in the world at the time). The cities were laid out in rectangular grids and contained a hundred-odd walled "blocks" inside their walls. Like the gates of the city, the gates of each block were locked at night.

In these cosmopolitan cities, knowledge of the outside world was stimulated by the presence of envoys, merchants, and pilgrims who came from neighboring states in Central Asia, Japan, Korea, Tibet, and Southeast Asia. Because of the presence of foreign merchants, many religions were practiced, including Nestorian Christianity, Manichaeism, Zoroastrianism, Judaism, and Islam, although none of them spread into the Chinese population the way Buddhism had a few centuries earlier. Foreign fashions in hair and clothing were often copied, and foreign amusements such as the Persian game of polo found followings among the well-to-do. The introduction of new musical instruments and tunes from India, Iran, and Central Asia brought about a major transformation in Chinese music.

The Tang Dynasty was the great age of Chinese poetry. Skill in composing poetry was tested in the civil service examinations, and educated men had to be able to compose poems at social gatherings. The pain of parting, the joys of nature, and the pleasures of wine and friendship were all common poetic topics. One of Li Bo's (701–762) most famous poems describes an evening of drinking with only the moon and his shadow for company:

A cup of wine, under the flowering trees;
I drink alone, for no friend is near.
Raising my cup I beckon the bright moon,
For he, with my shadow, will make three men.
The moon, alas, is no drinker of wine;
Listless, my shadow creeps about at
  my side.
…
Now we are drunk, each goes his way.
May we long share our odd, inanimate feast,
And we meet at last on the cloudy River of the sky.[7]

> " How can I govern these people and lead them aright? I cannot even understand what they say. But at least I am glad, now that the taxes are in, To learn that in my province there is no discontent. "
>
> **BO JUYI**

The poet Bo Juyi (772–846) often wrote of more serious subjects. At times he worried about whether he was doing his job justly and well:

From these high walls I look at the town below
Where the natives of Pa cluster like a swarm of flies.
How can I govern these people and lead them aright?
I cannot even understand what they say.
But at least I am glad, now that the taxes
  are in,
To learn that in my province there is no
  discontent.[8]

In Tang times Buddhism fully penetrated Chinese daily life. Stories of Buddhist origin became widely known, and Buddhist festivals, such as the festival for feeding hungry ghosts in the summer, became among the most popular holidays. Buddhist monasteries became an important part of everyday life. They ran schools for children. In remote areas they provided lodging for travelers. Merchants entrusted their money and wares to monasteries for safekeeping, in effect transforming the monasteries into banks and warehouses. The wealthy often donated money or land to support temples and monasteries, making monasteries among the largest landlords.

At the intellectual and religious level, Buddhism was developing in distinctly Chinese directions. Two schools that thrived were Pure Land and Chan. **Pure Land** appealed to laypeople because its simple act of calling on the Buddha Amitabha

Five-Stringed Pipa/Biwa
This musical instrument, decorated with fine wood marquetry, was probably presented by the Tang court to a Japanese envoy. It was among the objects placed in a Japanese royal storage house (Shōsōin) in 756. (Kyodo)

and his chief helper, the compassionate bodhisattva Guanyin, could lead to rebirth in Amitabha's paradise, the Pure Land. Among the educated elite the **Chan** school (known in Japan as Zen) also gained popularity. Chan teachings rejected the authority of the scriptures and claimed the superiority of mind-to-mind transmission of Buddhist truths. The "northern" Chan tradition emphasized meditation and monastic discipline. The "southern" tradition was even more iconoclastic, holding that enlightenment could be achieved suddenly through insight into one's own true nature, even without prolonged meditation.

Opposition to Buddhism re-emerged in the late Tang period. In addition to concerns about the fiscal impact of removing so much land from the tax rolls and so many men from the labor service force, there were concerns about Buddhism's foreign origins. As China's international position weakened, xenophobia surfaced. During the persecution of 845, more than 4,600 monasteries and 40,000 temples and shrines were destroyed, and more than 260,000 Buddhist monks and nuns were forced to return to secular life. Although this ban was lifted after a few years, the monastic establishment never fully recovered. Buddhism retained a strong hold among laypeople, and basic Buddhist ideas like karma and reincarnation had become fully incorporated into everyday Chinese thinking. But Buddhism was never again as central to Chinese life.

The East Asian Cultural Sphere

☐ What elements of Chinese culture were adopted by Koreans, Vietnamese, and Japanese, and how did they adapt them to their own circumstances?

During the millennium from 200 B.C.E. to 800 C.E. China exerted a powerful influence on its immediate neighbors, who began forming states of their own. By Tang times China was surrounded by independent states in Korea, Manchuria, Tibet, the area that is now Yunnan province, Vietnam, and Japan. All of these states were much smaller than China in area and population, making China by far the dominant force politically and culturally until the nineteenth century. Nevertheless, each of these separate states developed a strong sense of uniqueness and independent identity. In the case of Tibet, cultural borrowing was more often from neighboring India than from China.

The earliest information about each of these countries is found in Chinese sources. Han armies brought Chinese culture to Korea and Vietnam, but even in those cases much cultural borrowing was entirely voluntary as the elite, merchants, and craftsmen adopted the techniques, ideas, and practices they found appealing. In Japan much of the process of absorbing elements of Chinese culture was mediated via Korea. In Korea, Japan, and Vietnam the fine arts—painting, architecture, and ceramics in particular—were all strongly influenced by Chinese models. Tibet, though a thorn in the side of Tang China, was as much in the Indian sphere of influence as in the Chinese and thus followed a somewhat different trajectory. Most significantly, it never adopted Chinese characters as its written language, nor was it as influenced by Chinese artistic styles as other areas. Moreover the form of Buddhism that became dominant in Tibet came directly from India, not through Central Asia and China.

In each area, Chinese-style culture was at first adopted by elites, but in time many Chinese products and ideas, ranging from written language to chopsticks and soy sauce, became incorporated into everyday life. By the eighth century the written Chinese language was used by educated people throughout East Asia. Educated Vietnamese, Koreans, and Japanese could communicate in writing when they could not understand each other's spoken languages, and envoys to Chang'an could in this way carry out "brush conversations" with each other. The books that educated people read included the Chinese classics, histories, and poetry, as well as Buddhist sutras translated into Chinese. The great appeal of Buddhism known primarily through Chinese translation was a powerful force promoting cultural borrowing.

Vietnam

Vietnam is today classed with the countries to its west as part of Southeast Asia, but its ties are at least as strong to China, and its climate is much like that of southernmost China—subtropical, with abundant rain and rivers. The Vietnamese first appear in Chinese sources as a people of south China called the Yue, who gradually migrated farther south as the Chinese state expanded. The people of the Red River Valley in northern Vietnam had achieved a relatively advanced level of Bronze Age civilization by the first century B.C.E. The bronze heads of their arrows often were dipped in poison to facilitate killing large animals such as elephants, whose tusks were traded to China for iron. Power was held by hereditary tribal chiefs who served as civil, religious, and military leaders, with the king as the most powerful chief.

The collapse of the Qin Dynasty in 206 B.C.E. had an impact on this area because a former Qin general, Zhao Tuo (Trieu Da in Vietnamese), finding himself in the

• **Chan** A school of Buddhism (known in Japan as Zen) that rejected the authority of the sutras and claimed the superiority of mind-to-mind transmission of Buddhist truths.

far south, set up his own kingdom of Nam Viet (Nan Yue in Chinese). This kingdom covered much of south China and was ruled by Trieu Da from his capital near the present site of Guangzhou. Its population consisted chiefly of the Viet people. After killing all officials loyal to the Chinese emperor, Trieu Da adopted the customs of the Viet and made himself the ruler of a vast state that extended as far south as modern-day Da Nang.

After almost a hundred years of diplomatic and military duels between the Han Dynasty and Trieu Da and his successors, Nam Viet was conquered in 111 B.C.E. by Chinese armies. Chinese administrators were assigned to replace the local nobility. Chinese political institutions were imposed, and Confucianism was treated as the official ideology. The Chinese language was introduced as the medium of official and literary expression, and Chinese characters were adopted as the written form for the Vietnamese spoken language. The Chinese built roads, waterways, and harbors to facilitate communication within the region and to ensure that they maintained administrative and military control over it. Chinese art, architecture, and music had a powerful impact on their Vietnamese counterparts.

Chinese innovations that were beneficial to the Vietnamese were readily integrated into the indigenous culture, but the local elite were not reconciled

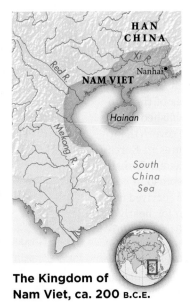

The Kingdom of Nam Viet, ca. 200 B.C.E.

to Chinese political domination. The most famous early revolt took place in 39 C.E., when two widows of local aristocrats, the Trung sisters, led an uprising against foreign rule. After overwhelming Chinese strongholds, they declared themselves queens of an independent Vietnamese kingdom. Three years later a powerful army sent by the Han emperor re-established Chinese rule.

China retained at least nominal control over northern Vietnam through the Tang Dynasty, and there were no real borders between China proper and Vietnam during this time. The local elite became culturally dual, serving as brokers between the Chinese governors and the native people.

Korea

Korea is a mountainous peninsula some 600 miles long extending south from Manchuria and Siberia. At its tip it is about 120 miles from Japan (Map 7.4). Archaeological, linguistic, and anthropological evidence indicates that the Korean people share a common ethnic origin with other peoples of North Asia, including those of Manchuria, Siberia, and Japan. Linguistically, Korean is not related to Chinese.

Korea began adopting elements of technology from China in the first millennium B.C.E., including bronze and iron technology. Chinese-Korean contact expanded

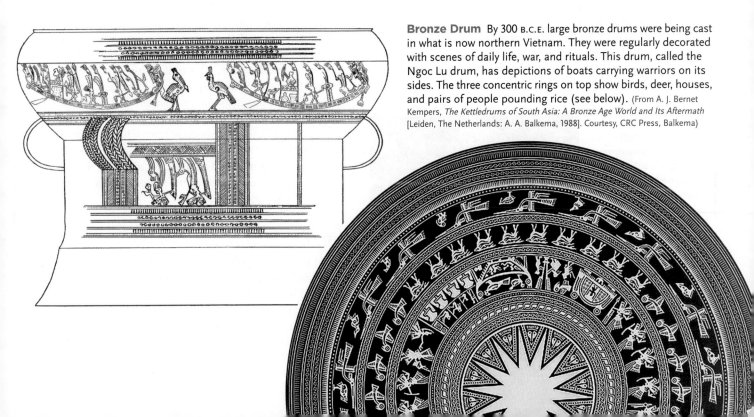

Bronze Drum By 300 B.C.E. large bronze drums were being cast in what is now northern Vietnam. They were regularly decorated with scenes of daily life, war, and rituals. This drum, called the Ngoc Lu drum, has depictions of boats carrying warriors on its sides. The three concentric rings on top show birds, deer, houses, and pairs of people pounding rice (see below). (From A. J. Bernet Kempers, *The Kettledrums of South Asia: A Bronze Age World and Its Aftermath* [Leiden, The Netherlands: A. A. Balkema, 1988]. Courtesy, CRC Press, Balkema)

during the Warring States Period when the state of Yan extended into part of Korea. In about 194 B.C.E. Wiman, an unsuccessful rebel against the Han Dynasty, fled to Korea and set up a state called Choson in what is now northwest Korea and southern Manchuria. In 108 B.C.E. this state was overthrown by the armies of the Han emperor Wu. Four prefectures were established there, and Chinese officials were dispatched to govern them.

The impact of the Chinese prefectures in Korea was similar to that of the contemporaneous Roman colonies in Britain in encouraging the spread of culture and political forms. The prefectures survived not only through the Han Dynasty, but also for nearly a century after the fall of the dynasty, to 313 C.E. The Chinese never controlled the entire Korean peninsula, however. The Han commanderies coexisted with the native Korean kingdom of Koguryŏ, founded in the first century B.C.E. Chinese sources describe this kingdom as a society of aristocratic tribal warriors who had under them a mass of serfs and slaves, mostly from conquered tribes. After the Chinese colonies were finally overthrown, the kingdoms of Paekche and Silla emerged farther south on the peninsula in the third and fourth centuries C.E., leading to what is called the Three Kingdoms Period (313–668 C.E.). In all three Korean kingdoms Chinese was used as the language of government and learning. Each of the three kingdoms had hereditary kings, but their power was curbed by the existence of very strong hereditary elites.

Buddhism was officially introduced in Koguryŏ from China in 372 and in the other states not long after. Buddhism connected Korea to societies across Asia. Buddhist monks went back and forth between China and Korea. One even made the journey to India and back, and others traveled on to Japan to aid in the spread of Buddhism there.

When the Sui Dynasty finally reunified China in 589, it tried to establish control of at least a part of Korea. But the Korean kingdoms were much stronger than their predecessors in Han times, and they repeat-

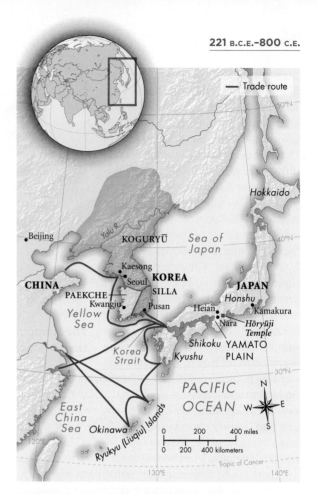

MAP 7.4 Korea and Japan, ca. 600 Korea and Japan are of similar latitude, but Korea's climate is more continental, with harsher winters. Of Japan's four islands, Kyushu is closest to Korea and mainland Asia.

edly repulsed Chinese attacks. The Tang government then tried allying itself with one state, Silla, to fight the others. Silla and Tang jointly destroyed Paekche in 660 and Koguryŏ in 668. With its new resources Silla was able to repel Tang efforts to make Korea a colony but agreed to vassal status. The unification under Silla marked the first political unification of Korea.

For the next century Silla embarked on a policy of wholesale borrowing of Chinese culture and institutions. Annual embassies were sent to Chang'an, and large numbers of students studied in China. The Silla government was modeled on the Tang, although modifications were made to accommodate Korea's more aristocratic social structure.

Japan

Japan does not touch China as do Korea, Tibet, and Vietnam. The heart of Japan is four mountainous islands off the coast of Korea (see Map 7.4). Since the land is rugged and lacking in navigable waterways, the Inland Sea, like the Aegean in Greece, was the easiest avenue of communication in early times. Hence the land bordering the Inland Sea — Kyushu, Shikoku, and

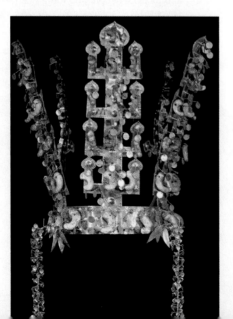

Gold Crown Excavated from a fifth- to sixth-century royal Silla tomb, this magnificent crown reflects metalwork traditions found in scattered places across the Eurasian steppe. The crown is decorated with dangling gold disks and comma-shaped beads of jadeite. The upright bars at the top are thought to represent deer antlers. (Courtesy, Gyeonju National Museum)

Honshu — developed as the political and cultural center of early Japan. Geography also blessed Japan with a moat — the Korea Strait and the Sea of Japan. Consequently, the Japanese for long periods were free to develop their way of life without external interference.

Japan's early development was closely tied to that of the mainland, especially to Korea. Physical anthropologists have discerned several major waves of immigrants into Japan. People of the Jōmon culture, established by about 10,000 B.C.E. after an influx of people from Southeast Asia, practiced hunting and fishing and fashioned clay pots. New arrivals from northeast Asia brought agriculture and a distinct culture called Yayoi (ca. 300 B.C.E.–300 C.E.). Later Yayoi communities were marked by complex social organization with rulers, soldiers, artisans, and priests. During the Han Dynasty objects of Chinese and Korean manufacture found their way into Japan, an indication that people were traveling back and forth as well. In the third century C.E. Chinese histories begin to report on the land called Wa made up of mountainous islands. It had numerous communities, markets, granaries, tax collection, and class distinctions. The people ate with their fingers, used body paint, purified themselves by bathing after a funeral, and liked liquor.

One of the most distinctive features of early Japan was its women rulers. A Chinese historian wrote:

> The country formerly had a man as ruler. For some seventy or eighty years after that there were disturbances and warfare. Thereupon the people agreed upon a woman for their ruler. Her name was Himiko. She occupied herself with magic and sorcery, bewitching the people. Though mature in age, she remained unmarried. She had a younger brother who assisted her in ruling the country. After she became the ruler, there were few who saw her. She had one thousand women as attendants, but only one man. He served her food and drink and acted as a medium of communication. . . .
>
> When Himiko passed away, a great mound was raised, more than a hundred paces in diameter. Over a hundred male and female attendants followed her to the grave. Then a king was placed on the throne, but the people would not obey him. Assassination and murder followed; more than one thousand were thus slain.
>
> A relative of Himiko named Iyo, a girl of thirteen, was then made queen and order was restored.[9]

During the fourth through sixth centuries, new waves of migrants from Korea brought the language that evolved into Japanese. They also brought sericulture (silkmaking), bronze swords, crossbows, iron plows, and the Chinese written language. In this period a social order similar to Korea's emerged, dominated by a warrior aristocracy organized into clans. Clad in helmet and armor, these warriors wielded swords, battle-axes, and often bows, and some rode into battle on horseback. Those vanquished in battle were made slaves. Each clan had its own chieftain, who marshaled clansmen for battle and served as chief priest. Over time the clans fought with each other, and their numbers were gradually reduced through conquest and alliance. By the fifth century the chief of the clan that claimed descent from the sun-goddess, located in the Yamato plain around modern Osaka, had come to occupy the position of Great King — or Queen, for as the quotation above shows, female rulers were not uncommon in this period.

The Yamato rulers used their religion to subordinate the gods of their rivals, much as Hammurabi had used Marduk in Babylonia (see page 42). They established the chief shrine of the sun-goddess near the seacoast, where she could catch the first rays of the rising sun. Cults to other gods also were supported as long as they were viewed as subordinate to the sun-goddess. This native religion was later termed **Shinto**, the Way of the Gods. Buddhism was formally introduced in 538 C.E. and coexisted with the Shinto reverence for the spirits of ancestors and all living things.

In the sixth century Prince Shōtoku (574–622) undertook a sweeping reform of the state designed to strengthen Yamato rule by adopting Chinese-style bureaucratic practices (though not the recruitment of officials by examination). His "Seventeen Principles" of 604 drew from both Confucian and Buddhist teachings. In it he likened the ruler to Heaven and instructed officials to put their duty to the ruler above the interest of their families. He instituted a ladder of official ranks similar to China's, admonished the nobility to avoid strife and opposition, and urged adherence to Buddhist precepts. Near his seat of government, Prince Shōtoku built the magnificent Hōryūji Temple and staffed it with monks from Korea. He also opened direct relations with China, sending four missions during the brief Sui Dynasty. (See "Viewpoints: Chinese and Japanese Principles of Good Government, ca. 650," page 200.)

State-building efforts continued through the seventh century and culminated in the establishment in 710 of Japan's first long-term true city, the capital at **Nara**, north of modern Osaka. Nara, which was modeled on the Tang capital of Chang'an, gave its name to an era that lasted until 794 and that was characterized by the avid importation of Chinese ideas and methods. Seven times missions with five hundred to six hundred men were sent on the dangerous sea crossing and long overland journey to Chang'an. As Buddhism developed a stronghold in Japan, it inspired many trips to China

• **Shinto** The Way of the Gods, it was the native religion espoused by the Yamato rulers in Japan.

• **Nara** Japan's capital and first true city; it was established in 710 and modeled on the Tang capital of Chang'an.

Viewpoints

Chinese and Japanese Principles of Good Government, ca. 650

• *Confucian principles of government, first developed in the Han dynasty, in time had considerable influence beyond China's borders, especially in Korea and Japan. The two seventh-century texts below look at good government from different sides. The first comes from an essay written in 648 in China by the Tang emperor Taizong, addressed to the heir apparent to encourage him to aspire to the Confucian understanding of the ideal ruler. The second text, issued by Prince Shōtoku in Japan in about the same period, is addressed to his officials. In both cases only the first item is included in full, but the titles of the other items are listed.*

Taizong's Plan for an Emperor

1. The Body of the Sovereign: The people are the origin of the state. The state is the foundation of the sovereign. The body of the lord of men should be like the great holy peaks, lofty and towering and unmovable. It should be like sun and moon, constant in their brilliance, and illuminating all alike. He is the one to whom the myriad people look up, to whom the entire empire turns. His will should be broad and magnanimous, sufficient to bind them together. His heart should be impartial and just, sufficient for him to make forceful decisions. Without awesome power, he will have no means to affect the most distant regions: without benign liberality he will have no means to cherish his people. He must comfort the nine grades of his kinsfolk by humanity. He must bind his great ministers to him by the rites. In serving his ancestors, he must bear in mind his filial obligations: in occupying his position [as ruler] he must remember to be reverent. He must repress his own [personal interests] and toil diligently, so as to put into practice virtue and righteousness. Such then is the body of the sovereign.
2. Establishing One's Kinsmen. . . .
3. Seeking Sage-Worthies. . . .
4. Carefully Examine Candidates for Offices. . . .
5. Accepting Remonstrance. . . .
6. Ridding Yourself of Flatterers. . . .
7. Guarding Against Excess. . . .
8. Esteem Frugality. . . .
9. Rewards and Punishments. . . .
10. Giving Due Attention to Agriculture. . . .
11. Reviewing Preparations for War. . . .
12. Honoring Learning. . . .

Prince Shōtoku's Seventeen-Article Edict

1. Harmony is to be valued, and contentiousness avoided. All men are inclined to partisanship and few are truly discerning. Hence there are some who disobey their lords and fathers or who maintain feuds with the neighboring villages. But when those above are harmonious and those below are conciliatory and there is concord in the discussion of all matters, the disposition of affairs comes about naturally. Then what is there that cannot be accomplished?
2. Sincerely reverence the Three Treasures [The Buddha, the Law, and the Sangha]. . . .
3. When you receive the imperial commands, fail not scrupulously to obey them. . . .
4. The ministers and functionaries should make ritual decorum their leading principle, for the leading principle in governing the people consists in ritual decorum. . . .
5. Ceasing from gluttony and abandoning covetous desires, deal impartially with the suits which are submitted to you. . . .
6. Chastise that which is evil and encourage that which is good. . . .
7. Let every man have his own charge, and let not the spheres of duty be confused. . . .
8. Let the ministers and functionaries attend the court early in the morning, and retire late. . . .
9. Trustworthiness is the foundation of right. . . .
10. Let us cease from wrath and refrain from angry looks. . . .
11. Give clear appreciation to merit and demerit, and deal out to each its sure reward or punishment. . . .
12. Let not the provincial authorities or the local nobles levy exaction on the people. . . .
13. Let all persons entrusted with office attend equally to their functions. . . .
14. Ye ministers and functionaries! Be not envious. . . .
15. To turn away from that which is private and to set our faces toward that which is public—this is the path of a minister. . . .
16. Let the people be called up for labor service only at seasonable times. . . .
17. Matters should not be decided by one person alone. . . .

Sources: Denis Twitchett, "*How to Be an Emperor*: T'ang T'ai-tsung's Vision of His Role," *Asia Major* 3d ser. 9.1–2 (1996), 57–58. Reprinted by permission of the Institute of History and Philology of Academic Sinica, Taipei, Taiwan; Prince Shōtoku adapted from W. G. Aston, *Nihongi: Chronicles of Japan from the Earliest Times to* A.D. *697* (London: Kegan Paul, Trench and Trübner, 1896), II, 128–133.

QUESTIONS FOR ANALYSIS

1. What similarities do you see in these two documents? In what sense can both be considered Confucian?
2. What differences in these documents can you attribute to the differences between China and Japan in the seventh century?

to acquire sources and to study at Chinese monasteries. Chinese and Korean craftsmen were often brought back to Japan, especially to help with the decoration of the many Buddhist temples then under construction. Musical instruments and tunes were imported as well, many originally from Central Asia. Chinese practices were instituted, such as the compilation of histories and law codes, the creation of provinces, and the appointment of governors to collect taxes from them. By 750 some seven thousand men staffed the central government.

Increased contact with the mainland had unwanted effects as well. In contrast to China and Korea, both part of the Eurasian landmass, Japan had been relatively isolated from many deadly diseases, so when diseases arrived with travelers, people did not have immunity. The great smallpox epidemic of 735–737 is thought to have reduced the population of about 5 million by 30 percent. (Smallpox did not become an endemic childhood disease in Japan until the tenth or eleventh century, measles until even later.)

The Buddhist monasteries that ringed Nara were both religious centers and wealthy landlords, and the monks were active in the political life of the capital. Copying the policy of the Tang Dynasty in China, the government ordered every province to establish a Buddhist temple with twenty monks and ten nuns to chant sutras and perform other ceremonies on behalf of the emperor and the state. When an emperor abdicated in 749 in favor of his daughter, he became a Buddhist priest-monk, a practice many of his successors would later follow.

Many of the temples built during the Nara period still stand, the wood, clay, and bronze statues in them exceptionally well preserved. The largest of these temples was the Tōdaiji, with its huge bronze statue of

□ Picturing the Past

Hōryūji Temple Japanese Buddhist temples, like those in China and Korea, consisted of several buildings within a walled compound. The buildings of the Hōryūji Temple (built between 670 and 711, after Prince Shōtoku's original temple burned down) include the oldest wooden structures in the world and house some of the best early Buddhist sculpture in Japan. The three main buildings depicted here are the pagoda, housing relics; the main hall, with the temple's principal images; and the lecture hall, for sermons. The five-story pagoda could be seen from far away, much like the steeples of cathedrals in medieval Europe. (Michael Hitoshi/ The Image Bank/Getty Images)

ANALYZING THE IMAGE How are the buildings arranged? How large is the compound? Do you see anything interesting about the roofs?

CONNECTIONS Was this temple laid out primarily for the convenience of monks who resided there or more for lay believers coming to worship? How would their needs differ?

the Buddha, which stood fifty-three feet tall and was made from more than a million pounds of metal. When the temple and statue were completed in 752, an Indian monk painted the eyes, and the ten thousand monks present for the celebration had a magnificent vegetarian feast. Objects from the dedication ceremony were placed in a special storehouse, the Shōsōin, and about ten thousand of them are still there, including books, weapons, mirrors, screens, and objects of gold, lacquer, and glass, most made in China but some coming from Central Asia and Persia via the Silk Road.

CONNECTIONS

East Asia was transformed in the years between the Qin unification in 221 B.C.E. and the end of the eighth century. The Han Dynasty and four centuries later the Tang Dynasty had proved that a centralized, bureaucratic monarchy could bring peace and prosperity to populations of 50 million or more spread across China proper. By 800 C.E. neighboring societies along China's borders, from Korea and Japan on the east to the Uighurs and Tibetans to the west, had followed China's lead, forming states and building cities. Buddhism had transformed the lives of all of these societies, bringing new ways of thinking about life and death and new ways of pursuing spiritual goals.

In the same centuries that Buddhism was adapting to and simultaneously transforming the culture of much of eastern Eurasia, comparable processes were at work in western Eurasia, where Christianity continued to spread, and in India where Brahmanism evolved into Hinduism. The spread of these religions was aided by increased contact between different cultures, facilitated in Eurasia by the merchants traveling the Silk Road or sailing the Indian Ocean. Where contact between cultures wasn't as extensive, as in Africa (discussed in Chapter 10), religious beliefs were more localized. The collapse of the Roman Empire in the west during this period was not unlike the collapse of the Han Dynasty, but in Europe the empire was never put back together at the level that it was in China, where the Tang Dynasty by many measures was more splendid than the Han. The story of these centuries in western Eurasia are taken up in the next two chapters, which trace the rise of Christianity and Islam and the movement of peoples throughout Europe and Asia. Before returning to the story of East Asia after 800 in Chapter 13, we will also examine the empires in Africa (Chapter 10) and the Americas (Chapter 11).

CHAPTER REVIEW

KEY TERMS

Great Wall (p. 177)
Confucian classics (p. 178)
Records of the Grand Historian (p. 180)
Silk Road (p. 181)
tributary system (p. 182)

eunuchs (p. 187)
Age of Division (p. 187)
Grand Canal (p. 193)
Pure Land (p. 195)
Chan (p. 196)
Shinto (p. 199)
Nara (p. 199)

□ What were the social, cultural and political consequences of the unification of China under the strong centralized governments of the Qin and Han empires? (p. 176)

After unifying China in 221 B.C.E., the Qin Dynasty created a strongly centralized government that abolished noble privilege and kept ordinary people in place through strictly enforced laws. The First Emperor of Qin standardized script, coinage, weights, and measures. Building roads for the army facilitated trade and helped establish China as a world power. During the four centuries of the subsequent Han Dynasty, the harsher laws and taxes of the Qin were lifted, though a strong centralized government was retained. The government sent huge armies against the nomadic Xiongnu, who regularly raided settlements in the north, but the Xiongnu remained a potent foe. The Han government promoted internal peace by providing relief in cases of floods, droughts, and famines and by keeping land taxes low for the peasantry. As a result, the population grew, reaching 58 million. Han armies expanded Chinese territory both to the south and into Central Asia, which helped trade along the Silk Road. Confucian teachers attracted many students, and popular religion flourished as people spread stories of gods and immortals and their paradises. The invention of paper reduced the cost of keeping records and aided the circulation of books.

□ How did Buddhism find its way into East Asia, and what was its appeal and impact? (p. 188)

In the final years of the Han Dynasty, Buddhism reached China from Central Asia. Conquest had little to do with the spread of Buddhism in East Asia (in contrast to the spread of Christianity and Islam, which often followed a change of rulers). Rather it was merchants and missionaries who brought Bud-

dhism, especially Mahayana Buddhism, across the Silk Road. Buddhism brought much that was new to China: a huge body of scriptures, celibate monks and nuns, traditions of depicting Buddhas and bodhisattvas in statues and paintings, and a strong proselytizing tradition. Buddhism was intellectually appealing to the educated, and rulers welcomed it as a tool to unite Chinese and non-Chinese citizens. It posed no threat to the social order, and people from all classes were drawn to its emphasis on kindness and charity. Buddhism offered new opportunities to women as nuns and let them pursue enlightenment on terms almost equal to men.

□ What were the lasting accomplishments of the Sui and Tang Dynasties? (p. 192)

After centuries of division, China was reunified in 589 C.E. by the Sui Dynasty. The Sui strengthened the central control of government by limiting the power of local officials to appoint their own subordinates. The competitive written exams that the Sui instituted for the selection of officials would dominate China and other parts of East Asia in the centuries to come. The building of the Grand Canal strengthened China internally and connected the north to the maritime trade with Southeast Asia and India. The Tang built upon Sui accomplishments, establishing government schools to prepare men for service as officials. China regained overlordship along the Silk Road into Central

Asia and once again had to deal with powerful northern neighbors, this time the Turks and Uighurs. In the wake of a huge internal rebellion, eunuchs gained power at court, and military governors treated their provinces as hereditary kingdoms. The Tang period was one of cultural flowering, especially in music and poetry. The introduction of new instruments and music from India, Iran, and Central Asia transformed Chinese music.

◻ What elements of Chinese culture were adopted by Koreans, Vietnamese, and Japanese, and how did they adapt them to their own circumstances? (p. 196)

From 200 B.C.E. to 800 C.E., China's neighbors, especially Korea, Japan, and Vietnam, began to adopt elements of China's material, political, and religious culture, including the Chinese writing system. Force of arms helped bring Chinese culture to both Korea and Vietnam, but military might was not the primary means by which culture spread in this period. Particularly in Korea and Japan, ambitious rulers sought Chinese expertise and Chinese products — such as, sericulture, bronze swords, crossbows, iron plows, and Chinese-style centralized governments — believing the adoption of the most advanced ideas and technologies to be to their advantage. In more isolated Japan, Koreans played a large role in the spread of Chinese culture. Korea, Vietnam, and Japan all retained many features of their earlier cultures even as they adopted Chinese practices, in the process developing distinctive national styles. For example, in Korea the government was modeled on the Tang, but was modified to accommodate Korea's aristocratic social structure.

SUGGESTED READING

Barfield, Thomas. *Perilous Frontier: Nomadic Empires and China, 221 B.C.–A.D. 1757.* 1989. A bold interpretation of the relationship between the rise and fall of dynasties in China and the rise and fall of nomadic confederations that derived resources from them.

Elvin, Mark. *The Pattern of the Chinese Past.* 1973. Analyzes the military dimensions of China's unification.

Farris, Wayne. *Population, Disease, and Land in Early Japan, 645–900.* 1985. Shows the impact of the eighth-century introduction of smallpox to Japan on the government and rural power structure.

Hardy, Grant. *Worlds of Bronze and Bamboo: Sima Qian's Conquest of History.* 1999. An excellent introduction to the methods of China's earliest historian. Although Sima Qian seems to present just the facts, Hardy shows how he brings out different perspectives and interpretations in different chapters.

Holcomb, Charles. *The Genesis of East Asia, 221 B.C.–A.D. 907.* 2001. A thought-provoking analysis of the connections between China and Korea, Japan, and Vietnam that emphasizes the use of the Chinese script.

Lee, Peter H. *Sourcebook of Korean Civilization.* 1993. Excellent collection of primary sources.

Lewis, Mark Edward. *China's Cosmopolitan Empire: The Tang Dynasty.* 2009. This accessible and lively survey complements the author's works on the Han Dynasty (*The Early Chinese Empires*) and the period of division (*China Between Empires*).

Schafer, Edward. *The Golden Peaches of Samarkand.* 1963. Draws on Tang literature to show the place of the western regions in Tang life and imagination.

Seth, Michael J. *A Concise History of Korea: From the Neolithic Period Through the Nineteenth Century.* 2006. An up-to-date and well-balanced introduction to Korean history.

Totman, Conrad. *A History of Japan.* 1999. A broad and up-to-date history of Japan.

Varley, H. Paul. *Japanese Culture.* 2000. An accessible introduction to Japanese history and culture.

Waley, Arthur. *The Life and Times of Po Chu-i, 772–846 A.D.* 1949. A lively biography of a Tang official, that draws heavily on his poetry.

Watt, James C. Y. *China: Dawn of a Golden Age 200–750 A.D.* 2004. A well-illustrated catalogue of a major art and archaeological exhibition.

Wright, Arthur. *Buddhism in Chinese History.* 1959. This short book remains a good introduction to China's encounter with Buddhism and the ways Buddhism was adapted to China.

NOTES

1. Li Yuning, ed., *The First Emperor of China* (White Plains, N.Y.: International Arts and Sciences Press, 1975), pp. 275–276, slightly modified.
2. Burton Watson, trans., *Records of the Grand Historian of China*, vol. 2 (New York: Columbia University Press, 1961), p. 496.
3. Ibid., p. 499.
4. From Patricia Buckley Ebrey, ed., *Chinese Civilization: A Sourcebook*, 2d ed. (New York: The Free Press, 1993), p. 62.
5. Patricia Buckley Ebrey, *The Cambridge Illustrated History of China* (Cambridge: Cambridge University Press, 1996), p. 74.
6. W. F. Jenner, *Memories of Loyang: Yang Hsüan-chih and the Lost Capital (493–534)* (Oxford: Clarendon Press, 1981), p. 208.
7. Arthur Waley, trans., *More Translations from the Chinese* (New York: Knopf, 1919), p. 27. Reprinted by permission of the Arthur Waley Estate.
8. Ibid., p. 71.
9. *Sources of Japanese Tradition*, by William Theodore de Bary, Donald Keene, George Tanabe, and Paul Varley, eds. Copyright © 2001 by Columbia University Press. Reproduced with permission of the publisher.

For practice quizzes and other study tools, visit the **Online Study Guide** at bedfordstmartins.com/mckayworld.

For primary sources from this period, see *Sources of World Societies*, **Second Edition**.

For Web sites, images, and documents related to topics in this chapter, visit **Make History** at bedfordstmartins.com/mckayworld.

• **French Reliquary of Sainte Foy** Preachers who spread Christianity often told stories of spiritually heroic saints and martyrs, and placed their remains in reliquaries for people to venerate. This jeweled ninth-century French reliquary contains the bones of Sainte Foy, a young woman thought to have been martyred centuries earlier. (Erich Lessing/Art Resource, NY)

From the third century onward the Western Roman Empire slowly disintegrated. The last Roman emperor in the West, Romulus Augustus, was deposed by the Ostrogothic chieftain Odoacer (OH-duh-way-suhr) in 476, but much of the empire had already come under the rule of various barbarian tribes well before this. Scholars have long seen this era as one of the great turning points in Western history, but during the last several decades focus has shifted to continuities as well as changes. What is now usually termed "late antiquity" has been recognized as a period of creativity and adaptation in Europe and western Asia, not simply of decline and fall.

Continuity and Change in Europe and Western Asia

200–850

The two main agents of continuity were the Eastern Roman (or Byzantine) Empire and the Christian Church. The Byzantine Empire lasted until 1453, a thousand years longer than the Western Roman Empire, and preserved and transmitted much of Greco-Roman law, philosophy, and institutions. Missionaries and church officials spread Christianity within and far beyond the borders of what had been the Roman Empire, transforming a small sect into the most important and wealthiest institution in Europe. The main agent of change in late antiquity was the migration of barbarian groups throughout much of Europe and western Asia. They brought different social, political, and economic structures with them, but as they encountered Roman and Byzantine culture and became Christian, their own ways of doing things were also transformed. •

The Byzantine Empire
☐ How was the Byzantine Empire able to survive for so long, and what were its most important achievements?

The Growth of the Christian Church
☐ What factors enabled the Christian Church to expand and thrive?

Christian Ideas and Practices
☐ How did Christian thinkers and missionaries adapt Greco-Roman ideas to Christian theology and develop effective techniques for converting barbarian peoples?

Migrating Peoples
☐ How did the barbarians shape social, economic, and political structures in Europe and western Asia?

The Byzantine Empire

☐ How was the Byzantine Empire able to survive for so long, and what were its most important achievements?

The emperor Constantine (see page 169) had tried to maintain the unity of the Roman Empire, but during the fifth and sixth centuries the western and eastern halves drifted apart. From Constantinople, Eastern Roman emperors worked to hold the empire together and to reconquer at least some of the West from barbarian tribes. Justinian (r. 527–565) waged long wars against the Ostrogoths (members of a Germanic barbarian tribe) and temporarily regained Italy and North Africa, but the costs were high. Justinian's wars exhausted the resources of the state, destroyed Italy's economy, and killed a large part of Italy's population.

By the late sixth century, after Justinian's death, a weakened Italy had fallen easily to another Germanic tribe, the Lombards. With this defeat, the lands that had been the Western Roman Empire were again under Germanic sway.

However, the Roman Empire continued in the East. The Eastern Roman or Byzantine Empire (Map 8.1) preserved the institutions and traditions of the old Roman Empire. Byzantium passed the intellectual heritage of Greco-Roman civilization on to later cultures as it also developed its own distinctive characteristics.

Sources of Byzantine Strength

Byzantine emperors traced their lines back past Constantine to Augustus (see page 154). While evolving into a Christian and Greek-speaking state with a mul-

MAP 8.1 The Byzantine and Sassanid Empires, ca. 600 Both the Byzantine and Sassanid Empires included territory that had earlier been part of the Roman Empire. The Sassanid Persians fought Roman armies before the founding of the Byzantine Empire. Later Byzantium and the Sassanids engaged in a series of wars that weakened both and brought neither lasting territorial acquisitions.

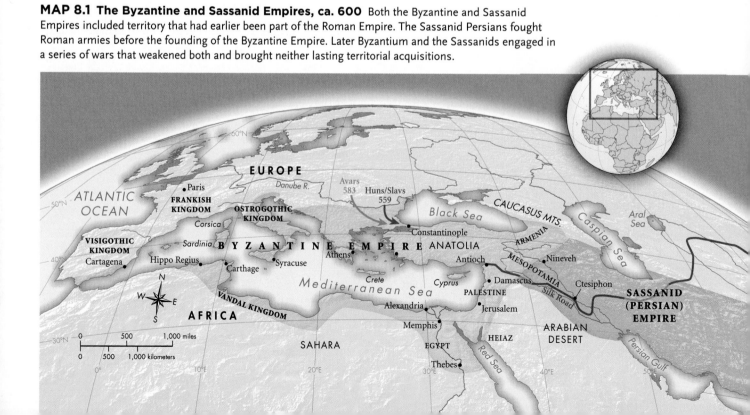

tiethnic population centered in the eastern Mediterranean and the Balkans, the Byzantines retained the legal and administrative system of the empire centered at Rome. (In fact, the Byzantines called themselves "Romans" and their state the "Roman Empire"; only in the sixteenth century did people begin to use the term "Byzantine Empire.") Thus, the senate that sat in Constantinople carried on the traditions and preserved the glory of the old Roman senate. The army that defended the empire was the direct descendant of the old Roman legions.

That army was kept very busy, for the Byzantine Empire survived waves of attacks. In 559 a force of Xiongnu (whom the Greeks and Romans called Huns) and Slavs reached the gates of Constantinople. In 583 the Avars, a mounted Mongol people who had swept across Russia and the Balkans, seized Byzantine forts along the Danube and also reached the walls of Constantinople. Between 572 and 630 the Greeks were repeatedly at war with the Sassanid Persians (see page 208). In 632 the Arabs began pressuring the Greek empire. Why didn't one or a combination of these enemies capture Constantinople, as the Germanic tribes had taken Rome? The answer lies, first, in the strong military leadership the Greeks possessed. General Priskos (d. 612) skillfully led Byzantine armies to a decisive victory over the Avars in 601. Then, after a long war, the well-organized emperor Heraclius I (r. 610–641) crushed the Persians at Nineveh in Mesopotamia (now Iraq).

Second, the city's location and excellent fortifications proved crucial. Constantinople had the most powerful defenses in the ancient world. One defense was natural: the sea that surrounded Constantinople on three sides. The other defense was the walls that surrounded the city, protecting it from invasions by both land and sea. Massive triple walls protected the city from sea invasion. Within the walls huge cisterns provided water, and vast gardens and grazing areas supplied vegetables and meat. Such strong fortifications and provisions meant that if attacked by land or sea, Constantinople's defenders could hold out far longer than a besieging army. In essence, the site chosen for the imperial capital in the fourth century enabled Con-

Sassanid Cameo In this cameo—a type of jewelry made by carving into a multicolored piece of rock—the Sassanid king Shapur and the Byzantine emperor Valerian fight on horseback, each identifiable by his distinctive clothing and headgear. This does not record an actual hand-to-hand battle, but uses the well-muscled rulers as symbols of their empires. (Erich Lessing/Art Resource, NY)

stantinople to survive longer than it might have otherwise. Because the city survived, the empire, though reduced in territory, endured.

The Sassanid Empire and Conflicts with Byzantium

For several centuries the Sassanid empire of Persia was Byzantium's most regular foe. In 226 Ardashir I (r. 226–243) founded the Sassanid dynasty, which lasted until 651, when it was overthrown by the Muslims. Ardashir expanded his territory and absorbed the Roman province of Mesopotamia.

Centered in the fertile Tigris-Euphrates Valley, but with access to the Persian Gulf and extending south to Meshan (modern Kuwait), the Sassanid empire depended on agriculture for its economic prosperity; its location also proved well suited for commerce (see Map 8.1). A lucrative caravan trade from Ctesiphon (TE-suh-fahn) north to Merv and then east to Samarkand linked the Sassanid empire to the Silk Road and China (see page 184). Persian metalwork, textiles, and glass were exchanged for Chinese silks, and this trade brought about considerable cultural contact between the Sassanids and the Chinese.

Whereas the Parthians (who fell to the Sassanids in 226) had tolerated many religions, the Sassanid Persians made Zoroastrianism the official state religion. Religion and the state were inextricably tied together. The king's power rested on the support of nobles and Zoroastrian priests, who monopolized positions in the court and in the imperial bureaucracy. A highly elaborate court ceremonial and ritual exalted the status of the king and emphasized his semidivine pre-eminence over his subjects. (The Byzantine monarchy, the Roman papacy, and the Muslim caliphate subsequently copied aspects of this Persian ceremonial.)

Adherents to religions other than Zoroastrianism, such as Jews and Christians, faced discrimination. The Jewish population in the Sassanid empire was sizable because the Romans had forced many Jews out of Israel and Judaea after a series of revolts against Roman rule, a dispersal later termed the diaspora. Jews suffered intermittent persecution under the Sassanids, as did Christians, whom followers of Zoroastrianism saw as being connected to Rome and Constantinople.

An expansionist foreign policy brought Persia into frequent conflict with Byzantium, and neither side was able to achieve a clear-cut victory. The long wars financed by higher taxation, on top of the arrival of the plague (see page 209), compounded discontent in both Byzantine and Persian societies. Moreover, internal political instability weakened the Sassanid dynasty,

> " Slaves become our property by the Law of Nations when they are either taken from the enemy, or are born of our female slaves. "
>
> JUSTINIAN'S *Digest*

and in the seventh century Persian territories were absorbed into the Islamic caliphate (see page 237).

The Law Code of Justinian

Byzantine emperors organized and preserved Roman law, making a lasting contribution to the medieval and modern worlds. Roman law had developed from many sources — decisions by judges, edicts of emperors, legislation passed by the senate, and opinions of jurists expert in the theory and practice of law. By the fourth century Roman law had become a huge, bewildering mass. Its sheer bulk made it almost unusable.

To address this problem, the emperor Justinian appointed a committee of eminent jurists to sort through and organize the laws. The result was the *Code*, which distilled the legal genius of the Romans into a coherent whole, eliminated outmoded laws and contradictions, and clarified the law itself.

Justinian next set about bringing order to the equally huge body of Roman jurisprudence, the science or philosophy of law. To harmonize the often differing opinions of Roman jurists, Justinian directed his jurists to clear up disputed points and to issue definitive rulings. Accordingly, in 533 his lawyers published the *Digest*, which codified Roman legal thought and contained provisions such as these on slavery:

> Slaves are brought under our ownership either by the Civil Law or by that of Nations. This is done by the Civil Law where anyone who is over twenty years of age permits himself to be sold for the sake of sharing in his own price [that is, for debt]. Slaves become our property by the Law of Nations when they are either taken from the enemy, or are born of our female slaves. . . .
>
> He who conceals a fugitive slave is a thief. . . . And the magistrates are very properly notified to detain fugitive slaves carefully in custody to prevent their escape. . . . Careful custody permits the use of leg irons.[1]

Finally, Justinian's lawyers compiled a handbook of civil law, the *Institutes*. These three works — the *Code*, the *Digest*, and the *Institutes* — are the backbone of the **corpus juris civilis**, the "body of civil law," which is the foundation of law for nearly every modern European nation.

Byzantine Intellectual Life

Just as they valued the law, the Byzantines prized education, and because of them many masterpieces of an-

---

• **corpus juris civilis** The "body of civil law," it is composed of the *Code*, the *Digest*, and the *Institutes*.

Greek Fire In this illustration from a twelfth-century manuscript, sailors shoot Greek fire toward an attacking ship from a pressurized tube that looks strikingly similar to a modern flamethrower. The exact formula for Greek fire has been lost, but it was probably made from a petroleum product because it continued burning on water. Greek fire was particularly important in Byzantine defenses of Constantinople from Muslim forces in the late seventh century. (Prado, Madrid/The Bridgeman Art Library)

cient Greek literature survived to influence the intellectual life of the modern world. The literature of the Byzantine Empire was predominately Greek, although Latin was long spoken by top politicians, scholars, and lawyers. Among members of the large reading public, history was a favorite subject.

The most remarkable Byzantine historian was Procopius (ca. 500–ca. 562), who left a rousing account of Justinian's reconquest of North Africa and Italy. Procopius's *Secret History*, on the other hand, is a vicious and uproarious attack on Justinian and his wife, the empress Theodora, which continued the wit and venom of earlier Greek and Roman writers. (See "Individuals in Society: Theodora of Constantinople," page 210.)

In mathematics and science the Byzantines discovered little that was new, though they passed Greco-Roman learning on to the Arabs. The best-known Byzantine scientific discovery was an explosive compound known as "Greek fire" made of crude oil mixed with resin and sulfur, which were heated and propelled by a pump through a bronze tube. As the liquid jet left the tube, it was ignited, somewhat like a modern flamethrower. Greek fire saved Constantinople from Arab assault in 678.

The Byzantines devoted a great deal of attention to medicine, and their general level of medical compe-

tence was far higher than that of western Europeans, for they could read about and use Hellenistic methods of treating illness and relieving pain. Yet Byzantine physicians could not cope with the terrible disease, often called "the Justinian plague," that swept through the Byzantine Empire and parts of western Europe between 541 and 543. Probably originating in northwestern India and carried to the Mediterranean region by ships, the disease was similar to the bubonic plague. Characterized by high fevers, chills, delirium, and enlarged lymph nodes, or by inflammation of the lungs that caused hemorrhages of black blood, the plague carried off tens of thousands of people. The epidemic had profound political as well as social consequences. It weakened Justinian's military resources, thus hampering his efforts to restore unity to the Mediterranean world. Losses from the plague also further weakened Byzantine and Persian forces that had long been fighting each other, contributing to their inability to offer more than token opposition to Muslim armies (see page 237).

Life in Constantinople

By the tenth century Constantinople was the greatest city in the Christian world: the seat of the imperial court and administration, a large population center,

Individuals in Society

Theodora of Constantinople

THE MOST POWERFUL WOMAN IN BYZANTINE history was the daughter of a bear trainer for the circus. Theodora (ca. 497–548) grew up in what her contemporaries regarded as an undignified and morally suspect atmosphere, and she worked as a dancer and actress, both dishonorable occupations in the Roman world. Despite her background, she caught the eye of Justinian, who was then a military leader and whose uncle (and adoptive father) Justin had himself risen from obscurity to become the ruler of the Byzantine Empire. Under Justinian's influence, Justin changed the law to allow an actress who had left her disreputable life to marry whom she liked, and Justinian and Theodora married in 525. When Justinian was proclaimed co-emperor with his uncle Justin on April 1, 527, Theodora received the rare title of *augusta*, empress. Thereafter her name was linked with Justinian's in the exercise of imperial power.

Most of our knowledge of Theodora's early life comes from the *Secret History*, a tell-all description of the vices of Justinian and his court written by Procopius around 550. Procopius was the official court historian and thus spent his days praising those same people. In the *Secret History*, however, he portrays Theodora and Justinian as demonic, greedy, and vicious, killing courtiers to steal their property. In scene after detailed scene, Procopius portrays Theodora as particularly evil, sexually insatiable, and cruel, a temptress who used sorcery to attract men, including the hapless Justinian.

In one of his official histories, *The History of the Wars of Justinian*, Procopius presents a very different Theodora. Riots between the supporters of two teams in chariot races had turned deadly, and Justinian wavered in his handling of the perpetrators. Both sides turned against the emperor, besieging the palace while Justinian was inside it. Shouting "*Nika!*" (Victory), the rioters swept through the city, burning and looting. Justinian's counselors urged flight, but, according to Procopius, Theodora rose and declared:

> For one who has reigned, it is intolerable to be an exile. . . . If you wish, O Emperor, to save yourself, there is no difficulty: we have ample funds and there are the ships. Yet reflect whether, when you have once escaped to a place of security, you will not prefer death to safety. I agree with an old saying

● **A sixth-century mosaic of the empress Theodora, made of thousands of tiny cubes of glass, shows her with a halo—a symbol of power—and surrounded by officials, priests, and court ladies.** (Scala/Art Resource, NY)

that the purple [that is, the color worn only by emperors] is a fair winding sheet [to be buried in].

Justinian rallied, ordered more than thirty thousand men and women executed, and crushed the revolt.

Other sources describe or suggest Theodora's influence on imperial policy. Justinian passed a number of laws that improved the legal status of women, such as allowing women to own property and to be guardians over their own children. He forbade the exposure of unwanted infants, which happened more often to girls than to boys, since boys were valued more highly. Theodora presided at imperial receptions for Arab sheiks, Persian ambassadors, Germanic princesses from the West, and barbarian chieftains from southern Russia. When Justinian fell ill from the bubonic plague in 542, Theodora took over his duties. Justinian is reputed to have consulted her every day about all aspects of state policy, including religious policy regarding the doctrinal disputes that continued throughout his reign.

Theodora's influence over her husband and her power in the Byzantine state continued until she died, perhaps of cancer, twenty years before Justinian. Her influence may have even continued after death, for Justinian continued to pass reforms favoring women and, at the end of his life, accepted an interpretation of Christian doctrine she had favored. Institutions that she established, including hospitals and churches, continued to be reminders of her charity and piety.

Theodora has been viewed as a symbol of the use of beauty and cleverness to attain position and power, and also as a strong and capable co-ruler who held the empire together during riots, revolts, and deadly epidemics. Just as she fascinated Procopius, she continues to intrigue writers today, who make her a character not only in historical works, but also in science fiction and fantasy

QUESTIONS FOR ANALYSIS

1. How would you assess the complex legacy of Theodora?
2. Since Procopius's public and private views of the empress are so different, should he be trusted at all as a historical source? Why?

and the pivot of a large volume of international trade. Given that the city was a natural geographical connecting point between East and West, its markets offered goods from many parts of the world. Furs and timber flowed across the Black Sea from the Rus (Russia) to the capital, as did slaves across the Mediterranean from northern Europe and the Balkans via Venice. Spices, silks, jewelry, and other luxury goods came to Constantinople from India and China by way of Arabia, the Red Sea, and the Indian Ocean. In return, the city exported glassware, mosaics, gold coins, silk cloth, carpets, and a host of other products, with much foreign trade in the hands of Italian merchants. At the end of the eleventh century Constantinople may have been the world's third largest city, with only Córdoba in Spain and Kaifeng in China larger.

Although merchants could become fabulously wealthy, as in western Europe and China, the landed aristocracy always held the dominant social position. By contrast, merchants and craftsmen, even when they acquired considerable wealth, never won social prominence. Aristocrats and monasteries usually invested their wealth in real estate, which involved little risk but brought little gain.

Constantinople did not enjoy constant political stability. Between the accession of Emperor Heraclius in 610 and the fall of the city to western Crusaders in 1204 (see page 407), four separate dynasties ruled at Constantinople. Imperial government involved such intricate court intrigue, assassination plots, and military revolts that the word *byzantine* is sometimes used in English to mean extremely entangled and complicated politics.

What do we know about private life in Constantinople? Research has revealed a fair amount about the Byzantine *oikos* (OY-kohs), or household. The typical household in the city included family members and servants, some of whom were slaves. Artisans lived and worked in their shops, while clerks, civil servants, minor officials, and businesspeople — those who today would be called middle class — commonly dwelled in multistory buildings perhaps comparable to the apartment complexes of modern American cities. Wealthy aristocrats resided in freestanding mansions that frequently included interior courts, galleries, large reception halls, small sleeping rooms, reading and writing rooms, baths, and chapels.

In the homes of the upper classes, the segregation of women seems to have been the first principle of interior design. As in ancient Athens, private houses contained a *gynaeceum* (jihn-uh-SEE-um), or women's apartment, where women were kept strictly separated from the outside world. The fundamental reason for this segregation was the family's honor: "An unchaste daughter is guilty of harming not only herself but also her parents and relatives. That is why you should keep your daughters under lock and key, as if proven guilty or imprudent, in order to avoid venomous bites," as an eleventh-century Byzantine writer put it.[2]

Marriage was part of a family's strategy for social advancement. Both the immediate family and the larger kinship group participated in the selection of a bride or a groom, choosing a spouse who might enhance the family's wealth or prestige.

The Growth of the Christian Church

☐ What factors enabled the Christian Church to expand and thrive?

As the Western Roman Empire disintegrated, the Christian Church survived and grew, becoming the most important institution in Europe. The church gained strength by taking more authority over religious issues away from the state. Also, the church's western realm, increasingly left to its own devices after the imperial capital moved from Rome to Constantinople, gained more power. Even so, the state continued to intervene in theological disputes. Meanwhile, new Christian orders emphasizing asceticism arose and made important contributions to religious and secular society.

The Evolution of Church Leadership and Orthodoxy

Believers in early Christian communities elected their leaders, but as the centuries passed appointment by existing church leaders or secular rulers became the common practice. During the reign of Diocletian (r. 284–305), the Roman Empire had been divided for administrative purposes into geographical units called **dioceses**, and Christianity adopted this pattern. Each diocese was headed by a bishop, who was responsible for delegating responsibilities for preaching and teaching, organizing preaching, overseeing the community's goods, and maintaining orthodox (established or correct) doctrine. The center of a bishop's authority was his cathedral, a word deriving from the Latin *cathedra*, meaning "chair."

Some bishops brought significant administrative skills to the early Christian Church. Bishop Ambrose of Milan (339–397), for example, had a solid education, was a trained lawyer, and had once been the governor

---

• **dioceses** Geographic administrative districts of the church, each under the authority of a bishop and centered around a cathedral.

> ❝It is written, God's to God and Caesar's to Caesar. The palace is the Emperor's, the churches are the Bishop's.❞

BISHOP AMBROSE OF MILAN

of a province. He was typical of the Roman aristocrats who held high public office, were converted to Christianity, and subsequently became bishops. He had a strong sense of his authority and even stood up to Emperor Theodosius (r. 379–395), who had ordered Ambrose to hand over his major church—called a basilica—to the emperor:

> At length came the command, "Deliver up the Basilica"; I reply, "It is not lawful for us to deliver it up, nor for your Majesty to receive it. By no law can you violate the house of a private man, and do you think that the house of God may be taken away? . . . But do not burden your conscience with the thought that you have any right as Emperor over sacred things. . . . It is written, God's to God and Caesar's to Caesar. The palace is the Emperor's, the churches are the Bishop's. To you is committed jurisdiction over public, not over sacred buildings."[3]

The emperor relented, and Ambrose's assertion that the church was supreme in spiritual matters and the state in secular issues remained the Christian leadership's position on church-state relations for centuries. Because of his strong influence Ambrose came to be regarded as one of the fathers of the church, and his authority was regarded as second only to the Bible's in later centuries. Although conflicts like these between religious and secular leaders were frequent, the church also received support from the emperors. In return the emperors expected the Christian Church's support in maintaining order and unity.

In the fourth century, disputes also arose within the Christian community, though these concerned theological issues. Some disagreements had to do with the nature of Christ. For example, **Arianism**, which originated with Arius (ca. 250–336), a priest of Alexandria, held that Jesus was created by the will of God the Father and thus was not co-eternal with him. Arius also reasoned that Jesus the Son must be inferior to God the Father, because the Father was incapable of suffering and did not die. Arian Christianity attracted many followers, including Greeks, Romans, and especially barbarian migrants to Europe who were converted by Arian Christian missionaries.

Emperor Constantine, who legalized Christianity in 312, rejected the Arian interpretation and decided that religious disagreement meant civil disorder. In 325 he summoned a council of church leaders to Nicaea in Asia Minor and presided over it personally. The council produced the Nicene Creed, which defined the orthodox position that Christ is "eternally begotten of the Father" and of the same substance as the Father. Arius and those who refused to accept the creed were banished, the first case of civil punishment for heresy. This participation of the emperor in a theological dispute within the church paved the way for later emperors to claim that they could do the same. The Nicene interpretation was modified slightly by councils later in the fourth century, but it eventually became the most widely held understanding of the nature of Christ. (It is accepted today by the Roman Catholic Church, the Eastern Orthodox churches, and most Protestant churches.) Although Arian Christianity slowly died out among Greeks and Romans, it remained the most

Sarcophagus of Helena This marble sarcophagus was made for Helena, the mother of Emperor Constantine, at her death. Its detailed carvings show victorious Roman horsemen and barbarian prisoners. Like her son, Helena became a Christian, and she was sent by Constantine on a journey to bring sacred relics from Jerusalem to Constantinople as part of his efforts to promote Christianity in the empire. (Vanni/Art Resource, NY)

common form of Christianity among barbarian groups for centuries.

In 380 Theodosius went even further than Constantine and made Christianity the official religion of the empire. He stripped Roman pagan temples of statues, made the practice of the old Roman state religion a treasonable offense, and persecuted Christians who dissented from orthodox doctrine. Most significantly, he allowed the church to establish its own courts and develop its own body of law, called canon law. These courts, not the Roman government, had jurisdiction over the clergy and ecclesiastical disputes. The foundation for later growth in church power had thus been laid.

The Western Church and the Eastern Church

The leader of the church in the West, the bishop of Rome, became more powerful than his counterpart in the Byzantine East for a variety of reasons. The change began in the fourth century with the move of the imperial capital and the emperor from Rome to Constantinople. Because the bishop of Rome no longer had any real competition for leadership in the West, he began to exercise more influence there.

The power of successive bishops of Rome increased as they repeatedly called on the emperors at Constantinople for military support against barbarian invaders. Because the emperors had no troops to spare, they rarely could send such support. The Western Church thus became less dependent on the emperors' power and gradually took over political authority in central Italy, charging taxes, sending troops, and enforcing laws.

The bishops of Rome also stressed their special role within the church. They pointed to words spoken by Jesus to one of his disciples, Peter, and the fact that, according to tradition, Peter had lived in Rome and been its first bishop, to assert a privileged position in the church hierarchy, an idea called the Petrine Doctrine. As successors of Peter, they stated, the bishops of Rome — known as **popes**, from the Latin word *papa*, meaning "father" — should be supreme over other Christian communities. They urged other churches to appeal to Rome for the resolution of disputed issues. (The Christian Church headed by the pope in Rome was generally called the Roman Church in this era, and later the Roman Catholic Church. The word *catholic* derives from a Greek word meaning "general," "universal," or "worldwide.")

By contrast, in the East the emperor's jurisdiction over the church was fully acknowledged, even though the bishops of Antioch, Alexandria, Jerusalem, and Constantinople had more power than other bishops. As in Rome, there was a head of the church in Constantinople, called the patriarch, but he did not develop the same powers that the pope did in the West because there was never a similar power vacuum into which he needed to step. He and other high church officials were appointed by the emperor. The Eastern emperors looked on religion as a branch of the state, and they considered it their duty to protect the faith not only against heathen outsiders but also against heretics within the empire. Following the pattern set by Constantine, the emperors summoned councils of bishops and theologians to settle doctrinal disputes. They and the Eastern bishops did not accept Rome's claim to primacy, and gradually the Eastern Christian Church, generally called the **Orthodox Church**, and the Roman Church began to diverge. (*Orthodoxy* with a capital *O* refers to the Eastern Church, and *orthodoxy* with a small *o* means correct doctrine as defined by church leaders.)

The Iconoclastic Controversy

In the centuries after Constantine the most serious dispute within the Orthodox Church concerned icons — images or representations of God the Father, Jesus, and the saints in a painting, bas-relief, or mosaic. Since the third century the church had allowed people to venerate icons. Although all prayer had to be directed to God the Father, Christian teaching held that icons representing the saints fostered reverence and that Jesus and the saints could most effectively plead a cause to God the Father. (For more about the role of saints, see page 219.) Iconoclasts, those who favored the destruction of icons, argued that people were worshipping the image itself rather than what it signified. This, they claimed, constituted idolatry, a violation of one of the Ten Commandments, a religious and moral code sacred to Christians.

The result of this dispute was a terrible theological conflict, the **iconoclastic controversy**, that split the Byzantine world for a century. In 730 the emperor Leo III (r. 717–741) ordered the destruction of icons. The removal of these images from Byzantine churches provoked a violent reaction: entire provinces revolted, and the empire and Roman papacy severed relations. Since Eastern monasteries were the fiercest defenders of icons, Leo's son Constantine V (r. 741–775),

- **Arianism** A theological belief, originating with Arius, a priest of Alexandria, that denied that Christ was co-eternal with God the Father.
- **popes** Heads of the Roman Catholic Church, who became political as well as religious authorities. The period of a pope's term in office is called a "pontificate."
- **Orthodox Church** Another name for the Eastern Christian Church, over which emperors continued to have power.
- **iconoclastic controversy** The conflict over the veneration of religious images in the Byzantine Empire.

nicknamed "Copronymous" ("Dung-name") by his enemies, took the war to the monasteries. He seized their property, executed some of the monks, and forced other monks into the army. Theological disputes and civil disorder over the icons continued intermittently until 843, when the icons were restored.

The implications of the iconoclastic controversy extended far beyond strictly theological issues. Iconoclasm raised the question of the right of the emperor to intervene in religious disputes — a central problem in the relations between church and state. Iconoclasm antagonized the pope and served to encourage him in his quest for an alliance with the Frankish monarchy (see page 225). This further divided the two parts of Christendom, and in 1054 a theological disagreement led the pope in Rome and the patriarch of Constantinople to excommunicate each other. The outcome was a continuing schism, or split, between the Roman Catholic and the Orthodox Churches.

From a cultural perspective, the acceptance of icons profoundly influenced subsequent religious art within Christianity. That art rejected the Judaic and Islamic prohibition against images of religious figures and continued the Greco-Roman tradition of giving these figures human forms.

Christian Monasticism

Like the great East Asian religions of Jainism and Buddhism (see pages 74–79), Christianity began and spread as a city religion. With time, however, some especially pious Christians started to feel that a life of asceticism (extreme material sacrifice, including fasting and the renunciation of sex) was a better way to show their devotion to Christ's teachings. Asceticism was — and is — a common part of many religious traditions, either as a temporary practice during especially holy times or as a permanent way of life.

Ascetics often separate themselves from their families and normal social life, and this is what Christian ascetics did. Individuals and small groups withdrew from cities and moved to the Egyptian desert, where they sought God through prayer in caves and shelters in the desert or mountains. These individuals were called "hermits," from the Greek word *eremos*, meaning "desert," or "monks," from the Greek word *monos*, meaning "alone." Gradually, large groups of monks emerged in the deserts of Upper Egypt, creating a style of life known as "monasticism." Many devout women also were attracted to this eremitical type of monasticism, becoming nuns. Although monks and nuns led isolated lives, ordinary people soon recognized them as holy people and sought them as spiritual guides.

Church leaders did not really approve of eremitical life. Hermits sometimes claimed to have mystical experiences — direct communications with God. If hermits could communicate directly with the Lord, what need had they for priests, bishops, and the institutional church? The church hierarchy instead encouraged those who wanted to live ascetic lives of devotion to do so in communities. Communal living in a monastery, they argued, provided an environment for training the aspirant in the virtues of charity, poverty, and freedom from self-deception. Consequently, in the fourth, fifth, and sixth centuries many different kinds of communal monasticism developed in Gaul, Italy, Spain, Anglo-Saxon England, and Ireland.

In 529 Benedict of Nursia (ca. 480–547), who had experimented with both the eremitical and the communal forms of monastic life, wrote a brief set of regulations for the

Saint Benedict Holding his *Rule* in his left hand, the seated and hooded patriarch of Western monasticism blesses a monk with his right hand. His monastery, Monte Cassino, is in the background. (Biblioteca Apostolica Vaticana)

monks who had gathered around him at Monte Cassino, between Rome and Naples. Benedict's guide for monastic life, known as *The Rule of Saint Benedict,* slowly replaced all others, and it has influenced all forms of organized religious life in the Roman Church. The guide outlined a monastic life of regularity, discipline, and moderation in an atmosphere of silence. Under Benedict's regulations, monks spent part of each day in formal prayer, chanting psalms and other prayers from the Bible. The rest of the day was passed in manual labor, study, and private prayer.

Why did the Benedictine form of monasticism eventually replace other forms of western monasticism? The monastic life as conceived by Saint Benedict struck a balance between asceticism and activity. It thus provided opportunities for men of entirely different abilities and talents—from mechanics and gardeners to literary scholars. The Benedictine form of religious life also proved congenial to women. Five miles from Monte Cassino at Plombariola, Benedict's twin sister Scholastica (ca. 480–543) adapted *The Rule of Saint Benedict* for her community of nuns.

Another reason for Benedictine monasticism's dominance was its material success. In the seventh and eighth centuries Benedictine monasteries pushed back forests and wastelands, drained swamps, and experimented with crop rotation, making a significant contribution to the agricultural development of Europe. In the process they earned immense wealth. The communal nature of their organization, whereby property was held in common and profits were pooled and reinvested, made their contributions to agriculture possible.

Monasteries also conducted schools for local young people. Some learned about prescriptions and herbal remedies and went on to provide medical treatment for their localities. Others copied manuscripts and wrote books. Local and royal governments drew on the services of the literate men and able administrators the monasteries produced.

Because all monasteries followed rules, men who lived a communal monastic life came to be called regular clergy, from the Latin word *regulus* (rule). In contrast, priests and bishops who staffed churches in which people worshipped and who were not cut off from the world were called secular clergy. According to official church doctrine, women were not members of the clergy, but this distinction was not clear to most people.

Monasticism in the Greek Orthodox world differed in fundamental ways from the monasticism that evolved in western Europe. First, while *The Rule of Saint Benedict* gradually became the universal guide for all western European monasteries, each monastic house in the Byzantine world developed its own set of rules for organization and behavior. Second, education never became a central feature of the Greek houses. Monks and nuns had to be literate to perform the services of the choir, and children destined for the monastic life were taught to read and write, but no monastery assumed responsibility for the general training of the local young. Since bishops and patriarchs of the Greek Church were recruited only from the monasteries, Greek houses did, however, exercise a cultural influence.

Christian Ideas and Practices

◻ How did Christian thinkers and missionaries adapt Greco-Roman ideas to Christian theology and develop effective techniques for converting barbarian peoples?

The growth of Christianity was tied not just to institutions such as the papacy and monasteries, but also to ideas. Initially, Christians rejected Greco-Roman culture. Gradually, however, Christian leaders and thinkers developed ideas that drew on classical influences. At the same time missionaries sponsored by bishops and monasteries spread Christian ideas and institutions far beyond the borders of the Roman and Byzantine Empires, often adapting them to local spiritual beliefs and practices as they assimilated pagan peoples to Christianity.

Christian Beliefs and the Greco-Roman Tradition

In the first century Christians believed that Christ would soon fulfill his promise to return and that the end of the world was near; therefore, they saw no point in devoting time to learning. By the second century, however, these apocalyptic expectations were diminishing, and church leaders began to incorporate elements of Greek and Roman philosophy and learning into Christian teachings (see page 168). They found support for this incorporation in the written texts that circulated among Christians. In the third and fourth centuries these texts were brought together as the New Testament of the Bible, with general agreement about most of what should be included but sharp disputes about some books. Although some of Jesus's sermons as recorded in the Gospels (see page 166) urged followers to avoid worldly attachments, other parts of the Bible advocated acceptance of existing social, economic, and political structures. Christian thinkers built on these, adapting Christian teachings to fit with Roman realities and Roman ideas to fit with Christian aims.

Procession to a New Church In this sixth-century ivory carving, two men in a wagon, accompanied by a procession of people holding candles, carry relics of a saint to a Christian church under construction. New churches often received holy items when they were dedicated, and processions were common ways in which people expressed community devotion. (Cathedral Treasury, Trier. Photo: Ann Muenchow)

Saint Jerome (340–419), a distinguished theologian and linguist regarded as a father of the church, translated the Bible's Old Testament and New Testament from Hebrew and Greek, respectively, into vernacular Latin (a form of Latin common among Christians of the time). Called the "Vulgate," his edition of the Bible served as the official translation until the sixteenth century, and scholars rely on it even today. Familiar with the writings of classical authors such as Cicero and Virgil, Saint Jerome believed that Christians should study the best of ancient thought because it would direct their minds to God. He maintained that the best ancient literature should be interpreted in light of the Christian faith.

Christian attitudes toward gender and sexuality provide a good example of the ways early Christians challenged and then adopted the views of their contemporary world, modifying these as they did. In his plan of salvation Jesus considered women the equal of men. He attributed no disreputable qualities to women and did not refer to them as inferior creatures. On the contrary, women were among his earliest and most faithful converts.

Accordingly, women took an active role in the spread of Christianity, preaching, acting as missionaries, being martyred alongside men, and perhaps even baptizing believers. Because early Christians believed that the second coming of Christ was imminent, they devoted their energies to their new spiritual family of co-believers. Also, they often met in people's homes and called one another brother and sister, a metaphorical use of family terms that was new to the Roman Empire. Some women embraced the ideal of virginity and either singly or in monastic communities declared themselves "virgins in the service of Christ." All this made Christianity seem dangerous to many Romans, especially when becoming Christian led some young people to avoid marriage, which was viewed by Romans as the foundation of society and a necessity for maintaining the power of the paterfamilias (see page 151).

Not all Christian teachings represented a radical break from Roman tradition, however. In the first century male church leaders began to place restrictions on female believers. Paul (see page 168) and later writers forbade women to preach, and women were gradually excluded from holding official positions in Christianity other than in women's monasteries. In so limiting the activities of female believers Christianity was following well-established social patterns, just as it modeled its official hierarchy after that of the Roman Empire.

Christian teachings about sexuality also built on and challenged classical models. The church's unfavorable view of sexual activity involved an affirmation of the importance of a spiritual life, but it also incorporated hostility toward the body found in some Hellenistic philosophies. Just as spirit was superior to matter, the thinking went, the mind was superior to the body. Though Christian teachings affirmed that God had created the material world and sanctioned marriage, most Christian thinkers also taught that celibacy was the better life and that anything that distracted one's attention from the spiritual world performed an evil function. Most church fathers saw women as just such a distraction and temptation, and in some of their writings women are portrayed as evil. Thus these writings contain a strong streak of misogyny (hatred of women), which was passed down to later Christian thinkers. Same-sex relations — which were generally acceptable in the Greco-Roman world, especially if they were between socially unequal individuals — were also evil in the eyes of church fathers. Their misogyny and hostility toward sexuality had a greater influence on the formation of later attitudes than did the relatively egalitarian actions and words of Jesus.

Saint Augustine

One thinker had an especially strong role in shaping Christian views about sexual activity and many other issues: Saint Augustine of Hippo (354–430), the most influential church father in the West. Augustine was born into an urban family in what is now Algeria in North Africa. His father, a minor civil servant, was a pagan; his mother, Monica, a devout Christian. It was not until adulthood that he converted to his mother's religion, eventually becoming bishop of the city of Hippo Regius. Augustine gained renown as a preacher, a vigorous defender of orthodox Christianity, and the author of more than ninety-three books and treatises.

Augustine's autobiography, *The Confessions*, is a literary masterpiece and one of the most influential books in history. Written in the rhetorical style and language of late Roman antiquity, it nonetheless challenges Greco-Roman views of human behavior and morality. *The Confessions* describes Augustine's moral struggle, the conflict between his spiritual aspirations and his sensual self. Many Greek and Roman philosophers had taught that knowledge and virtue are the same: a person who knows what is right will do what is right. Augustine rejected this idea, arguing that people do not always act on the basis of rational knowledge. Instead, the basic or dynamic force in any individual is the will. When Adam ate the fruit forbidden by God in the Garden of Eden (Genesis 3:6), he committed the "original sin" and corrupted the will, wrote Augustine. Adam's sin was not simply his own but was passed on to all later humans through sexual intercourse; even infants were tainted. Augustine viewed sexual desire as the result of the disobedience of Adam and Eve (who also ate the forbidden fruit), linking sexuality even more clearly with sin than had earlier church fathers. According to Augustine, because Adam disobeyed God, all human beings have an innate tendency to sin: their will is weak. But Augustine held that God restores the strength of the will through grace, which is transmitted in certain rituals that the church defined as **sacraments**. Augustine's ideas on sin, grace, and redemption became the foundation of all subsequent Western Christian theology, Protestant as well as Catholic.

Missionary Activity

Christ had said that his teaching was for all peoples, and Christians sought to make their faith catholic — that is, worldwide or believed everywhere. The Mediterranean served as the highway over which Christianity spread to the cities of the Byzantine Empire (Map 8.2). From there missionaries took Christian teachings to the countryside, and then to areas beyond the borders of the empire.

Because the religion of a region's chieftain or king determined the religion of the people, missionaries concentrated their initial efforts on these leaders and members of their families, and the leaders then ordered their people to convert. Queens and other female members of the royal family were often the first converts in an area, and they influenced their husbands and brothers. Barbarian kings accepted Christianity because they believed that the Christian God was more powerful than pagan gods and that the Christian God — either the Arian or the Nicene version — would deliver victory in battle, because Christianity taught obedience to (kingly) authority, or because Christian priests possessed knowledge and a charisma that could be associated with kingly power.

Many barbarian groups were converted by Arian missionaries, who also founded dioceses. Even before Saint Jerome translated the Bible into Latin, one of these Arian missionaries, Bishop Ulfilas (ca. 310–383), an Ostrogoth himself, translated the Bible from Greek into the Gothic language, creating a new Gothic script in order to write it down. Over the next several centuries this text was recopied many times and carried with the Gothic tribes as they migrated throughout southern Europe. In the sixth and seventh centuries most Goths and other Germanic tribes converted to Roman Christianity, sometimes peacefully and sometimes as a result of conquest. Ulfilas's Bible — and the Gothic script he invented — were forgotten and rediscovered only a thousand years later.

Tradition identifies the conversion of Ireland with Saint Patrick (ca. 385–461). After a vision urged him to Christianize Ireland, Patrick studied in Gaul and in 432 was consecrated a bishop. He then returned to Ireland, where he converted the Irish tribe by tribe, first baptizing the king.

The Christianization of the English really began in 597, when Pope Gregory I (pontificate 590–604) sent a delegation of monks to England. The conversion of the English had far-reaching consequences because Britain later served as a base for the Christianization of Germany and other parts of northern Europe (see

• **sacraments** Certain rituals of the church believed to act as a conduit of God's grace, such as the Eucharist and baptism.

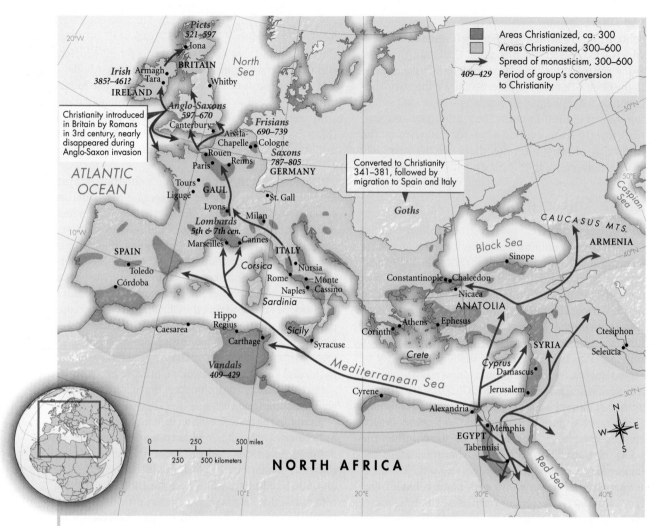

□ Mapping the Past

MAP 8.2 The Spread of Christianity, ca. 300–800 Originating in the area near Jerusalem, Christianity spread throughout the Roman world.

ANALYZING THE MAP Based on the map, how did the roads and sea-lanes of the Roman Empire influence the spread of Christianity?

CONNECTIONS How does the map support the conclusion that Christianity began as an urban religion and then spread into more rural areas?

Map 8.2). Between the fifth and tenth centuries the majority of people living on the European continent and the nearby islands accepted the Christian religion — that is, they received baptism, though baptism in itself did not automatically transform people into Christians.

In eastern Europe missionaries traveled far beyond the boundaries of the Byzantine Empire. In 863 the emperor Michael III (r. 842–867) sent the brothers Cyril (826–869) and Methodius (815–885) to preach Christianity in Moravia (an eastern region of the modern Czech Republic). Other missionaries succeeded in converting the Russians in the tenth century. Another

Byzantine influence on Russia was the Slavic alphabet invented by Cyril (called the "Cyrillic alphabet"). This made possible the birth of Russian literature, and it is still in use today. Similarly, Byzantine art and architecture became the basis of and inspiration for Russian forms, particularly in the creation of religious icons.

Conversion and Assimilation

When a ruler marched his people to the waters of baptism, the work of Christianization had only begun. Christian kings could order their subjects to be bap-

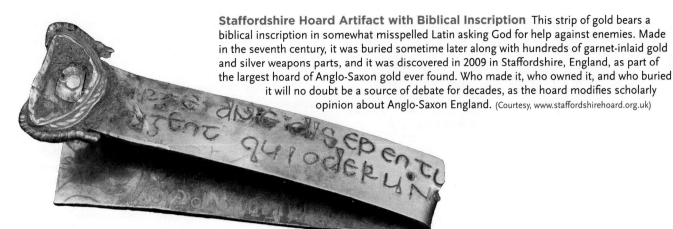

Staffordshire Hoard Artifact with Biblical Inscription This strip of gold bears a biblical inscription in somewhat misspelled Latin asking God for help against enemies. Made in the seventh century, it was buried sometime later along with hundreds of garnet-inlaid gold and silver weapons parts, and it was discovered in 2009 in Staffordshire, England, as part of the largest hoard of Anglo-Saxon gold ever found. Who made it, who owned it, and who buried it will no doubt be a source of debate for decades, as the hoard modifies scholarly opinion about Anglo-Saxon England. (Courtesy, www.staffordshirehoard.org.uk)

tized, married, and buried in Christian ceremonies, which they did increasingly across Europe. Churches could be built, and people could be required to attend services and belong to parishes, but the church could not compel people to accept Christian beliefs, many of which, such as "love your enemies," seemed strange or radical.

How, then, did missionaries and priests get masses of pagan and illiterate peoples to understand and become more accepting of Christian ideals and teachings? They did it through preaching, assimilation, the ritual of penance, and veneration of the saints.

Preaching aimed at presenting the basic teachings of Christianity and strengthening the newly baptized in their faith through stories about the lives of Christ and the saints. Deeply ingrained pagan customs and practices, however, could not be stamped out by words alone or even by imperial edicts. Thus Christian missionaries often pursued a policy of assimilation, easing the conversion of pagan men and women by stressing similarities between their customs and beliefs and those of Christianity. In the same way that classically trained scholars such as Jerome and Augustine blended Greco-Roman and Christian ideas, missionaries and converts mixed barbarian pagan ideas and practices with Christian ones. For example, bogs and lakes sacred to Germanic gods became associated with saints (discussed in more detail below), as did various aspects of ordinary life, such as traveling, planting crops, and worrying about a sick child. Aspects of existing midwinter celebrations, which often centered on the return of the sun as the days became longer, were incorporated into celebrations of Christmas. Spring rituals involving eggs and rabbits (both symbols of fertility) were added to celebrations of Easter.

The ritual of **penance** was also instrumental in teaching Christian beliefs, in this case concerning sins, actions and thoughts that went against God's commands. Christianity taught that only by confessing sins and asking forgiveness could a sinning believer be reconciled with God. Confession was initially a public ritual, but by the fifth century individual confession to a parish priest was more common. During this ritual the individual knelt before the priest, who questioned him or her about sins he or she might have committed. The priest then set a penance, such as fasting or saying specific prayers, to allow the person to atone for the sin. Penance gave new converts a sense of the behavior expected of Christians, encouraged the private examination of conscience, and offered relief from the burden of sinful deeds.

Although confession became mostly a private affair, most religious observances continued to be community matters, as they had been in the ancient world. People joined with family members, friends, and neighbors to celebrate baptisms and funerals, presided over by a priest.

Veneration of **saints**, people who had lived (or died) in a way that was spiritually heroic or noteworthy, was another way that Christians formed stronger connections with their religion. Saints were understood to provide protection and assistance to worshippers, and parish churches often housed saints' relics, that is, bones, articles of clothing, or other objects associated with them. The relics served as links between the material world and the spiritual, and miracle stories about saints and their relics were an important part of Christian preaching and writing. For example, Gregory of Tours (ca. 538–594), a bishop in the Frankish kingdom, described his father's faith in relics:

Because my father wished himself to be protected by relics of saints, he asked a cleric to grant him something from these relics, so that with their protection he might be kept safe as he set out on this long journey. He put the sacred ashes in a gold medallion and

---

• **penance** Ritual in which Christians asked a priest for forgiveness for sins, and the priest set certain actions to atone for the sins.

• **saints** People who were venerated for having lived or died in a way that was spiritually heroic or noteworthy.

> "He claimed that often, because of the powers of these relics, he had avoided the violence of bandits, the dangers of floods, the threats of turbulent men, and attacks from swords."

GREGORY OF TOURS

carried it with him. Although he did not even know the names of the blessed men, he was accustomed to recount that he had been rescued from many dangers. He claimed that often, because of the powers of these relics, he had avoided the violence of bandits, the dangers of floods, the threats of turbulent men, and attacks from swords.[4]

Christians came to venerate the saints as powerful and holy. They prayed to saints or to the Virgin Mary to intercede with God, or they simply asked the saints to assist and bless them. The entire village participated in processions marking saints' days or important points in the agricultural year, often carrying images of saints or their relics around the houses and fields. Although the decision to adopt Christianity was often made first by an emperor or king, actual conversion was a local matter, as people came to feel that the parish priest and the saints provided them with benefits in this world and the world to come. Christianity became an important means through which barbarian groups migrating into Europe gained access to at least some of Greco-Roman culture.

Migrating Peoples

☐ How did the barbarians shape social, economic, and political structures in Europe and western Asia?

The migration of peoples from one area to another has been a continuing feature of world history. One of the most enduring patterns of migration was the movement of peoples west and south from Central Asia and northern Europe beginning in the second century C.E. (Map 8.3). The Greeks who encountered these peoples called them *barbaros* because they seemed to the Greeks to be speaking nonsense syllables — bar, bar, bar. ("Bar-bar" is the Greek equivalent of "blah-blah" or "yada-yada.") Although *barbaros* originally meant someone who did not speak Greek, gradually people labeled as such were also seen as unruly, savage, and more primitive than members of the advanced civilization of

Greece. (See "Viewpoints: Roman and Byzantine Views of Barbarians," page 222.) The word brought this broader meaning with it when it came into Latin and other European languages.

Barbarians included many different ethnic groups with social and political structures, languages, laws, and beliefs developed in central and northern Europe and western Asia over many centuries. Among the largest barbarian groups were the Celts (whom the Romans called Gauls) and Germans; Germans were further subdivided into various tribes, such as Ostrogoths, Visigoths, Burgundians, and Franks. *Celt* and *German* are often used as ethnic terms, but they are better understood as linguistic terms, a Celt being a person who spoke a Celtic language, an ancestor of the modern Gaelic or Breton languages, and a German one who spoke a Germanic language, an ancestor of modern German, Dutch, Danish, Swedish, and Norwegian. Celts, Germans, and other barbarians brought their customs and traditions with them when they moved south and west, and these gradually combined with classical and Christian customs and beliefs to form a new type of society. From this cultural mix the Franks emerged as an especially strong and influential force, and they built a lasting empire (see page 225).

Social and Economic Structures

Barbarians generally had no notion of the state as we use the term today; they thought in social, not political, terms. The basic social unit was the tribe, made up of kin groups, and tribe members believed that they were all descended from a common ancestor. Blood united them; kinship protected them. Kin groups were made up of families, which were responsible for the debts and actions of their members and for keeping the peace in general.

Barbarian groups usually resided in small villages, and climate and geography determined the basic patterns of agricultural and pastoral life. Many groups settled on the edges of clearings where they raised barley, wheat, oats, peas, and beans. Men and women tilled their fields with simple scratch plows, which broke the soil with wooden spikes, and harvested their grain with small iron sickles. The kernels of grain were eaten as porridge, ground up for flour, or fermented into strong, thick beer. Most of people's caloric intake came from grain in some form.

Within the small villages, there were great differences in wealth and status. Free men and their families constituted the largest class, and the number of cattle these men possessed indicated their wealth and determined their social status. Free men also took part in tribal warfare. Slaves (prisoners of war) worked as farm laborers, herdsmen, and household servants.

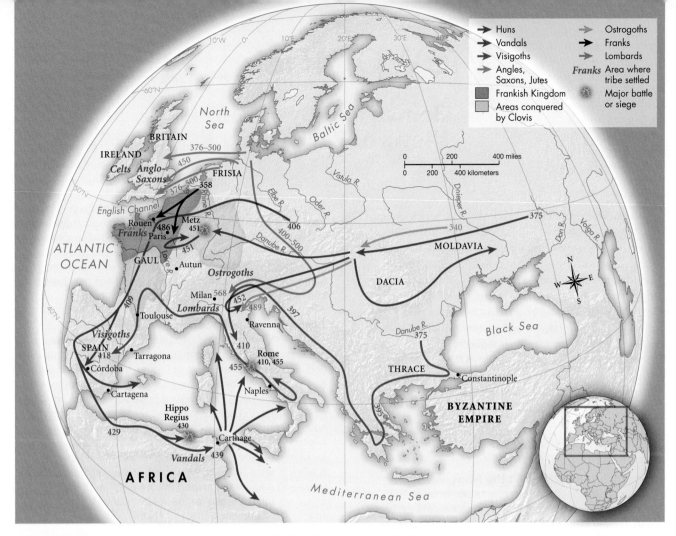

MAP 8.3 The Barbarian Migrations, ca. 340–500 Various barbarian groups migrated throughout Europe and western Asia in late antiquity, pushed and pulled by a number of factors. Many of them formed loosely structured states, of which the Frankish kingdom would become the most significant.

Barbarian society was patriarchal: within each household the father had authority over his wife, children, and slaves. Some wealthy and powerful men had more than one wife, a pattern that continued even after they became Christian, but polygamy was not widespread among ordinary people. A woman was considered to be under the legal guardianship of a man, and she had fewer rights to own property than did Roman women in the late empire. However, once they were widowed (and there must have been many widows in such a violent, warring society), women sometimes assumed their husbands' rights over family property and took guardianship of their children.

Chiefs, Warriors, and Laws

Barbarian tribes were led by chieftains, the tribe members recognized as the strongest and bravest in battle. Each chief was elected from among the male members of the strongest family. He led the tribe in war, settled disputes among its members, conducted negotiations

with outside powers, and offered sacrifices to the gods. As barbarian groups migrated into and conquered parts of the Western Roman Empire, their chiefs became even more powerful. Often chiefs adopted the title of king, though this title implies broader power than they actually had.

Closely associated with the chief in some tribes was the comitatus (kuhm-ee-TAH-tuhs), or "war band." The warriors swore loyalty to the chief and fought alongside him in battle. Warriors may originally have been relatively equal to one another, but during the migrations and warfare of the second through the fourth centuries, the war band was transformed into a system of stratified ranks. When tribes settled down, warriors also began to acquire land as both a mark of prestige and a means to power. Social inequalities emerged and gradually grew stronger. These inequalities help explain the origins of the European noble class.

Early barbarian tribes had no written laws. Instead, law was custom — preserved in the minds of tribal elders and handed down by word of mouth from

Viewpoints

Roman and Byzantine Views of Barbarians

• *The earliest written records about the barbarian groups that migrated, attacked, and sometimes conquered the more urbanized and densely populated areas of Europe and western Asia all come from the pens of educated Greeks, Romans, and Byzantines. They provide us with important information about barbarians, but always from the perspective of outsiders with a particular point of view. The selections below are typical of such commentary. The first is from the fourth-century Roman general and historian Ammianus Marcellinus, who fought in Roman armies against Germanic tribes, the Huns, and the Persians, and later wrote a history of the Roman Empire. The second is from the sixth-century Byzantine historian Agathias, describing recent encounters between the forces of the Byzantine emperor Justinian and various Germanic tribes.*

Ammianus Marcellinus on the Huns, ca. 380

"The people of the Huns, but little known from ancient records, dwelling beyond the Maeotic Sea near the ice-bound ocean, exceed every degree of savagery. . . . They all have compact, strong limbs and thick necks, and are so monstrously ugly and misshapen, that one might take them for two legged-beasts or for the stumps, rough-hewn into images, that are used in putting sides to bridges. But although they have the form of men, however ugly, they are so hardy in their mode of life that they have no need of fire nor of savory food, but eat the roots of wild plants and the half-raw flesh of any kind of animal whatever, which they put between their thighs and the backs of their horses, and thus warm a little. They are never protected by any buildings, but they avoid these like tombs. . . . They are not at all adapted to battles on foot, but they are almost glued to their horses, which are hardy, it is true, but ugly. . . . They fight from a distance with missiles having sharp bone [points], instead of the usual (metal) parts, joined to the shafts with wonderful skill; then they gallop over the intervening spaces and fight hand to hand with swords, regardless of their

own lives. . . . No one in their country ever plows a field or touches a plow-handle. They are all without fixed abode, without hearth, or law, or settled mode of life, and keep roaming from place to place, like fugitives, accompanied by wagons in which they live; in wagons their wives weave for them their hideous garments, in wagons they cohabit with their husbands, bear children, and rear them to the age of puberty."

Agathias on the Franks

"The Franks are not nomads, as indeed some barbarian peoples are, but their system of government, administration and laws are modelled more or less on the Roman pattern, apart from which they uphold similar standards with regard to contracts, marriage, and religious observance. They are in fact all Christians and adhere to the strictest orthodoxy. They also have magistrates in their cities and priests and celebrate the feasts in the same way we do, and, for a barbarian people, strike me as extremely well-bred and civilized and as practically the same as ourselves except for their uncouth style of dress and peculiar language. I admire them for their other attributes and especially for the spirit of justice and harmony which prevails amongst them."

QUESTIONS FOR ANALYSIS

1. What qualities of the Huns does Ammianus Marcellinus find admirable? What does he criticize?

2. What qualities of the Franks does Agathias praise? Why does he find these qualities admirable?

3. How does the fact that both Ammianus Marcellinus and Agathias come from agricultural societies with large cities shape their views of barbarians?

generation to generation. Beginning in the late sixth century, however, some tribal chieftains began to collect, write, and publish lists of their customs at the urging of Christian missionaries. The churchmen wanted to understand barbarian ways in order to assimilate the tribes to Christianity. Moreover, by the sixth century many barbarian chieftains needed regulations for the Romans under their jurisdiction as well as for their own people.

Barbarian law codes often included clauses designed to reduce interpersonal violence. Any crime that involved a personal injury, such as assault, rape, and murder, was given a particular monetary value, called the **wergeld** (WUHR-gehld) (literally "man-money" or "money to buy off the spear"), that was to be paid by a person accused of a crime to the victim or the victim's family. If the accused agreed to pay the wergeld and if the victim or his or her family accepted the payment,

Visigothic Work and Play
This page comes from one of the very few manuscripts from the time of the barbarian invasions to have survived, a copy of the first five books of the Old Testament—the Pentateuch—made around 600, perhaps in Visigothic Spain or North Africa. The top shows biblical scenes, while the bottom shows people engaged in everyday activities—building a wall, drawing water from a well, and trading punches. (Bibliothèque nationale de France)

there was peace. If the accused refused to pay the wergeld or if the victim or family refused to accept it, a blood feud ensued.

The wergeld varied according to the severity of the crime and also the social status and gender of the victim, as shown in these clauses from the law code of the Salian Franks, one of the barbarian tribes.

> If any person strike another on the head so that the brain appears, and the three bones which lie above the brain shall project, he shall be sentenced to 1200 denars, which make 300 shillings....
>
> If any one have killed a free woman after she has begun bearing children, he shall be sentenced to 2400 denars, which make 600 shillings.[5]

In other codes as well, a crime against a woman of childbearing years often carried a wergeld as substantial as that for a man of higher stature, suggesting that

barbarians were concerned about maintaining their population levels.

Like Greeks, Romans, and Hindus, barbarians worshipped hundreds of gods and goddesses with specialized functions. They regarded certain mountains, lakes, rivers, or groves of trees as sacred because these were linked to deities. Rituals to honor the gods were held outdoors rather than in temples or churches, often at certain points in the yearly agricultural cycle. Among the Celts, religious leaders called druids had legal and educational as well as religious functions, orally passing down laws and traditions from generation to generation. Bards singing poems and ballads also passed down myths and stories of heroes and gods, which were written down much later.

• **wergeld** Compensatory payment for death or injury set in many barbarian law codes.

Migrations and Political Change

Migrating groups that the Romans labeled barbarians had pressed along the Rhine-Danube frontier of the Roman Empire since about 150 C.E. (see page 169). In the third and fourth centuries increasing pressures on the frontiers from the east and north placed greater demands on Roman military manpower, which plague and a declining birthrate had reduced. Roman generals therefore recruited refugees and barbarian tribes allied with the Romans to serve in the Roman army, and some rose to the highest ranks.

Anglo-Saxon Helmet This ceremonial bronze helmet from seventh-century England was found inside a ship buried at Sutton Hoo. The nearly 100-foot-long ship was dragged overland before being buried completely. It held one body and many grave goods, including swords, gold buckles, and silver bowls made in Byzantium. The unidentified person who was buried here was clearly wealthy and powerful, and so was very likely a chief. (Courtesy of the Trustees of the British Museum)

Why did the barbarians migrate? In part, they were searching for more regular supplies of food, better farmland, and a warmer climate. Conflicts within and among barbarian groups also led to war and disruption, which motivated groups to move. Franks fought Alemanni (another Germanic tribe) in Gaul, while Visigoths fought Vandals in the Iberian peninsula and across North Africa. Roman expansion led to further movement of barbarian groups but also to the blending of cultures.

The spread of the Celts presents a good example of both conflict and assimilation. Celtic-speaking peoples had lived in central Europe since at least the fifth century B.C.E. and had spread out from there to the Iberian peninsula in the west, Hungary in the east, and the British Isles in the north. As Julius Caesar advanced northward into what he termed Gaul (present-day France), he defeated many Celtic tribes (see page 154). Celtic peoples conquered by the Romans often assimilated to Roman ways, adopting the Latin language and many aspects of Roman culture. Also, Celts and Romans intermarried, and many Celtic men became Roman citizens and joined the Roman army. By the fourth century C.E., however, Gaul and Britain were under pressure from Germanic groups moving westward. Roman troops withdrew from Britain, and Celtic-speaking peoples clashed with Germanic-speaking invaders, of whom the largest tribes were the Angles and the Saxons. Some Celtic-speakers moved farther west, to Brittany (modern northwestern France), Wales, Scotland, and Ireland. Others remained and intermarried with Germanic peoples, their descendants forming a number of small Anglo-Saxon kingdoms.

In eastern Europe, a significant factor in barbarian migration and the merging of various Germanic groups was pressure from nomadic steppe peoples from central Asia. These included the Alans, Avars, Bulghars, Khazars, and most prominently the Huns, who attacked the Black Sea area and the Eastern Roman Empire beginning in the fourth century. Under the leadership of their warrior-king Attila, the Huns swept into central Europe in 451, attacking Roman settlements in the Balkans and Germanic settlements along the Danube and Rhine Rivers. After Attila turned his army southward and crossed the Alps into Italy, a papal delegation, including Pope Leo I himself, asked him not to attack Rome. Though papal diplomacy was later credited with stopping the advance of the Huns, dwindling food supplies for Hunnic troops, as well as a plague that had spread among them, were probably much more important factors. The Huns retreated from Italy, and within a year Attila was dead. Later leaders were not as effective, and the Huns never again played a significant role in European history. Their conquests had pushed many Germanic groups together, however, which transformed smaller bands of people into larger, more unified groups that could more easily pick the Western Roman Empire apart.

After they conquered an area, barbarians generally established rulership under kings (chieftains). The kingdoms did not have definite geographical borders, and their locations shifted as tribes moved. Eventually, barbarian kingdoms came to include Italy itself. The Western Roman emperors increasingly relied on barbarian commanders and their troops to maintain order. In 476 the barbarian chieftain Odoacer deposed Romulus Augustus, the last person to have the title of Roman emperor in the West. Odoacer did not take the title of emperor, calling himself instead the king of Italy, so that this date marks the official end of the Roman Empire in the West. From Constantinople, Eastern Roman emperors such as Justinian (see page 208) worked to reconquer at least some of the West from barbarian tribes. They were occasionally successful but could not hold the empire together for long.

The Frankish Kingdom

Most barbarian kingdoms did not last very long, but one that did, and that came to have a decisive role in history, was that of the Franks. The Franks were a confederation of Germanic peoples who came from the marshy lowlands north and east of the northernmost part of the Roman Empire. In the fourth and fifth centuries they settled within the empire and allied with the Romans, some attaining high military and civil positions. The Franks believed that Merovech, a semi-legendary figure, founded their ruling dynasty, which was thus called **Merovingian** (mehr-uh-VIHN-jee-uhn).

The reign of Clovis (ca. 481–511) was decisive in the development of the Franks as a unified people. Through military campaigns, Clovis acquired the central provinces of Roman Gaul and began to conquer southern Gaul from other Germanic tribes. His wife Clotild, a Roman Christian, converted her husband and supported the founding of churches and monasteries. Her actions typify the role women played in the Christianization of barbarian kingdoms. (See "Listening to the Past: Gregory of Tours, The Conversion of Clovis," page 226.) Clotild, and other Frankish queens, frequently influenced events, for they had a say in how royal funds were spent and often spent long periods as regents for their sons until they came of age.

Clovis's conversion to Roman Christianity brought him the crucial support of the bishops of Gaul in his campaigns against tribes that were still pagan or had accepted the Arian version of Christianity. As the defender of Roman Christianity against heretical tribes,

Clovis went on to conquer the Visigoths, extending his domain to include much of what is now France and southwestern Germany.

When Clovis died his kingdom was divided among his four sons, following Frankish custom. For the next two centuries rulers of the various kingdoms fought one another in civil wars, and other military leaders challenged their authority. So brutal were these wars that historians used to use the term *Dark Ages* to apply to the entire Merovingian period, although more recently they have noted that the Merovingians also developed new political institutions, so the era was not uniformly bleak.

Merovingian kings based some aspects of their government on Roman principles. For example, they adopted the Roman concept of the *civitas* — Latin for a city and its surrounding territory. A count presided over the civitas, raising troops, collecting royal revenues, and providing justice on the basis of local, not royal, law. At the king's court — that is, wherever the king was present — an official called the mayor of the palace supervised legal, financial, and household officials; the mayor of the palace also governed in the king's absence. In the seventh century that position was held by members of an increasingly powerful family, the **Carolingians** (ka-ruh-LIHN-jee-uhns), who advanced themselves through advantageous marriages, a well-earned reputation for military strength, and the help of the church.

Eventually the Carolingians replaced the Merovingians as rulers of the Frankish kingdom, cementing their authority when the Carolingian Charles Martel defeated Muslim invaders in 732 at the Battle of Poitiers (pwah-ty-AY) in central France. Muslims and Christians have interpreted the battle differently. Muslims considered it a minor skirmish and attributed the Frankish victory to Muslim difficulties in maintaining supply lines over long distances and to ethnic conflicts and unrest in Islamic Spain. Charles Martel and later Carolingians used the victory to portray themselves as defenders of Christendom against the Muslims.

The Battle of Poitiers helped the Carolingians acquire more support from the church, perhaps their most important asset. They further strengthened their ties to the church by supporting the work of missionaries who preached Christian principles — including the duty to obey secular authorities — to pagan peoples, and

- **Merovingian** A dynasty founded in 481 by the Frankish chieftain Clovis in what is now France. *Merovingian* derives from *Merovech*, the name of the semi-legendary leader from whom Clovis claimed descent.
- **Carolingian** A dynasty of rulers that took over the Frankish kingdom from the Merovingians in the seventh century; *Carolingian* derives from the Latin word for "Charles," the name of several members of this dynasty.

Listening to the Past

Gregory of Tours, The Conversion of Clovis

Modern Christian doctrine holds that conversion is a process, the gradual turning toward Jesus and the teachings of the Christian Gospels. But in the early medieval world, conversion was perceived more as a one-time event determined by the tribal chieftain. If he accepted baptism, the mass conversion of his people followed. The selection here about the Frankish king Clovis is from The History of the Franks *by Gregory, bishop of Tours (ca. 504–594), written about a century after the events it describes.*

"The first child which Clotild bore for Clovis was a son. She wanted to have her baby baptized, and she kept urging her husband to agree to this. "The gods whom you worship are no good," she would say.

"They haven't even been able to help themselves, let alone others. . . . Take your Saturn, for example, who ran away from his own son to avoid being exiled from his kingdom, or so they say; and Jupiter, that obscene perpetrator of all sorts of mucky deeds, who couldn't keep his hands off other men, who had his fun with all his female relatives and couldn't even refrain from intercourse with his own sister. . . .

"You ought instead to worship Him who created at a word and out of nothing heaven, and earth, the sea and all that therein is, who made the sun to shine, who lit the sky with stars, who peopled the water with fish, the earth with beasts, the sky with flying creatures, by whose hand the race of man was made, by whose gift all creation is constrained to serve in deference and devotion the man He made." However often the Queen said this, the King came no nearer to belief. . . .

The Queen, who was true to her faith, brought her son to be baptized. . . . The child was baptized; he was given the name Ingomer; but no sooner had he received baptism than he died in his white robes. Clovis was extremely angry. He began immediately to reproach his Queen. "If he had been dedicated in the name of my gods," he said, "he would have lived without question; but now that he has been baptized in the name of your God he has not been able to live a single day!"

"I give thanks to Almighty God," replied Clotild, "the Creator of all things who has not found me completely unworthy, for He has deigned to welcome into his Kingdom a child conceived in my womb. . . ."

Some time later Clotild bore a second son. He was baptized Chlodomer. He began to ail and Clovis said, "What else do you expect? It will happen to him as it happened to his brother: no sooner is he baptized in the name of your Christ than he will die!" Clotild prayed to the Lord and at His commands the baby recovered.

Queen Clotild continued to pray that her husband might recognize the true God and give up his idol-worship. Nothing could persuade him to accept Christianity. Finally war broke out against the Alemanni and in this conflict he was forced by necessity to accept what he had refused of his own free will. It so turned out that when the two armies met on the battlefield there was a great slaughter and the troops of Clovis were rapidly being annihilated. He raised his eyes to heaven when he saw this, felt compunction in his heart and was moved to tears. "Jesus Christ," he said, "you who Clotild maintains to be the Son of the living God, you who deign to give help to those in travail and victory to those who trust in you, in faith I beg the glory of your help. If you will give me victory over my enemies, and if I may have evidence to that miraculous power which the people dedicated to your name say that they have experienced, then I will believe in you and I will be baptized in your name. I have called upon my own gods, but, as I see only too clearly, they have no intention of helping me. I therefore cannot believe that they possess any power for they do not come to the assistance of those who trust them. I now call upon you. I want to believe in you, but I must first be saved from my enemies." Even as he said this the Alemanni turned their backs and began to run away. As soon as they saw that their King was killed, they submitted to Clovis. "We beg you," they said, "to put an end to

---

by allying themselves with the papacy against other Germanic tribes.

Charlemagne

The most powerful of the Carolingians was Charles the Great (r. 768–814), generally known as Charlemagne (SHAHR-luh-mayn). In the autumn of the year 800, Charlemagne visited Rome, where on Christmas Day Pope Leo III crowned him emperor. The event had momentous consequences. In taking as his motto *Renovatio romani imperi* (Revival of the Roman Empire), Charlemagne was deliberately perpetuating old Roman imperial ideas while identifying with the new Rome of the Christian Church. From Baghdad, the Abbasid Empire's caliph, Harun al-Rashid (r. 786–809), congratulated Charlemagne on his coronation with the gift of an elephant. The elephant survived for nearly a

this slaughter. We are prepared to obey you." Clovis stopped the war. He made a speech in which he called for peace. Then he went home. He told the Queen how he had won a victory by calling on the name of Christ. This happened in the fifteenth year of his reign (496).

The Queen then ordered Saint Remigius, Bishop of the town of Rheims, to be summoned in secret. She begged him to impart the word of salvation to the King. The Bishop asked Clovis to meet him in private and began to urge him to believe in the true God, Maker of heaven and earth, and to forsake his idols, which were powerless to help him or anyone else. The King replied: "I have listened to you willingly, holy father. There remains one obstacle. The people under my command will not agree to forsake their gods. I will go and put to them what you have just said to me." He arranged a meeting with his people, but God in his power had preceded him, and before he could say a word all those present shouted in unison: "We will give up worshipping our mortal gods, pious King, and we are prepared to follow the immortal God about whom Remigius preaches." This news was reported to the Bishop. He was greatly pleased and he ordered the baptismal pool to be made ready.... The baptistry was prepared, sticks of incense gave off clouds of perfume, sweet-smelling candles gleamed bright and the holy place of baptism was filled with divine fragrance. God filled the hearts of all present with such grace that they imagined themselves to have been transported to some perfumed paradise. King Clovis asked that he might be baptized first by the Bishop.

Like some new Constantine he stepped forward to the baptismal pool, ready to wash away the sores of his old leprosy and to be cleansed in flowing water from the sordid stains which he had borne so long.

King Clovis confessed his belief in God Almighty, three in one. He was baptized in the name of the Father, the Son, and the Holy Ghost, and marked in holy chrism [an anointing oil] with the sign of the Cross of Christ. More than three thousand of his army were baptized at the same time. ”

Source: Gregory of Tours, from *The History of the Franks*, translated with an introduction by Lewis Thorpe, pp. 141–144. Copyright © Lewis Thorpe, 1974, London. Reproduced by permission of Penguin Books Ltd.

QUESTIONS FOR ANALYSIS

1. Who took the initiative in urging Clovis's conversion? What can we deduce from that?

2. According to this account, why did Clovis ultimately accept Christianity?

3. How does Gregory of Tours portray the workings of divine power in Clovis's conversion?

4. On the basis of this selection, do you consider *The History of the Franks* reliable? Why?

decade, though like everyone else at Charlemagne's capital of Aachen (on the western border of modern Germany), it lived in a city that was far less sophisticated, healthy, and beautiful than Abbasid Baghdad. Although the Muslim caliph recognized Charlemagne as a fellow sovereign, the Byzantines regarded his papal coronation as rebellious and Charlemagne as a usurper. His crowning as emperor thus marks a decisive break between Rome and Constantinople.

Charlemagne's most striking characteristic was his phenomenal energy, which helps explain his great military achievements. Continuing the expansionist policies of his ancestors, he fought more than fifty campaigns, and by around 805 the Frankish kingdom included all of continental Europe except Spain, Scandinavia, southern Italy, and the Slavic fringes of the East.

▫ Picturing the Past

Charlemagne and His Wife This illumination from a ninth-century manuscript portrays Charlemagne with one of his wives. Marriage was an important tool of diplomacy for Charlemagne, and he had a number of wives and concubines. (Erich Lessing/Art Resource, NY)

ANALYZING THE IMAGE What does Charlemagne appear to be doing? How would you characterize his wife's reaction?

CONNECTIONS Does this depiction of a Frankish queen match what you've read about female rulers in this era, such as Theodora and Clotild?

For administrative purposes, Charlemagne divided his entire kingdom into counties. Each of the approximately six hundred counties was governed by a count, who had full military and judicial power and held his office for life but could be removed by the emperor for misconduct. As a link between local authorities and the central government, Charlemagne appointed officials called *missi dominici*, "agents of the lord king." Each year beginning in 802 two missi, usually a count and a bishop or abbot, visited assigned districts. They checked up on the counts and their districts' judicial, financial, and clerical activities.

It is ironic that Charlemagne's most enduring legacy was the stimulus he gave to scholarship and learning. Barely literate, preoccupied with the control of vast territories, and much more a warrior than a thinker, Charlemagne nevertheless set in motion a cultural revival that later historians called the "Carolingian Renaissance." The Carolingian Renaissance was a rebirth of interest in, study of, and preservation of the language, ideas, and achievements of classical Greece and Rome. Scholars at Aachen copied Greco-Roman and Christian books and manuscripts and built up libraries. Furthermore, Charlemagne urged monasteries to promote Christian learning, and both men's and

• **Treaty of Verdun** A treaty ratified in 843 that divided Charlemagne's territories among his three surviving grandsons; their kingdoms set the pattern for the modern states of Germany, France, and Italy.

Charlemagne's Conquests, ca. 768-814

Members of the nobility engaged in plots and open warfare against the emperor, often allying themselves with one of Louis's three sons. In 843, shortly after Louis's death, those sons agreed to the **Treaty of Verdun**, which divided the empire into three parts: Charles the Bald received the western part, Lothair the middle and the title of emperor, and Louis the eastern part, from which he acquired the title "the German." Though of course no one knew it at the time, this treaty set the pattern for political boundaries in Europe that has been maintained to today. Other than brief periods under Napoleon and Hitler, Europe would never again see as large a unified state as it had under Charlemagne, which is one reason he has become a symbol of European unity in the twenty-first century.

The Treaty of Verdun, 483

The weakening of central power was hastened by invasions and migrations from the north, south, and east. Thus Charlemagne's empire ended in much the same way that the Roman Empire had earlier, from a combination of internal weakness and external pressure.

women's houses produced beautiful illustrated texts, preserving Christian and classical works for subsequent generations.

Charlemagne left his vast empire to his sole surviving son, Louis the Pious (r. 814–840), who attempted to keep the empire intact. This proved to be impossible.

CONNECTIONS

For centuries the end of the Roman Empire in the West was seen as a major turning point in history, the fall of the sophisticated and educated classical world to uncouth and illiterate tribes. Over the last several decades, however, many historians have put a greater emphasis on continuities. Barbarian kings relied on officials trained in Roman law, and Latin remained the language of scholarly communication and the Christian Church. Greco-Roman art and architecture still adorned the land, and people continued to use Roman roads, aqueducts, and buildings. In eastern Europe and western Asia, the Byzantine Empire preserved the traditions of the Roman Empire and protected the intellectual heritage of Greco-Roman culture for another millennium.

Very recently, however, some historians and archaeologists have returned to an emphasis on change. They note that people may have traveled on Roman roads after the end of the Roman Empire, but the roads were rarely maintained, and travel itself was much less secure than during the empire. Merchants no longer traded over long distances, so people's access to goods produced outside their local area plummeted. Knowledge about technological processes such as the making of glass and roof tiles declined or disappeared. Although there was intermarriage and cultural assimilation among Romans and barbarians, there was also violence and great physical destruction, even in Byzantium.

In the middle of the era covered in this chapter, a new force emerged that had a dramatic impact on much of Europe and western Asia—Islam. In the seventh and eighth centuries Sassanid Persia, much of the Byzantine Empire, and the barbarian kingdoms in the Iberian peninsula fell to Arab forces carrying this new religion. As we have seen in this chapter, a reputation as victors over Islam helped the Franks establish the most powerful state in Europe. As we will see in Chapter 14, Islam continued to shape European culture and politics in subsequent centuries. In terms of world history, the expansion of Islam may have been an even more dramatic turning point than the fall of the Roman Empire. Here, too, however, there were continuities, as the Muslims adopted and adapted Greek, Byzantine, and Persian political and cultural institutions.

◻ CHAPTER REVIEW

KEY TERMS

corpus juris civilis (p. 208)	sacraments (p. 217)
dioceses (p. 211)	penance (p. 219)
Arianism (p. 212)	saints (p. 219)
popes (p. 213)	wergeld (p. 222)
Orthodox Church (p. 213)	Merovingian (p. 225)
iconoclastic controversy (p. 213)	Carolingian (p. 225)
	Treaty of Verdun (p. 229)

◻ **How was the Byzantine Empire able to survive for so long, and what were its most important achievements? (p. 206)**

During the sixth and seventh centuries the Byzantine Empire survived waves of attacks, owing to effective military leadership and to fortifications around Constantinople. From this strong position Byzantine emperors organized and preserved Roman institutions, and the Byzantine Empire survived until 1453, nearly a millennium longer than the Roman Empire in the West. In particular, the emperor Justinian oversaw creation of the *Code*, which distilled the legal genius of the Romans into a coherent whole, eliminated outmoded laws and contradictions, and clarified the law itself. Just as they valued the law, the Byzantines prized education, and because of them many masterpieces of ancient Greek literature survived to influence the intellectual life of the modern world. In mathematics and science, the Byzantines passed Greco-Roman learning on to the Arabs, and they discovered an explosive compound, "Greek fire," that saved Constantinople from Arab assault. The Byzantines also devoted a great deal of attention to medicine, and their general level of medical competence was far higher than that of western Europeans.

◻ **What factors enabled the Christian Church to expand and thrive? (p. 211)**

Christianity gained the support of the fourth-century emperors and gradually adopted the Roman system of hierarchical organization. The church possessed able administrators and leaders whose skills were tested in the chaotic environment of the end of the Roman Empire in the West. Bishops expanded their activities, and in the fifth century the bishops of Rome, taking the title "pope," began to stress their supremacy over other Christian communities. Monasteries offered opportunities for individuals to develop deeper spiritual devotion and also provided a model of Christian living, methods that advanced agricultural development, and places for education and learning.

◻ **How did Christian thinkers and missionaries adapt Greco-Roman ideas to Christian theology and develop effective techniques for converting barbarian peoples? (p. 215)**

Christian thinkers reinterpreted the classics in a Christian sense, incorporating elements of Greek and Roman philosophy and of various pagan religious groups into Christian teachings. Of these early thinkers, Augustine of Hippo was the most influential. His ideas about sin, free will, and sexuality shaped western European thought from the fifth century on. Missionaries and priests got pagan and illiterate peoples to understand and become more accepting of Christianity by preaching the basic teachings of the religion, stressing similarities between pagan customs and beliefs and those of Christianity, and introducing the ritual of penance and the veneration of saints.

◻ **How did the barbarians shape social, economic, and political structures in Europe and western Asia? (p. 220)**

The barbarian groups that, beginning in the second century, migrated throughout Europe and Central Asia brought with them customs and traditions that combined with classical and Christian customs and beliefs. Barbarians generally had no notion of the state as we use the term today; they thought in social, not political, terms. The basic social unit was the tribe, made up of kin groups formed by families. Family groups lived in small agriculture-based villages, where there were great differences in wealth and status. Most barbarian kingdoms were weak and short-lived, though the kingdom of the Franks was relatively more unified and powerful. Rulers first in the Merovingian Dynasty, and then in the Carolingian, used military victories, strategic marriage alliances, and the help of the church to enhance their authority. Carolingian government reached the peak of its power under Charlemagne, who continued the expansionist policies of his ancestors, extending the Frankish kingdom to include all of continental Europe except Spain, Scandinavia, southern Italy, and the Slavic areas of the East.

SUGGESTED READING

Barbero, Allesandro. *Charlemagne: Father of a Continent.* 2004. A wonderful biography of Charlemagne and a study of the times in which he lived that argues for the complexity of his legacy.

Brown, Peter. *Augustine of Hippo*, rev. ed. 2000. The best biography of Saint Augustine, which treats him as a symbol of change.

Brown, Peter. *The World of Late Antiquity*, A.D. 150–750, rev. ed. 1989. A lavishly illustrated survey that stresses social and cultural change and has clearly written introductions to the entire period.

Burns, Thomas S. *Rome and the Barbarians, 100 B.C.– 400 A.D.* 2003. Argues that Germanic and Roman cultures assimilated more than they conflicted.

Cameron, Averil. *The Mediterranean World in Late Antiquity, A.D. 395–600.* 1993. Focuses especially on political and economic changes.

Clark, Gilian. *Women in Late Antiquity: Pagan and Christian Lifestyles.* 1994. Explores law, marriage, and religious life.

Dunn, Marilyn. *The Emergence of Monasticism: From the Desert Fathers to the Early Middle Ages.* 2003. Focuses on the beginnings of monasticism.

Fletcher, Richard. *The Barbarian Conversion: From Paganism to Christianity.* 1998. A superbly written analysis of conversion to Christianity.

Herrin, Judith. *Byzantium: The Surprising Life of a Medieval Empire.* 2009. An examination of many aspects of Byzantine culture that focuses on people and demonstrates Byzantium's continuing significance for world history.

Herrin, Judith. *The Formation of Christendom.* 1987. The best synthesis of the development of the Christian Church from the third to the ninth centuries.

Pelikan, Jaroslav. *The Excellent Empire: The Fall of Rome and the Triumph of the Church.* 1987. Describes how interpretations of the fall of Rome have influenced our understanding of Western culture.

Riche, Pierre. *Daily Life in the World of Charlemagne*, trans. JoAnn McNamara. 1978. A detailed study of many facets of Carolingian society.

Todd, Malcolm. *The Early Germans*, 2d ed. 2004. Uses archaeological and literary sources to analyze Germanic social structure, customs, and religion and to suggest implications for an understanding of migration and ethnicity.

Ward-Perkins, Bryan. *The Fall of Rome and the End of Civilization.* 2006. Uses material evidence to trace the physical destruction and economic dislocation that accompanied the barbarian migrations.

Wells, Peter S. *The Barbarians Speak: How the Conquered Peoples Shaped Roman Europe.* 1999. Presents extensive evidence of Celtic and Germanic social and technical development.

Wickham, Chris. *Framing the Early Middle Ages: Europe and the Mediterranean, 400–800.* 2007. A massive, yet accessible survey of economic and social changes in many regions, with great attention to ordinary people.

NOTES

1. S. P. Scott, trans., *Corpus Juris Civilis: The Civil Law* (Cincinnati: The Central Trust, 1932), sections 1.5.5, 11.4.1.

2. Quoted in E. Patlagean, "Byzantium in the Tenth and Eleventh Centuries," in *A History of Private Life*. Vol. 1: *From Pagan Rome to Byzantium*, ed. P. Ariès and G. Duby (Cambridge, Mass.: Harvard University Press, 1987), p. 573.

3. R. C. Petry, ed., *A History of Christianity: Readings in the History of Early and Medieval Christianity* (Englewood Cliffs, N.J.: Prentice Hall, 1962), p. 70.

4. Gregory of Tours, *The Glory of the Martyrs*, trans. Raymond Van Dam (Liverpool: Liverpool University, 1988), p. 108. Used by permission of Liverpool University Press.

5. E. F. Henderson, ed., *Select Historical Documents of the Middle Ages* (London: G. Bell and Sons, 1912), pp. 176, 189.

• **Egyptian Man** Life remained gracious in the great cities of North Africa and the Middle East even as Islam brought new traditions. This image of a man wearing a turban and holding a cup is from a wall painting. Found in Egypt, it dates to the eleventh century, during the Fatimid caliphate. (Museum of Islamic Art, Cairo/Gianni Dagli Orti/The Art Archive)

Around 610 in the city of Mecca in what is now Saudi Arabia, a merchant called Muhammad had a religious vision that inspired him to preach God's revelations to the people of Mecca. By the time he died in 632, he had many followers in Arabia, and a century later his followers controlled what is now Syria, Palestine, Egypt, Iraq, Iran, northern India, northern Africa, Spain, and southern France. Within another century Muhammad's beliefs had been carried across Central Asia to the borders of China and India. The speed with which Islam spread is one of the most amazing stories in world history, and scholars have pointed to many factors that must have contributed to its success. Military victories were rooted in strong military organization and the practice of establishing garrison cities in newly conquered territories. The religious zeal of new converts certainly played an important role. So too did the political weakness of many of the governments then holding power in the lands where Islam extended, such as the Byzantine government centered in Constantinople. Commerce and trade also spread the faith of Muhammad.

The Islamic World

600-1400

Although its first adherents were nomads, Islam developed and flourished in a mercantile milieu. By land and sea, Muslim merchants transported a rich variety of goods across Eurasia. On the basis of the wealth that trade generated, a gracious, sophisticated, and cosmopolitan culture developed with centers at Baghdad and Córdoba. During the ninth, tenth, and eleventh centuries, the Islamic world witnessed enormous intellectual vitality and creativity. Muslim scholars produced important work in many disciplines, especially mathematics, medicine, and philosophy. This brilliant civilization profoundly influenced the development of both Eastern and Western civilizations. •

The Origins of Islam

□ From what kind of social and economic environment did Muhammad arise, and what did he teach?

The Arabian peninsula, about a third of the size of Europe or the United States, covers about a million square miles, much but not all of the land desert. By the seventh century C.E. farming prevailed in the southwestern mountain valleys with their ample rainfall. In other areas scattered throughout the peninsula, oasis towns sustained sizable populations including artisans, merchants, and religious leaders. Outside the towns were Bedouin (BEH-duh-uhn) nomadic tribes who moved from place to place, grazing their sheep, goats, and camels. Though always small in number, Bedouins were the most important political and military force in the region because of their toughness, solidarity, fighting traditions, possession of horses and camels, and ability to control trade and lines of communication. Mecca became the economic and cultural center of western Arabia, in part because pilgrims came to visit the Ka'ba, a temple containing a black stone thought to be a god's dwelling place as well as other holy objects connected to other gods. Muhammad's roots were in this region.

Arabian Social and Economic Structure

The basic social unit of the Bedouins and other Arabs was the tribe. Consisting of people connected through kinship, tribes provided protection and support and in turn expected members' total loyalty. Like the Germanic peoples in the age of their migrations (see pages 220–229), Arab tribes were not static entities but rather continually evolving groups. A particular tribe might include both nomadic and sedentary members.

As in other nomadic societies, nomads in Arabia depended on agriculturally productive communities for food they could not produce, cloth, metal products, and weapons. Nomads paid for these goods with livestock, milk and milk products, hides, and hair, items in demand in oasis towns. Nomads acquired additional income by serving as desert guides and as guards for caravans, or by creating the need for guards by plundering caravans and extorting protection money.

Page from the Qur'an The aesthetic appeal of Arabic calligraphy is easy to recognize in this thirteenth-century Qur'an. (Museum of Islamic Art, Cairo/Gianni Dagli Orti/The Art Archive)

In northern and central Arabia in the early seventh century, tribal confederations with their warrior elite were dominant. In the southern parts of the peninsula, however, religious aristocracies tended to hold political power. Many oasis or market towns contained members of one holy family who served the deity of the town and acted as guardians of the deity's shrine. At the shrine, a cultic leader tried to settle disputes among warring tribes. All Arabs respected the shrines because they served as neutral places for such arbitration.

The power of the northern warrior class rested on its fighting skills. The southern religious aristocracy, by contrast, depended on its religious and economic power. Located in agricultural areas that were also commercial centers, the religious aristocracy had a stronger economic base than did the warrior-aristocrats. The political genius of Muhammad was to bind together these different tribal groups into a strong, unified state.

Muhammad's Rise as a Religious Leader

Much like the earliest sources for Jesus, the earliest account of the life of Muhammad (ca. 570–632) comes from oral traditions passed down among followers and not written down for several decades or generations. According to these traditions, Muhammad was orphaned at the age of six and brought up by his paternal uncle. As a young man, he became a merchant in the caravan trade that crisscrossed the Arabian desert. Later he entered the service of a wealthy widow, Khadija, and their subsequent marriage brought him financial security. Muhammad was extremely pious and devoted to contemplation. At about age forty, in a cave in the hills near Mecca where he was accustomed to praying, Muhammad had a vision of an angelic being who commanded him to preach the revelations that God would be sending him. Muhammad began to preach to the people of Mecca, urging them to give up their idols and to submit to the one indivisible God. During his lifetime, Muhammad's followers jotted down his revelations haphazardly on animal bones and skins (paper was very scarce) and committed them to memory. After his death, scribes organized the revelations into chapters. In 651 they published the version of them that Muslims consider authoritative, the **Qur'an** (kuh-RAHN). Muslims revere the Qur'an for its sacred message and for the beauty of its Arabic language.

For the first two or three centuries after the death of Muhammad, there was considerable debate about theological issues, such as the oneness of God, the role of angels, the prophets, the Scriptures, and Judgment Day, as well as about political issues, such as the authority of Muhammad and that of the caliph (KAY-lif; political ruler, successor to Muhammad). Likewise, religious scholars had to sort out and assess the **hadith** (huh-DEETH), collections of the sayings of or anecdotes about Muhammad. Controversies over the authenticity of particular sayings continued for centuries. Muhammad's example as revealed in the hadith became the legal basis for the conduct of every Muslim. The life of Muhammad, who is also known as the Prophet, provides the "normative example," or **Sunna**, for the Muslim believer. Once Islamic theology and law had developed into a religious system, Muhammad was revealed as the perfect man, the embodiment of

- **Qur'an** The sacred book of Islam.
- **hadith** Collections of the sayings of and anecdotes about Muhammad.
- **Sunna** An Arabic term meaning "trodden path." The term refers to the deeds and sayings of Muhammad, which constitute the obligatory example for Muslim life.

the will of God. Muhammad's example became central to the Muslim way of life.

The Tenets of Islam

Islam, the strict monotheistic faith that is based on the teachings of Muhammad, rests on the principle of the oneness and omnipotence of God (Allah). The word *Islam* means "surrender to God," and *Muslim* means "a person who submits." Muslims believe that Muhammad was the last of the prophets, completing the work begun by Abraham, Moses, and Jesus. According to the Qur'an, the coming of the final prophet was acknowledged by both Jewish and Christian authorities. The Qur'an asserts that the Prophet Muhammad descended from Adam, the first man, and that the Prophet Abraham built the Ka'ba. The Qur'an holds that the holy writings of both Jews and Christians represent divine revelation, but it claims that both Jews and Christians tampered with the books of God.

Muslims believe that they worship the same God as Jews and Christians. Monotheism had flourished in Middle Eastern Semitic and Persian cultures for centuries before Muhammad. Islam appropriates much of the Old and New Testaments of the Bible but often retells the narratives with significant shifts in meaning. Islam recognizes Moses's laws about circumcision, ritual bathing, and restrictions on eating pork and shellfish, and the Qur'an calls Christians "nearest in love" to Muslims. Muhammad insisted that he was not preaching a new message; rather, he was calling people back to the one true God, urging his contemporaries to reform their lives, to return to the faith of Abraham, the first monotheist.

Unlike the Old Testament, much of which is a historical narrative, or the New Testament, which is a collection of essays on the example and teachings of Jesus, the Qur'an is a collection of directives issued in God's name. Its organization is not strictly topical or chronological. To deal with seeming contradictions, later commentators explained the historical circumstances behind each revelation.

The Qur'an prescribes a strict code of moral behavior. A Muslim must recite the profession of faith in God and in Muhammad as his prophet: "There is no God but God, and Muhammad is his Prophet." A believer must also pray five times a day, fast and pray during the sacred month of Ramadan, make a pilgrimage (hajj) to the holy city of Mecca once during his or her lifetime, and give alms to the Muslim poor. These fundamental obligations are known as the **Five Pillars of Islam**.

Dome of the Rock, Jerusalem Completed in 691 and revered by Muslims as the site where Muhammad ascended to Heaven, the Dome of the Rock is the oldest surviving Islamic sanctuary and, after Mecca and Medina, the holiest place in Islam. Although influenced by Byzantine and Persian architecture, it also has distinctly Arabic features, such as the 700 feet of carefully selected Qur'anic inscriptions and vegetal motifs that grace the top of the outer walls. (imagebroker.net/SuperStock)

Islam forbids alcoholic beverages and gambling. It condemns usury in business — that is, lending money and charging the borrower interest — and taking advantage of market demand for products by charging high prices. Most scholars hold that compared with earlier Arab standards, the Qur'an set forth a strict sexual code. Muslim jurisprudence condemned licentious behavior by both men and women and specified the same punishments for both. (By contrast, contemporary Frankish law punished prostitutes, but not their clients.)

Islam warns about Judgment Day and the importance of the life to come. Like the Christian Judgment Day, on that day God will separate the saved and the damned. The Qur'an describes in detail the frightful tortures with which God will punish the damned and the heavenly rewards of the saved and the blessed.

Islamic States and Their Expansion

☐ What made possible the spread of Islam, and what forms of government were established to rule Muslim lands?

According to Muslim tradition, Muhammad's preaching at first did not appeal to many people. Legend has it that for the first three years he attracted only fourteen believers. In preaching a transformation of the social order and calling for the destruction of the idols in the Ka'ba, Muhammad challenged the power of the local elite and the pilgrimage-based local economy. As a result, the townspeople of Mecca turned against him, and he and his followers were forced to flee to Medina. This *hijra* (hih-JIGH-ruh), or emigration, occurred in 622, and Muslims later dated the beginning of their era from that event.

At Medina, Muhammad attracted increasing numbers of believers, and his teachings began to have an impact. His followers supported themselves by raiding caravans en route to Mecca, setting off a violent conflict between Mecca and Medina. After eight years of strife, Mecca capitulated. Thus, by the time he died in 632, Muhammad had welded together all the Bedouin tribes.

Muhammad displayed genius as both a political strategist and a religious teacher. He gave Arabs the idea of a unique and unified **umma** (UH-muh), or community, that consisted of all those whose primary identity and bond was a common religious faith and commitment, not a tribal tie. The umma was to be a religious and political community led by Muhammad for the achievement of God's will on earth. In the early seventh century the southern Arab tribal confederations lacked cohesiveness and were constantly warring. The Islamic notion of an absolute higher authority transcended the boundaries of individual tribal units and fostered the political consolidation of the tribal confederations. All authority came from God through Muhammad. Within the umma, the law of God was discerned and applied through Muhammad.

Islam's Spread Beyond Arabia

After the Prophet's death, Islam spread far beyond Arabia (Map 9.1). In the sixth century two powerful empires divided the Middle East: the Greek-Byzantine empire centered at Constantinople and the Persian-Sassanid empire concentrated at Ctesiphon (near Baghdad in present-day Iraq). The Byzantine Empire stood for Hellenistic culture and championed Christianity (see Chapter 8). The Sassanid empire espoused Persian cultural traditions and favored the religious faith known as Zoroastrianism (see pages 61, 208). Although each empire maintained an official state religion, neither possessed religious unity. Both had sizable Jewish populations, and within Byzantium sects that Orthodox Greeks considered heretical — Monophysites and Nestorians — were politically divisive forces. During the fourth through sixth centuries these two empires fought each other fiercely, each trying to expand its territories at the expense of the other and to control and tax the rich trade coming from Arabia and the Indian Ocean region. Many peripheral societies were drawn into the conflict. The resulting disorder facilitated the growth of Muslim states.

The second and third successors of Muhammad, Umar (r. 634–644) and Uthman (r. 644–656), launched a two-pronged attack against the Byzantine and Sassanid empires. One force moved north from Arabia against the Byzantine provinces of Syria and Palestine, and the Greek armies there could not halt them (see page 207). From Syria, the Muslims conquered the rich province of Egypt, taking the commercial and intellectual hub of Alexandria in 642. Simultaneously, Arab armies swept into the Sassanid empire. The Muslim defeat of the Persians at Nihawand in 642 signaled the collapse of this empire (see Map 9.1).

The Muslims continued their drive eastward. In the mid-seventh century they occupied the province of Khurasan, where the city of Merv became the center

- **Five Pillars of Islam** The basic tenets of the Islamic faith; they include reciting a profession of faith in God and in Muhammad as God's prophet, praying five times daily, fasting and praying during the month of Ramadan, making a pilgrimage to Mecca once in one's lifetime, and contributing alms to the poor.

- **umma** A community of people who share a religious faith and commitment rather than a tribal tie.

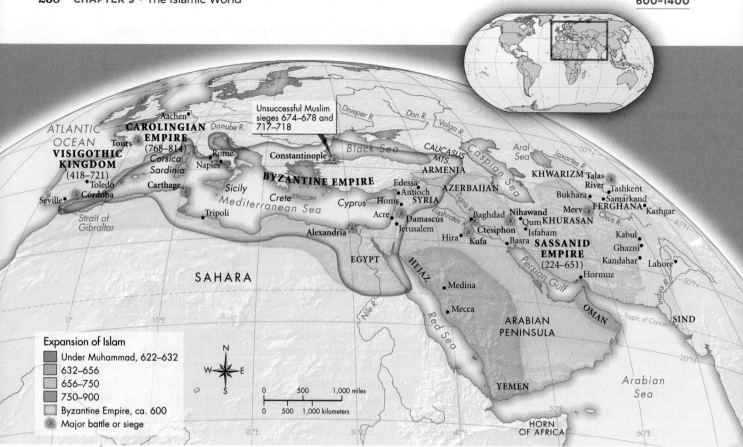

Mapping the Past

MAP 9.1 The Expansion of Islam, 622–900 The rapid expansion of Islam in a relatively short span of time testifies to the Arabs' superior fighting skills, religious zeal, and economic ambition as well as to their enemies' weakness. Plague, famine, and political troubles in Sassanid Persia contributed to Muslim victory there.

ANALYZING THE MAP Trace the routes of the spread of Islam by time period. How fast did it spread? How similar were the climates of the regions that became Muslim?

CONNECTIONS Which were the most powerful and populous of the societies that were absorbed into the Muslim world? What regions or societies were more resistant?

of Muslim control over eastern Persia and the base for campaigns farther east. By 700 the Muslims had crossed the Oxus River and swept toward Kabul, today the capital of Afghanistan. They then penetrated Kazakhstan and then seized Tashkent, one of the oldest cities in Central Asia. The clash of Muslim horsemen with a Chinese army at the Talas River in 751 marked the farthest Islamic penetration into Central Asia (see Map 9.1). From southern Persia, a Muslim force marched into the Indus Valley in northern India and in 713 founded an Islamic community there. Beginning in the eleventh century Muslim dynasties from Ghazni in Afghanistan carried Islam deeper into the Indian subcontinent (see page 349).

Likewise, to the west Arab forces moved across North Africa and crossed the Strait of Gibraltar. In 711

at the Guadalete River they easily defeated the Visigothic kingdom of Spain. A few Christian princes supported by Merovingian rulers held out in the Cantabrian Mountains, but the Muslims controlled most of Spain until the thirteenth century. Advances into France were stopped in 732 when the Franks defeated Arab armies in a battle near the city of Tours, and Muslim occupation of parts of southern France did not last long.

Reasons for the Spread of Islam

By the beginning of the eleventh century the crescent of Islam flew from the Iberian heartlands to northern India. How can this rapid and remarkable expansion be explained? The internal view of Muslim historians was that God supported the Islamic faith and aided its spread. The external, especially European, view used to be that religious fervor was the main driving force; the Muslim concept of jihad (JEE-hahd), or struggle, seemed the key element. The Qur'an does not precisely explain jihad. Some Muslim scholars hold that it signifies the individual struggle against sin and toward perfection on "the straight path" of Islam. Others claim that jihad has a social and communal implication — a militancy as part of a holy war against unbelievers living in territories outside the control of the Muslim community. The Qur'an states, "Fight those in the way of God who fight you" (Qur'an 4:74).[1] Just as Christians have a missionary duty to spread their faith, so Muslims have the obligation, as individuals and as a community, to extend the power of Islam.

Today, few historians emphasize religious zeal alone but rather point to a combination of Arab military advantages and the political weaknesses of their opponents. The Byzantine and Sassanid empires had just fought a grueling century-long war and had also been weakened by the plague, which hit urban, stationary populations harder than nomadic populations. Equally important are the military strength and tactics of the Arabs. For example, rather than scattering as landlords of peasant farmers over conquered lands, Arab soldiers remained together in garrison cities, where their Arab ethnicity, tribal organization, religion, and military success set them apart. All soldiers were registered in the **diwān** (dih-WAHN), an administrative organ adopted from the Persians or Byzantines. Soldiers received a monthly ration of food for themselves and their families and an annual cash stipend. In return, they had to be available for military service. Fixed salaries, regular pay, and the lure of battlefield booty attracted rugged tribesmen from Arabia. Except for the Berbers of North Africa, whom the Arabs could not pacify, Muslim armies initially did not seek to convert or recruit warriors from conquered peoples. In later campaigns to the east, many recruits were recent converts to Islam from Christian, Persian, and Berber backgrounds. The assurance of army wages secured the loyalty of these very diverse men.

The Arab commanders recognized the economic benefits of capturing the major cities of the region. Arab caravans frequented the market towns of southern Syria and the rich commercial centers of the north, such as Edessa, Aleppo, and Damascus. Syria's economic prosperity probably attracted the Muslims, and perhaps Muhammad saw the land as a potential means of support for the poor who flooded into Medina. Syria also contained sites important to the faith: Jerusalem, where Jesus and other prophets mentioned in the Qur'an had lived and preached, and Hebron, the traditional burial place of Abraham, the father of monotheism.

How did the conquered peoples make sense of their new subordinate situations? Jews and Christians tried to minimize the damage done to their former status and played down the gains of their new masters. Whereas Christians regarded the conquering Arabs as God's punishment for their sins, Jews saw the Arabs as instruments for their deliverance from Greek and Sassanid persecution.

While the conquered peoples figured out their situations as subordinates, Muslims had to figure out how to rule their new territories after Muhammad's death. The government they established is called the caliphate.

The Caliphate and the Split Between Shi'a and Sunni Alliances

When Muhammad died in 632, he left a large Muslim umma, but this community stood in danger of disintegrating into separate tribal groups. How was the vast empire that came into existence within one hundred years of his death to be governed? Neither the Qur'an nor the Sunna offered guidance for the succession.

In this crisis, according to tradition, a group of Muhammad's ablest followers elected Abu Bakr (573–634), a close supporter of the Prophet and his father-in-law, and hailed him as caliph, a term combining the ideas of leader, successor, and deputy (of the Prophet). This election marked the victory of the concept of a universal community of Muslim believers.

Because the law of the Qur'an was to guide the community, there had to be an authority to enforce the law, and the caliph assumed this responsibility. Muslim teaching holds that the law is paramount. God is the sole source of the law, and the ruler is bound to obey the law. Government exists not to make law but to enforce it. Islam draws no distinction between the temporal and spiritual domains: social law is a basic strand in the fabric of comprehensive religious law. Religious leaders and institutions nevertheless act as a check on political leaders who drift too far from religious standards. The creation of Islamic law in an institutional sense took three or four centuries and is one of the great achievements of medieval Islam.

In the two years of his rule (632–634), Abu Bakr governed on the basis of his personal prestige within the Muslim umma. He sent out military expeditions, collected taxes, dealt with tribes on behalf of the entire community, and led the community in prayer. Gradually, under Abu Bakr's first three successors, Umar, Uthman, and Ali (r. 656–661), the caliphate emerged as an institution. Umar succeeded in exerting his

---

• **diwān** A unit of government.

authority over the Bedouin tribes involved in ongoing conquests. Uthman asserted the right of the caliph to protect the economic interests of the entire umma. Also, Uthman's publication of the definitive text of the Qur'an showed his concern for the unity of the umma. However, Uthman was from a Mecca family that had resisted the Prophet until the capitulation of Mecca in 630, and he aroused resentment when he gave favors to members of his family. Opposition to Uthman coalesced around Ali, and when Uthman was assassinated in 656, Ali was chosen to succeed him.

The issue of responsibility for Uthman's murder raised the question of whether Ali's accession was legitimate. Uthman's cousin Mu'awiya, a member of the Umayyad family who had built a power base as governor of Syria, refused to recognize Ali as caliph. In the ensuing civil war, Ali was assassinated, and Mu'awiya (r. 661–680) assumed the caliphate. Mu'awiya founded the Umayyad Dynasty and shifted the capital of the Islamic state from Medina in Arabia to Damascus in Syria. Although electing caliphs remained the Islamic ideal, beginning with Mu'awiya, the office of caliph increasingly became hereditary. Two successive dynasties, the Umayyad (661–750) and the Abbasid (750–1258), held the caliphate.

From its inception the caliphate rested on the theoretical principle that Muslim political and religious unity transcended tribalism. Mu'awiya sought to enhance the power of the caliphate by making tribal leaders dependent on him for concessions and special benefits. At the same time, his control of a loyal and well-disciplined army enabled him to take the caliphate in an authoritarian direction. Through intimidation he forced the tribal leaders to accept his son Yazid as his heir, thereby establishing the dynastic principle of succession. By distancing himself from a simple life within the umma and withdrawing into the palace that he built at Damascus, and by surrounding himself with symbols and ceremony, Mu'awiya laid the foundations for an elaborate caliphal court. Many of Mu'awiya's innovations were designed to protect him from assassination. A new official, the *hajib*, or chamberlain, restricted access to the caliph, who received visitors while he was seated on a throne surrounded by bodyguards.

The assassination of Ali and the assumption of the caliphate by Mu'awiya had another profound consequence. It gave rise to a fundamental division in the umma and in Muslim theology. Ali had claimed the caliphate on the basis of family ties — he was Muhammad's cousin and son-in-law. When Ali was murdered, his followers argued that Ali had been the Prophet's designated successor — partly because of the blood tie, partly because Muhammad had designated Ali **imam** (ih-MAHM), or leader in community prayer. These supporters of Ali were called **Shi'a** (SHEE-uh), meaning "supporters" or "partisans" of Ali (Shi'a are also known as Shi'ites). In succeeding generations, opponents of the Umayyad Dynasty emphasized their blood descent from Ali and claimed to possess divine knowledge that Muhammad had given them as his heirs.

Those who accepted Mu'awiya as caliph insisted that the central issue was adhering to the practices and beliefs of the umma based on the precedents of the Prophet. They came to be called **Sunnis** (SOO-neez), which derived from *Sunna* (examples from Muhammad's life). When a situation arose for which the Qur'an offered no solution, Sunni scholars searched for a precedent in the Sunna, which gained an authority comparable to the Qur'an itself.

Both Sunnis and Shi'a maintain that authority within Islam lies first in the Qur'an and then in the Sunna. Who interprets these sources? Shi'a claim that the imam does, for he is invested with divine grace and insight. Sunnis insist that interpretation comes from the consensus of the **ulama**, the group of religious scholars.

Throughout the Umayyad period the Shi'a constituted a major source of discontent. They condemned the Umayyads as worldly and sensual rulers, in contrast to the pious true successors of Muhammad. The Abbasid (uh-BA-suhd) clan, which based its claim to the caliphate on the descent of Abbas, Muhammad's uncle, exploited the situation. The Abbasids agitated the Shi'a, encouraged dissension among tribal factions, and contrasted Abbasid piety with the pleasure-loving style of the Umayyads.

The Abbasid Caliphate

In 747 Abu' al-Abbas led a rebellion against the Umayyads, and in 750 he won general recognition as caliph. Damascus had served as the headquarters of Umayyad rule. Abu' al-Abbas's successor, al-Mansur (r. 754–775), founded the city of Baghdad in 762 and made it his capital. Thus the geographical center of the caliphate shifted eastward to former Sassanid territories. The first three Abbasid caliphs crushed their opponents, turned against many of their supporters, and created a new ruling elite drawn from newly converted Persian families that had traditionally served the ruler. The Abbasid revolution established a basis for rule and

- **imam** The leader in community prayer.
- **Shi'a** Arabic term meaning "supporters of Ali"; they make up one of the two main divisions of Islam.
- **Sunnis** Members of the larger of the two main divisions of Islam; the division between Sunnis and Shi'a began in a dispute about succession to Muhammad, but over time many differences in theology developed.
- **ulama** A group of religious scholars whom Sunnis trust to interpret the Qur'an and the Sunna.

citizenship more cosmopolitan and Islamic than the narrow, elitist, and Arab basis that had characterized Umayyad government.

The Abbasids worked to identify their rule with Islam. They patronized the ulama, built mosques, and supported the development of Islamic scholarship. Moreover, during the Abbasid caliphate, provincial governors gradually won semi-independent power, whereas under the Umayyads the Muslim state had been a federation of regional and tribal armies. Although at first Muslims represented only a small minority of the conquered peoples, Abbasid rule provided the religious-political milieu in which Islam gained, over time, the allegiance of the vast majority of the populations from Spain to Afghanistan.

The Abbasids also borrowed heavily from Persian culture. Following Persian tradition, the Abbasid caliphs claimed to rule by divine right, as reflected in the change of their title from "successor of the Prophet" to "deputy of God." A majestic palace with hundreds of attendants and elaborate court ceremonies deliberately isolated the caliph from the people he ruled. Subjects had to bow before the caliph, kissing the ground, a symbol of his absolute power.

Under the third caliph, Harun al-Rashid (r. 786–809), Baghdad emerged as a flourishing commercial, artistic, and scientific center—the greatest city in Islam and one of the most cosmopolitan cities in the world. Its population of about a million people—an astoundingly large size for preindustrial times—created a huge demand for goods and services, and Baghdad became an entrepôt (trading center) for textiles, slaves, and foodstuffs coming from Oman, East Africa, and India. The city also became intellectually influential. Harun al-Rashid organized the translation of Greek medical and philosophical texts. As part of this effort the Christian scholar Hunayn ibn Ishaq (808–873) translated Galen's medical works into Arabic and made Baghdad a center for the study and practice of medicine. Likewise, impetus was given to the study of astronomy, and through a program of astronomical observations, Muslim astronomers sought to correct and complement Ptolemaic astronomy, which held that the earth is a stationary object at the center of the universe. Above all, studies in Qur'anic textual analysis, history, poetry, law, and philosophy—all in Arabic— reflected the development of a distinctly Islamic literary and scientific culture.

An important innovation of the Abbasids was the use of slaves as soldiers. The caliph al-Mu'taṣim (r. 833–842) acquired several thousand Turkish slaves who were converted to Islam and employed in military service. Scholars have offered varied explanations for this practice: that the use of slave soldiers was a response to a manpower shortage; that as highly skilled horsemen, the Turks had military skills superior to those

Abbasid Wooden Doors These ninth-century wooden doors are thought to come from Samarra, a city about 125 miles upstream from Baghdad, which briefly served as the capital in the ninth century. (Image copyright © The Metropolitan Museum of Art/Art Resource, NY)

of the Arabs and other peoples; and that al-Mu'taṣim felt he could trust the Turks more than the Arabs, Persians, Khurasans, and other recruits. In any case, slave soldiers—later including Slavs, Indians, and sub-Saharan blacks—became a standard feature of Muslim armies in the Middle East down to the twentieth century.

Administration of the Islamic Territories

The Islamic conquests brought into being a new imperial system. The Muslims adopted the patterns of administration used by the Byzantines in Egypt and Syria and by the Sassanids in Persia. Specifically, Arab **emirs**, or governors, were appointed and given overall responsibility for public order, maintenance of the armed forces, and tax collection. Below them, experienced native officials — Greeks, Syrians, and Copts (Egyptian Christians) — remained in office. Thus there was continuity with previous administrations.

The Umayyad caliphate witnessed the further development of the imperial administration. At the head stood the caliph, who led military campaigns against unbelievers. Theoretically, he had the ultimate responsibility for the interpretation of the sacred law. In practice, however, the ulama interpreted the law as revealed in the Qur'an and the Sunna. In the course of time, the ulama's interpretations constituted a rich body of law, the **shari'a** (shuh-REE-uh), which covered social, criminal, political, commercial, and religious matters. The ulama enjoyed great prestige in the Muslim community and were consulted by the caliph on difficult legal and spiritual matters. The *qadis* (KAH-dees), or

judges, who were well versed in the sacred law, carried out the judicial functions of the state. Nevertheless, Muslim law prescribed that all people have access to the caliph, and he set aside special times for hearing petitions and for directly redressing grievances.

The central administrative organ was the diwān, which collected the taxes that paid soldiers' salaries (see page 239) and financed charitable and public works, such as aid to the poor and the construction of mosques, irrigation works, and public baths. Another important undertaking was a relay network established to convey letters and intelligence reports rapidly between the capital and distant outposts. The relay system made it possible for the caliph to respond quickly when news reached him of revolts by emirs and other officials far from the capital.

The early Abbasid period witnessed considerable economic expansion and population growth, complicating the work of government. New and specialized departments emerged, each with a hierarchy of officials. The most important new official was the **vizier** (vuh-ZEER), a position that the Abbasids adopted from the Persians. The vizier was the caliph's chief assistant, advising the caliph on matters of general policy, supervising the bureaucratic administration, and, under the caliph, overseeing the army, the provincial governors, and relations with foreign governments. Depending on the caliph's personality, viziers could acquire extensive power, and some used their offices for personal gain. Although some viziers' careers ended with their execution, there were always candidates seeking the job.

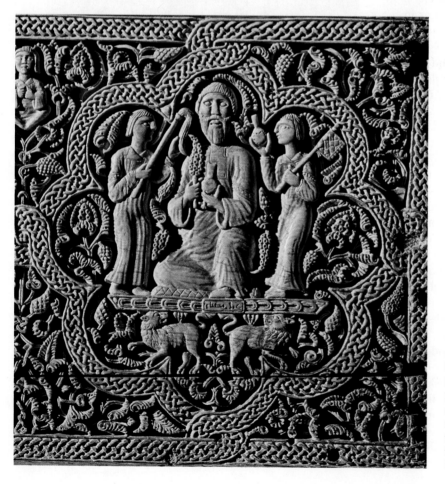

Ivory Chest of Pamplona, Spain The court of the Spanish Umayyads prized small, intricately carved ivory chests, often made in a royal workshop and used to store precious perfumes. This exquisite side panel depicts an eleventh-century caliph flanked by two attendants. An inscription on the front translates as "In the Name of God. Blessings from God, goodwill, and happiness." (Museo Navarra, Pamplona/Institut Amatller d'Art Hispanic)

Fragmentation and Military Challenges, 900–1400

☐ How were the Muslim lands governed from 900 to 1400, and what new challenges did rulers face?

In theory, the caliph and his central administration governed the whole empire, but in practice, the many parts of the empire enjoyed considerable local independence. As long as public order was maintained and taxes were forwarded, the central government rarely interfered. At the same time, the enormous distance between many provinces and the imperial capital, and the long time it took to travel this distance by horse or camel, made it difficult for the caliph to prevent provinces from breaking away. Local, ethnic, or tribal loyalties, combined with fierce ambition, led to the creation of regional dynasties in much of the Islamic world, including Spain, Persia, Central Asia, northern India, and Egypt. None of these states repudiated Islam, but they did stop sending tax revenues to Baghdad. Moreover, most states became involved with costly wars against their neighbors in their attempts to expand. Sometimes these conflicts were worsened by Sunni-Shi'a antagonisms. All these developments, as well as invasions by Turks and Mongols, posed challenges to central Muslim authority.

Breakaway Territories and Shi'a Gains

One of the first territories to break away from the Baghdad-centered caliphate was Spain. In 755 an Umayyad prince who had escaped death at the hands of the triumphant Abbasids and fled to Spain set up an independent regime at Córdoba (see Map 9.1). Other territories soon followed. In 800 the emir in Tunisia in North Africa set himself up as an independent ruler and refused to place the caliph's name on the local coinage. And in 820 Tahir, the son of a slave, was rewarded with the governorship of Khurasan because he had supported the caliphate. Once he took office, Tahir ruled independently of Baghdad, not even mentioning the caliph's name in the traditional Friday prayers in recognition of caliphal authority.

In 946 a Shi'a Iranian clan overran Iraq and occupied Baghdad. The caliph was forced to recognize the clan's leader as commander-in-chief and to allow the celebration of Shi'a festivals — though the caliph and most of the people were Sunnis. A year later the caliph was accused of plotting against his new masters, snatched from his throne, dragged through the streets,

The Patio of the Lions at Alhambra, Fourteenth Century The fortress that the Moorish rulers of Spain built at Granada is considered one of the masterpieces of Andalusian art, notable for the fine carving of geometrical designs and Arabic calligraphy. (George Holton/ Photo Researchers, Inc.)

- **emirs** Arab governors who were given overall responsibility for public order, maintenance of the armed forces, and tax collection.
- **shari'a** Muslim law, which covers social, criminal, political, commercial, and religious matters.
- **vizier** The caliph's chief assistant.

and blinded. Blinding was a practice adopted from the Byzantines as a way of rendering a ruler incapable of carrying out his duties. This incident marked the practical collapse of the Abbasid caliphate. Abbasid caliphs, however, remained as puppets of a series of military commanders and symbols of Muslim unity until the Mongols killed the last Abbasid caliph in 1258 (see page 245).

In another Shi'a advance, the Fatimids, a Shi'a dynasty that claimed descent from Muhammad's daughter Fatima, conquered North Africa then expanded into the Abbasid province of Egypt, founding the city of Cairo as their capital in 969. For the next century or so, Shi'a were in ascendancy in much of the western Islamic world.

The Ascendancy of the Turks

In the mid-tenth century the Turks began to enter the Islamic world in large numbers. First appearing in Mongolia in the sixth century, groups of Turks gradually appeared across the grasslands of Eurasia. Skilled horsemen, they became prime targets for Muslim slave raids, as they made good slave soldiers. Once they understood that Muslims could not be captured for slaves, more and more of them converted to Islam (and often became *ghazi*, frontier raiders, who attacked unconverted Turks to capture slaves). The first to convert accepted Sunni Islam near Bukhara, then a great Persian commercial and intellectual center.

In the 1020s and 1030s Seljuk Turks overran Persia then pushed into Iraq and Syria. Baghdad fell to them on December 18, 1055, and the caliph became a puppet of the Turkish sultan—literally, "he with authority." The Turkic elite rapidly gave up pastoralism and took up the sedentary lifestyle of the people they governed.

The Fatimid Caliphate, 909–1171

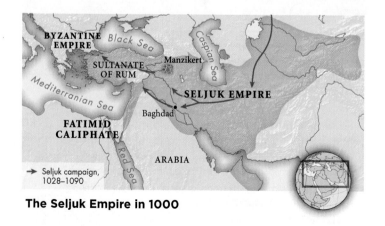

The Seljuk Empire in 1000

The Turks brought badly needed military strength to the Islamic world. They played a major part in recovering Jerusalem after it was held for nearly a century, from 1099 to 1187, by the European Crusaders (who had fought to take Christian holy lands back from the Muslims; see pages 405–408). They also were important in preventing the later Crusades from accomplishing much. Moreover, the Turks became staunch Sunnis and led a campaign against Shi'a.

The influx of Turks from 950 to 1100 also helped provide a new expansive dynamic. At the battle of Manzikert in 1071, Seljuk Turks broke through Byzantine border defenses, opening Anatolia to Turkish migration. Over the next couple of centuries, perhaps a million Turks entered the area—including bands of ghazis and dervishes (Sufi brotherhoods). Seljuk Turks set up the Sultanate of Rum in Anatolia, which lasted until the Mongols invaded in 1243. With the Turks came many learned men from the Persian-speaking East. Over time, many of the Christians in Anatolia converted to Islam and became fluent in Turkish.

The Mongol Invasions

In the early thirteenth century the Mongols arrived in the Middle East. Originally from the grasslands of Mongolia, in 1206 they proclaimed Chinggis Khan (1162–1227) as their leader, and he welded Mongol, Tatar, and Turkish tribes into a strong confederation that rapidly subdued neighboring settled societies (see pages 336–345). After conquering much of north China, the Mongols swept westward, leaving a trail of blood and destruction. They used terror as a weapon, and out of fear many cities surrendered without a fight.

In 1219–1221, when the Mongols first reached the Islamic lands, the areas from Persia through the Central Asian cities of Herat and Samarkand were part of the kingdom of Khwarizm. The ruler—the son of a Turkish slave who had risen to governor of a province—was a conqueror himself, having conquered much of Persia. He had the audacity to execute Chinggis's envoy, and Chinggis retaliated with a force of a hundred thousand soldiers that sacked city after city, often slaughtering the residents or enslaving them and sending them to Mongolia. Millions are said to have died. The irrigation systems that were needed for agriculture in this dry region had been neglected for some time, and with the Mongol invasions suffered a fatal blow.

Great Mosque at Isfahan in Persia
Begun in the late eighth century and added to over the centuries, the Great Mosque in Isfahan is one of the masterpieces of Islamic architecture. The huge dome and the vaulted niches around the courtyard are covered with blue, turquoise, white, and yellow tile. (© Roger Wood/Corbis)

Not many Mongol forces were left in Persia after the campaign of 1219–1221, and another army, sent in 1237, captured the Persian city of Isfahan. In 1251 the decision was taken to push farther west. Chinggis Khan's grandson, Hülegü (1217–1265) led an attack on the Abbasids in Baghdad, sacking and burning the city and killing the last Abbasid caliph in 1258. The fall of Damascus followed in 1260. Mamluk soldiers from Egypt, however, were able to withstand the Mongols and win a major victory at Ayn Jalut in Syria, which has been credited with saving Egypt and the Muslim lands in North Africa and perhaps Spain. At any rate, the desert ecology of the region did not provide suitable support for the Mongol armies, which required five horses for each soldier. Moreover, in 1260 the Great Khan (ruler of Mongolia and China) died, and the top Mongol generals withdrew to Mongolia for the selection of the next Great Khan.

Hülegü and his descendants ruled the central Muslim lands (referred to as the Il-Khanate) for eighty years. In 1295 his descendant Ghazan embraced Islam and worked for the revival of Muslim culture. As the Turks had done earlier, the Mongols, once converted, injected new vigor into the faith and spirit of Islam. In the Il-Khanate, the Mongols governed through Persian viziers and native financial officials.

Muslim Society: The Life of the People

☐ What social distinctions were important in Muslim society?

When the Prophet appeared, Arab society consisted of independent Bedouin tribal groups loosely held together by loyalty to a strong leader and by the belief that all members of a tribe were descended from a common ancestor. Heads of families elected the *sheik*, or tribal chief. He was usually chosen from among elite warrior families who believed their bloodlines made them superior. According to the Qur'an, however, birth counted for nothing; piety was the only criterion for honor: "O ye folk, verily we have created you male and female. . . . Verily the most honourable of you in the sight of God is the most pious of you."[2] The idea of social equality was a basic Muslim doctrine.

When Muhammad defined social equality, he was thinking about equality among Muslims alone. But even among Muslims, a sense of pride in ancestry could not be destroyed by a stroke of the pen. Claims based on birth remained strong among the first Muslims, and after Islam spread outside of Arabia, full-blooded Arab tribesmen regarded themselves as superior to foreign converts.

The Social Hierarchy

In the Umayyad period, Muslim society was distinctly hierarchical. At the top of the hierarchy were the caliph's household and the ruling Arab Muslims. Descended from Bedouin tribespeople and composed of warriors, veterans, governing officials, and town settlers, this class constituted the ruling elite. Because birth continued to determine membership, it was more a caste than a class. It was also a relatively small group, greatly outnumbered by Muslim villagers and country people.

Converts constituted the second class in Islamic society, one that grew slowly over time. Converts to Islam had to attach themselves to one of the Arab tribes in a subordinate capacity. Many resented having to do this, since they believed they represented a culture superior to that of Arab tribespeople. From the Muslim converts eventually came the members of the commercial and learned professions — merchants, traders, teachers, doctors, artists, and interpreters of the shari'a. Second-class citizenship led some Muslim converts to adopt Shi'ism (see page 240). Even so, over the centuries, Berber, Copt, Persian, Aramaean, and other converts to Islam intermarried with their Muslim conquerors. Gradually, assimilation united peoples of various ethnic backgrounds.

Dhimmis (zih-MEEZ) — including Jews, Christians, and Zoroastrians — formed the third stratum. Considered "protected peoples" because they worshipped only one God, they were allowed to practice their religions, maintain their houses of worship, and conduct their business affairs as long as they gave unequivocal recognition to Muslim political supremacy and paid a small tax. Because many Jews and Christians were well educated, they were often appointed to high positions in provincial capitals as well as in Damascus and Baghdad. Restrictions placed on Christians and Jews were not severe, and outbursts of violence against them were rare. However, their social position deteriorated during the Crusades and the Mongol invasions, when there was a general rise of religious loyalties. At those times, Muslims suspected the dhimmis, often rightly, of collaborating with the enemies of Islam.

How did the experience of Jews under Islam compare with that of Jews living in Christian Europe? Recent scholarship shows that in Europe Jews were first marginalized in the Christian social order then completely expelled from it. In Islam Jews, though marginalized, participated fully in commercial and professional activities, some attaining economic equality with their Muslim counterparts. (See "Viewpoints: Jews in Muslim Lands," page 247.) The seventeenth Sura (chapter) of the Qur'an, titled Bani Isra'il, "The Children of Israel," accords to the Jews a special respect because they were "the people of the Book." Also, Islamic culture was urban and commercial and gave the merchant considerable respect; medieval Christian culture was basically rural and agricultural and did not revere the businessperson.

Slavery

Slavery had long existed in the ancient Middle East, and the Qur'an accepted slavery much the way the Old and New Testaments did. But the Qur'an prescribes just and humane treatment of slaves, saying that a master should feed and clothe his slaves adequately; give them moderate, not excessive, work; and not punish them severely. The Qur'an also explicitly encourages the freeing of slaves and urges owners whose slaves ask for their freedom to give them the opportunity to buy it. In fact, the freeing of slaves was thought to pave the way to paradise.

Muslim expansion ensured a steady flow of slaves captured in war. The great Muslim commander Musa ibn Nusayr (640–716), himself the son of a Christian enslaved in Iraq, is reputed to have taken 300,000 prisoners of war in his North African campaigns and 30,000 virgins from the Visigothic nobility of Spain. (These numbers are surely inflated, as most medieval numbers are.) Every soldier, from general to private, had a share of slaves from captured prisoners.

Women slaves worked as cooks, cleaners, laundresses, and nursemaids. A few performed as singers, musicians, dancers, and reciters of poetry. Many female slaves also served as concubines. Not only rulers but also high officials and rich merchants owned many concubines. Down the economic ladder, artisans and tradesmen often had a few concubines who assumed domestic as well as sexual duties.

According to tradition, the seclusion of women in a harem protected their virtue (see page 252), and when men had the means the harem was secured by eunuch (castrated) guards. The use of eunuch guards seems to have been a practice Muslims adopted from the Byzantines and Persians. Early Muslim law forbade castration, so in the early Islamic period Muslims secured eunuchs from European, African, and Central Asian slave markets. In contrast to China, where only the emperor could have eunuch servants, the well-to-do in the Muslim world could purchase them to guard their harems.

• **dhimmis** A term meaning "protected peoples"; they included Jews, Christians, and Zoroastrians.

Viewpoints

Jews in Muslim Lands

• *Under Islam, Jews were considered protected people whose religion was tolerated as long as they abided by rules such as refraining from proselytizing. Often Jews rose to high positions in government service. The two documents below, both written by Jews, show some of the possibilities open to Jews as well as some of the difficulties. The first document is one of the thousands of medieval Jewish documents found in the nineteenth century at a synagogue in Cairo. It is addressed to Abu Sad al-Tustari (d. 1047), a Jew then powerful at court through his connection to the caliph's mother. The second document was written by the eminent Jewish philosopher Maimonides (1137 or 1138– 1204). In it he explains how busy he was kept as a physician by both the court and the populace at large after he moved from Spain to Egypt.*

Letter from the Congregation of a Synagogue in Tripoli to Abu Sad al-Tustari

We the entire congregation of Tripoli send our greetings to our Lord, the honorable Elder, and ask the Lord our God, Who hears the cry of the downtrodden, to grant you eternal life. We wish to inform your Excellency that we are in great distress because we have no place to pray. Everywhere else, the synagogues have been returned to the House of Israel— except in our town. The reason for this is that our synagogue was converted into a mosque. We are, therefore, petitioning our Master to show us kindness with an edict from the Government permitting us to build for ourselves a synagogue—as has been done everywhere else—on one of our ruined properties on which servants of the ruler dwell without paying any rent. We may point out to our Lord that this very year the congregation in [the port city of] Jubayl rebuilt their synagogue, and no Muslim said anything. We also wish to inform our Lord that we will pay an annual rent for the place to the Gentiles.

There is no need to mention that this is a matter which would be pleasing to God. Your welfare and blessings will increase forever. Selah.

May salvation come swiftly.

Maimonides, On His Life as a Jewish Physician in Cairo

I live in Fustat, and the king lives in Cairo, and between the two places there is a distance of [about 1½ miles]. With the king I have a very heavy program. It is impossible for me not to see him first thing every day. If he suffers any indisposition, or if any of his sons or concubines falls sick, I cannot leave Cairo, and I spend most of my day in the palace. It may also happen that one or two of his officers fall sick, and I must attend to them. In short, I go to Cairo early every morning, and if there is no mishap and nothing new, I return to Fustat in the afternoon, and certainly not before then. By then I am hungry, and I find the anterooms all filled with people: Gentiles and Jews, great and small, judges and bailiffs, friends and enemies, a mixed multitude, who await the moment of my return. I dismount from my beast and wash my hands and go to them to soothe them and placate them and beg them to excuse me and wait while I eat a quick meal, my only one in the whole day. Then I go out to treat them and write prescriptions and instructions for their illnesses. They come and go without a break until night, and sometimes, I swear by my faith in the Torah, until two hours of the night or more. I talk to them and instruct them and converse with them, lying on my back from exhaustion. By nightfall I am so worn out that I cannot speak. In fine, no Jew can speak to me or keep company with me or have private conversation with me except on the Sabbath.

Sources: Norman A. Stillman, *The Jews of Arab Lands: A History and Source Book* (Philadelphia: The Jewish Publication Society of America, 1979), p. 204: Reprinted with permission from the Jewish Publication Society. © 1979, Norman Stillman; Bernard Lewis, ed. and trans., *Islam from the Prophet Muhammad to the Capture of Constantinople* (Oxford University Press, 1987), pp. 228–229. Used by permission of Oxford University Press, Inc.

QUESTIONS FOR ANALYSIS

1. Why would a Jewish community member appeal to a Jew with connections at court rather than to the ruler himself?

2. How does Maimonides talk about himself? Does he see his court appointment as an honor or a burden?

3. Taking these two documents together, what would you infer about Jewish communities under Islam?

Slaves Dancing A few women slaves performed as dancers, singers, and musicians, usually before an elite audience of rulers, officials, and wealthy merchants. This reconstructed wall-painting from the ninth century adorned a harem in a royal palace in Samarra. (Bildarchiv Preussischer Kulturbesitz/Art Resource, NY)

Muslims also employed eunuchs as secretaries, tutors, and commercial agents, possibly because eunuchs were said to be more manageable and dependable than men with ordinary desires. Male slaves, eunuchs or not, were also set to work as longshoremen on the docks, as oarsmen on ships, in construction crews, in workshops, and in gold and silver mines.

As already noted, male slaves also fought as soldiers. Any free person could buy a slave, but only a ruler could own military slaves. In the ninth century the rulers of Tunisia formed a special corps of black military slaves, and at the end of that century the Tulunid rulers of Egypt built an army of 24,000 white and 45,000 black slaves. The Fatimid rulers of Egypt (969–1171) raised large black battalions, and a Persian visitor to Cairo between 1046 and 1049 estimated an army of 100,000 slaves, of whom 30,000 were black soldiers.

Slavery in the Islamic world differed in at least two fundamental ways from the slavery later practiced in the Americas. First, race had no particular connection to slavery among Muslims, who were as ready to take slaves from Europe as from Africa. Second, slavery in the Islamic world was not the basis for plantation agriculture, as it was in the southern United States, the Caribbean, and Brazil in the eighteenth and nineteenth centuries. True, in the tenth century large numbers of black slaves worked on date plantations in northeastern Arabia. But massive revolts of black slaves called Zanj from East Africa (see pages 288–289), provoked by mercilessly harsh labor conditions in the salt flats and on the sugar and cotton plantations of southwestern Persia, erupted in 869. Gathering momentum, the Zanj captured the rich cities of Ahwaz, Basra, and Wasit and threatened Baghdad. Only the strenuous efforts of the commander of the caliph's armies, which were composed of Turkish slaves and included naval as well as land forces, halted and gradually crushed the Zanj in 883. The long and destructive Zanj revolt ended the Muslim experiment with plantation agriculture.

Slavery was rarely hereditary in the Muslim world. Most slaves who were taken from non-Muslim peoples later converted, which often led to emancipation. The children of female slaves by Muslim masters were by definition Muslim and thus free. To give Muslim slavery the most positive possible interpretation, one could say that it provided a means to fill certain socioeconomic and military needs and that it assimilated rather than segregated outsiders.

Women in Classical Islamic Society

Before Islam, Arab tribal law gave women virtually no legal status. Girls were sold into marriage by their guardians, and their husbands could terminate the union at will. Also, women had virtually no property or succession rights. Seen from this perspective, the Qur'an sought to improve the social position of women.

The hadith — records of what Muhammad said and did, and what believers in the first two centuries after his death believed he said and did (see page 235) — provide information about the Prophet's wives. Some hadith portray them as subject to common human frailties, such as jealousy; others report miraculous events in their lives. Most hadith describe the wives as "mothers of the believers" — models of piety and righteousness whose every act illustrates their commitment to promoting God's order on earth by personal example.

Although the hadith usually depict women in terms of moral virtue, domesticity, and saintly ideals, they also show some prominent women in political roles. For example, Aisha, daughter of the first caliph and probably Muhammad's favorite wife, played a leading role in rallying support for the movement opposing Ali, who succeeded Uthman in 656 (see page 240). Likewise, Umm Salama, a member of a wealthy and prominent clan in Mecca, first supported Ali, then switched sides and supported the Umayyads.[3] (See "Listening to the Past: Abu Hamid Al-Ghazali, The Etiquette of Marriage," page 250.)

The Qur'an, like the religious writings of other traditions, represents moral precept rather than social practice, and the texts are open to different interpretations. Modern scholars tend to agree that the Islamic sacred book intended women to be the spiritual and sexual equals of men and gave them considerable economic rights. In the early Umayyad period, moreover, women played active roles in the religious, economic, and political life of the community. They owned property. They had freedom of movement and traveled widely. They participated with men in public religious rituals and observances. But this Islamic ideal of women and men having equal value to the community did not last, and, as Islamic society changed, the precepts of the Qur'an were interpreted in more patriarchal ways.

By the Abbasid period, the status of women had declined. The practices of the Byzantine and Persian lands that had been conquered, including seclusion of women, were absorbed. The supply of slave women increased substantially. Some scholars speculate that as wealth replaced ancestry as the criterion of social status, men more and more viewed women as possessions, as a form of wealth.

Men were also seen as dominant in their marriages. The Qur'an states that "men are in charge of women because Allah hath made the one to excel the other, and because they (men) spend of their property (for the support of women). So good women are obedient, guarding in secret that which Allah hath guarded."[4] A tenth-century interpreter, Abu Ja'far Muhammad ibn-Jarir al-Tabari, commented on that passage this way:

> Men are in charge of their women with respect to disciplining (or chastising) them, and to providing them with restrictive guidance concerning their duties toward God and themselves (i.e., the men), by virtue of that by which God has given excellence (or preference) to the men over their wives: i.e., the payment of their dowers to them, spending of their wealth on them, and providing for them in full.[5]

A thirteenth-century commentator on the same Qur'anic passage goes into more detail and argues that women are incapable of and unfit for any public duties, such as participating in religious rites, giving evidence in the law courts, or being involved in any public political decisions. This view came to be accepted, and later interpreters further categorized the ways in which men were superior to women.

Separating Men and Women in a Mosque In this mid-sixteenth-century illustration of the interior of a mosque, a screen separates the women, who are wearing veils and tending children, from the men. The women can hear what is being said, but the men cannot see them. (Bodleian Library, University of Oxford, Ms. Ouseley Add 24, fol. 55v)

Listening to the Past

Abu Hamid Al-Ghazali, The Etiquette of Marriage

Abu Hamid Al-Ghazali (1058–1111) was a Persian philosopher, theologian, jurist, and Sufi, and a prolific author of more than seventy books. His magnum opus, the Revival of the Religious Sciences, *is divided into four parts:* Acts of Worship, Norms of Daily Life, The Ways to Perdition, *and* The Ways of Salvation. *The passages on marriage presented here are only a small part of* Norms of Daily Life, *a lengthy treatise full of quotations from the Qur'an and traditions about the words and actions of Muhammad. His writings reflect the trend toward more patriarchal readings of Muslim teachings.*

"There are five advantages to marriage: procreation, satisfying sexual desire, ordering the household, providing companionship, and disciplining the self in striving to sustain them. The first advantage—that is, procreation—is the prime cause, and on its account marriage was instituted. The aim is to sustain lineage so that the world would not want for humankind. . . .

It was for the purpose of freeing the heart that marriage with the bondmaid was permitted when there was fear of hardship, even though it results in enslaving the son, which is a kind of attrition; such marriage is forbidden to anyone who can obtain a free woman. However, the enslaving of a son is preferable to destroying the faith, for enslavement affects temporarily the life of the child, while committing an abomination results in losing the hereafter; in comparison to one of its days the longest life is insignificant. . . .

It is preferable for a person with a temperament so overcome by desire that one woman cannot curb it to have more than one woman, up to four. For God will grant him love and mercy, and will appease his heart by them; if not, replacing them is recommended. Seven nights after the death of Fatimah, Ali got married. It is said that al-Hasan, the son of Ali, was a great lover having married more than two hundred women. Perhaps he would marry four at a time, and perhaps he would divorce four at a time replacing them with others. . . .

The fourth advantage [of marriage]: being free from the concerns of household duties, as well as of preoccupation with cooking, sweeping, making beds, cleaning utensils, and means for obtaining support. . . .

Ali used to say, "The worst characteristics of men constitute the best characteristics of women; namely, stinginess, pride, and cowardice. For if the woman is stingy, she will preserve her own and her husband's possessions; if she is proud, she will refrain from addressing loose and improper words to everyone; and if she is cowardly, she will dread everything and will therefore not go out of her house and will avoid compromising situations for fear of her husband. . . ."

Some God-fearing men as a precaution against delusion would not marry off their daughters until they are seen. Al-Amash said, "Every marriage occurring without looking ends in worry and sadness." It is obvious that looking does not reveal character, religion, or wealth; rather, it distinguishes beauty from ugliness. . . .

The Messenger of God declared that "The best women are those whose faces are the most beautiful and whose dowries are the smallest." He enjoined against excessiveness in dowries. The Messenger of God married one of his wives for a dowry of ten dirhams and household furnishings that consisted of a hand mill, a jug, a pillow made of skin stuffed with palm fibers, and a stone; in the case of another, he feasted with two measures of barley; and for another, with two measures of dates and two of mush. . . .

It is incumbent upon the guardian also to examine the qualities of the husband and to look after his daughter so as not to give her in marriage to one who is ugly, ill-mannered, weak in faith, negligent in upholding her rights, or unequal to

The Sunni aphorism "There shall be no monkery in Islam" captures the importance of marriage in Muslim culture and the Muslim belief that a sexually frustrated person is dangerous to the community. Islam had no roles for the celibate. In the Muslim world, as in China, every man and woman is expected to marry unless physically incapable or financially unable. Marriage is seen as a safeguard of virtue, essential to the stability both of the family and of society.

As in medieval Europe and traditional India and China, marriage in Muslim society was considered too important an undertaking to be left to the romantic emotions of the young. Families or guardians, not the prospective bride and groom, identified suitable partners and finalized the contract. The official wedding ceremony consisted of an offer and its acceptance by representatives of the bride's and groom's parents at a meeting before witnesses. A wedding banquet at which men and women feasted separately followed; the quality of the celebration, of the gifts, and of the food depended on the relative wealth of the two families. Because it was absolutely essential that the bride be a virgin, marriages were arranged shortly after the onset of the girl's menstrual period at age twelve or

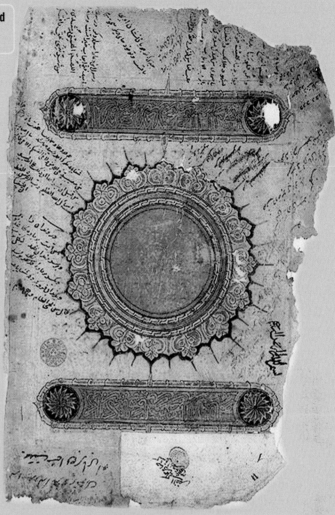
her in descent. The Prophet has said, "Marriage is enslavement; let one, therefore, be careful in whose hands he places his daughter." . . .

The Prophet asked his daughter Fatimah, "What is best for a woman?" She replied, "That she should see no man, and that no man should see her." So he hugged her and said they were "descendants one of another" [Qur'an 3:33]. Thus he was pleased with her answer. . . .

The Prophet permitted women to go to the mosques; the appropriate thing now, however, is to prevent them [from doing so], except for the old [ones]. Indeed such [prevention] was deemed proper during the days of the companions; A'ishah declared, "If the Prophet only knew of the misdeeds that women would bring about after his time, he would have prevented them from going out." . . .

If [a man] has several wives, then he should deal equitably with them and not favor one over the other; should he go on a journey and desire to have one [of his wives] accompany him, he should cast lots among them, for such was the practice of the Messenger. If he cheats a woman of her night, he should make up for it, for making up for it is a duty upon him. . . .

Let [a man] proceed with gentle words and kisses. The Prophet said, "Let none of you come upon his wife like an animal, and let there be an emissary between them." He was asked, "What is this emissary, O Messenger of God?" He said, "The kiss and [sweet] words."

One should not be overjoyed with the birth of a male child, nor should he be excessively dejected over the birth of a female child, for he does not know in which of the two his blessings lie. Many a man who has a son wishes he did not have him, or wishes that he were a girl. The girls give more tranquility and [divine] remuneration, which are greater.

Concerning divorce, let it be known that it is permissible; but of all permissible things, it is the most detestable to Almighty God. 🙶

Source: Madelain Farah, *Marriage and Sexuality in Islam: A Translation of Al-Ghazāli's Book on the Etiquette of Marriage from the Ihyā'* (Salt Lake City: University of Utah Press, 1984), pp. 53, 63, 64, 66, 85–86, 88–89, 91, 95–96, 100, 103, 106, 113, 116, slightly modified.

QUESTIONS FOR ANALYSIS

1. In what ways are the views toward marriage and gender expressed by Al-Ghazali similar to those seen in other traditions?

2. Were there situations in which the author did not think it was appropriate to do what Muhammad and his early followers did? What was his reasoning?

thirteen. Husbands were perhaps ten to fifteen years older. Youthful marriages ensured a long period of fertility.

A wife's responsibilities depended on the wealth and occupation of her husband. A farmer's wife helped in the fields, ground the corn, carried water, prepared food, and did the myriad of tasks necessary in rural life. Shopkeepers' wives in the cities sometimes helped in business. In an upper-class household, the lady supervised servants, looked after all domestic arrangements, and did whatever was needed for her husband's comfort.

In every case, children were the wife's special domain. A mother exercised authority over her children and enjoyed their respect. A Muslim tradition asserts that "Paradise is at the mother's feet." Thus, as in Chinese culture, the prestige of the young wife depended on the production of children—especially sons—as rapidly as possible. A wife's failure to have children was one of the main reasons for a man to take a second wife or to divorce his wife entirely.

Like the Jewish tradition, Muslim law permits divorce. The law prescribes that if a man intends to divorce his wife, he should avoid hasty action and not have intercourse with her for three months; it is hoped that during that time they will reconcile. If the woman turns out to be pregnant, her husband knows that he is the father. Although divorce is allowed, it is not encouraged. One commentator cited the Prophet as saying, "The lawful thing which God hates most is divorce."[6]

In contrast to the traditional Christian view of sexual activity as something inherently shameful and only a cure for lust even within marriage, Islam maintains a healthy acceptance of sexual pleasure for both males and females. The Qur'an permits a man to have four wives, provided that all are treated justly. Some modern Muslim commentators link this provision to a surplus of women that resulted from the wars during the Prophet's lifetime. As in other societies that allowed men to take several wives, only wealthy men could afford to do so. The vast majority of Muslim males were monogamous because they had difficulty enough supporting one wife.

In many present-day Muslim cultures, few issues are more sensitive than the veiling and seclusion of women. These practices have their roots in pre-Islamic times, and they took firm hold in classical Islamic society. As Arab conquerors subjugated various peoples, they adopted some of the vanquished peoples' customs. Veiling was probably of Byzantine or Persian origin. The head veil seems to have been the mark of freeborn urban women; wearing it distinguished them from slave women. Country and desert women did not wear veils because they interfered with work. The veil also indicated respectability and modesty. The Qur'an contains no specific rule about the veil, but its few vague references have been interpreted as sanctioning the practice. Gradually, the custom of covering women extended beyond the veil. Eventually, all parts of a woman's body were considered best covered in public.

An even greater restriction on women than veiling was the practice of purdah, literally, seclusion behind a screen or curtain—the harem system. The English word *harem* comes from the Arabic *haram*, meaning "forbidden" or "sacrosanct," which the women's quarters of a house or palace were considered to be. The practice of secluding women in a harem also derives from Arabic contacts with Persia and other Eastern cultures. Scholars do not know precisely when the harem system began, but by 800 women in more prosperous households stayed out of sight. The harem became another symbol of male prestige and prosperity, as well as a way to distinguish upper-class women from peasants.

Trade and Commerce

☐ Why did trade thrive in Muslim lands?

Islam looked favorably on profit-making enterprises. From 1000 to 1500 there was less ideological resistance to striving for profit in trade and commerce in the Muslim world than in the Christian West or the Confucian East. Also in contrast to the social values of the medieval West and the Confucian East, Muslims tended to look with disdain on agricultural labor. Muhammad had earned his living in business as a representative of the city of Mecca, which carried on a brisk trade from southern Palestine to southwestern Arabia. According to the sayings of the Prophet: "The honest, truthful Muslim merchant will stand with the martyrs on the Day of Judgment. I commend the merchants to you, for they are the couriers of the horizons and God's trusted servants on earth."[7]

> "The honest, truthful Muslim merchant will stand with the martyrs on the Day of Judgment."
>
> **THE PROPHET MUHAMMAD**

The Qur'an, moreover, has no prohibition against trade with Christians or other unbelievers. In fact, non-Muslims, including the Jews of Cairo and the Armenians in the central Islamic lands, were prominent in mercantile networks.

Waterways served as the main commercial routes of the Islamic world (Map 9.2). They included the Mediterranean and Black Seas; the Caspian Sea and the Volga River, which gave access deep into Russia; the Aral Sea, from which caravans departed for China; the Gulf of Aden; and the Arabian Sea and the Indian Ocean, which linked the Persian Gulf region with eastern Africa, the Indian subcontinent, and eventually Indonesia and the Philippines.

Cairo was a major Mediterranean entrepôt for intercontinental trade. Foreign merchants from Central Asia, Persia, Iraq, northern Europe (especially Venice), the Byzantine Empire, and Spain sailed up the Nile to the Aswan region, traveled east from Aswan by caravan to the Red Sea, and then sailed down the Red Sea to Aden, where they entered the Indian Ocean on their way to India. They exchanged textiles, glass, gold, silver, and copper for Asian spices, dyes, and drugs and for Chinese silks and porcelains. Muslim and Jewish merchants dominated the trade with India, and all spoke and wrote Arabic. Their commercial practices included the *sakk*, an Arabic word that is the root of the English *check*, an order to a banker to pay money held on account to a third party; the practice can be traced to Roman Palestine. Muslims also developed other business innovations, such as the bill of exchange, a writ-

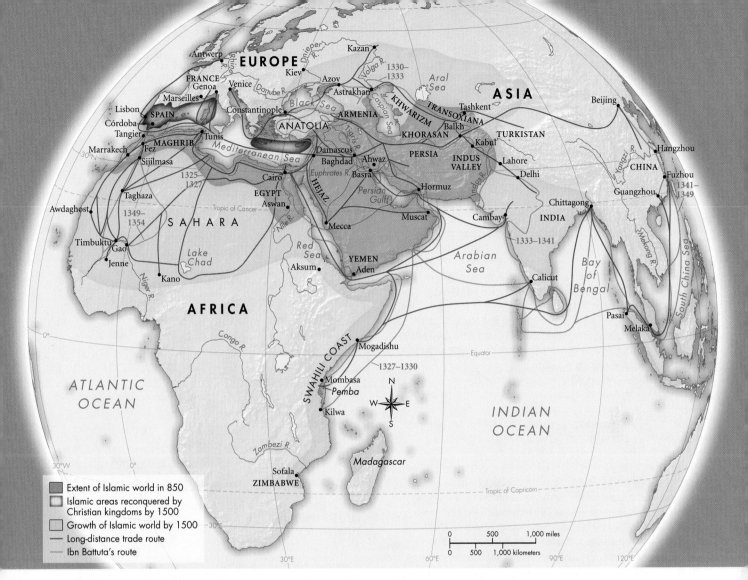

MAP 9.2 The Expansion of Islam and Its Trading Networks in the Thirteenth and Fourteenth Centuries By 1500 Islam had spread extensively in North and East Africa, and into the Balkans, the Caucasus, Central Asia, India, and island Southeast Asia. Muslim merchants played a major role in bringing their religion as they extended their trade networks. They were active in the Indian Ocean long before the arrival of Europeans.

ten order from one person to another to pay a specified sum of money to a designated person or party, and the idea of the joint stock company, an arrangement that lets a group of people invest in a venture and share its profits (and losses) in proportion to the amount each has invested.

Trade also benefited from improvements in technology. The adoption from the Chinese of the magnetic compass, an instrument for determining directions at sea by means of a magnetic needle turning on a pivot, greatly helped navigation of the Arabian Sea and the Indian Ocean. The construction of larger ships led to a shift in long-distance cargoes from luxury goods such as pepper, spices, and drugs to bulk goods such as sugar, rice, and timber. Venetian galleys sailing the Mediterranean came to carry up to 250 tons of cargo, but the

Arab and Persian ships plying the Indian Ocean were built to carry up to 400 tons. The teak forests of western India supplied the wood for Arab ships.

In this period Egypt became the center of Muslim trade, benefiting from the decline of Iraq caused by the Mongol capture of Baghdad and the fall of the Abbasid caliphate (see page 245). Beginning in the late twelfth century Persian and Arab seamen sailed down the east coast of Africa and established trading towns between Somalia and Sofala (see pages 286–291). These thirty to fifty urban centers — each merchant-controlled, fortified, and independent — linked Zimbabwe in southern Africa with the Indian Ocean trade and the Middle Eastern trade.

A private ninth-century list mentions a great variety of commodities transported into and through the

Individuals in Society

Ibn Battuta

IN 1354 THE SULTAN OF MOROCCO APPOINTED a scribe to write an account of the travels of Abu 'Abdallah Ibn Battuta (1304–1368), who between 1325 and 1354 had traveled through most of the Islamic world. The two men collaborated. The result was a travel book written in Arabic and later hailed as the richest eyewitness account of fourteenth-century Islamic culture. It has often been compared to the slightly earlier *Travels* of the Venetian Marco Polo (see page 346).

Ibn Battuta was born in Tangiers to a family of legal scholars. As a youth, he studied Muslim law, gained fluency in Arabic, and acquired the qualities considered essential for a civilized Muslim gentleman: courtesy, manners, and the social polish that eases relations among people.

At age twenty-one he left Tangiers to make the *hajj* (pilgrimage) to Mecca. He crossed North Africa and visited Alexandria, Cairo, Damascus, and Medina. Reaching Mecca in October 1326, he immediately praised God for his safe journey, kissed the Holy Stone at the Ka'ba, and recited the ritual prayers. There he decided to see more of the world.

In the next four years Ibn Battuta traveled to Iraq and to Basra and Baghdad in Persia, then returned to Mecca before sailing down the coast of Africa as far as modern Tanzania. On the return voyage he visited Oman and the Persian Gulf region, then traveled by land across central Arabia to Mecca. Strengthened by his stay in the holy city, he decided to go to India by way of Egypt, Syria, and Anatolia; across the Black Sea to the plains of western Central Asia, detouring to see Constantinople; back to the Asian steppe; east to Khurasan and Afghanistan; and down to Delhi in northern India.

For eight years Ibn Battuta served as a judge in the service of the sultan of Delhi. In 1341 the sultan chose him to lead a diplomatic mission to China. After the expedition was shipwrecked off the southeastern coast of India, Ibn Battuta traveled through southern India, Sri Lanka, and the Maldive Islands. Then he went to China, stopping in Bengal and Sumatra before reaching the southern coast of China, then under Mongol rule. Returning to Mecca in 1346, he set off for home, getting to Morocco in 1349. After a brief trip across the Strait of Gibraltar to Granada, he undertook his last journey, by camel caravan across the Sahara to Mali in the west African Sudan (see page 280), returning home in 1354. Scholars estimate that he had traveled about seventy-five thousand miles.

Ibn Battuta had a driving intellectual curiosity to see and understand the world. At every stop, he sought the learned jurists and pious men at the mosques and madrasas. He marveled at the Lighthouse of Alexandria, then in ruins; at the

• **A traveler, perhaps Ibn Battuta, as depicted on a 1375 European map.** (The Granger Collection, New York)

vast harbor at Kaffa (in southern Ukraine on the Black Sea), whose two hundred Genoese ships were loaded with silks and slaves for the markets at Venice, Cairo, and Damascus; and at the elephants in the sultan's procession in Delhi, which carried machines that tossed gold and silver coins to the crowds.

Ibn Battuta must have had an iron constitution. Besides walking long distances on his land trips, he endured fevers, dysentery, malaria, the scorching heat of the Sahara, and the freezing cold of the steppe. His thirst for adventure was stronger than his fear of nomadic warriors and bandits on land and the dangers of storms and pirates at sea.

Source: R. E. Dunn, *The Adventures of Ibn Battuta: A Muslim Traveler of the Fourteenth Century* (Berkeley: University of California Press, 1986).

QUESTIONS FOR ANALYSIS

1. Trace the routes of Ibn Battuta's travels on Map 9.2 (page 253).

2. How did a common Muslim culture facilitate Ibn Battuta's travels?

Arab Trade and Commerce A mariner's compass determines direction at sea. Arab traders brought this Chinese south-pointing compass (right) to the West, probably in the twelfth century. In 1984 archaeologists unearthed these coins (left) on the island of Pemba, off the coast of modern Kenya. Deriving from Tunisian, Egyptian, and Syrian mints and bearing Arabic scripts, the coins testify to Muslim trade with the Swahili city-states. (compass: Ontario Science Center, Toronto; coins: Courtesy, Dr. Mark Horton, Department of Archaeology and Anthropology, University of Bristol, Bristol, UK)

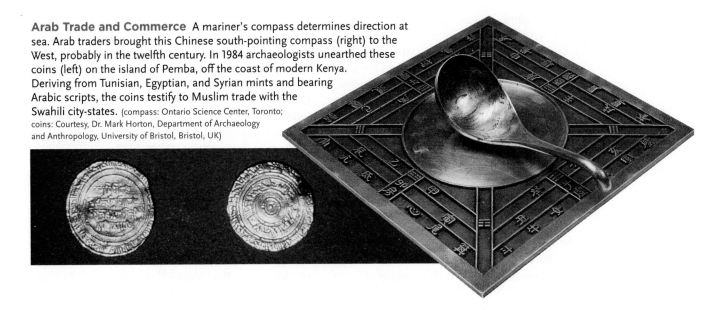

Islamic world by land and by sea:

> Imported from India: tigers, leopards, elephants, leopard skins, red rubies, white sandal-wood, ebony, and coconuts
>
> From China: aromatics, silk, porcelain, paper, ink, peacocks, fiery horses, saddles, felts, cinnamon
>
> From the Byzantines: silver and gold vessels, embroidered cloths, fiery horses, slave girls, rare articles in red copper, strong locks, lyres, water engineers, specialists in plowing and cultivation, marble workers, and eunuchs
>
> From Egypt: ambling donkeys, fine cloths, papyrus, balsam oil, and, from its mines, high-quality topaz
>
> From the Khazars [a people living on the northern shore of the Black Sea]: slaves, slave women, armor, helmets, and hoods of mail
>
> From Ahwaz [a city in southwestern Persia]: sugar, silk brocades, castanet players and dancing girls, kinds of dates, grape molasses, and candy.[8]

Did Muslim economic activity amount to a kind of capitalism? If capitalism is defined as private (not state) ownership of the means of production, the production of goods for sale, profit as the main motive for economic activity, competition, and a money economy, then, unquestionably, the medieval Muslim economy had capitalistic features. Until the sixteenth century much more world trade went through Muslim than European hands.

One by-product of the extensive trade through Muslim lands was the spread of useful plants. Cotton, sugar cane, and rice spread from India to other places with suitable climates. Citrus fruits made their way to Muslim Spain from Southeast Asia and India. The value of this trade contributed to the prosperity of the Abbasid era.

Cultural Developments

☐ What new ideas and practices emerged in the arts, sciences, education, and religion?

Long-distance trade provided the wealth that made possible a gracious and sophisticated culture in the cities of the Muslim world. (See "Individuals in Society: Ibn Battuta," page 254.) Education helped foster achievements in the arts and sciences, and Sufism brought a new spiritual and intellectual tradition.

The Cultural Centers of Baghdad and Córdoba

Although cities and mercantile centers dotted the entire Islamic world, the cities of Baghdad and Córdoba, at their peak in the tenth century, stand out as the finest examples of cosmopolitan Muslim civilization. On Baghdad's streets thronged a kaleidoscope of races, creeds, costumes, and cultures, an almost infinite variety of peoples: returning travelers, administrative officials, slaves, visitors, and merchants from Asia, Africa, and Europe. Shops and marketplaces offered a dazzling and exotic array of goods from all over the world.

The caliph Harun al-Rashid presided over a glamorous court. He invited writers, dancers, musicians, poets, and artists to live in Baghdad, and he is reputed to have rewarded one singer with 100,000 silver pieces for a single song. This brilliant era provided the background for the tales that appear in *The Thousand and One Nights*.

The central story of this fictional collection concerns the attempt of a new bride, Scheherazade, to keep her husband, Shahyar, legendary king of Samarkand, from killing her out of certainty that she will be unfaithful like his first wife. In efforts to delay her execution, she entertains him with one tale a night for 1,001 nights. In the end, Scheherazade's efforts succeed, and her husband pardons her. Among the tales she tells him are such famous ones as "Aladdin and His Lamp," "Sinbad the Sailor," and "Ali Baba and the Forty Thieves." Though filled with folklore, the *Arabian Nights* (as it is also called) has provided many of the images through which Europeans have understood the Islamic world.

Córdoba in southern Spain competed with Baghdad for the cultural leadership of the Islamic world. In the tenth century no city in Asia or Europe could equal dazzling Córdoba. Its streets were well paved and lighted, and the city had an abundant supply of fresh water. With a population of about 1 million, Córdoba contained 1,600 mosques, 900 public baths, 213,177 houses for ordinary people, and 60,000 mansions for generals, officials, and the wealthy. In its 80,455 shops, 13,000 weavers produced silks, woolens, and brocades that were internationally famous. Córdoba was also a great educational center with 27 free schools and a library containing 400,000 volumes. (By contrast, the great Benedictine abbey of Saint-Gall in Switzerland had about 600 books.) Moreover, Córdoba's scholars made contributions in chemistry, medicine and surgery, music, philosophy, and mathematics. It was through Córdoba and Persia that the Indian game of chess entered western Europe. The contemporary Saxon nun Hroswitha of Gandersheim (d. 1000) described Córdoba as the "ornament of the world."[9]

Education and Intellectual Life

Muslim culture valued learning, especially religious learning, because knowledge provided the guidelines by which men and women should live. Parents, thus, established elementary schools for the training of their children. After the caliph Uthman (see page 240) ordered the preparation of an approved text of the Qur'an and had copies of it made, the Qur'an became the basic text. From the eighth century onward formal education for young men involved reading, writing, and the study of the Qur'an, believed essential for its religious message and for its training in proper grammar and syntax.

Teachers Disputing in a Madrasa Although Islamic education relied heavily on memorization of the Qur'an, religious scholars frequently debated the correct interpretation of a particular text. Listening to this lively disputation, the students illustrated in this 1222 book are learning to think critically and creatively. (Bibliothèque nationale de France, Ms. Arabe 6094, fol. 16)

Islam is a religion of the law, and the institution for instruction in Muslim jurisprudence was the **madrasa** (muh-DRA-suh), the school for the study of Muslim law and religion. Many madrasas were founded between 1000 and 1350. By 1193 thirty madrasas existed in Damascus, with sixty more established there between 1200 and 1250. Aleppo, Jerusalem, Alexandria, and above all Cairo also witnessed the foundation of madrasas.

Schools were urban phenomena. Wealthy merchants endowed them, providing salaries for teachers, stipends for students, and living accommodations for both. The teacher served as a guide to the correct path of living. All Islamic higher education rested on a close relationship between teacher and students, so in selecting a teacher, the student (or his father) considered the character and intellectual reputation of the teacher, not that of the institution. Students built their subsequent careers on the reputation of their teachers.

Learning depended heavily on memorization. In primary school, which was often attached to an institution of higher learning, a boy began his education by memorizing the entire Qur'an. Normally, he achieved this feat by the time he was seven or eight! In adolescence a student learned by heart an introductory work in one of the branches of knowledge, such as jurisprudence or grammar. Later he analyzed the texts in detail. Memorizing four hundred to five hundred lines a day was considered outstanding. Every class day, the teacher examined the student on the previous day's learning and determined whether the student fully understood what he had memorized. Students, of course, learned to write, for they had to record the teacher's commentary on a particular text. But the overwhelming emphasis was on the oral transmission of knowledge.

Because Islamic education focused on particular books, when the student had mastered a text to his teacher's satisfaction, the teacher issued the student a certificate stating that he had studied the book or collection of traditions with his teacher. The certificate allowed the student to transmit a text to the next generation on the authority of his teacher.

As the importance of books suggests, the Muslim transmission and improvement of papermaking techniques had special significance to education. For centuries the Chinese had been making paper from rags and from the fibers of hemp, jute, bamboo, and other plants. After these techniques spread westward, Muslim papermakers improved on them by adding starch to fill the pores in the surfaces of the sheets. Muslims carried this new method to Baghdad in Iraq, Damascus in Syria, Cairo in Egypt, and the Maghrib (North Africa), from which it entered Spain. Even before the invention of printing, papermaking had a revolutionary impact on the collection and diffusion of knowledge and thus on the transformation of society.

Mechanical Hand Washer Building on the work of the Greek engineer and inventor Archimedes (see page 138), the Arab scientist Ibn al-Razzaz al-Raziri (ca. 1200) designed practical devices to serve general social needs and illustrated them in a mechanical engineering handbook. In this diagram, a device in the form of a servant pours water with its right hand and offers a towel with its left. The device resembles a modern faucet that releases water when hands are held under it. (Freer Gallery of Art, Smithsonian Institution, Washington, D.C./The Bridgeman Art Library)

Muslim higher education, apart from its fundamental goal of preparing men to live wisely and in accordance with God's law, aimed at preparing them to perform religious and legal functions as Qur'an — or hadith — readers; as preachers in the mosques; as professors, educators, or copyists; and especially as judges. Judges issued fatwas, or legal opinions, in the public courts; their training was in the Qur'an, hadith, or some text forming part of the shari'a.

What educational opportunities were available to women? Although tradition holds that Muhammad

• **madrasa** A school for the study of Muslim law and religious science.

said, "The seeking of knowledge is a duty of every Muslim," Islamic culture was ambivalent on the issue of female education. Because of the basic Islamic principle that "Men are the guardians of women, because God has set the one over the other," the law excluded women from participating in the legal, religious, or civic occupations for which the madrasa prepared young men. Moreover, educational theorists insisted that men should study in a sexually isolated environment because feminine allure would distract them. Nevertheless, many young women received substantial educations from their parents or family members; the initiative invariably rested with their fathers or older brothers. The daughter of Ali ibn Muhammad al-Diruti al Mahalli, for example, memorized the Qur'an, learned to write, and received instruction in several sacred works. According to one biographical dictionary covering the lives of 1,075 women, 411 of them had memorized the Qur'an, studied with a particular teacher, and received a certificate. After marriage, responsibility for a woman's education belonged to her husband.

How does Islamic higher education during the twelfth through fourteenth centuries compare with that available in Europe or China at the same time (see pages 412–413, 373–378)? There are some striking

similarities and some major differences. In both Europe and the Islamic countries, religious authorities ran most schools, while in China the government, local villages, and lineages ran schools, and private tutoring was very common. In the Islamic world, as in China, the personal relationship of teacher and student was seen as key to education. In Europe the reward for satisfactorily completing a course of study was a degree granted by the university. In China, at the very highest levels, the state ran a civil service examination system that rewarded achievement with appointments in the state bureaucracy. In Muslim culture, by contrast, it was not the school or the state but the individual teacher whose evaluation mattered and who granted certificates.

Still, there were also some striking similarities in the practice of education. Students in all three cultures had to master a sacred language (Latin, Arabic, or classical Chinese). In all three cultures education rested heavily on the study of basic religious, legal, or philosophical texts: the Old and New Testaments or the Justinian *Code* in Europe; the Confucian classics and commentaries in China; the Qur'an, hadith, and legal texts deriving from them in the Muslim world. Also in all three cultures memorization played a large role in

Pharmacist Preparing Drugs The translation of Greek scientific treatises into Arabic, combined with considerable botanical experimentation, gave Muslims virtually unrivaled medical knowledge. Many ailments were treated with prescription drugs. In this thirteenth-century illustration a pharmacist prepares a drug in a cauldron over a brazier. It has been said that the pharmacy as an institution is an Islamic invention. (Image copyright © The Metropolitan Museum of Art/Art Resource, NY)

the acquisition and transmission of learning. Furthermore, teachers in all three societies lectured on particular passages, and leading teachers might disagree fiercely about the correct interpretations of a particular text, forcing students to question, to think critically, and to choose among divergent opinions. All these similarities in educational practice contributed to cultural cohesion and ties among the educated living in scattered localities.

In the Muslim world the spread of the Arabic language, not only among the educated classes but also among all the people, was the decisive element in the creation of a common culture. Recent scholarship demonstrates that after the establishment of the Islamic empire, the major influence in the cultural transformation of the Byzantine–Sassanid–North African and the Central Asian worlds was language. The Arabic language proved more important than religion in this regard. Whereas conversion to Islam was gradual, linguistic conversion went much faster. Arabic became the official language of the state and its bureaucracies in former Byzantine and Sassanid territories, and Muslim conquerors forbade Persian-speaking people to use their native language. Islamic rulers required tribute from monotheistic peoples—the Persians and Greeks—but they did not force them to change their religions. Conquered peoples were, however, compelled to submit to a linguistic conversion—to adopt the Arabic language. In time Arabic produced a cohesive and "international" culture over a large part of the Eurasian world.

As a result of Muslim creativity and vitality, modern scholars consider the years from 800 to 1300 to be one of the most brilliant periods in the world's history. Near the beginning of this period the Persian scholar al-Khwarizmi (d. ca. 850) harmonized Greek and Indian findings to produce astronomical tables that formed the basis for later Eastern and Western research. Al-Khwarizmi also studied mathematics, and his textbook on algebra (from the Arabic *al-Jabr*) was the first work in which the word *algebra* is used to mean the "transposing of negative terms in an equation to the opposite side."

Muslim medical knowledge far surpassed that of the West. The Baghdad physician al-Razi (865–925), the first physician to make the clinical distinction between measles and smallpox, produced an encyclopedic treatise on medicine that was translated into Latin and circulated widely in the West. In Córdoba the great surgeon al-Zahrawi (d. 1013) produced an important work in which he discussed the cauterization of wounds (searing them with a branding iron) and the crushing of stones in the bladder. Muslim science reached its peak in the work of Ibn Sina of Bukhara (980–1037), known in the West as Avicenna. His *al-Qanun* codified all Greco-Arabic medical thought, described the contagious nature of tuberculosis and the spreading of diseases, and listed 760 drugs.

Muslim scholars also wrote works on geography, jurisprudence, and philosophy. Al-Kindi (d. ca. 870) was the first Muslim thinker to try to harmonize Greek philosophy and the religious precepts of the Qur'an. He sought to integrate Islamic concepts of human beings and their relations to God and the universe with the principles of ethical and social conduct discussed by Plato and Aristotle. Inspired by Plato's *Republic* and Aristotle's *Politics*, the distinguished philosopher al-Farabi (d. 950) wrote a political treatise describing an ideal city whose ruler is morally and intellectually perfect and who has as his goal the citizens' complete happiness. Avicenna maintained that the truths found by human reason cannot conflict with the truths revealed in the Qur'an. Ibn Rushid, or Averroës (1126–1198), of Córdoba, a judge in Seville and later the royal court physician, paraphrased and commented on the works of Aristotle. He insisted on the right to subject all knowledge, except the dogmas of faith, to the test of reason and on the essential harmony of religion and philosophy.

The Mystical Tradition of Sufism

Like the world's other major religions—Buddhism, Hinduism, Judaism, and Christianity—Islam also developed a mystical tradition: Sufism (SOO-fizm). It arose in the ninth and tenth centuries as a popular reaction to the materialism and worldliness of the later Umayyad regime. Sufis sought a personal union with God—divine love and knowledge through intuition rather than through rational deduction and study of the shari'a. The earliest of the Sufis followed an ascetic routine (denial of physical desires to achieve a spiritual goal), dedicating themselves to fasting, prayer, meditation on the Qur'an, and the avoidance of sin.

The woman mystic Rabi'a (717–801) epitomized this combination of renunciation and devotion. An attractive woman who refused marriage so that nothing would distract her from a total commitment to God, Rabi'a attracted followers, whom she served as a spiritual guide. One of her poems captures her deep devotion: "O my lord, if I worship thee from fear of hell, and if I worship thee in hope of paradise, exclude me thence,

> "O my lord, if I worship thee from fear of hell, and if I worship thee in hope of paradise, exclude me thence, but if I worship thee for thine own sake, then withhold not from me thine eternal beauty."

RABI'A

but if I worship thee for thine own sake, then withhold not from me thine eternal beauty."[10]

Between the tenth and the thirteenth centuries groups of Sufis gathered around prominent leaders called *shaykhs*; members of these groups were called *dervishes*. Dervishes entered hypnotic or ecstatic trances, either through the constant repetition of certain prayers or through physical exertions such as whirling or dancing (hence the English phrase "whirling dervish" for one who dances with abandonment).

Some Sufis acquired reputations as charismatic holy men to whom ordinary Muslims came seeking spiritual consolation, healing, charity, or political mediation between tribal and factional rivals. Other Sufis became known for their writings. Probably the most famous medieval Sufi was the Spanish mystic-philosopher Ibn al'Arabi (1165–1240). He traveled widely in Spain, North Africa, and Arabia seeking masters of Sufism. In Mecca he received a "divine commandment" to begin his major work, *The Meccan Revelation*, which

◻ Picturing the Past

Sufi Collective Ritual Collective or group rituals, in which Sufis tried through ecstatic experiences to come closer to God, have always fascinated outsiders, including non-Sufi Muslims. Here the sixteenth-century Persian painter Sultan Muhammad illustrates the writing of the fourteenth-century lyric poet Hafiz. Notice the various musical instruments and the delicate floral patterns so characteristic of Persian art. (Edinburgh University Library, Scotland/With kind permission of the University of Edinburgh/The Bridgeman Art Library)

ANALYZING THE IMAGE What sort of architectural space is depicted here? What distinctions do you see among the people in terms of how they dress and what they are doing?

CONNECTIONS How common are music and dance in religion? What do they provide?

evolved into a personal encyclopedia of 560 chapters. Also at Mecca the wisdom of a beautiful young girl inspired him to write a collection of love poems, *The Interpreter of Desires*, for which he composed a mystical commentary. In 1223, after visits to Egypt, Anatolia, Baghdad, and Aleppo, Ibn al'Arabi concluded his pilgrimage through the Islamic world at Damascus, where he produced *The Bezels [Edges] of Wisdom*, considered one of the greatest works of Sufism.

Muslim-Christian Encounters

☐ How did Muslims and Christians come into contact with each other, and how did they view each other?

During the early centuries of its development, Islam came into contact with the other major religions of Eurasia—Hinduism in India, Buddhism in Central Asia, Zoroastrianism in Persia, and Judaism and Christianity in western Asia and Europe. However, the relationship that did the most to define Muslim identity was the one with Christianity. To put this another way, the most significant "other" to Muslims in the heartland of Islam was Christendom. The close physical proximity and the long history of military encounters undoubtedly contributed to making the Christian-Muslim encounter so important to both sides.

European Christians and Middle Eastern Muslims shared a common cultural heritage from the Judeo-Christian past. In the classical period of Islam, Muslims learned about Christianity from the Christians they met in conquered territories; from the Old and New Testaments; from Jews; and from Jews and Christians who converted to Islam. Before 1400 a wide spectrum of Muslim opinion about Jesus and Christians existed. At the time of the Crusades and of the Christian reconquest of Muslim Spain (the *reconquista*, 722–1492), polemical anti-Christian writings appeared. In other periods, Muslim views were more positive.

In the medieval period Christians and Muslims met frequently in business and trade. Commercial contacts, especially when European merchants resided for a long time in the Muslim East, gave Europeans, notably the Venetians, familiarity with Muslim art and architecture. Likewise, when in the fifteenth century Muslim artists in the Ottoman Empire and in Persia became acquainted with Western artists, such as Gentile Bellini, they admired and imitated them. Also, Christians very likely borrowed aspects of their higher education practices from Islam.

In the Christian West, Islam had the greatest cultural impact in Andalusia in southern Spain. Between roughly the eighth and twelfth centuries, Muslims, Christians, and Jews lived in close proximity in Andalusia, and some scholars believe the period represents a remarkable era of interfaith harmony. Many Christians adopted Arabic patterns of speech and dress, gave up the practice of eating pork, and developed a special appreciation for Arabic music and poetry. Some Christian women of elite status chose the Muslim practice of going out in public with their faces veiled. Records describe Muslim and Christian youths joining in celebrations and merrymaking. These assimilated Christians, called **Mozarabs** (moh-ZAR-uhbz), did not attach much importance to the doctrinal differences between the two religions.

However, Mozarabs soon faced the strong criticism of both Muslim scholars and Christian clerics. Muslim teachers feared that close contact between people of the two religions would lead to Muslim contamination and become a threat to the Islamic faith. Christian bishops worried that a knowledge of Islam would lead to confusion about essential Christian doctrines. Both Muslim scholars and Christian theologians argued that assimilation led to moral decline.

Thus, beginning in the late tenth century, Muslim regulations closely defined what Christians and Muslims could do. A Christian, however much assimilated, remained an unbeliever, a word that carried a pejorative connotation. Because of their status as unbelievers, Mozarabs had to live in special sections of cities; could not learn the Qur'an, employ Muslim workers or servants, or build new churches; and had to be buried in their own cemeteries. A Muslim who converted to Christianity immediately incurred a sentence of death. By about 1250 the Christian reconquest of Muslim Spain had brought most of the Iberian peninsula under Christian control. With their new authority Christian kings set up schools that taught both Arabic and Latin to train missionaries.

Beyond Andalusian Spain, mutual animosity limited contact between people of the two religions. The Muslim assault on Christian Europe in the eighth and ninth centuries—with villages burned, monasteries sacked, and Christians sold into slavery—left a legacy of bitter hostility. Christians felt threatened by a faith that acknowledged God as creator of the universe but denied the Trinity (the doctrine of God as the union of a holy father, his son, and the holy spirit); that accepted Jesus as a prophet but denied his divinity; and that believed in the Last Judgment but seemed to make

• **Mozarabs** Christians who adopted some Arabic customs but did not convert.

sensuality Heaven's greatest reward. Europeans' perception of Islam as a menace helped inspire the Crusades of the eleventh through thirteenth centuries (see pages 404–408).

Despite the conflicts between the two religions, Muslim scholars often wrote sympathetically about Jesus. For example, the great historian al Tabari (d. 923), relying on Arabic sources, wrote positively of Jesus's life, focusing on his birth and crucifixion. Also, Ikhwan al-Safa, an eleventh-century Islamic brotherhood, held that in his preaching Jesus deliberately rejected the harsh punishments reflected in the Jewish Torah and tried to be the healing physician teaching by parables and trying to touch people's hearts by peace and love. In terms of more critical views of Christianity, al Tabari used Old Testament books to prove Muhammad's prophethood. The prominent theologian and qadi (judge) of Teheran, Abd al-Jabbar (d. 1024), though not critical of Jesus, argued that Christians had rejected Jesus's teachings: they failed to observe the ritual purity of prayer, substituting poems by Christian scholars for scriptural prayers; they gave up circumcision, the sign of their covenant with God and Abraham; they moved the Sabbath from Saturday to Sunday; they allowed the eating of pork and shellfish; and they adopted a Greek idea, the Trinity, defending it by quoting Aristotle. Thus, al-Jabbar maintained — and he was followed later by many other Muslim theologians and scholars — that Christians failed to observe the laws of Moses and Jesus and distorted Jesus's message.

In the Christian West, both positive and negative views of Islam appeared in literature. The Bavarian knight Wolfram von Eschenbach's *Parzival* and the En-

Mozarabic Bible In this page from a tenth-century Mozarabic Bible, Moses is depicted closing the passage through the Red Sea, thus drowning the Egyptians. (Real Collegiata San Isidoro de León/Gianni Dagli Orti/The Art Archive)

glishman William Langland's *Piers the Plowman* — two medieval poems that survive in scores of manuscripts, suggesting that they circulated widely — reveal broadmindedness and tolerance toward Muslims. Some travelers in the Middle East were impressed by the kindness and generosity of Muslims and with the strictness and devotion with which Muslims observed their faith. Frequently, however, Christian literature portrayed Muslims as the most dreadful of Europe's enemies, guilty of every kind of crime. In his *Inferno,* for example, the great Florentine poet Dante (1265–1321) placed the Muslim philosophers Avicenna and Averroës with other virtuous "heathens," among them Socrates and Aristotle, in the first circle of Hell, where they endured only moderate punishment. Muhammad, however, Dante consigned to the ninth circle, near Satan himself, where he was condemned as a spreader of discord and scandal and suffered perpetual torture.

Even when they rejected each other most forcefully, the Christian and Muslim worlds had a significant impact on each other. Art styles, technology, and even institutional practices spread in both directions. During the Crusades Muslims adopted Frankish weapons and methods of fortification. Christians in contact with Muslim scholars recovered ancient Greek philosophical texts that survived only in Arabic translation.

CONNECTIONS

During the five centuries that followed Muhammad's death, his teachings came to be revered in large parts of the world from Spain to Afghanistan. Although in some ways similar to the earlier spread of Buddhism out of India and Christianity out of Palestine, in the case of Islam, military conquests played a large part in the extension of Muslim lands. Still, conversion was never complete; both Christians and Jews maintained substantial communities within Muslim lands. Moreover, cultural contact among Christians, Jews, and Muslims was an important element in the development of each culture.

Muslim civilization in these centuries drew from many sources, including Persia and Byzantium, and in turn had broad impact beyond its borders. Muslim scholars preserved much of early Greek philosophy and science through translation into Arabic. Trade connected the Muslim lands both to Europe and to India and China.

During the first and second centuries after Muhammad, Islam spread along the Mediterranean coast of North Africa, which had been part of the Roman world. The next chapter explores other developments in the enormous and diverse continent of Africa during this time. Many of the written sources that tell us about the African societies of these centuries were written in Arabic by visitors from elsewhere in the Muslim world. Muslim traders traveled through many of the societies in Africa north of the Congo, aiding the spread of Islam to the elites of many of these societies. Ethiopia was an exception, as Christianity spread there from Egypt before the time of Muhammad and retained its hold in subsequent centuries. Africa's history is introduced in the next chapter.

□ CHAPTER REVIEW

□ From what kind of social and economic environment did Muhammad arise, and what did he teach? (p. 234)

Muhammad was born in the Arabian peninsula among farmers, traders, merchants, and herders, where tribes were the basic social unit. After experiencing a religious vision, Muhammad began to preach to the people, urging them to give up their idols and submit to the one indivisible God. He taught strict monotheism — that there is one and only one God and that believers must submit to God's will. This God is the same God of the Christians and Jews, and Islam, the religion based on Muhammad's teachings, appropriates much of the Old and New Testaments of the Bible. Through his religious teaching, Muhammad helped to bind different tribal groups into a strong, unified state by emphasizing commitment to a common religious faith over tribal ties. After Muhammad's death, religious leaders organized his revelations into chapters, eventually producing the Qur'an, which prescribes a strict code of moral behavior.

□ What made possible the spread of Islam, and what forms of government were established to rule Muslim lands? (p. 237)

A mixture of religious zeal, desire for plunder, and the weakness of their neighbors pushed Muslims to carry their faith from the Arabian peninsula through the Middle East, to North Africa and Spain, and to the borders of China and northern India — all within the relatively short span of a century. Successors to Muhammad established the caliphate, which through two successive dynasties — the Umayyad, centered at Damascus in Syria, and the Abbasid, with its capital at Baghdad in Iraq — coordinated rule over Muslim lands through emirs (governors), qadi (judges), and viziers (chief assistants to caliphs). A key challenge faced by the caliphate was a fundamental division in Muslim theology between the Sunnis and the Shi'a.

□ How were the Muslim lands governed from 900 to 1400, and what new challenges did rulers face? (p. 243)

In theory, the caliph and his central administration governed the whole Muslim empire, but in practice, the many parts of the empire enjoyed considerable local independence. Local, ethnic, or tribal loyalties, combined with fierce ambition, led to the creation of regional dynasties in much of the Islamic world. As a result, various territories, including Spain, began to break away from the Baghdad-centered caliphate. In

this situation, Turks played more and more important roles in the armies and came to be the effective rulers in many places. They were succeeded by the Mongols who invaded the Middle East in the thirteenth century and ruled the central Muslim lands for eighty years.

□ What social distinctions were important in Muslim society? (p. 245)

In the Umayyad period Muslim society was distinctly hierarchical. At the top of the hierarchy were the caliph's household and the ruling Arab Muslims. Next were converts to Islam, including the Copts, Berbers, Persians, and Aramaeans. Below the converts were Jews, Christians, and Zoroastrians, recognized as protected people because they recognized only one God, who were allowed to continue practicing their religions. In addition there were a substantial number of slaves, many of whom were war captives. Slaves normally were converted to Islam and might come to hold important positions, especially in the army. Distinctions between men and women in Islamic society were strict. In the Qur'an men were said to be in charge of women because God "made the one to excel the other," and women were enjoined to be obedient. In time, the seclusion and veiling of women became common practices, especially among the well-to-do.

□ Why did trade thrive in Muslim lands? (p. 252)

Muhammad was said to see merchants as "God's trusted servants on earth," and Islam did not discourage profit-making. Merchants were respected and treated well. By land and sea Muslim merchants transported a rich variety of goods across Asia, the Middle East, Africa, and western Europe. As trade thrived, innovations such as money orders to bankers, bills of exchange, and joint stock companies aided the conduct of business.

□ What new ideas and practices emerged in the arts, sciences, education, and religion? (p. 255)

Trade provided the wealth that made possible a gracious and sophisticated culture in the cities of the Muslim world. Urban culture, with centers at Baghdad and Córdoba, also thrived because of the strong foundation provided by education (at madrasas and other institutions). Education fostered achievements in the arts and sciences and in other intellectual pursuits, and as a result of Muslim creativity and vitality, modern scholars consider the years from 800 to 1300 one of the most brilliant periods in world history. During this period Muslim scholars produced important work in many disciplines, especially mathematics, medicine, and philosophy. As the larger culture blossomed, a new spiritual and intellectual tradition arose in the mystical practices of Sufism. Sufis sought a personal union with God — divine love and knowledge through intuition rather than through rational deduction and study of the shari'a.

◻ How did Muslims and Christians come into contact with each other, and how did they view each other? (p. 261)

European Christians and Middle Eastern Muslims shared a common cultural heritage from the Judeo-Christian past. In the classical period of Islam, Muslims learned about Christianity from the Christians they met in conquered territories, from the Old and New Testaments, from Jews, and from Jews and Christians who converted to Islam. Before 1500 a wide spectrum of Muslim opinion about Jesus and Christians existed. At the time of the Crusades and of the Christian reconquest of Muslim Spain, polemical anti-Christian writings appeared. In other periods Muslim views were more positive. For their part some Christians, such as the Mozarabs, assimilated into Muslim culture, while others, including writers of certain literary works, saw Muslims as enemies and criminals.

SUGGESTED READING

Ahmed, Leila. *Women and Gender in Islam.* 1993. Links modern issues to their historical roots.

Berkey, Jonathan. *The Transmission of Knowledge in Medieval Cairo.* 1992. A study of religious education and its social context.

Bulliet, Richard W. *Cotton, Climate, and Camels in Early Islamic Iran.* 2009. Links a cooling of the climate to a decline in the Iranian cotton industry and cross-breeding of one- and two-hump camels.

Cohen, Mark R. *Under Crescent and Cross: The Jews in the Medieval Ages.* 1994. Argues that Jews were less marginalized and persecuted under Islamic states than under Christian states.

Constable, Olivia Remie. *Trade and Traders in Muslim Spain: The Commercial Realignment of the Iberian Peninsula, 900–1500.* 1994. An excellent study of Muslim trade and commerce drawing on a wide range of both Western and Arabic sources.

Ettinghausen, Richard, Oleg Grabar, and Marilyn Jenkins-Madina. *The Art and Architecture of Islam, 650–1250.* 2001. A stunningly illustrated overview of Islamic art.

Fletcher, Richard. *The Cross and the Crescent.* 2003. A balanced, fascinating, and lucidly written short account of the earliest contacts between Christians and Muslims.

Hourani, Albert, and Malise Ruthven. *A History of the Arab Peoples,* 2d ed. 2003. An important synthesis.

Lewis, Bernard, ed. and trans. *Islam from the Prophet Muhammad to the Capture of Constantinople: Religion and Society.* 1987. A collection of original sources on many topics.

Lewis, Bernard. *Race and Slavery in the Middle East.* 1990. Explores the culture of slavery beginning from before Islam, with particular attention to slaves from Africa.

Long, Pamela O. *Technology and Society in the Medieval Centuries: Byzantium, Islam, and the West, 500–1300.* 2003. A useful survey of Arab scientific and military developments.

Peters, F. E. *The Hajj: The Muslim Pilgrimage to Mecca and the Holy Places.* 1994. Covers the social, commercial, and political significance of the obligatory Muslim pilgrimage to Mecca.

Sells, Michael. *Approaching the Qur'an.* 2007. Includes selected translations set in historical and cultural context.

Stowasser, Barbara Freyer. *Women in the Qur'an: Traditions and Interpretation.* 1994. A fine analysis of the Qur'an's statement on women.

Turner, Howard R. *Science in Medieval Islam: An Illustrated Introduction.* 1995. A fascinating exploration of Islamic science with chapters on astronomy, medicine, geography, alchemy, mathematics, and other topics.

NOTES

1. F. E. Peters, *A Reader on Classical Islam* (Princeton: Princeton University Press, 1994), pp. 154–155.
2. Quoted in R. Levy, *The Social Structure of Islam*, 2d ed. (Cambridge: Cambridge University Press, 1957), p. 56.
3. See B. F. Stowasser, *Women in the Qur'an, Traditions, and Interpretation* (New York: Oxford University Press, 1994), pp. 94–118.
4. Quoted in B. F. Stowasser, "The Status of Women in Early Islam," in *Muslim Women,* ed. F. Hussain (New York: St. Martin's Press, 1984), p. 25.
5. Quoted ibid., pp. 25–26.
6. Peters, *A Reader on Classical Islam,* p. 250.
7. Quoted in B. Lewis, ed. and trans., *Islam from the Prophet Muhammad to the Capture of Constantinople,* vol. 2: *Religion and Society* (New York: Harper & Row, 1975), p. 126.
8. Ibid, pp. 154–157. Used by permission of Oxford University Press, Inc.
9. R. Hillenbrand, "Cordoba," in *Dictionary of the Middle Ages,* vol. 3, ed. J. R. Strayer (New York: Scribner's, 1983), pp. 597–601.
10. Margaret Smith, *Readings from the Mystics of Islam* (London: Luzac and Co., 1950), p. 11.

For practice quizzes and other study tools, visit the **Online Study Guide** at bedfordstmartins.com/mckayworld.

For primary sources from this period, see ***Sources of World Societies*, Second Edition**.

For Web sites, images, and documents related to topics in this chapter, visit **Make History** at bedfordstmartins.com/mckayworld.

• **Ife Ruler** West African rulers, such as the one shown in this bronze head of a Yoruban king, or *Oni*, from the thirteenth or fourteenth century, were usually male. (© Jerry Thompson)

10

Until fairly recently, most of the outside world knew little about the African continent, its history, or its people. The sheer size of the continent, along with tropical diseases and the difficulty of navigating Africa's rivers inland, limited travel there to a few intrepid Muslim adventurers such as Ibn Battuta. Ethnocentrism and racism became critical factors with the beginning of the Atlantic slave trade in the 1500s, followed in the nineteenth century by European colonialism, which distorted and demeaned knowledge and information about Africa. But recent scholarship has allowed us to learn more about early African civilizations, and we are able to appreciate the richness, diversity, and dynamism of those cultures. We know now that between about 400 and 1500 some highly centralized, bureaucratized, and socially stratified civilizations developed in Africa alongside communities with a looser form of social organization that were often held together simply through common bonds of kinship.

African Societies and Kingdoms
1000 B.C.E.–1500 C.E.

In West Africa there arose during this period several large empires that were closely linked to the trans-Saharan trade in salt, gold, cloth, ironware, ivory, and other goods. After 700 this trade connected West Africa with the Muslim societies of North Africa and the Middle East. Vast stores of new information, contained in books and carried by visiting scholars, now arrived from an Islamic world that was experiencing a Golden Age.

Meanwhile, Bantu-speaking peoples carried ironworking and the domestication of crops and animals from modern Cameroon to Africa's southern tip. They established kingdoms, such as Great Zimbabwe, in the interior, while one group, the Swahili, established large and prosperous city-states along the Indian Ocean coast. •

The Land and Peoples of Africa

□ How did Africa's geography shape its history and contribute to its diverse population, and how has this fueled the debate over who is African?

The world's second largest continent (after Asia), Africa covers 20 percent of the earth's land surface. The student beginning the study of African history should bear in mind the enormous diversity of African peoples and cultures both within and across regions. It is difficult and often wrong to make broad generalizations about African life. Statements that begin "African culture is . . ." or "African people are . . ." are virtually meaningless. African peoples are not now and never have been homogeneous. This rich diversity helps explain why the study of African history is so exciting and challenging.

Africa's Geographical and Human Diversity

Five main climatic zones roughly divide the continent (Map 10.1). Fertile land with unpredictable rainfall borders parts of the Mediterranean coast in the north and the southwestern coast of the Cape of Good Hope in the south. Inland from these areas lies dry steppe country with little plant life. The steppe gradually gives way to Africa's great deserts: the Sahara in the north and the Namib (NAH-mihb) and Kalahari in the south. The vast Sahara—3.5 million square miles—takes its name from the Arabic word for "tan," the color of the desert. (Folk etymology ascribes the word *Sahara* to an ancient Arabic word that sounds like a parched man's gasp for water.) The Sahara's southern subdesert fringe is called the Sahel (SA-hihl), from the Arabic word for "shore." The savanna—flat grassland—extends in a swath across the widest part of the continent, across parts of south-central Africa, and along the eastern coast. It is one of the richest habitats in the world and accounts for perhaps 55 percent of the African continent. Dense, humid tropical rain forests stretch along coastal West Africa and on both sides of the equator in central Africa. Africa's climate is mostly tropical, with subtropical climates limited to the northern and southern coasts and to regions of high elevation. Rainfall is seasonal on most of the continent and is very sparse in desert and semidesert areas.

Geography and climate have significantly shaped African economic development. In the eastern African plains the earliest humans hunted wild animals. The drier steppe regions favored herding. Wetter savanna regions, like the Nile Valley, encouraged grain-based agriculture. Tropical forests favored hunting and gathering and, later, root-based agriculture. Root crops, such as yams, potatoes, and cassava, are high in carbohydrates and are usually grown in areas that are not suitable for grains. Rivers and lakes supported economies based on fishing.

Africa's peoples are as diverse as the continent's topography. In North Africa contacts with Asian and European civilizations date back to the ancient Phoenicians, Greeks, and Romans (see Chapters 5 and 6). Groups living on the coast or along trade routes had the greatest degree of contact with outside groups. The native Berbers of North Africa, living along the Mediterranean, intermingled with many different peoples—with Muslim Arabs, who first conquered North Africa in the seventh and eighth centuries C.E. (see page 238); with Spanish Muslims and Jews, many of whom settled in North Africa after their expulsion from Spain in 1492 (see page 440); and with sub-Saharan blacks with whom they traded across the Sahara Desert. The peoples living along the Swahili coast in East Africa developed a maritime civilization and had rich commercial contacts with southern Arabia, the Persian Gulf, India, China, and the Malay Archipelago.

Black Africans inhabited the region south of the Sahara, an area of savanna and rain forest. The ancient Greeks called them *Ethiopians*, which means "people with burnt faces." The Berbers also described this region based on its inhabitants, coining the term *Akal-n-Iquinawen,* which survives today as *Guinea.* Similarly, the Arabs used the term *Bilad al-Sudan,* which survives as *Sudan.* The Berber and Arab terms both mean "land of the blacks." Short-statured peoples, sometimes inaccurately referred to as Pygmies, inhabited the equatorial rain forests. South of those forests, in the continent's southern third, lived the Khoisan (KOY-sahn), a small people with yellow-brown skin color who primarily were hunters but also had domesticated livestock.

Egypt, Race, and Being African

When Europeans first started exploring sub-Saharan Africa's interior in the nineteenth century they were amazed at the quality of the art and architecture they came across, which included the ruins at Great Zimbabwe and the Nok heads, both of which are discussed in this chapter. In response they developed the **Hamitic thesis**, which argued that Africans were not capable of such work, so a "Hamitic race" related to the Caucasian race must have settled in Africa in the distant past, practiced their advanced technologies, including ironworking, and then blended into nearby African populations or departed. Although completely discredited today, the Hamitic thesis survived throughout much of the twentieth century.

As is evident from the nineteenth century's artificial construction of a Hamitic race, popular usage of the term *race* has often been imprecise and inaccurate. The application of general characteristics and patterns of behavior to peoples based on perceptions of physical differences is one of the legacies of imperialism and colonialism. Anthropologists have long insisted that when applied to geographical, national, religious, linguistic, or cultural groups, the concept of race is inappropriate and has been refuted by the scientific data. But race remains an essential category in the popular psyche, and the issue of race continues to engender fierce debate. Nowhere in African studies has this debate been more strident than over questions relating to Egyptian identity and civilization, and Africa's contribution to European civilization.

Geographically, Egypt, located in North Africa, is part of the African continent. But from the days of the ancient Greek historian Herodotus, who visited Egypt in the fifth century B.C.E. (see page 123), down to the present, scholars have vigorously, even violently,

ca. 1000 B.C.E.–1500 C.E.	Bantu-speakers expand across central and southern Africa
ca. 600 C.E.	Christian missionaries convert Nubian rulers
642 C.E.	Muslim conquest of Egypt; Islam introduced to Africa
650–1500 C.E.	Slave trade from sub-Saharan Africa to the Mediterranean
700–900 C.E.	Berbers develop caravan routes
ca. 900–1100 C.E.	Kingdom of Ghana; bananas and plantains arrive in Africa from Asia
ca. 1100–1400 C.E.	Great Zimbabwe is built, flourishes
ca. 1200–1450 C.E.	Kingdom of Mali
ca. 1312–1337 C.E.	Reign of Mansa Musa in Mali
1314–1344 C.E.	Reign of Amda Siyon in Ethiopia
1324–1325 C.E.	Mansa Musa's pilgrimage to Mecca

Nok Woman Hundreds of terra-cotta sculptures such as the head of this woman survive from the Nok culture, which originated in the central plateau of northern Nigeria in the first millennium B.C.E. (Werner Forman/Art Resource, NY)

• **Hamitic thesis** A nineteenth-century concept, tied to scientific racism, that a subgroup of the Caucasian race, the Hamites, brought superior technology and knowledge to Africa in the ancient past; now completely discredited.

MAP 10.1 The Geography of Africa Africa's climate zones have always played a critical role in the history of the continent and its peoples. These zones mirror each other north and south of the equator: tropical forest, savanna, sub-desert, desert, and Mediterranean climate.

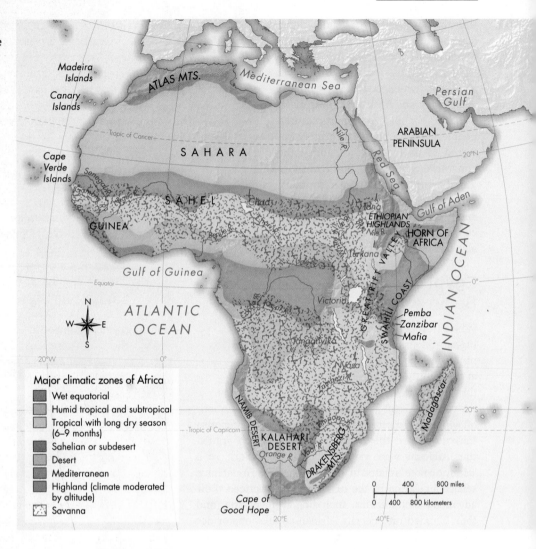

Major climatic zones of Africa

- Wet equatorial
- Humid tropical and subtropical
- Tropical with long dry season (6–9 months)
- Sahelian or subdesert
- Desert
- Mediterranean
- Highland (climate moderated by altitude)
- Savanna

debated whether racially and culturally Egypt is part of the Mediterranean world or part of the African world. More recently, the debate has also included the question of whether Egyptians of the first century B.C.E. made such contributions to the Western world as architecture (the pyramids), mathematics, philosophy, science, and religion (the idea of divine kingship), and, if so, whether they were black people.

Some African and African American scholars have argued that much Western historical writing since the eighteenth century has been a "European racist plot" to destroy evidence that would recognize African accomplishments. They have amassed architectural and linguistic evidence, as well as a small mountain of quotations from Greek and Roman writers and from the Bible, to insist that the ancient Egyptians belonged to the black race. The late Senegalese scholar Cheikh Anta Diop claimed to have examined the skin of ancient Egyptian mummies and said that it "was pigmented in the same way as that of all other (sub-Saharan) Afri-

can negroes."[1] Similarly, in 1987 the English historian Martin Bernal argued that Egypt and therefore Africa had never received enough credit for their contributions to Greek civilization.[2]

Against this view, another group of scholars holds that the ancient Egyptians were Caucasians. They believe that Phoenician, Berber, Libyan, Hebrew, and Greek peoples populated Egypt and created its civilization. Whereas Diop relied on the book of Genesis to support his thesis, his detractors argue that the Hebrew Scriptures are not an anthropological treatise but a collection of Hebrew, Mesopotamian, and Egyptian legends concerned with the origins of all human peoples, not racial groups in the twentieth-century sense. They point out that the pharaohs of the first century B.C.E. descended from the (white) Macedonian generals whom Alexander the Great had placed over Egypt.

A third proposition, perhaps the most plausible, holds that ancient Egypt, at the crossroads of three continents, was a melting pot of different cultures and peoples. To attribute Egyptian civilization to any one group is blatant racism and ultimately extremist. Many diverse peoples contributed to the great achievements of Egyptian culture. Moderate scholars believe that black Africans resided in ancient Egypt, primarily in Upper Egypt (south of what is now Cairo), but that other racial groups constituted the majority of the population. The argument put forward by Bernal and others that Egypt significantly contributed to Greek civilization has been critically challenged by a number of these scholars, including Mary Lefkowitz and Guy MacLean Rogers, for the selective gathering of evidence and poor historical and linguistic scholarship.[3] On these complex issues, the jury remains out.[4]

Early African Societies

☐ How did settled agriculture affect life among the early societies in the western Sudan and among the Bantu-speaking societies of central and southern Africa?

The introduction of new crops from Asia and methods of settled agriculture profoundly changed many African societies, although the range of possibilities was greatly dependent on local variations in climate and geography. Bantu-speakers took the knowledge of domesticated livestock and agriculture and the iron-working skills that developed in northern and western Africa and spread them south across central and southern Africa. The most prominent feature of early West African society was a strong sense of community based on blood relationships and on religion. Extended families made up the villages that collectively formed small kingdoms.

Settled Agriculture and Its Impact

Agriculture began very early in Africa. Knowledge of plant cultivation moved west from ancient Judaea (southern Palestine), arriving in the Nile Delta in Egypt about the fifth millennium B.C.E. Settled agriculture then traveled down the Nile Valley and moved west across the Sahel to the central and western Sudan. By the first century B.C.E. settled agriculture existed in West Africa. From there it spread to the equatorial forests. African farmers learned to domesticate plants, including millet, sorghum, and yams. Cereal-growing people probably taught forest people to plant grains on plots of land cleared by a method known as "slash and burn." Gradually most Africans evolved a sedentary way

of life: living in villages, clearing fields, relying on root crops such as yams and cassava, and fishing. Hunting-and-gathering societies survived only in scattered parts of Africa, particularly in the central rain forest region and in southern Africa.

Between 1500 and 1000 B.C.E. settled agriculture also spread southward from Ethiopia along the Great Rift Valley of present-day Kenya and Tanzania. Archaeological evidence reveals that the peoples of this region grew cereals, raised cattle, and used wooden and stone tools. Cattle raising spread more quickly than did planting, prospering on the open savannas that are free of tsetse flies, which are devastating to cattle. The early African peoples of this region prized cattle highly. Many trading agreements, marriage alliances, political compacts, and treaties were negotiated in terms of cattle.

Cereals such as millet and sorghum are indigenous to Africa. Scholars speculate that traders brought bananas, taros (a type of yam), sugarcane, and coconut palms to Africa from Southeast Asia. Because tropical forest conditions were ideal for banana plants, their cultivation spread rapidly. Throughout sub-Saharan Africa native peoples also domesticated donkeys, pigs, chickens, geese, and ducks.

The evolution from a hunter-gatherer life to a settled life had profound effects. In contrast to nomadic conditions, settled societies made shared or common needs more apparent, and those needs strengthened ties among extended families. Agricultural and pastoral populations also increased, though scholars speculate that this increase was not steady, but rather fluctuated over time. Nor is it clear that the growth in numbers of people was accompanied by a commensurate increase in agricultural output.

Early African societies were similarly influenced by the spread of ironworking, though scholars dispute the route by which this technology spread to sub-Saharan Africa. Some believe the Phoenicians brought the iron-smelting technique to northwestern Africa, from where it spread southward. Others insist it spread westward from the Meroë (MEHR-oh-ee) region on the Nile. Most of West Africa had acquired knowledge of ironworking by 250 B.C.E., however, and archaeologists believe Meroë achieved pre-eminence as an iron-smelting center only in the first century B.C.E. Thus a stronger case can probably be made for the Phoenicians. The great trans-Saharan trade routes (see page 274) may have carried ironworking south from the Mediterranean coast. In any case, ancient iron tools found at the village of Nok on the Jos Plateau in present-day Nigeria seem to prove a knowledge of ironworking in West Africa by at least 700 B.C.E. The Nok culture, which enjoys enduring fame for its fine terra-cotta (baked clay) sculptures, flourished from about 800 B.C.E. to 200 C.E.

Tassili Rock Painting
This scene of cattle grazing near a group of huts (repre-sented on the left by ovals) reflects the domestication of animals and the development of settled pastoral agriculture in Africa. Women and children seem to perform most of the domestic chores. Tassili is a mountainous region in the Sahara where over 15,000 of these paintings have been cata-logued, with the oldest dating back 9,000–10,000 years. (Photo: Henri Lhote. Courtesy, Irene Lhote)

Bantu Migrations

The spread of ironworking is linked to the migrations of Bantu-speaking peoples. Today the overwhelming majority of the 70 million people living south of the Congo River speak a **Bantu** language. Because very few Muslims or Europeans penetrated into the inte-rior, and few Bantu-speakers, except the Swahili, for example, wrote down their languages, very few written sources for the early history of central and southern Africa survive. Lacking written sources, modern schol-ars have tried to reconstruct the history of the Bantu-speakers on the basis of linguistics, oral traditions (rarely reliable beyond three hundred years back), ar-chaeology, and anthropology. Botanists and zoologists have played particularly critical roles in providing in-formation about early diets and environments.

The word *Bantu* is a linguistic classification, and lin-guistics (the study of the nature, structure, and modifi-cation of human speech) has helped scholars explain the migratory patterns of African peoples east and south of the equatorial forest. There are hundreds of Bantu languages, including Zulu, Sotho, and Tswana, which are part of the southern African linguistic and cultural nexus, and Swahili, which is spoken in east-ern, and to a limited extent central, Africa.

Bantu-speaking peoples originated in the Benue re-gion, the borderlands of modern Cameroon and Nige-ria. In the second millennium B.C.E. they began to spread south and east into the forest zone of equatorial Africa.

Why they began this movement is still a matter of dis-pute among historians. Some hold that rapid population growth sent people in search of land. Others believe that the evolution of centralized kingdoms allowed rul-ers to expand their authority, while causing newly sub-jugated peoples to flee in the hope of regaining their independence.

Since the early Bantu-speakers had words for fish-ing, fishhooks, fish traps, dugout canoes, paddles, yams, and goats, linguists assume that they were fishermen and that they cultivated roots. Because initially they lacked words for grains and cattle herding, they proba-bly were not involved in grain cultivation or the do-mestication of cattle. During the next fifteen hundred years, however, Bantu-speakers migrated throughout the savanna, adopted mixed agriculture, and learned ironworking. Mixed agriculture (cultivating cereals and raising livestock) and ironworking were practiced in western East Africa (the region of modern Burundi) in the first century B.C.E. In the first millennium C.E. Bantu-speakers migrated into eastern and southern Africa. Here the Bantu-speakers, with their iron weap-ons, either killed, drove off, or assimilated the hunting-gathering peoples they met. Some of the earlier assimi-lated inhabitants gradually adopted a Bantu language, contributing to the spread of Bantu culture.

The settled cultivation of cereals, the keeping of live-stock, and the introduction of new crops such as the banana — together with Bantu-speakers' intermarriage with indigenous peoples — led over a long time to considerable population increases and the need to migrate farther. The so-called Bantu migrations should not be seen as a single movement sweeping across Africa from west to east to south and displacing all peoples in their path. Rather, those migrations were a series of group interactions between Bantu-speakers and pre-existing peoples in which bits of culture, languages, economies, and technologies were shared and exchanged to produce a wide range of cultural variation across central and southern Africa.[5]

Bantu Migrations, ca. 1000 B.C.E.–1500 C.E.

The Bantu-speakers' expansion and subsequent land settlement that dominated eastern and southern African history in the first fifteen hundred years of the Common Era was uneven. Enormous differences in the quality of the environment determined settlement patterns. Some regions were well watered; others were very arid. This situation resulted in very uneven population distribution. The largest concentration of people seems to have been in the region bounded on the west by the Congo River and on the north, south, and east by Lakes Edward and Victoria and Mount Kilimanjaro, comprising parts of modern Uganda, Rwanda, and Tanzania. There the agricultural system rested on sorghum and yam cultivation. Between 900 and 1100 bananas and plantains (a starchy form of the banana) arrived from Asia. Because little effort was needed for their cultivation and the yield was much higher than for yams, bananas soon became the Bantu people's staple crop. The rapid growth of the Bantu-speaking population led to further migration southward and eastward. By the eighth century the Bantu-speaking people had crossed the Zambezi River and had begun settling in the region of present-day Zimbabwe, and by the fifteenth century they had reached Africa's southeastern coast.

Life in the Kingdoms of the Western Sudan, ca. 1000 B.C.E.–800 C.E.

The **Sudan** is the region bounded by the Sahara to the north, the Gulf of Guinea to the south, the Atlantic Ocean to the west, and the mountains of Ethiopia to the east (see Map 10.1). In the savanna of the western Sudan—where the Bantu migrations originated—a series of dynamic kingdoms emerged in the millennium before European intrusion began in the 1400s and 1500s.

Between 1000 B.C.E. and 200 C.E. the peoples of the western Sudan made the momentous shift from nomadic hunting to settled agriculture. The rich savanna proved ideally suited to the production of cereals, es-

pecially rice, millet, and sorghum. People situated near the Senegal River and Lake Chad supplemented their diet with fish. Food supply affects population, and the peoples of the region—known as the Mande-speakers and the Chadic-speakers, or Sao (sowl)—increased dramatically in number. By 400 C.E. the entire savanna, particularly the areas around Lake Chad, the Niger River bend, and present-day central Nigeria (see Map 10.1), had a large population.

Families and clans affiliated by blood kinship lived together in villages or small city-states. The basic social unit was the extended family. A chief, in consultation with a council of elders, governed a village. Some villages seem to have formed kingdoms. Village chiefs were responsible to regional heads, who answered to provincial governors, who in turn were responsible to a king. The chiefs and their families formed an aristocracy.

Kingship in the Sudan may have emerged from the priesthood, whose members were believed to make rain and to have contact with spirit powers. African kings always had religious sanction or support for their authority and were often considered divine. In this respect, early African kingship bears a strong resemblance to Germanic kingship of the same period (discussed in Chapter 14): the king's authority rested in part on the ruler's ability to negotiate with outside powers, such as the gods.

Among the Asante in modern-day Ghana, one of the most prominent West African peoples, the king was considered divine but shared some royal power with the Queen Mother. She was a full member of the governing council and enjoyed full voting power in various matters of state. The future king was initially chosen by the Queen Mother from eligible royal candidates, and then had to be approved by both his elders and by the commoners. Among the Yoruba in modern Nigeria the Queen Mother held the royal insignia and could refuse it if the future king did not please her. It was she who also placed the royal beaded crown on the king's head. Although the Mende in modern Sierra Leone was one of the few African societies to be led by female rulers, women exercised significant power and autonomy in many African societies. The institutions of female chiefs, known as *iyalode* among the Yoruba and *omu* among the Igbo in modern Nigeria, were established to

---

- **Bantu** Speakers of a Bantu language living south and east of the Congo River.

- **Sudan** The African region surrounded by the Sahara, the Gulf of Guinea, the Atlantic Ocean, and the mountains of Ethiopia.

represent women in the political process. The *omu* was even considered a female co-ruler with the male chief.

Religious practices in the western Sudan, like African religions elsewhere, were animistic and polytheistic. Most people believed that a supreme being had created the universe and was the source of all life. Most African religions also recognized ancestral spirits, which people believed might seek God's blessings for the prosperity and security of their families and communities as long as these groups behaved appropriately. If not, the ancestral spirits might not protect them from harm, and illness and misfortune could result. Some African religions believed as well that nature spirits lived in such things as the sky, forests, rocks, and rivers. These spirits controlled the forces of nature and had to be appeased. During the annual agricultural cycle, for example, all the spirits had to be propitiated from the time of clearing the land through sowing the seed to the final harvest. Because special ceremonies were necessary to satisfy the spirits, special priests with the knowledge and power to communicate with them through sacred rituals were needed. The heads of families and villages were often priests. Each family head was responsible for ceremonies honoring the dead and living members of the family.[6]

In some societies of West Africa oracles who spoke for the gods were particularly important. Some of the most famous oracles were those among the Ibo in modern Nigeria. These were female priestesses who were connected with a particular local deity that resided in a sacred cave or other site, as is vividly described in the Nigerian author Chinua Achebe's 1958 novel *Things Fall Apart.* All the members of the surrounding villages would come to the priestess to seek advice about such matters as crops and harvests, war, marriage, legal issues, and religion. Clearly, these priestesses held much power and authority, even over the local male rulers.

Kinship patterns and shared religious practices helped to bind together the early African kingdoms of the western Sudan. The spread of Islam across the Sahara by at least the ninth century C.E., however, created a north-south religious and cultural divide in the western Sudan. Islam advanced across the Sahel into modern Mauritania, Mali, Burkina Faso, Niger, northern Nigeria, and Chad, but halted when it reached the savanna and forest zones of West Africa. The societies in the south maintained their traditional animistic religious practices. Muslim empires lying along the great northern bend of the Niger River evolved into formidable powers ruling over sizable territory as they seized control of the southern termini of the trans-Saharan trade. What made this long-distance trade possible was the "ship of the desert," the camel.

The Trans-Saharan Trade

☐ What characterized trans-Saharan trade, and how did it affect West African society?

The expression "trans-Saharan trade" refers to the north-south trade across the Sahara (see Map 10.2). The camel had an impact on this trade comparable to the very important impact of horses and oxen on European agriculture. Although scholars dispute exactly when the camel was introduced from Central Asia — first into North Africa, then into the Sahara and the Sudan — they agree that it was before 200 C.E. Camels can carry about five hundred pounds as far as twenty-five miles a day and can go for days without drinking, living on the water stored in their stomachs. Temperamental and difficult to work with, camels had to be loaded on a daily, sometimes twice-daily, basis, and much of the cargo for a long trip was made up of provisions for the journey itself. Nevertheless, camels proved more efficient for desert transportation than horses or oxen. The trans-Saharan trade brought lasting economic and social change to Africa, facilitating the spread of Islam via Muslim Arab traders, and affected the development of world commerce.

The Berbers of North Africa

Sometime in the fifth century C.E. the North African **Berbers** fashioned a saddle for use on the camel. This saddle had no direct effect on commercial operations, for a merchant usually walked and guided the camel on foot. But the saddle gave the Berbers and later the region's Arabian inhabitants maneuverability on the

Trans-Saharan Trade A Berber caravan driver adjusts the salt block on his camel in a timeless ritual of the trans-Saharan trade. (© James Michael Dorsey)

animal and thus a powerful political and military advantage: they came to dominate the desert and to create lucrative routes across it. The Berbers determined who could enter the desert, and they extracted large sums of protection money from merchant caravans in exchange for a safe trip.

Between 700 and 900 C.E. the Berbers developed a network of caravan routes between the Mediterranean coast and the Sudan (see Map 10.2). The long expedition across the Sahara testifies to the spirit of the traders and to their passion for wealth. Because of the blistering sun and daytime temperatures reaching 110 degrees, caravan drivers preferred night travel, when temperatures might drop to the low 20s. Ibn Battuta, an Arab traveler in the fourteenth century when the trade was at its height, left one of the best descriptions of the trans-Saharan traffic. (See "Individuals in Society: Ibn Battuta," page 254.) It took Ibn Battuta twenty-five days to travel from Sijilmasa to the oasis of Taghaza and another sixty-five days to travel from Taghaza to the important market town of Walata.

Nomadic raiders, the Tuareg (TWAH-reg), posed a serious threat to trans-Saharan traders. The Tuareg were Berbers who lived in the desert uplands and preyed on the caravans as a way of life. To avoid being victimized, merchants made safe-conduct agreements with them and selected guides from among them. Large numbers of merchants crossed the desert together to discourage attack; caravans of twelve thousand camels were reported in the fourteenth century. Blinding sandstorms often separated part of a line of camels and on at least one recorded occasion buried alive some camels and drivers. Water was the biggest problem. To satisfy normal thirst and to compensate for constant sweating, each person required a gallon of water per day. Desperate thirst sometimes forced the traders to kill camels and drink the foul, brackish water in their stomachs. The Tuareg used this problem to their advantage, sometimes poisoning wells to wipe out caravans and steal their goods.

The Arab Berber merchants from North Africa who controlled the caravan trade carried dates, salt (essential in tropical climates to replace the loss from perspiration) from the Saharan salt mines, and some manufactured goods—silk and cotton cloth, beads, mirrors—to the Sudan. These products were exchanged for the much-coveted commodities of the West African savanna—gold, ivory, gum, kola nuts (eaten as a stimulant), and enslaved West African men and women who were sold to Muslim slave markets in Morocco, Algiers, Tripoli, and Cairo.

Effects of Trade on West African Society

The steady growth of trans-Saharan trade had three important effects on West African society. First, trade

TABLE 10.1 Estimated Magnitude of Trans-Saharan Slave Trade, 650–1500		
YEARS	**ANNUAL AVERAGE OF SLAVES TRADED**	**TOTAL**
650–800	1,000	150,000
800–900	3,000	300,000
900–1100	8,700	1,740,000
1100–1400	5,500	1,650,000
1400–1500	4,300	430,000

Source: R. A. Austen, "The Trans-Saharan Slave Trade: A Tentative Census," in *The Uncommon Market: Essays in the Economic History of the Atlantic Slave Trade*, ed. H. A. Gemery and J. S. Hogendorn (New York: Academic Press, 1979). Used with permission.

stimulated gold mining. Parts of modern-day Senegal, Nigeria, and Ghana contained rich veins of gold. Both sexes shared in mining it. Men hacked out gold-bearing rocks and crushed them, separating the gold from the soil. Women washed the gold in gourds. Alluvial gold (mixed with soil, sand, or gravel) was separated from the soil by panning. Scholars estimate that by the eleventh century nine tons of gold were exported to the Mediterranean coast and Europe annually—a prodigious amount for the time, since even with modern machinery and sophisticated techniques, the total gold exports from the same region in 1937 amounted to only twenty-one tons. Some of this metal went to Egypt. From there it was transported down the Red Sea and eventually to India (see Map 9.2 on page 253) to pay for the spices and silks demanded by Mediterranean commerce. In this way, African gold linked the entire world, exclusive of the Western Hemisphere.

Second, trade in gold and other goods created a desire for slaves. Slaves were West Africa's second most valuable export (after gold). Slaves worked the gold and salt mines, and in Muslim North Africa, southern Europe, and southwestern Asia there was a high demand for household slaves among the elite. African slaves, like their early European and Asian counterparts, seem to have been peoples captured in war. Recent research suggests, moreover, that large numbers of black slaves were also recruited for Muslim military service through the trans-Saharan trade. High death rates from disease, manumission, and the assimilation of some blacks into Muslim society meant that the demand for slaves remained high for centuries. Table 10.1 shows the scope of the trans-Saharan slave trade. The total number of blacks enslaved over an 850-year period may be tentatively estimated at more than 4 million.[7]

Slavery in Muslim societies, as in European and Asian countries before the fifteenth century, was not

Berbers North African peoples who controlled the caravan trade between the Mediterranean and the Sudan.

based on skin color. Muslims also enslaved Caucasians who had been purchased, seized in war, or kidnapped from Europe. Wealthy Muslim households in Córdoba, Alexandria, and Tunis often included slaves of a number of races, all of whom had been completely cut off from their cultural roots. Likewise, West African kings who sold blacks to northern traders also bought a few white slaves—Slavic, British, and Turkish—for their own domestic needs. Race had little to do with the phenomenon of slavery.

The third important effect on West African society was the role of trans-Saharan trade in stimulating the development of urban centers. Scholars date the growth of African cities from around the early ninth century. Families that had profited from trade tended to congregate in the border zones between the savanna and the Sahara. They acted as middlemen between the miners to the south and Muslim merchants from the north. By the early thirteenth century these families had become powerful black merchant dynasties. Muslim traders from the Mediterranean settled permanently in the trading depots, from which they organized the trans-Saharan caravans. The concentration of people stimulated agriculture and the craft industries. Gradually cities of sizable population emerged. Jenne, Gao, and Timbuktu, which enjoyed commanding positions on the Niger River bend, became centers of the export-import trade. Sijilmasa grew into a thriving market center. Koumbi Saleh, with between fifteen thousand and twenty thousand inhabitants, was probably the largest city in the western Sudan in the twelfth century. (By European standards, Koumbi Saleh was a metropolis; London and Paris achieved this size only in the late thirteenth century.) Between 1100 and 1400 these cities played a dynamic role in the commercial life of West Africa and Europe and became centers of intellectual creativity.

The Spread of Islam in Africa

Perhaps the most influential consequence of the trans-Saharan trade was the introduction of Islam to West African society. In the eighth century Arab invaders overran all of coastal North Africa. They introduced the Berbers living there to the religion of Islam (see page 238), and gradually the Berbers became Muslims. As traders, these Berbers carried Islam to sub-Saharan West Africa. From the eleventh century onward militant Almoravids, a coalition of fundamentalist western Saharan Berbers, preached Islam to the rulers of Ghana, Mali, Songhai, and Kanem-Bornu, who, admiring

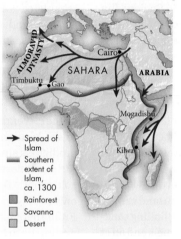

The Spread of Islam in Africa

Muslim administrative techniques and wanting to protect their kingdoms from Muslim Berber attacks, accepted Islamic conversion. Some merchants also sought to preserve their elite mercantile status with the Berbers by adopting Islam. By the tenth century Muslim Berbers controlled the north-south trade routes to the savanna. By the eleventh century African rulers of Gao and Timbuktu had accepted Islam. The king of Ghana was also influenced by Islam. Muslims quickly became integral to West African government and society. Hence in the period from roughly 1000 to 1400, Islam in West Africa was a class-based religion with conversion inspired by political or economic motives. Rural people in the Sahel region and the peoples of the savanna and forest regions farther south, however, largely retained their traditional animism.

Conversion to Islam introduced West Africans to a rich and sophisticated culture. By the late eleventh century Muslims were guiding the ruler of Ghana in the operation of his administrative machinery. The king of Ghana adopted the Muslim diwān, the agency for keeping financial records (see page 239). Because efficient government depends on the preservation of records, the arrival of Islam in West Africa marked the advent of written documents there. Arab Muslims also taught the rulers of Ghana how to manufacture bricks, and royal palaces and mosques began to be built of brick. African rulers corresponded with Arab and North African Muslim architects, theologians, and other intellectuals, who advised them on statecraft and religion. Islam accelerated the development of the West African empires of the ninth through fifteenth centuries.

After the Muslim conquest of Egypt in 642 (see page 237), Islam spread southward from Egypt up the Nile Valley and west to Darfur and Wadai. This Muslim penetration came not by military force but, as in the trans-Saharan trade routes in West Africa, by gradual commercial passage.

Muslim expansion from the Arabian peninsula across the Red Sea to the Horn of Africa, then southward along the coast of East Africa, represents a third direction of Islam's growth in Africa. From ports on the Red Sea and the Gulf of Aden, maritime trade carried the Prophet's teachings to East Africa and the Indian Ocean. Muslims founded the port city of **Mogadishu**, today Somalia's capital. In the twelfth century Mogadishu developed into a Muslim sultanate, a monarchy that employed a slave military corps against foreign and domestic enemies. Archaeological evidence, confirmed by Arabic sources, reveals a rapid Islamic expansion along Africa's east coast in the thirteenth century as far south as Kilwa, where Ibn Battuta came across a center for Islamic law during a visit in 1331.

African Kingdoms and Empires, ca. 800–1500

☐ How were the East African city-states, Aksum, and Great Zimbabwe different from and similar to the kingdoms of the western Sudan?

All African societies shared one basic feature: a close relationship between political and social organization. Ethnic or blood ties bound clan members together. What scholars call **stateless societies** were culturally homogeneous ethnic societies, generally organized around kinship groups. The smallest ones numbered fewer than a hundred people and were nomadic hunting groups. Larger stateless societies of perhaps several thousand people, such as the Tiv in modern central Nigeria, lived a settled and often agricultural or herding life. These societies lacked a central authority figure, such as a king, capital city, or military; hence their designation by some historians as decentralized societies. A village or group of villages might recognize a chief who held very limited powers and whose position was not hereditary, but more commonly they were governed by local councils, whose members were either elders or persons of merit. Although stateless societies functioned successfully, their weakness lay in their inability to organize and defend themselves against attack by the powerful armies of neighboring kingdoms or by the European powers of the colonial era.

While stateless societies were relatively common in Africa, the period from about 800 to 1500 is best known as the age of Africa's great empires (Map 10.2). It witnessed the flowering of several powerful African states. In the western Sudan the large empires of Ghana, Mali, and Songhai developed, complete with sizable royal bureaucracies. On the east coast emerged powerful city-states based on sophisticated mercantile activities and, like Sudan, very much influenced by Islam. In Ethiopia, in central East Africa, kings relied on the Christian faith of their people to strengthen political authority. In southern Africa the empire of Great Zimbabwe, built on the gold trade with the east coast, flourished.

The Kingdom of Ghana, ca. 900–1100

So remarkable was the kingdom of **Ghana** during the age of Africa's great empires that Arab and North African visitors praised it as a model for other rulers. Even in modern times, ancient Ghana holds a central place in Africa's historical consciousness. When the Gold Coast colony gained its independence from British colonial rule in 1957, its new political leaders paid tribute to this glorious heritage by naming their new country Ghana. Although modern Ghana lies far from the site of the old kingdom, the name was selected to signify the rebirth of ancient Ghana's illustrious past in black Africa.

The nucleus of the territory that became the kingdom of Ghana was inhabited by Soninke people who called their ruler *ghana*, or war chief. By the late eighth century Muslim traders and other foreigners applied the king's title to the region where the Soninke lived, the black kingdom south of the Sahara. The Soninke themselves called their land Wagadou (WAH-guh-doo). Only the southern part of Wagadou received enough rainfall to be agriculturally productive, and it was in this area that the civilization of Ghana developed (see Map 10.2). Skillful farming and an efficient system of irrigation led to the production of abundant crops, which eventually supported a population of as many as two hundred thousand.

The Soninke name for their king — war chief — aptly describes the king's major preoccupation in the tenth century. In 992 Ghana captured the Berber town of Awdaghost, strategically situated on the trans-Saharan trade route. Thereafter Ghana controlled the southern portion of a major caravan route. Before the year 1000 the rulers of Ghana had extended their influence almost to the Atlantic coast and had captured a number of small kingdoms in the south and east. By the early eleventh century the Ghanaian king exercised sway over a territory approximately the size of Texas. No other power in the West African region could successfully challenge him.

Throughout this vast West African area, all authority sprang from the king. Religious ceremonies and court rituals emphasized the king's sacredness and were intended to strengthen his authority. The king's position was hereditary in the matrilineal line — that is, the ruling king's heir was one of the king's sister's sons (presumably the eldest or fittest for battle). According to the eleventh-century Spanish Muslim geographer al-Bakri (1040?–1094), "This is their custom . . . the kingdom is inherited only by the son of the king's sister. He the king has no doubt that his successor is a son of his sister, while he is not certain that his son is in fact his own."[8]

- **Mogadishu** A Muslim port city in East Africa founded between the eighth and tenth centuries; today it is the capital of Somalia.
- **stateless societies** African societies bound together by ethnic or blood ties rather than being political states.
- **Ghana** From the word for ruler, the name of a large and influential African kingdom inhabited by the Soninke people.

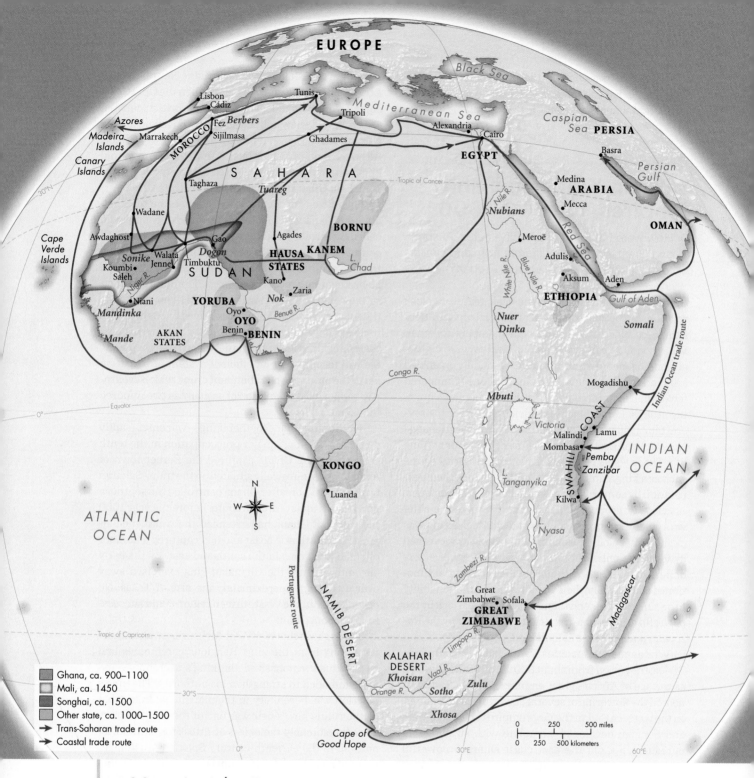

□ Mapping the Past

MAP 10.2 African Kingdoms and Trade, ca. 800–1500 Throughout world history powerful kingdoms have generally been closely connected to far-flung trade networks.

ANALYZING THE MAP Which kingdoms, empires, and city-states were linked to the trans-Saharan trade network? Which were connected to the Indian Ocean trade network? To the Portuguese route?

CONNECTIONS How were the kingdoms, empires, and city-states shown on this map shaped by their proximity to trade routes?

A council of ministers assisted the king in the work of government, and from the ninth century on most of these ministers were Muslims. Detailed evidence about the early Ghanaian bureaucracy has not survived, but scholars suspect that separate agencies were responsible for taxation, royal property, foreigners, forests, and the army. The royal administration was well served by ideas, skills, and especially literacy brought from the North African and Arab Muslim worlds. The king and his people, however, clung to their ancestral religion and basic cultural institutions.

The king of Ghana held his court in the large and vibrant city of **Koumbi Saleh**, which al-Bakri actually describes as two towns — one in which the king and the royal court lived, and the other Muslim. Al-Bakri provides a valuable picture of the Muslim part of the town in the eleventh century:

The city of Ghana consists of two towns lying on a plain, one of which is inhabited by Muslims and is large, possessing twelve mosques — one of which is a congregational mosque for Friday prayer; each has its imam, its muezzin and paid reciters of the Quran. The town possesses a large number of jurisconsults and learned men.[9]

Either for their own protection or to preserve their special identity, the Muslims of Koumbi Saleh lived separate from the African artisans and tradespeople. The Muslim community in Ghana must have been large and prosperous to have supported twelve mosques. Muslim religious leaders exercised civil authority over their fellow Muslims. The imam was the religious leader who conducted the ritual worship, especially the main prayer service on Fridays (see page 240). The muezzin led the prayer responses after the imam; he needed a strong voice so that those at a distance and the women in the harems, or enclosures, could hear (see page 252). The presence of the religious leaders and of other learned Muslims suggests that Koumbi Saleh was a city of vigorous intellectual activity.

Al-Bakri also described the royal court:

The town inhabited by the king is six miles from the Muslim one and is called Al Ghana. . . . The residence of the king consists of a palace and a number of dome-shaped dwellings, all of them surrounded by a strong enclosure, like a city wall. In the town . . . is a mosque, where Muslims who come on diplomatic missions to the king pray.[10]

The king adorns himself, as do the women here, with necklaces and bracelets; on their heads they wear caps decorated with gold, sewn on material of fine cotton stuffing. When he holds court in order to hear the people's complaints and to do justice, he sits in a pavilion around which stand ten horses wearing golden trappings; behind him ten

> "When [the king] holds court . . . he sits in a pavilion around which stand ten horses wearing golden trappings . . . ; at his right are the sons of the chiefs of the country, splendidly dressed and with their hair sprinkled with gold."
>
> **AL-BAKRI**

pages stand, holding shields and swords decorated with gold; at his right are the sons of the chiefs of the country, splendidly dressed and with their hair sprinkled with gold. . . . When the king's coreligionists appear before him, they fall on their knees and toss dust on their heads — this is their way of greeting their sovereign. Muslims show respect by clapping their hands.[11]

Justice derived from the king, who heard cases at court or on his travels throughout his kingdom. As al-Bakri recounts:

When a man is accused of denying a debt or of having shed blood or some other crime, a headman (village chief) takes a thin piece of wood, which is sour and bitter to taste, and pours upon it some water which he then gives to the defendant to drink. If the man vomits, his innocence is recognized and he is congratulated. If he does not vomit and the drink remains in his stomach, the accusation is accepted as justified.[12]

This appeal to the supernatural for judgment was similar to the justice by ordeal that prevailed among the Germanic peoples of western Europe at the same time (discussed in Chapter 14). Complicated cases were appealed to the king, who often relied on the advice of Muslim legal experts.

The king's elaborate court, the administrative machinery he built, and the extensive territories he governed were all expensive. To support the kingdom, the royal estates — some hereditary, others conquered in war — produced annual revenue, mostly in the form of foodstuffs for the royal household. The king also received tribute annually from subordinate chieftains. Customs duties on goods entering and leaving the country generated revenues. Salt was the largest import. Berber merchants paid a tax to the king on the cloth, metalwork, weapons, and other goods that they brought into the country from North Africa; in return these traders received royal protection from bandits. African traders bringing gold into Ghana from the south also paid the customs duty.

• **Koumbi Saleh** The city in which the king of Ghana held his court.

Finally, the royal treasury held a monopoly on the export of gold. The gold industry was undoubtedly the king's largest source of income. It was on gold that the fame of medieval Ghana rested. The ninth-century Persian geographer al-Ya-qubi wrote, "Its king is mighty, and in his lands are gold mines. Under his authority are various other kingdoms — and in all this region there is gold."[13]

The governing aristocracy — the king, his court, and Muslim administrators — occupied the highest rung on the Ghanaian social ladder. On the next rung stood the merchant class. Considerably below the merchants stood the farmers, cattle breeders, gold mine supervisors, and skilled craftsmen and weavers — what today might be called the middle class. Some merchants and miners must have enjoyed great wealth, but, as in all aristocratic societies, money alone did not suffice. High status was based on blood and royal service. On the social ladder's lowest rung were slaves, who worked in households, on farms, and in the mines. As in Asian and European societies of the time, slaves accounted for only a small percentage of the population.

Apart from these social classes stood the army. According to al-Bakri, "the king of Ghana can put 200,000 warriors in the field, more than 40,000 being armed with bow and arrow." Like most medieval estimates, this is probably a gross exaggeration. The king of Ghana, however, was not called "war chief" for nothing. He maintained at his palace a standing force of a thousand men, comparable to the bodyguards of the emperors of the Roman republic. These thoroughly disciplined, well-armed, totally loyal troops protected the king and the royal court. They lived in special compounds, enjoyed the king's favor, and sometimes acted as his personal ambassadors to subordinate rulers. In wartime this regular army was augmented by levies of soldiers from conquered peoples and by the use of slaves and free re-

> " Its king is mighty, and in his lands are gold mines. Under his authority are various other kingdoms — and in all this region there is gold. "
>
> **AL-YA-QUBI**

serves. The force that the king could field was sizable, if not as huge as al-Bakri estimated.

The reasons for ancient Ghana's decline are still a matter of much debate. By al-Bakri's time there were other increasingly powerful neighbors, such as the Mandinke, to challenge Ghana's influence in the region. The most commonly accepted theory for Ghana's rapid decline held, however, that the Berber Almoravid dynasty of North Africa invaded and conquered Ghana around 1100 and forced its rulers and people to convert to Islam. A close study of this question has recently concluded that while Almoravid and Islamic pressures certainly disrupted the empire, weakening it enough for its incorporation into the rising Mali empire, there was no Almoravid military invasion and subsequent forced conversion to Islam.[14]

The Kingdom of Mali, ca. 1200–1450

There can be no doubt that Ghana and its capital of Koumbi Saleh were in decline between 1100 and 1200, and a cloud of obscurity hung over the western Sudan. The kingdom of Ghana split into several small kingdoms that feuded among themselves. One people, the Mandinka, from the kingdom of Kangaba on the upper Niger River, gradually asserted their dominance over these kingdoms. The Mandinka had long been part of the Ghanaian empire, and the Mandinka and Soninke belonged to the same language group. Kangaba formed the core of the new empire of Mali. Building on Ghanaian foundations, Mali developed into a better-organized and more powerful state than Ghana.

The kingdom of Mali owed its greatness to two fundamental assets. First, its strong agricultural and commercial base provided for a large population and enormous wealth. Second, Mali had two rulers, Sundiata (soon-JAH-tuh) and Mansa Musa, who combined military success with exceptionally creative personalities.

The earliest surviving evidence about the Mandinka, dating from the early eleventh century, indicates that they were extremely successful at agriculture. Consistently large harvests throughout the twelfth and thirteenth centuries meant a plentiful supply of food, which encouraged steady population growth. The geographical location of Kangaba also placed the Mandinka in an ideal position in West African trade. Earlier, during the period of Ghanaian hegemony, the Mandinka had acted as middlemen in the gold and salt traffic flowing north and south. In the thirteenth century Mandinka traders

The Expansion of Mali, ca. 1200–1450

Walata
Timbuktu
Gao
Koumbi Saleh
Jenne
Niani

ATLANTIC OCEAN

Senegal R.
Gambia
Niger R.
Volta R.

Territory of Mali
- ca. 1100
- ca. 1350
- ca. 1500

formed companies, traveled widely, and gradually became a major force in the entire West African trade.

The founder of Mali, Sundiata (r. ca. 1230–1255) set up his capital at Niani, transforming the city into an important financial and trading center. He then embarked on a policy of imperial expansion. Through a series of military victories, Sundiata and his successors absorbed into Mali other territories of the former kingdom of Ghana and established hegemony over the trading cities of Gao, Jenne, and Walata.

These expansionist policies were continued in the fourteenth century by Sundiata's descendant Mansa Musa (r. ca. 1312–1337), early Africa's most famous ruler. In the language of the Mandinke, *mansa* means "emperor." Mansa Musa fought many campaigns and checked every attempt at rebellion. Ultimately his influence extended northward to several Berber cities in the Sahara, eastward to the trading cities of Timbuktu and Gao, and westward as far as the Atlantic Ocean. Throughout his territories, he maintained strict royal control over the rich trans-Saharan trade. Thus this empire, roughly twice the size of the Ghanaian kingdom and containing perhaps 8 million people, brought Mansa Musa fabulous wealth.

Mansa Musa built on the foundations of his predecessors. The stratified aristocratic structure of Malian society perpetuated the pattern set in Ghana, as did the system of provincial administration and annual tribute. The emperor took responsibility for the territories that formed the heart of the empire and appointed governors to rule the outlying provinces or dependent kingdoms. But Mansa Musa made a significant innovation: in a practice strikingly similar to a system used in both China and France at the time, he appointed members of the royal family as provincial governors. He could count on their loyalty, and they received valuable experience in the work of government.

In another aspect of administration, Mansa Musa also differed from his predecessors. He became a devout Muslim. Although most of the Mandinke clung to their ancestral animism, Islamic practices and influences in Mali multiplied.

The most celebrated event of Mansa Musa's reign was his pilgrimage to Mecca in 1324–1325, during which he paid a state visit to the sultan of Egypt. Mansa Musa's entrance into Cairo was magnificent. Preceded by five hundred slaves, each carrying a six-pound staff of gold, he followed with a huge host of retainers, including one hundred elephants each bearing one hundred pounds of gold. The emperor lavished his wealth on the citizens of the Egyptian capital. Writing twelve years later, al-Omari, one of the sultan's officials, recounts:

This man Mansa Musa spread upon Cairo the flood of his generosity: there was no person, officer of the court, or holder of any office of the Sultanate who did not receive a sum of gold from him. The people of Cairo earned incalculable sums from him, whether by buying and selling or by gifts. So much gold was current in Cairo that it ruined the value of money.[15]

The Great Friday Mosque, Jenne The mosque at Jenne was built in the form of a parallelogram. Inside, nine long rows of adobe columns run along a north-south axis and support a flat roof of palm logs. A pointed arch links each column to the next in its row, forming nine east-west archways facing the *mihrab*, the niche in the wall of the mosque indicating the direction of Mecca and from which the imam speaks. This mosque (rebuilt in 1907 on a thirteenth-century model) testifies to the considerable wealth, geometrical knowledge, and manpower of Mali. (© Gavin Hellier/Alamy)

For the first time, the Mediterranean world gained concrete knowledge of Mali's wealth and power, and the black kingdom began to be known as one of the world's great empires. Mali retained this international reputation into the fifteenth century. Musa's pilgrimage also had significant consequences within Mali. He gained some understanding of the Mediterranean countries and opened diplomatic relations with the Muslim rulers of Morocco and Egypt. His zeal for the Muslim faith and Islamic culture increased. Musa brought back from Arabia the distinguished architect al-Saheli, whom he commissioned to build new mosques at Timbuktu and other cities. These mosques served as centers for the conversion of Africans to Islam. Musa employed Muslim engineers to build in brick. He also encouraged Malian merchants and traders to wear the distinctive flowing robes and turbans of Muslim males.

Timbuktu began as a campsite for desert nomads, but under Mansa Musa, it grew into a thriving trading post, or entrepôt (AHN-truh-poh), attracting merchants and traders from North Africa and all parts of the Mediterranean world. They brought with them cosmopolitan attitudes and ideas. In the fifteenth century Timbuktu developed into a great center for scholarship and learning. Architects, astronomers, poets, lawyers, mathematicians, and theologians flocked there. One hundred fifty schools, for men only, were devoted to Qur'anic studies. The school of Islamic law enjoyed a distinction in Africa comparable to the prestige of the school at Cairo (see page 257). The vigorous traffic in books that flourished in Timbuktu made them the most common items of trade. Timbuktu's tradition and reputation for African scholarship lasted until the eighteenth century.

Moreover, in the fourteenth and fifteenth centuries many Arab and North African Muslim intellectuals and traders married native African women. These unions brought into being a group of racially mixed people. The necessity of living together harmoniously, the traditional awareness of diverse cultures, and the cosmopolitan atmosphere of Timbuktu all contributed to a rare degree of racial toleration and understanding. After visiting the court of Mansa Musa's successor in 1352–1353, Ibn Battuta observed:

[T]he Negroes possess some admirable qualities. They are seldom unjust, and have a greater abhorrence of injustice than any other people. Their sultan shows no mercy to anyone who is guilty of the least act of it. There is com-plete security in their country. Neither traveler nor inhabitant in it has anything to fear from robbers. . . . They do not confiscate the property of any white man who dies in their country, even if it be uncounted wealth. On the contrary, they give it into the charge of some trustworthy person among the whites.[16]

The third great West African empire, Songhai, succeeded Mali in the fourteenth century. It encompassed the old empires of Ghana and Mali and extended its territory farther north and east to become one of the largest African empires in history (see Map 10.2).

Ethiopia: The Christian Kingdom of Aksum

Just as the ancient West African empires were significantly affected by Islam and the Arab culture that accompanied it, the African kingdoms that arose in modern Sudan and Ethiopia in northeast Africa were heavily influenced by Egyptian culture, and they influenced it in return. This was particularly the case in ancient Nubia. Nubia's capital was at Meroë (see Map 10.2); thus the country is often referred to as the Nubian kingdom of Meroë.

As part of the Roman Empire, Egypt was subject to Hellenistic and Roman cultural forces, and it became an early center of Christianity. Nubia, however, was never part of the Roman Empire; its people clung to ancient Egyptian religious ideas. Christian missionaries went to the Upper Nile region and succeeded in converting the Nubian rulers around 600 C.E. By that time, there were three separate Nubian states, of which the kingdom of Nobatia, centered at Dongola, was the

The Kingdom of Aksum, ca. 600

strongest. The Christian rulers of Nobatia had close ties with the kingdom of **Aksum** in Ethiopia, and through this relationship Egyptian culture spread to Ethiopia.

Two-thirds of the country consists of the Ethiopian highlands, the rugged plateau region of East Africa. The Great Rift Valley divides this territory into two massifs (mountain masses), of which the Ethiopian Plateau is the larger. Sloping away from each side of the Great Rift Valley are a series of mountains and valleys. Together with this mountainous environment, the three Middle Eastern religions—Judaism, Christianity, and Islam—have influenced Ethiopian society, bringing symbols of its cultural identity via trade and contact with it neighbors in the Upper Nile,

Christianity and Islam in Ethiopia The prolonged contest between the two religions in Ethiopia was periodically taken to the battlefield. This drawing from the eighteenth century by an Ethiopian artist shows his countrymen (left) advancing victoriously and celebrates national military success. (© British Library Board. OR 533 f50v)

including Nobatia, and via its proximity to the Middle East.

By the first century C.E. the kingdom of Aksum in northwestern Ethiopia was a sizable trading state. Merchants at Adulis, its main port on the Red Sea, sold ivory, gold, emeralds, rhinoceros horns, shells, and slaves to the Sudan, Arabia, Yemen, and various cities across the Indian Ocean in exchange for glass, ceramics, fabrics, sugar, oil, spices, and precious gems. Adulis contained temples, stone-built houses, and irrigated agriculture. Between the first and eighth centuries Aksum served as the capital of an empire extending over much of what is now northern Ethiopia. The empire's prosperity rested on trade. Aksum even independently minted specie (coins) modeled on the Roman *solidus;* at that time, only the Roman Empire, Persia, and some Indian states issued coins that circulated in Middle Eastern trade. It was the first and only sub-Saharan African state to have its own currency, and the last after its decline until the Swahili city-state of Kilwa minted gold coins beginning perhaps as early as the eleventh century.

The expansion of Islam into northern Ethiopia in the eighth century (see page 276) weakened Aksum's commercial prosperity. The Arabs first ousted the Greek Byzantine merchants who traded on the Dahlak Archipelago (in the southern Red Sea) and converted the islands' inhabitants. Then, Muslims attacked and destroyed Adulis. Some Aksumites converted to Islam; many others found refuge in the rugged mountains north of the kingdom, where they were isolated from outside contacts. Thus began the insularity that characterized later Ethiopian society.

Tradition ascribes to Frumentius (ca. 300–380 C.E.), a Syrian Christian trader, the introduction of Coptic Christianity, an Orthodox form of Christianity that originated in Egypt, into Ethiopia. Kidnapped as a young boy en route from India to Tyre (in southern Lebanon), Frumentius was taken to Aksum, given his freedom, and appointed tutor to the future king, Ezana. Upon Ezana's accession to the throne, Frumentius went to Alexandria, Egypt, where he was consecrated the first bishop of Aksum around 340 C.E. He then returned to Ethiopia with some priests to spread Christianity. Shortly after members of the royal court accepted Christianity, it became the Ethiopian state religion. Ethiopia's future was to be inextricably tied up with Christianity, a unique situation in black Africa.

- **Timbuktu** Originally a campsite for desert nomads, it grew into a thriving city under Mansa Musa, king of Mali and Africa's most famous ruler.
- **Aksum** A kingdom in northwestern Ethiopia that was a sizable trading state and the center of Christian culture.

Ethiopia's acceptance of Christianity led to the production of ecclesiastical documents and royal chronicles, making Ethiopia the first black African society that can be studied from written records. The Scriptures were translated into Ge'ez (gee-EHZ), an ancient language and script used in Ethiopia and Aksum. Pagan temples were dedicated to Christian saints; and, as in early medieval Ireland and in the Orthodox Church of the Byzantine world, the monasteries were the main cultural institutions of the Christian faith in Ethiopia. Monks went out from the monasteries to preach and convert the people, who resorted to the monasteries in times of need. As the Ethiopian state expanded, vibrant monasteries provided inspiration for the establishment of convents for nuns, as in medieval Europe (see page 400).

Monastic records provide fascinating information about early Ethiopian society. Settlements were made on the warm and moist plateau lands, not in the arid lowlands or the river valleys. Farmers used a scratch plow (unique in sub-Saharan Africa) to cultivate wheat and barley, and they regularly rotated those cereals. Plentiful rainfall seems to have helped produce abundant crops, which in turn led to population growth. In contrast to people in most of sub-Saharan Africa, both sexes probably married young. Because of ecclesiastical opposition to polygyny, monogamy was the norm, other than for kings and the very rich. The abundance of land meant that young couples could establish independent households. Widely scattered farms, with the parish church as the central social unit, seem to have been the usual pattern of existence.

Above the broad class of peasant farmers stood warrior-nobles. Their wealth and status derived from their fighting skills, which kings rewarded with grants of estates and with the right to collect tribute from the peasants. To acquire lands and to hold warriors' loyalty, Ethiopian kings had to pursue a policy of constant territorial expansion. (See "Individuals in Society: Amda Siyon," page 285.) Nobles maintained order in their regions, supplied kings with fighting men, and displayed their superior status by the size of their households and their generosity to the poor.

Sometime in the fourteenth century six scribes in the Tigrayan highlands of Ethiopia combined oral tradition, Jewish and Islamic commentaries, apocryphal (noncanonical) Christian texts, and the writings of the early Christian Church fathers to produce the *Kebra Negast* (The Glory of Kings). This history served the authors' goals: it became an Ethiopian national epic, glorifying a line of rulers descended from the Hebrew king Solomon (see page 53), arousing patriotic feelings, and linking Ethiopia's identity to the Judeo-Christian tradition. The book mostly deals with the origins of Emperor Menilek I of Ethiopia in the tenth century B.C.E.

The *Kebra Negast* asserts that Queen Makeda of Ethiopia (called Sheba in the Jewish tradition) had little governmental experience when she came to the throne. So she sought the advice and wise counsel of King Solomon (r. 961–922 B.C.E.) in Jerusalem. Makeda learned Jewish statecraft, converted to Judaism, and expressed her gratitude to Solomon with rich gifts of spices, gems, and gold. Desiring something more precious, Solomon prepared a lavish banquet for his attractive pupil. Satiated with spicy food and rich wines, Makeda fell asleep. In the middle of the night Solomon tricked Makeda into allowing him into her bed. Their son, Menilek, was born some months later. When Menilek reached maturity, he visited Solomon in Jerusalem. There Solomon anointed him crown prince of Ethiopia and sent a retinue of young Jewish nobles to accompany him home as courtiers. Unable to face life without the Hebrews' Ark of the Covenant, the courtiers stole the cherished wooden chest, which the Hebrews believed contained the Ten Commandments. God apparently approved the theft, for he lifted the youths, pursued by Solomon's army, across the Red Sea and into Ethiopia. Thus, according to the *Kebra Negast*, Menilek avenged his mother's shame, and God gave his legal covenant to Ethiopia, Israel's successor.[17] Although written around twenty-three hundred years after the events, the myths and legends contained in the *Kebra Negast* effectively served the purpose of building nationalistic fervor.

Consuming a spiked drink may not be the most dignified or auspicious way to found an imperial dynasty, but from the tenth to the sixteenth centuries, and even in the Ethiopian constitution of 1955, rulers of Ethiopia claimed that they belonged to the Solomonic line of succession. Thus the church and state in Ethiopia were inextricably linked.

Ethiopia's high mountains isolated the kingdom and hindered access from the outside, but through trade word gradually spread about the Christian devotion of this African kingdom. Twelfth-century Crusaders returning from the Middle East told of a powerful Christian ruler, Prester John, whose lands lay behind Muslim lines and who was eager to help restore the Holy Land to Christian control. The story of Prester John sparked European imagination and led to exploration aimed at finding his legendary kingdom, which was eventually identified with Ethiopia. In the later thirteenth century the dynasty of the Solomonic kings witnessed a literary and artistic renaissance particularly notable for works of hagiography (biographies of saints), biblical exegesis (critical explanation or interpretation of the bible), and manuscript illumination. The most striking feature of Ethiopian society in the period from 500 to 1500 was the close relationship between the church and the state. Christianity inspired

Amda Siyon

SCHOLARS CONSIDER AMDA SIYON (r. 1314–1344) the greatest ruler of Ethiopia's Solomonic dynasty. Yet we have no image or representation of him. We know nothing of his personal life, though if he followed the practice of most Ethiopian kings, he had many wives and children. Nor do we know anything about his youth and education. The evidence of what he did, however, suggests a tough military man who personified the heroic endurance and physical pain expected of warriors. According to a chronicle of Siyon's campaign against the Muslim leader of Ifat, he

> clove the ranks of the rebels and struck so hard that he transfixed two men as one with the blow of his spear, through the strength of God. Thereupon the rebels scattered and took to flight, being unable to hold their ground in his presence.

Amda Siyon reinforced control over his kingdom's Christian areas. He then expanded into neighboring regions of Shewa, Gojam, and Damot. Victorious there, he gradually absorbed the Muslim states of Ifat and Hedya to the east and southeast. These successes gave him effective control of the central highlands and also the Indian Ocean trade routes to the Red Sea (see Map 10.2). He governed in a quasi-feudal fashion. Theoretically the owner of all land, he assigned *gults*, or fiefs, to his ablest warriors. In return for nearly complete authority in their regions, these warrior-nobles conscripted soldiers for the king's army, required agricultural services from the farmers working on their land, and collected taxes in kind.

Ethiopian rulers received imperial coronation at Aksum, but their kingdom had no permanent capital. Rather, the ruler and court were peripatetic. They constantly traveled around the country to check the warrior-nobles' management of the gults, to crush revolts, and to impress ordinary people with royal dignity.

Territorial expansion had important economic and religious consequences. Amda Siyon concluded trade agreements with Muslims by which they were allowed to trade with his country in return for Muslim recognition of his authority, and their promise to accept his administration and pay taxes. Economic growth followed. As a result of these agreements, the flow of Ethiopian gold, ivory, and slaves to Red Sea ports for export to the Islamic heartlands and to South Asia accelerated. Profits from commercial exchange improved people's lives, or at least the lives of the upper classes.

Monk-missionaries from traditional Christian areas flooded newly conquered regions, stressing that Ethiopia was a new Zion, or second Israel; a Judeo-Christian nation defined by religion. Ethiopian Christianity focused on the divinity of the Old Testament Jehovah, rather than on the humanity of the New Testament Jesus. Jewish dietary restrictions, such as the avoidance of pork and shellfish, shaped behavior, and the holy Ark of the Covenant had a prominent place in the liturgy. But the monks also taught New Testament values, especially the importance of charity and spiritual reform. Following

the Byzantine pattern, the Ethiopian priest-king claimed the right to summon church councils and to issue doctrinal degrees. Christianity's stress on monogamous marriage, however, proved hard to enforce. As in other parts of Africa (and in Islamic lands, China, and South Asia), polygyny remained common, at least among the upper classes.

QUESTIONS FOR ANALYSIS

1. What features mark Ethiopian culture as unique and distinctive among early African societies?
2. Referring to Solomonic Ethiopia, assess the role of legend in history.

Sources: G. W. B. Huntingford, ed., *The Glorious Victories of Amda Seyon* (Oxford: Oxford University Press, 1965), pp. 89–90; H. G. Marcus, *A History of Ethiopia*, updated ed. (Berkeley: University of California Press, 2002); J. Iliffe, *Africans: The History of a Continent*, 2d ed. (New York: Cambridge University Press, 2007).

● Colorful biblical scenes adorn the interior of the Urai Kidane Miharet Church, one of the many monasteries established by Amda Siyon.
(Ariadne Van Zandberger/The Africa Image Library, photographersdirect.com)

□ Picturing the Past

The Queen of Sheba and King Solomon Sheba, Queen Makeda, figured prominently in European as well as Ethiopian art. Created in about 1180 by a French artist as part of a series of biblical scenes for an abbey in Austria, this image shows Solomon receiving gifts from Sheba's servants. The inscription surrounding the scene reads "Solomon joins himself to the Queen of Sheba and introduces her to his faith." (Erich Lessing/Art Resource, NY)

ANALYZING THE IMAGE What are King Solomon and Queen Sheba wearing and holding? How are the other figures depicted, and what are they doing?

CONNECTIONS What does the style of this image suggest about the background of the artist and about the audience for whom the image was intended?

fierce devotion and tended to equate doctrinal heresy with political rebellion, thus reinforcing central monarchical power.

The East African City-States

Like Ethiopia, the city-states of East Africa were shaped by their proximity to the trade routes of the Red Sea and Indian Ocean. In the first century C.E. a merchant seaman from Alexandria in Egypt sailed down the Red Sea and out into the Indian Ocean, where he stopped at seaports along the coasts of East Africa, Arabia, and India. He took careful notes on all he observed, and the result, *Periplus of the Erythraean Sea* ("Red Sea" in Greek, but the word can designate the Indian Ocean as well), is the earliest surviving literary evidence of the

city-states of the East African coast. (See "Viewpoints: Early Descriptions of Africa," page 287.) Although primarily preoccupied with geography and navigation, the *Periplus* includes accounts of the local East African peoples and their commercial activities. Since the days of the Roman emperors, the *Periplus* testifies, the East African coast had strong commercial links with India and the Mediterranean.

Greco-Roman ships traveled from Adulis on the Red Sea around the tip of the Gulf of Aden and down the portion of the East African coast that the Greeks called Azania in modern-day Kenya and Tanzania (see Map 10.2). These ships carried manufactured goods — cotton cloth, copper and brass, iron tools, and gold and silver plate. At the African coastal emporiums, Mediterranean merchants exchanged these goods for

Viewpoints

Early Descriptions of Africa

• One of the earliest surviving documents describing any part of Africa is the Periplus of the Erythraean Sea. Written in Greek around 70 C.E., probably by an Egyptian merchant from Alexandria, the Periplus provides a detailed account of the author's sea voyage for use by future travelers. The excerpt below describes the East African coast.

Over fourteen hundred years after the Periplus, a Portuguese mariner named Gomes Eannes de Azarar left the first account of the people and places along the West African coast. The selection here recounts the capture of the first slaves of the Atlantic slave trade along the West African coast in 1441 by two Portuguese ship captains, Antam Gonçalvez and Nuno Tristam.

Periplus of the Erythraean Sea

15. . . . [A]fter two courses of a day and night along the Ausanitic coast,* is the island Menuthias, about three hundred stadia from the mainland, low and wooded, in which there are rivers and many kinds of birds and the mountain-tortoise. There are no wild beasts except the crocodiles; but there they do not attack men. In this place there are sewed boats, and canoes hollowed from single logs, which they use for fishing and catching tortoise. In this island they also catch them in a peculiar way, in wicker baskets, which they fasten across the channel-opening between the breakers.

16. Two days' sail beyond, there lies the very last market-town of the continent of Azania, which is called Rhapta. . . . Along this coast live men of piratical habits, very great in stature, and under separate chiefs for each place. The . . . chief governs it under some ancient right that subjects it to the sovereignty of the state that is become first in Arabia. And the people of Muza now hold it under his authority and send thither many large ships; using Arab captains and agents, who are familiar with the natives and intermarry with them, and who know the whole coast and understand the language.

17. There are imported into these markets the lances made at Muza especially for this trade, and hatchets and daggers and awls, and various kinds of glass; and at some places a little wine, and wheat, not for trade, but to serve for getting the good-will of the savages. There are exported from these places a great quantity of ivory, but inferior to that of Adulis, and rhinoceros-horn and tortoise-shell (which is in best demand after that from India), and a little palm-oil.

Gomes Eannes de Azarar

Thereupon [Nuno Tristam] caused Antam Gonçalvez to be called . . . "You", said he, "my friend Antam Gonçalvez, are not ignorant of the will of the Infant† our Lord, and you know that . . . he hath toiled in vain in this part of the world, never being able to arrive at any certainty as to the people of this land, under what law or lordship they do live. And although you are carrying off these two captives, and by their means the Infant may come to know something about this folk, yet that doth not prevent what is still better, namely, for us to carry off many more; for, besides the knowledge which the Lord Infant will gain by their means, profit will also accrue to him by their service or ransom. Wherefore, it seemeth to me that we should do well to act after this manner. That is to say, in this night now following, you should choose ten of your men and I another ten of mine . . . and let us then go together and seek those whom you have found. . . ."

And so it chanced that in the night they came to where the natives lay scattered in two encampments. . . . And when our men had come nigh to them, they attacked them very lustily, shouting at the top of their voices, "Portugal" . . . the fright of which so abashed the enemy, that it threw them all into disorder. And so, all in confusion, they began to fly without any order or carefulness. Except indeed that the men made some show of defending themselves . . . , especially one of them who fought face to face with Nuno Tristam, defending himself till he received his death. And besides this one, . . . the others killed three and took ten prisoners, what of men, women and boys.

Sources: W. H. Schoff, trans. and ed., *The Periplus of the Erythraean Sea: Travel and Trade in the Indian Ocean by a Merchant of the First Century* (London, Bombay, and Calcutta, 1912), pp. 27–29; Gomes Eannes de Azurara, *The Chronicle of the Discovery and Conquest of Guinea*, vol. 1, trans. C. R. Beazley and E. Prestage (New York: Burt Franklin, 1963), pp. 46–48.

QUESTIONS FOR ANALYSIS

1. What aspects of the East African coast did the author of the *Periplus* write about, and how might these details benefit future travelers to the region?

2. What reasons are given in the second document for enslaving the ten Africans?

3. What are the main concerns of the authors of these documents?

*Coast of modern Zanzibar.

†Portuguese term for any prince other than the eldest; here it refers to Prince Henry the Navigator (see page 466).

Listening to the Past

A Tenth-Century Muslim Traveler Describes Parts of the East African Coast

Other than Ethiopia, early African societies left no written accounts of their institutions and cultures, so modern scholars rely for information on the chronicles of travelers and merchants. Outsiders, however, come with their own preconceptions, attitudes, and biases. They tend to measure what they visit and see by the conditions and experiences with which they are familiar.

Sometime in the early tenth century the Muslim merchant-traveler Al Mas'udi (d. 945 c.e.), in search of African ivory, visited Oman, the southeast coast of Africa, and Zanzibar. He referred to all the peoples he encountered as Zanj, a term that was also applied to the maritime Swahili culture of the area's towns. Al Mas'udi's report, excerpted here, offers historians a wealth of information about these peoples.

66 Omani seamen cross the strait [of Berbera, off northern Somalia] to reach Kanbalu island [perhaps modern Pemba], located in the sea of Zanj. The island's inhabitants are a mixed population of Muslims and idolatrous Zanj. . . . I have sailed many seas, the Chinese sea, the Rum sea [Mediterranean], the Khazar [Caspian Sea], the Kolzom [Red Sea], and the sea of Yemen. I have encountered dangers without number, but I know no sea more perilous than the sea of Zanj. Here one encounters a fish called el-Owal [whale]. . . . The sailors fear its approach, and both day and night they strike pieces of wood together or beat drums to drive it away. . . . The Zanj sea also contains many other fish species possessing the most varied shapes and forms. . . . Ambergris* is found in great quantities along the Zanj coast and also along the coastline of Shihr in Arabia. . . . The best ambergris is found in the islands and on the shores of the Zanj sea: it is round, of a pale blue tint, sometimes the size of an ostrich egg, sometimes a little less. Lumps of it are swallowed by the whale. . . . When the sea becomes very rough the whale vomits up large rock size balls of ambergris. When it tries to gulp them down again it chokes to death and its body floats to the surface. Quickly the men of Zanj, or from other lands, who have been waiting for a favorable moment, draw the fish near with harpoons and tackle, cut open its stomach, and extract the ambergris. The pieces found in its intestines emit a nauseating odor, and Iraqi and Persian chemists call these *nedd:* but the fragments found near the back are much purer as these have been longer inside the body. . . .

The lands of the Zanj provide the people with wild leopard skins that they wear and that they export to Muslim countries. These are the largest leopard skins and make the most beautiful saddles. The Zanj also export tortoise-shell for making combs, and ivory is likewise employed for this purpose. The giraffe is the most common animal found in these lands. . . . They [the Zanj] settled in this country and spread south to Sofala, which marks the most distant frontier of this land and the terminus of the ship voyages made from Oman and Siraf on the Zanj sea. Just as the China sea ends with the land of Japan, the limits of the sea of Zanj are the lands of Sofala and the Waqwaq, a region with a warm climate and fertile soil that produces gold in abundance and many other marvelous things. This is where the Zanj built their capital and chose their king, whom they call *Mfalme*, the traditional title for their sovereigns. The *Mfalme* rules over all other Zanj kings and commands 300,000 cavalrymen. The Zanj employ the ox as a beast of burden, for their country contains no horses, mules, or camels, and they do not even know of these animals. Nor do they know of snow or hail. . . . The territory of the Zanj commences where a branch diverts from the upper Nile and continues to the land of Sofala and the Waqwaq. Their villages extend for about 700 parasangs in length and breadth along the coast. The country is divided into valleys, mountains, and sandy deserts. It abounds in wild elephants but you will not see a single tame one. The Zanj employ them neither for war nor for anything else. . . . When they want to catch them, they throw into the water the leaves, bark, and branches of a particular tree that grows in their country: then they hide in ambush until the elephants come to drink. The tainted water burns them and makes them drunk, causing them to fall down and be unable to get up. The Zanj then rush upon them, armed with very long spears, and kill them for their tusks. Indeed, the lands of the Zanj produce tusks each weighing fifty pounds

cinnamon, myrrh and frankincense, captive slaves, and animal byproducts such as ivory, rhinoceros horns, and tortoise shells. The ships then headed back north and, somewhere around Cape Guardafui on the Horn of Africa, caught the monsoon winds eastward to India, where ivory was in great demand.

In the early centuries of the Common Era many merchants and seamen from the Mediterranean set-tled in East African coastal towns. Succeeding centuries saw the arrival of more traders. The great emigration from Arabia after the death of Muhammad accelerated Muslim penetration of the area, which the Arabs called the Zanj, "land of the blacks," a land inhabited by a Bantu-speaking peoples also called the Zanj. Along the coast, Arabic Muslims established small trading colonies whose local peoples were ruled and more. They generally go to Oman, and are then sent on to China and India. These are the two primary destinations, and if they were not, ivory would be abundant in Muslim lands.

In China the kings and military and civil officers ride in ivory palanquins:† no official or dignitary would dare to enter the royal presence in an iron palanquin. Only ivory can serve on this occasion. Thus they prefer straight tusks to curved. . . . They also burn ivory before their idols and incense their altars with its perfume, just as Christians use the Mary incense and other scents in their churches. The Chinese derive no other benefit from the elephant and believe it brings bad fortune when used for domestic purposes or war. In India ivory is much in demand. There dagger handles, as well as curved sword-scabbards, are fashioned from ivory. But ivory is chiefly used in the manufacture of chessmen and backgammon pieces. . . .

Although the Zanj are always hunting the elephant and collecting its ivory, they still make no use of ivory for their own domestic needs. For their finery they use iron rather than gold and silver, and oxen, as we mentioned above, as beasts of burden or for war, as we use camels or horses. The oxen are harnessed like horses and run at the same speed.

To return to the Zanj and their kings, these are known as *Wfalme*, meaning son of the Great Lord. They refer thus to their king because he has been selected to govern them fairly. As soon as he exerts tyrannical power or strays from the rule of law they put him to death and exclude his descendants from accession to the throne. They claim that through his wrongful actions he ceases to be the son of the Master, that is, the King of Heaven and Earth. They give God the name *Maliknajlu*, meaning the Sovereign Master.

The Zanj express themselves eloquently and have preachers in their own language. Often a devout man will stand in the center of a large crowd and exhort his listeners to render themselves agreeable to God and to submit to his commands. He depicts for them the punishments their disobedience exposes them to, and recalls the example of their ancestors and former kings. These people possess no religious code: their kings follow custom and govern according to traditional political practices.

The Zanj eat bananas, which are as abundant as they are in India; but the staples in their diets are millet and a plant called *kalari* that is pulled from the earth like truffles. It is similar to the cucumber of Egypt and Syria. They also eat honey and meat. Every man worships what he pleases, be it a plant, an animal or a mineral.‡ The coconut grows on many of the islands: its fruit is eaten by all the Zanj peoples. One of these islands, situated one or two days' sail off the coast, contains a Muslim population and a hereditary royal family. This is the island of Kanbalu, which we have already mentioned. 99

● **The merchant trade along the East African coast still relies on dhows, whose design has remained virtually unchanged since Al Mas'udi's time.** (Ken Welsh/age footstock/Robert Harding World Imagery)

Source: Al Mas'udi, *Les Prairies d'Or*, trans. Arab to French by C. Barbier de Meynard and Pavet de Courteille (Paris: Imperial Printers, 1861, 1864), vol. I: pp. 231, 234, 333–335; vol. III: pp. 2, 3, 5–9, 26–27, 29, 30–31. Trans. French to English by Roger B. Beck.

QUESTIONS FOR ANALYSIS

1. What does Al Mas'udi's report tell us about the Zanj peoples and their customs? How would you describe his attitude toward them?

2. What commodities were most sought after by Muslim traders? Why? Where were they sold?

*A solid, waxy, flammable substance, produced in the digestive system of sperm whales, not swallowed as Mas'udi purports. Principally used in perfumery, and not to be confused with amber, the fossil resin used in the manufacture of ornamental objects such as beads and women's combs.
†An enclosed litter attached to poles that servants supported on their shoulders.
‡These are forms of animism.

by kings and practiced various animistic religions. Eventually — whether through Muslim political hegemony or gradual assimilation — the coastal peoples slowly converted to Islam. Indigenous African religions, however, remained strong in the continent's interior. (See "Listening to the Past: A Tenth-Century Muslim Traveler Describes Parts of the East African Coast," above.)

Migrants from the Arabian peninsula and the Malay Archipelago had a profound influence on the lives of the coastal people of East Africa. Beginning in the late twelfth century fresh waves of Arabs and of Persians from Shiraz poured down the coast, first settling at Mogadishu, then pressing southward to Kilwa. Everywhere they landed, they introduced Islamic culture to the indigenous population. Similarly, from the first to

Great Mosque at Kilwa Built between the thirteenth and fifteenth centuries to serve the Muslim commercial aristocracy of Kilwa on the Indian Ocean, the mosque attests to the wealth and power of the East African city-states. (Karen Samson Photography)

the fifteenth centuries Indonesians crossed the Indian Ocean and settled on the African coast and on the large island of Madagascar, or Malagasy, an Indonesian name. All these immigrants intermarried with Africans, and the resulting society combined Asian, African, and especially Islamic traits. The East African coastal culture was called **Swahili**, after a Bantu language whose vocabulary and poetic forms exhibit a strong Arabic influence. The thirteenth-century Muslim mosque at Mogadishu and the fiercely Muslim populations of Mombasa and Kilwa in the fourteenth century attest to strong Muslim influence.

By the late thirteenth century **Kilwa** had become the most powerful city on the coast, exercising political hegemony as far north as Pemba and as far south as Sofala (see Map 10.2). In the fourteenth and fifteenth centuries the coastal cities were great commercial empires comparable to the Italian city-state of Venice (discussed in Chapter 14). Like Venice, Swahili cities such as Kilwa, Mombasa, and Pemba were situated on offshore islands. The tidal currents that isolated them from the mainland also protected them from landside attack.

Much current knowledge about life in the East African trading societies rests on the account of Ibn Battuta. When he arrived at Kilwa, he found "a large

city on the seacoast, most of whose inhabitants are Zinj, jet-black in colour. They have tattoo marks on their faces. . . . The city of Kilwa is one of the finest and most substantially built towns; all the buildings are of wood, and the houses are roofed with al-dis [reeds]."[18] On the mainland were fields and orchards of rice, millet, oranges, mangoes, and bananas and pastures and yards for cattle, sheep, and poultry. Yields were apparently high; Ibn Battuta noted that the rich enjoyed three enormous meals a day and were very fat.

From among the rich mercantile families that controlled the coastal cities arose a ruler who by the fourteenth century had taken the Arabic title *sheik*. The sheik governed both the island city of Kilwa and the nearby mainland. Farther inland, tribal chiefs ruled with the advice of councils of elders.

Approaching the East African coastal cities in the late fifteenth century, Portuguese traders were astounded at their enormous wealth and prosperity. This wealth rested on the sheik's monopolistic control of all trade in the area. Some coastal cities manufactured goods for export: Mogadishu produced cloth for the Egyptian market; Mombasa and Malindi processed iron tools; and Sofala made cottons for the interior trade. The bulk of the cities' exports, however, consisted of animal products — leopard skins, tortoise shell, ambergris, ivory—and gold. The gold originated in the Mutapa region south of the Zambezi River, where the Bantu mined it. As in tenth-century Ghana, gold was a royal monopoly in the fourteenth-century coastal city-states. The Mutapa kings received it as annual tribute, prohibited outsiders from entering the mines or participating in the trade, and controlled shipments down the Zambezi to the coastal markets. Kilwa's prosperity rested on its traffic in gold.

African goods satisfied the global aristocratic demand for luxury goods. In Arabia leopard skins were made into saddles, shells were made into combs, and ambergris was used in the manufacture of perfumes. Because African elephants' tusks were larger and more durable than the tusks of Indian elephants, African ivory was in great demand in India for sword and dagger handles, carved decorative objects, and the ceremonial bangles used in Hindu marriage rituals. Wealthy Chinese valued African ivory for use in the construction of sedan chairs.

In exchange for these natural products, the Swahili cities bought in, among many other items, incense, glassware, glass beads, and carpets from Arabia; textiles, spices, rice, and cotton from India; and grains, fine porcelain, silk, and jade from China. Swahili kings imposed enormous duties on imports, perhaps more than 80 percent of the value of the goods themselves. Even so, traders who came to Africa made fabulous profits.

Slaves were another export from the East African coast. Reports of slave trading in East Africa began with the publication of the *Periplus*. The trade accelerated with the establishment of Muslim settlements in the eighth century and continued down to the arrival of the Portuguese in the late fifteenth century, who provided a market for African slaves in the New World (discussed in Chapter 15). In fact, the global market for slaves would fuel the East African coastal slave trade until at least the beginning of the twentieth century.

As in West Africa, traders obtained slaves primarily through raids and kidnapping. As early as the tenth century Arabs from Oman enticed hungry children with dates. When the children accepted the sweet fruits, they were abducted and enslaved. Profit was the traders' motive.

The Arabs called the northern Somalia coast *Ras Assir* (Cape of Slaves). From there, Arab traders transported slaves northward up the Red Sea to the markets of Arabia and Persia. Muslim dealers also shipped blacks from the region of Zanzibar across the Indian Ocean to markets in India. Rulers of the Deccan Plateau in central India used large numbers of black slave soldiers in their military campaigns. Slaves also worked on the docks and dhows (typical Arab lateen-rigged

Copper Coin from Mogadishu, Twelfth Century Islamic proscriptions against representation of the human form prevented the use of rulers' portraits on coinage, unlike the practice of the Romans, Byzantines, and Sassanids. Instead, Islamic coins since the Umayyad period were decorated exclusively with writing. Sultan Haran ibn Sulayman of Kilwa on the East African coast minted this coin, a symbol of the region's Muslim culture and of its rich maritime trade. (Courtesy of the Trustees of the British Museum)

ships) in the Muslim-controlled Indian Ocean and as domestic servants and concubines throughout South and East Asia.

As early as the tenth century sources mention persons with "lacquer-black bodies" in the possession of wealthy families in Song China.[19] In 1178 a Chinese official noted in a memorial to the emperor that Arab traders were shipping thousands of blacks from East Africa to the Chinese port of Guangzhou (Canton) by way of the Malay Archipelago. The Chinese employed these slaves as household servants, as musicians, and, because East Africans were often expert swimmers, as divers to caulk the leaky seams of ships below the water line.

By the thirteenth century Africans living in many parts of South and East Asia had made significant economic and cultural contributions to their societies. It appears, however, that in Indian, Chinese, and East African markets, slaves were never as valuable a commodity as ivory. Thus the volume of the Eastern slave trade did not approach that of the trans-Saharan slave trade.[20]

Southern Africa and Great Zimbabwe

Southern Africa, bordered on the northwest by the Kalahari Desert and on the northeast by the Zambezi River (see Map 10.2), enjoys a mild and temperate climate. Desert conditions prevail along the Atlantic coast, which gets less than five inches of annual rainfall. Eastward toward the Indian Ocean, rainfall increases, amounting to between fifty to ninety inches a year in some places. Temperate grasslands characterize the highlands in the interior. Considerable variations in climate occur throughout much of southern Africa from year to year.

- **Swahili** The East African coastal culture, named after a Bantu language whose vocabulary and poetic forms exhibit strong Arabic influences.

- **Kilwa** The most powerful city on the east coast of Africa by the late thirteenth century.

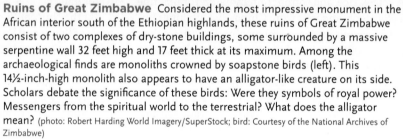

Ruins of Great Zimbabwe Considered the most impressive monument in the African interior south of the Ethiopian highlands, these ruins of Great Zimbabwe consist of two complexes of dry-stone buildings, some surrounded by a massive serpentine wall 32 feet high and 17 feet thick at its maximum. Among the archaeological finds are monoliths crowned by soapstone birds (left). This 14½-inch-high monolith also appears to have an alligator-like creature on its side. Scholars debate the significance of these birds: Were they symbols of royal power? Messengers from the spiritual world to the terrestrial? What does the alligator mean? (photo: Robert Harding World Imagery/SuperStock; bird: Courtesy of the National Archives of Zimbabwe)

Southern Africa has enormous mineral resources: gold, copper, diamonds, platinum, and uranium. Preindustrial peoples mined some of these deposits in open excavations down several feet, but fuller exploitation required modern technology. (Today, gold mining operations can penetrate two miles below the surface.)

Located at the southern extremity of the Afroeurasian landmass, southern Africa has a history that is very different from the histories of West Africa, the Nile Valley, and the East African coast. Unlike the rest of coastal Africa, southern Africa remained far removed from the outside world until the Portuguese arrived in the late fifteenth century — with one important exception. Bantu-speaking people reached southern Africa in the eighth century. They brought skills in ironworking and mixed farming (settled crop production plus cattle and sheep raising) and immunity to the kinds of diseases that later decimated the Amerindians of South America (discussed in Chapter 16).

The earliest residents of southern Africa were hunters and gatherers. In the first millennium C.E. new farming techniques from the north arrived. Lack of water and timber (both needed to produce the charcoal used in iron smelting) slowed the spread of iron technology and tools and thus of crop production in southwestern Africa. These advances reached the western coastal region by 1500. By that date, Khoisan-speakers were farming in the arid western regions. The area teemed with wild game — elephants, buffalo, lions, hippopotamuses, leopards, zebras, and many varieties of antelope. To the east, descendants of Bantu-speaking immigrants grew sorghum, raised cattle and sheep, and fought with iron-headed spears. However, disease-bearing insects such as the tsetse (SET-see) fly, which causes sleeping sickness, attacked the cattle and sheep and retarded their domestication.

The nuclear family was the basic social unit among early southern African peoples, who practiced polygyny and traced descent in the male line. Several families formed bands numbering between twenty and eighty people. Such bands were not closed entities; people in neighboring territories identified with bands speaking the same language. As in most preindustrial societies, a division of labor existed whereby men hunted and women cared for children and raised edible plants. People lived in caves or in camps made of portable material, and they moved from one watering or hunting region to another as seasonal or environmental needs required.

In 1871 a German explorer came upon the ruined city of **Great Zimbabwe** southeast of what is now Masvingo in Zimbabwe. Archaeologists consider Great Zimbabwe the most impressive monument in Africa south of the Nile Valley and the Ethiopian highlands.

The ruins consist of two vast complexes of dry-stone buildings, a fortress, and an elliptically shaped enclosure commonly called the Temple. Stone carvings, gold and copper ornaments, and Asian ceramics once decorated the buildings. The ruins extend over sixty acres and are encircled by a massive wall. The entire city was built from local granite between the eleventh and fifteenth centuries without any outside influence.

These ruins tell a remarkable story. Great Zimbabwe was the political and religious capital of a vast empire. During the first millennium C.E. settled crop cultivation, cattle raising, and work in metal led to a steady buildup in population in the Zambezi-Limpopo region. The area also contained a rich gold-bearing belt. Gold ore lay near the surface; alluvial gold lay in the Zambezi River tributaries. In the tenth century the inhabitants collected the alluvial gold by panning and washing; after the year 1000, the gold was worked in open mines with iron picks. Traders shipped the gold eastward to Sofala (see Map 10.2). Great Zimbabwe's wealth and power rested on this gold trade.

Great Zimbabwe declined in the fifteenth century, perhaps because the area had become agriculturally exhausted and could no longer support the large population. Some people migrated northward and settled in the Mazoe River Valley, a tributary of the Zambezi. This region also contained gold, and the settlers built a new empire in the tradition of Great Zimbabwe. This empire's rulers were called "Mwene Mutapa," and their power was also based on the gold trade down the Zambezi River to Indian Ocean ports. It was this gold that the Portuguese sought when they arrived on the East African coast in the late fifteenth century.

• **Great Zimbabwe** A ruined South African city discovered by a German explorer in 1871; it is considered the most powerful monument south of the Nile Valley and Ethiopian highlands.

CONNECTIONS

Because our ancestors first evolved in Africa, Africa's archaeological record is rich with material artifacts, such as weapons, tools, ornaments, and eating utensils. But its written record is much less complete, and thus the nonmaterial dimensions of human society — human interaction in all its facets — is much more difficult to reconstruct. The only exception is in Egypt, where hieroglyphic writings give us a more complete picture of Egyptian society than of nearly any other ancient culture.

Not until the Phoenicians, Greeks, and Romans were there written accounts of the peoples of North and East Africa. These accounts document Africa's early connections and contributions to the vast trans-Saharan and Indian Ocean trading networks that stretched from Europe to China. This trade brought wealth to the kingdoms, empires, and city-states that developed alongside the routes. But the trade in ideas most profoundly connected the growing African states to the wider world, most notably through Islam, which arrived by the eighth century, and Christianity, which developed a foothold in Ethiopia.

Prior to the late fifteenth century Europeans had little knowledge about African societies. All this would change during the European Age of Discovery. Chapter 16 traces the expansion of Portugal from a small and poor European nation to an overseas empire, as it established trading posts and gained control of the African gold trade. Portuguese expansion led to competition, spurring Spain and then England to strike out for gold of their own in the Americas. The acceleration of this conquest would forever shape the history of Africa and the Americas (discussed in Chapters 11 and 15) and intertwine them via the African slave trade that fueled the labor needs of the colonies in the Americas.

◻ CHAPTER REVIEW

◻ How did Africa's geography shape its history and contribute to its diverse population, and how has this fueled the debate over who is African? (p. 268)

Africa is a huge continent with many different climatic zones and diverse geography. The peoples of Africa are as diverse as the topography. Groups relying on herd animals developed in the drier, disease-free steppe regions well-suited to domesticated animals, while agricultural settlements developed in the wetter savanna regions. In the tropical forests of central Africa and arid zones of southern Africa, hunter-gatherers dominated. Along the coasts and by lakes and rivers, maritime communities grew whose inhabitants relied on fishing and trade for their livelihood.

The peoples of North Africa were closely connected with the Middle Eastern and European civilizations of the Mediterranean basin. Similarly, the peoples of the Swahili coast participated in trade with Arabia, the Persian Gulf, India, China, and the Malay Archipelago. Black Africans living in the Sahel zone of West Africa traded across the Sahara and became part of the larger world of Islam. Because the peoples south of the Sahara are generally described as black Africans, the inappropriate concept of race has engendered fierce debate over just who is African. Since the days of ancient Greece, historians have debated whether Egypt, because of its proximity to the Mediterranean, should be identified as part of Africa or part of the Mediterranean world. Race as a concept for determining one's "Africanness" has been discredited as extremist.

◻ How did settled agriculture affect life among the early societies in the western Sudan and among the Bantu-speaking societies of central and southern Africa? (p. 271)

With the introduction of new crops from Asia and settled agriculture, early societies across the western

KEY TERMS

Hamitic thesis (p. 269)	Ghana (p. 277)
Bantu (p. 272)	Koumbi Saleh (p. 279)
Sudan (p. 273)	Timbuktu (p. 282)
Berbers (p. 274)	Aksum (p. 282)
Mogadishu (p. 276)	Swahili (p. 290)
stateless societies (p. 277)	Kilwa (p. 290)
	Great Zimbabwe (p. 293)

Sudan were profoundly affected as they switched from hunting and gathering in small bands to form settled farming communities. Populations increased significantly in this rich savanna zone that was ideally suited for grain production. Blood kinship brought together families in communities governed by chiefs or local councils. Animistic religions that recognized ancestral and nature spirits developed. The nature spirits were thought to dwell in nearby streams, forests, mountains, or caves.

The migrations of the Bantu-speakers over a two-thousand-year period began in modern Cameroon and Nigeria, and spread across all of central and southern Africa. Possessing iron tools and weapons, domesticated livestock, and a knowledge of settled agriculture, these Bantu-speakers assimilated, killed, or drove away all the previous inhabitants of these regions.

◻ What characterized trans-Saharan trade, and how did it affect West African society? (p. 274)

The most essential component in the trans-Saharan trade was the camel. The camel made it possible for great loads to be hauled across vast stretches of hot, dry desert. The Berbers of North Africa endured these long treks south and then north again across the Sahara. To control this trade they fashioned camel saddles that gave them great political and military advantage. The primary items of trade were salt from the north and gold from the south, although textiles, fruit, ivory, kola nuts, gum, beads, and other goods were also prized by one side or the other. Enslaved West Africans, males and females, were also traded north to slave markets in Morocco, Algiers, Tripoli, and Cairo.

The trans-Saharan trade had three important effects on West African society. First, it stimulated gold mining. Second, it increased the demand for West Africa's second most important commodity, slaves. Third, the trans-Saharan trade stimulated the development of large urban centers in West Africa, such as Gao, Timbuktu, Koumbi Saleh, Sijilmasa, and Jenne.

☐ How were the East African city-states, Aksum, and Great Zimbabwe different from and similar to the kingdoms of the western Sudan? (p. 277)

East African city-states were centered on individual cities, such as Kilwa and Mogadishu. Their existence was based on Indian Ocean commercial networks, in which they traded African products for luxury items from Arabia, Southeast Asia, and East Asia. Like East Africa, South Africa was made up of city-states, chief among them Great Zimbabwe. Located at the southernmost reach of the Indian Ocean trade network, these city-states exchanged their gold for the riches of Arabia and Asia. Somewhat more isolated, the kingdom of Aksum in Ethiopia utilized its access to the Red Sea to trade north to the Mediterranean and south to the Indian Ocean. While Ghana and Mali in the western Sudan also owed their prosperity to trade — primarily the trade of gold — they were great empires whose kings ruled over millions of people.

The East African city-states and the kingdoms of the western Sudan were both part of the world of Islam. Arabian merchants brought Islam with them as they settled along the East African coast, and Berber traders brought Islam to West Africa. Differing from its neighbors, Ethiopia formed a unique enclave of Christianity in the midst of Islamic societies. The Bantu-speaking peoples of Great Zimbabwe were neither Islamic nor Christian, and they practiced indigenous forms of worship such as animism.

SUGGESTED READING

Allen, J. de Vere. *Swahili Origins*. 1993. A study of the problem of Swahili identity.

Austen, Ralph. *African Economic History*. 1987. Classic study of Africa's economic history.

Austen, Ralph. *Trans-Saharan Africa in World History*. 2010. Excellent new introduction to the Sahara region and the trans-Saharan trade that gave it life.

Beck, Roger B. *The History of South Africa*. 2000. Introduction to this large and important country.

Bouvill, E. W., and Robin Hallett. *The Golden Trade of the Moors: West African Kingdoms in the Fourteenth Century*. 1995. Classic description of the trans-Saharan trade.

Bulliet, R. W. *The Camel and the Wheel*. 1995. The importance of the camel to African trade.

Ehret, Christopher. *An African Classical Age: Eastern and Southern Africa in World History, 1000 B.C. to A.D. 400*. 2001. Solid introduction by a renowned African scholar.

Ehret, Christopher. *The Civilizations of Africa: A History to 1800*. 2002. The best study of pre-1800 African history.

Gilbert, Erik, and Jonathan Reynolds. *Africa in World History*. 2007. Groundbreaking study of Africa's place in world history.

Iliffe, John. *Africans: The History of a Continent*, 2d ed. 2007. Thoughtful introduction to African history.

Levtzion, Nehemia, and Randall L. Pouwels. *History of Islam in Africa*. 2000. Comprehensive survey of Islam's presence in Africa.

Marcus, H. G. *A History of Ethiopia*. 2002. Standard introduction to Ethiopian history.

Mitchell, Peter. *African Connections: Archaeological Perspectives on Africa and the Wider World*. 2005. Places ancient Africa and its history in a global context.

Newman, J. L. *The Peopling of Africa: A Geographic Interpretation*. 1995. Explores population distribution and technological change down to the late nineteenth century.

Schmidt, Peter R. *Historical Archaeology in Africa: Representation, Social Memory, and Oral Traditions*. 2006. An excellent introduction to archaeology and the reconstruction of Africa's history.

NOTES

1. C. A. Diop, "The African Origins of Western Civilization," and R. Mauny, "A Review of Diop," in *Problems in African History: The Precolonial Centuries*, ed. R. O. Collins et al. (New York: Markus Weiner Publishing, 1994), pp. 32–40, 41–49; the quotations are from p. 42.

2. Martin Bernal, *Black Athena: Afroasiatic Roots of Classical Civilization*, Volume I: *The Fabrication of Ancient Greece, 1785–1965* (New Brunswick, N.J.: Rutgers University Press, 1987).

3. Mary R. Lefkowitz and Guy MacLean Rogers, *Black Athena Revisited* (Chapel Hill: University of North Carolina Press, 1996).

4. Mauny, "A Review of Diop." For contrasting views of Afrocentrism in American higher education, see T. Martin, *The Jewish Onslaught: Dispatches from the Wellesley Battlefront* (Dover, Mass.: The Majority Press, 1993), and M. Lefkowitz, *Not Out of Africa: How Afrocentrism Became an Excuse to Teach Myth as History* (New York: Basic Books, 1996).

5. T. Spear, "Bantu Migrations," in *Problems in African History: The Precolonial Centuries*, p. 98.

6. J. S. Trimingham, *Islam in West Africa* (Oxford: Oxford University Press, 1959), pp. 6–9.

7. R. A. Austen, "The Trans-Saharan Slave Trade: A Tentative Census," in *The Uncommon Market: Essays in the Economic History of the Atlantic Slave Trade*, ed. H. A. Gemery and J. S. Hogendorn (New York: Academic Press, 1979), pp. 1–71, esp. p. 66.

8. Quoted in J. O. Hunwick, "Islam in West Africa, A.D. 1000–1800," in *A Thousand Years of West African History*, ed. J. F. Ade Ajayi and I. Espie (New York: Humanities Press, 1972), pp. 244–245.

9. Quoted in A. A. Boahen, "Kingdoms of West Africa, c. A.D. 500–1600," in *The Horizon History of Africa* (New York: American Heritage, 1971), p. 183.

10. Al-Bakri, *Kitab al-mughrib fdhikr bilad Ifriqiya wa'l-Maghrib (Description de l'Afrique Septentrionale)*, trans. De Shane (Paris: Adrien-Maisonneuve, 1965), pp. 328–329.

11. Quoted in R. Oliver and C. Oliver, eds., *Africa in the Days of Exploration* (Englewood Cliffs, N.J.: Prentice-Hall, 1965), p. 10.

12. Quoted in Boahen, "Kingdoms of West Africa," p. 184.

13. This quotation and the next appear in E. J. Murphy, *History of African Civilization* (New York: Delta, 1972), pp. 109, 111.

14. Pekka Masonen and Humphrey J. Fisher, "Not Quite Venus from the Waves: The Almoravid Conquest of Ghana in the Modern Historiography of Western Africa," *History in Africa* 23 (1996): 197–232.

15. Quoted in Murphy, *History of African Civilization*, p. 120.

16. Quoted in Oliver and Oliver, *Africa in the Days of Exploration*, p. 18.

17. See H. G. Marcus, *A History of Ethiopia*, updated ed. (Berkeley: University of California Press, 2002), pp. 17–20.

18. Ibn Battuta, *The Travels of Ibn Battuta, A.D. 1325–1354*, vol. 1, ed. H.A.R. Gibb (London: University Press, 1972), pp. 379–380.

19. Austen, "The Trans-Saharan Slave Trade," p. 65; J. H. Harris, *The African Presence in Asia* (Evanston, Ill.: Northwestern University Press, 1971), pp. 3–6, 27–30; P. Wheatley, "Analecta Sino-Africana Recensa," in Neville Chittick and Robert Rotberg, *East Africa and the Orient* (New York: Africana Publishing, 1975), p. 109.

20. I. Hrbek, ed., *General History of Africa*, vol. 3, *Africa from the Seventh to the Eleventh Century* (Berkeley: University of California Press; New York: UNESCO, 1991), pp. 294–295, 346–347.

For practice quizzes and other study tools, visit the **Online Study Guide** at bedfordstmartins.com/mckayworld.

For primary sources from this period, see *Sources of World Societies*, **Second Edition**.

For Web sites, images, and documents related to topics in this chapter, visit **Make History** at bedfordstmartins.com/mckayworld.

• **Moche Portrait Vessel** A Moche artist captured the commanding expression of a ruler in this ceramic vessel. The Moche were one of many cultures in Peru that developed technologies that were simultaneously useful and beautiful, including brightly colored cloth, hanging bridges made of fiber, and intricately fit stone walls. (Private Collection/Photo © Boltin Picture Library/The Bridgeman Art Library)

The first humans settled in the Americas
between 40,000 and 15,000 B.C.E. after emigrating
from Asia. The melting of glaciers 13,000 to 11,000
years ago separated the Americas and Afroeurasia,
and the Eastern and Western Hemispheres developed in isolation from one another. There were
many parallels, however. In both areas people initially gathered and hunted their food, and then some groups began to plant crops, adapting
plants that were native to the areas they settled. Techniques of plant domestication spread,
allowing for population growth because harvested crops provided a more regular food supply than did gathered food. In certain parts of
both hemispheres, efficient production and
transportation of food supplies led to the
growth of cities, with monumental buildings
honoring divine and human power, specialized production of a wide array of products,
and marketplaces where those products
were exchanged. New products included improved military equipment, which leaders
used to enhance their authority and build up the large political entities we call kingdoms
and empires. The power of those leaders also often rested on religious ideas, so that providing service to a king or obeying the laws he set forth was viewed as a way to honor the gods.
In the Western Hemisphere strong and prosperous empires developed first in Mesoamerica — consisting of present-day Mexico and Central America — and then in the Andes.   •

The Americas
2500 B.C.E.–1500 C.E.

The First Peoples of the Americas

☐ How did early peoples in the Americas adapt to their environment as they created technologies of food production and economic systems?

As in the development of early human cultures worldwide, the environment shaped the formation of settlements in the Americas. North America includes arctic tundra, dry plains, coastal wetlands, woodlands, deserts, and temperate rain forests. **Mesoamerica** is dominated by high plateaus with a temperate climate and good agricultural land bounded by coastal plains. The Caribbean coast of Central America—modern Belize, Guatemala, Honduras, Nicaragua, El Salvador, Costa Rica, and Panama—is characterized by thick jungle lowlands, heavy rainfall, and torrid heat. South America has extremely varied terrain. The entire western coast is edged by the Andes, the highest mountain range in the Western Hemisphere, while three-fourths of the continent—almost the whole interior—is lowland plains. South America's Amazon River, at four thousand miles the second-longest river in the world, is bordered by tropical lowland rain forests with dense growth and annual rainfall in excess of eighty inches. Not surprisingly, the varied environments of the Americas contributed to the great diversity of peoples, cultures, and linguistic groups. While all these environments have supported extensive human settlement at various times, it is easier to learn about those people who lived in drier areas, such as the high mountains of the Andes or the deserts of southwestern North America, because artifacts survive longer there.

Describing the Americas and Their Peoples

The environment shaped the history of the Americas, but history shaped the words we use to describe the lands and peoples of these areas. Perhaps more than anywhere else in the world, these words resulted from errors and misunderstandings, and they are often controversial.

About a decade after Christopher Columbus's first voyage in 1492, another Italian explorer and adventurer, Amerigo Vespucci, wrote a letter to his old employers, the Medici rulers in Italy, trumpeting the wonders of the "new world" he had seen. He claimed to have been the first explorer to travel to what is now Venezuela in 1497, a year before Columbus got to the South American mainland. This letter was published many times in many different languages, and the name "New World" began to show up on world maps around 1505. Shortly after that, the word *America*, meaning "the

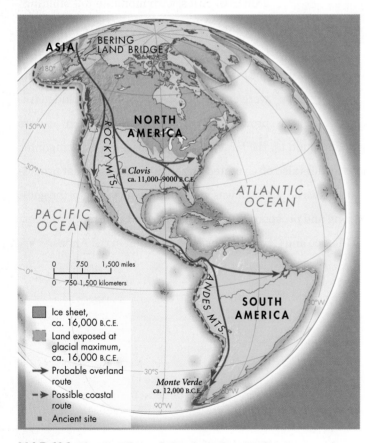

MAP 11.1 The Settling of the Americas Before 10,000 B.C.E. Genetic evidence is currently providing new information about the ways that people migrated across the Bering Strait through the region known as Beringia. It suggests that this occurred in waves, that people settled in Beringia for a while before going on, and that people also migrated back to Asia.

land of Amerigo," also appeared, because mapmakers read and believed Vespucci's letter. But by just a few years later, mapmakers and others knew that Columbus had been the first to this new world. They wanted to omit the label "America" from future maps, but the name had already stuck.

Our use of the word *Indian* for the indigenous peoples of the Americas stems from another mistake. Columbus was trying to reach Asia by sailing west and thought he was somewhere in the East Indies when he landed, which is why he called the people he met "Indians." They apparently called themselves "Tainos," and people who lived on nearby islands called themselves other things. In many cases native people died so fast from the germs brought by Europeans that we have no idea what they called themselves, so the words we use for various indigenous groups come from other indigenous groups or from European languages, and some were originally derogatory nicknames. Many indigenous groups are returning to designations from their own languages, and scholars are attempting to use terminology that is historically accurate, so certain groups are known by multiple names. The use of the word *Indian* is itself highly controversial, and various other terms are often used, including Native Americans, Amerindians, and (in Canada) First Peoples. Each of these substitutes has supporters and opponents, including people who are themselves of indigenous background. No single term for all the indigenous inhabitants of the Western Hemisphere is universally accepted, though in the United States "American Indians" is now becoming more common. The many peoples of the Americas did not think of themselves as belonging to a single group, any more than the peoples living in Europe at Columbus's time thought of themselves as Europeans.

Settling the Americas

The traditions of many American Indian peoples teach that their group originated independently, often through the actions of a divine figure. Many creation accounts, including that of the book of Genesis in the Bible, begin with people who are created out of earth and receive assistance from supernatural beings who set out certain ways the people are supposed to behave. Both Native American and biblical creation accounts continue to have deep spiritual importance for many people.

□ CHRONOLOGY

ca. 40,000–13,000 b.c.e. Initial human migration to the Americas (date disputed)

ca. 8000 b.c.e. Beginnings of agriculture

ca. 2500 b.c.e. First cities in Norte Chico region of Peru; earliest mound building in North America

ca. 1500–300 b.c.e. Olmec culture

ca. 1200 b.c.e. Emergence of Chavin culture

ca. 200 b.c.e.–600 c.e. Hopewell culture

ca. 100–800 c.e. Moche culture

ca. 450 c.e. Peak of Teotihuacán's influence

ca. 600–900 c.e. Peak of Maya culture

ca. 1050–1250 c.e. Construction of mounds at Cahokia

ca. 1325 c.e. Construction of Aztec city of Tenochtitlán begins

ca. 1450 c.e. Height of Aztec culture

ca. 1500 c.e. Inca Empire reaches its largest extent

Archaeological and DNA evidence indicates that the earliest humans came to the Americas from Siberia and East Asia, but exactly when and how this happened is hotly debated. The traditional account is that people crossed the Bering Strait from what is now Russian Siberia to what is now Alaska sometime between 15,000 and 13,000 b.c.e., mostly by walking (Map 11.1). This was the end of the last Ice Age, so more of the world's water was frozen and ocean levels were much lower than they are today. (This situation is the opposite of what is occurring today; global warming is melting polar ice, which is raising water levels around the world.) The migrants traveled southward through North America between two large ice sheets that were slowly melting and retreating. They lived by gathering and hunting, using spears with distinctive fluted stone tips that archaeologists term "Clovis points" after the town in New Mexico where they were first discovered.

Clovis points have been found widely throughout the Americas, and archaeologists used to see the Clovis people who first created these spear points about 11,000 b.c.e as the ancestors of most indigenous people in the Western Hemisphere. Within the last several decades, however, sites in many places have yielded stone tools that appear to predate Clovis.

• **Mesoamerica** The term used by scholars to designate the area of present-day Mexico and Central America.

Archaeologists working at Monte Verde along the coast of Chile have excavated a site that they date to at least 12,000 B.C.E., which would have required a very fast walk from the Bering land bridge. Other sites have been excavated in Brazil, Colombia, Chile, Venezuela, and in many parts of the United States. The pre-Clovis dating of many of these sites has been controversial, in part because the number of objects found at any one site has been small. But in 2011 more than fifteen thousand artifacts were found at one site in Texas, dating to between 11,200 B.C.E. and 13,500 B.C.E. A large group of prominent archaeologists affirmed that this site provides compelling evidence there were humans in the Americas before the Clovis people.

These new archaeological discoveries are leading increasing numbers of archaeologists to conclude that migrants over the land bridge were preceded by people coming originally from Asia who traveled along the coast in skin boats, perhaps as early as 40,000 years ago. They lived by gathering and fishing in the rich coastal estuaries and kelp beds, and they slowly worked their way southward. The coasts that they traveled along are today far under water, and so archaeological evidence is difficult to obtain, but DNA and other genetic evidence have lent support to the theory of coastal migration.

However and whenever people got to the Western Hemisphere — and a consensus about this may emerge in the next decade — they lived by gathering, fishing, and hunting, as did everyone throughout the world at that point. Some groups were nomadic and followed migrating game, while others did not have to travel to be assured of a regular food supply. Coastal settlements from the Pacific Northwest to the southern end of South America relied on fish and shellfish, and some also hunted seals and other large marine mammals.

The Development of Agriculture

About 8000 B.C.E. people in some parts of the Americas began raising crops as well as gathering wild produce. As in the development of agriculture in Afroeurasia, people initially planted the seeds of native plants. Pumpkins and other members of the gourd family were among the earliest crops, as were chilies, beans, and avocados. At some point people living in what is now southern Mexico also began raising what would become the most important crop in the Americas — maize, which we generally call corn. Exactly how this happened is not clear. In contrast to other grains such as wheat and rice, the kernels of maize — which are the seeds as well as the part that is eaten for food — are wrapped in a husk, so the plant cannot propagate itself easily. In addition, no wild ancestor of maize has been found. What many biologists now think happened is that a related grass called "teosinte" developed mutant forms with large kernels enclosed in husks, and people living in the area quickly realized the benefits of these new forms. They began to intentionally plant kernels from them and crossbred the results to get better crops each year.

People bred various types of maize for different purposes and for different climates, making it the staple food throughout the highlands of Mesoamerica. They often planted maize along with squash, beans, and other crops in a field called a milpa (MIHL-puh); the beans use the maize stalks for support as they grow and also fix nitrogen in the soil, acting as a natural fertilizer. Crops can be grown in milpas year after year, in contrast to single-crop planting in which rotation is needed so as not to exhaust the soil.

Inca Terraces In order to create more land for farming and limit soil erosion, Andean peoples built terraces up steep slopes. Later the Incas built systems of aqueducts and canals to bring water to terraced fields. (Wolfgang Kaehler/Corbis)

Maize was viewed as the source of human life and therefore came to have a symbolic and religious meaning. It featured prominently in sculptures of gods and kings, and it was often associated with a specific deity, the corn god. Ceremonies honoring this god were held regularly. In them, people asked for good harvests, as in this Mexica (meh-SHEE-kah) hymn, recorded in the sixteenth century:

> The god of corn, born in Paradise,
> where flowers bloom,
> on the day One Flower . . .
> The god of corn,
> born in the region of rain and mist,
> where the children of men are conceived.[1]

In central Mexico, along with milpas, people also built *chinampas* (chee-NAHM-pahs), floating gardens. They dredged soil from the bottom of a lake or pond, placed the soil on mats of woven twigs, and then planted maize and other crops in the soil. Chinampas were enormously productive, yielding up to three harvests a year.

Knowledge of maize cultivation and maize seeds themselves spread from Mesoamerica into both North and South America. By 3000 B.C.E. farmers in what is now Peru and Uruguay were planting maize, and by 2000 B.C.E. farmers in southwest North America were as well. The crop then spread into the Mississippi Valley and to northeastern North America, where farmers bred slightly different variants for the different growing conditions. After 1500 C.E. maize cultivation spread to Europe, Africa, and Asia as well, becoming an essential food crop there. (In the twentieth century maize became even more successful; about one-quarter of the nearly fifty thousand items in the average American supermarket now contains corn.)

The expansion of maize was the result of contacts between different groups that can be traced through trade goods as well. Copper from the Great Lakes, used for jewelry and ornaments, was a particularly valuable item and was traded throughout North America, reaching Mexico by 3000 B.C.E. Obsidian from the Rocky Mountains, used for blades, was traded widely, as were shells and later pottery.

Various cultivars of maize were developed for many different climates, but maize was difficult to grow in high altitudes. Thus in the high Andes, people relied on potatoes, with the ear-

“The god of corn, born in Paradise, where flowers bloom.”

MEXICA HYMN

liest evidence of people eating potatoes dating from about 11,000 B.C.E. in Monte Verde. Potatoes first grew wild and then were cultivated, and selective breeding produced many different varieties. The slopes on which potatoes were grown were terraced with stone retaining walls, keeping the hillsides from sliding. High-altitude valleys were connected to mountain life and vegetation to form a single interdependent agricultural system, called "vertical archipelagos," capable of supporting large communities. Such vertical archipelagos often extended more than thirty-seven miles from top to bottom. The terraces were shored up with earthen walls to retain moisture, enabling the production of bumper crops of potatoes. Potatoes ordinarily cannot be stored for long periods, but Andean peoples developed a product called *chuñu*, freeze-dried potatoes made by subjecting potatoes alternately to nightly frosts and daily sun. Chuñu will keep unspoiled for several years. Coca (the dried leaves of a plant native to the Andes from which cocaine is derived), chewed in moderation as a dietary supplement, enhanced people's stamina and their ability to withstand the cold that was part of living at high altitudes.

Maize will also not grow well in hot, wet climates. In the Amazon rain forest manioc, a tuber that can be cooked in many ways, became the staple food instead. It was planted along with other crops, including fruits, nuts, and various types of palm trees such as domesticated peach palms, which produce fruit, pulp that is made into flour, heart of palm that is eaten raw, and juice that can be fermented into beer. Just how many people Amazonian agriculture supported before the introduction of European diseases (see "Connections" on page

Lime Container from the Andes This 9-inch gold bottle for holding lime, made between 500 C.E. and 1000 C.E., shows a seated female figure with rings in her ears and beads across her forehead and at her neck, wrists, knees, and ankles. Lime helped release the active ingredients in coca, which was used by many peoples of South America in rituals and to withstand bodily discomfort. Pieces of coca leaves were placed in the mouth with small amounts of powdered lime made from seashells and then chewed. (Image © The Metropolitan Museum of Art/Art Resource, NY)

327) is hotly debated by anthropologists, but increasing numbers see the original tropical rain forest not as a pristine wilderness, but as an ecosystem managed effectively by humans for thousands of years.

Farming in the Americas was not limited to foodstuffs. Beginning about 2500 B.C.E. people living along the coast of Peru used irrigation to raise cotton, and textiles became an important part of Peruvian culture. Agriculture in the Americas was extensive, though it was limited by the lack of an animal that could be harnessed to pull a plow. People throughout the Americas domesticated dogs for hunting, and in the Andes they domesticated llamas and alpacas to carry loads through the mountains. But no native species allowed itself to be harnessed as horses, oxen, and water buffalo did in Asia and Europe, which meant that all agricultural labor was human-powered.

Early Societies

◻ What physical, social, and intellectual features characterized early societies in the Americas?

Agricultural advancement had definitive social and political consequences. Careful cultivation of the land brought a reliable and steady food supply, which contributed to a relatively high fertility rate. As a result, population in the Americas grew steadily and may have reached about 15 million by the first century B.C.E. This growth in population allowed for the creation of the first urban societies.

Mounds, Towns, and Trade in North and South America

By 2500 B.C.E. some groups in North America began to build massive earthworks, mounds of earth and stone serving a variety of purposes (see page 311). Some mounds were conical, others elongated or wall-like, others pyramidical, and still others, called effigy mounds, in serpentine, bird, or animal form. The Ohio and Mississippi River Valleys contain the richest concentration of mounds, but these earthworks have been found from the Great Lakes down to the Gulf of Mexico (see Map 11.1). One early large mound at Poverty Point, Louisiana, on the banks of the Mississippi dates from about 1300 B.C.E. It consists of six octagonal ramparts, one within the other, that measure six feet high and more than four hundred yards across. The area was home to perhaps five thousand people and was inhabited for hundreds of years, with trade goods brought in by canoe and carved stone beads exported.

Large structures for political and religious purposes began to be built earlier in South America than in North America. By about 2500 B.C.E. cities grew along river valleys on the coast of Peru in the region called Norte Chico (NAWR-tay CHEE-koh). Stepped pyramids, some more than ten stories high, dominated these settlements, and they were built at about the same time as the pyramids in Egypt. Cities in Norte Chico often used irrigation to produce squash, beans, cotton, and other crops. People who lived along the coast relied extensively on fish and shellfish, which they traded with residents of inland cities for the cotton needed to make nets. The largest city, Caral, had many plazas, houses, and temples built with large pieces of quarried stone, supported by woven cotton and grass bags filled with smaller stones. Cotton was used in Norte Chico for many other things, including the earliest example yet discovered of a **khipu** (also spelled *quipu*), a collection of knotted strings that was used to record information. Later Peruvian cultures, including the Incas, developed ever more complex khipu, using the colors of the string and the style and position of the knots to represent tax obligations, census records, and other numeric data.

Along with khipu, Norte Chico culture also developed religious ideas and representations of deities. Dating to about 2250 B.C.E. the oldest religious image yet found in the Americas, a piece of gourd with a drawing of a fanged god holding a staff, comes from Norte Chico. This staff god became a major deity in many Andean cultures, one of a complex pantheon of deities. Religious ceremonies, as well as other festivities, in Norte Chico likely involved music, as a large number of bone flutes have been discovered.

The earliest cities in the Andes were built by the Chavin people beginning about 1200 B.C.E. These people built pyramids and other types of monumental architecture, quarrying and trimming huge blocks of stone and assembling them without mortar. They worked gold and silver into human and animal figurines, trading these and other goods to coastal peoples.

Olmec Agriculture, Technology, and Religion

The **Olmecs** created the first society with cities in Mesoamerica. The word *Olmec* comes from an Aztec term for the peoples living in southern Veracruz and western Tabasco, Mexico, between about 1500 and 300 B.C.E. Until 1993 knowledge of the Olmecs rested on archaeological evidence — pyramids, jade objects, axes, figurines, and stone monuments — but that year two linguists deciphered Olmec writing. Since then, un-

• **khipu** An intricate system of knotted and colored strings used by early Peruvian cultures to store information such as census and tax records.

• **Olmecs** The oldest of the early advanced Mesoamerican civilizations.

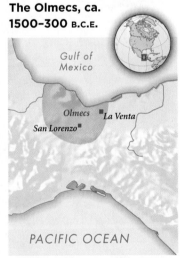

Inca Khipu, ca. 1400 C.E. This khipu, a collection of colored, knotted strings, recorded numeric information and allowed Inca administrators to keep track of the flow of money, goods, and people in their large empire. Every aspect of the khipu—the form and position of the knots, the colors and spin of the string—may have provided information. Administrators read them visually and by running their hands through them, as Braille text is read today. (Museo Arqueologico Rafael Larco Herrera, Lima, Peru)

derstanding of Olmec and other contemporary Meso-american cultures such as the Zapotecs also has come from the written records they left.

The Olmecs cultivated maize, squash, beans, and other plants and supplemented that diet with wild game and fish. They engaged in long-distance trade, exchanging rubber, cacao (from which chocolate is made), pottery, figurines, jaguar pelts, and the services of painters and sculptors for obsidian (a hard, black volcanic glass from which paddle-shaped weapons were made), basalt, iron ore, shells, and various perishable goods. Trading networks extended as far away as central and western Mexico and the Pacific coast.

Originally the Olmecs lived in egalitarian societies that had few distinctions based on status or wealth. After 1500 B.C.E., however, more complex, hierarchical societies evolved. Most Olmecs continued to live in small villages along the rivers of the region, while their leaders resided in large cities, including those today known as San Lorenzo and La Venta. These cities contained palaces (large private houses) for the elite, large plazas, temples (ritual centers), water reservoirs, and carved stone drains for the disposal of wastes. They also contained special courts on which men played a game with a hard rubber ball that was both religious ritual and sport.

Later Mesoamerican groups played a similar ball game, and they also adopted other aspects of Olmec culture: large pyramid-shaped buildings, huge stone heads of rulers or gods, sacrifice at sacred ceremonial sites, and a calendar that traced celestial phenomena, which they believed influenced human life. The need to record time led the Olmecs to develop a symbolic writing system, which they also passed down.

Around 900 B.C.E. San Lorenzo, the center of early Olmec culture, was destroyed, probably by migrating peoples from the north, and power passed to La Venta in Tabasco. Archaeological excavation at La Venta has uncovered a huge volcano-shaped pyramid. Standing 110 feet high at an inaccessible site on an island in the Tonala River, the so-called Great Pyramid was the center of the Olmec religion. The upward thrust of this monument, like ziggurats in Mesopotamia or cathedrals in medieval Europe, may have represented the human effort to get closer to the gods. Built of huge stone slabs, the Great Pyramid required, scholars estimate, some eight hundred thousand hours of human labor. It testifies to the region's good harvests, which were able to support a labor force large enough to build such a monument.

The Olmecs, ca. 1500–300 B.C.E.

Gulf of Mexico

Olmecs   La Venta
San Lorenzo

PACIFIC OCEAN

Classical Era Mesoamerica and North America, 300–900 C.E.

☐ How did Mesoamerican and North American peoples develop prosperous and stable societies in the classical era?

The urban culture of the Olmecs and other Mesoamerican peoples influenced subsequent Mesoamerican societies. Especially in what became known as the classical era (300–900 C.E.), various groups developed large states centered on cities, with high levels of technological and intellectual achievement. The city-states established by the **Maya** were the longest lasting, but others were significant as well. Peoples living in North America built communities that, although smaller than those in Mesoamerica, featured significant achieve-

Palace Doorway Lintel at Yaxchilan, Mexico Lady Xoc, principal wife of King Shield-Jaguar, who holds a torch over her, pulls a thorn-lined rope through her tongue to sanctify with her blood the birth of a younger wife's child—reflecting the importance of blood sacrifice in Maya culture. The elaborate headdresses and clothes of the couple show their royal status. (Photograph K2887 © Justin Kerr)

ments, such as the use of irrigation to enhance agricultural production.

Maya Agriculture and Trade

The word *Maya* seems to derive from *Zamna*, the name of a Maya god. Linguistic evidence suggests that the first Maya were a small North American Indian group that emigrated from the area that is now southern Oregon and northern California to the western highlands of Guatemala. Between the third and second millennia B.C.E. various groups, including the Cholans and Tzeltalans, broke away from the parent group and moved north and east into the Yucatán peninsula. The Cholan-speaking Maya, who occupied the area during the time of great cultural achievement, apparently created the culture.

Maya communities relied on agriculture. The staple crop in Mesoamerica was maize, often raised in multiple-crop milpas with other foodstuffs, including beans, squash, chili peppers, some root crops, and fruit trees. The Maya also practiced intensive agriculture in raised, narrow, rectangular plots that they built above the low-lying, seasonally flooded land bordering rivers.

The raised-field and milpa systems yielded food sufficient to support large population centers. The entire Maya region could have had as many as 14 million inhabitants. At Uxmal, Uaxactún, Copán, Piedras Negras, Tikal, Palenque, and Chichén Itzá (Map 11.2), archaeologists have uncovered the palaces of nobles, elaborate pyramids where nobles were buried, engraved pillars, masonry temples, altars, sophisticated polychrome pottery, and courts for games played with a rubber ball. The largest site, Tikal, may have had forty thousand people and served as a religious and ceremonial center.

At these population centers, public fairs for trading merchandise accompanied important religious festivals. Jade, obsidian, beads of red spiny oyster shell, lengths of cloth, and cacao beans—all in high demand in the Mesoamerican world—served as media of exchange. The extensive trade among Maya communities, plus a common language, promoted unity among the peoples of the region and gave them a common sense of identity. Merchants trading beyond Maya regions, such as with the Zapotecs of the Valley of Oaxaca and with the Teotihuacános of the central valley of Mexico, were considered state ambassadors bearing "gifts" to royal neighbors, who reciprocated with their own "gifts." Since this long-distance trade played an important part in international relations, the merchants conducting it were high nobles or even members of the royal family.

The extensive networks of rivers and swamps in the area ruled by the Maya were the main arteries of transportation; over them large canoes carved out of hardwood trees carried cargoes of cloth and maize. Wide roads also linked Maya centers; on the roads merchants and lords were borne in litters, goods and produce on human backs. Trade produced considerable wealth that seems to have been concentrated in a noble class, for the Maya had no distinctly mercantile class. They did have a sharply defined hierarchical society. A hereditary elite owned private land, defended society, carried on commercial activities, exercised political power, and directed religious rituals. Artisans and scribes made up the next social level. The rest of the people were farmers, unskilled laborers, and slaves, the latter including prisoners of war.

Wars were fought in Maya society for a variety of reasons. Long periods without rain caused crop failure, which led to famine and then war with other centers for food. Certain cities, such as Tikal, extended their authority over larger areas through warfare with neighboring cities. Within the same communities, domestic strife between factions over the succession to the kingship or property led to violence.

Maya Science and Religion

The Maya developed the most complex writing system in the Americas, a script with nearly a thousand characters that represent concepts and sounds. With this script important events and observations were re-

MAP 11.2 The Maya World, 300–900 C.E.
The Maya built dozens of cities linked together in trading networks of roads and rivers. Only the largest of them are shown here.

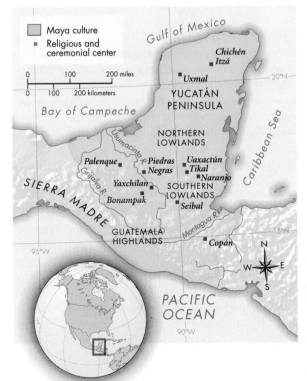

> "In the year 3114 B.C. my forefathers were present, during the Creation of the World."
>
> **MAYA STELE FROM TIKAL**

corded in books made of bark paper and deerskin, on stone pillars archaeologists term "steles," on pottery, and on the walls of temples and other buildings. The deciphering of this writing over the last fifty years has demonstrated that the inscriptions are historical documents recording the births, accessions, marriages, wars, and deaths of Maya kings and nobles, in contrast to the earliest writings from Mesopotamia, which are tax records for payments to the temple (see page 39). As was common for elites everywhere, Maya leaders often stressed the ancient ancestry of their families. "In the year 3114 B.C. my forefathers were present, during the Creation of the World," reads one stele in the city of Tikal, recording the lineage of the Maya Lord Kan Boar.[2] The writing and pictorial imagery often represent the same events, allowing for a fuller understanding of Maya dynastic history.

Learning about Maya religion through written records is more difficult. In the sixteenth century Spanish religious authorities ordered all books of Maya writing to be destroyed, viewing them as demonic. Only three (and part of a fourth) survived, because they were already in Europe. These texts provide information about religious rituals and practices, as well as astronomical calculations. Further information comes from the ***Popul Vuh*** (poh-POHL VOO), or *Book of Council*, a book of mythological narratives and dynastic history written in the middle of the sixteenth century in the Maya language but in European script, which Spanish friars had taught to Maya students. Like the Bible in Judeo-Christian tradition, the *Popul Vuh* gives the Maya view of the creation of the world, concepts of good and evil, and the entire nature and purpose of the living experience. (See "Viewpoints: Creation in the *Popul Vuh* and in Okanogan Tradition," page 308.) Because almost all religious texts from Mesoamerica—not just Maya texts but also those from other cultures—were destroyed by Spanish Christian authorities, this book's significance is enormous.

Maya religious practice emphasized performing rituals at specific times, which served as an impetus for further refinements of the calendar. From careful

- **Maya** A highly developed Mesoamerican culture centered in the Yucatán peninsula of Mexico. The Maya created the most intricate writing system in the Western Hemisphere.
- ***Popul Vuh*** The *Book of Council*, a collection of mythological narratives and dynastic histories that constitutes the primary record of the Maya civilization.

Viewpoints

Creation in the *Popul Vuh* and in Okanogan Tradition

> • *Every people of the world appears to have had a creation account that describes the way the world and the people within it came to be. These are excerpts from the accounts of the Maya people, as recorded in the sixteenth century in the* Popul Vuh, *and of the Okanogan people of the Pacific Northwest, as recorded in the twentieth century from oral traditions.*

Popul Vuh

"Heart of Sky arrived here with Sovereign and Quetzal Serpent [three creator gods] in the darkness, in the night. . . . They thought and they pondered. They reached an accord, bringing together their words and their thoughts. . . . Then the earth was created by them. Merely their word brought about the creation of it. In order to create the earth, they said, "Earth," and immediately it was created. . . . Then were conceived the animals of the mountains, the guardians of the forest, and all that populate the mountains—the deer and the birds, the puma and the jaguar, the serpent and the rattlesnake. . . . This, then, is the beginning of the conception of humanity, when that which would become the flesh of mankind was sought. Then spoke they who are called She Who Has Borne Children and He Who Has Begotten Sons, the Framer and the Shaper [four other gods associated with creation], Sovereign and Quetzal Serpent: "The dawn approaches, and our work is not completed. A provider and a sustainer have yet to appear—a child of light, a son of light. Humanity has yet to appear to populate the face of the earth," they said. Thus they gathered together and joined their thoughts in the darkness, in the night. They searched and they sifted. Here they thought and they pondered. Their thoughts came forth bright and clear. They discovered and established that which would become the flesh of humanity. . . . Thus their frame and shape were given expression by our first Mother and our first Father. Their flesh was merely yellow ears of maize and white ears of maize. . . . And so there were four who were made, and mere food was their flesh. . . . Then their companions, their wives, also came to be. It was the gods who conceived them as well."

Okanogan Tradition

"The earth was once a human being: Old One made her out of a woman. "You will be the mother of all people," he said.

Earth is alive yet, but she has been changed. The soil is her flesh, the rocks are her bones, the wind is her breath, trees and grass are her hair. She lives spread out, and we live on her. When she moves, we have an earthquake.

After taking the woman and changing her to earth, Old One gathered some of her flesh and rolled it into balls, as people do with mud or clay. He made the first group of these balls into the ancients, the beings of the early world. . . .

Besides the ancients, real people and real animals lived on the earth at that time. Old One made the people out of the last balls of mud he took from the earth. He rolled them over and over, shaped them like Indians, and blew on them to bring them alive. They were so ignorant that they were the most helpless of all the creatures Old One had made.

Old One made people and animals into males and females so that they might breed and multiply. Thus all living things came from the earth. When we look around, we see part of our mother everywhere."

Sources: Allen Christensen, trans., *Popul Vuh: The Sacred Book of the Maya* (Winchester, U.K.: O Books, 2003), pp. 70, 71, 74, 192, 195, 201. Used by permission of O Books; "Creation of the Animal People" from Ella C. Clark, *Indian Legends of the Pacific Northwest*. Copyright © 1981 by Ella C. Clark. Reprinted by permission of the University of California Press.

QUESTIONS FOR ANALYSIS

1. Who carries out the creation of the world and human beings in each of these accounts? How does the process of creation combine the spiritual and the material world?

2. How are humans created? What does this process suggest about the relations between humans and the rest of creation?

---

observation of the earth's movements around the sun, the Maya devised a calendar of eighteen 20-day months and one 5-day month, for a total of 365 days. They also used a second calendar with a cycle of 260 days, perhaps inherited from the Olmecs. When these two cyclical calendars coincided, which happened once every fifty-two years, the Maya celebrated with a period of feasting, ball-game competitions, and religious observance. These observances—and those at other times as well—included human sacrifice to honor the gods and demonstrate the power of earthly kings. The actions of those kings were recorded using yet a third calendar, which counted in a linear fashion forward from a specific date.

Using a system of bars (— = 5) and dots (o = 1), the Maya devised a form of mathematics based on the vigesimal (20) rather than the decimal (10) system. More unusual was their use of the number zero, which

Maya Ballplayers and Writing This model of a ball court, made in Mesoamerica sometime before 250 C.E., shows the widely played game in which players used their hips, protected by padding, to hit a rubber ball through a vertical ring high on the wall. Spectators watched and bet on the games, which were also religious rituals and could result in death for the loser. The stone disk showing a player with an elaborate feather headdress comes from a Maya ball court built in 591 C.E. Maya glyphs rim the edge of the disk. (ball court: Yale University Art Gallery/Art Resource, NY; stone disk: National Anthropological Museum Mexico/The Art Archive)

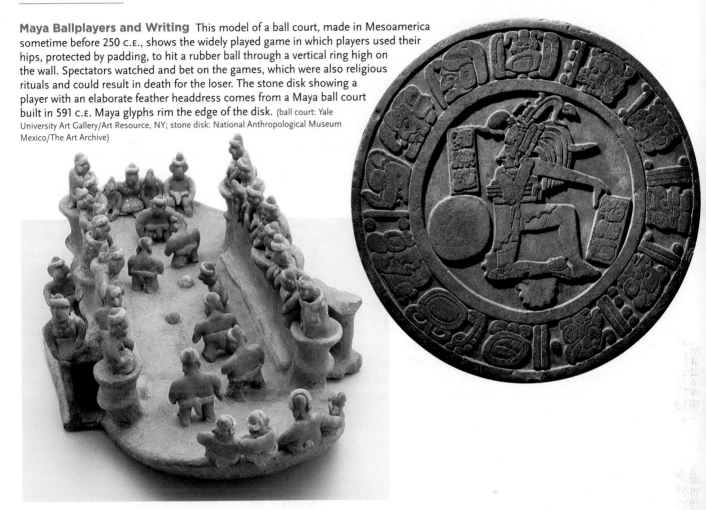

allows for more complex calculations than are possible in number systems without it. The zero may have actually been discovered by the Olmecs, who used it in figuring their calendar, but the Maya used it mathematically as well. (At about the same time, mathematicians in India also began using zero.) The Maya's proficiency with numbers made them masters of abstract knowledge—notably in astronomy, mathematics, calendric development, and the recording of history.

Maya civilization lasted about a thousand years, reaching its peak between approximately 600 and 900 C.E., the period when the Tang Dynasty was flourishing in China, Islam was spreading in the Middle East, and Carolingian rulers were extending their sway in Europe. Between the eighth and tenth centuries the Maya abandoned their cultural and ceremonial centers, and Maya civilization collapsed. Archaeologists and historians attribute the decline to a combination of agricultural failures due to land exhaustion and drought; overpopulation; disease; and constant wars fought to achieve economic and political goals. These wars brought widespread destruction, which aggravated agrarian problems. Royalty also suffered from the decline in Maya civilization: just as in good times

kings attributed moral authority and prosperity to themselves, so in bad times, when military, economic, and social conditions deteriorated, they were blamed.

Growth and Assimilation of the Teotihuacán and Toltec Cultures

The Maya were not alone in creating a complex culture in Mesoamerica during the classic period. In the isolated valley of Oaxaca at modern-day Monte Albán in southern Mexico, Zapotecan-speaking peoples established a great religious center whose temples and elaborately decorated tombs testify to the wealth of the nobility. To the north of Monte Albán, Teotihuacán (tay-oh-tee-wah-KAHN) in central Mexico witnessed the flowering of a remarkable civilization built by a new people from regions east and south of the Valley of Mexico. In about 450 C.E. the city of Teotihuacán had a population of over two hundred thousand—more than any European city at the time. The inhabitants were stratified into distinct social classes. The rich and powerful resided in houses of palatial splendor in a special precinct. Ordinary working people, tradespeople, artisans, and obsidian craftsmen lived in apartment compounds, or barrios, on the edge of the city. Agricultural laborers lived outside the city. Teotihuacán became the center of trade and culture for all of Mesoamerica.

In the center of the city stood several great pyramids, which the Aztecs later referred to as the Pyramids of the Sun and the Moon. The Pyramid of the Sun, built of sun-dried bricks and faced with stone, is the world's third-largest pyramid, only a bit smaller than the largest ancient Egyptian pyramid. (The world's largest pyramid is also in Mesoamerica: the great pyramid of Cholula in Puebla, Mexico, built at about the same time as the pyramids of Teotihuacán.) Exactly what deities were worshipped there is unknown, although they appear to have included the feathered serpent god worshipped by many Mesoamerican peoples, called Quetzalcoatl (kwet-suhl-kuh-WAH-tuhl) or "quetzal serpent" by the Aztecs, named for the brilliant plumage of the quetzal bird.

Around 750 C.E. less-developed peoples from the southwest burned Teotihuacán, and the city-state fell

The Toltecs, ca. 900–1200 C.E.

Gulf of Mexico

Tula • Toltecs
■ Teotihuacan
L. Texcoco

Zapotecs
Monte Albán ■

■ Toltec site
■ Other site
PACIFIC OCEAN

apart. This collapse, plus that of the Maya in about 900 B.C.E., marks the end of the classical period in Mesoamerica for most scholars, just as the end of the Roman Empire in the West marks the end of the classical era in Europe (see Chapter 6). As in Europe, a period of disorder, militarism, and domination by smaller states followed.

Whereas nature gods and their priests seem to have governed the great cities of the earlier period, militant gods and warriors dominated the petty states that now arose. Among these states, the most powerful heir to Teotihuacán was the Toltec confederation, a weak union of strong states. The Toltecs admired the culture of their predecessors and sought to absorb and preserve it. Through intermarriage, they assimilated with the Teotihuacán people. In fact, every new Mesoamerican confederation became the cultural successor of earlier confederations.

Under Topiltzin (r. ca. 980–1000), the Toltecs extended their hegemony over most of central Mexico. Topiltzin established his capital at Tula, and its splen-

The Pyramid of the Sun at Teotihuacán Built in several stages beginning in about 100 C.E., the Pyramid of the Sun has sides measuring 700 feet long and 200 feet high. Originally it was covered with lime plaster decorated with brightly colored murals. Smaller pyramids surround it in what was the heart of the bustling city of Teotihuacán. (© age footstock/SuperStock)

Great Serpent Mound, Adams County, Ohio Made by people in the Hopewell culture, this 1,254-foot-long mound in the form of a writhing snake has its "head" at the highest point, suggesting an open mouth ready to swallow a huge egg formed by a heap of stones. (Georg Gerster/ Photo Researchers, Inc.)

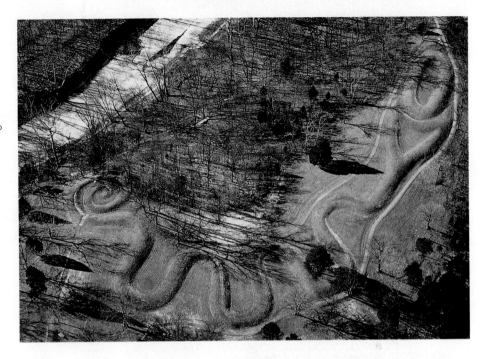

dor and power became legendary during his reign. After the reign of Topiltzin, troubles beset the Toltec state. Drought led to crop failure. Northern peoples, the Chichimecas, attacked the borders in waves. Weak, incompetent rulers could not quell domestic uprisings. When the last Toltec king committed suicide in 1174, the Toltec state collapsed.

Hohokam, Hopewell, and Mississippian Societies

Mesoamerican trading networks extended into southwestern North America, where by 300 B.C.E. the Hohokam people and other groups were using irrigation canals, dams, and terraces to enhance their farming of the arid land (Map 11.3). The Hohokam built platforms for ceremonial purposes and, like the Olmecs and other Mesoamerican peoples, played games with rubber balls. The balls themselves were imported, for rubber trees do not grow in the desert, and turquoise and other precious stones were exported in return. Religious ideas came along with trade goods. Along with local divinities who created, preserved, and destroyed, the feathered serpent god became important to desert peoples. They planted desert crops such as agave, as well as cotton and maize that came from Mexico. Other groups, including the Anasazi (ah-nuh-SAH-zee), the Yuma, and later the Pueblo and Hopi also built settlements in this area, using large sandstone blocks and masonry to construct thick-walled houses that offered protection from the heat. Mesa Verde, the largest Anasazi town, had a population of about twenty-five hundred living in houses built into and on cliff walls. Roads connected Mesa Verde to other Anasazi towns, allow-

ing timber and other construction materials to be brought in more easily. Drought, deforestation, and soil erosion led to decline in both the Hohokam and Anasazi cultures, increasing warfare between towns.

To the east, the mound building introduced at settlements along the Mississippi River around 2000 B.C.E. spread more widely in the valleys of other rivers. One of the most important mound-building cultures was that of the Hopewell (200 B.C.E.–600 C.E.), named for a town in Ohio near where the most extensive mounds were built. Some mounds were burial chambers for priests, leaders, and other high-status individuals, or for thousands of more average people. Others were platforms for the larger houses of important people. Still others were simply huge mounds of earth shaped like animals or geometric figures, which may have served some sort of ceremonial purpose. Mound building thus had many purposes: to honor the gods, to remember the dead, and to make distinctions between leaders and common folk.

Hopewell earthworks also included canals that enabled trading networks to expand, bringing products from the Caribbean far into the interior. Those trading networks also carried maize, allowing more intensive agriculture to spread throughout the eastern woodlands of North America.

At Cahokia (kuh-HOE-kee-uh), near the confluence of the Mississippi and Missouri Rivers in Illinois, archaeologists have uncovered the largest mound of all, part of a ceremonial center and city that housed perhaps thirty-eight thousand people. Work on this complex of mounds, plazas, and houses — which covered five and a half square miles — began about 1050 C.E. and was completed about 1250 C.E. A fence of wooden posts

□ Mapping the Past

MAP 11.3 Major North American Agricultural Societies, ca. 600–1500 C.E.
Many North American groups used agriculture to increase the available food supply and allow greater population density and the development of urban centers. Shown here are three of these cultures: the Mississippian, Anasazi, and Hohokam.

ANALYZING THE MAP How did the location of the Mississippian and other mound-building cultures facilitate trade?

CONNECTIONS The climate and natural vegetation of North America in this period did not differ significantly from those of today. What different types of challenges might these have posed for crop-raising in the three societies shown here?

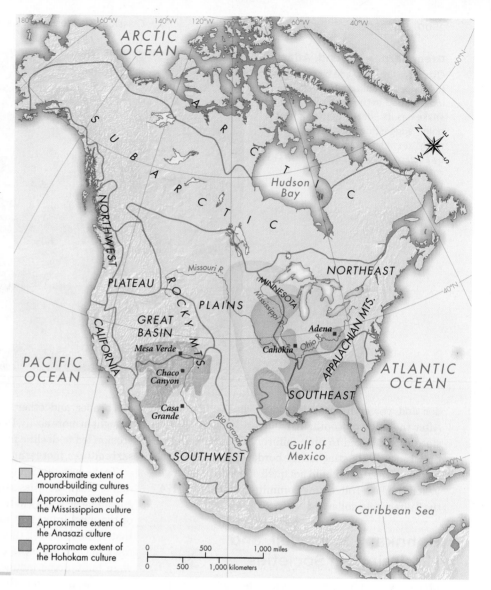

Approximate extent of mound-building cultures

Approximate extent of the Mississippian culture

Approximate extent of the Anasazi culture

Approximate extent of the Hohokam culture

surrounded the center of the complex. Several hundred rectangular mounds inside and outside the fence served as tombs and as the bases for temples and palaces. Within the fence, the largest mound rose in four stages to a height of one hundred feet and was nearly one thousand feet long. On its top stood a large building, used perhaps as a temple.

The mounds at Cahokia are the most impressive physical achievement of the **Mississippian** mound builders, who built cities and mounds throughout much of the eastern United States. What do the mounds tell us about Mississippian societies? The largest mounds served as burial chambers for leaders and, in many cases, for the leaders' male and female servants, who were sacrificed in order to assist the leader in the after-

life. Mounds also contain valuable artifacts, such as jewelry made from copper from Michigan, mica (a mineral used in building) from the Appalachians, obsidian from the Rocky Mountains, conch shells from the Caribbean, and pipestone from Minnesota.

From these burial items, archaeologists have deduced that mound culture was hierarchical and that power was increasingly centralized. The leader had religious responsibilities and also managed long-distance trade and gift-giving. The exchange of goods was not perceived as a form of commerce but as a means of showing respect and of establishing bonds among diverse groups. Large towns housed several thousand inhabitants and served as political and ceremonial centers. They controlled surrounding villages of a few hundred people but did not grow into large, politically unified city-states the way Tikal and Teotihuacán did.

Mississippian mound builders relied on agriculture to support their complex cultures, and by the time Cahokia was built, maize agriculture had spread to the Atlantic coast. Particularly along riverbanks and the

• **Mississippian** An important mound-building culture that thrived between 800 and 1500 C.E. in a territory that extended from the Mississippi River to the Appalachian Mountains. The largest mound produced by this culture is found at Cahokia, Illinois.

• **Nahuatl** The language of both the Toltecs and the Aztecs.

Engraved Mississippian Copper Plate This ornamental copper plate was excavated in Etowah Mound, Georgia, a Mississippian site first settled in about 1000 C.E. The copper may have been mined along the shore of Lake Superior in what is now northern Michigan, the largest source of copper in North America. Falcons were associated with success in warfare and long life among Mississippians, and warriors with falcon wings were frequently shown in the handiworks of this culture. (Catalogue No. A91117, Department of Anthropology, Smithsonian Institution; photo by D. E. Hurlbert)

coastline, fields of maize, beans, and squash surrounded large, permanent villages containing many houses, all surrounded by walls made of earth and timber. Hunting and fishing provided animal protein, but the bulk of people's food came from farming. For recreation, people played various ball games and chunkey, a game in which spears were thrown at a disk rolled across the ground. As in Mesoamerica, these games were sometimes played in large arenas with many spectators, who frequently gambled on the outcome.

Mississippian people's religious ideas are revealed in pottery in the form of bowls, jars, and bottles; in effigy pipes in various shapes; and in engraved shells, decorated copper plates, and carved stone statues. Along with the visible world, the Mississippian cosmos included an Overworld and an Underworld filled with supernatural beings; the three worlds were linked together by an axis usually portrayed as a tree or a striped pole. The forces and beings of both spiritual worlds, which often took the form of falcons, serpents, panthers, or creatures that combined parts from various animals, were honored through ceremonies and rituals, and they offered supernatural power to humans who performed these rites correctly.

At its peak in about 1150 Cahokia was the largest city north of Mesoamerica. However, construction of the interior wooden fence denuded much of the surrounding countryside of trees, which made spring floods worse and eventually destroyed much of the city. An earthquake at the beginning of the thirteenth century furthered the destruction, and the city never recovered. The worsening climate of the fourteenth century that brought famine to Europe probably also contributed to Cahokia's decline, and the site's population dispersed. Throughout Mississippian areas the fifteenth century brought increased warfare, as evidenced by the building of walls and defensive works around towns, and more migration. Iroquois-speaking peoples in particular migrated south from what is now New York into the valleys of the Ohio River and its

tributaries, sometimes displacing groups that had been living in these areas through warfare. In the fifteenth or early sixteenth century a group of Iroquois nations formed an association known as the Iroquois League to lessen intergroup violence. This league was a powerful force when European colonists first entered these areas.

The Aztecs

☐ How did the Aztecs both build on the achievements of earlier Mesoamerican cultures and develop new traditions to create their large empire?

The Aztecs provide a spectacular example of a culture that adopted many things from earlier peoples and also adapted them to create an even more powerful state. Around 1300 a group of **Nahuatl**-speaking people are believed to have migrated southward from what is now northern Mexico, settling on the shores and islands of Lake Texcoco in the central valley of Mexico (Map 11.4). Here they built the twin cities of Tenochtitlán (tay-nawch-teet-LAHN) and Tlatelolco, which by 1500 were probably larger than any city in Europe except

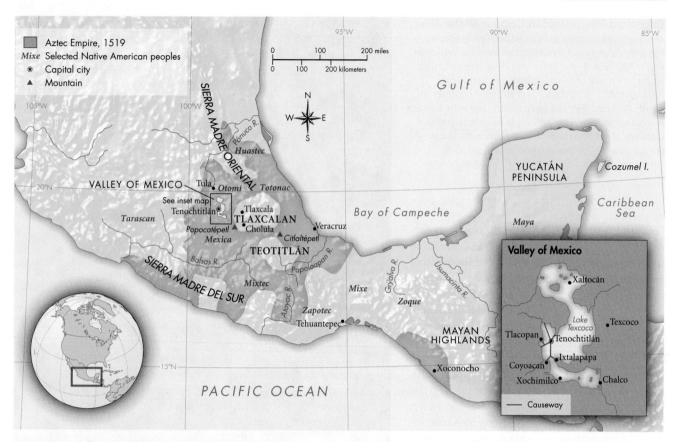

MAP 11.4 The Aztec (Mexica) Empire in 1519 The Mexica migrated into the central valley of what is now Mexico from the north, conquering other groups and establishing an empire, later called the Aztec Empire. The capital of the Aztec Empire was Tenochtitlán, built on islands in Lake Texcoco.

Istanbul. As they migrated, these people, who were later called the Aztecs, conquered many neighboring city-states and established an empire later termed the Aztec Empire. The word *Aztec* was not used at the time, however, and most scholars now prefer the term **Mexica** to refer to the empire and its people; we use both terms here.

Religion and War in Aztec Society

In Mexica society, religion was the dynamic factor that transformed other aspects of the culture: economic security, social mobility, education, and especially war. War was an article of religious faith. The state religion of the Aztecs initially gave them powerful advantages over other groups in central Mexico; it inspired them to conquer vast territories in a remarkably short time. War came to be seen as a religious duty; through it

nobles, and occasionally commoners, honored the gods, gained prestige, and often acquired wealth.

The Mexicas worshipped a number of gods and goddesses as well as some deities that had dual natures as both male and female. The basic conflict in the world was understood as being between order and disorder, though the proper life was seen as balancing these two, because disorder could never be completely avoided. Disorder was linked to dirt and uncleanness, so temples, shrines, and altars were kept very clean; rituals of purification often involved sweeping or bathing. Like many polytheists, Mexicas took the deities of people they encountered into their own pantheon or mixed their attributes with those of existing gods. Quetzalcoatl, for example, the feathered serpent god found among many Mesoamerican groups, was generally revered by the Mexicas as a creator deity and a source of knowledge.

Among the deities venerated by Mexica and other Mesoamerican groups was Huitzilopochtli (weet-zeel-oh-POHCH-tlee), a young warrior-god whose name translates fully as "Blue Hummingbird of the South" (or "Blue Hummingbird on the Left") and who symbolized the sun blazing at high noon. The sun, the source

• **Mexica** The dominant ethnic group of what is now Mexico, which created an empire based on war and religion that reached its height in the mid-1400s; in the nineteenth century the people became known as Aztecs.

of all life, had to be kept moving in its orbit if darkness was not to overtake the world. To keep it moving, Aztecs believed, the sun had to be frequently fed precious fluids — that is, human blood. Therefore, human sacrifice was seen as a sacred duty, essential for the preservation and prosperity of humankind. (See "Individuals in Society: Tlacaélel," page 316.)

Most victims were war captives, for the Aztecs controlled their growing empire by sacrificing prisoners seized in battle, by taking hostages from among defeated peoples as ransom against future revolt, and by demanding that subject states provide an annual tribute of people to be sacrificed to Huitzilopochtli. In some years it was difficult to provide enough war captives, so other types of people, including criminals and slaves, were sacrificed as well. Additionally, unsuccessful generals, corrupt judges, and careless public officials — even people who accidentally entered forbidden precincts of the royal palaces — were routinely sacrificed. Non-captive victims had a lower status than did captives, however, and Mexicas engaged in special wars simply to provide victims for sacrifices, termed "flower (or flowery) wars." Flowers were frequently associated metaphorically with warfare in Mexica culture, with blood described as a flower of warfare, swords and banners as blooming like flowers, and a warrior's life as being as fleeting as a flower's blooming. The objective of flower wars was to capture warriors from the other side, not to kill them.

The Mexica state religion required constant warfare for two basic reasons. One was to meet the gods' needs for human sacrifice; the other was to acquire warriors for the next phase of imperial expansion. Moreover, defeated peoples had to pay tribute in foodstuffs to support rulers, nobles, warriors, and the imperial bureaucracy. The vanquished supplied laborers for agriculture, the economic basis of Mexica society. Likewise, conquered peoples had to produce workers for the construction and maintenance of the entire Aztec infrastructure — roads, dike systems, aqueducts, causeways, and royal palaces. Finally, merchants also benefited from warfare, for it opened new markets for traders' goods in subject territories.

Social Distinctions Among Aztecs

A wealth of information has survived about fifteenth- and sixteenth-century Mexico. The Aztecs wrote many books recounting their history, geography, and religious practices, and they loved making speeches, which scribes wrote down. The Aztecs also preserved records of their legal disputes, which alone amounted to vast files. The Spanish conquerors subsequently destroyed much of this material, but enough documents remain to construct a picture of the Mexica people at the time of the Spanish intrusion.

Few sharp social distinctions existed among the Aztecs during their early migrations, but by the early sixteenth century Aztec society had changed. A stratified social structure had come into being, and the warrior aristocracy exercised great authority. Men who had

Huitzilopochtli This painting of the hummingbird god of war carrying a shield in one hand and serpent-headed knife in the other was made by Aztec priests in a book written on bark paper about the time of the Spanish conquest. He is shown descending from a step-pyramid, perhaps a reference to the great pyramid in the center of Tenochtitlán, where he was worshipped.
(© Foundation for the Advancement of Mesoamerican Studies, Inc., www.famsi.org)

Individuals in Society

Tlacaélel

THE HUMMINGBIRD GOD HUITZILOPOCHTLI
was originally a somewhat ordinary god of war and of young
men, but in the fifteenth century he was elevated in status
among the Mexica. He became increasingly associated with
the sun and gradually became the Mexicas' most important
deity. This change appears to have been primarily the work of
Tlacaélel, the very long-lived chief adviser to the emperors
Itzcóatl (r. 1427–1440), Montezuma I (r. 1440–1469), and
Axayacatl (r. 1469–1481). Tlacaélel first gained influence
during wars in the 1420s in which the Mexicas defeated the
rival Tepanecs, after which he established new systems of
dividing military spoils and enemy lands. At the same time, he
advised the emperor that new histories were needed in which
the destiny of the Mexica people was made clearer. Tlacaélel
ordered the destruction of older historical texts, and under his
direction the new chronicles connected Mexicas' fate directly
to Huitzilopochtli. Mexica writing was primarily pictographic,
drawn and then read by specially trained scribes who used
written records as an aid to oral presentation, especially for
legal issues, historical chronicles, religious and devotional
poetry, and astronomical calculations.

According to these new texts, the Mexicas had been guided
to Lake Texcoco by Huitzilopochtli; there they saw an eagle
perched on a cactus, which a prophecy foretold would mark the
site of their new city. Huitzilopochtli kept the world alive by bringing the sun's warmth, but to do this he required the Mexicas,
who increasingly saw themselves as the "people of the sun," to
provide a steady offering of human blood.

The worship of Huitzilopochtli became linked to cosmic
forces as well as daily survival. In Nahua tradition, the
universe was understood to exist in a series of five suns,
or five cosmic ages. Four ages had already passed, and
their suns had been destroyed; the fifth sun, the age in
which the Mexicas were now living, would also be
destroyed unless the Mexicas fortified the sun with the
energy found in blood. Warfare thus not only brought new
territory under Mexica control but also provided sacrificial
victims to nourish the sun god. With these ideas, Tlacaélel
created what Miguel León-Portilla, a leading contemporary scholar of Nahuatl religion and philosophy, has
termed a "mystico-militaristic" conception of Aztec destiny.

Human sacrifice was practiced in many cultures of
Mesoamerica, including the Olmec and the Maya as well
as the Mexica, before the changes introduced by
Tlacaélel, but the number of victims is believed to have
increased dramatically during the last period of Mexica
rule. A huge pyramid-shaped temple in the center of
Tenochtitlán, dedicated to Huitzilopochtli and the water
god Tlaloc, was renovated and expanded many times, the
last in 1487. Each expansion was dedicated by priests
sacrificing war captives. Similar ceremonies were held
regularly throughout the year on days dedicated to
Huitzilopochtli and were attended by many observers,
including representatives from neighboring states as well as
masses of Mexicas. According to many accounts, victims were
placed on a stone slab, and their hearts were cut out with an
obsidian knife; the officiating priest then held the heart up as
an offering to the sun. Sacrifices were also made to other gods
at temples elsewhere in Tenochtitlán, and perhaps in other
cities controlled by the Mexicas.

Estimates of the number of people sacrificed to Huitzilopochtli
and other Mexica gods vary enormously and are impossible to
verify. Both Mexica and later Spanish accounts clearly exaggerated the numbers, but most historians today assume that
between several hundred and several thousand people were
killed each year.

Sources: Miguel León-Portilla, *Pre-Columbian Literatures of Mexico* (Norman:
University of Oklahoma Press, 1969); Inga Clendinnen, *Mexicas: An Interpretation* (Cambridge: Cambridge University Press, 1991).

QUESTIONS FOR ANALYSIS

1. How did the worship of Huitzilopochtli contribute to Aztec
   expansion? To hostility toward the Aztecs?

2. Why might Tlacaélel have seen it as important to destroy
   older texts as he created this new Aztec mythology?

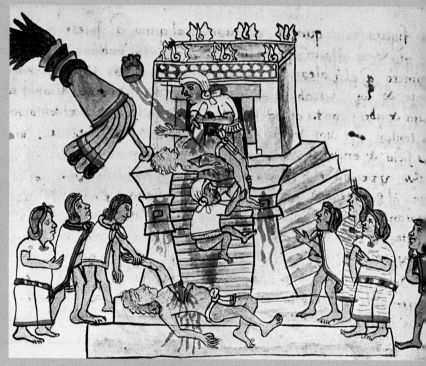

**Tlacaélel emphasized human sacrifice as one of the Aztecs'
religious duties.** (Scala/Art Resource, NY)

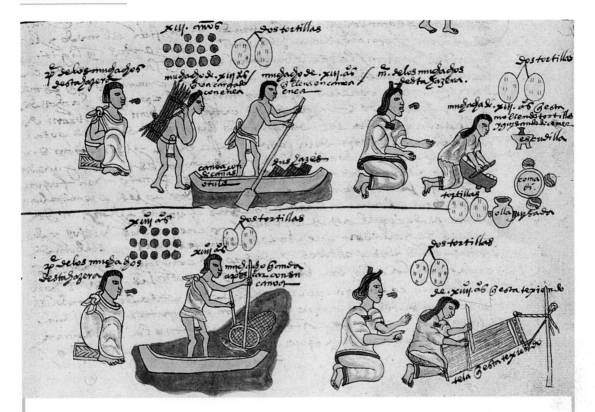

◻ Picturing the Past

Aztec Adolescents This scene of adults supervising the tasks that young people at each age (indicated by dots) were expected to learn appeared in a painted book made by Mexica artists in the middle of the sixteenth century. It includes Nahuatl and Spanish words, including "dos [two] tortillas," the basic amount of food the artists thought was appropriate for these adolescents. (The Bodleian Library, University of Oxford, MS Arch. Selden. A.1, fol. 60r)

ANALYZING THE IMAGE What tasks are boys expected to learn? What tasks are girls expected to learn? What do these differences suggest about Aztec society?

CONNECTIONS This painting was made about a generation after the Spanish conquest so that in some ways it represents an idealized past rather than current reality. How might this have shaped the artists' views of adolescence?

distinguished themselves in war occupied the highest military and social positions in the state. Generals, judges, and governors of provinces were appointed by the emperor from among his servants who had earned reputations as war heroes. These great lords, or te-cuhtli (teh-COOT-lee), dressed luxuriously and lived in palaces. Acting as provincial governors, they exercised full political, judicial, and military authority on the emperor's behalf. In their territories they maintained order, settled disputes, and judged legal cases; oversaw the cultivation of land; and made sure that tribute — in food or gold — was paid. The governors also led troops in wartime. These functions resembled those of feudal lords in western Europe during the Middle Ages. Just as only nobles in France and England could wear fur and carry swords, just as gold jewelry and

elaborate hairstyles for women distinguished royal and noble classes in African kingdoms, so in Mexica societies only the tecuhtli could wear jewelry and embroidered cloaks. As the empire expanded, the growth of a strong mercantile class led to an influx of tropical wares and luxury goods: cotton, feathers, cocoa, skins, turquoise jewelry, and gold. These goods contributed to the elegant and extravagant lifestyle that the upper classes enjoyed.

Beneath the great nobility of military leaders and imperial officials was the class of warriors. Theoretically, every free man could be a warrior, and parents dedicated their male children to war, burying a male child's umbilical cord with some arrows and a shield on the day of his birth. In actuality the sons of nobles were more likely to become warriors because of their fathers' positions and influence in the state. At the age of six boys entered a school that trained them for war. They were taught to fight with a *ma-cana*, a paddle-shaped wooden club edged with bits of obsidian. Youths were also trained in the use of spears, bows and arrows, lances fitted with obsidian points, and atlatls, notched throwing sticks made of bone, wood, or antler. They learned to live on little food and sleep and to accept pain without complaint. At about age eighteen a warrior fought his first campaign. If he captured a prisoner for ritual sacrifice, he acquired the title *iyac*, or warrior. If in later campaigns he succeeded in killing or capturing four of the enemy, he became a *tequiua*—one who shared in the booty and thus was a member of the nobility. If a young man failed in several campaigns to capture the required four prisoners, he became a *macehualli* (plural *macehualtin*), a commoner.

> "O great Lord of All Things, remember your servant who has gone to exalt your honor and the greatness of your name. He will offer blood in that sacrifice that is war."
>
> **PRAYER TO HUITZILOPOCHTLI**

The macehualtin were the ordinary citizens—the backbone of Aztec society and the vast majority of the population. The word *macehualli* means "worker" and implies boorish speech and vulgar behavior. Members of this class performed all sorts of agricultural, military, and domestic services and carried heavy public burdens not required of noble warriors. Government officials assigned them work on the temples, roads, and bridges. Army officers called them up for military duty, but Mexica considered this an honor and a religious rite, not a burden. Unlike nobles, priests, orphans, and slaves, macehualtin paid taxes. Macehualtin in the capital, however, possessed certain rights: they held their plots of land for life, and they received a small share of the tribute paid by the provinces to the emperor.

Beneath the macehualtin were the *tlalmaitl*, the landless workers or serfs. Some social historians speculate that this class originated during the period of migrations and upheavals following the end of the classical period (see page 306), when weak and defenseless people placed themselves under the protection of strong warriors, just as European peasants had become serfs after the end of the Roman Empire (see Chapter 6). The tlalmaitl provided agricultural labor, paid rents in kind, and were bound to the soil—they could not move off the land. In many ways the tlalmaitl resembled the serfs of western Europe, but unlike serfs they performed military service when called on

to do so. They enjoyed some rights as citizens and generally were accorded more respect than slaves.

Slaves were the lowest social class. Like Asian, European, and African slaves, most were prisoners captured in war or kidnapped from enemy tribes. But Aztecs who stole from a temple or private house or plotted against the emperor could also be enslaved, and people in serious debt sometimes voluntarily sold themselves into slavery. Female slaves often became their masters' concubines. Mexica slaves differed fundamentally from European ones, for they could possess goods; save money; buy land, houses, and even slaves for their own service; and purchase their freedom. If a male slave married a free woman, their offspring were free, and a slave who escaped and managed to enter the emperor's palace was automatically free. Most slaves eventually gained their freedom. Mexica slavery, therefore, had some humane qualities and resembled slavery in Islamic societies (see pages 246–248).

Women of all social classes played important roles in Mexica society, but those roles were restricted largely to the domestic sphere. As the little hands of the newborn male were closed around a tiny bow and arrow indicating his warrior destiny, so the infant female's hands were wrapped around miniature weaving instruments and a small broom: weaving was a sacred and exclusively female art; the broom signaled a female's responsibility for the household shrines and for keeping the home swept and free of contamination. Almost all Mexica people married, men at about twenty and women several years earlier. As in premodern Asian and European societies, parents selected their children's spouses, using neighborhood women as go-betweens. Save for the few women vowed to the service of the temple, marriage and the household were a woman's fate, and marriage represented social maturity for both sexes. Pregnancy became the occasion for family and neighborhood feasts, and a successful birth launched celebrations lasting from ten to twenty days.

Women were expected to pray for their husbands' success in battle while they were gone. One prayer to Huitzilopochtli went:

> O great Lord of All Things, remember your servant
> Who has gone to exalt your honor and the greatness
>   of your name.
> He will offer blood in that sacrifice that is war.
> Behold, Lord, that he did not go out to work for me
> Or for his children. . . . He went for your sake,
> In your name, to obtain glory for you. . . .
> Give him victory in this war so that he may return
> To rest in his home and so that my children and I
>   may see
> His countenance again and feel his presence.[3]

Alongside the secular social classes stood the temple priests. Huitzilopochtli and each of the numerous

---

• **Tenochtitlán** A large and prosperous Aztec city that was built starting in 1325. It was admired by the Spanish when they entered in 1519.

lesser gods were attended to by many priests who oversaw the upkeep of the temple, assisted at religious ceremonies, and performed ritual sacrifices. The priests also did a brisk business in foretelling the future from signs and omens. Aztecs consulted priests on the selection of wives and husbands, on the future careers of newborn babies, and before leaving on journeys or for war. Temples possessed enormous wealth in gold and silver ceremonial vessels, statues, buildings, and land. From the temple revenues and resources, the priests supported schools, aided the poor, and maintained hospitals. The chief priests had the ear of the emperor and often exercised great power and influence.

The emperor stood at the peak of the social pyramid. Aztec historians contradict one another about the origin of the imperial dynasty, but modern scholars tend to accept the verdict of one sixteenth-century authority that the "custom has always been preserved among the Mexicans (that) the sons of kings have not ruled by right of inheritance but by election."[4] A small oligarchy of the chief priests, warriors, and state offi-

cials made the selection. If none of the sons of the previous emperor proved satisfactory, a brother or nephew of the emperor was chosen, but election was always restricted to the royal family.

The Aztec emperor was expected to be a great warrior who had led Mexica and allied armies into battle. All his other duties pertained to the welfare of his people. It was up to the emperor to see that justice was done; he was the final court of appeal. He also held ultimate responsibility for ensuring an adequate food supply. The emperor Montezuma I (r. 1440–1469) distributed twenty thousand loads of stockpiled grain when a flood hit Tenochtitlán. This deed and other recorded actions show that the Aztec emperors took their public duties seriously.

The City of Tenochtitlán

When the Spanish entered **Tenochtitlán** (which they called Mexico City) in November 1519, they could not believe their eyes. According to Bernal Díaz, one of

The Aztec Capital of Tenochtitlán This 1524 map of Tenochtitlán, made by a European mapmaker, was included with a Latin edition of one of the letters of Cortés, printed in Germany. It was based on Cortés's written description of the city and shows the city laid out in concentric circles, with causeways and people paddlng canoes. The administrative and religious buildings were at the heart of the city, surrounded by residential quarters. The smaller map at the left shows the Gulf of Mexico as Cortés understood it, with Yucatan as an island instead of a peninsula. This map has north at the bottom, and if you rotate it 180 degrees, you will see some familiar landmarks, including the mouth of the Mississippi River (which the Spanish called Río del Espíritu Santo) and Florida. This was the first printed map on which the name "Florida" appeared. (The Newberry Library)

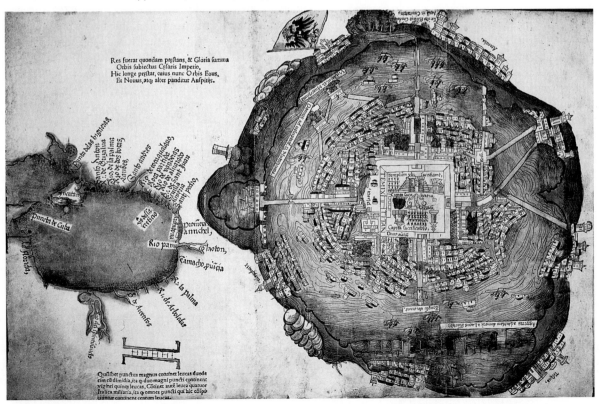

Cortés's companions:

> When we saw all those cities and villages built in the water, and other great towns on dry land, and that straight and level causeway leading to Mexico, we were astounded. These great towns and cues (temples) and buildings rising from the water, all made of stone, seemed like an enchanted vision. . . . Indeed, some of our soldiers asked whether it was not all a dream.[5]

As of 1500 Tenochtitlán had about 60,000 households and a total population of around 250,000, making it one of the largest cities in the world. At the time, no European city and few Asian cities could boast a population even half that size. The total Aztec Empire has been estimated at around 5 million inhabitants, with the total population of Mesoamerica at between 20 and 30 million.

Originally built on salt marshes, Tenochtitlán was approached by four great causeways that connected it with the mainland. Openings in the causeways, covered by bridges, provided places for boats to pass through. Stone and adobe walls surrounded the city itself, making it (somewhat like medieval Constantinople; see page 207) highly defensible and capable of resisting a prolonged siege. Wide, straight streets as well as canals plied by boats and canoes crisscrossed the city. Lining the roads and canals stood thousands of rectangular one-story houses of mortar faced with stucco. Although space was limited, many small gardens and parks were alive with the colors and scents of flowers.

A large aqueduct whose sophisticated engineering astounded Cortés carried pure water from distant springs and supplied fountains in the parks. Streets and canals opened onto public squares and marketplaces, where tradespeople offered every kind of merchandise. Butchers hawked turkeys, ducks, chickens, rabbits, and deer; grocers sold kidney beans, squash, avocados, maize, and all kinds of peppers. Artisans sold intricately designed gold, silver, and feathered jewelry, while seamstresses offered various items of clothing customarily worn by ordinary people: sandals, loincloths and cloaks for men, and blouses and long skirts for women. The seamstresses also provided embroidered robes and cloaks for the rich. Slaves for domestic service, wood for building, herbs for seasoning and

medicine, honey and sweets, knives, jars, smoking tobacco, even human excrement used to cure animal skins — all these wares added to the dazzling spectacle.

At one side of the central square of Tenochtitlán stood the great temple of Huitzilopochtli. Built as a pyramid and approached by three flights of 120 steps each, the temple was about one hundred feet high and dominated the city's skyline. According to Cortés, it was "so large that within the precincts, which are surrounded by a very high wall, a town of some five hundred inhabitants could easily be built. All round inside this wall there are very elegant quarters with very large rooms and corridors where their priests live."[6]

Travelers, perhaps inevitably, compare what they see abroad with what is familiar to them at home. Tenochtitlán thoroughly astounded Cortés, and in his letter to the emperor Charles V he describes the city in comparison to his homeland: "the market square," where sixty thousand people a day came to buy and sell, "was twice as big as Salamanca"; the beautifully constructed "towers," as the Spaniards called the pyramids, rose higher "than the cathedral at Seville"; Montezuma's palace was "so marvelous that it seems to me to be impossible to describe its excellence and grandeur[;] . . . in Spain there is nothing to compare with it." Accustomed to the squalor and filth of their own cities, the Spaniards were dumbfounded by the cleanliness of Tenochtitlán and by all the evidence of its ordered and elegant planning.[7] Unfortunately their amazement was not matched by an ability to maintain the city's splendor. Very shortly after the Spanish conquered the city in 1521 (see page 474), disease killed off most of its residents, much of its treasure was shipped back to Spain, and its temples and palaces were demolished.

The Incas

☐ What were the sources of strength and prosperity, and of problems, for the Incas as they created their enormous empire?

In the center of Peru rise the cold highlands of the Andes. Six valleys of fertile and wooded land at altitudes ranging from eight thousand to eleven thousand feet punctuate highland Peru. The largest of these valleys are the Huaylas, Cuzco, and Titicaca. It was there that Inca civilization developed and flourished. Like the Aztecs, the Incas started as a small militaristic group. But they grew in numbers and power as they conquered surrounding groups, eventually establishing one of the most extraordinary empires in the world. Gradually, Inca culture spread throughout Peru.

• **Moche** A Native American culture that thrived along Peru's northern coast between 100 and 800 C.E. The culture existed as a series of city-states and is distinguished by an extraordinarily rich and diverse pottery industry.

• **Incas** The Andean people who created a large empire that was at its peak around 1500 and was held together by an extensive system of roads.

Earlier Peruvian Cultures

Inca achievements built on those of cultures that preceded them in the Andes and on the Peruvian coast. These included the Chavin civilization (see page 304) and the **Moche** (MO-cheh) civilization, which flourished along a 250-mile stretch of Peru's northern coast between 100 and 800 C.E. Rivers that flowed out of the Andes into the valleys allowed the Moche people to develop complex irrigation systems, with which they raised food crops and cotton. Each Moche valley contained a large ceremonial center with palaces and pyramids surrounded by settlements of up to ten thousand people. Their dazzling gold and silver artifacts, elaborate headdresses, and ceramic vessels display a remarkable skill in metalwork and pottery.

Politically, Moche civilization was made up of a series of small city-states rather than one unified state, and warfare was common among them. As in Aztec culture, war provided victims for human sacrifice, frequently portrayed on Moche pottery. Beginning about 500, the Moche suffered several severe El Niños, the changes in ocean current patterns in the Pacific that bring both searing drought and flooding. Their leaders were not able to respond effectively to the devastation, and the cities lost population.

The Moche civilization was one of several that were able to carve out slightly larger empires than their predecessors, the Chavin. These newer civilizations built cities around large public plazas, with temples, palaces, and elaborate stonework. Using terraces and other means to increase the amount of arable soil, they grew potatoes and other crops, even at very high altitudes. Enough food was harvested to feed not only the farmers themselves but also massive armies, administrative bureaucracies, and thousands of industrial workers. These cultures were skilled at using fibers for a variety of purposes, including building boats to use on Lake Titicaca and hanging bridges to take humans and pack llamas across steep valleys.

Inca Imperialism and Its Religious Basis

Who were the **Incas**? *Inca* was originally the name of the governing family of a group that settled in the basin

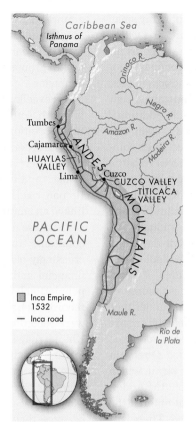

The Inca Empire, 1532

of Cuzco. From that family, the name was gradually extended to all peoples living in the Andes valleys. The Incas themselves used the word to identify their ruler or emperor. Here the term is used for both the ruler and the people. As with the Aztecs, so with the Incas: religious ideology was the force that transformed the culture, and it also created pressure for imperialist expansion.

The Incas believed their ruler descended from the sun-god and that the health and prosperity of the state depended on him. Dead rulers were thought to link the people to the sun-god. When the ruler died, his corpse was preserved as a mummy in elaborate clothing and housed in a sacred and magnificent chamber. A sixteenth-century account of the death of the emperor Pachacuti Inca (r. 1438–1471) in 1471 described the practices for burying him and honoring him after his death:

He was buried by putting his body in the earth in a large new clay urn, with him very well dressed. Pachacuti Inca [had] ordered that a golden image made to resemble him be placed on top of his tomb. And it was to be worshiped in place of him by the people who went there. . . . [He had] ordered those of his own lineage to bring this statue out for the feasts that were held in Cuzco. When they brought it out like this, they sang about the things that the Inca did in his life, both in the wars and in his city. Thus they served and revered him, changing its garments as he used to do, and serving it as he was served when he was alive.[8]

As a group, the descendants of a dead ruler managed his lands and sources of income and used the revenues to care for his mummy, maintain his cult, and support themselves. The costs of maintaining the cult were high; therefore, the next ruler had to find new sources of income through higher taxes or imperial expansion, as the account about Pachacuti Inca points out:

Word should be sent to all the land, and from all the provinces and towns they should bring again all that is necessary for the service of the new lord [the successor to Pachacuti Inca], including gold, silver, livestock, clothing, and the rest of the things needed to replenish all the storehouses that, because of his death, had been emptied for the sacrifices and things he ordered to be done.[9]

Around 1000 C.E. the Incas were one of many small groups fighting among themselves for land and water. The cult of royal mummies provided the impetus for expanding Inca power. The desire for conquest provided incentives for courageous (or ambitious) nobles: those who were victorious in battle and gained new territories for the state could expect lands, additional wives, servants, herds of llamas, gold, silver, fine clothes, and other symbols of high status. Even common soldiers who distinguished themselves in battle could be rewarded with booty and raised to noble status. The imperial interests of the emperor paralleled those of other social groups. Under Pachacuti Inca and his successors, Inca domination was gradually extended by warfare to the frontier of present-day Ecuador and Colombia in the north and to the Maule River in present-day Chile in the south, an area of about 350,000 square miles. Eighty provinces, scores of ethnic groups, and 16 million people came under Inca control. A remarkable system of roads held the empire together. Conquered peoples were forced to adopt the Inca language, which the Spanish called **Quechua** (KEH-chuh-wuh), and this was another way in which the Inca way of life was spread throughout the Andes. Before Inca civilization, each group that entered the Andes valleys had its own distinct language. These languages were not written and have become extinct. Scholars will probably never understand the linguistic condition of Peru before the fifteenth century, when Pachacuti made Quechua the official language of his people and administration. Though not written until the Spanish in Peru adopted it as a second official language, Quechua had replaced local languages by the seventeenth and eighteenth centuries and is still spoken by most Peruvians today.

Both the Aztecs and the Incas ruled very ethnically diverse peoples. Whereas the Aztecs tended to control their subject peoples through terror, the Incas governed by means of imperial unification. They imposed not only their language but also their entire panoply of gods. Magnificent temples scattered throughout the expanding empire housed images of these gods. Priests led prayers and elaborate rituals, and on such occasions as a terrible natural disaster or a great military victory, they sacrificed human beings to the gods.

Imperial unification was also achieved through the forced participation of local chieftains in the central bureaucracy and through a policy of colonization. To prevent rebellion in newly conquered territories, Pachacuti Inca and subsequent rulers transferred all the inhabitants of these territories to other parts of the empire, replacing them with workers who had lived longer under Inca rule. The rulers also drafted men from conquered territories for distant wars, breaking up kin groups that had existed in Andean society for centuries.

An excellent system of roads — averaging three feet in width, some paved and others not — facilitated the transportation of armies and the rapid communication of royal orders by runners. The roads followed straight lines wherever possible but also crossed pontoon bridges and tunneled through hills. Like Persian and Roman roads, these great feats of Inca engineering linked an empire.

On these roads, Inca officials, tax collectors, and accountants traveled throughout the empire, using increasingly elaborate khipus (see page 304) to record financial and labor obligations, the output of fields, population levels, land transfers, and other numerical records. Scholars have deciphered the way numbers were recorded on khipus, finding a base-ten system. Khipus may also have been used to record narrative history, but this theory is more speculative, as knowledge of how to read them died out after the Spanish conquest. Just as the Spanish destroyed books in Mesoamerica, they also destroyed khipus in the Andes because they thought they might contain religious messages and encourage people to resist Spanish authority. About 750 Inca khipus survive today, more than half in museums in Europe.

Although the pressure for growth of the Inca empire continued unabated, it produced stresses. For example, open lands began to be scarce, so the Incas attempted to penetrate the tropical Amazon forest east of the Andes, an effort that led to repeated military disasters. Traditionally, the Incas waged wars with highly trained armies drawn up in massed formation and fought pitched battles on level ground, often engaging in hand-to-hand combat. But in dense jungles the troops could not maneuver or maintain order against enemies using guerrilla tactics and sniping at them with deadly blowguns. Another source of stress was revolts among subject peoples in conquered territories. Even the system of roads and message-carrying runners couldn't keep up with the administrative needs of the empire. The average runner could cover about 50 leagues, or 175 miles, per day — a remarkable feat of physical endurance, especially at a high altitude — but the larger the empire became, the greater the distances to be covered. The roundtrip from the capital at Cuzco to Quito in Ecuador, for example, took from ten to twelve days, so that an emperor might have to base urgent decisions on incomplete or out-of-date information. The empire was overextended.

When the Inca Huayna Capac died in 1525, his throne was bitterly contested by two of his sons,

• Quechua First deemed the official language of the Incas under Pachacuti, it is still spoken by most Peruvians today.

Machu Picchu The Inca city of Machu Picchu, surrounded by mountains in the clouds, clings to a spectacular crag in upland Peru. It was built around 1450, when the Inca Empire was at its height, and abandoned about a century later. (Will McIntyre/Photo Researchers, Inc.)

The Clan-Based Structure of Inca Society

Huascar and Atahualpa. Huascar's threat to do away with the cult of royal mummies led the nobles — who often benefited from managing land and wealth for a deceased ruler — to throw their support behind Atahualpa. In the civil war that began in 1532, Atahualpa's veteran warriors easily defeated Huascar's green recruits, but the conflict weakened the Incas. On his way to his coronation at Cuzco, Atahualpa encountered Pizarro and 168 Spaniards who had recently entered the kingdom. The Spaniards quickly became the real victors in the Inca kingdom (see pages 475–476).

The *ayllu* (EYE-yoo), or clan, served as the fundamental social unit of Inca society. All members of the ayllu owed allegiance to the *curacas*, or clan leaders, who conducted relations with outsiders. The ayllu held specific lands granted by village or provincial authorities on a long-term basis, and individual families tended to work the same plots for generations. Cooperation in the cultivation of the land and intermarriage among members of the ayllu wove people into a tight web of connections. (See "Listening to the Past: Felipe Guaman Poma de Ayala, *The First New Chronicle and Good Government*," page 324.)

Listening to the Past

Felipe Guaman Poma de Ayala, *The First New Chronicle and Good Government*

According to his own self-description, Felipe Guaman Poma de Ayala (1550?–1620?) was a member of an indigenous noble family in Peru. His native language was Quechua, but he was baptized as a Christian, learned to read and write Spanish, and served as an assistant to a Spanish friar and a Spanish judge. He saw and experienced firsthand the abuses of the Spanish authorities in what had been the Inca Empire. In the early seventeenth century he began writing and illustrating what became his masterpiece, a handwritten book of almost eight hundred pages of text and nearly four hundred line drawings addressed to the king of Spain that related the history of the Inca Empire and the realities of Spanish rule. Finishing in about 1615, he hoped to send the book to Spain, where it would convince the king to make reforms that would bring about the "good government" of the book's title. (The book apparently never reached the king, though it did make it to Europe. It was discovered in the Danish Royal Library in Copenhagen in 1908; how it got there is unknown.) Guaman Poma's descriptions of Inca life before the conquest are shaped by his purpose, but they also portray some important aspects of Andean culture that appear from other sources to have been quite accurate. In the following section, Guaman Poma sets out certain traditional age-group categories of Inca society, which he terms "paths," ten for men and ten for women. Through these, he gives us a glimpse of Inca values and every-day activities, and suggests that this orderly structure underlay Inca power.

❝The first path was that of the brave men, the soldiers of war. They were thirty-three years of age (they entered this path as young as twenty-five, and left it at fifty). These brave men were held very much apart and distinguished in every manner possible. The Inca [the Inca ruler] selected some of these Indians to serve in his battles and wars. He selected some from among these brave Indians to settle as *mitmacs* (foreigners) in other provinces, giving them more than enough land, both pasture and cropland, to multiply, and giving each of them a woman from the same land. He did this to keep his kingdom secure; they served as overseers. He selected some of these brave Indians to serve as plowmen and as skilled workers in every task that was necessary for the Inca and the other lords, princes, noblemen, and ladies of this kingdom; those selected in this way were called *mitmac* (foreigners). Others of these

brave men were selected to work in the mines and for other labor, toil, and obligations. . . .

The Fifth Path was that of the *sayapayac* [those who stand upright]. These were the Indians of the watch, aged from eighteen to twenty years. They served as messenger boys between one pueblo and another, and to other nearby places in the valley. They also herded flocks, and accompanied the Indians of war and the great lords and captains. They also carried food. . . .

The Eighth Path was that of boys aged from five to nine years. These were the "boys who play" (*puellacoc wamracuna*). They served their mothers and fathers in whatever ways they could, and bore many whippings and thumpings; they also served by playing with the toddlers and by rocking and watching over the babies in cradles. . . .

The Tenth Path was that of those called *wawa quirawpi cac* (newborn babies at the breast, in cradles), from the age of one month. It is right for others to serve them; their mothers must necessarily serve them for no other person can give milk to these children. . . .

The First Path was that of the married women and widows called *auca camayocpa warmin* [the warriors' women], whose occupation is weaving fine cloth for the Inca, the other lords, the captains, and the soldiers. They were thirty-three years of age when they married; up until then, they remained virgins and maidens. . . . These wives of brave men were not free [from tribute obligations]. These women had the occupation of weaving fine *awasca* cloth and spinning yarn; they assisted the commons in their pueblos and provinces, and they assisted with everything their titled noble lords decreed. . . .

The Sixth Path was that of those called *coro tasquicunas*, *rotusca tasqui*, which means "young girls with short-cropped hair." They were from twelve to eighteen years of age and served their fathers, mothers, and grandmothers. They also began to serve the great ladies so that they could learn to spin yarn and weave delicate materials. They served as animal herders and workers in the fields, and in making *chica* [corn beer] for their fathers and mothers, and they assisted in other occupations insofar as they could, helping out . . . they were filled with obedience and respect, and were taught to cook, spin, and weave. Their hair was kept cropped until they reached the age of thirty, when they were married and given the dowry of their destitution and poverty.

The Seventh Path was that of the girls called flower pickers. . . . They picked flowers to dye wool for *cumpis*, cloth, and other things, and they picked the edible herbs mentioned above, which they dried out and stored in the warehouse to be

CAPÍ PRIME CALLE VECI:GEÑE
AVCACAMAIOC

PRIMERA CALLE
AVACOCVARMI

• Guaman Poma's line drawings show a man and woman on the "first path," the man a warrior holding an obsidian blade in one hand and the severed head of an enemy in the other, and the woman weaving fine cloth on a back-strap loom. (Nick Saunders/Barbara Heller Photo Library, London/Art Resource, NY)

eaten the following year. These girls were from nine to twelve years of age. . . .

The Ninth Path was that of the girls aged one and two, who were called *llucac warmi wawa* ("young girls who crawl"). They do nothing; instead, others serve them. Better said, they ought to be served by their mothers, who should be exempt [from tribute] because of the work of raising their children. Their mothers have to walk around carrying them, and never let go of their hands. 99

Source: Felipe Guaman Poma de Ayala, *The First New Chronicle and Good Government*, selected, translated and annotated by David Frye, pp. 70, 72, 74, 75, 77, 80, 81, 82. Copyright © 2006 by Hackett Publishing Company, Inc. Reprinted by permission of Hackett Publishing Company, Inc. All rights reserved.

QUESTIONS FOR ANALYSIS

1. The "first path" among both men and women is the one with the highest status. Judging by the way Guaman Poma describes these, what do the Incas especially value? How do his descriptions of other paths support your conclusions about this?

2. In what ways are the paths set out for boys and men different from those for girls and women? In what ways are they similar? What does this suggest about Inca society?

3. Guaman Poma wrote this about eighty years after the Spanish conquest of Peru. How does the date and the colonial setting affect our evaluation of this work as a source?

In return for the land, every family had to provide crops for the Inca nobles, bureaucracy, and religious personnel, and also send a person to work a certain number of days per year at other tasks. These included providing military service; building and maintaining palaces, temples, roads, and irrigation systems; terracing and irrigating new arable land; acting as runners on the post roads; weaving and dying cotton cloth; and excavating imperial gold, silver, and copper mines. This labor tax, called the *mit'a* (MEE-tuh), was rotated among households in an ayllu throughout the year, and it was similar to the labor obligations required of peasant families in Europe. The government also made an ayllu responsible for maintaining state-owned granaries, which distributed grain in times of shortage and famine, and supplied assistance in natural disasters.

As the Inca Empire expanded, it imposed this pattern of social and labor organization on newly conquered indigenous peoples. After the conquest, the Spaniards adopted the Incas' ways of organizing their economy and administration, just as the Incas (and, in Mesoamerica, the Aztecs) had built on earlier cultures.

The state required everyone to marry and even decided when and sometimes whom a person should marry. Women married in their late teens, men when they were a little older. The marriage ceremony consisted of the joining of hands and the exchange of a pair of sandals. This ritual was followed by a large wedding feast at which the state presented the bride and groom with two sets of clothing, one for everyday wear and the other for festive occasions. Sometimes, marriage was used as a symbol of conquest; Inca rulers and nobles married the daughters of elite families among the peoples they conquered. Very high-ranking Inca men sometimes had many wives, but marriage among common people was generally monogamous.

An Inca Cape Inca artisans could produce gorgeous textiles, and on ceremonial occasions nobles proudly paraded in brightly colored feathers or in garments made of luxurious alpaca wool. This exquisite cape is fashioned from the feathers of a blue and yellow macaw; the pattern, befitting aristocratic tastes, features lordly pelicans carried on litters by less exalted birds. (The Textile Museum, Washington, D.C., 91.395. Acquired by George Hewitt Myers in 1941)

The backbreaking labor of ordinary people in the fields and mines made possible the luxurious lifestyle of the great Inca nobility. The nobles — called *orejones,* or "big ears," by the Spanish because they pierced their ears and distended the lobes with heavy jewelry — were the ruling Inca's kinsmen. Lesser nobles included the curacas, royal household servants, public officials, and religious leaders.

In the fifteenth century Inca rulers ordered that allegiance be paid to the ruler at Cuzco rather than to the curacas, and they relocated the entire populations of certain regions and disrupted clan groups, which led to resentment. As the empire expanded, there arose a noble class of warriors, governors, and local officials whose support the ruling Inca secured with gifts of land, precious metals, and llamas and alpacas (llamas were used as beasts of burden; alpacas were raised for their long, fine wool). The nobility was exempt from agricultural work and from other kinds of public service.

CONNECTIONS

Research on all the cultures discussed in this chapter is providing new information every year, provoking vigorous debates among scholars. Archaeologists are discovering new objects and reinterpreting the sites where they were found; historians are learning to better read indigenous writing systems; biologists are using more complex procedures to study genetic linkages; anthropologists are integrating information from oral histories and preserved traditions, and scholars in other disciplines are using both traditional and new methods to expand their understanding. In no other chapter of this book are the basic outlines of what most people agree happened changing as fast as they are for the Americas. Together the various fields of study have produced a history of the Western Hemisphere in the centuries before 1500 that looks more like the history of the Eastern Hemisphere than it did twenty years ago. We now know that there were large, settled agricultural communities in many parts of North and South America that traded ideas and goods with one another, and that the empires of Mesoamerica and the Andes were as rich and powerful as any in Asia, Africa, or Europe.

The parallel paths of the two hemispheres were radically changed by Columbus's arrival and the events that followed, however. The greater availability of metals, especially iron, in the Eastern Hemisphere meant that the military technology of the Europeans who came to the Western Hemisphere was more deadly than anything indigenous peoples had developed. Even more deadly, however, were the germs Europeans brought with them, from which the people of the Western Hemisphere died in astounding numbers. In some cases one or two indigenous people who had made contact with Europeans would spread disease throughout the native population. As a result, when Europeans arrived in the home areas of these people they would find deserted villages with only a few residents. Often, they could not imagine how so few people could have built huge earth mounds or massive stone works. Therefore, they speculated that that these structures must have been built by wandering Egyptians or Israelites, a tribe of giants, or (in the early twentieth century) space aliens, giving rise to myths that have been slow to die.

□ CHAPTER REVIEW

□ How did early peoples in the Americas adapt to their environment as they created technologies of food production and economic systems? (p. 300)

The environment shaped the history of human settlements in the Americas, but later history shaped the way the lands and peoples of these areas have been described. Early peoples crossed into the Western Hemisphere from Asia, although exactly when this happened is hotly debated. All the highly varied environments, from polar tundra to tropical rain forests, came to support human settlement. About 8000 B.C.E., people in some parts of the Americas began raising crops as well as gathering wild produce. Maize became the most important crop, with knowledge about its cultivation spreading from Mesoamerica into North and South America.

□ What physical, social, and intellectual features characterized early societies in the Americas? (p. 304)

Agricultural advancement led to an increase in population, which allowed greater concentrations of people and the creation of the first urban societies. In certain parts of North and South America, towns dependent on agriculture flourished. Some groups in North America began to build large earthwork mounds, while others in Mesoamerica and South America practiced irrigation. The Olmecs created the first society with cities in Mesoamerica, with large ceremonial buildings, an elaborate calendar, and a symbolic writing.

□ How did Mesoamerican and North American peoples develop prosperous and stable societies in the classical era? (p. 306)

The urban culture of the Olmecs and other Mesoamerican peoples influenced subsequent societies. Especially in what became known as the classical era (300–900 C.E.), various groups developed large states centered on cities, with high levels of technological and intellectual achievement. Of these, the Maya were the longest-lasting, creating a complex written language, multiple-crop milpas and raised beds for agriculture, roads connecting population centers, trading practices that built unity among Maya communities as well as wealth, and striking art. Peoples living in North America built communities that were smaller than those in Mesoamerica, but many also used irrigation techniques to enhance agricultural production and continued to build earthwork mounds for religious purposes.

□ How did the Aztecs both build on the achievements of earlier Mesoamerican cultures and develop new traditions to create their large empire? (p. 313)

The Aztecs, also known as the Mexica, built a unified culture based heavily on the heritage of earlier Mesoamerican societies and distinguished by achievements in engineering, sculpture, and architecture, including the streets, canals, public squares, and aqueduct of Tenochtitlán, the most spectacular and one of the largest cities in the world in 1500. In Mexica society, religion was the dynamic factor that transformed other aspects of the culture: economic security, social mobility, education, and especially war. War was an article of religious faith, providing riches and land, sacrificial victims for ceremonies honoring the Aztec gods, warriors for imperial expansion, and laborers. Aztec society was hierarchical, with nobles and priests having special privileges.

□ What were the sources of strength and prosperity, and of problems, for the Incas as they created their enormous empire? (p. 320)

Inca achievements built on those of cultures that preceded theirs in the Andes, including the Moche and Chavin civilizations. Moche, Chavin, and Inca cultures made their home in the valleys along the Peruvian coast and in the Andean highlands, cultivating food crops and cotton. The Incas, who began as a small militaristic group, eventually created the largest empire in South America and conquered surrounding groups. The Incas' far-flung empire stretched along the Andes, kept together through a system of roads, along which moved armies and administrators. The Incas achieved imperial unification by imposing their gods on conquered peoples, forcing local chieftains to participate in the central bureaucracy, and pursuing a policy of colonization. The imperial expansion that increased the Incas' strength also caused stress. Andean society was dominated by clan groups, and Inca measures to disrupt these groups and move people great distances created resentment.

SUGGESTED READING

Carassco, David, and Scott Sessions. *Daily Life of the Aztecs: People of the Sun and Earth.* 2008. An overview of Aztec culture designed for general readers.

Clendinnen, Inga. *Aztecs: An Interpretation.* 1992. Pays particular attention to the role that rituals and human sacrifice played in Aztec culture.

Coe, Michael D. *The Maya.* 2005. A new edition of a classic survey that incorporates the most recent scholarship.

Conrad, G. W., and A. A. Demarest. *Religion and Empire: The Dynamics of Aztec and Inca Expansionism.* 1993. Compares the two largest American empires.

D'Altroy, Terence. *The Incas.* 2003. Examines the ways in which the Incas drew on earlier traditions to create their empire; by a leading scholar.

Freidel, David. *A Forest of Kings: The Untold Story of the Ancient Maya.* 1990. A splendidly illustrated work providing expert treatment of the Maya world.

Kehoe, Alice Beck. *America Before the European Invasion.* 2002. An excellent survey of North America before the coming of the Europeans, by an eminent anthropologist.

Knight, Alan. *Mexico: From the Beginnings to the Spanish Conquest.* 2002. Provides information on many Mesoamerican societies.

León-Portilla, Miguel. *The Aztec Image of Self and Society: An Introduction to Nahua Culture.* 1992. The best appreciation of Aztec religious ritual and symbolism.

Mann, Charles C. *1491: New Revelations of the Americas Before Columbus.* 2005. A thoroughly researched overview of all the newest scholarship, written for a general audience.

Milner, George R. *The Moundbuilders: Ancient Peoples of Eastern North America.* 2005. Beautifully illustrated book that discusses the mounds and the societies that built them; could also be used as a tourist guide.

Wright, Ronald. *Time Among the Maya: Travels in Belize, Guatemala, and Mexico.* 1989. A highly readable account of Maya agricultural and religious calendars and their influence on modern Maya culture.

NOTES

1. Florentine Codex, Book 2, trans. John M. Curl, author of *Ancient American Poets.* Reprinted by permission.
2. "Maya Writing," Authentic Maya, http://www.authenticmaya.com/maya_writing.htm.
3. Fray Diego Durán, *Mexicas: The History of the Indies of New Spain,* trans. with notes, by Doris Heyden and Fernand Horcasitas (New York: Orion Press, 1964), p. 203. Copyright © 1994 by the University of Oklahoma Press. Reprinted with permission of the publisher.
4. Quoted in J. Soustelle, *Daily Life of the Aztecs on the Eve of the Spanish Conquest,* trans. P. O'Brian (Stanford, Calif.: Stanford University Press, 1970), p. 89.
5. Bernal Díaz, *The Conquest of New Spain,* trans. J. M. Cohen (New York: Penguin Books, 1978), p. 214.
6. Quoted in J. H. Perry, *The Discovery of South America* (New York: Taplinger, 1979), pp. 161–163.
7. Quoted in Inga Clendinnen, *Aztecs: An Interpretation* (New York: Cambridge University Press, 1992), pp. 16–17.
8. *Narrative of the Incas by Juan de Betanzos,* trans. and ed. Roland Hamilton and Dana Buchanan from the Palma de Mallorca manuscript, p. 138. Copyright © 1996. By permission of the University of Texas Press.
9. Ibid.

• **Mongol Woman** Women played influential roles among the Mongols. The Mongol woman portrayed in this painting is Chabi, wife of Khubilai Khan. Like other Mongols, she maintained Mongol dress even though she spent much of her time in China. (National Palace Museum, Taipei, Taiwan)

12

The large expanse of Asia treated in this chapter underwent profound changes during the centuries examined here. The north saw the rise of nomadic pastoral societies, first the Turks, then more spectacularly the Mongols. The nomads' mastery of the horse and mounted warfare gave them a military advantage that agricultural societies could rarely match. From the fifth century on, groups of Turks appeared along the fringes of the settled societies of Eurasia, from China and Korea to India and Persia. Often Turks were recruited as auxiliary soldiers; sometimes they gained the upper hand. By the tenth century many were converting to Islam.

Cultural Exchange in Central and Southern Asia
to 1400

Much more dramatic was the rise of the Mongols under the charismatic leadership of Chinggis Khan in the late twelfth and early thirteenth centuries. A military genius, with a relatively small army Chinggis subdued one society after another from Byzantium to the Pacific. For a century Mongol hegemony fostered unprecedented East-West trade and contact. More Europeans made their way east than ever before, and Chinese inventions such as printing and the compass made their way west.

Over the course of several centuries Arab and Turkish armies brought Islam to India, but the Mongols never gained power there. In the Indian subcontinent during these centuries, regional cultures flourished. Although Buddhism declined, Hinduism continued to flourish. India continued to be the center of a very active seaborne trade, and this trade helped carry Indian ideas and practices to Southeast Asia. Buddhism was adopted in much of Southeast Asia, along with other ideas and techniques from India. The maritime trade in spices and other goods brought increased contact with the outside world to all but the most isolated of islands in the Pacific. •

Central Asian Nomads

☐ What aspects of nomadic life gave the nomads of Central Asia military advantages over nearby settled civilizations?

Chinggis Khan and the Mongol Empire

☐ How did Chinggis Khan and his successors conquer much of Eurasia, and how did the Mongol conquests change the regions affected?

East-West Communication During the Mongol Era

☐ How did the Mongol conquests facilitate the spread of ideas, religions, inventions, and diseases?

India, Islam, and the Development of Regional Cultures, 300–1400

☐ What was the result of India's encounters with Turks, Mongols, and Islam?

Southeast Asia, the Pacific Islands, and the Growth of Maritime Trade

☐ How did states develop along the maritime trade routes of Southeast Asia and beyond?

Manichean Priests Many religions spread through Central Asia before it became predominantly Muslim after 1300. This fragment of a tenth- to twelfth-century illustrated document, found at the Silk Road city of Turfan, is written in the Uighur language and depicts Manichean priests. (Archives Charmet/The Bridgeman Art Library)

Central Asian Nomads

☐ What aspects of nomadic life gave the nomads of Central Asia military advantages over nearby settled civilizations?

One experience Rome, Persia, India, and China all shared was conflict with **nomads** who came from the very broad region referred to as Central Asia. This region was dominated by the **steppe**, arid grasslands that stretched from modern Hungary, through southern Russia and across Central Asia (today's Tajikistan, Turkmenistan, Kazakhstan, Kyrgyzstan, and Uzbekistan) and adjacent parts of China, to Mongolia and parts of today's northeast China. Initially small in number, the nomadic peoples of this region would use their military superiority to conquer first other nomads, then the settled societies they encountered. In the process, they created settled empires of their own that drew on the cultures they absorbed.

Nomadic Society

Easily crossed by horses but too dry for crop agriculture, the grasslands could support only a thin population of nomadic herders who lived off their flocks of sheep, goats, camels, horses, or other animals. Following the seasons, they would break camp at least twice a year and move their animals to new pastures, going north in the spring and south in the fall.

In their search for water and good pastures, nomadic groups often came into conflict with other nomadic groups pursuing the same resources, which the two would then fight over, as there was normally no higher political authority able to settle disputes. Groups on the losing end, especially if they were small, faced the threat of extermination or slavery, which prompted them to make alliances with other groups or move far away. Groups on the winning end of intertribal conflicts could exact tribute from those they defeated, sometimes so much that they could devote themselves entirely to war, leaving the work of tending herds to their slaves and vassals.

To get the products of nearby agricultural societies, especially grain, woven textiles, iron, tea, and wood, nomadic herders would trade their own products, such as horses and furs. When trade was difficult, they would turn to raiding to seize what they needed. Much of the time nomadic herders raided other nomads, but nearby agricultural settlements were common targets as well. The nomads' skill as horsemen and archers made it difficult for farmers and townsmen to defend against them. It was largely to defend against the raids of the Xiongnu nomads, for example, that the Chinese built the Great Wall.

Political organization among nomadic herders was generally very simple. Clans—members of an extended family—had chiefs, as did tribes (coalitions of clans). Leadership within a group was based on military prowess and was often settled by fighting. Occasionally a charismatic leader would emerge who was able to extend alliances to form confederations of tribes. From the point of view of the settled societies, which have left most of the records about these nomadic groups, large confederations were much more of a threat, since they could plan coordinated attacks on cities and towns. Large confederations rarely lasted more than a century or so, however, and when they broke up, tribes again spent much of their time fighting with each other, relieving some of the pressure on their settled neighbors.

The three most wide-ranging and successful confederations were those of the Xiongnu—Huns, as they were known in the West—who emerged in the third century B.C.E. in the area near China; the Turks, who had their origins in the same area in the fourth and fifth centuries C.E.; and the Mongols, who did not become important until the late twelfth century. In all three cases, the entire steppe region was eventually swept up in the movement of peoples and armies.

The Turks

The Turks were the first of the Inner Asian peoples to have left a written record in their own language; the earliest Turkish documents date from the eighth century. Turkic languages may have already been spoken

□ CHRONOLOGY

ca. 320–480	Gupta Empire in India
ca. 380–450	Life of India's greatest poet, Kalidasa
ca. 450	White Huns invade northern India
ca. 500	Srivijaya gains control of Strait of Malacca
ca. 500–1400	India's medieval age; caste system reaches its mature form
552	Turks rebel against Rouruan and rise to power in Central Asia
ca. 780	Borobudur temple complex begun in Srivijaya
802–1432	Khmer Empire of Cambodia
ca. 850–1250	Kingdom of the Uighurs
1030	Turks control north India
ca. 1100–1200	Buddhism declines in India
ca. 1200–1300	Easter Island society's most prosperous period
1206	Temujin proclaimed Chinggis Khan; Mongol language recorded; Delhi sultanate established
ca. 1240	*The Secret History of the Mongols*
1276	Mongol conquest of Song China
ca. 1300	Plague spreads throughout Mongol Empire
1398	Timur takes control of the Delhi sultanate

in dispersed areas of the Eurasian steppe when the Turks first appeared; today these languages are spoken by the Uighurs in western China; the Uzbeks, Kazakhs, Kyrghiz, and Turkmens of Central Asia; and the Turks of modern Turkey. The original religion of the Turks was shamanistic and involved worship of Heaven, making it similar to the religions of many other groups in the steppe region.

In 552 a group called Turks who specialized in metalworking rebelled against their overlords, the Rouruan, whose empire dominated the region from the eastern Silk Road cities of Central Asia through Mongolia. The Turks quickly supplanted the Rouruan as overlords of the Silk Road in the east. When the first Turkish khagan (ruler) died a few years later, the Turkish empire was divided between his younger brother, who took the western part (modern Central Asia), and

- **nomads** Groups of people who move from place to place in search of food, water, and pasture for their animals, usually following the seasons.
- **steppe** Grasslands that are too dry for crops but support pasturing animals; they are common across much of the center of Eurasia.

• **333**

his son, who took the eastern part (modern Mongolia). Sogdians — who were influential merchants along the Silk Road — convinced them to send a delegation to both the Persian (see Chapter 9) and the Byzantine courts (see Chapter 8). Repeated diplomatic overtures in both directions did not prevent hostilities, however, and in 576 the Western Turks captured the Byzantine city of Bosporus in the Crimea.

The Eastern Turks frequently raided China and just as often fought among themselves. The Chinese history of the Sui Dynasty records that "The Turks prefer to destroy each other rather than to live side-by-side. They have a thousand, nay ten thousand clans who are hostile to and kill one another. They mourn their dead with much grief and swear vengeance."[1] In the early seventh century the empire of the Eastern Turks ran up against the growing military might of the Tang Dynasty in China and soon broke apart.

In the eighth century a Turkic people called the Uighurs formed a new empire based in Mongolia that survived about a century. It had close ties to Tang China, providing military aid but also extracting large payments in silk. During this period many Uighurs adopted religions then current along the Silk Road, notably Buddhism, Nestorian Christianity, and Manichaeism. In the ninth century this Uighur empire was destroyed by another Turkic people from north of Mongolia called the Kyrghiz (KIHR-guhz). Some fled to what is now western China. Setting up their capital city in Kucha, these Uighurs created a remarkably stable and prosperous kingdom that lasted four centuries (ca. 850–1250). Because of the dry climate of the region, many buildings, wall paintings, and manuscripts written in a variety of languages have been preserved from this era. They reveal a complex urban civilization in which Buddhism, Manichaeism, and Christianity existed side by side, practiced by Turks as well as by Tokharians, Sogdians, and other Iranian peoples.

Farther west in Central Asia other groups of Turks, such as the Karakhanids, Ghaznavids, and Seljuks, rose to prominence. Often local Muslim forces would try to capture them, employ them as slave soldiers, and convert them. By the mid- to late tenth century many were serving in the Islamic Abbasid armies. Also in the tenth century Central Asian Turks began converting to Islam (which protected them from being abducted as slaves). Then they took to raiding unconverted Turks.

In the mid-eleventh century the Turks had gained the upper hand in the caliphate, and the caliphs became little more than figureheads. From there Turkish power was extended into Syria, Palestine, and Asia Minor. (Asia Minor is now called Turkey because Turks mi-

grated there by the thousands over several centuries.) In 1071 Seljuk Turks inflicted a devastating defeat on the Byzantine army in eastern Anatolia (see page 244). Other Turkish confederations established themselves in Afghanistan and extended their control into north India (see page 352).

In India, Persia, and Anatolia, the formidable military skills of nomadic Turkish warriors made it possible for them to become overlords of settled societies. By the end of the thirteenth century nomad power prevailed through much of Eurasia. Just as the Uighurs developed a hybrid urban culture along the eastern end of the Silk Road, adopting many elements from the mercantile Sogdians, the Turks of Central and West Asia created an Islamic culture that drew from both Turkish and Iranian sources. Often Persian was used as the administrative language of the states they formed. Nevertheless, despite the presence of Turkish overlords all along the southern fringe of the steppe, no one group of Turks was able to unite them all into a single political unit. That feat had to wait for the next major power on the steppe, the Mongols.

The Mongols

In the twelfth century ambitious Mongols did not aspire to match the Turks or other groups that had migrated west, but rather wanted to be successors to the Khitans and Jurchens, nomadic groups that had stayed in the east and mastered ways to extract resources from China, the largest and richest country in the region. In the tenth and eleventh centuries the Khitans had accomplished this; in the twelfth century the Jurchens had overthrown the Khitans and extended their reach even deeper into China. The Khitans and Jurchens formed hybrid nomadic-urban states, with northern sections where tribesmen continued to live in the traditional way and southern sections politically controlled by the non-Chinese rulers but settled largely by taxpaying Chinese. The Khitans and Jurchens had scripts created to record their languages and adopted many Chinese governing practices. They built cities in pastoral areas that served as trading centers and places to enjoy their newly acquired wealth. In both cases, their elite became culturally dual, adept in Chinese ways as well as in their own traditions.

The Mongols lived north of these hybrid nomadic-settled societies and maintained their traditional ways. Chinese, Persian, and European observers have all left descriptions of the daily life of the Mongols, which they found strikingly different from their own. The daily life of the peasants of China, India, Vietnam, and Japan, all tied to the soil, had much more in common with each other than with the Mongol pastoralists. Before considering the military conquests of the Mongols, it is useful to look more closely at their way of life.

• **yurts** Tents in which the pastoral nomads lived; they could be quickly dismantled and loaded onto animals or carts.

Mongol Daily Life

Before their great conquests the Mongols, like other steppe nomads, did not have cities, towns, or villages. Rather, they moved with their animals between winter and summer pastures. To make their settlements portable, the Mongols lived in tents called **yurts** rather than in houses. The yurts, about twelve to fifteen feet in diameter, were constructed of light wooden frames covered by layers of wool felt, greased to make them waterproof. Yurts were round, since this shape held up better against the strong winds that blew across the treeless grasslands. They could be dismantled and loaded onto pack animals or carts in a short time. The floor of a yurt was covered first with dried grass or straw, then with felt, skins, or rugs. In the center, directly under the smoke hole, was the hearth. The master's bed was on the north. Goat horns attached to the frame of the yurt were used as hooks to hang joints of meat, cooking utensils, bows, quivers of arrows, and the like. A group of families traveling together would set up their yurts in a circle open to the south and draw up their wagons in a circle around the yurts for protection.

Because the steppe was too cold and dry for agriculture, the Mongol diet consisted mostly of animal products. Without granaries to store food, the Mongols' survival was endangered when weather or diseases of their animals threatened their food supply. The most common meat was mutton, supplemented with wild game. When grain or vegetables could be obtained through trade, they were added to the diet. Wood was scarce, so dried animal dung or grasses fueled the cook fires.

The Mongols milked sheep, goats, cows, and horses and made cheese and fermented alcoholic drinks from the milk. A European visitor to Mongolia in the 1250s described how they milked mares, a practice unfamiliar to Europeans:

> They fasten a long line to two posts standing firmly in the ground, and to the line they tie the young colts of the mares which they mean to milk. Then come the mothers who stand by their foals, and allow themselves to be milked. And if any of them be too unruly, then one takes her colt and puts it under her, letting it suck a while, and presently taking it away again, and the milker takes its place.[2]

He also described how they made the alcoholic drink koumiss from the milk, a drink that "goes down very pleasantly, intoxicating weak brains."[3]

Because of the intense cold of the winter, the Mongols made much use of furs and skins for clothing. Both men and women usually wore silk trousers and tunics (the silk obtained from China). Over these they wore robes of fur, for the very coldest times in two layers — an inner layer with the hair on the inside and an outer layer with the hair on the outside. Hats were of felt or fur, boots of felt or leather. Men wore leather belts to which their bows and quivers could be attached. Women of high rank wore elaborate headdresses decorated with feathers.

Mongol Yurt A Chinese artist in the thirteenth or fourteenth century captured the essential features of a Mongol yurt to illustrate the story of a Chinese woman who married a nomad. (Image © The Metropolitan Museum of Art/Art Resource, NY)

Mongol women had to work very hard and had to be able to care for the animals when the men were away hunting or fighting. They normally drove the carts and set up and dismantled the yurts. They also milked the sheep, goats, and cows and made the butter and cheese. In addition, they made the felt, prepared the skins, and sewed the clothes. Because water was scarce, clothes were not washed with water, nor were dishes. Women, like men, had to be expert riders, and many also learned to shoot. They participated actively in family decisions, especially as wives and mothers. In *The Secret History of the Mongols*, a work written in Mongolian in about 1240, the mother and wife of the Mongol leader Chinggis Khan frequently make impassioned speeches on the importance of family loyalty. (See "Listening to the Past: The Abduction of Women in *The Secret History of the Mongols*," page 338.)

Mongol men kept as busy as the women. They made carts and wagons and the frames for the yurts. They also made harnesses for the horses and oxen, leather saddles, and the equipment needed for hunting and war, such as bows and arrows. Men also had charge of the horses, and they milked the mares. Young horses were allowed to run wild until it was time to break them in. Catching them took great skill in the use of a long springy pole with a noose at the end. One specialist among the nomads was the blacksmith, who made stirrups, knives, and other metal tools.

Kinship underlay most social relationships among the Mongols. Normally each family occupied a yurt, and groups of families camping together were usually related along the male line (brothers, uncles, nephews, and so on). More distant patrilineal relatives were recognized as members of the same clan and could call on each other for aid. People from the same clan could not marry each other, so men had to get wives from other clans. When a woman's husband died, she would be inherited by another male in the family, such as her husband's brother or his son by another woman. Tribes were groups of clans, often distantly related. Both clans and tribes had chiefs who would make decisions on where to graze and when to retaliate against another tribe that had stolen animals or people. Women were sometimes abducted for brides. When tribes stole men from each other, they normally made them into slaves, and slaves were forced to do much of the heavy work. They would not necessarily remain slaves their entire lives, however, as their original tribes might be able to recapture them or make exchanges for them, or their masters might free them.

Even though population was sparse in the regions where the Mongols lived, conflict over resources was endemic, and each camp had to be on the alert for

attacks. Defending against attacks and retaliating against raids was as much a part of the Mongols' daily life as caring for their herds and trading with nearby settlements.

Mongol children learned to ride at a young age, first on goats. The horses they later rode were short and stocky, almost like ponies, but nimble and able to endure long journeys and bitter cold. Even in the winter the horses survived by grazing, foraging beneath the snow. The prime weapon boys had to learn to use was the compound bow, which had a pull of about 160 pounds and a range of more than 200 yards, well suited for using on horseback, giving Mongol soldiers an advantage in battle. Other commonly used weapons were small battle-axes and lances fitted with hooks to pull enemies off their saddles.

From their teenage years Mongol men participated in battles, and among the Mongols courage in battle was essential to male self-esteem. Hunting was a common form of military training. Each year tribes would organize one big hunt; mounted hunters would form a vast ring perhaps ten or more miles in circumference, then gradually shrink it down, trapping all the animals before killing them. On military campaigns a Mongol soldier had to be able to ride for days without stopping to cook food; he ate from a supply of dried milk curd and cured meat, which could be supplemented by blood let from the neck of his horse. When time permitted, the soldiers would pause to hunt, adding dogs, wolves, foxes, mice, and rats to their food.

As with the Turks and other steppe nomads, religious practices centered around the shaman, a religious expert believed to be able to communicate with the gods. The high god of the Mongols was Heaven/Sky, but they recognized many other gods as well. Some groups of Mongols, especially those closer to settled communities, converted to Buddhism, Nestorian Christianity, or Manichaeism.

Chinggis Khan and the Mongol Empire

☐ How did Chinggis Khan and his successors conquer much of Eurasia, and how did the Mongol conquests change the regions affected?

In the mid-twelfth century the Mongols were just one of many peoples in the eastern grasslands, neither particularly numerous nor especially advanced. Why then did the Mongols suddenly emerge as an overpowering force on the historical stage? One explanation is ecological. A drop in the mean annual temperature created a subsistence crisis. As pastures shrank, the Mon-

• **Chinggis Khan** The title given to the Mongol ruler Temujin in 1206 and later to his successors; it means Great Ruler.

gols and other nomads had to look beyond the steppe to get more of their food from the agricultural world. A second reason for their sudden rise was the appearance of a single individual, the brilliant but utterly ruthless Temujin (ca. 1162–1227), later and more commonly called Chinggis Khan (sometimes spelled Genghis or Ghengis).

Chinggis Khan

What we know of Temujin's early career was recorded in *The Secret History of the Mongols*, written within a few decades of his death. In Temujin's youth his father had built a modest tribal following. When Temujin's father was poisoned by a rival, his followers, not ready to follow a boy of twelve, drifted away, leaving Temujin and his mother and brothers in a vulnerable position. Temujin slowly collected followers. In 1182 Temujin was captured and carried in a cage to a rival's camp. After a daring midnight escape, he led his followers to join a stronger chieftain whom his father had once aided. With the chieftain's help, Temujin began avenging the insults he had received.

Temujin proved to be a natural leader, and as he subdued the Tartars, Kereyids, Naimans, Merkids, and other Mongol and Turkish tribes, he built up an army of loyal followers. He mastered the art of winning allies through displays of personal courage in battle and generosity to his followers. To those who opposed him, he could be merciless. He once asserted that nothing gave more pleasure than massacring one's enemies, seizing their horses and cattle, and ravishing their women. Sometimes Temujin would kill all the men in a defeated tribe to prevent later vendettas. At other times he would take them on as soldiers in his own armies. Courage impressed him. One of his leading generals, Jebe, first attracted his attention when he held his ground against overwhelming opposition and shot Temujin's horse out from under him. Another prominent general, Mukhali, became Temujin's personal slave at age twenty-seven after his tribe was defeated by Temujin in 1197. Within a few years he was leading a corps of a thousand men from his own former tribe.

In 1206, at a great gathering of tribal leaders, Temujin was proclaimed **Chinggis Khan**, or Great Ruler. Chinggis decreed that Mongol, until then an

The Tent of Chinggis Khan In this fourteenth-century Persian illustration from Rashid al-Din's *History of the World*, two guards stand outside while Chinggis is in his tent. (The Granger Collection, New York)

Listening to the Past

The Abduction of Women in
The Secret History of the Mongols

Within a few decades of Chinggis Khan's death, oral traditions concerning his rise were written down in the Mongolian language. They begin with the cycles of revenge among the tribes in Mongolia, many of which began when women were abducted for wives. These passages relate how Temujin's (Chinggis Khan's) father Yesugei seized Hogelun, Temujin's future mother, from a passing Merkid tribesman; how twenty years later three Merkids in return seized women from Temujin; and Temujin's revenge.

❝ That year Yesugei the Brave was out hunting with his falcon on the Onan. Yeke Chiledu, a nobleman of the Merkid tribe, had gone to the Olkhunugud people to find himself a wife, and he was returning to the Merkid with the girl he'd found when he passed Yesugei hunting by the river. When he saw them riding along Yesugei leaned forward on his horse. He saw it was a beautiful girl. Quickly he rode back to his tent and just as quick returned with his two brothers, Nekun Taisi and Daritai Odchigin. When Chiledu saw the three Mongols coming he whipped his dun-colored horse and rode off around a nearby hill with the three men behind him. He cut back around the far side of the hill and rode to Lady Hogelun, the girl he'd just married, who stood waiting for him at the front of their cart. "Did you see the look on the faces of those three men?" she asked him. "From their faces it looks like they mean to kill you. As long as you've got your life there'll always be girls for you to choose from. There'll always be women to ride in your cart. As long as you've got your life you'll be able to find some girl to marry. When you find her, just name her Hogelun for me, but go now and save your own life!" Then she pulled off her shirt and held it out to him, saying: "And take this to remember me, to remember my scent." Chiledu reached out from his saddle and took the shirt in his hands. With the three Mongols close behind him he struck his dun-colored horse with his whip and took off down the Onan River at full speed.

The three Mongols chased him across seven hills before turning around and returning to Hogelun's cart. Then Yesugei the Brave grasped the reins of the cart, his elder brother Nekun Taisi rode in front to guide them, and the younger brother Daritai Odchigin rode along by the wheels. As they rode her back toward their camp, Hogelun began to cry, . . . and she cried till she stirred up the waters of the Onan River, till she shook the trees in the forest and the grass in the valleys. But as the party approached their camp Daritai, riding beside her, warned her to stop: "This fellow who held you in his arms, he's already ridden over the mountains. This man who's lost you, he's crossed many rivers by now. You can call out his name, but he can't see you now even if he looks back. If you tried to find him now you won't even find his tracks. So be still now," he told her. Then Yesugei took Lady Hogelun to his tent as his wife. . . .

[Some twenty years later] one morning just before dawn Old Woman Khogaghchin, Mother Hogelun's servant, woke with a start, crying: "Mother! Mother! Get up! The ground is shaking, I hear it rumble. The Tayichigud must be riding back to attack us. Get up!"

Mother Hogelun jumped from her bed, saying: "Quick, wake my sons!" They woke Temujin and the others and all ran for the horses. Temujin, Mother Hogelun, and Khasar each took a horse. Khachigun, Temuge Odchigin, and Belgutei each took a horse. Bogorchu took one horse and Jelme another. Mother Hogelun lifted the baby Temulun onto her saddle. They saddled the last horse as a lead and there was no horse left for [Temujin's wife] Lady Borte. . . .

Old Woman Khogaghchin, who'd been left in the camp, said: "I'll hide Lady Borte." She made her get into a black covered cart. Then she harnessed the cart to a speckled ox. Whipping the ox, she drove the cart away from the camp down the Tungelig. As the first light of day hit them, soldiers rode up and told them to stop. "Who are you?" they asked her, and Old Woman Khogaghchin answered: "I'm a servant of Temujin's. I've just come from shearing his sheep. I'm on my way back to my own tent to make felt from the wool." Then they asked her: "Is Temujin at his tent? How far is it from here?" Old Woman Khogaghchin said: "As for the tent, it's not far. As for Temujin, I couldn't see whether he was there or not. I was just shearing his sheep out back." The soldiers rode off toward the camp, and Old Woman Khogaghchin whipped the ox. But as the cart moved faster its axletree snapped. "Now we'll have to run for the woods on foot," she thought, but before she could start the soldiers returned. They'd made [Temujin's half brother] Belgutei's mother their captive, and had her slung over one of their horses with her feet swinging down. They rode up to the old woman shouting: "What have you got in that cart!" "I'm just carrying wool," Khogaghchin replied, but an old soldier turned to the younger ones and said, "Get off your horses and see what's in there." When they opened the door of the cart they found Borte inside. Pulling her out, they forced Borte and Khogaghchin to ride on their horses, then they all set out after Temujin. . . .

The men who pursued Temujin were the chiefs of the three Merkid clans, Toghtoga, Dayin Usun, and Khagatai Darmala. These three had come to get their revenge, saying: "Long ago Mother Hogelun was stolen from our brother, Chiledu." When they couldn't catch Temujin they said to each other: "We've got our revenge. We've taken their wives from them," and they rode down from Mount Burkhan Khaldun back to their homes. . . .

Having finished his prayer Temujin rose and rode off with Khasar and Belgutei. They rode to [his father's sworn brother] Toghoril Ong Khan of the Kereyid camped in the Black Forest on the Tula River. Temujin spoke to Ong Khan, saying: "I was attacked by surprise by the three Merkid chiefs. They've stolen my wife from me. We've come to you now to say, 'Let my father the Khan save my wife and return her.'" . . .

[Temujin and his allies] moved their forces from Botoghan Bogorjin to the Kilgho River where they built rafts to cross over to the Bugura Steppe, into [the Merkid] Chief Toghtoga's land. They came down on him as if through the smoke-hole of his tent, beating down the frame of his tent and leaving it flat, capturing and killing his wives and his sons. They struck at his door-frame where his guardian spirit lived and broke it to pieces. They completely destroyed all his people until in their place there was nothing but emptiness. . . .

As the Merkid people tried to flee from our army running down the Selenge with what they could gather in the darkness, as our soldiers rode out of the night capturing and killing the Merkid, Temujin rode through the retreating camp shouting out: "Borte! Borte!"

Lady Borte was among the Merkid who ran in the darkness and when she heard his voice, when she recognized Temujin's voice, Borte leaped from her cart. Lady Borte and Old Woman Khogaghchin saw Temujin charge through the crowd and they ran to him, finally seizing the reins of his horse. All about them was moonlight. As Temujin looked down to see who had stopped him he recognized Lady Borte. In a moment he was down from his horse and they were in each other's arms, embracing. **"**

Source: Paul Kahn, trans., *The Secret History of the Mongols: The Origin of Chinghis Khan.* Copyright © 1984. Reprinted with permission of Paul Kahn.

QUESTIONS FOR ANALYSIS

1. What do you learn from these stories about the Mongol way of life?

2. "Marriage by capture" has been practiced in many parts of the world. Can you infer from these stories why such a system would persist? What was the impact of such practices on kinship relations?

3. Can you recognize traces of the oral origins of these stories?

Chinggis and his wife Borte are seated together at a feast in this fourteenth-century Persian illustration. (Bibliothèque nationale de France/The Bridgeman Art Library)

unwritten language, be written down in the script used by the Uighur Turks. With this script a record was made of the Mongol laws and customs, ranging from the rules for the annual hunt to punishments of death for robbery and adultery. Another measure adopted at this assembly was a postal relay system to send messages rapidly by mounted courier, suggesting that Chinggis already had ambitions to rule a vast empire.

With the tribes of Mongolia united, the energies previously devoted to infighting and vendettas were redirected to exacting tribute from the settled populations nearby, starting with the Jurchen (Jin) state that extended into north China (see Map 13.2, page 372). Because of his early experiences with intertribal feuding, Chinggis mistrusted traditional tribal loyalties, and as he fashioned a new army, he gave it a new, non-tribal structure. He conscripted soldiers from all the tribes and assigned them to units that were composed of members from different tribes. He selected commanders for each unit whom he could remove at will, although he allowed commanders to pass their posts to their sons. Marco Polo, the famous European traveler who later attended the Mongol court of Chinggis's grandson, explained the decimal hierarchy of his armies this way:

> When one of the great Tartar chiefs proceeds on an expedition, he puts himself at the head of an army of a hundred thousand horses, and organizes them in the following manner. He appoints an officer to the command of every ten men, and others to command a hundred, a thousand, and ten thousand men, respectively. Thus ten of the officers commanding ten men take their orders from him who commands a hundred; of these, each ten, from him who commands a thousand; and each ten of these latter, from him who commands ten thousand. By this arrangement each officer has only to attend to the management of ten men or ten bodies of men.[4]

After Chinggis subjugated a city, he would send envoys to cities farther out to demand submission and threaten destruction. Those who opened their city gates and submitted without fighting could become allies and retain local power, but those who resisted faced the prospect of mass slaughter. He despised city dwellers and would sometimes use them as living shields in the next battle. After the Mongol armies swept across north China in 1212–1213, ninety-odd cities lay in rubble. Beijing, captured in 1215, burned for more than a month. Not surprisingly many governors of cities and rulers of small states hastened to offer submission.

Chinggis preferred conquest to administration and did not stay in north China to set up an administrative structure. He left that to subordinates and turned his attention westward, to Central Asia and Persia, then dominated by different groups of Turks. In 1218 Chinggis proposed to the Khwarizm shah of Persia that he accept Mongol overlordship and establish trade relations. The shah, to show his determination to resist, ordered the envoy and the merchants who had accompanied him killed. The next year Chinggis led an army of one hundred thousand soldiers west to retaliate. Mongol forces destroyed the shah's army and sacked one Persian city after another, demolishing buildings and massacring hundreds of thousands of people.

After returning from Central Asia, Chinggis died in 1227 during the siege of a city in northwest China. Before he died, he instructed his sons not to fall out among themselves but instead to divide the spoils.

Chinggis's Successors

Although Mongol leaders traditionally had had to win their positions, after Chinggis died the empire was divided into four states called **khanates**, with one of the lines of his descendants taking charge of each one (Map 12.1). Chinggis's third son, Ögödei, assumed the title of khan, and he directed the next round of invasions.

In 1237 representatives of all four lines led 150,000 Mongol, Turkish, and Persian troops into Europe. During the next five years they gained control of Moscow and Kievan Russia and looted cities in Poland and Hungary. They were poised to attack deeper into Europe when they learned of the death of Ögödei in 1241. To participate in the election of a new khan, the army returned to the Mongols' new capital city, Karakorum.

Once Ögödei's son was certified as his successor, the Mongols turned their attention to Persia and the Middle East. In 1256 a Mongol army took northwest Iran, then pushed on to the Abbasid capital of Baghdad. When it fell in 1258, the last Abbasid caliph was murdered, and the population was put to the sword. The Mongol onslaught was successfully resisted, however, by both the Delhi sultanate (see page 353) and the Mamluk rulers in Egypt (see page 245).

Under Chinggis's grandson Khubilai Khan (r. 1260–1294) the Mongols completed their conquest of China. South China had never been captured by non-Chinese, in large part because horses were of no strategic advantage in a land of rivers and canals. Perhaps because they were entering a very different type of terrain, the Mongols proceeded deliberately. First they surrounded the Song empire in central and south China (discussed in Chapter 13) by taking its westernmost province in 1252, as well as Korea to its east in 1258, destroying the Nanzhao kingdom in modern Yunnan in 1254, and then

• **khanates**   The states ruled by a khan; the four units into which Chinggis divided the Mongol Empire.

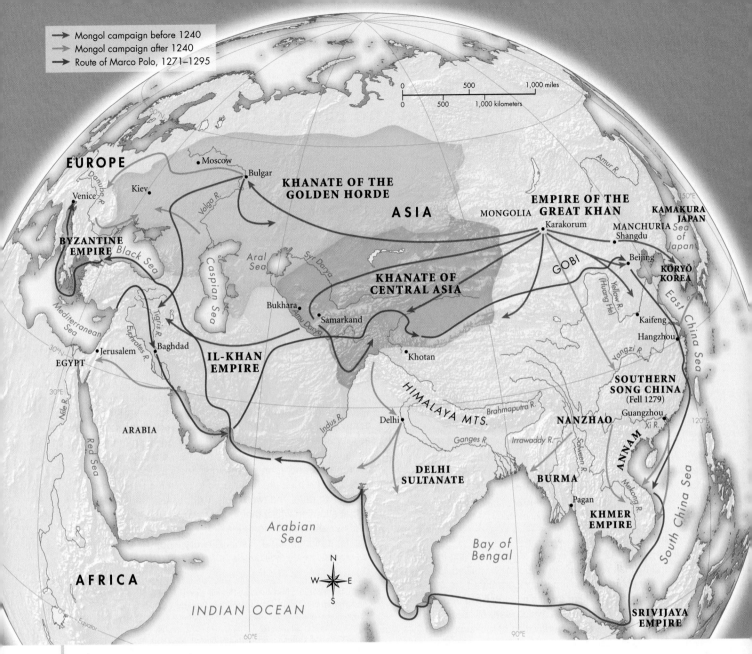

Mongol campaign before 1240
Mongol campaign after 1240
Route of Marco Polo, 1271–1295

□ Mapping the Past

MAP 12.1 The Mongol Empire The creation of the vast Mongol Empire facilitated communication across Eurasia and led to both the spread of deadly plagues and the transfer of technical and scientific knowledge. After the death of Chinggis Khan in 1227, the empire was divided into four khanates ruled by different lines of his successors. In the 1270s the Mongols conquered southern China, but most of their subsequent campaigns did not lead to further territorial gains.

ANALYZING THE MAP Trace the campaigns of the Mongols. Which ones led to acquisition of territory, and which ones did not?

CONNECTIONS Would the division of the Mongol Empire into separate khanates have made these areas easier for the Mongols to rule? What drawbacks might it have had from the Mongols' point of view?

continuing south and taking Annam (northern Vietnam) in 1257. A surrendered Song commander advised them to build a navy to attack the great Song cities located on rivers. During the five-year siege of a central Chinese river port, both sides used thousands of boats and tens of thousands of troops. The Mongols employed experts in naval and siege warfare from all over their empire — Chinese, Korean, Jurchen, Uighur, and Persian. Catapults designed by Muslim engineers launched a barrage of rocks weighing up to a hundred pounds

Viewpoints

Chinese and European Accounts About the Mongol Army

• *The Mongols received little attention from historians until they were united under Chinggis and began their military conquests. The following documents offer different perspectives on the Mongol army. The first, one of the earliest surviving accounts, was written about 1220 by a Chinese historian, Li Xinchuan, living in south China under the Song Dynasty. He would have learned of the Mongols secondhand, as the Song had diplomatic relations with Jin, then under attack by the Mongols. He reported how the Tartars — referring to the Mongols — gained control of north China in 1213–1214. The second excerpt refers to the time that the state of Song in South China sustained its first major attack by the Mongols in 1236, when Mongol armies entered the western province of Sichuan and destroyed major cities like Chengdu. A man who survived the slaughter, Zhu Sisun, later reported what he went through. Marco Polo, encountering the Mongols a half century later after most of their conquests through Eurasia were complete, had a different view of the warriors.*

Li Xinchuan

"In the spring of 1213 [the Tartars] attacked Yanjing [modern Beijing] and that fall Yunji [the Jin emperor] was killed. Chinggis left Samohe in charge of Yanjing and incorporated the 46 divisions of the surrendered [Jin] armies of Yang Boyu and Liu Bolin into the great Tartar armies, which were divided into three divisions to conquer the prefectural cities of [the circuits of] River North, River East, and Mountains East. . . . At this time the troops of the various circuits of north China pulled back to defend the region west of the mountains, but there were not enough troops, so commoners were drafted as soldiers and put on the tops of the city walls to defend them. The Tartars drove their family members to attack them, and fathers and sons or brothers often got close enough to recognize and call out to each other. Because of this, [the drafted soldiers] were not firmly resolved, and all of the cities surrendered as soon as the fighting began. From the twelfth month of 1213 to the first month of 1214, more than ninety prefectures fell. Every place the armies passed through was devastated. For several thousand *li*, throughout River East, River North, and Mountains East, the people were slaughtered. Gold and silk, boys and girls, oxen and sheep, horses and other animals were all "rolled up" and taken away. Houses were burnt down and defensive walls smashed."

Zhu Sisun

"Here is how the people of Sichuan went to their deaths: groups of fifty people were clustered together, and the Mongols impaled them all with swords and piled up the corpses. At sunset, those who did not appear dead were again stabbed. Sisun lay at the bottom of a pile of corpses, and by chance the evening stabbing did not reach him. The blood of the corpses above him dripped steadily into his mouth. Halfway through the night Sisun began to revive, and crawling into the woods he made his escape."

Marco Polo

"They are brave in battle, almost to desperation, setting little value upon their lives, and exposing themselves without hesitation to all manner of danger. Their disposition is cruel. They are capable of supporting every kind of privation, and when there is a necessity for it, can live for a month on the milk of their mares, and upon such wild animals as they may chance to catch. The men are habituated to remain on horseback during two days and two nights, without dismounting, sleeping in that situation whilst their horses graze. No people on earth can surpass them in fortitude under difficulties, nor show greater patience under wants of every kind."

Sources: Li Xinchuan, *Jianyan yilai chaoye zaji* (Beijing: Zhonghua shuju, 2000), pp. 847–851, translated by Patricia Ebrey; Paul J. Smith, "Family, Landsmann, and Status-Group Affinity in Refugee Mobility Strategies: The Mongol Invasions and the Diaspora of Sichuanese Elites, 1230–1330," *Harvard Journal of Asiatic Studies* 52.2 (1992), 671–672, slightly modified; *The Travels of Marco Polo, the Venetian*, ed. Manuel Komroff (New York: Boni and Liveright, 1926), p. 93.

QUESTIONS FOR ANALYSIS

1. How would you explain the differences in what these writers chose to mention?

2. If you were writing a history of the Mongols, would you consider these sources as equally valid evidence, or do you find some more reliable than others? Does anything in the accounts seem exaggerated? How can you judge?

each. During their advance toward the Chinese capital of Hangzhou, the Mongols ordered the total slaughter of the people of the major city of Changzhou, and in 1276 the Chinese empress dowager surrendered in hopes of sparing the people of the capital a similar fate.

Having overrun China and Korea, Khubilai turned his eyes toward Japan. In 1274 a force of 30,000 soldiers and support personnel sailed from Korea to Japan. In 1281 a combined Mongol and Chinese fleet of about 150,000 made a second attempt to conquer Japan. On both occasions the Mongols managed to land but were beaten back by Japanese samurai armies. Each time fierce storms destroyed the Mongol fleets. The Japanese claimed that they had been saved by the *kamikaze*, the "divine wind" (which later lent its name to the thousands of Japanese aviators who crashed their airplanes into American warships during World War II). A decade later, in 1293, Khubilai tried sending a fleet to the islands of Southeast Asia, including Java, but it met with no more success than the fleets sent to Japan.

Why were the Mongols so successful against so many different types of enemies? Even though their population was tiny compared to the populations of the large agricultural societies they conquered, their tactics, their weapons, and their organization all gave them advantages. Like other nomads before them, they were superb horsemen and excellent archers. Their horses were extremely nimble, able to change direction quickly, thus allowing the Mongols to maneuver easily and ride through infantry forces armed with swords, lances, and javelins. Usually only other nomadic armies, like the Turks, could stand up well against the Mongols. (See "Viewpoints: Chinese and European Accounts About the Mongol Army," page 342.)

The Mongols were also open to trying new military technologies. To attack walled cities, they learned how to use catapults and other engines of war. At first they employed Chinese catapults, but when they learned that those used by the Turks in Afghanistan were more powerful, they adopted the better model. The Mongols also used exploding arrows and gunpowder projectiles developed by the Chinese.

◻ MONGOL CONQUESTS

1206	Temujin made Chinggis Khan
1215	Fall of Beijing (Jurchens)
1219–1220	Fall of Bukhara and Samarkand in Central Asia
1227	Death of Chinggis
1237–1241	Raids into eastern Europe
1257	Conquest of Annam (northern Vietnam)
1258	Conquest of Abbasid capital of Baghdad; conquest of Korea
1260	Khubilai succeeds to khanship
1274	First attempt at invading Japan
1276	Surrender of Song Dynasty (China)
1281	Second attempt at invading Japan
1293	Mongol fleet unsuccessful in invasion of Java
mid-14th century	Decline of Mongol power

The 1258 Fall of Baghdad This illustration from a fourteenth-century Persian manuscript shows the Mongol army attacking the walled city of Baghdad. Note the use of catapults on both sides. (Bildarchiv Preussischer Kulturbesitz/Art Resource, NY)

The Mongols made good use of intelligence and tried to exploit internal divisions in the countries they attacked. Thus, in north China they appealed to the Khitans, who had been defeated by the Jurchens a century earlier, to join them in attacking the Jurchens. In Syria they exploited the resentment of Christians against their Muslim rulers.

The Mongols as Rulers

The success of the Mongols in ruling vast territories was due in large part to their willingness to incorporate other ethnic groups into their armies and governments. Whatever their original country or religion, those who served the Mongols loyally were rewarded. Uighurs, Tibetans, Persians, Chinese, and Russians came to hold powerful positions in the Mongol government. Chinese helped breach the walls of Baghdad in the 1250s, and Muslims operated the catapults that helped reduce Chinese cities in the 1270s. Mongol armies incorporated the armies they vanquished and in time had large numbers of Turkish troops.

Since, in Mongol eyes, the purpose of fighting was to gain riches, they regularly would loot the settlements they conquered, taking whatever they wanted, including the residents. Land would be granted to military commanders, nobles, and army units to be governed and exploited as the recipients wished. Those working the land would be given to them as serfs. The Mongols built a capital city called Karakorum in modern Mongolia, and to bring it up to the level of the cities they conquered, they transported skilled workers from those cities. For instance, after Bukhara and Samarkand were captured in 1219–1220, some thirty thousand artisans

were seized and transported to Mongolia. Sometimes these slaves gradually improved their status. A French goldsmith from Budapest named Guillaume Boucher was captured by the Mongols in 1242 and taken to Karakorum, where he gradually won favor and was put in charge of fifty workers to make gold and silver vessels for the Mongol court.

The traditional nomad disdain for farmers led some commanders to suggest turning north China into a gigantic pasture after it was conquered. In time, though, the Mongols came to realize that simply appropriating the wealth and human resources of the settled lands was not as good as extracting regular revenue from them. A Chinese-educated Khitan who had been working for the Jurchens in China explained to the Mongols that collecting taxes from farmers would be highly profitable: they could extract a revenue of 500,000 ounces of silver, 80,000 bolts of silk, and more than 20,000 tons of grain from the region by taxing it. The Mongols gave this a try, but soon political rivals convinced the khan that he would gain even more by letting Central Asian Muslim merchants bid against each other for licenses to collect taxes any way they could, a system called **tax-farming**. Ordinary Chinese found this method of tax collecting much more oppressive than traditional Chinese methods, since there was little to keep the tax collectors from seizing everything they could.

By the second half of the thirteenth century there was no longer a genuine pan-Asian Mongol Empire. Much of Asia was in the hands of Mongol successor states, but these were generally hostile to each other. Khubilai was often at war with the khanate of Central Asia, then held by his cousin Khaidu, and he had little contact with the khanate of the Golden Horde in south Russia. The Mongols adapted their methods of government to the existing traditions of each place they ruled, and the regions now went their separate ways.

In China the Mongols resisted assimilation and purposely avoided many Chinese practices. The rulers conducted their business in the Mongol language and spent their summers in Mongolia. Khubilai discouraged Mongols from marrying Chinese and took only Mongol women into the palace. Some Mongol princes preferred to live in yurts erected on the palace grounds rather than in the grand palaces constructed at Beijing. Chinese were treated as legally inferior not only to the Mongols but also to all other non-Chinese. In cases of assault the discrepancy was huge, as a Mongol

Gold Belt Plaques Like earlier nomads, the Mongols favored art with animal designs, such as these two gold belt plaques, which depict deer under trees or flowers. Belts and horses were often exchanged to seal or commemorate an alliance. (Nasser D. Khalili Collection of Islamic Art, © Nour Foundation, Courtesy of the Khalili Family Trust)

who murdered a Chinese could get off with a fine, but a Chinese who hit a Mongol to defend himself would face severe penalties.

In Central Asia, Persia, and Russia the Mongols tended to merge with the Turkish groups already there and, like them, converted to Islam. Russia in the thirteenth century was not a strongly centralized state, and the Mongols allowed Russian princes and lords to continue to rule their territories as long as they turned over adequate tribute (thus adding to the burden on peasants). The city of Moscow became the center of Mongol tribute collection and grew in importance. In the Middle East the Mongol Il-khans (as they were known in Persia) were more active as rulers, again continuing the traditions of the caliphate. In Mongolia itself, however, Mongol traditions were maintained.

Mongol control in each of the khanates lasted about a century. In the mid-fourteenth century the Mongol dynasty in China deteriorated into civil war, and in the 1360s the Mongols withdrew back to Mongolia. There was a similar loss of Mongol power in Persia and Central Asia. Only on the south Russian steppe did the Golden Horde maintain its hold for another century.

As Mongol rule in Central Asia declined, a new conqueror emerged, Timur, also known as Tamerlane (Timur the Lame). Not a nomad but a highly civilized Turkish noble, Timur in the 1360s struck out from his base in Samarkand into Persia, north India (see page 353), southern Russia, and beyond. His armies used the terror tactics that the Mongols had perfected, massacring the citizens of cities that resisted. In the decades after his death in 1405, however, Timur's empire went into decline.

East-West Communication During the Mongol Era

☐ How did the Mongol conquests facilitate the spread of ideas, religions, inventions, and diseases?

The Mongol governments did more than any earlier political entities to encourage the movement of people and goods across Eurasia. With these vast movements came cultural accommodation as the Mongols, their conquered subjects, and their trading partners learned from one another. This cultural exchange included both physical goods and the sharing of ideas, including the introduction of new religious beliefs and the adoption of new ways to organize and rule the Mongol empire. It also facilitated the spread of the plague and the unwilling movement of enslaved captives.

The Movement of Peoples

The Mongols had never looked down on merchants the way the elites of many traditional states did, and they welcomed the arrival of merchants from distant lands. Even when different groups of Mongols were fighting among themselves, they usually allowed caravans to pass without harassing them.

The Mongol practice of transporting skilled people from the lands they conquered also brought people into contact with each other in new ways. Besides those forced to move, the Mongols recruited administrators from all over. Chinese, Persians, and Arabs served the Mongols, and the Mongols often sent them far from home. Especially prominent were the Uighur Turks of Chinese Central Asia, whose familiarity with Chinese civilization and fluency in Turkish were extremely valuable in facilitating communication. Literate Uighurs staffed much of the Mongol administration.

One of those who served the Mongols was Rashid al-Din (ca. 1247–1318). A Jew from Persia and the son of an apothecary, Rashid al-Din converted to Islam at the age of thirty and entered the service of the Mongol Il-khan of Persia as a physician. He rose in government service, traveled widely, and eventually became prime minister. Rashid al-Din became friends with the ambassador from China, and together they arranged for translations of Chinese works on medicine, agronomy, and statecraft. He had ideas on economic management that he communicated to Mongol officials in Central Asia and China. Aware of the great differences between cultures, he believed that the Mongols should try to rule in accord with the moral principles of the majority in each land. On that basis he convinced the Mongol khan of Persia to convert to Islam. Rashid al-Din undertook to explain the great variety of cultures by writing a world history more comprehensive than any previously written.

The Mongols were remarkably open to religious experts from all the lands they encountered. More Europeans made their way as far as Mongolia and China in the Mongol period than ever before. Popes and kings sent envoys to the Mongol court in the hope of enlisting the Mongols on their side in their long-standing conflict with Muslim forces over the Holy Land. European visitors were also interested in finding Christians who had been cut off from the West by the spread of Islam, and in fact there were considerable numbers of Nestorian Christians in Central Asia. In 1245 Pope Innocent IV wrote two letters to the "King and people of the Tartars" asking him to become a Christian and cease attacks against Europe. They were delivered to a Mongol general in Armenia. The next year another

• **tax-farming** Assigning the collection of taxes to whoever bids the most for the privilege.

our own eyes, to which they reduce all peoples who have submitted to them."[5]

A few years later, in 1253, Flemish friar William of Rubruck set out with the permission of King Louis IX of France as a missionary to convert the Mongols. He too made his way to Karakorum, where he found many Europeans. At Easter, Hungarians, Russians, Georgians, Armenians, and Alans all took communion in a Nestorian church. Rubruck also recorded information he heard about China while in Mongolia, such as the Chinese practice of writing with a brush.

The most famous European visitor to the Mongol lands was the Venetian Marco Polo (ca. 1254–1324). In his famous *Travels*, Marco Polo described all the places he visited or learned about during his seventeen years away from home. He reported being warmly received by Khubilai, who impressed him enormously. He was also awed by the wealth and splendor of Chinese cities and spread the notion of Asia as a land of riches. In Marco Polo's lifetime, some skeptics did not believe his tale, and even today some scholars speculate that he may have learned about China from Persian merchants he met in the Middle East without actually going to China. But Mongol scholars staunchly defend Marco Polo, even though they admit that he stretched the truth to make himself look good in several places. Regardless of the final verdict on Marco Polo's veracity, there is no doubt that the great popularity of his book contributed to European interest in finding new routes to Asia.

The Spread of Disease, Goods, and Ideas

The rapid transfer of people and goods across Central Asia spread more than ideas and inventions. It also spread diseases, the most deadly of which was the plague known in Europe as the Black Death, which most scholars identify today as the bubonic plague. In the early fourteenth century, transmitted by rats and fleas, the plague began to spread from Central Asia into West Asia, the Mediterranean, and western Europe. When the Mongols were assaulting the city of Kaffa in the Crimea in 1346, they were infected by the plague and had to withdraw. In retaliation, they purposely spread the disease to their enemy by catapulting the bodies of victims into the city of Kaffa. Soon the disease was carried from port to port throughout the Mediterranean by ship. The confusion of the mid-fourteenth century that led to the loss of Mongol power in China, Iran, and Central Asia undoubtedly owes something to the effect of the spread of the plague and other diseases. (For more on the Black Death, see Chapter 14.)

Traditionally, the historians of each of the countries conquered by the Mongols portrayed them as a scourge.

Depictions of Europeans The Mongol Empire, by facilitating travel across Asia, increased knowledge of faraway lands. Rashid al-Din's *History of the World* included a history of the Franks, illustrated here with images of Western popes (left) conferring with Byzantine emperors (right). (Topkapi Saray Museum, Ms. H.1654, fol. 303a)

envoy, Giovanni di Pian de Carpine, reached the Volga River and the camp of Batu, the khan of the Golden Horde. Batu sent him on to the new Great Khan in Karakorum with two Mongol guides, riding so fast that they had to change horses five to seven times a day. Their full journey of more than three thousand miles took a remarkably short five and a half months. Carpine spent four months at the Great Khan's court but never succeeded in convincing the khan to embrace Christianity or drop his demand that the pope appear in person to tender his submission to the khan. When Carpine returned home, he wrote a report that urged preparation for a renewed Mongol attack on Europe. The Mongols had to be resisted "because of the harsh, indeed intolerable, and hitherto unheard-of slavery seen with

Russian historians, for instance, saw this as a period of bondage that set Russia back and cut it off from western Europe. Among contemporary Western historians, it is now more common to celebrate the genius of the Mongol military machine and treat the spread of ideas and inventions as an obvious good, probably because we see global communication as a good in our own world. There is no reason to assume, however, that people benefited equally from the improved communications and the new political institutions of the Mongol era. Merchants involved in long-distance trade prospered, but those enslaved and transported hundreds or thousands of miles from home would have seen themselves not as the beneficiaries of opportunities to encounter cultures different from their own, but rather as the most pitiable of victims.

The places that were ruled by Mongol governments for a century or more—China, Central Asia, Persia, and Russia—do not seem to have advanced at a more rapid rate during that century than they did in earlier centuries, either economically or culturally. By Chinese standards Mongol imposition of hereditary status distinctions was a step backward from a much more mobile and open society, and placing Persians, Arabs, or Tibetans over Chinese did not arouse interest in foreign cultures. Much more foreign music and foreign styles in clothing, art, and furnishings were integrated into Chinese civilization in Tang times than in Mongol times.

In terms of the spread of technological and scientific ideas, Europe seems to have been by far the main beneficiary of increased communication, largely because in 1200 it lagged farther behind than the other areas. Chinese inventions such as printing, gunpowder, and the compass spread westward. Persian and Indian expertise in astronomy and mathematics also spread. In terms of the spread of religions, Islam probably gained the most. It came to dominate in Chinese Central Asia, which had previously been Buddhist.

Another element promoting Eurasian connection was maritime trade, which linked all the societies of the Indian Ocean and East Asia. The products of China and other areas of the East introduced to Europe by merchants like Marco Polo whetted the appetites of Europeans for goods from the East, and the demand for Asian goods eventually culminated in the great age of European exploration and expansion (discussed in Chapter 16). By comparison, in areas the Mongols had directly attacked, protecting their own civilization became a higher priority than drawing from the outside to enrich or enlarge it.

India, Islam, and the Development of Regional Cultures, 300–1400

☐ What was the result of India's encounters with Turks, Mongols, and Islam?

South Asia, although far from the heartland of the steppe, still felt the impact of the arrival of the Turks in Central Asia. Over the course of many centuries, horsemen from both the east and the west (Scythians, Huns, Turks, and Mongols) all sent armies south to raid or invade north India. After the Mauryan Empire broke apart in 185 B.C.E. (see page 85), India was politically divided into small kingdoms for several centuries. Only the Guptas in the fourth century would emerge to unite much of north India, though their rule was cut short by the invasion of the Huns in about 450. In the centuries that followed, India witnessed the development of regional cultures and was profoundly shaped by Turkish nomads from Central Asia who brought their culture and, most importantly, Islam to India. Despite these

Horse and Groom Zhao Mengfu (1254–1322), the artist of this painting and a member of the Song imperial family, took up service under the Mongol emperor Khubilai. The Mongol rulers, great horsemen themselves, would likely have appreciated this depiction of a horse buffeted by the wind. (National Palace Museum, Taipei, Taiwan)

> "I see your body in the sinuous creeper, your gaze in the startled eyes of deer, your cheek in the moon."
>
> **KALIDASA**

events, the lives of most Indians remained unchanged, with the majority of the people living in villages in a society defined by caste.

The Gupta Empire, ca. 320–480

In the early fourth century a state emerged in the Ganges plain that was able to bring large parts of north India under its control. The rulers of this Indian empire, the Guptas, consciously modeled their rule after that of the Mauryan Empire, and the founder took the name of the founder of that dynasty, Chandragupta. Although the Guptas never controlled as much territory as the Mauryans had, they united north India and received tribute from states in Nepal and the Indus Valley, thus giving large parts of India a period of peace and political unity.

The Gupta Empire, ca. 320–480

The Guptas' administrative system was not as centralized as that of the Mauryans. In the central regions they drew their revenue from a tax on agriculture of one-quarter of the harvest and maintained monopolies on key products such as metals and salt (reminiscent of Chinese practice). They also exacted labor service for the construction and upkeep of roads, wells, and irrigation systems. More distant areas were assigned to governors who were allowed considerable leeway, and governorships often became hereditary. Areas still farther away were encouraged to become vassal states, able to participate in the splendor of the capital and royal court in subordinate roles and to engage in profitable trade, but not required to turn over much in the way of revenue.

The Gupta kings were patrons of the arts. Poets composed epics for the courts of the Gupta kings, and other writers experimented with prose romances and popular tales. India's greatest poet, Kalidasa (ca. 380–450), like Shakespeare, wrote poems as well as plays in verse. His most highly esteemed play, *Shakuntala*, con-

cerns a daughter of a hermit who enthralls a king who is out hunting. The king sets up house with her, then returns to his court and, owing to a curse, forgets her. Only much later does he acknowledge their child as his true heir. Equally loved is Kalidasa's one-hundred-verse poem "The Cloud Messenger" about a demigod who asks a passing cloud to carry a message to his wife, from whom he has long been separated. At one point he instructs the cloud to tell her: "I see your body in the sinuous creeper, your gaze in the startled eyes of deer, your cheek in the moon, your hair in the plumage of peacocks, and in the tiny ripples of the river I see your sidelong glances, but alas, my dearest, nowhere do I see your whole likeness."[6]

In mathematics, too, the Gupta period could boast of impressive intellectual achievements. The so-called Arabic numerals are actually of Indian origin. Indian mathematicians developed the place-value notation system, with separate columns for ones, tens, and hundreds, as well as a zero sign to indicate the absence of units in a given column. This system greatly facilitated calculation and spread as far as Europe by the seventh century.

The Gupta rulers were Hindus, but they tolerated all faiths. Buddhist pilgrims from other areas of Asia reported that Buddhist monasteries with hundreds or even thousands of monks and nuns flourished in the cities. The success of Buddhism did not hinder Hinduism with its many gods, which remained popular among ordinary people.

The great crisis of the Gupta Empire was the invasion of the Huns (Xiongnu). The migration of these nomads from Central Asia shook much of Eurasia. Around 450 a group of them known as the White Huns thundered into India. Mustering his full might, the Gupta ruler Skandagupta (r. ca. 455–467) threw back the invaders. Although the Huns failed to uproot the Gupta Empire, they dealt the dynasty a fatal blow.

India's Medieval Age and the First Encounter with Islam

After the decline of the Gupta Empire, India once again broke into separate kingdoms that were frequently at war with each other. Most of the dynasties of India's medieval age (ca. 500–1400) were short-lived, but a balance of power was maintained between the major regions of India, with none gaining enough of an advantage to conquer the others. Particularly notable are the Cholas, who dominated the southern tip of the peninsula, Sri Lanka, and much of the eastern Indian Ocean to the twelfth century (Map 12.2).

Political division fostered the development of regional cultures. Literature came to be written in India's regional languages, among them Marathi, Bengali, and Assamese. Commerce continued as before, and the

Wall Painting at Ajanta Many of the best surviving examples of Gupta period painting are found at the twenty-nine Buddhist cave temples at Ajanta in central India. The walls of these caves were decorated in the fifth and sixth centuries with scenes from the former lives of the Buddha. These two scenes, showing a royal couple on the right and a princess and her attendants on the left, offer glimpses of what the royal courts of the period must have looked like. (Benoy K. Behl)

coasts of India remained important in the sea trade of the Indian Ocean.

The first encounters with Islam occurred in this period. In 711, after pirates had plundered a richly laden Arab ship near the mouth of the Indus, the Umayyad governor of Iraq sent a force with six thousand horses and six thousand camels to seize the Sind area in western India (modern day Pakistan). The western part of India remained part of the caliphate for centuries, but Islam did not spread much beyond this foothold. During the ninth and tenth centuries Turks from Central Asia moved into the region of to-day's northeastern Iran and western Afghanistan, then known as Khurasan. Converts to Islam, they first served as military forces for the caliphate in Baghdad, but as its authority weakened (see pages 243–244), they made themselves rulers of an effectively independent Khurasan and frequently sent raiding parties into north India. Beginning in 997, Mahmud of Ghazni (r. 997–1030) led seventeen annual forays into India from his base in modern Afghanistan. His goal was plunder to finance his wars against other Turkish rulers in Central Asia. Toward this end, he systematically looted Indian palaces and temples, viewing religious statues as infidels' idols. Eventually even the Arab conquerors of the Sind fell to the Turks. By 1030 the Indus Valley, the Punjab, and the rest of northwest India were in the grip of the Turks.

The new rulers encouraged the spread of Islam, but the Indian caste system (see page 71) made it difficult to convert higher-caste Indians. Al-Biruni (d. 1048), a Persian scholar who spent much of his later life at the court of Mahmud and learned Sanskrit, wrote of the obstacles to Hindu-Muslim communication. The most basic barrier was language, but the religious gulf was also fundamental:

They totally differ from us in religion, as we believe in nothing in which they believe, and vice versa. On the whole, there is very little disputing about theological topics among them; at the utmost they fight with words, but they will never stake their soul or body or property on religious controversy. . . . They call foreigners impure and forbid having any connection with them, be it by intermarriage or any kind of relationship, or by sitting, eating, and drinking with them, because thereby, they think, they would be polluted.[7]

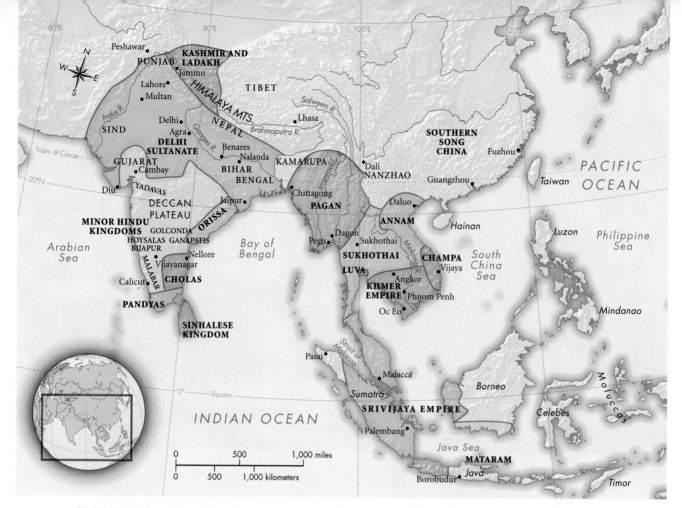

MAP 12.2 South and Southeast Asia in the Thirteenth Century The extensive coastlines of South and Southeast Asia and the predictable monsoon winds aided seafaring in this region. Note the Strait of Malacca, through which most east-west sea trade passed.

After the initial period of raids and destruction of temples, the Muslim Turks came to an accommodation with the Hindus, who were classed as a **protected people**, like the Christians and Jews, and allowed to follow their religion. They had to pay a special tax but did not have to perform military service. Local chiefs and rajas were often allowed to remain in control of their domains as long as they paid tribute. Most Indians looked on the Muslim conquerors as a new ruling caste, capable of governing and taxing them but otherwise peripheral to their lives. The myriad castes largely governed themselves, isolating the newcomers.

Nevertheless, over the course of several centuries Islam gained a strong hold on north India, especially in the Indus Valley (modern Pakistan) and in Bengal at the mouth of the Ganges River (modern Bangladesh). Moreover, the sultanate seems to have had a positive effect on the economy. Much of the wealth confiscated

from temples was put to more productive use, and India's first truly large cities emerged. The Turks also were eager to employ skilled workers, giving new opportunities to low-caste manual and artisan labor.

The Muslim rulers were much more hostile to Buddhism than to Hinduism, seeing Buddhism as a competitive proselytizing religion. In 1193 a Turkish raiding party destroyed the great Buddhist university at Nalanda in Bihar. Buddhist monks were killed or forced to flee to Buddhist centers in Southeast Asia, Nepal, and Tibet. Buddhism, which had thrived for so long in peaceful and friendly competition with Hinduism, went into decline in its native land.

Hinduism, however, remained as strong as ever. South India was largely unaffected by these invasions, and traditional Hindu culture flourished there under native kings ruling small kingdoms. (See "Individuals in Society: Bhaskara the Teacher," page 351.) Temple-centered Hinduism flourished, as did devotional cults and mystical movements. This was a great age of religious art and architecture in India. Extraordinary temples covered with elaborate bas-relief were built in many areas. Sexual passion and the union of men and

Individuals in Society

Bhaskara the Teacher

IN INDIA, AS IN MANY OTHER SOCIETIES, astronomy and mathematics were closely linked, and many of the most important mathematicians served their rulers as astronomers. Bhaskara (1114–ca. 1185) was such an astronomer-mathematician. For generations his Brahmin family had been astronomers at the Ujjain astronomical observatory in north-central India, and his father had written a popular book on astrology.

Bhaskara was a highly erudite man. A disciple wrote that he had thoroughly mastered eight books on grammar, six on medicine, six on philosophy, five on mathematics, and the four Vedas. Bhaskara eventually wrote six books on mathematics and mathematical astronomy. They deal with solutions to simple and quadratic equations and show his knowledge of trigonometry, including the sine table and relationships between different trigonometric functions, and even some of the basic elements of calculus. Earlier Indian mathematicians had explored the use of zero and negative numbers. Bhaskara developed these ideas further, in particular improving on the understanding of division by zero.

A court poet who centuries later translated Bhaskara's book titled *The Beautiful* explained its title by saying Bhaskara wrote it for his daughter named Beautiful (Lilavati) as consolation when his divination of the best time for her to marry went awry.

> • **The observatory where Bhaskara worked in Ujjain today stands in ruins.** (Dinodia Photo Library)

Whether Bhaskara did or did not write this book for his daughter, many of the problems he provides in it have a certain charm:

> On an expedition to seize his enemy's elephants, a king marched two yojanas the first day. Say, intelligent calculator, with what increasing rate of daily march did he proceed, since he reached his foe's city, a distance of eighty yojanas, in a week?*
>
> Out of a heap of pure lotus flower, a third part, a fifth, and a sixth were offered respectively to the gods Siva, Vishnu, and the Sun; and a quarter was presented to Bhavani. The remaining six lotuses were given to the venerable preceptor. Tell quickly the whole number of lotus.†
>
> If eight best variegated silk scarfs, measuring three cubits in breadth and eight in length, cost a hundred nishkas, say quickly, merchant, if thou understand trade, what a like scarf, three and a half cubits long and half a cubit wide will cost.‡

In the conclusion to *The Beautiful*, Bhaskara wrote:

> Joy and happiness is indeed ever increasing in this world for those who have *The Beautiful* clasped to their throats, decorated as the members are with neat reduction of fractions, multiplication, and involution, pure and perfect as are the solutions, and tasteful as is the speech which is exemplified.

Bhaskara had a long career. His first book on mathematical astronomy, written in 1150 when he was thirty-six, used mathematics to calculate solar and lunar eclipses or planetary conjunctions. Thirty-three years later he was still writing on the subject, this time providing simpler ways to solve problems encountered before. Bhaskara wrote his books in Sanskrit, already a literary language rather than a vernacular language, but even in his own day some of them were translated into other Indian languages.

Within a couple of decades of his death, a local ruler endowed an educational institution to study Bhaskara's works, beginning with his work on mathematical astronomy. In the text he had inscribed at the site, the ruler gave the names of Bhaskara's ancestors for six generations, as well as of his son and grandson, who had continued in his profession.

QUESTIONS FOR ANALYSIS

1. What might have been the advantages of making occupations like astronomer hereditary in India?
2. How does Bhaskara link joy and happiness to mathematical concepts?

*Quotations from Haran Chandra Banerji, *Colebrooke's Translation of the Lilanvanti*, 2d ed. (Calcutta: The Book Co., 1927), pp. 80–81, 30, 51, 200. The answer is that each day he must travel 22/7 yojanas farther than the day before.
†The answer is 120.
‡The answer, from the formula $x = (1 \times 7 \times 1 \times 100) / (8 \times 3 \times 8 \times 2 \times 2)$, is given in currencies smaller than the nishka: 14 drammas, 9 panas, 1 kakini, and 6⅔ cowry shells. (20 cowry shells = 1 kakini, 4 kakini = 1 pana, 16 panas = 1 dramma, and 16 drammas = 1 nishka.)

Kandariyâ Mahâdeva Hindu Temple Built around 1050 by a local king in central India, this is one of the best preserved Hindu temples from the medieval period. The main spire rises 100 feet, and the sides are decorated with more than 600 stone statues. (Yvan Travert/akg images)

women were frequently depicted, symbolically representing passion for and union with the temple god.

The Delhi Sultanate

In the twelfth century a new line of Turkish rulers arose in Afghanistan, led by Muhammad of Ghur (d. 1206). Muhammad captured Delhi and extended his control nearly throughout north India. When he fell to an assassin in 1206, one of his generals, the former slave Qutb-ud-din, seized the reins of power and established a government at Delhi, separate from the government in Afghanistan. This sultanate of Delhi lasted for three centuries, even though dynasties changed several times.

The North African Muslim world traveler Ibn Battuta (1304–1368; see page 254), served for several years as a judge at the court of one of the Delhi sultans. He praised the sultan for his insistence on the observance of ritual prayers and many acts of generosity to those in need, but he also considered the sultan overly violent. Here is just one of many examples he offered of how quick the sultan was to execute:

During the years of the famine, the Sultan had given orders to dig wells outside the capital, and have grain crops sown in those parts. He provided the cultivators with the seed, as well as with all that was necessary for cultivation in the way of money and supplies, and required them to cultivate these crops for the [royal] grain-store. When the jurist 'Afif al-Din heard of this, he said, "This crop will not produce what is hoped for." Some informer told the Sultan what he had said, so the Sultan jailed him, and said to him, "What reason have you to meddle with the government's business?" Some time later he released him, and as 'Afif al-Din went to his house he was met on the way by two friends of his, also jurists, who said to him, "Praise be to God for your release," to which our jurist replied, "Praise be to God who has delivered us from the evildoers." They then separated, but they had not reached their houses before this was reported to the Sultan, and he commanded all three to be fetched and brought before him. "Take out this fellow," he said, referring to 'Afif al-Din, "and cut off his head baldrickwise," that is, the head is cut off along with an arm and part of the chest, "and behead the other two." They said to him, "He deserves punishment, to be sure, for what he said, but in our case for what crime are you killing us?" He replied, "You heard what he said and did not disavow it, so you as good as agreed with it." So they were all put to death, God Most High have mercy on them.[8]

A major accomplishment of the Delhi sultanate was holding off the Mongols. Chinggis Khan and his troops entered the Indus Valley in 1221 in pursuit of the shah of Khurasan. The sultan wisely kept out of the way, and when Chinggis Khan left some troops in the area, the sultan made no attempt to challenge them. Two generations later, in 1299, a Mongol khan launched a campaign into India with two hundred thousand men, but the sultan of the time was able to defeat them. Two years later the Mongols returned and camped at Delhi for two months, but they eventually left without taking the sultan's fort. Another Mongol raid in 1306–1307 also was successfully repulsed.

Although the Turks by this time were highly cosmopolitan and no longer nomadic, they had retained their martial skills and understanding of steppe warfare. They were expert horsemen, and horses thrived in northwest India. The south and east of India, however, like the south of China, were less hospitable to raising horses, and generally people had to import them. In India's case, though, the climate of the south and east was well suited to elephants, which had been used as weapons of war in India since early times. Rulers in the northwest imported elephants from more tropical regions. The Delhi sultanate is said to have had as many as one thousand war elephants at its height.

During the fourteenth century, however, the Delhi sultanate was in decline and proved unable to ward off the armies of Timur (see page 345), who took Delhi in 1398. Timur's chronicler reported that when the troops drew up for battle outside Delhi, the sultanate had 10,000 horsemen, 20,000 foot soldiers, and 120 war elephants. Though alarmed at the sight of the elephants, Timur's men dug trenches to trap them and shot at their drivers. The sultan fled, leaving the city to surrender. Timur took as booty all the elephants, loading them with treasures seized from the city. Ruy Gonzalez de Clavijo, an ambassador from the king of Castile (now part of Spain), who arrived in Samarkand in 1403, was greatly impressed by these well-trained elephants. "When all the elephants together charged abreast, it seemed as though the solid earth itself shook at their onrush," he observed, noting that he thought each elephant was worth a thousand foot soldiers in battle.[9]

Timur's invasion left a weakened sultanate. The Delhi sultanate endured under different rulers until 1526, when it was conquered by the Mughals, a Muslim dynasty that would rule over most of northern Indian from the sixteenth into the nineteenth century.

Life in Medieval India

Local institutions played a much larger role in the lives of the overwhelming majority of people in medieval India than did the state. Craft guilds oversaw conditions of work and trade; local councils handled law and

> "When all the elephants together charged abreast, it seemed as though the solid earth itself shook at their onrush."
>
> **RUY GONZALEZ DE CLAVIJO**

order at the town or village level; and local castes gave members a sense of belonging and identity.

Like peasant societies elsewhere, including in China, Japan, and Southeast Asia, agricultural life in India ordinarily meant village life. The average farmer worked a small plot of land outside the village. All the family members pooled their resources — human, animal, and material — under the direction of the head of the family. These joint efforts strengthened family solidarity.

The agricultural year began with spring plowing. The traditional plow, drawn by two oxen wearing yokes and collars, had an iron-tipped share and a handle with which the farmer guided it. Rice, the most important and popular grain, was sown at the beginning of the long rainy season. Beans, lentils, and peas were the farmer's friends, for they grew during the cold season and were harvested in the spring, when fresh food was scarce. Cereal crops such as wheat, barley, and millet provided carbohydrates and other nutrients. Sugar cane was another important crop. Some families cultivated vegetables, spices, fruit trees, and flowers in their gardens.

Farmers also raised livestock. Most highly valued were cattle, which were raised for plowing and milk, hides, and horns, but Hindus did not slaughter them for meat. Like the Islamic and Jewish prohibition on the consumption of pork, the eating of beef was forbidden among Hindus.

Local craftsmen and tradesmen lived and worked in specific parts of a town or village. They were frequently organized into guilds, with guild heads and guild rules. The textile industries were particularly well developed. Silk (which had entered India from China), linen, wool, and cotton fabrics were produced in large quantities and traded throughout India and beyond. The cutting and polishing of precious stones was another industry associated closely with foreign trade.

In the cities shops were open to the street; families lived on the floors above. The busiest tradesmen dealt in milk and cheese, oil, spices, and perfumes. Equally prominent but disreputable were tavern keepers. Indian taverns were haunts of criminals and con artists, and in the worst of them fighting was as common as drinking. In addition to these tradesmen and merchants, a host of peddlers shuffled through towns and villages selling everything from needles to freshly cut flowers.

The Chinese Buddhist pilgrim Faxian (FAH-shen), during his six years in Gupta India, described it as a

Men at Work This stone frieze from the Buddhist stupa in Sanchi depicts Indian men doing a variety of everyday jobs. Although the stone was carved to convey religious ideas, we can use it as a source for such details of daily life as the sort of clothing men wore while working and how they carried loads. (Dinodia Photo Library)

peaceful land where people could move about freely without needing passports and where the upper castes were vegetarians. He was the first to make explicit reference to "untouchables," remarking that they hovered around the margins of Indian society, carrying gongs to warn upper-caste people of their polluting presence.

In this period the caste system reached its mature form. Within the broad division into the four *varna* (strata) of Brahmin, Kshatriya, Vaishya, and Shudra (see page 71), the population was subdivided into numerous castes, or **jati**. Each caste had a proper occupation. In addition, its members married only within the caste and ate only with other members. Members of high-status castes feared pollution from contact with lower-caste individuals and had to undertake rituals of purification to remove the taint.

Eventually Indian society comprised perhaps as many as three thousand castes. Each caste had its own governing body, which enforced the rules of the caste. Those incapable of living up to the rules were expelled,

becoming outcastes. These unfortunates lived hard lives, performing tasks that others considered unclean or lowly.

Villages were often walled, as in north China and the Middle East. The streets were unpaved, and the rainy season turned them into a muddy soup. Cattle and sheep roamed as freely as people. Some families kept pets, such as cats or parrots. Half-wild mongooses served as effective protection against snakes. The pond outside the village was its main source of water and also a spawning ground for fish, birds, and mosquitoes. Women drawing water frequently encountered water buffalo wallowing in the shallows. After the farmers returned from the fields in the evening, the village gates were closed until morning.

The life of the well-to-do is described in the *Kama-sutra* (Book on the Art of Love). Comfortable surroundings provided a place for men to enjoy poetry, painting, and music in the company of like-minded friends. Courtesans well-trained in entertaining men added to the pleasures of wealthy men. A man who had more than one wife was advised not to let one wife speak ill of the other and to try to keep each of them happy by taking them to gardens, giving them presents, telling them secrets, and loving them well.

• **jati** The thousands of Indian castes.

• **sati** A practice whereby a high-caste Hindu woman would throw herself on her husband's funeral pyre.

For all members of Indian society regardless of caste, marriage and family were the focus of life. As in China, the family was under the authority of the eldest male, who might take several wives, and ideally sons stayed home with their parents after they married. The family affirmed its solidarity by the religious ritual of honoring its dead ancestors — a ritual that linked the living and the dead, much like ancestor worship in China (see pages 95–96). People commonly lived in extended families: grandparents, uncles and aunts, cousins, and nieces and nephews all lived together in the same house or compound.

Children were viewed as a great source of happiness. The poet Kalidasa described children as the greatest joy of their father's life:

> With their teeth half-shown in causeless laughter,
> and their efforts at talking so sweetly uncertain,
> when children ask to sit on his lap
> a man is blessed, even by the dirt on their bodies.[10]

Children in poor households worked as soon as they were able. Children in wealthier households faced the age-old irritations of learning reading, writing, and arithmetic. Less attention was paid to daughters than to sons, though in more prosperous families they were often literate. Because girls who had lost their virginity could seldom hope to find good husbands and thus would become financial burdens and social disgraces to their families, daughters were customarily married as children, with consummation delayed until they reached puberty.

A wife was expected to have no life apart from her husband. A widow was expected to lead the hard life of the ascetic, sleeping on the ground; eating only one simple meal a day, without meat, wine, salt, or honey; wearing plain undyed clothes without jewelry; and shaving her head. She was viewed as inauspicious to everyone but her children, and she did not attend family festivals. Among high-caste Hindus, a widow would be praised for throwing herself on her husband's funeral pyre. Buddhist sects objected to this practice, called **sati**, but some Hindu religious authorities declared that by self-immolation a widow could expunge both her own and her husband's sins, so that both would enjoy eternal bliss in Heaven.

Within the home the position of a wife often depended on her own intelligence and strength of character. Wives were supposed to be humble, cheerful, and diligent even toward worthless husbands. As in other patriarchal societies, however, occasionally a woman ruled the household. For women who did not want to accept the strictures of married life, the main way out was to join a Buddhist or Jain religious community (see pages 190–191).

Southeast Asia, the Pacific Islands, and the Growth of Maritime Trade

☐ How did states develop along the maritime trade routes of Southeast Asia and beyond?

Much as Roman culture spread to northern Europe and Chinese culture spread to Korea, Japan, and Vietnam, in the first millennium C.E. Indian learning, technology, and material culture spread to Southeast Asia, both mainland and insular. The spread of Indian culture was facilitated by the growth of maritime trade, but this interchange did not occur uniformly, and by 1400 there were still isolated societies in this region, most notably in the Pacific islands east of Indonesia.

Southeast Asia is a tropical region that is more like India than China, with temperatures hovering around 80°F and rain falling dependably throughout the year. The topography of mainland Southeast Asia is marked by north-south mountain ranges separated by river valleys. It was easy for people to migrate south along these rivers but harder for them to cross the heavily forested mountains that divided the region into areas that had limited contact with each other. The indigenous population was originally mostly Malay, but migrations over the centuries brought many other peoples, including speakers of Austro-Asiatic (such as Vietnamese and Cambodian), Austronesian (such as Malay and Polynesian), and Sino-Tibetan-Burmese (such as Burmese and possibly Thai) languages, some of whom moved to the islands offshore and farther into the Pacific Ocean.

State Formation and Indian Influences

Southeast Asia was long a crossroads. Traders from China, India, Africa, and Europe either passed through the region when traveling from the Indian to the Pacific Ocean, or came for its resources, notably spices. (See "Global Trade: Spices," page 356.)

The northern part of modern Vietnam was under Chinese political control off and on from the second century B.C.E. to the tenth century C.E. (see pages 196–197), but Indian influence was of much greater significance for the rest of Southeast Asia. The first state to appear in historical records, called Funan by Chinese visitors, had its capital in southern Vietnam. In the first to sixth centuries C.E. Funan extended its control over much of Indochina and the Malay Peninsula. Merchants from northwest India would offload their goods and carry them across the narrowest part of the Malay Peninsula. The ports of Funan offered food and

Global Trade

Spices were a major reason from ancient times on for both Europeans and Chinese to trade with South and Southeast Asia. Pepper, nutmeg, cloves, cinnamon, and other spices were in high demand not only because they could be used to flavor food but also because they were thought to have positive pharmacological properties. Unlike other highly desired products of India and farther east—such as sugar, cotton, rice, and silk—no way was found to produce the spices close to where they were in demand. Because of the location where these spices were produced, this trade was from earliest times largely a maritime trade conducted through a series of middlemen. The spices were transported from where they were grown to nearby ports, and from there to major entrepôts (trading centers), where merchants would take them in many different directions.

Two types of pepper grew in India and Southeast Asia. Black pepper is identical to our familiar peppercorns. "Long pepper," from a related plant, was hotter. The Mediterranean world imported its pepper from India; China imported it from Southeast Asia. After the discovery of the New World, the importation of long pepper declined, as the chili pepper found in Mexico was at least as spicy and grew well in Europe and China.

By Greek and Roman times trade in pepper was substantial. According to the Greek geographer Strabo (64 B.C.E.–24 C.E.), 120 ships a year made the trip to India to acquire pepper, the round

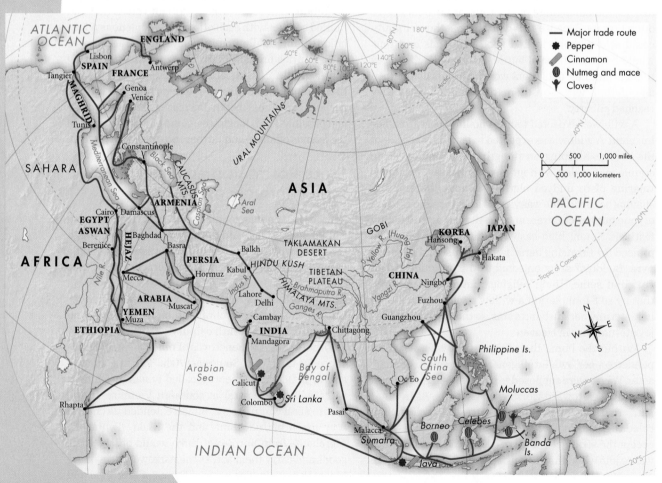

MAP 12.3 The Spice Trade, ca. 100 B.C.E.–**1500** C.E.

trip taking a year because sailors had to wait for the monsoon winds to shift direction. Pliny in about 77 C.E. complained that the Roman Empire wasted fifty million sesterces per year on long pepper and white and black pepper combined.

Cloves and nutmeg entered the repertoire of spices somewhat later than pepper. They are interesting because they could be grown in only a handful of small islands in the eastern part of the Indonesian archipelago. Merchants in China, India, Arab lands, and Europe got them through intermediaries and did not know where they were grown. An Arab source from about 1000 C.E. reported that cloves came from an island near India that had a Valley of Cloves, and that they were acquired by a silent barter. The sailors would lay the items they were willing to trade out on the beach, and the next morning they would find cloves in their place.

The demand for these spices in time encouraged Chinese, Indian, and Arab seamen to make the trip to the Strait of Malacca or east Java. Malay seamen in small craft such as outrigger canoes would bring the spices the thousand or more

A fifteenth-century Italian painter depicted a bag of cinnamon bark nearly as large as the merchant holding it. (Biblioteca Estense, Modena, Italy/The Bridgeman Art Library)

miles to the major ports where foreign merchants would purchase them. This trade was important to the prosperity of the Srivijaya kingdom. The trade was so profitable, however, that it also attracted pirates.

In the Mongol era travelers like Marco Polo, Ibn Battuta, and Odoric of Pordenone (in modern Italy) reported on the cultivation and marketing of spices in the various places they visited. Ibn Battuta described pepper plants as vines planted to grow up coconut palms. He also reported seeing the trunks of cinnamon trees floated down rivers in India. Odoric reported that pepper was picked like grapes from groves so huge it would take eighteen days to walk around them. Marco Polo referred to the 7,459 islands in the China Sea that local mariners could navigate and that produced a great variety of spices as well as aromatic wood. He also reported that spices, including pepper, nutmeg, and cloves, could be acquired at the great island of Java, perhaps not understanding that they had often been shipped from the innumerable small islands to Java.

Gaining direct access to the spices of the East was one of the motivations behind Christopher Columbus's voyages. Not long after, Portuguese sailors did reach India by sailing around Africa, and soon the Dutch were competing with them for control of the spice trade and setting up rival trading posts. Pepper was soon successfully planted in other tropical places, including Brazil. India, however, has remained the largest exporter of spices to this day.

▫ Picturing the Past

Bayan Relief, Angkor Among the many relief sculptures at the temples of Angkor are depictions of royal processions, armies at war, trade, cooking, cockfighting, and other scenes of everyday life. In the relief shown here, the boats and fish convey something of the significance of the sea to life in Southeast Asia.
(Robert Wilson, photographer)

READING THE IMAGE Find the boat. What do the people on it seem to be doing? What fish and animals do you see in the picture? Can you find the alligator eating a fish?

CONNECTIONS Why would a ruler devote so many resources to decorating the walls of a temple? Why include scenes like this one?

lodging to the merchants as they waited for the winds to shift to continue their voyages. Brahmin priests and Buddhist monks from India settled along with the traders, serving the Indian population and attracting local converts. Rulers often invited Indian priests and monks to serve under them, using them as foreign experts knowledgeable about law, government, architecture, and other fields.

Sixth-century Chinese sources report that the Funan king lived in a multistory palace and the common people lived in houses built on piles with roofs of bamboo leaves. The king rode around on an elephant, but narrow boats measuring up to ninety feet long were a more important means of transportation. The people enjoyed both cockfighting and pig fighting. Instead of drawing water from wells, as the Chinese did, they made pools, from which dozens of nearby families would draw water.

After the decline of Funan, maritime trade continued to grow, and petty kingdoms appeared in many places. Indian traders frequently established small settlements, generally located on the coast. Contact with the local populations led to intermarriage and the creation of hybrid cultures. Local rulers often adopted Indian customs and values, embraced Hinduism and Buddhism, and learned **Sanskrit**, India's classical literary language. Sanskrit gave different peoples a common mode of written expression, much as Chinese did in East Asia and Latin did in Europe.

When Indian traders, migrants, and adventurers entered mainland Southeast Asia, they encountered both

- **Sanskrit** India's classical literary language.
- **Srivijaya** A maritime empire that held the Strait of Malacca and the waters around Sumatra, Borneo, and Java.

long-settled peoples and migrants moving southward from the frontiers of China. As in other such extensive migrations, the newcomers fought one another as often as they fought the native populations. In 939 the north Vietnamese became independent of China and extended their power southward along the coast of present-day Vietnam. The Thais had long lived in what is today southwest China and north Burma. In the eighth century the Thai tribes united in a confederacy and expanded northward against Tang China. Like China, however, the Thai confederacy fell to the Mongols in 1253. Still farther west another tribal people, the Burmese, migrated to the area of modern Burma in the eighth century. They also established a state, which they ruled from their capital, Pagan, and came into contact with India and Sri Lanka.

The most important mainland state was the Khmer (kuh-MAIR) Empire of Cambodia (802–1432), which controlled the heart of the region. The Khmers were indigenous to the area. Their empire eventually extended south to the sea and the northeast Malay Peninsula. Indian influence was pervasive; the impressive temple complex at Angkor Wat built in the early twelfth century was dedicated to the Hindu god Vishnu. Social organization, however, was modeled not on the Indian caste system but on indigenous traditions of social hierarchy. A large part of the population was of slave status, many descended from non-Khmer mountain tribes defeated by the Khmers. Generally successful in a long series of wars with the Vietnamese, the Khmers reached the peak of their power in 1219 and then gradually declined.

The Srivijaya Maritime Trade Empire

Far different from these land-based states was the maritime empire of **Srivijaya**, based on the island of Sumatra in modern Indonesia. From the sixth century on, it held the important Strait of Malacca, through which most of the sea traffic between China and India passed. This state, held together as much by alliances as by direct rule, was in many ways like the Gupta state of the same period in India, securing its prominence and binding its vassals and allies through its splendor and the promise of riches through trade.

Much as the Korean and Japanese rulers adapted Chinese models (see pages 199–201), the Srivijayan rulers drew on Indian traditions to justify their rule and organize their state. The Sanskrit writing system was used for government documents, and Indians were often employed as priests, scribes, and administrators.

Angkor Wat Temple The Khmers built several stone temple complexes at Angkor. This aerial view catches something of the scale of the largest of these complexes, Angkor Wat. (Roy Garner/Alamy)

Using Sanskrit overcame the barriers raised by the many different native languages of the region. Indian mythology took hold, as did Indian architecture and sculpture. Kings and their courts, the first to embrace Indian culture, consciously spread it to their subjects. The Chinese Buddhist monk Yixing (d. 727) stopped at Srivijaya for six months in 671 on his way to India and for four years on his return journey. He found a thousand monks there, some of whom helped him translate Sanskrit texts.

After several centuries of prosperity, Srivijaya suffered a stunning blow in 1025. The Chola state in south India launched a large naval raid and captured the Srivijayan king and capital. Unable to hold their gains, the Indians retreated, but the Srivijaya Empire never regained its vigor.

During the era of the Srivijayan kingdom, other kingdoms flourished as well in island Southeast Asia. Borobudur, the magnificent Buddhist temple complex, was begun under patronage of Javan rulers in around 780. This stone monument depicts the ten tiers of Buddhist cosmology. When pilgrims made the three-mile-long winding ascent, they passed numerous sculpted reliefs depicting the journey from ignorance to enlightenment.

Buddhism became progressively more dominant in Southeast Asia after 800. Mahayana Buddhism became important in Srivijaya and Vietnam, but Theravada Buddhism, closer to the original Buddhism of early India, became the dominant form in the rest of mainland Southeast Asia. Buddhist missionaries from India and Sri Lanka played a prominent role in these developments. Local converts continued the process by making pilgrimages to India and Sri Lanka to worship and to observe Indian life for themselves.

The Spread of Indian Culture in Comparative Perspective

The social, cultural, and political systems developed in India, China, and Rome all had enormous impact on neighboring peoples whose cultures were originally not as technologically advanced. Some of the mechanisms for cultural spread were similar in all three cases, but differences were important as well.

In the case of Rome and both Han and Tang China, strong states directly ruled outlying regions, bringing their civilizations with them. India's states, even its largest empires, such as the Mauryan and Gupta, did not have comparable bureaucratic reach. Outlying areas tended to be in the hands of local lords who had consented to recognize the overlordship of the stronger state. Moreover, most of the time India was politically divided.

The expansion of Indian culture into Southeast Asia thus came not from conquest and extending direct political control, but from the extension of trading networks, with missionaries following along. This made it closer to the way Japan adopted features of Chinese culture, often through the intermediary of Korea. In both cases, the cultural exchange was largely voluntary, as the Japanese or Southeast Asians sought to adopt more up-to-date technologies (such as writing) or were persuaded of the truth of religious ideas they learned from foreigners.

The Settlement of the Pacific Islands

Through most of Eurasia, societies became progressively less isolated over time. But in 1400 there still remained many isolated societies, especially in the islands east of modern Indonesia. As discussed in Chapter 1, *Homo sapiens* began settling the western Pacific islands very early, reaching Australia by 50,000 years ago and New Guinea by 35,000 years ago. The process did not stop there, however. The ancient Austronesians (speakers of Austronesian languages) were skilled mariners who used double-canoes and brought pottery, the root vegetable taro, pigs, and chickens to numerous islands of the Pacific in subsequent centuries, generally following the coasts. Their descendants, the Polynesians, learned how to sail into the open ocean with only the stars, currents, wind patterns, paths of birds, and perhaps paths of whales and dolphins to help them navigate. They reached Tahiti and the Marquesas Islands in the central Pacific by about 200 c.e. Undoubtedly, seafarers were sometimes blown off their intended course, but communities would not have developed unless the original groups had included women as well as men, so probably in many cases they were looking for new places to live.

After reaching the central Pacific, Polynesians continued to fan out, in some cases traveling a thousand or more miles away. They reached the Hawaiian Islands in about 300 c.e., Easter Island in perhaps 1000, and New Zealand not until about 1000–1300. There even were groups who sailed west, eventually settling in Madagascar between 200 and 500.

In the more remote islands, such as Hawai'i, Easter Island, and New Zealand, the societies that developed were limited by the small range of domesticated plants and animals that the settlers brought with them and those that were indigenous to the place. Easter Island is perhaps the most extreme case. Only 15 miles wide at its widest point (only 63 square miles in total area), it is 1,300 miles from the nearest inhabited island (Pitcairn) and 2,240 miles from the coast of South America. At some point there was communication with South America, as sweet potatoes originally from there made their way to Easter Island. The community that developed on the island raised chickens and cultivated sweet potatoes, taro, and sugarcane. The inhabitants also engaged in deep-sea fishing, catching dolphins and tuna. Their tools were made of stone, wood, or bone.

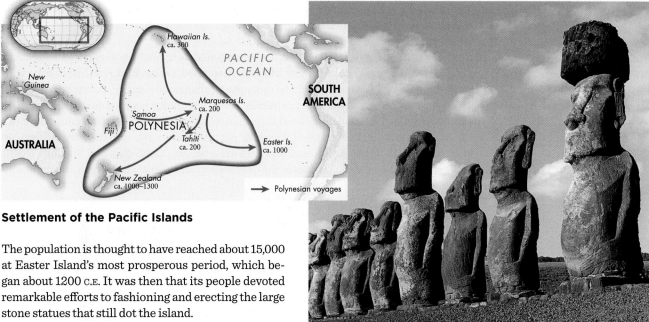

Settlement of the Pacific Islands

The population is thought to have reached about 15,000 at Easter Island's most prosperous period, which began about 1200 C.E. It was then that its people devoted remarkable efforts to fashioning and erecting the large stone statues that still dot the island.

What led the residents of such a small island to erect more than eight hundred statues, most weighing around ten tons and standing twenty to seventy feet tall? When the first Europeans arrived in 1722, no statues had been erected for several generations, and the local residents explained them as representing ancestors. One common theory is that they were central to the islanders' religion and that rival clans competed with each other to erect the most impressive statues. The effort they had to expend to carve them with stone tools, move them to the chosen site, and erect them would have been formidable.

After its heyday, Easter Island suffered severe environmental stress with the decline of its forests. Whether the rats that came with the original settlers ate too many of the trees' seeds or the islanders cut down too many of the trees to transport the stone statues, the impact of deforestation was severe. The islanders could not make boats to fish in the ocean, and bird colonies shrank, as nesting areas decreased, also reducing the food supply. Scholars still disagree on how much weight to give the many different elements that contributed to a decline in the prosperity of Easter Island from the age when the statues were erected.

Easter Island Statues Archaeologists have excavated and restored many of Easter Island's huge statues, which display remarkable stylistic consistency, with the head disproportionately large and the legs not visible. (JP De Mann/Robert Harding World Imagery)

Certainly, early settlers of an island could have drastic impact on its ecology. When Polynesians first reached New Zealand, they found large birds up to ten feet tall. They hunted them so eagerly that within a century the birds had all but disappeared. Hunting seals and sea lions also led to their rapid depletion. But the islands of New Zealand were much larger than Easter Island, and in time the Maori (the indigenous people of New Zealand) found more sustainable ways to feed themselves, depending more and more on agriculture.

The societies of Eurasia became progressively more connected to each other during the centuries discussed in this chapter. One element promoting connection was the military superiority of the nomadic warriors of the steppe, first the Turks, then the Mongols, who conquered many of the settled civilizations near them. Through conquest they introduced their culture and, in the case of the Turks, the religion of Islam to India.

Another element was maritime trade, which connected all the societies of the Indian Ocean and East Asia. As the Mongol Empire declined, maritime trading routes became an even more important part of the African, European, and Asian economic integration, with long-lasting consequences for the Afro-Eurasian trading world (see Chapter 16). Maritime trade was also one of the key elements in the spread of Indian culture to both mainland and insular Southeast Asia. Other elements connecting these societies included Sanskrit as a language of administration and missionaries who brought both Hinduism and Buddhism far beyond their homelands. Some societies did remain isolated, probably none more than the remote islands of the Pacific, such as Hawai'i, Easter Island, and New Zealand.

East Asia was a key element in both the empires created by nomadic horsemen and the South Asian maritime trading networks. As discussed in Chapter 13, before East Asia had to cope with the rise of the Mongols, it experienced one of its most prosperous periods, during which China, Korea, and Japan became more distinct culturally. China's economy boomed during the Song Dynasty, and the scholar-official class, defined through the civil service examination, came more and more to dominate culture. In Korea and Japan, by contrast, aristocrats and military men gained ascendancy. Although China, Korea, and Japan all drew on both Confucian and Buddhist teachings, they ended up with elites as distinct as the Chinese scholar-official, the Korean aristocrat, and the Japanese samurai.

□ CHAPTER REVIEW

KEY TERMS

nomads (p. 332)	protected people
steppe (p. 332)	(p. 350)
yurts (p. 335)	jati (p. 354)
Chinggis Khan	sati (p. 355)
(p. 337)	Sanskrit (p. 358)
khanates (p. 340)	Srivijaya (p. 359)
tax-farming (p. 344)	

□ **What aspects of nomadic life gave the nomads of Central Asia military advantages over nearby settled civilizations? (p. 332)**

The nomadic pastoral societies that stretched across Eurasia had the great military advantage of being able to raise horses in large numbers and support themselves from their flocks. Their mastery of the horse and mounted archery allowed them repeatedly to overawe or conquer their neighbors. On military campaigns, Mongol horsemen were able to travel without stopping for days. Nomadic pastoralists generally were organized on the basis of clans and tribes that selected chiefs for their military talent. Much of the time these tribes fought with each other, but several times in history leaders formed larger confederations capable of coordinated attacks on cities and towns. From the fifth to the twelfth centuries the most successful nomadic groups on the Eurasian steppes were Turks of one sort or another.

□ **How did Chinggis Khan and his successors conquer much of Eurasia, and how did the Mongol conquests change the regions affected? (p. 336)**

In the early thirteenth century, through his charismatic leadership and military genius, Chinggis Khan was able to lead victorious armies from one side of Eurasia to another. To avoid tribal feuding, he gave his army a non-tribal structure. He rewarded loyalty and displays of courage, but he could be merciless to those who opposed him. His initial conquests were quite destructive, with the inhabitants of many cities enslaved or killed. Those who opened their city gates and submitted without fighting could become allies and retain local power, but those who resisted faced the prospect of mass slaughter. After the empire was divided into four khanates ruled by different lines of Chinggis's descendants, more stable forms of government were developed. The Mongols gave important positions to people willing to serve them faithfully, and they did not try to change the cultures or religions of the countries they conquered. In Mongolia and China the Mongol rulers welcomed those learned in all religions. In Central Asia and Persia the Mongol khans converted to Islam and gave it the support earlier rulers there had done.

□ **How did the Mongol conquests facilitate the spread of ideas, religions, inventions, and diseases? (p. 345)**

For a century the Mongol Empire fostered unprecedented East-West contact. The Mongols encouraged trade and often moved craftsmen and other specialists from one place to another. Missionaries were tolerated, as were all religions. As more Europeans made their way east than ever before, Chinese inventions such as printing and the compass made their way west. Because Europe was further behind in 1200, it benefited most from the spread of technical and scientific ideas. Diseases also spread, including the Black Death, carried by fleas and rats that found their way into the goods of merchants and other travelers.

❑ What was the result of India's encounters with Turks, Mongols, and Islam? (p. 347)

India was invaded by the Mongols, but not conquered. After the fall of the Gupta Empire in about 480, India was for the next millennium ruled by small kingdoms, which allowed regional cultures to flourish. The north and northwest were frequently raided by Turks from Afghanistan or Central Asia, and for several centuries Muslim Turks ruled a state in north India called the Delhi sultanate. Over time Islam gained adherents throughout South Asia. Hinduism continued to flourish, but Buddhism went into decline.

❑ How did states develop along the maritime trade routes of Southeast Asia and beyond? (p. 355)

Throughout the medieval period India continued to be the center of a very active seaborne trade, and this trade helped carry Indian ideas and practices to Southeast Asia. Local rulers used experts from India to establish strong states, such as the Khmer kingdom in modern Cambodia and the Srivijaya kingdom in modern Malaysia and Indonesia. Buddhism became the dominant religion throughout the region, though Hinduism also played an important role. Indian influences did not spread uniformly, and the Pacific islands east of Indonesia remained isolated culturally for centuries.

SUGGESTED READING

Abu-Lughod, Janet L. *Before European Hegemony: The World System A.D. 1250–1350.* 1989. Examines the period of Mongol domination from a global perspective.

Ali, Daud. *Courtly Culture and Political Life in Early Medieval India.* 2004. Explores the growth of royal households and the development of a courtly worldview in India from 350 to 1200.

Beckwith, Christopher I. *Empires of the Silk Road: A History of Central Eurasia from the Bronze Age to the Present.* 2009. Makes Central Asia the center of Eurasian history.

Chaudhuri, K. N. *Asia Before Europe.* 1990. Discusses the economy and civilization of cultures within the basin of the Indian Ocean.

Di Cosmo, Nicola, Allen J. Frank, and Peter B. Golden. *The Cambridge History of Inner Asia: The Chinggisid Age.* 2009. Authoritative account of the Mongols and their successors in Central Asia.

Findley, Carter Vaughn. *The Turks in World History.* 2005. Covers both the early Turks and the connections between the Turks and the Mongols.

Fischer, Steven Roger. *A History of the Pacific Islands.* 2002. A broad-ranging history, from early settlement to modern times.

Franke, Herbert, and Denis Twitchett, eds. *The Cambridge History of China,* vol. 6, *Alien Regimes and Border States.* 1994. Clear and thoughtful accounts of the Mongols and their predecessors in East Asia.

Jackson, Peter. *The Delhi Sultanate.* 2003. Provides a close examination of north India in the thirteenth and fourteenth centuries.

Jackson, Peter. *The Mongols and the West, 1221–1410.* 2005. A close examination of many different types of connections between the Mongols and both Europe and the Islamic lands.

Lane, George. *Daily Life in the Mongol Empire.* 2006. Treats many topics, including food, health, dwellings, women, and folktales.

Liberman, Victor. *Strange Parallels: Southeast Asia in Global Context, c. 800–1830,* 2 vols. 2003, 2009. Ambitious and challenging effort to see Southeast Asia as a part of Eurasia.

Ratchnevsky, Paul. *Genghis Khan: His Life and Legacy.* 1992. A reliable account by a leading Mongolist.

Rossabi, Morris. *Khubilai Khan: His Life and Times.* 1988. Provides a lively account of the life of one of the most important Mongol rulers.

Shaffer, Lynda. *Maritime Southeast Asia to 1500.* 1996. A short account of early Southeast Asia from a world history perspective.

NOTES

1. Trans. in Denis Sinor, "The Establishment and Dissolution of the Türk Empire," in *The Cambridge History of Early Inner Asia,* ed. Denis Sinor (Cambridge: Cambridge University Press, 1990), p. 307.
2. Manuel Komroff, ed., *Contemporaries of Marco Polo* (New York: Dorset Press, 1989), p. 65.
3. Ibid.
4. *The Travels of Marco Polo, the Venetian,* ed. Manuel Komroff (New York: Boni and Liveright, 1926), pp. 93–94.
5. Cited in John Larner, *Marco Polo and the Discovery of the World* (New Haven, Conn.: Yale University Press, 1999), p. 22.
6. Quoted in A. L. Basham, *The Wonder That Was India,* 2d ed. (New York: Grove Press, 1959), p. 420. Copyright © A. L. Basham. All quotations from this work are reprinted by permission of Pan Macmillan, London, and Namita Catherine Basham.
7. Edward C. Sachau, *Alberuni's India,* vol. 1 (London: Kegan Paul, 1910), pp. 19–20, slightly modified.
8. H. A. R. Gibb, *The Travels of Ibn Battuta* (Cambridge: Cambridge University Press for the Hakluyt Society, 1971), pp. 700–701. Reprinted by permission of David Higham Associates on behalf of the Hakluyt Society.
9. Guy le Strang, trans., *Clavijo, Embassy to Tamerlane, 1403–1406* (London: Routledge, 1928), pp. 265–266.
10. Quoted in Basham, *The Wonder That Was India,* p. 161.

For practice quizzes and other study tools, visit the **Online Study Guide** at bedfordstmartins.com/mckayworld.

For primary sources from this period, see *Sources of World Societies*, **Second Edition**.

For Web sites, images, and documents related to topics in this chapter, visit **Make History** at bedfordstmartins.com/mckayworld.

• **First Song Emperor** China enjoyed a period of great cultural and economic development under the Song Dynasty, whose founder, Taizu, is depicted in this painting. (The Granger Collection, New York)

13

During the six centuries between 800 and 1400, East Asia was the most advanced region of the world. For several centuries the Chinese economy had grown spectacularly, and China's methods of production were highly advanced in fields as diverse as rice cultivation, the production of iron and steel, and the printing of books. Philosophy and the arts all flourished. China's system of government was also advanced for its time. In the Song period the principle that the government should be in the hands of highly educated scholar-officials, selected through competitive written civil service examinations, became well established. Song China's great wealth and sophisticated government did not give it military advantage, however, and in this period China had to pay tribute to militarily more powerful northern neighbors, the Khitans, the Jurchens, and finally the Mongols, who conquered all of China in 1279.

During the previous millennium basic elements of Chinese culture had spread beyond China's borders, creating the East Asian cultural sphere based on the use of Chinese as the language of civilization. Beginning around 800, however, the pendulum shifted toward cultural differentiation as Japan, Korea, and China developed in distinctive ways. In both Korea and Japan, for several centuries court aristocrats were dominant both politically and culturally, and then aristocrats lost out to generals with power in the countryside. By 1200 Japan was dominated by warriors — known as samurai — whose ethos was quite unlike China's literati elite. In both Korea and Japan, Buddhism retained a very strong hold, one of the ties that continued to link the countries of East Asia. In addition, China and Korea both had to deal with the same menacing neighbors to the north. Even Japan had to mobilize its resources to fend off two seaborne Mongol attacks. •

States and Cultures in East Asia
800–1400

The Medieval Chinese Economic Revolution, 800–1100

☐ What made possible the expansion of the Chinese economy, and what were the outcomes of this economic growth?

China During the Song and Yuan Dynasties, 960–1368

☐ How did the civil service examinations and the scholar-official class shape Chinese society and culture, and what impact did the Mongol conquest have on them?

Korea Under the Koryŏ Dynasty, 935–1392

☐ How did Korean society and culture develop in an age when its northern neighbors were Khitans, Jurchens, and Mongols?

Japan's Heian Period, 794–1185

☐ How did the Heian form of government contribute to the cultural flowering of Japan in the period?

The Samurai and the Kamakura Shogunate, 1185–1333

☐ What were the causes and consequences of military rule in Japan?

The Medieval Chinese Economic Revolution, 800–1100

☐ What made possible the expansion of the Chinese economy, and what were the outcomes of this economic growth?

Chinese historians traditionally viewed dynasties as following a standard cyclical pattern. Founders were vigorous men able to recruit capable followers to serve as officials and generals. Externally they would extend China's borders; internally they would bring peace. They would collect low but fairly assessed taxes. Over time, however, emperors born in the palace would get used to luxury and lack the founders' strength and wisdom. Families with wealth or political power would find ways to avoid taxes, forcing the government to impose heavier taxes on the poor. As a result, impoverished peasants would flee; the morale of those in the government and armies would decline; and the dynasty would find itself able neither to maintain internal peace nor to defend its borders.

Viewed in terms of this theory of the **dynastic cycle**, by 800 the Tang Dynasty (see pages 193–196) was in decline. It had ruled China for nearly two centuries, and its high point was in the past. A massive rebellion had wracked it in the mid-eighth century, and the Uighur Turks and Tibetans were menacing its borders. Many of the centralizing features of the government had been abandoned, with power falling more and more to regional military governors.

Historically, Chinese political theorists always assumed that a strong, centralized government was better than a weak one or than political division, but if anything the Tang toward the end of its dynastic cycle seems to have been both intellectually and economically more vibrant than the early Tang had been. Less control from the central government seems to have stimulated trade and economic growth.

A government census conducted in 742 shows that China's population was still approximately 50 million, very close to what it had been in 2 C.E. Over the next three centuries, with the expansion of wet-field rice cultivation in central and south China, the country's food supply steadily increased, and so did its popula-

Chinese Paper Money Chinese paper currency indicated the unit of currency and the date and place of issue. The Mongols continued the use of paper money, as this note from the Mongol period attests. (© Cultural Relics Press)

tion, which reached 100 million by 1100. China was certainly the largest country in the world at the time; its population probably already exceeded that of all the Islamic countries of the time or that of all the countries of Europe put together.

Agricultural prosperity and denser settlement patterns aided commercialization of the economy. Peasants in Song China no longer merely aimed at self-sufficiency. They had found that producing for the market made possible a better life. Peasants sold their surpluses and used their profits to buy charcoal, tea, oil, and wine. In many places farmers specialized in commercial crops, such as sugar, oranges, cotton, silk, and tea. (See "Global Trade: Tea," page 368.) The need to transport the products of interregional trade stimulated the inland and coastal shipping industries, providing employment for shipbuilders and sailors and business opportunities for enterprising families with enough capital to purchase a boat. Marco Polo, the Venetian merchant who wrote of his visit to China from about 1275 to 1292, was astounded at the boat traffic on the Yangzi River. He claimed to have seen no fewer than fifteen thousand vessels at one city on the river, "and yet there are other towns where the number is still greater."[1]

As marketing increased, demand for money grew enormously, leading eventually to the creation of the world's first paper money. The decision by the late Tang government to abandon the use of bolts of silk as supplementary currency had increased the demand for copper coins. By 1085 the output of coins had increased tenfold to more than 6 billion coins a year. To avoid the weight and bulk of coins for large transactions, local merchants in late Tang times started trading receipts from deposit shops where they had left money or goods. The early Song authorities awarded a small set of these shops a monopoly on the issuing of these certificates of deposit, and in the 1120s the government took over the system, producing the world's first government-issued paper money. Marco Polo was amazed:

> The coinage of this paper money is authenticated with as much form and ceremony as if it were actually of pure gold or silver; for to each note a number of officers, specially appointed, not only subscribe their names, but affix their signets also; and when this has been regularly done by the whole of them,

> "The coinage of this paper money is authenticated with as much form and ceremony as if it were actually of pure gold or silver."
>
> **MARCO POLO**

the principal officer . . . having dipped into vermilion the royal seal committed to his custody, stamps with it the piece of paper, so that the form of the seal tinged with the vermilion remains impressed upon it.[2]

With the intensification of trade, merchants became progressively more specialized and organized. They set up partnerships and joint stock companies, with a separation of owners (shareholders) and managers. In the large cities merchants were organized into guilds according to the type of product sold, and they arranged sales from wholesalers to shop owners and periodically set prices. When government officials wanted to

• **dynastic cycle** The theory that Chinese dynasties go through a predictable cycle from early vigor and growth to subsequent decline as administrators become lax and the well-off find ways to avoid paying taxes, cutting state revenues.

Global Trade

Tea is made from the young leaves and leaf buds of *Camellia sinensis*, a plant native to the hills of southwest China. As an item of trade, tea has a very long history. Already by Han times (206 B.C.E.–220 C.E.) tea was being grown and drunk in southwest China, and for several centuries thereafter it was looked on as a local product of the region with useful pharmacologic properties, such as countering the effects of wine. By Tang times (608–907) it was being widely cultivated in the Yangzi River Valley and was a major item of interregional trade. Tea was common enough in Tang life that poets often mentioned it in their poems. In the eighth century the Chinese poet Lu Yu wrote an entire treatise on the wonders of tea.

The most intensive time for tea production was the harvest season, since young leaves were of much more value than mature ones. Mobilized for about a month each year, women would come out to help pick the tea. Not only were Chinese tea merchants among the wealthiest merchants, but from the late eighth century on, taxes on tea became a major source of government revenue.

Tea circulated in several forms, loose and compressed (brick), powder and leaf. The cost of tea varied both by form and by region of origin. In Song times (960–1279), the cheapest tea could cost as little as 18 cash per catty, the most expensive 275. In Kaifeng in the 1070s the most popular type was loose tea powdered at water mills. The tea exported from Sichuan to Tibet, however, was formed into solid bricks for ease of transport.

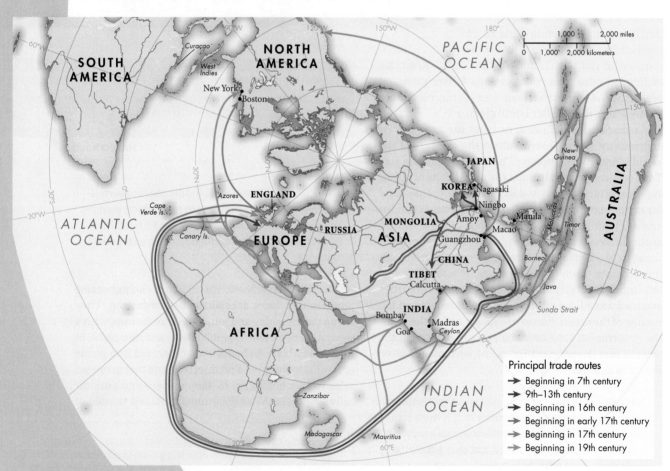

MAP 13.1 The Tea Trade

The Song Dynasty established a government monopoly on tea. Only those who purchased government licenses could legally trade in tea. The dynasty also used its control of tea to ensure a supply of horses, needed for military purposes. The government could do this because the countries on its borders that produced the best horses—Tibet, Central Asia, Mongolia, and so on—were not suitable for growing tea. Thus the Song government insisted on horses for tea.

Tea reached Korea and Japan as a part of Buddhist culture. Buddhist monks drank it to help them stay awake during long hours of recitation or meditation. The priest Saichō, patriarch of Tendai Buddhism, visited China in 804 and reportedly brought back tea seeds. Tea drinking did not become widespread in Japan, however, until the twelfth century, when Zen monasteries popularized its use. By the fourteenth century tea imported from China was still prized, but the Japanese had already begun to appreciate the distinctive flavors of teas from different regions of Japan. With the development of the tea ceremony, tea drinking became an art in Japan, with much attention to the selection and handling of tea utensils. In both Japan and Korea, offerings of tea became a regular part of offerings to ancestors, as they were in China.

Tea drinkers were fastidious about the utensils they used, the temperature of the water, and how the tea was prepared. In this detail from a Song period painting, a gentleman is supervising three servants who are preparing tea outdoors for his guests. The fourteenth-century Chinese tea-leaf jar (right) was imported to Japan, where it was treasured as an art object and used by tea masters. (ceremony: National Palace Museum, Taipei, Taiwan; jar: Tokugawa Art Museum, Nagoya)

Tea did not become important in Europe until the seventeenth century. Tea first reached Russia in 1618, when a Chinese embassy presented some to the tsar. Under agreements between the Chinese and Russian governments, camel trains would arrive in China laden with furs and would return carrying tea, taking about a year for the round trip. By 1700 Russia was receiving more than 600 camel loads of tea annually. By 1800 it was receiving more than 6,000 loads, amounting to more than 3.5 million pounds. Tea reached western Europe in the sixteenth century, both via Arabs and via Jesuit priests traveling on Portuguese ships.

In Britain, where tea drinking would become a national institution, tea was first drunk in coffeehouses. In his famous diary Samuel Pepys recorded having his first cup of tea in 1660. By the end of the seventeenth century tea made up more than 90 percent of China's exports to England. In the eighteenth century tea drinking spread to homes and tea gardens. Queen Anne (r. 1702–1714) was credited with starting the custom of drinking tea instead of ale for breakfast. Afternoon tea became a central feature of British social life in the nineteenth century.

Already by the end of the eighteenth century Britain imported so much tea from China that it worried about the outflow of silver to pay for it. Efforts to balance trade with China involved promoting the sale of Indian opium to China and efforts to grow tea in British colonies. Using tea seeds collected in China and a tea plant indigenous to India's Assam province, both India and Sri Lanka eventually grew tea successfully. By the end of the nineteenth century huge tea plantations had been established in India, and India surpassed China as an exporter of tea.

The spread of the popularity of drinking tea also stimulated the desire for fine cups to drink it from. Importation of Chinese ceramics, therefore, often accompanied adoption of China's tea customs.

requisition supplies or assess taxes, they dealt with the guild heads.

Foreign trade also flourished in the Song period. In 1225 the superintendent of customs at the coastal city of Quanzhou wrote an account of the foreign places Chinese merchants visited. It includes sketches of major trading cities from Srivijaya and Malabar in Southeast Asia to Cairo and Baghdad in the Middle East. Pearls were said to come from the Persian Gulf, ivory from the Red Sea port of Aden, pepper from the Indonesian islands of Java and Sumatra, and cotton from the various kingdoms of India. In this period Chinese ships began to displace Indian and Arab merchants in the South Seas. Ship design was improved in several ways. Watertight bulkheads improved buoyancy and protected cargo. Stern-mounted rudders improved steering. Some of the ships were powered by both oars and sails and were large enough to hold several hundred men.

Also important to oceangoing travel was the perfection of the **compass**. The way a magnetic needle would point north had been known for some time, but in Song times the needle was reduced in size and attached to a fixed stem (rather than floated in water). In some cases it was put in a small protective case with a glass top, making it suitable for sea travel. The first reports of a compass used in this way date to 1119.

The Song also witnessed many advances in industrial techniques. Heavy industry, especially iron, grew astoundingly. With advances in metallurgy, iron production reached around 125,000 tons per year in 1078, a sixfold increase over the output in 800. At first charcoal was used in the production process, leading to deforestation of parts of north China. By the end of the eleventh century, however, bituminous coke had largely taken the place of charcoal. Much of the iron was put to military purposes. Mass-production methods were used to make iron armor in small, medium, and large sizes. High-quality steel for swords was made through high-temperature metallurgy. Huge bellows, often driven by water wheels, were used to superheat the molten ore. The needs of the army also brought Chinese engineers to experiment with the use of gunpowder. In the twelfth-century wars against the Jurchens (see page 334), those defending a besieged city used gunpowder to propel projectiles at the enemy.

The quickening of the economy fueled the growth of cities. Dozens of cities had fifty thousand or more residents, and quite a few had more than a hundred thousand — very large populations compared to other places in the world at the time. Both the capitals, Kaifeng (kigh-fuhng) and Hangzhou (hahng-joh), are estimated to have had in the vicinity of a million residents. Marco Polo described Hangzhou as the finest and most splendid city in the world. He reported that it had ten marketplaces, each half a mile long, where forty thousand to fifty thousand people would shop on any given day. There were also bathhouses; permanent shops selling things such as spices, drugs, and pearls; and innumerable courtesans — "adorned in much finery, highly

City Life A well-developed system of river and canal transport kept the Song capital well supplied with goods from across China, as shown in this detail from a 17-foot-long hand scroll painted in the twelfth century. (Palace Museum, Beijing)

Transplanting Rice To get the maximum yield per plot and to make it possible to grow two crops in the same field, Chinese farmers grew rice seedlings in a seed bed and then, when a field was free, transplanted the seedlings into the flooded field. Because the Song government wanted to promote up-to-date agricultural technology, in the twelfth century it commissioned a set of twelve illustrations of the steps to be followed. This painting comes from a later version of those illustrations. (Freer Gallery of Art, Smithsonian Institution, Washington, D.C., Purchase F1949.9b, F1954.20)

perfumed, occupying well-furnished houses, and attended by many female domestics."³

The medieval economic revolution shifted the economic center of China south to the Yangzi River drainage area. This area had many advantages over the north China plain. Rice, which grew in the south, provides more calories per unit of land and therefore allows denser settlement. The milder temperatures often allowed two crops to be grown on the same plot of land, first a summer and then a winter crop. The abundance of rivers and streams facilitated shipping, which reduced the cost of transportation and thus made regional specialization economically more feasible. In the first half of the Song Dynasty, the capital was still at Kaifeng in the north, close to the Grand Canal (see page 193), which linked the capital to the rich south.

The economic revolution of Song times cannot be attributed to intellectual change, as Confucian scholars did not reinterpret the classics to defend the morality of commerce. But neither did scholar-officials take a unified stand against economic development. As officials they had to work to produce revenue to cover government expenses such as defense, and this was much easier to do when commerce was thriving.

Ordinary people benefited from the Song economic revolution in many ways. There were more opportunities for the sons of farmers to leave agriculture and find work in cities. Those who stayed in agriculture had a better chance to improve their situations by taking up sideline production of wine, charcoal, paper, or textiles. Energetic farmers who grew cash crops such as sugar, tea, mulberry leaves (for silk), and cotton (recently introduced from India) could grow rich. Greater interregional trade led to the availability of more goods at the rural markets held every five or ten days.

Of course, not everyone grew rich. Poor farmers who fell into debt had to sell their land, and if they still owed money they could be forced to sell their daughters as maids, concubines, or prostitutes. The prosperity of the cities created a huge demand for women to serve the rich in these ways, and Song sources mention that criminals would kidnap girls and women to sell in distant cities at huge profits.

China During the Song and Yuan Dynasties, 960–1368

☐ How did the civil service examinations and the scholar-official class shape Chinese society and culture, and what impact did the Mongol conquest have on them?

In the tenth century Tang China broke up into separate contending states, some of which had non-Chinese rulers. The two states that proved to be long-lasting were the Song, which came to control almost all of China proper south of the Great Wall, and the Liao, whose ruling house was Khitan and which held the territory of modern Beijing and areas north (Map 13.2). Although the Song Dynasty had a much larger population, the Liao was militarily the stronger of the two. In

• **compass** A tool developed in Song times to aid in navigation at sea; it consisted of a magnetic needle that would point north that was placed in a small protective case.

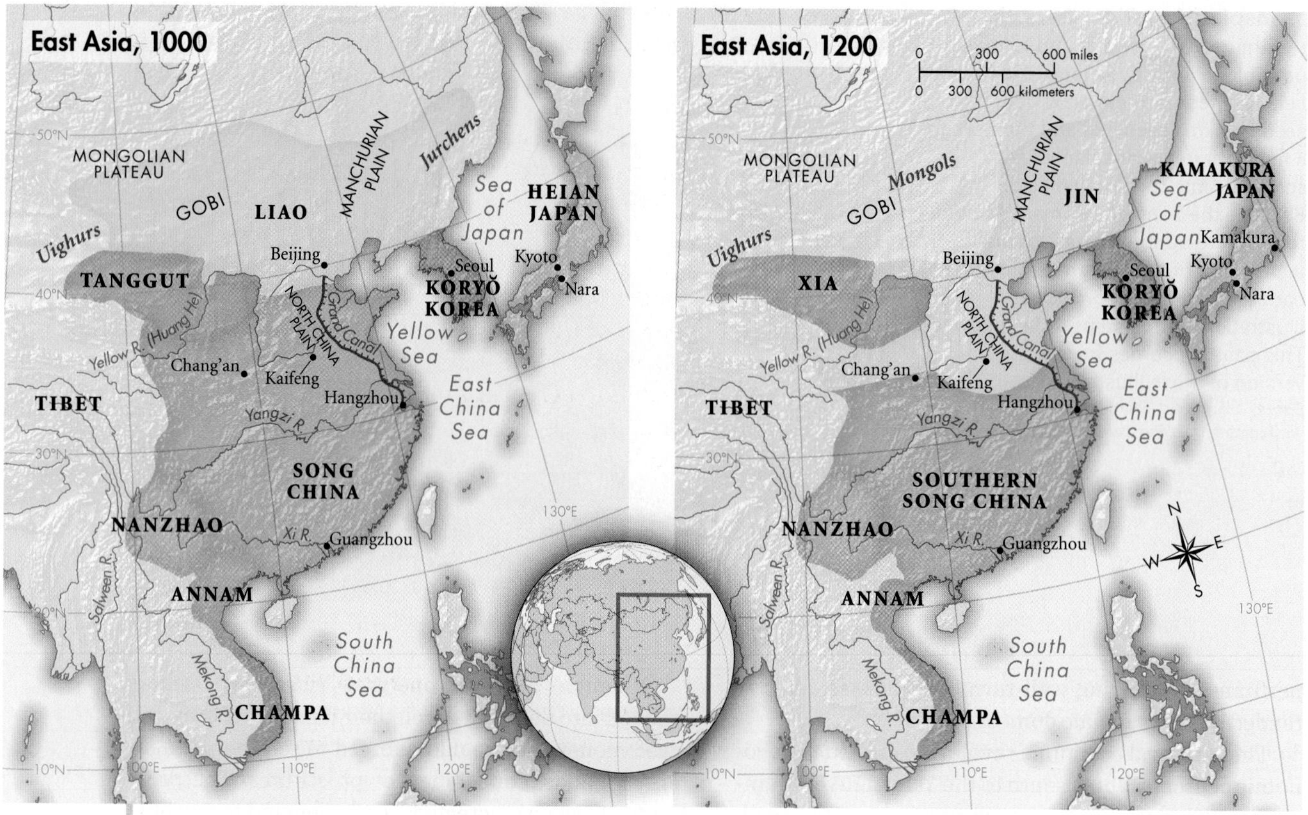

East Asia, 1000

East Asia, 1200

▫ Mapping the Past

MAP 13.2 East Asia in 1000 and 1200 The Song Empire did not extend as far as its predecessor, the Tang, and faced powerful rivals to the north—the Liao Dynasty of the Khitans and the Xia Dynasty of the Tanguts. Koryŏ Korea maintained regular contact with Song China, but Japan, by the late Heian period, was no longer deeply involved with the mainland. By 1200 military families dominated both Korea and Japan, but the borders were little changed. On the mainland, the Liao Dynasty had been overthrown by the Jurchens' Jin Dynasty, which also seized the northern third of the Song Empire. Because the Song relocated its capital to Hangzhou in the south, this period is called the Southern Song period.

ANALYZING THE MAP What are the countries of East Asia in 1000? What are the major differences in 1200?

CONNECTIONS What connections do you see between the length of their northern borders and the histories of China, Korea, and Japan?

the early twelfth century the Liao state was defeated by the Jurchens, another non-Chinese people, who founded the Jin Dynasty and went on to conquer most of north China, leaving Song to control only the south. After a century the Jurchens' Jin Dynasty was defeated by the Mongols who extended their Yuan Dynasty to control all of China by 1276.

The Song Dynasty

The founder of the Song Dynasty, Taizu (r. 960–976), was a general whose troops elevated him to emperor (somewhat reminiscent of Roman practice). Taizu worked to make sure that such an act could not happen

in the future by placing the armies under central government control. To curb the power of his generals, he retired or rotated them and assigned civil officials to supervise them. In time these civil bureaucrats came to dominate every aspect of Song government and society. The civil service examination system established during the Sui Dynasty (see page 192) was greatly expanded to provide the dynasty with a constant flow of men trained in the Confucian classics.

Curbing the generals' power ended warlordism but did not solve the military problem of defending against the nomadic Khitans's Liao Dynasty to the north. After several attempts to push the Liao back beyond the Great Wall, the Song concluded a peace treaty with them. The Song agreed to make huge annual payments of gold and silk to the Khitans, in a sense paying them not to invade. Even so, the Song rulers had to maintain a standing army of more than a million men. By the middle of the eleventh century military expenses consumed half the government's revenues. Song had the industrial base to produce swords, armor, and arrowheads in huge quantities, but had difficulty maintaining enough horses and well-trained horsemen. Even though China was the economic powerhouse of the region, with by far the largest population, the horse was a major weapon of war in this period, and it was not easy to convert wealth to military advantage.

In the early twelfth century the military situation rapidly worsened when the Khitan state was destroyed by another tribal confederation led by the Jurchens. Although the Song allied with the Jurchens, the Jurchens quickly realized how easy it would be to defeat the Song. When they marched into the Song capital in 1126, they captured the emperor and took him and his entire court hostage, and he died eight years later in captivity. Song forces rallied around one of his sons who escaped capture, and this prince reestablished a Song court in the south at Hangzhou (see Map 13.2). This Southern Song Dynasty controlled only about two-thirds of the former Song territories, but the social, cultural, and intellectual life there remained vibrant until the Song fell to the Mongols in 1279.

The Scholar-Officials and Neo-Confucianism

The Song period saw the full flowering of one of the most distinctive features of Chinese civilization, the **scholar-official class** certified through highly competitive civil service examinations. This elite was both broader and better educated than the elites of earlier periods in Chinese history. Once the **examination system** was fully developed, aristocratic habits and prejudices largely disappeared. Ancestry did not matter as much when office depended more on study habits than on connections.

The examination system came to carry such prestige that the number of scholars entering each competition escalated rapidly, from fewer than 30,000 early in the eleventh century, to nearly 80,000 by the end of that century, to about 400,000 by the dynasty's end. To prepare for the examinations, men had to memorize the classics in order to be able to recognize even the most obscure passages. They also had to master specific forms of composition, including poetry, and be ready to discuss policy issues, citing appropriate historical examples. Those who became officials this way had usually tried the exams several times and were on average a little over thirty years of age when they succeeded. Because the competition was so fierce, the

great majority of those who devoted years to preparing for the exams never became officials.

The invention of printing should be given some credit for the trend toward a better-educated elite. Tang craftsmen developed the art of carving words and pictures into wooden blocks, inking the blocks, and pressing paper onto them. Each block held an entire page of text and illustrations. Such whole-page blocks were used for printing as early as the middle of the ninth century, and in the eleventh century **movable type** (one piece of type for each character) was invented, but it was rarely used because whole-block printing was cheaper. In China as in Europe a couple of centuries later, the introduction of printing dramatically lowered the price of books, thus aiding the spread of literacy.

Among the upper class the availability of cheaper books enabled scholars to amass their own libraries. Song publishers printed the classics of Chinese literature in huge editions to satisfy scholarly appetites. Works on philosophy, science, and medicine also were avidly consumed, as were Buddhist texts. Han and Tang poetry and historical works became the models for Song writers. One popular literary innovation was the encyclopedia, which first appeared in the Song period, at least five centuries before the publication of the first European encyclopedia.

The life of the educated man involved more than study for the civil service examinations and service in office. Many took to refined pursuits such as collecting antiques or old books and practicing the arts—especially poetry writing, calligraphy, and painting. For many individuals these cultural interests overshadowed any philosophical, political, or economic concerns; others found in them occasional outlets for creative activity and aesthetic pleasure. In the Song period the engagement of the elite with the arts led to extraordinary achievement in calligraphy and painting, especially landscape painting. A large share of the social life of upper-class men was centered on these refined pastimes, as they gathered to compose or criticize poetry, to view each other's art treasures, and to patronize young talents.

The new scholar-official elite produced some extraordinary men able to hold high court offices while pursuing diverse intellectual interests. (See "Individuals in Society: Shen Gua," page 375.) Ouyang Xiu spared

---

- **scholar-official class** Chinese educated elite that included both scholars and officials. The officials had usually gained office by passing the highly competitive civil service examination. Scholars without office had often studied for the examinations but failed repeatedly.

- **examination system** A system of selecting officials based on competitive written examinations.

- **movable type** A system of printing in which one piece of type is used for each unique character.

◻ Picturing the Past

On a Mountain Path in Spring With spare, sketchy strokes, the court painter Ma Yuan (ca. 1190–1225) depicts a scholar on an outing accompanied by his boy servant carrying a lute. The scholar gazes into the mist, his eyes attracted by a bird in flight. The poetic couplet was inscribed by Emperor Ningzong (r. 1194–1124), at whose court Ma Yuan served. It reads: "Brushed by his sleeves, wild flowers dance in the wind. / Fleeing from him, hidden birds cut short their songs." (National Palace Museum, Taipei, Taiwan)

ANALYZING THE IMAGE Find the key elements in this picture: the scholar, the servant boy, the bird, the willow tree. Are these elements skillfully conveyed? Are there other elements in the painting that you find hard to read?

CONNECTIONS What do you think is the reason for writing a poetic couplet on this painting? Does it enhance the experience of viewing the painting or detract from it?

time in his busy official career to write love songs, histories, and the first analytical catalogue of rubbings of ancient stone and bronze inscriptions. Sima Guang, besides serving as prime minister, wrote a narrative history of China from the Warring States Period (403–221 B.C.E.) to the founding of the Song Dynasty. Su Shi wrote more than twenty-seven hundred poems and eight hundred letters while active in opposition politics. He was also an esteemed painter, calligrapher, and theorist of the arts. Su Song, another high official, constructed an eighty-foot-tall mechanical clock. He adapted the water-powered clock invented in the Tang period by adding a chain-driven mechanism. The clock told not only the time of day but also the day of the month, the phase of the moon, and the position of certain stars and planets in the sky. As in Renaissance Europe a couple of centuries later (discussed in Chapter 15), gifted men made advances in a wide range of fields.

These highly educated men accepted the Confucian responsibility to aid the ruler in the governing of the country. In this period, however, this commitment tended to embroil them in unpleasant factional politics. In 1069 the chancellor Wang Anshi proposed a series of sweeping reforms designed to raise revenues and help small farmers. Many well-respected scholars and officials thought that Wang's policies would do more harm than good and resisted enforcing them. Animosities grew as critics were assigned offices far from the capital. Later, when they returned to power, they retaliated against those who had pushed them out, escalating the conflict.

Individuals in Society

Shen Gua

IN THE ELEVENTH CENTURY IT WAS NOT RARE for Chinese men of letters to have broad interests, but few could compare to Shen Gua (1031–1095), a man who tried his hand at everything from mathematics, geography, economics, engineering, medicine, divination, and archaeology to military strategy and diplomacy.

In his youth Shen Gua traveled widely with his father, who served as a provincial official, which added to his knowledge of geography. In 1063 he passed the civil service examinations, and in 1066 he received a post in the capital, just before Wang Anshi's rise to power. He generally sided with Wang in the political disputes of the day. He eventually held high astronomical, ritual, and financial posts and became involved in waterworks and the construction of defense walls. He was sent as an envoy to the Khitans in 1075 to try to settle a boundary dispute. When a military campaign that he advised failed in 1082, he was demoted and later retired to write.

It is from his book of notes that we know the breadth of his interests. In one note Shen describes how, on assignment to inspect the frontier, he made a relief map of wood and glue-soaked sawdust to show the mountains, roads, rivers, and passes. The emperor was so impressed when he saw it that he ordered all the border prefectures to make relief maps. Elsewhere Shen describes the use of petroleum and explains how to make movable type from clay. Shen Gua often applied a mathematical approach to issues that his contemporaries did not think of in those terms. He once computed the total number of possible situations on a Go board, and another time he calculated the longest possible military campaign given the limits of human carriers, who had to carry their own food as well as food for the soldiers.

Shen Gua is especially known for his scientific explanations. He explained the deflection of the compass from due south. He identified petrified bamboo and from its existence argued that the region where it was found must have been much warmer and more humid in ancient times. He argued against the theory that tides are caused by the rising and setting of the sun, demonstrating that they correlate with the cycles of the moon. He proposed switching from a lunar calendar to a solar one of 365 days, saying that even though his contemporaries would reject his idea, "surely in the future some will adopt my idea." To convince his readers that the sun and the moon were spherical, not flat, he suggested that they cover a ball with fine powder on one side and then look at it obliquely. The powder was the part of the moon illuminated by the sun, and as the viewer looked at it obliquely, the white part would be crescent shaped, like a waxing moon. Shen Gua, however, did not realize that the sun and moon had entirely different orbits, and he explained why they did not collide by positing that both were composed of *qi* (vital energy) and had form but not substance.

Shen Gua also wrote on medicine and criticized his contemporaries for paying more attention to old treatises than to clinical experience. Yet he, too, was sometimes stronger on theory than on observation. In one note he argued that longevity pills could be made from cinnabar. He reasoned that if cinnabar could be transformed in one direction, it ought to be susceptible to transformation in the opposite direction as well. Therefore, since melted cinnabar causes death, solid cinnabar should prevent death.

QUESTIONS FOR ANALYSIS

1. How did Shen Gua's travels add to his curiosity about the material world?

2. In what ways could Shen Gua have used his scientific interests in his work as a government official?

3. How does Shen Gua's understanding of the natural world compare to that of the early Greeks? (See Chapter 5, pages 128–131.)

• **Shen Gua played Go with white and black markers on a grid-like board like this one.**
(Library of Congress, LC-USZC4-8471/8472)

Besides politics, scholars also debated issues in ethics and metaphysics. For several centuries Buddhism had been more vital than Confucianism. Beginning in the late Tang period Confucian teachers began claiming that the teachings of the Confucian sages contained all the wisdom one needed and that a true Confucian would reject Buddhist teachings. During the eleventh century many Confucian teachers urged students to set their sights not on exam success but on the higher goals of attaining the wisdom of the sages. Metaphysical theories about the workings of the cosmos in terms of *li* (principle) and *qi* (vital energy) were developed in response to the challenge of the sophisticated metaphysics of Buddhism.

Neo-Confucianism, as this movement is generally termed, was more fully developed in the twelfth century by the immensely learned Zhu Xi (joo shee) (1130–1200). Besides serving in office, he wrote, compiled, or edited almost a hundred books; corresponded with dozens of other scholars; and still regularly taught groups of disciples, many of whom stayed with him for years at a time. Although he was treated as a political threat during his lifetime, within decades of his death his writings came to be considered orthodox, and in subsequent centuries candidates for the examinations had to be familiar with his commentaries on the classics. (See "Viewpoints: Zhu Xi and Yuan Cai on Family Management," page 377.)

Women's Lives in Song Times

Thanks to the spread of printing, more books survive from the Song period than from earlier periods, giving us more glimpses of women's lives. Song stories, documents, and legal cases show us widows who ran inns, maids sent out by their mistresses to do errands, midwives who delivered babies, pious women who spent their days chanting Buddhist sutras, nuns who called on such women to explain Buddhist doctrine, girls who learned to read with their brothers, farmers' daughters who made money by weaving mats, child-

less widows who accused their nephews of stealing their property, wives who were jealous of the concubines their husbands brought home, and women who used part of their own large dowries to help their husbands' sisters marry well.

Families who could afford it usually tried to keep their wives and daughters within the walls of the house, rather than let them work in the fields or in shops or inns. At home there was plenty for them to do. Not only was there the work of tending children and preparing meals, but spinning, weaving, and sewing were considered women's work and took a great deal of time. Families that raised silkworms also needed women to do much of the work of coddling the worms and getting them to spin their cocoons. Within the home women generally had considerable say and took active interest in issues such as the selection of marriage partners for their children.

Women tended to marry between the ages of sixteen and twenty. Their husbands were, on average, a couple of years older than they were. Marriages were arranged by their parents, who would have either called on a professional matchmaker (most often an older woman) or turned to a friend or relative for suggestions. Before a wedding took place, written agreements were exchanged, listing the prospective bride's and groom's birth dates, parents, and grandparents; the gifts that would be exchanged; and the dowry the bride would bring. The goal was to match families of approximately equal status, but a young man who had just passed the civil service exams would be considered a good prospect even if his family had little wealth.

A few days before the wedding the bride's family sent her dowry to the groom's family, which at a minimum contained boxes full of clothes and bedding. In better-off families, the dowry also included items of substantial value, such as gold jewelry or deeds to land. On the day of the wedding the groom and some of his friends and relatives went

Woman Attendant The Song emperors were patrons of a still-extant temple in northern China that enshrined a statue of the "holy mother," the mother of the founder of the ancient Zhou Dynasty. The forty-two maids who attend her, one of whom is shown here, seem to have been modeled on the palace ladies who attended Song emperors. (© Cultural Relics Press)

• **Neo-Confucianism** The revival of Confucian thinking that began in the eleventh century, characterized by the goal of attaining the wisdom of the sages, not exam success.

Viewpoints

Zhu Xi and Yuan Cai on Family Management

• *The Confucian tradition put considerable emphasis on the correct way for family members to treat each other and on the rituals that should govern family life. Filial piety was considered a central virtue in Confucius's* Analects, *and the early Confucian text, the* Greater Learning, *argued that a man who wanted to serve the ruler or bring peace to the realm had to first manage his own family.*

What could one do to attain harmony in his family? Zhu Xi (1130–1200), one of the leading Neo-Confucian philosophers of his day, placed emphasis on ritual. His discussion of the importance of setting up an ancestral shrine is the first item in his influential Family Rituals. *Other parts of this book detail the steps to be taken in funerals, weddings, coming-of-age ceremonies, and ancestral rites. His contemporary Yuan Cai (ca. 1140–ca. 1190) was a local government official whose views about how to attain family harmony seem to have come from his personal experience rather than the study of Confucian texts. His book also gives advice on arranging marriages, managing servants, and avoiding bankruptcy These two books, while written in Chinese, circulated in Korea and Japan as well as China, with Zhu Xi's* Family Rituals *becoming especially important in Korea.*

Zhu Xi on the Offering Hall

When a man of virtue builds a house his first task is always to set up an offering hall to the east of the main room of his house. For this hall four altars to hold the spirit tablets of the ancestors are made; collateral relatives who died without descendants may have associated offerings made to them there according to their generational seniority. Sacrificial fields should be established and sacrificial utensils prepared. Once the hall is completed, early each morning the master enters the outer gate to pay a visit. All comings and goings are reported there. On New Year's Day, the solstices, and each new and full moon, visits are made. On the customary festivals, seasonal foods are offered, and when an event occurs, reports are made. Should there be flood, fire, robbers, or bandits, the offering hall is the first thing to be saved. The spirit tablets, inherited manuscripts, and then the sacrificial utensils should be moved; only afterward may the family's valuables be taken. As one generation succeeds another, the spirit tablets are reinscribed and moved to their new places.

Yuan Cai on Forbearance

People say that lasting harmony in families begins with the ability to forbear. But knowing how to forbear without knowing how to live with forbearing can lead to a great many errors. Some seem to think that forbearance means to repress anger; that is, when someone offends you, you repress your feelings and do not reveal them. If this happens only once or twice it would be all right. But if it happens repeatedly the anger will come bursting forth like an irrepressible flood.

A better method is to dissipate anger as the occasion arises instead of hiding it in your chest. Do this by saying to yourself, "He wasn't thinking," "He doesn't know any better," "He made a mistake," "He is narrow in his outlook," "How much harm can this really do?" If you keep the anger from entering your heart, then even if someone offends you ten times a day, neither your speech nor your behavior will be affected. You will then see the magnitude of the benefits of forbearance.

Yuan Cai on Dislike Among Relatives

Dislike among blood relatives may start from a very minor incident but end up ingrained. It is just that once two people take a dislike to each other they become irascible, and neither is willing to be the first to cool off. When they are in each other's company day in and day out, they cannot help but irritate each other. If, having reached this state, one of them would be willing to take the initiative in cooling off and would talk to the other, then the other would reciprocate, and the situation would return to normal. This point is worth deep consideration.

Sources: Patricia Buckley Ebrey, trans., *Family and Property in Sung China: Yuan Ts'ai's* Precepts for Social Life (Princeton, N.J.: Princeton University Press, 1984), pp. 186–187. Reprinted by permission of Princeton University Press; Patricia Buckley Ebrey, trans., *Chu Hsi's* Family Rituals: *A Twelfth-Century Chinese Manual for the Performance of Cappings, Weddings, Funerals, and Ancestral Rites* (Princeton, N.J.: Princeton University Press, 1991), p. 5. Reprinted by permission of Princeton University Press.

QUESTIONS FOR ANALYSIS

1. Would attention to the details of ancestral rites of the sort Zhu Xi outlines help avoid the sorts of problems among relatives that Yuan Cai discusses, or could it make them worse?
2. The ideal Chinese family was one that did not divide during the parents' lifetimes, so that adult brothers and their families all lived together with their elderly parents. What can you infer about problems connected to such large, complex families from these two authors?

to the bride's home to get her. She would be elaborately dressed and would tearfully bid farewell to everyone in her family. She was carried to her new home in a fancy sedan chair to the sound of music, alerting everyone on the street that a wedding was taking place. Meanwhile the groom's family's friends and relatives had gathered at his home, ready to greet the bridal party. The bride would kneel and bow to her new parents-in-law and later also to the tablets representing her husband's ancestors. A classical ritual still practiced was for the new couple to drink wine from the same cup. A ritual that had become popular in Song times was to attach a string to the bride and groom, literally tying them together. Later they were shown to their new bedroom, where the bride's dowry had already been placed, and people tossed beans or rice on the bed, symbolizing the desired fertility. After teasing them, the guests left them alone and went out to the courtyard for a wedding feast.

The young bride's first priority was to try to win over her mother-in-law, since everyone knew that mothers-in-law were hard to please. One way to do this was to quickly bear a son for the family. Within the patrilineal system, a woman fully secured her position in the family by becoming the mother of one of the men. Every community had older women skilled in midwifery who were called to help when a woman went into labor. If the family was well-to-do, arrangements might be made for a wet nurse to help her take care of the newborn.

Women frequently had four, five, or six children, but likely one or more would die in infancy. If a son reached adulthood and married before the woman herself was widowed, she would be considered fortunate, for she would have always had an adult man who could take care of business for her — first her husband, then her grown son. But in the days when infectious diseases took many people in their twenties and thirties, it was not uncommon for a woman to be widowed while in her twenties, when her children were still very young.

A woman with a healthy and prosperous husband faced another challenge in middle age: her husband could bring home a **concubine** (and more than one if he could afford it). Moralists insisted that it was wrong for a wife to be jealous of her husband's concubines, but contemporary documents suggest that jealousy was very common. Wives outranked concubines and could give them orders in the house, but a concubine had her own ways of getting back through her hold on the husband. The children born to a concubine were considered just as much children of the family as the wife's children, and if the wife had had only daughters and the concubine had a son, the wife would find herself dependent on the concubine's son in her old age.

As a woman's children grew up, she would start thinking of suitable marriage partners. Many women liked the idea of bringing other women from their families of birth — perhaps a brother's daughter — to be their daughters-in-law. No matter who was selected, a woman's life became easier once she had a daughter-in-law to do the cooking and cleaning. Many found more time for religious devotions at this stage of their lives. Their sons, still living with them, could be expected to look after them and do their best to make their late years comfortable.

Neo-Confucianism is sometimes blamed for a decline in the status of women in Song times, largely because one of the best known of the Neo-Confucian teachers, Cheng Yi, once told a follower that it would be better for a widow to die of starvation than to lose her virtue by remarrying. In later centuries this saying was often quoted to justify pressuring widows, even very young ones, to stay with their husbands' families and not remarry. In Song times, however, widows frequently remarried.

It is true that **foot binding** began during the Song Dynasty, but it was not recommended by Neo-Confucian teachers; rather it was associated with the pleasure quarters and with women's efforts to beautify themselves. Mothers bound the feet of girls aged five to eight with long strips of cloth to keep them from growing and to bend the four smaller toes under to make the foot narrow and arched. The hope was that the girl would be judged more beautiful. Foot binding spread gradually during Song times but was probably still largely an elite practice. In later centuries it became extremely common in north and central China, eventually spreading to all classes. Women with bound feet were less mobile than women with natural feet, but only those who could afford servants bound their feet so tightly that walking was difficult.

China Under Mongol Rule

As discussed in Chapter 12, the Mongols conquered China in stages, gaining much of north China by 1215 and all of it by 1234, but not taking the south till the 1270s. The north suffered the most devastation. The non-Chinese rulers in the north, the Jin Dynasty of the Jurchen — with 150,000 cavalry, mostly Jurchen, and more than 300,000 Chinese infantrymen — thought they had the strongest army known to history, and they certainly had one of the largest. Yet Mongol tactics frustrated them. The Mongols would take a city, plunder it, and then withdraw, letting the Jin take it back and deal with the resulting food shortages and destruction.

• **concubine** A woman contracted to a man as a secondary spouse; although subordinate to the wife, her sons were considered legitimate heirs.

• **foot binding** The practice of binding the feet of girls with long strips of cloth to keep them from growing large.

Under these circumstances, Jurchen power rapidly collapsed.

Not until Khubilai was Great Khan was the Song Dynasty defeated and south China brought under the control of the Mongol's Yuan Dynasty. Non-Chinese rulers had gained control of north China several times in Chinese history, but none of them had been able to secure control of the region south of the Yangzi River, which required a navy. By the 1260s Khubilai had put Chinese shipbuilders to work building a fleet, crucial to his victory over Song (see page 341).

Life in China under the Mongols was much like life in China under earlier alien rulers. Once order was restored, people did their best to get on with their lives. Some were deprived of their land, business, or freedom and suffered real hardship. Yet people still spoke Chinese, followed Chinese customary practices in arranging their children's marriages or dividing their family property, made offerings at local temples, celebrated the new year and other customary festivals, and turned to local landowners when in need. Teachers still taught students the classics; scholars continued to write books; and books continued to be printed.

The Mongols, like other foreign rulers before them, did not see anything particularly desirable in the social mobility of Chinese society. Preferring stability, they assigned people hereditary occupations such as farmer, Confucian scholar, physician, astrologer, soldier, artisan, salt producer, miner, and Buddhist monk; the occupations came with obligations to the state. Besides these occupational categories, the Mongols classified the population into four grades, with the Mongols occupying the top grade. Next came various non-Chinese, such as the Uighurs and Persians. Below them were Chinese former subjects of the Jurchen, called the Han. At the bottom were the former subjects of the Song, called southerners.

The reason for codifying ethnic differences this way was to preserve the Mongols' privileges as conquerors. Chinese were not allowed to take Mongol names, and great efforts were made to keep them from passing as Mongols or marrying Mongols. To keep Chinese from rebelling, they were forbidden to own weap-

ons or congregate in public. Khubilai even prohibited Chinese from dealing in bamboo because it could be used to make bows and arrows.

As the Mongols captured Chinese territory, they recruited Chinese into their armies and government. Although some refused to serve the Mongols, others argued that the Chinese would fare better if Chinese were the administrators and could shield Chinese society from the most brutal effects of Mongol rule. A few Confucian scholars devoted themselves to the task of patiently teaching Mongol rulers the principles of Confucian government.

Nevertheless, government service, which had long been central to the identity and income of the educated elite in China, was not as widely available under the Mongols. The Mongols reinstituted the civil service examinations in 1315, but filled only about 2 percent of the positions in the bureaucracy through it and reserved half of those places for Mongols.

The scholar-official elite without government employment turned to alternative ways to support themselves. Those who did not have land to live off of found work as physicians, fortune-tellers, children's teachers, Daoist priests, publishers, booksellers, or playwrights. Many took leadership roles at the local level, such as founding academies for Confucian learning or promoting local charitable ventures. Through such

Blue-and-White Jars of the Yuan Period
Chinese ceramics had long been in demand outside of China, and an innovation of the Mongol period—decorating white porcelain with underglaze designs in blue—proved especially popular. Persia imported large quantities of Chinese blue-and-white ceramics, and Korean, Japanese, and Vietnamese potters took up versions of the style themselves. (© The Trustees of the British Museum/Art Resource, NY)

activities, scholars out of office could assert the importance of civil over military values and see themselves as trustees of the Confucian tradition.

Since the Mongols wanted to extract wealth from China, they had every incentive to develop the economy. They encouraged trade both within China and beyond its borders and tried to keep paper money in circulation. They repaired the Grand Canal, which had been ruined during their initial conquest of north China. Chinese industries with strong foreign markets, such as porcelain, thrived. Nevertheless, the economic expansion of late Tang and Song times did not continue under the alien rule of the Jurchen and Mongols. The economy of north China, with its strong iron industry, contracted under the Jurchen, and the destruction of cities was extensive during the first five decades of Mongol rule of the north. Although the Mongols did not discourage commerce, they were not as experienced in controlling currency, leading to serious inflation. The combination of war, disease, and a shrinking economy led to a population decline, probably of tens of millions.

The Mongols' Yuan Dynasty began a rapid decline in the 1330s as disease, rebellions, and poor leadership led to disorder throughout the country. When a Chinese strongman succeeded in consolidating the south, the Mongol rulers retreated to Mongolia before he could take Beijing. By 1368 the Yuan Dynasty had given way to a new Chinese-led dynasty: the Ming.

Korea Under the Koryŏ Dynasty, 935–1392

☐ How did Korean society and culture develop in an age when its northern neighbors were Khitans, Jurchens, and Mongols?

During the Silla period Korea was strongly tied to Tang China and avidly copied China's model (see page 198). This changed along with much else in North Asia between 800 and 1400. In this period Korea lived more in the shadows of the powerful nomad states of the Khitans, Jurchens, and Mongols than of the Chinese.

The Silla Dynasty began to decline after the king was killed in a revolt in 780. For the next 155 years the

The Koryŏ Dynasty, 935-1392

Mongol invasion
Wall

kings were selected from several collateral lines, and the majority of them met violent deaths. Rebellions and coups d'état followed one after the other, as different groups of nobles placed their candidates on the throne and killed as many of their opponents as they could. As conditions deteriorated, serfs absconded in large numbers, and independent merchants and seamen of humble origins came to dominate the three-way trade between China, Korea, and Japan.

The dynasty that emerged from this confusion was called Koryŏ (KAW-ree-oh) (935–1392). (The English word *Korea* derives from the name of this dynasty.) During this time Korea developed more independently of the China model than it had in Silla times, just as contemporary Japan was doing (see the next section). This was not because the Chinese model was rejected; the Koryŏ capital was laid out on the Chinese model, and the government was closely patterned on the Tang system. But despite Chinese influence, Korean society remained deeply aristocratic.

The founder of the dynasty, Wang Kon (877–943), was a man of relatively obscure maritime background, and he needed the support of the old aristocracy to maintain control. His successors introduced civil service examinations on the Chinese model, as well as examinations for Buddhist clergy, but because the aristocrats were the best educated and the government schools admitted only the sons of aristocrats, this system served primarily to solidify their control. Politics was largely the competition among aristocratic clans for influence at court and marriage of their daughters to the royal princes. Like the Heian aristocrats in Japan (see pages 382–386), the Koryŏ aristocrats wanted to stay in the capital and only reluctantly accepted posts in the provinces.

At the other end of the social scale, the number of people in the serf-slave stratum seems to have increased. This lowborn stratum included not only privately held slaves but also large numbers of government slaves as well as government workers in mines, porcelain factories, and other government industries. Sometimes entire villages or groups of villages were considered lowborn. There were occasional slave revolts, and some manumitted (freed) slaves did rise in status, but prejudice against anyone with slave ancestors was so strong that the law provided that "only if there is no evidence of lowborn status for eight generations in one's official household registration may one receive a position in the government."[4] In China and

Wooden Blocks for Printing
The Heainsa Buddhist Temple in Korea has preserved the 80,000 woodblocks used to print the huge Buddhist canon in the thirteenth century. The monk shown here is replacing a block. All the blocks are carved on both sides and stabilized by wooden frames that have kept them from warping. (© OUR PLACE THE WORLD HERITAGE COLLECTION, www. ourplaceworldheritage.com)

Japan, by contrast, slavery was a much more minor element in the social landscape.

The commercial economy declined in Korea during this period, showing that it was not closely linked to China's then booming economy. Except for the capital, there were no cities of commercial importance, and in the countryside the use of money declined. One industry that did flourish was ceramics. Connoisseurs have long appreciated the elegance of the pale green Koryŏ celadon pottery, decorated with designs executed in inlaid white or gray clay.

Buddhism remained strong throughout Korea, and monasteries became major centers of art and learning. As in Song China and Kamakura Japan, Chan (Zen) and Tiantai (Tendai) were the leading Buddhist teachings (see pages 196, 385). The founder of the Koryŏ Dynasty attributed the dynasty's success to the Buddha's protection, and he and his successors were ardent patrons of the church. The entire Buddhist canon was printed in the eleventh century and again in the thirteenth. (The 81,258 individual woodblocks used to print it still survive in a monastery in southern Korea.) As in medieval Europe, aristocrats who entered the church occupied the major abbacies. Monasteries played the same roles as they did in China and Japan, such as engaging in money lending and charitable works. As in Japan (but not China), some monasteries accumulated military power.

Not all cultural advances were connected to monasteries or Buddhism. The most important literary work of the Koryŏ period is *The History of the Three Kingdoms*, compiled in 1145 in Chinese. Modeled on Chinese histories, it is the best source of information on early Korean history.

The Koryŏ Dynasty was preserved in name long after the ruling family had lost most of its power. In 1170 the palace guards massacred the civil officials at court and placed a new king on the throne. The coup leaders scrapped the privileges that had kept the aristocrats in power and appointed themselves to the top posts. After incessant infighting among the generals and a series of coups, in 1196 the general Ch'oe Ch'ung-hon took control. Ch'oe had a private army of about three thousand warrior-retainers and an even larger number of slaves. The domination of Korea by the Ch'oe family was much like the contemporaneous situation in Japan, where warrior bands were seizing power. Moreover, because the Ch'oe were content to dominate the government while leaving the Koryŏ king on the throne, they had much in common with the Japanese shoguns, who followed a similar strategy.

Although Korea adopted many ideas from China, it could not so easily adopt the Chinese assumption that it was the largest, most powerful, and most advanced society in the world. Korea, from early times, recognized China as being in many ways senior to it, but when strong non-Chinese states emerged to its north in Manchuria, Korea was ready to accommodate them as well. Koryŏ's first neighbor to the north was the Khitan state of Liao, which in 1010 invaded and sacked the capital. To avoid destruction, Koryŏ acceded to vassal status, but Liao invaded again in 1018. This time Koryŏ was able to repel the nomadic Khitans. Afterward a defensive wall was built across the Korean peninsula south of the Yalu River. When the Jurchens and their Jin Dynasty supplanted the Khitans's Liao Dynasty, Koryŏ agreed to send them tribute as well.

As mentioned in Chapter 12, Korea was conquered by the Mongols, and the figurehead Koryŏ kings were moved to Beijing, where they married Mongol princesses, their descendants becoming more Mongol than Korean. This was a time of hardship for the Korean people. In the year 1254 alone, the Mongols enslaved two hundred thousand Koreans and took them away. Ordinary people in Korea suffered grievously when their land was used as a launching pad for the huge Mongol invasions of Japan: nine hundred ships and the provisions for the soldiers on them had to be procured from the Korean countryside. In this period Korea also suffered from frequent attacks by Japanese pirates, somewhat like the depredations of the Vikings in Europe a little earlier (see page 394). The Mongol overlords did little to provide protection, and the harried coastal people had little choice but to retreat inland.

When Mongol rule in China fell apart in the mid-fourteenth century, it declined in Korea as well. Chinese rebels opposing the Mongols entered Korea and even briefly captured the capital in 1361. When the Ming Dynasty was established in China in 1368, the Koryŏ court was unsure how to respond. In 1388 a general, Yi Song-gye, was sent to oppose a Ming army at the northwest frontier. When he saw the strength of the Ming, he concluded that making an alliance was more sensible than fighting, and he led his troops back to the capital, where in 1392 he usurped the throne, founding the Choson Dynasty.

Japan's Heian Period, 794–1185

☐ How did the Heian form of government contribute to the cultural flowering of Japan in the period?

As described in Chapter 7, during the seventh and eighth centuries the Japanese ruling house pursued a vigorous policy of adopting useful ideas, techniques, and policies from the more advanced civilization of China. The rulers built a splendid capital along Chinese lines in Nara and fostered the growth of Buddhism. Monasteries grew so powerful in Nara, however, that in less than a century the court decided to move away from them and encourage other sects of Buddhism.

The new capital was built about twenty-five miles away at Heian (HAY-ahn; modern Kyoto). Like Nara, Heian was modeled on the Tang capital of Chang'an (although neither of the Japanese capitals had walls, a major feature of Chinese cities). For the first century at Heian the government continued to follow Chinese models, but it turned away from them with the decline of the Tang Dynasty in the late ninth century. The last official embassy to China made the trip in 894. During the Heian period (794–1185) Japan witnessed a literary and cultural flowering under the rule of the Fujiwara family.

Fujiwara Rule

Only the first two Heian emperors were much involved in governing. By 860 political management was taken over by a series of regents from the Fujiwara family, who supplied most of the empresses in this period. The emperors continued to be honored, even venerated, because of their presumed divine descent, but the Fujiwaras ruled. Fujiwara dominance represented the privatization of political power and a return to clan politics. Political history thus took a very different course in Japan than in China, where, when a dynasty weakened, military strongmen would compete to depose the emperor and found their own dynasties. In Japan for the next thousand years, political contenders sought to manipulate the emperors rather than supplant them.

The Fujiwaras reached the apogee of their glory under Fujiwara Michinaga (r. 995–1027). Like many aristocrats of the period, he was learned in Buddhism, music, poetry, and Chinese literature and history. He dominated the court for more than thirty years as the father of four empresses, the uncle of two emperors, and the grandfather of three emperors. He acquired great landholdings and built fine palaces for himself and his family. After ensuring that his sons could continue to rule, he retired to a Buddhist monastery, all the while continuing to maintain control.

By the end of the eleventh century several emperors who did not have Fujiwara mothers found a device to counter Fujiwara control: they abdicated but continued to exercise power by controlling their young sons on the throne. This system of rule has been called **cloistered government** because the retired emperors took Buddhist orders, while maintaining control of the government from behind the scenes. Thus for a time the imperial house was a contender for political power along with other aristocratic groups.

Aristocratic Culture

A brilliant aristocratic culture developed in the Heian period. It was strongly focused on the capital at Heian, where nobles, palace ladies, and imperial family members lived a highly refined and leisured life. In their society niceties of birth, rank, and breeding counted for everything. From their diaries we know of the pains

The Tale of Genji
In this scene from a twelfth-century painting illustrating *The Tale of Genji*, Genji has his inkstone and brushes ready to respond to the letter he is reading. (Tokugawa Reimeikai Foundation, Tokyo, Japan/Photo AISA/The Bridgeman Art Library)

aristocratic women took in their dress, selecting the color combinations of the kimonos they wore, layer upon layer. Even among men, presentation and knowing how to dress tastefully were more important than skill with a horse or sword. The elegance of one's calligraphy and the allusions in one's poems were matters of intense concern to both men and women at court. Courtiers did not like to leave the capital, and some like the court lady Sei Shonagon shuddered at the sight of ordinary working people. In her *Pillow Book*, she wrote of encountering a group of commoners on a pilgrimage: "They looked like so many basket-worms as they crowded together in their hideous clothes, leaving hardly an inch of space between themselves and me. I really felt like pushing them all over sideways."[5] (See "Listening to the Past: *The Pillow Book* of Sei Shonagon," page 384.)

In this period a new script was developed for writing Japanese phonetically. Each symbol was based on a simplified Chinese character and represented one of the syllables used in Japanese (such as *ka, ki, ku, ke, ko*). Although "serious" essays, histories, and government documents continued to be written in Chinese, less formal works such as poetry and memoirs were written in Japanese. Mastering the new writing system took much less time than mastering writing in Chinese and aided the spread of literacy, especially among women in court society.

> "They looked like so many basket-worms as they crowded together in their hideous clothes, leaving hardly an inch of space between themselves and me. I really felt like pushing them all over sideways."
>
> **SEI SHONAGON**

In the Heian period women played important roles at all levels of society. Women educated in the arts and letters could advance at court as attendants to the ruler's empress and other consorts. Women could inherit property from their parents, and they would compete with their brothers for shares of the family property. In political life, marrying a daughter to an emperor or shogun (see page 386) was one of the best ways to gain power, and women often became major players in power struggles.

The literary masterpiece of this period is **The Tale of Genji**, written in Japanese by Lady Murasaki over several years (ca. 1000–1010). This long narrative

• **cloistered government** A system in which an emperor retired to a Buddhist monastery but continued to exercise power by controlling his young son on the throne.

• **The Tale of Genji** A Japanese literary masterpiece about court life written by Lady Murasaki.

Listening to the Past

The Pillow Book of Sei Shonagon

Beginning in the late tenth century Japan produced a series of great women writers. At the time women were much freer than men to write in vernacular Japanese, giving them a large advantage. Lady Murasaki, author of the novel The Tale of Genji, *is the most famous of the women writers of the period, but her contemporary Sei Shonagon is equally noteworthy. Sei Shonagon served as a lady in waiting to Empress Sadako during the last decade of the tenth century (990–1000). Her only known work is* The Pillow Book, *a collection of notes, character sketches, anecdotes, descriptions of nature, and eccentric lists such as boring things, awkward things, hateful things, and things that have lost their power.*

The Pillow Book *portrays the lovemaking/marriage system among the aristocracy more or less as it is depicted in* The Tale of Genji. *Marriages were arranged for family interests, and a man could have more than one wife. Wives and their children commonly stayed in their own homes, where their husbands and fathers would visit them. But once a man had an heir by his wife, there was nothing to prevent him from establishing relations with other women. Some relationships were long-term, but many were brief, and men often had several lovers at the same time. Some women became known for their amorous conquests, others as abandoned women whose husbands ignored them. The following passage from* The Pillow Book *looks on this lovemaking system with amused detachment.*

"It is so stiflingly hot in the Seventh Month that even at night one keeps all the doors and lattices open. At such times it is delightful to wake up when the moon is shining and to look outside. I enjoy it even when there is no moon. But to wake up at dawn and see a pale sliver of a moon in the sky—well, I need hardly say how perfect that is.

I like to see a bright new straw mat that has just been spread out on a well-polished floor. The best place for one's three-foot curtain of state is in the front of the room near the veranda. It is pointless to put it in the rear of the room, as it is most unlikely that anyone will peer in from that direction.

It is dawn and a woman is lying in bed after her lover has taken his leave. She is covered up to her head with a light mauve robe that has a lining of dark violet; the colour of both the outside and the lining is fresh and glossy. The woman, who appears to be asleep, wears an unlined orange robe and a dark crimson skirt of stiff silk whose cords hang loosely by her side, as if they have been left untied. Her thick tresses tumble over each other in cascades, and one can imagine how long her hair must be when it falls freely down her back.

Nearby another woman's lover is making his way home in the misty dawn. He is wearing loose violet trousers, an orange hunting costume, so lightly coloured that one can hardly tell whether it has been dyed or not, a white robe of still silk, and a scarlet robe of glossy, beaten silk. His clothes, which are damp from the mist, hang loosely about him. From the dishevelment of his side locks one can tell how negligently he must have tucked his hair into the black lacquered headdress when he got up. He wants to return and write his next-morning letter before the dew on the morning glories has had time to vanish; but the path seems endless, and to divert himself he hums "the sprouts in the flax fields."

As he walks along, he passes a house with an open lattice. He is on his way to report for official duty, but cannot help stopping to lift up the blind and peep into the room. It amuses him to think that a man has probably been spending the night here and has only recently got up to leave, just as happened to himself. Perhaps that man too had felt the charm of the dew.

Looking around the room, he notices near the woman's pillow an open fan with a magnolia frame and purple paper; and at the foot of her curtain of state he sees some narrow

depicts a cast of characters enmeshed in court life, with close attention to dialogue and personality. Murasaki also wrote a diary that is similarly revealing of aristocratic culture. In one passage she tells of an occasion when word got out that she had read the Chinese classics:

Worried what people would think if they heard such rumors, I pretended to be unable to read even the inscriptions on the screens. Then Her Majesty asked me to read to her here and there from the collected

works of [the Tang Chinese poet] Bo Juyi, and, because she evinced a desire to know much more about such things, we carefully chose a time when other women would not be present and, amateur that I was, I read with her the two books of Bo Juyi's New Ballads in secret; we started the summer before last.[6]

Despite the reluctance of Murasaki and the lady she served to let others know of their learning, there were, in fact, quite a few women writers in this period. The wife of a high-ranking court official wrote a poetic mem-

strips of Michinoku paper and also some other paper of a faded colour, either orange-red or maple.

The woman senses that someone is watching her and, looking up from under her bedclothes, sees a gentleman leaning against the wall by the threshold, a smile on his face. She can tell at once that he is the sort of man with whom she need feel no reserve. All the same, she does not want to enter into any familiar relations with him, and she is annoyed that he should have seen her asleep.

"Well, well, Madam," says the man, leaning forward so that the upper part of his body comes behind her curtains, "what a long nap you're having after your morning adieu! You really are a lie-abed!"

"You call me that, Sir," she replied, "only because you're annoyed at having had to get up before the dew had time to settle."

Their conversation may be commonplace, yet I find there is something delightful about the scene.

Now the gentleman leans further forward and, using his own fan, tries to get hold of the fan by the woman's pillow. Fearing his closeness, she moves further back into her curtain enclosure, her heart pounding. The gentleman picks up the magnolia fan and, while examining it, says in a slightly bitter tone, "How standoffish you are!"

But now it is growing light; there is a sound of people's voices, and it looks as if the sun will soon be up. Only a short while ago this same man was hurrying home to write his next-morning letter before the mists had time to clear. Alas, how easily his intentions have been forgotten!

While all this is afoot, the woman's original lover has been busy with his own next-morning letter, and now, quite unexpectedly, the messenger arrives at her house. The letter is attached to a spray of bush-clover, still damp with dew, and the paper gives off a delicious aroma of incense. Because of the new visitor, however, the woman's servants cannot deliver it to her.

Finally it becomes unseemly for the gentleman to stay any longer. As he goes, he is amused to think that a similar scene may be taking place in the house he left earlier that morning. 99

Source: Ivan Morris, trans., *The Pillow Book of Sei Shonagon* (New York: Penguin Books, 1970), pp. 60–62. © Ivan Morris 1967. Reprinted by permission of Oxford University Press and Columbia University Press.

QUESTIONS FOR ANALYSIS

1. What sorts of images does Sei Shonagon evoke to convey an impression of a scene?

2. What can you learn from this passage about the material culture of Japan in this period?

3. Why do you think Sei Shonagon was highly esteemed as a writer?

oir of her unhappy twenty-year marriage to him and his rare visits. A woman wrote both an autobiography that related her father's efforts to find favor at court and a love story of a hero who travels to China. Another woman even wrote a history that concludes with a triumphal biography of Fujiwara Michinaga.

Buddhism remained very strong throughout the Heian period. A mission sent to China in 804 included two monks in search of new texts. One of the monks, Saichō, spent time at the monasteries on Mount Tiantai and brought back the Buddhist teachings associated with that mountain (called Tendai in Japanese). Tendai's basic message is that all living beings share the Buddha nature and can be brought to salvation. Tendai practices include strict monastic discipline, prayer, textual study, and meditation. Once back in Japan, Saichō established a monastery on Mount Hiei outside Kyoto, which grew to be one of the most important monasteries in Japan. By the twelfth century this monastery and its many branch temples had vast lands and a powerful army of monk-soldiers to protect its interests. Whenever the monastery felt that its interests were at risk, it sent the monk-soldiers into the capital to parade its sacred symbols in an attempt to intimidate the civil authorities.

Kūkai, the other monk on the 804 mission to China, came back with texts from another school of Buddhism — Shingon, "True Word," a form of **Esoteric Buddhism**. Esoteric Buddhism is based on the idea that teachings containing the secrets of enlightenment had been secretly transmitted from the Buddha. An adept (expert) can gain access to these mysteries through initiation into the mandalas (cosmic diagrams), mudras (gestures), and mantras (verbal formulas). On his return to Japan, Kūkai attracted many followers and was allowed to establish a monastery at Mount Kōya, south of Osaka. The popularity of Esoteric Buddhism was a great stimulus to Buddhist art.

The Samurai and the Kamakura Shogunate, 1185–1333

▢ What were the causes and consequences of military rule in Japan?

The gradual rise of a warrior elite over the course of the Heian period finally brought an end to the domination of the Fujiwaras and other Heian aristocratic families. In 1156 civil war broke out between the Taira and Minamoto warrior clans based in western and eastern Japan, respectively. Both clans relied on skilled warriors, later called samurai, who were rapidly becoming a new social class. A samurai and his lord had a double bond: in return for the samurai's loyalty and service, the lord granted him land or income. From 1159 to 1181 a Taira named Kiyomori dominated the court, taking the position of prime minister and marrying his daughter to the emperor. His relatives became governors of more than thirty provinces, managed some five hundred tax-exempt estates, and amassed a fortune in the trade with Song China and Koryŏ Korea. Still, the Minamoto clan managed to defeat the Taira, and the Minamoto leader, Yoritomo, became **shogun**, or general-in-chief. With him began the Kamakura Shogunate (1185–1333). This period is often referred to as Japan's feudal period

because it was dominated by a military class whose members were tied to their superiors by bonds of loyalty and supported by landed estates rather than salaries.

Military Rule

The similarities between military rule in Japan and feudalism in medieval Europe during roughly the same period have fascinated scholars, as have the very significant differences. In Europe feudalism emerged out of the fusion of Germanic and Roman social institutions and flowered under the impact of Muslim and Viking invasions. In Japan military rule evolved from a combination of the native warrior tradition and Confucian ethical principles of duty to superiors.

The emergence of the samurai was made possible by the development of private landholding. The government land allotment system, copied from Tang China, began breaking down in the eighth century (much as it did in China). By the ninth century local lords began escaping imperial taxes and control by commending (formally giving) their land to tax-exempt entities such as monasteries, the imperial family, and certain high-ranking officials. The local lord then received his land back as a tenant and paid his protector a small rent. The monastery or privileged individual received a steady income from the land, and the local lord escaped imperial taxes and control. By the end of the thirteenth century most land seems to have been taken off the tax rolls this way. Each plot of land could thus have several people with rights to shares of its produce, ranging from the cultivator, to a local lord, to an estate manager working for him, to a regional strongman, to a noble or temple in the capital. Unlike peasants in medieval Europe, where similar practices of commendation occurred, those working the land in Japan never became serfs. Moreover, Japanese lords rarely lived on the lands they had rights in, unlike English or French lords who lived on their manors.

Samurai resembled European knights in several ways. Both were armed with expensive weapons, and both fought on horseback. Just as the knight was supposed to live according to the chivalric code, so Japanese samurai were expected to live according to **Bushido** (or "way of the warrior"), a code that stressed military honor, courage, stoic acceptance of hardship, and, above all, loyalty. Physical hardship was accepted as routine, and soft living was despised as weak and unworthy. Disloyalty brought social disgrace, which the samurai could avoid only through *seppuku*, ritual suicide by slashing his belly.

The Kamakura Shogunate derives its name from Kamakura, a city near modern Tokyo that was the seat of the Minamoto clan. The founder, Yoritomo, ruled the country much the way he ran his own estates, appoint-

- **Esoteric Buddhism** A sect of Buddhism that maintains that the secrets of enlightenment have been secretly transmitted from the Buddha and can be accessed through initiation into the mandalas, mudras, and mantras.

- **shogun** The Japanese general-in-chief, whose headquarters was the shogunate.

- **Bushido** Literally, the "way of the warrior"; the code of conduct by which samurai were expected to live.

ing his retainers to newly created offices. To cope with the emergence of hard-to-tax estates, he put military land stewards in charge of seeing to the estates' proper operation. To bring order to the lawless countryside, he appointed military governors to oversee the military and enforce the law in the provinces. They supervised the conduct of the land stewards in peacetime and commanded the provincial samurai in war.

Yoritomo's wife Masako protected the interests of her own family, the Hōjōs, especially after Yoritomo died. She went so far as to force her first son to abdicate when he showed signs of preferring the family of his wife to the family of his mother. She later helped her brother take power away from her father. Thus the process of reducing power holders to figureheads went one step further in 1219 when the Hōjō family reduced the shogun to a figurehead. The Hōjō family held the reins of power until 1333.

The Mongols' two massive seaborne invasions in 1274 and 1281 (see page 343) were a huge shock to the shogunate. The Kamakura government was hard-pressed to gather adequate resources for its defense. Temples were squeezed, farmers were taken away from their fields to build walls, and warriors were promised generous rewards in return for their service. Although the Hōjō regents, with the help of a "divine wind" (*kamikaze*), repelled the Mongols, they were unable to reward their vassals in the traditional way because little booty was found among the wreckage of the Mongol fleets. Discontent grew among the samurai, and by the fourteenth century the entire political system was breaking down. Both the imperial and the

Kamakura Shogunate, 1185–1333

shogunate families were fighting among themselves. As land grants were divided, samurai became impoverished and took to plunder and piracy, or shifted their loyalty to local officials who could offer them a better living.

The factional disputes among Japan's leading families remained explosive until 1331, when the emperor Go-Daigo tried to recapture real power. His attempt sparked an uprising by the great families, local lords, samurai, and even Buddhist monasteries, which had thousands of samurai retainers. Go-Daigo destroyed the Kamakura Shogunate in 1333 but soon lost the loyalty of his followers. By 1338 one of his most important military supporters, Ashikaga Takauji, had turned on him and established the Ashikaga Shogunate, which lasted until 1573. Takauji's victory was also a victory for the samurai, who took over civil authority throughout Japan.

Cultural Trends

The cultural distance between the elites and the commoners narrowed a little during the Kamakura period. Buddhism was vigorously spread to ordinary Japanese by energetic preachers. Honen (1133–1212) propagated the Pure Land teaching, preaching that

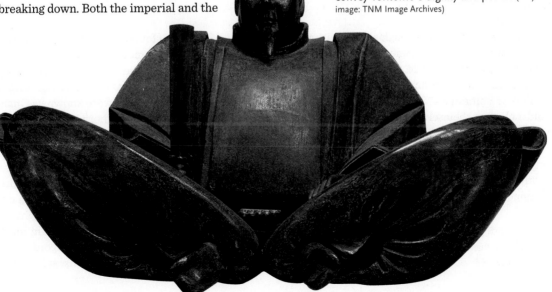

The Shogun Minamoto Yoritomo in Court Dress This wooden sculpture, 27.8 inches tall (70.6 cm), was made about a half century after Yoritomo's death for use in a shrine dedicated to his memory. The bold shapes convey Yoritomo's dignity and power. (Tokyo National Museum/ image: TNM Image Archives)

The Itinerant Preacher Ippen
The monk Ippen spread Pure Land teaching as he traveled through Japan urging people to call on the Amitabha Buddha through song and dance. This detail from a set of twelve paintings done in 1299, a decade after his death, shows him with his belongings on his back as he approaches a village. (Tokyo National Museum/image: TNM Image Archives)

paradise could be reached through simple faith in the Buddha and repeating the name of the Buddha Amitabha. Neither philosophical understanding of Buddhist scriptures nor devotion to rituals was essential. His follower Shinran (1173–1263) taught that monks should not shut themselves off in monasteries but should marry and have children. A different path was promoted by Nichiren (1222–1282), a fiery and intolerant preacher who proclaimed that to be saved people had only to invoke sincerely the Lotus Sutra, one of the most important of the Buddhist sutras. These lay versions of Buddhism found a receptive audience among ordinary people in the countryside.

It was also during the Kamakura period that **Zen** came to flourish in Japan. Zen teachings originated in Tang China, where they were known as Chan (see page 196). Rejecting the authority of the sutras, Zen teachers claimed the superiority of mind-to-mind transmission of Buddhist truth. When Japanese monks went to China in the twelfth century looking for ways to revitalize Japanese Buddhism, they were impressed by the rigorous monastic life of the Chan/Zen monasteries. One school of Zen held that enlightenment could be achieved suddenly through insight into one's own true nature. This school taught rigorous meditation and the use of kōan riddles to unseat logic and free

• **Zen** A school of Buddhism that emphasized meditation and truths that could not be conveyed in words.

the mind for enlightenment. This teaching found eager patrons among the samurai, who were attracted to its discipline and strong master-disciple bonds.

Buddhism remained central to the visual arts. Many temples in Japan still house fine sculptures done in this period. In painting, narrative hand scrolls brought to life the miracles that faith could bring and the torments of Hell awaiting unbelievers. All forms of literature were depicted in these scrolls, including *The Tale of Genji*, war stories, and humorous anecdotes.

During the Kamakura period war tales continued the tradition of long narrative prose works. *The Tale of the Heike* tells the story of the fall of the Taira family and the rise of the Minamoto clan. The tale reached a large and mostly illiterate audience because blind minstrels would chant sections to the accompaniment of a lute. The story is suffused with the Buddhist idea of the transience of life and the illusory nature of glory. Yet it also celebrates strength, courage, loyalty, and pride. The Minamoto warriors from the east are portrayed as the toughest. In one scene one of them dismisses his own prowess with the bow, claiming that other warriors from his region could pierce three sets of armor with their arrows. He then brags about the martial spirit of warriors from the east: "They are bold horsemen who never fall, nor do they let their horses stumble on the roughest road. When they fight they do not care if even their parents or children are killed; they ride over their bodies and continue the battle."[7] In this they stood in contrast to the warriors of the west, who in good Confucian fashion would retire from battle to mourn their parents.

> **"**They are bold horsemen who never fall, nor do they let their horses stumble on the roughest road. When they fight they do not care if even their parents or children are killed; they ride over their bodies and continue the battle.**"**
>
> *THE TALE OF THE HEIKE*

After stagnating in the Heian period, agricultural productivity began to improve in the Kamakura period, and the population grew, reaching perhaps 8.2 million by 1333. Much like farmers in contemporary Song China, Japanese farmers in this period adopted new strains of rice, often double-cropped in warmer regions, made increased use of fertilizers, and improved irrigation for paddy rice. Besides farming, ordinary people made their livings as artisans, traders, fishermen, and entertainers. Although trade in human beings was banned, those who fell into debt might sell themselves or their children, and professional slave traders kidnapped women and children. A vague category of outcastes occupied the fringes of society, in a manner reminiscent of India. Buddhist strictures against killing and Shinto ideas of pollution probably account for the exclusion of butchers, leatherworkers, morticians, and lepers, but other groups, such as bamboo whisk makers, were also traditionally excluded for no obvious reason.

CONNECTIONS

East Asia faced many internal and external challenges between 800 and 1400, and the ways the societies responded to them shaped their subsequent histories. In China the first four centuries of this period were a time of economic growth, urbanization, the spread of printing, and the expansion of the educated class. In Korea and Japan aristocracy and military rule were more typical of the era. All three areas, but especially China and Korea, faced an unprecedented challenge from the Mongols, with Japan less vulnerable because it did not share a land border. The challenges of the period did not hinder creativity in the literary and visual arts; among the greatest achievements of this era are the women's writings of Heian Japan, such as *The Tale of Genji*, and landscape painting of both Song and Yuan China.

Europe during these six centuries, the subject of the next chapter, also faced invasions from outside; in its case, the pagan Vikings were especially dreaded. Europe had a social structure more like that of Korea and Japan than of China, with less centralization and a more dominant place in society for military men. The centralized church in Europe, however, was unlike anything known in East Asian history. These centuries in Europe saw a major expansion of Christendom, especially to Scandinavia and eastern Europe, both through conversion and migration. Although there were scares that the Mongols would penetrate deeper into Europe, the greatest challenge in Europe was the Black Death and the huge loss of life that it caused.

CHAPTER REVIEW

□ What made possible the expansion of the Chinese economy, and what were the outcomes of this economic growth? (p. 366)

The loosening of the central government's control of the economy in the late Tang period seems to have stimulated trade and economic growth. In the period from 800 to 1100, China's population doubled to 100 million, reflecting in part the spread of wet-field rice cultivation, especially in the south. At the same time, the economy became increasingly commercialized. There was a huge increase in the use of money and the introduction of paper money to meet demand. Cities grew, and the economic center of China shifted from the north China plain to the south, the region drained by the Yangzi River. Merchants became more specialized, and foreign trade grew.

□ How did the civil service examinations and the scholar-official class shape Chinese society and culture, and what impact did the Mongol conquest have on them? (p. 371)

In the Song period the booming economy and the invention of printing allowed a great expansion in the size of the scholar-official class, which came to dominate the government. The life of the educated class was strongly shaped by the civil service examinations, which most educated men spent a decade or more studying for, often unsuccessfully. Their high levels of education fostered interest in literature, antiquities, philosophy, and art. Because there were more educated men, more books were written, and because of the spread of printing, a much greater share of them have survived to the present, making it possible to see dimensions of life poorly documented for earlier periods, such as the lives of women. China's great wealth and its elite's high levels of education could not be easily converted to military supremacy, and the Song had to pay tribute to its northern neighbors, eventually falling to the Mongols. During the Mongols' Yuan Dynasty, China's economic expansion came to an end. The Mongols instituted hereditary occupations, ending much of the social mobility that characterized the Song Dynasty. The status of scholars was made hereditary, but there were many fewer opportunities for them to serve in the government.

KEY TERMS

dynastic cycle (p. 366)
compass (p. 370)
scholar-official class
    (p. 373)
examination system
    (p. 373)
movable type (p. 373)
Neo-Confucianism
    (p. 376)
concubine (p. 378)
foot binding (p. 378)
cloistered government
    (p. 382)
The Tale of Genji
    (p. 383)
Esoteric Buddhism
    (p. 386)
shogun (p. 386)
Bushido (p. 386)
Zen (p. 388)

□ How did Korean society and culture develop in an age when its northern neighbors were Khitans, Jurchens, and Mongols? (p. 380)

During the Koryŏ dynasty Korea evolved more independently of China than it had for the past several centuries, in part because it had to placate powerful non-Chinese neighbors. The commercial economy declined, and an increasing portion of the population was unfree; slaves worked much of the agricultural land in the hands of aristocrats and local magnates, and the government compelled others to work for it in mines or factories. Buddhism continued to flourish. Military strongmen dominated the government, but the armies were no match for the much larger empires to their north and had to accede to often onerous demands, especially during the period of Mongol domination.

□ How did the Heian form of government contribute to the cultural flowering of Japan in the period? (p. 382)

In marked contrast to Song China, in Heian Japan a tiny aristocracy dominated government and society. More important than the emperors were a series of regents, most of them from the Fujiwara family and fathers-in-law of the emperors. The aristocratic court society put great emphasis on taste and refinement. Women were influential at the court and wrote much of the best literature of the period. Buddhism remained popular, and the teachings of Esoteric Buddhism were introduced from China, stimulating art. The Heian aristocrats had little interest in life in the provinces, which gradually came under the control of military clans.

□ What were the causes and consequences of military rule in Japan? (p. 386)

After a civil war between the two leading military clans, a military government, called the shogunate, was established in the east. The Kamakura Shogunate was dominated by a military class of samurais who were bound to their lord by loyalty and service in return for land and income. A change in landownership practices made possible the emergence of this warrior class. Emperors were still placed on the throne, but they had little power. A major crisis in military control was caused by the two invasions of the Mongols. Although both times the invaders were repelled, the costs of defense were high. During this period of military rule, culture was no longer so capital-centered, and Buddhism was vigorously spread to ordinary people. Arts that appealed to the samurai, such as war stories and Zen Buddhism, all flourished.

SUGGESTED READING

Bowring, Richard. *The Religious Traditions of Japan 500–1600.* 2005. A wide-ranging study that puts Buddhism in the context of local cults.

Chaffee, John W. *The Thorny Gates of Learning in Sung China: A Social History of Examinations.* 1985. Documents the wide-ranging impact of the examination system and the ways men could improve their chances.

Ebrey, Patricia Buckley. *The Inner Quarters: Marriage and the Lives of Chinese Women in the Sung Period.* 1993. Overview of the many facets of women's lives, from engagements to dowries, childrearing, and widowhood.

Ebrey, Patricia Buckley, Anne Walthall, and James B. Palais. 2009. *East Asia: A Cultural, Social, and Political History,* 2d ed. Textbook with strong coverage of this period.

Egan, Ronald. *Word, Image, and Deed in the Life of Su Shi.* 1994. A sympathetic portrait of one of the most talented men of the age.

Farris, Wayne W. *Heavenly Warriors.* 1992. Argues against Western analogies in explaining the dominance of the samurai.

Friday, Karl F. *Hired Swords.* 1992. Treats the evolution of state military development in connection with the emergence of the samurai.

Hansen, Valerie. *Changing the Gods in Medieval China, 1127–1276.* 1990. A portrait of the religious beliefs and practices of ordinary people in Song times.

Kuhn, Dieter. *The Age of Confucian Rule: The Song Transformation of China.* 2009. Accessible overview, especially strong on economic history and material culture.

Lorge, Peter. 2009. *War, Politics and Society in Early Modern China, 900–1795.* Examines dynasties as military powers.

Morris, Ivan. *The World of the Shining Prince: Court Life in Ancient Japan.* 1964. An engaging portrait of Heian culture based on both fiction and nonfiction sources.

Rossabi, Maurice. *China Among Equals.* 1983. Essays on Song, Liao, Jin, and Yuan, as well as Korea.

Souyri, Pierre François. *The World Turned Upside Down: Medieval Japanese Society.* 2001. A thought-provoking analysis of both the social system and the mentalities of Japan's Middle Ages.

NOTES

1. *The Travels of Marco Polo, the Venetian,* ed. Manuel Komroff (New York: Boni and Liveright, 1926), p. 227.
2. Ibid., p. 159.
3. Ibid., p. 235.
4. Peter H. Lee, ed., *Sourcebook of Korean Civilization* (New York: Columbia University Press, 1993), p. 327.
5. Ivan Morris, trans., *The Pillow Book of Sei Shonagon* (New York: Penguin Books, 1970), p. 258.
6. Quoted in M. Collcott, M. Jansen, and I. Kumakura, *Cultural Atlas of Japan* (New York: Facts on File, 1988), p. 82, slightly modified.
7. Ibid., p. 101.

For practice quizzes and other study tools, visit the **Online Study Guide** at bedfordstmartins.com/mckayworld.

For primary sources from this period, see ***Sources of World Societies*, Second Edition**.

For Web sites, images, and documents related to topics in this chapter, visit **Make History** at bedfordstmartins.com/mckayworld.

• **Hedwig of Bavaria** Noble women in medieval Europe played a wide variety of roles. Hedwig of Bavaria conducted diplomatic negotiations, ruled her husband's territory when he was away, founded monasteries, and worked to expand Christianity in eastern Europe. (The John Paul Getty Museum, Los Angeles, Ms Ludwig XI, fol.12v [detail], Court Atelier of Duke Ludwig I of Liegnitz and Brieg [illuminator], *Vita beatae Hedwigis*, 1353. Tempera colors, colored washes and ink bound between wood boards covered with red-stained pigskin, 34.1 x 24.8 cm)

14

By the fifteenth century scholars in the growing cities of northern Italy began to think that they were living in a new era, one in which the glories of ancient Greece and Rome were being reborn. What separated their time from classical antiquity, in their opinion, was a long period of darkness and barbarism, to which a seventeenth-century professor gave the name "Middle Ages." In this conceptualization, the history of Europe was divided into three periods — ancient, medieval, and modern — an organization that is still in use today. Later, the history of other parts of the world was sometimes fit into this three-period schema as well, with discussions of the "classical" period in Maya history, of "medieval" India and China, and of "modern" everywhere.

Today historians often question whether labels of past time periods for one culture work on a global scale, and some scholars are uncertain about whether "Middle Ages" is a just term even for European history. They assert that the Middle Ages was not simply a period of stagnation between two high points but rather a time of enormous intellectual energy and creative vitality. While agrarian life continued to dominate Europe, political structures that would influence later European history began to form, and Christianity continued to spread. People at the time did not know that they were living in an era that would later be labeled "middle" or sometimes even "dark," and we can wonder whether they would have shared this negative view of their own times. •

Europe in the Middle Ages

800–1450

Political Developments

☐ How did medieval rulers overcome internal divisions and external threats, and work to create larger and more stable territories?

The Christian Church

☐ How did the Christian Church enhance its power and create new institutions and religious practices?

The Crusades

☐ What were the motives, course, and consequences of the Crusades?

The Life of the People

☐ How did the lives of common people, nobles, and townspeople differ, and what new commercial developments increased wealth?

Learning and Culture

☐ What were the primary educational and cultural developments in medieval Europe?

Crises of the Later Middle Ages

☐ Why have the later Middle Ages been seen as a time of calamity and crisis?

Political Developments

☐ How did medieval rulers overcome internal divisions and external threats, and work to create larger and more stable territories?

Later scholars dated the beginning of the Middle Ages to the fifth century, the time of the fall of the Roman Empire in the West. However, the growth of Germanic kingdoms such as those of the Merovingians and the Carolingians (see Chapter 8) is generally viewed as the beginning of "medieval" politics in Europe, and that is why we begin this chapter with the ninth century. In 800 Charlemagne, the most powerful of the Carolingians, was crowned the Holy Roman emperor. After his death his empire was divided among his grandsons, and their kingdoms were weakened by nobles vying for power. In addition, beginning around 800 western Europe was invaded by several different groups. Local nobles were the strongest power, and common people turned to them for protection. By the eleventh century, however, rulers in some parts of Europe reasserted authority and slowly built centralized states.

Invasions and Migrations

From the moors of Scotland to the mountains of Sicily, there arose in the ninth century the prayer, "Save us, O God, from the violence of the Northmen." The Northmen were pagan Germanic peoples from Norway, Sweden, and Denmark who came to be known as Vikings. Some scholars believe that the name *Viking* derives from the Old Norse word *vik*, meaning "creek." A Viking was someone who waited in a creek or bay to attack passing vessels.

Viking assaults began around 800, and by the mid-tenth century the Vikings had brought large sections of continental Europe and Britain under their sway. In the east they sailed the rivers of Russia as far as the Black Sea. In the west they established permanent settlements in Iceland and short-lived ones in Greenland and Newfoundland in Canada (Map 14.1).

The Vikings were superb seamen with advanced methods of boatbuilding. Propelled either by oars or by sails, lacking decks, and about sixty-five-feet long, a Viking ship could carry between forty and sixty men — enough to harass an isolated monastery or village. Against these ships navigated by experienced and fearless sailors, the Carolingian Empire, with no navy, was helpless. At first the Vikings attacked and sailed off laden with booty. Later, on returning, they settled down and colonized the areas they had conquered, often marrying local women and adopting the languages and some of the customs of their new homes.

Along with the Vikings, groups of central European steppe peoples known as Magyars (MAG-yahrz) also raided villages in the late ninth century, taking plunder and captives and forcing leaders to pay tribute in an effort to prevent further looting and destruction. Moving westward, small bands of Magyars on horseback reached far into Europe. They subdued northern Italy, compelled Bavaria and Saxony to pay tribute, and penetrated into the Rhineland and Burgundy. Western Europeans thought of them as returning Huns, so the Magyars came to be known as Hungarians. They settled in the area that is now Hungary, became Christian, and in the eleventh century allied with the papacy.

From North Africa, the Muslims also began new encroachments in the ninth century. They already ruled most of Spain and now conquered Sicily, driving northward into central Italy and the south coast of France.

What was the impact of these invasions? From the perspective of those living in what had been

---

• **vassal** A knight who has sworn loyalty to a particular lord.

> *"Save us, O God, from the violence of the Northmen."*
>
> **NINTH-CENTURY PRAYER**

Charlemagne's empire, Viking, Magyar, and Muslim attacks contributed to increasing disorder and violence. Italian, French, and English sources often describe this period as one of terror and chaos. People in other parts of Europe might have had a different opinion. In Muslim Spain and Sicily scholars worked in thriving cities, and new crops such as cotton and sugar enhanced ordinary people's lives. In eastern Europe states such as Moravia and Hungary became strong kingdoms. A Viking point of view might be the most positive, for by 1100 descendants of the Vikings not only ruled their homelands in Norway, Sweden, and Denmark but also ruled northern France (a province known as Normandy, or land of the Northmen), England, Sicily, Iceland, and Russia, with an outpost in Greenland and occasional voyages to North America.

Feudalism and Manorialism

The large-scale division of Charlemagne's empire led to a decentralization of power at the local level. Civil wars weakened the power and prestige of kings, who could do little about regional violence. Likewise, the invasions of the ninth century, especially those of the Vikings, weakened royal authority. The Frankish kings were unable to halt the invaders, and the local aristocracy had to assume responsibility for defense. Thus, in the ninth and tenth centuries great aristocratic families increased their authority in their local territories, and distant and weak kings could not interfere. Common people turned for protection to the strongest power, the local nobles.

The most powerful nobles were those who gained warriors' allegiance, often symbolized in an oath-swearing ceremony of "homage and fealty" that grew out of earlier Germanic oaths of loyalty. In this ceremony a warrior (knight) swore his loyalty as a **vassal**—from a Celtic term meaning "servant"—to the more powerful individual, who became his lord. In return for the vassal's loyalty, aid,

Animal Headpost from a Viking Ship Skilled woodcarvers produced ornamental headposts for ships, sledges, wagons, and bedsteads. The fearsome quality of many carvings suggests that they were intended to ward off evil spirits and to terrify. (© University Museum of Cultural Heritage, Oslo. Photographer: Eirik Irgens Johnsen)

Mapping the Past

MAP 14.1 Invasions and Migrations of the Ninth Century This map shows the Viking, Magyar, and Arab invasions and migrations in the ninth century. Compare it with Map 8.3 (page 221) on the barbarian migrations of late antiquity to answer the following questions.

ANALYZING THE MAP What similarities do you see in the patterns of migration in these two periods? What significant differences?

CONNECTIONS How did Viking expertise in shipbuilding and sailing make their migrations different from those of earlier Germanic tribes? How did this set them apart from the Magyar and Muslim invaders of the ninth century?

and military assistance, the lord promised him protection and material support. This support might be a place in the lord's household but was more likely land of the vassal's own, called a **fief** (*feudum* in Latin). The fief, which might contain forests, churches, and towns, technically still belonged to the lord, and the vassal had only the use of it. Peasants living on a fief produced the food and other goods necessary to maintain the knight.

Though historians debate this, fiefs appear to have been granted extensively first by Charles Martel (688–741) and then by his successors, including Charlemagne

and his grandsons. These fiefs went to the most powerful nobles, who often took the title of count. As the Carolingians' control of their territories weakened, the practice of granting fiefs moved to the local level, with lay lords, bishops, and abbots as well as kings granting fiefs. This system, later named **feudalism**, was based on personal ties of loyalty cemented by grants of land rather than on allegiance to an abstract state or governmental system.

The economic power of the warrior class rested on landed estates, which were worked by peasants under

Homage and Fealty Although the rite of entering a feudal relationship varied widely across Europe and sometimes was entirely verbal, a few illustrations exist. Here the vassal kneels before the lord, places his clasped hands between those of the lord, and declares, "I become your man." Sometimes the lord handed over a clump of earth, representing the fief, and the ceremony concluded with a kiss, symbolizing peace between them. (Osterreichische Nationalbibliothek, Vienna #E 8.037-C/D [Cod. 2262, fol 174r])

a system of **manorialism**. Free farmers surrendered themselves and their land to the lord's jurisdiction in exchange for protection. The land was given back to them to farm, but they were tied to the land by various payments and services. Most significantly, a peasant lost his or her freedom and became a **serf**, part of the lord's permanent labor force. Unlike slaves, serfs were personally free, but they were bound to the land and unable to leave it without the lord's permission.

The transition from freedom to serfdom was slow, but by the year 800 perhaps 60 percent of the population of western Europe had been reduced to serfdom. Over the next several centuries unstable conditions and insecurity further increased the need for protection, so that by around 1000 the majority of western Europeans were serfs. While serfs ranged from the highly prosperous to the desperately poor, all had lost their freedom. In eastern Europe the transition was slower but longer lasting. Western European peasants began to escape from serfdom in the later Middle Ages, at the very point that serfs were more firmly tied to the land in eastern Europe, especially in eastern Germany, Poland, and Russia.

The Restoration of Order

The eleventh century witnessed the beginnings of political stability in western Europe. Foreign invasions gradually declined, and in some parts of Europe lords in control of large territories built up their power even

further, becoming kings over growing and slowly centralizing states. As rulers expanded their territories and extended their authority, they developed larger bureaucracies, armies, judicial systems, and other institutions to maintain control, as well as taxation systems to pay for them. These new institutions and practices laid the foundations for modern national states. Political developments in England, France, and Germany provide good examples of the beginnings of the national state in the central Middle Ages.

Under the pressure of Viking invasions in the ninth and tenth centuries, the seven kingdoms of Anglo-Saxon England united under one king. At the same time, England was divided into local shires, or counties, each under the jurisdiction of a sheriff appointed by the king. When Edward the Confessor (r. 1042–1066) died, his cousin, Duke William of Normandy, a French-speaking descendant of the Vikings, crossed the channel and won the English throne by defeating his Anglo-

---

• **fief** A portion of land, the use of which was given by a lord to a vassal in exchange for the latter's oath of loyalty.

• **feudalism** A medieval European political system that defines the military obligations and relations between a lord and his vassals and involves the granting of fiefs.

• **manorialism** The economic system that governed rural life in medieval Europe, in which the landed estates of a lord were worked by the peasants under the lord's jurisdiction in exchange for his protection.

• **serf** A peasant who lost his or her freedom and became permanently bound to the landed estate of a lord.

Saxon rival at the Battle of Hastings. Later dubbed "the Conqueror," William (r. 1066–1087) subdued the rest of the country, distributed land to his Norman followers, and required all feudal lords to swear an oath of allegiance to him as king. He retained the Anglo-Saxon institution of sheriff.

In 1085 William decided to conduct a systematic survey of the entire country to determine how much wealth there was and who had it. This process was described by a contemporary chronicler:

> He sent his men over all England into every shire and had them find out . . . what or how much everybody had who was occupying land in England, in land or cattle, and how much money it was worth. So very narrowly did he have it investigated, that there was no single . . . yard of land, nor indeed . . . one ox nor one cow nor one pig was there left out, and not put down in his record: and all these records were brought to him afterwards.[1]

The resulting record, called the *Domesday Book* (DOOMZ-day) from the Anglo-Saxon word *doom*, meaning "judgment," provided William and his descendants with vital information for governing the country. Completed in 1086, the book still survives, and it is an invaluable source of social and economic information about medieval England.

In 1128 William's granddaughter Matilda married a powerful French noble, Geoffrey of Anjou. Their son, who became Henry II of England, inherited provinces in northwestern France from his father. When Henry married the great heiress Eleanor of Aquitaine in 1152, he claimed lordship over Aquitaine and other provinces in southwestern France as well. The histories of England and France were thus closely intertwined in the Middle Ages.

In the early twelfth century France consisted of a number of nearly independent provinces, each governed by its local ruler. The work of unifying France began under Philip II (r. 1180–1223), called "Augustus" because he vastly enlarged the territory of the kingdom. By the end of his reign Philip was effectively master of northern France, and by 1300 most of the provinces of modern France had been added to the royal domain through diplomacy, marriage, war, and inheritance.

In central Europe the German king Otto I (r. 936–973) defeated many other lords to build up his power, based on an alliance with and control of the church.

The Norman Conquest, 1066

Otto asserted the right to control church appointments, and bishops and abbots had to perform feudal homage for the lands that accompanied their church positions. German rulers were not able to build up centralized power, however. Under Otto I and his successors, a loose confederation stretching from the North Sea to the Mediterranean developed. In this confederation, later called the Holy Roman Empire, the emperor shared power with princes, dukes, counts, city officials, archbishops, and bishops.

Frederick Barbarossa (r. 1152–1190) of the house of Hohenstaufen tried valiantly to make the Holy Roman Empire a united state. He made alliances with the high nobles and even compelled the great churchmen to become his vassals. When he tried to enforce his authority over the cities of northern Italy, however, they formed a league against him in alliance with the pope, and infantrymen from the cities defeated Frederick's mounted knights. Frederick's absence from the German part of his empire allowed the princes and other rulers of independent provinces to consolidate their power there as well.

Law and Justice

Throughout Europe in the twelfth and thirteenth centuries, the law was a hodgepodge of customs, feudal rights, and provincial practices. Rulers wanted to blend these elements into a uniform system of rules acceptable and applicable to all their peoples, though their success in doing so varied.

The French king Louis IX (r. 1226–1270) was famous in his time for his concern for justice. Each French province, even after being made part of the kingdom of France, retained its unique laws and procedures. But Louis IX created a royal judicial system, establishing the Parlement of Paris, a kind of supreme court that heard appeals from lower courts.

Under Henry II (r. 1154–1189), England developed and extended a common law—a law common to and accepted by the entire country. No other country in medieval Europe did so. Each year Henry sent out circuit judges (royal officials who traveled in a given circuit or district) to hear civil and criminal cases. Wherever the king's judges sat, there sat the king's court. Slowly, the king's court gained jurisdiction over all property disputes and criminal actions.

Henry's son John (r. 1199–1216) met with serious disappointment after taking the throne. He lost the

French province of Normandy to Philip Augustus in 1204 and spent the rest of his reign trying to win it back. Saddled with heavy debt from his father and brother Richard (r. 1189–1199), John tried to squeeze more money from nobles and town dwellers, creating an atmosphere of resentment. When John's military campaign failed in 1214, it was clear that the French lands that had once belonged to the English king were lost for good. His ineptitude as a soldier in a culture that idealized military glory turned the people against him. The barons revolted and in 1215 forced him to attach his seal to the Magna Carta — the "Great Charter," which became the cornerstone of English justice and law.

To contemporaries the Magna Carta was intended to redress the grievances that particular groups had against King John. It came to have much broader significance, however, and every English king in the Middle Ages reissued the Magna Carta as evidence of his promise to observe the law. It came to signify the principle that everyone, including the king and the government, must obey the law, and it gradually came to be seen as almost sacred. Some clauses of the Magna Carta contain the germ of the idea of due process of law: a person may not be arbitrarily arrested and held indefinitely in prison without being accused of crime and brought to trial.

Statements of legal principles such as the Magna Carta were not how most people experienced the law in medieval Europe. Instead they were involved in actual cases. Judges determined guilt or innocence in a number of ways. In some cases, particularly those in which there was little clear evidence, they ordered a trial by ordeal, in which the accused might be tied hand and foot and dropped in a lake or river. People believed that water was a pure substance and would reject anything foul or unclean, although God could always affect the outcome. Thus a person who sank was considered innocent, while a person who floated was found guilty. Trials by ordeal are fascinating to modern audiences, but they were relatively rare, and their use declined as courts increasingly favored more rational procedures, in which judges heard testimony, sought witnesses, and read written evidence if it was available. Violent crimes were often punished by public execution. Hanging was the most common method of execution, although nobles might be beheaded because hanging was seen as demeaning. Executioners were feared figures, but they were also well-paid public officials and were a necessary part of the legal structure.

The Christian Church

◻ How did the Christian Church enhance its power and create new institutions and religious practices?

Kings and emperors were not the only rulers consolidating their power in the eleventh and twelfth centuries; the papacy did as well, although the popes' efforts were sometimes challenged by medieval kings and emperors. Despite such challenges, monasteries continued to be important places for learning and devotion, and new religious orders were founded. Also, Christianity expanded into Europe's northern and eastern regions, and Christian rulers expanded their holdings in Muslim Spain.

Córdoba Mosque and Cathedral The huge arches of the Great Mosque at Córdoba dwarf the cathedral built in its center after the city was conquered by Christian armies in 1236. During the reconquista (see page 404), Christian kings often transformed mosques into churches, often by simply adding Christian elements such as crosses and altars to existing structures. (dbimages/Alamy)

Papal Reforms

During the ninth and tenth centuries the church came under the control of kings and feudal lords, who chose priests, bishops, abbots, and other church officials in their territories, granting them fiefs that provided an income and expecting loyalty and service in return. Church offices were sometimes sold outright — a practice called *simony*. Although the Roman Church encouraged clerical celibacy, many priests were married or living with women. Popes were chosen by wealthy Roman families from among their members, and after gaining the papal office they paid more attention to their families' political fortunes or their own pleasures than to the institutional or spiritual health of the church. Not surprisingly, clergy at all levels who had bought their positions or had been granted them for political reasons provided little spiritual guidance, and their personal lives were rarely models of high moral standards.

Serious efforts to change all this began in the eleventh century. A series of popes believed that secular or lay control over the church was largely responsible for the lack of moral leadership, so they proclaimed the church independent from secular rulers. The Lateran Council of 1059 decreed that the authority and power to elect the pope rested solely in the college of cardinals, a special group of priests from the major churches in and around Rome. The college retains that power today.

Pope Gregory VII (pontificate 1073–1085) vigorously championed reform and the expansion of papal power. He ordered all priests to give up their wives and children or face dismissal, invalidated the ordination of church officials who had purchased their offices, and placed nuns under firmer control of male authorities. He believed that the pope, as the successor of Saint Peter, was the vicar of God on earth and that papal orders were the orders of God. Thus he was the first pope to emphasize the political authority of the papacy. He ordered that any church official selected or appointed by a layperson should be deposed, and any layperson, including rulers, who appointed a church official should be excommunicated — cut off from the sacraments and the Christian community.

European rulers immediately protested this restriction of their power, and the strongest reaction came from Henry IV, the ruler of Germany who would later become the Holy Roman emperor. Henry continued to appoint officials, and Gregory responded by excommunicating bishops who supported Henry and threatening to depose him. In January 1077 Henry arrived at the pope's residence in Canossa in northern Italy and, according to legend, stood outside in the snow for three days seeking forgiveness. As a priest, Gregory was obliged to grant absolution and readmit the emperor into the Christian community. Although Henry bowed before the pope, he actually won a victory, maintaining authority over his subjects and in 1084 being crowned emperor. This victory was temporary, however, for high nobles within the empire took advantage of further conflicts with the pope to enhance their position, siding with the church to gain power. They subordinated lesser nobles, expanded restrictions on peasants, and prevented later emperors such as Frederick Barbarossa from unifying the empire.

Monastic Life

Although they were in theory cut off from the world (see page 214), monasteries and convents were deeply affected by issues of money, rank, and power. By the eighth century monasteries and convents dotted the European landscape, and during the ninth and tenth centuries they were often the target of Viking attacks or raids by local looters seeking valuable objects. Some religious communities fled and dispersed, while others fell under the control and domination of local feudal lords. Powerful laymen appointed themselves or their relatives as abbots, took the lands and goods of monasteries, and spent monastic revenues.

Medieval monasteries fulfilled the needs of the feudal system in other ways as well. They provided noble boys with education and opportunities for ecclesiastical careers. Although a few men who rose in the ranks of church officials were of humble origins, most were from high-status families. Social class also defined the kinds of religious life open to women. Kings and nobles usually established convents for their female relatives and other elite women, and the position of abbess, or head of a convent, became the most powerful position a woman could hold in medieval society. (See "Individuals in Society: Hildegard of Bingen," page 401.) People of lower social standing did live and work in monasteries, but as lay brothers and sisters who performed manual labor, not religious duties.

Routines within individual monasteries varied widely from house to house and from region to region. In every monastery, however, daily life centered on the liturgy or Divine Office, psalms, and other prayers, which monks and nuns said seven times a day and once during the night. Praying was looked on as a vital service, as crucial as the labor of peasants and the military might of nobles. Prayers were said for peace, rain, good harvests, the civil authorities, the monks' and nuns' families, and their benefactors. Monastic patrons in turn lavished gifts on the monasteries, which often became very wealthy, controlling large tracts of land and the peasants who farmed them.

The combination of lay control and wealth created problems for monasteries as monks and nuns concentrated on worldly issues and levels of spiritual observance and intellectual activity declined. Several waves

Individuals in Society

Hildegard of Bingen

THE TENTH CHILD OF A LESSER NOBLE FAMILY, Hildegard (1098–1179) was turned over to the care of an abbey in the Rhineland when she was eight years old. There she learned Latin and received a good education. She spent most of her life in various women's religious communities, two of which she founded herself. When she was a child, she began having mystical visions, often of light in the sky, but told few people about them. In middle age, however, her visions became more dramatic: "And it came to pass . . . when I was 42 years and 7 months old, that the heavens were opened and a blinding light of exceptional brilliance flowed through my entire brain. And so it kindled my whole heart and breast like a flame, not burning but warming . . . and suddenly I understood of the meaning of expositions of the books."* She wanted the church to approve of her visions and wrote first to St. Bernard of Clairvaux, who answered her briefly and dismissively, and then to Pope Eugenius, who encouraged her to write them down. Her first work was *Scivias* (Know the Ways of the Lord), a record of her mystical visions that incorporates extensive theological learning (see the illustration).

Obviously possessed of leadership and administrative talents, Hildegard left her abbey in 1147 to found the convent of Rupertsberg near Bingen. There she produced *Physica* (On the Physical Elements) and *Causa et Curae* (Causes and Cures), scientific works on the curative properties of natural elements; poems; a mystery play; and several more works of mysticism. She carried on a huge correspondence with scholars, prelates, and ordinary people. When she was over fifty, she left her community to preach to audiences of clergy and laity, and she was the only woman of her time whose opinions on religious matters were considered authoritative by the church.

Hildegard's visions have been explored by theologians and also by neurologists, who judge that they may have originated in migraine headaches, as she reports many of the same phenomena that migraine sufferers do: auras of light around objects, areas of blindness, feelings of intense doubt and intense euphoria. The interpretations that she develops come from her theological insight and learning, however, not from her illness. That same insight also emerges in her music, which is what she is best known for today. Eighty of her compositions survive—a huge number for a medieval composer—most of them written to be sung by the nuns in her convent, so they have strong lines for female voices. Many of her songs and chants have been recorded recently by various artists and are available on compact disk, as downloads, and on several Web sites.

QUESTIONS FOR ANALYSIS

1. Why do you think Hildegard might have kept her visions secret at first? Why do you think she eventually sought church approval for them?
2. In what ways were Hildegard's accomplishments extraordinary given women's general status in the Middle Ages?

*From *Scivias*, trans. Mother Columba Hart and Jane Bishop, *The Classics of Western Spirituality* (New York/Mahwah: Paulist Press, 1990).

Inspired by heavenly fire, Hildegard begins to dictate her visions to her scribe. The original of this elaborately illustrated copy of *Scivias* disappeared from Hildegard's convent during World War II, but fortunately a facsimile had already been made. (Private Collection/The Bridgeman Art Library)

Agricultural Work In this scene from a German manuscript written about 1190, men and women of different ages are sowing seeds and harvesting grain. All residents of a village, including children, engaged in agricultural tasks. (Rheinisches Landesmuseum, Bonn/The Bridgeman Art Library)

of reform improved the situation in some monasteries, but when deeply impressed laypeople showered gifts on monasteries with good reputations, monastic observance and spiritual fervor again declined. New religious orders, such as the Cistercians (sihs-TUHR-shuhnz), founded in 1098, attempted to solve the problem by establishing their houses in isolated areas, rejecting the traditional feudal sources of income (such as the possession of mills and serfs), and living very simply. Their innovative methods of farming, sheep-raising, and cloth production brought financial success, however, and by the late twelfth century economic prosperity and political power had begun to compromise the original Cistercian ideals.

In the thirteenth century the growth of cities provided a new challenge for the church. Many urban people thought that the church did not meet their spiritual needs. They turned instead to heresies — that is, to versions of Christianity outside of those approved by the papacy. Ironically, many of these belief systems denied the value of material wealth. Combating **heresy** became a principal task of new religious orders, most prominently the Dominicans and Franciscans, who preached and ministered to city dwellers; the Dominicans also staffed the papal Inquisition, a special court designed to root out heresy.

Popular Religion

Apart from the land, the weather, and local legal and social conditions, religion had the greatest impact on the daily lives of ordinary people in medieval Europe. Religious practices varied widely from country to country and even from province to province. But nowhere was religion a one-hour-a-week affair.

For Christians, the village church was the center of community life — social, political, and economic as well as religious — with the parish priest in charge of a host of activities. Every Sunday and on holy days the villagers stood at Mass or squatted on the floor (there were no chairs), breaking the painful routine of work. The feasts that accompanied baptisms, weddings, funerals, and other celebrations were commonly held in the churchyard. Popular religion consisted largely of rituals heavy with symbolism. For example, before slicing a loaf of bread, the pious woman tapped the sign of the cross on it with her knife. Before planting began on local lands, the village priest customarily went out and sprinkled the fields with water, symbolizing refreshment and life. Everyone participated in village processions. The entire calendar was designed with reference to Christmas, Easter, and Pentecost, events in the life of Jesus and his disciples.

The Christian calendar was also filled with saints' days. Saints were individuals who had lived particularly holy lives and were honored locally or more widely for their connection with the divine. The cult of the saints, which developed in a rural and uneducated en-

> **heresy** An opinion, belief, or action counter to doctrines that church leaders defined as correct; heretics could be punished by the church.

vironment, represents a central feature of popular culture in the Middle Ages. People believed that the saints possessed supernatural powers that enabled them to perform miracles, and each saint became the special property of the locality in which his or her relics — remains or possessions — rested. Relics such as the saint's bones, articles of clothing, tears, and saliva, and even the dust from his or her tomb, were enclosed in the church altar. In return for the saint's healing powers and support, peasants would offer prayers, loyalty, and gifts.

Just as they felt connections to saints, people had a strong sense of the presence of God. They believed that God rewarded the virtuous with peace, health, and material prosperity and punished sinners with disease, poor harvests, and war. Sin was caused by the Devil, who lurked everywhere and constantly incited people to evil deeds.

Most people in medieval Europe were Christian, but there were small Jewish communities scattered through many parts of Europe, as well as Muslims in the Iberian Peninsula, Sicily, other Mediterranean islands, and southeastern Europe. Increasing suspicion and hostility marked relations among believers in different religions throughout the Middle Ages, but there were also important similarities in the ways that European Christians, Jews, and Muslims understood and experienced their faiths. In all three traditions, every major life transition, such as marriage or the birth of a child, was marked by a ceremony that involved religious officials or spiritual elements. In all three faiths, death was marked by religious rituals, and the living had obligations to the dead, including prayers and special mourning periods.

The Expansion of Christianity

The eleventh and twelfth centuries saw not only reforms in monasticism and the papacy but also an expansion of Christianity into Scandinavia, the Baltic lands, eastern Europe, and Spain that had profound cultural consequences. The expansion was accomplished through wars, the establishment of new bishoprics, and the vast migration of Christian colonists into non-Christian territories. As it occurred, more and more Europeans began to think of themselves as belonging to a realm of Christianity that was political as well as religious, a realm they called Christendom.

Christian influences entered Scandinavia and the Baltic lands primarily through the creation of dioceses (church districts headed by bishops). This took place in Denmark in the tenth and eleventh centuries, and the institutional church spread rather quickly due to the support offered by the strong throne. Dioceses were established in Norway and Sweden in the eleventh century, and in 1164 Uppsala, Sweden, long the center of the pagan cults of Odin and Thor, became a Catholic archdiocese.

Otto I (see page 398) planted a string of dioceses along his northern and eastern frontiers, hoping to pacify the newly conquered Slavs in eastern Europe. However, frequent Slavic revolts illustrate the people's resentment of German lords and clerics and indicate that the church did not easily penetrate the region.

The church also moved into central Europe, first into Bohemia in the tenth century and from there into Poland and Hungary in the eleventh century. In the twelfth and thirteenth centuries thousands of settlers poured into eastern Europe from the west. These new

Baking Bread Bread and beer or ale were the main manorial products for local consumption. While women dominated the making of ale and beer, men and women cooperated in the making and baking of bread — the staple of the diet. Most people did not have ovens in their own homes because of the danger of fire; they used the communal manorial oven, which, like a modern pizza oven, could bake several loaves at once. (Bibliothèque nationale de France)

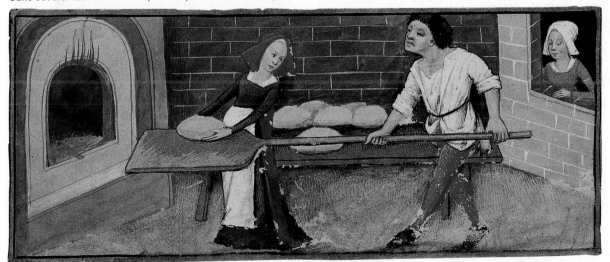

immigrants, German in descent, name, language, and law, settled in Silesia, Mecklenburg, Bohemia, Poland, Hungary, and Transylvania, where they established towns.

The Iberian Peninsula was another area of Christian expansion. About 950 Caliph Abd al-Rahman III (912–961) of the Umayyad Dynasty of Córdoba ruled most of the peninsula. Christian Spain consisted of the small kingdoms of Castile, León, Catalonia, Aragon, Navarre, and Portugal. When civil wars erupted among Rahman's descendants, Muslim lands were split among several small kingdoms, making it easier for Christians to take over these lands. By 1248 Christians held all of the peninsula save for the small state of Granada in the south. As the Christians advanced, they changed the face of Spanish cities, transforming mosques into cathedrals.

Fourteenth-century clerical propagandists would call the movement to expel the Muslims the **reconquista** (reconquest)—a sacred and patriotic crusade to wrest the country from "alien" Muslim hands from about 722 to 1492. This religious idea became part of Spanish political culture and of the national psychology. Rulers of the Christian kingdoms of Spain increasingly passed legislation discriminating against Muslims and Jews living under Christian rule, and they attempted to exclude anyone from the nobility who could not prove "purity of blood"—that is, that they had no Muslim or Jewish ancestors. As a consequence of the reconquista (ray-kon-KEES-tah), the Spanish and Portuguese also learned how to administer vast tracts of newly acquired territory. In the sixteenth century they used their claims about the rightful dominance of Christianity to justify their colonization of new territories in Mexico, Brazil, Peru, Angola, and the Philippines, and relied on their experiences at home to provide models of how to govern.

Date of Christian reconquest
- By 814
- By 910
- By 1037
- By 1097
- By 1150
- By 1190
- By 1275
- By 1492

FRANCE
LEÓN
NAVARRE
ARAGON
CASTILE
PORTUGAL
GRANADA
ATLANTIC OCEAN
Mediterranean Sea
AFRICA

The Reconquista, 722-1492

Spain was not the only place in Europe where "blood" became a way of understanding differences among people and a basis for discriminatory laws. When Germans moved into eastern Europe and English forces took over much of Ireland, they increasingly barred local people from access to legal courts and denied them positions in monasteries or craft guilds. They banned intermarriage between ethnic groups in an attempt to maintain ethnic purity, even though everyone was Christian. As Europeans later came into contact with people from Africa and Asia, and particularly as they developed co-

lonial empires there, these notions of blood also became a way of conceptualizing racial categories.

The Crusades

☐ What were the motives, course, and consequences of the Crusades?

The expansion of Christianity in the Middle Ages was not limited to Europe but extended to the eastern Mediterranean in what were later termed the **Crusades**. Occurring in the late eleventh and early twelfth centuries, the Crusades were wars sponsored by the papacy to recover the holy city of Jerusalem from the Muslims. The word *crusade* was not actually used at the time and did not appear in English until the late sixteenth century. It means literally "taking the cross," a vow to spread Christianity symbolized by the cross that soldiers sewed on their garments. Although people of all ages and classes participated in the Crusades, so many knights did that crusading became a distinctive feature of the upper-class lifestyle. In an aristocratic military society, men coveted reputations as Crusaders; the Christian knight who had been to Jerusalem enjoyed great prestige.

Background and Motives

In the eleventh century the papacy had strong reasons for wanting to launch an expedition against Muslims in the East. If the pope could muster a large army against the enemies of Christianity, his claim to be the leader of Christian society in the West would be strengthened. Moreover, in 1054 a serious theological disagreement had split the Greek Church of Byzantium and the Roman Church of the West. The pope believed that a crusade would lead to strong Roman influence in Greek territories and eventually the reunion of the two churches.

Popes and other church officials gained support for war in defense of Christianity by promising spiritual benefits to those who joined a campaign or died fighting. Church leaders said that these people would be forgiven for their sins without having to do penance, that is, without having to confess to a priest and carry out some action to make up for the sins. Preachers communicated these ideas widely and told stories about warrior-saints who slew hundreds of enemies.

Religious zeal led increasing numbers of people to go on pilgrimages to holy places, including Jerusalem. The Arabic Muslims who had ruled Jerusalem and the surrounding territory for centuries allowed Christian pilgrims to travel freely, but in the late eleventh century the Seljuk Turks took over Palestine, defeating

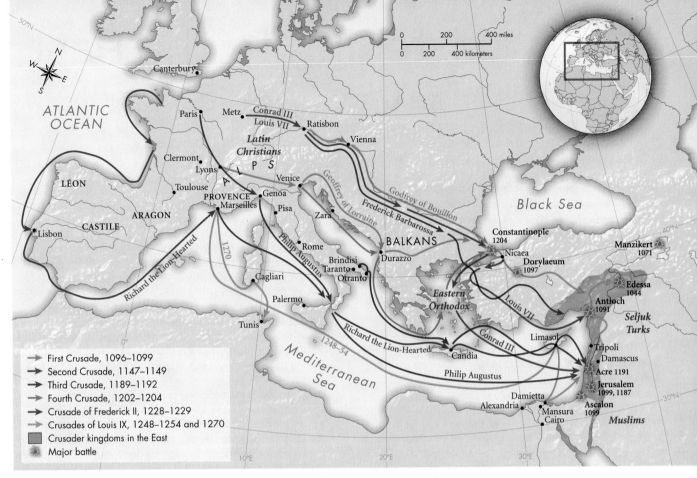

MAP 14.2 The Crusades, 1096–1270 The Crusaders took many different sea and land routes on their way to Jerusalem, often crossing the lands of the Byzantine Empire, which led to conflict with Eastern Christians. The Crusader kingdoms in the East lasted only briefly.

both Arabic and Byzantine armies, and pilgrimage became more difficult. The Byzantine emperor at Constantinople appealed to western European Christians for support. The emperor's appeal fit well with papal aims, and in 1095 Pope Urban II called for a great Christian holy war against the infidels. He urged Christian knights who had been fighting one another to direct their energies against those he claimed were the true enemies of God, the Muslims.

The Course of the Crusades

Thousands of people of all classes responded to Urban's call, streaming southward and then toward Jerusalem in what became known as the First Crusade. The First Crusade was successful, mostly because of the dynamic enthusiasm of the participants, who had little more than religious zeal. They knew little of the geography or climate of the Middle East, and although there were several counts with military experience, the Crusaders could never agree on a leader. Adding to these disadvantages, supply lines were never set up, starvation and disease wracked the army, and the Turks slaughtered hundreds of noncombatants. Nevertheless, the army pressed on, defeating the Turks in several battles,

and after a monthlong siege it took Jerusalem in July 1099 (Map 14.2). Fulcher of Chartres, a chaplain on the First Crusade, described the scene:

> Amid the sound of trumpets and with everything in an uproar they attacked boldly, shouting "God help us!" . . . They ran with the greatest exultation as fast as they could into the city and joined their companions in pursuing and slaying their wicked enemies without cessation. . . . If you had been there your feet would have been stained to the ankles in the blood of the slain. What shall I say? None of them were left alive. Neither women nor children were spared.[2]

With Jerusalem taken, some Crusaders regarded their mission as accomplished and set off for home, but the appearance of more Muslim troops convinced the Crusaders that they needed to stay. Slowly institutions were set up to rule local territories and the Muslim

- **reconquista** A fourteenth-century term used to describe the Christian crusade to wrest Spain back from the Muslims from 722 to 1492; clerics believed it was a sacred and patriotic mission.
- **Crusades** Holy wars sponsored by the papacy for the recovery of the Holy Land from the Muslims.

An Arab View of the Crusades

The Crusades helped shape the understanding that Arabs and Europeans had of each other and all subsequent relations between the Christian West and the Arab world. To medieval Christians, the Crusades were papally approved military expeditions to recover holy places in Palestine; to the Arabs, these campaigns were "Frankish wars" or "Frankish invasions" for the acquisition of territory.

Early in the thirteenth century, Ibn Al-Athir (1160–1223), a native of Mosul, an important economic and cultural center in northern Mesopotamia (modern Iraq), wrote a history of the First Crusade. He relied on Arab sources for the events he described. Here is his account of the Crusaders' capture of Antioch.

66 The power of the Franks first became apparent when in the year 478/1085–86* they invaded the territories of Islam and took Toledo and other parts of Andalusia [in Spain]. Then in 484/1091 they attacked and conquered the island of Sicily and turned their attention to the African coast. Certain of their conquests there were won back again, but they had other successes, as you will see.

In 490/1097 the Franks attacked Syria. This is how it all began: Baldwin, their King, a kinsman of Roger the Frank who had conquered Sicily, assembled a great army and sent word to Roger saying: "I have assembled a great army and now I am on my way to you, to use your bases for my conquest of the African coast. Thus you and I shall become neighbors."

Roger called together his companions and consulted them about these proposals. "This will be a fine thing for them and for us!" they declared, "for by this means these lands will be converted to the Faith!" At this Roger raised one leg and farted loudly, and swore that it was of more use than their advice. "Why?" "Because if this army comes here it will need quantities of provisions and fleets of ships to transport it to Africa, as well as reinforcements from my own troops. Then, if the Franks succeed in conquering this territory they will take it over and will need provisioning from Sicily. This will cost me my annual profit from the harvest. If they fail they will return here and be an embarrassment to me here in my own domain." . . .

He summoned Baldwin's messenger and said to him: "If you have decided to make war on the Muslims your best course will be to free Jerusalem from their rule and thereby win great honor. I am bound by certain promises and treaties of allegiance with the ruler of Africa." So the Franks made ready to set out to attack Syria.

Another story is that the Fatimids of Egypt were afraid when they saw the Seljuqids extending their empire through Syria as far as Gaza, until they reached the Egyptian border and Atsiz invaded Egypt itself. They therefore sent to invite the Franks to invade Syria and so protect Egypt from the Muslims.† But God knows best.

When the Franks decided to attack Syria they marched east to Constantinople, so that they could cross the straits and advance into Muslim territory by the easier, land route. When they reached Constantinople, the Emperor of the East refused them permission to pass through his domains. He said: "Unless you first promise me Antioch, I shall not allow you to cross into the Muslim empire." His real intention was to incite them to attack the Muslims, for he was convinced that the Turks, whose invincible control over Asia Minor he had observed, would exterminate every one of them. They accepted his conditions and in 490/1097 they crossed the Bosphorus at Constantinople. . . . They . . . reached Antioch, which they besieged.

When Yaghi Siyan, the ruler of Antioch, heard of their approach, he was not sure how the Christian people of the city would react, so he made the Muslims go outside the city on their own to dig trenches, and the next day sent the Christians out alone to continue the task. When they were ready to return home at the end of the day he refused to allow them. "Antioch is yours," he said, "but you will have to leave it to me until I see what happens between us and the Franks." "Who will protect our children and our wives?" they said. "I shall look after them for you." So they resigned themselves to their fate, and lived in the Frankish camp for nine months, while the city was under siege.

---

*Muslims traditionally date events from Muhammad's hegira, or emigration, to Medina, which occurred in 622 according to the Christian calendar.

†Although Muslims, Fatimids were related doctrinally to the Shi'ites, but the dominant Sunni Muslims considered the Fatimids heretics.

---

population. Four small "Crusader states" — Jerusalem, Edessa, Tripoli, and Antioch — were established, and castles and fortified towns were built in these states to defend against Muslim reconquest. Reinforcements arrived in the form of pilgrims and fighters from Europe, so that there was constant coming and going by land and more often by sea after the Crusaders conquered port cities.

Between 1096 and 1270 the crusading ideal was expressed in eight papally approved expeditions, though none after the First Crusade accomplished very much. The Muslim states in the Middle East were politically fragmented when the Crusaders first came, and it took them about a century to reorganize. They did so dramatically under Saladin (Salah al-Din), who unified Egypt and Syria. In 1187 the Muslims retook Jerusa-

Yaghi Siyan showed unparalleled courage and wisdom, strength and judgment. If all the Franks who died had survived they would have overrun all the lands of Islam. He protected the families of the Christians in Antioch and would not allow a hair of their heads to be touched.

After the siege had been going on for a long time the Franks made a deal with . . . a cuirass [breastplate]-maker called Ruzbih whom they bribed with a fortune in money and lands. He worked in the tower that stood over the riverbed, where the river flowed out of the city into the valley. The Franks sealed their pact with the cuirass-maker, God damn him! and made their way to the water-gate. They opened it and entered the city. Another gang of them climbed the tower with their ropes. At dawn, when more than 500 of them were in the city and the defenders were worn out after the night watch, they sounded their trumpets. . . . Panic seized Yaghi Siyan and he opened the city gates and fled in terror, with an escort of thirty pages. His army commander arrived, but when he discovered on enquiry that Yaghi Siyan had fled, he made his escape by another gate. This was of great help to the Franks, for if he had stood firm for an hour, they would have been wiped out. They entered the city by the gates and sacked it, slaughtering all the Muslims they found there. This happened in jumada I (491/April/May 1098). . . .

It was the discord between the Muslim princes . . . that enabled the Franks to overrun the country. "

Source: *Arab Historians of the Crusades*, selected and translated from the Arabic sources by Francesco Gabrieli. Translated from the Italian by E. J. Costello. © 1969 by Routledge & Kegan Paul Ltd. Reproduced by permission of Taylor & Francis Books UK and The University of California Press.

QUESTIONS FOR ANALYSIS

1. Most Christian histories of the Crusades begin with Pope Urban II's call in 1095. What does Ibn Al-Athir see as the beginning? How would this make his view of the Crusades different from that of Christian chroniclers?

2. How does Ibn Al-Athir characterize the Christian leaders Roger and Baldwin? How does this compare with his characterization of Yaghi Siyan, the Muslim ruler of Antioch?

3. To what does Ibn Al-Athir attribute the fall of Antioch? To what does he attribute Christian defeats of the Muslims more generally? What does this suggest about his view of Christian military capabilities?

lem, but the Christians kept their hold on port towns, and Saladin allowed pilgrims safe passage to Jerusalem. From that point on, the Crusader states were more important economically than politically or religiously, giving Italian and French merchants direct access to Eastern products such as perfumes and silk.

After the Muslims retook Jerusalem the crusading movement faced other setbacks. During the Fourth Crusade (1202–1204), Crusaders stopped in Constantinople, and when they were not welcomed they sacked the city and grabbed thousands of relics, which were later sold in Europe. The Byzantine Empire splintered into three parts and soon consisted of little more than the city of Constantinople. Moreover, the assault of one Christian people on another — when one of the goals of the Crusades was reunion of the Greek and Latin

Churches — made the split between the churches permanent and discredited the entire crusading movement in the eyes of many Christians.

The battles of the Crusades were typical of much medieval warfare, which consisted of the besieging of towns and castles. Help could not enter nor could anyone leave; the larger the number of besiegers, the greater was the chance the fortification would fall. Women swelled the numbers of besiegers. In the Crusades, women assisted in filling the moats surrounding fortified places with earth so that ladders and war engines could be brought close, provided water to fighting men, worked as washerwomen, foraged for food, and provided sexual services.

In the late thirteenth century Turkish armies, after gradually conquering all other Muslim rulers, turned against the Crusader states. In 1291 the Christians' last stronghold, the port of Acre, fell in a battle that was just as bloody as the first battle for Jerusalem two centuries earlier. Knights then needed a new battlefield for military actions, which some found in Spain, where the rulers of Aragon and Castile continued fighting Muslims until 1492.

Consequences of the Crusades

The Crusades testified to the religious enthusiasm of the High Middle Ages and the influence of the papacy, gave kings and the pope opportunities to expand their bureaucracies, and provided an outlet for nobles' dreams of glory. The Crusades also introduced some Europeans to Eastern luxury goods, but their immediate cultural impact on the West remains debatable. By the late eleventh century strong economic and intellectual ties with the East had already been made. However, the Crusades were a boon to Italian merchants, who profited from outfitting military expeditions as well as from the opening of new trade routes and the establishment of trading communities in the Crusader states.

Despite these advantages, the Crusades had some seriously negative sociopolitical consequences. For one thing, they proved to be a disaster for Jewish-Christian relations. Inspired by the ideology of holy war, Christian armies on their way to Jerusalem on the First Crusade joined with local mobs to attack Jewish families and communities, sometimes burning people alive in the synagogue or Jewish section of town. Later Crusades brought similar violence, enhanced by accusations that Jews engaged in the ritual murder of Christians to use their blood in religious rites.

Legal restrictions on Jews gradually increased throughout Europe. Jews were forbidden to have Christian servants or employees, to hold public office, to appear in public on Christian holy days, or to enter Christian parts of town without a badge marking them as Jews. They were prohibited from engaging in any trade with Christians except money-lending — which only fueled popular resentment — and were banished from England and France.

The Crusades also left an inheritance of deep bitterness in Christian-Muslim relations. Each side dehumanized the other, viewing those who followed the other religion as unbelievers. (See "Listening to the Past: An Arab View of the Crusades," page 406.) Whereas Europeans perceived the Crusades as sacred religious movements, Muslims saw them as expansionist and imperialistic. The ideal of a sacred mission to conquer or convert Muslim peoples entered Europeans' consciousness and became a continuing goal. When in 1492 Christopher Columbus sailed west, he used the language of the Crusades in his diaries, and he hoped to establish a Christian base in India from which a new crusade against Islam could be launched (see page 470).

The Life of the People

☐ How did the lives of common people, nobles, and townspeople differ, and what new commercial developments increased wealth?

In the late ninth century medieval intellectuals described Christian society as composed of those who pray (the monks), those who fight (the nobles), and those who work (the peasants). This image of society became popular in the Middle Ages, especially among people who were worried about the changes they saw around them. They asserted that the three categories of citizens had been established by God and that every person had been assigned a fixed place in the social order.

This three-category model does not fully describe medieval society; there were degrees of wealth and status within each group. Also, the model does not take townspeople and the emerging commercial classes into consideration, and it completely excludes those who were not Christian, such as Jews, Muslims, and pagans. Furthermore, those who used the model, generally bishops and other church officials, ignored the fact that each of these groups was made up of both women and men; they spoke only of warriors, monks, and farmers. Despite — or perhaps because of — these limitations, the model of the three categories was a powerful mental construct. Therefore, we can use it to organize our investigation of life in the Middle Ages, broadening it to include groups and issues that medieval authors did not. (See page 400 for a discussion of the life of monks and nuns — "those who pray.")

The Life and Work of Peasants

The men and women who worked the land in the Middle Ages made up probably more than 90 percent of the population. The evolution of localized feudal systems into more centralized states had relatively little impact on the daily lives of these peasants except when it involved warfare. While only nobles fought, their battles often destroyed the houses, barns, and fields of ordinary people, who might also be killed either directly or as a result of the famine and disease that often accompanied war. Villagers might seek protection in the local castle during times of war, but typically they worked and lived without paying much attention to political developments within castle walls.

This lack of attention went in the other direction as well. Since villagers did not perform what were considered "noble" deeds, the aristocratic monks and clerics who wrote the records that serve as historical sources did not spend time or precious writing materials on them. So it is more difficult to find information on the majority of Europeans who were peasants than on the small group at the top of society.

Medieval theologians lumped everyone who worked the land into the category of "those who work," but in fact there were many levels of peasants, ranging from slaves to free and very rich farmers. Most peasants were serfs, required to stay in the village and perform labor on the lord's land. The number of workdays varied, but serfs usually worked three days a week except in the planting or harvest seasons, when the number of days increased. Serfs frequently had to pay arbitrary levies, as for marriage or inheritance of property. A free person had to do none of these things. For his or her landholding, rent had to be paid to the lord, but a free person could move and live as he or she wished.

Serfdom was a hereditary condition. A person born a serf was likely to die a serf, though many serfs did secure their freedom, and the economic revival that began in the eleventh century (see pages 410–412) allowed many to buy their freedom. Further opportunities for increased personal freedom came when lords organized groups of villagers to migrate to sparsely settled frontier areas or to cut down forests or fill in swamps so that there was more land available for farming. Those who took on this extra work often gained a reduction in traditional manorial obligations and an improvement of their social and legal conditions.

In the Middle Ages most European peasants, free and unfree, lived in family groups in small villages that were part of a manor, the estate of a lord (see page 397). The manor was the basic unit of medieval rural organization and the center of rural life. Within the manors of western and central Europe, villages were made up of small houses for individual families, a church, and perhaps the large house of the lord. Peasant households consisted of one married couple, their children (including stepchildren), and perhaps one or two other relatives, such as a grandparent or unmarried aunt. In southern and eastern Europe, extended families were more likely to live in the same household or very near one another. Between one-third and one-half of children died before age five, though many people lived into their sixties.

The arable land of the manor was divided between the lord and the peasantry, with the lord's portion known as the demesne (dih-MAYN) or home farm. A peasant family's land was not usually one particular field but a scattering of strips across many fields, some of which would be planted in grain, some in other crops, and some left unworked to allow the soil to rejuvenate. That way if one field yielded little, strips in a different field might be more bountiful.

The peasants' work was typically divided according to gender. Men and boys were responsible for clearing new land, plowing, and caring for large animals; women and girls were responsible for the care of small animals, spinning, and food preparation. Both sexes harvested and planted, though often there were gender-specific tasks within each of these major undertakings. Women and men worked in the vineyards and in the harvest and preparation of crops needed by the textile industry — flax and plants used for dyeing cloth. Beginning in the eleventh century water mills and windmills aided in some tasks, especially grinding grain, and an increasing use of horses rather than oxen speeded up plowing.

The mainstay of the diet for peasants everywhere — and for all other classes — was bread. Peasants also ate vegetables, not because they appreciated their importance for good health but because there was usually little else available. Animals were too valuable to be used for food on a regular basis, but weaker animals were often slaughtered in the fall so that they did not need to be fed through the winter, and their meat was preserved with salt and eaten on great feast days such as Christmas and Easter. Ale was the universal drink of common people, and it provided needed calories and some relief from the difficult and monotonous labor that filled people's lives. In many places, severe laws forbidding hunting and trapping in the forests restricted deer and other game to the king and nobility.

The Life and Work of Nobles

The nobility, though a small fraction of the total population, strongly influenced all aspects of medieval culture. Despite political, scientific, and industrial revolutions, nobles continued to hold real political and social power in Europe into the nineteenth century.

In the early Middle Ages noble status was limited to a very few families, but in the eleventh century knights in service to kings began to claim such status because it gave them special legal privileges. Nobles generally paid few taxes, and they had power over the people living on their lands. They maintained order, resolved disputes, and protected their dependents from attacks. They appointed officials who oversaw agricultural production. The liberty and privileges of the noble were inheritable, perpetuated by blood and not by wealth alone.

Nobles did have military obligations to their lords, but by the mid-twelfth century their duty to fight was limited in most parts of western Europe to forty days a year. The noble was obliged to attend his lord's court on important occasions when the lord wanted to put on great displays, such as on religious holidays or the wedding of a son or daughter.

Originally, most knights focused solely on military skills, but gradually a different ideal of knighthood emerged, usually termed **chivalry**. Chivalry was a code of conduct originally devised by the clergy to transform the typically crude and brutal behavior of the knightly class. It may have originated in oaths administered to Crusaders in which fighting was declared to have a sacred purpose and knights vowed loyalty to the church as well as to their lords. Qualities other than loyalty gradually

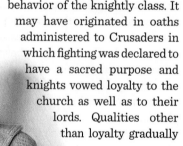

became part of chivalry: bravery, generosity, honor, graciousness, mercy, and eventually gallantry toward women. The chivalric ideal — and it was an ideal, not a standard pattern of behavior — created a new standard of masculinity for nobles, in which loyalty and honor remained the most important qualities, but graceful dancing and intelligent conversation were not considered unmanly.

Noblewomen played a large and important role in the functioning of the estate. They were responsible for managing the household's "inner economy" — cooking, brewing, spinning, weaving, and caring for yard animals. When the lord was away for long periods, his wife became the sole manager of the family properties. Often the responsibilities of the estate fell permanently to her if she became a widow.

Towns, Cities, and the Growth of Commercial Interests

The rise of towns and the growth of a new business and commercial class were a central part of Europe's recovery after the disorders of the tenth century. The growth of towns was made possible by several factors: a rise in population; increased agricultural output, which provided an adequate food supply for new town dwellers; and a minimum of peace and political stability, which allowed merchants to transport and sell goods. The development of towns was to lay the foundations for Europe's transformation, centuries later, from a rural agricultural society into an urban industrial society — a change with global implications.

Medieval towns had a few characteristics in common, one being that walls enclosed them. (The terms *burgher* and *bourgeois* derive from the Old English and Old German words *burg, burgh, borg,* and *borough* for "a walled or fortified place.") Most towns were first established as trading centers, with a marketplace in the middle, and they were likely to have a mint for coining money and a court for settling disputes. In each town, many people inhabited a small, cramped area. As population increased, towns rebuilt their walls, expanding the living space to accommodate growing numbers. Residents bargained with lords to make the town

Saint Maurice Some of the individuals who were held up to young men as models of ideal chivalry were probably real, but their lives were embellished with many stories. One such individual was Saint Maurice (d. 287), a soldier apparently executed by the Romans for refusing to renounce his Christian faith. He first emerges in the Carolingian period, and later he was held up as a model knight and declared a patron of the Holy Roman Empire and protector of the imperial army in wars against the pagan Slavs. His image was used on coins, and his cult was promoted by the archbishops of Magdeburg, who moved his relics to their cathedral. Until 1240 he was portrayed as a white man, but after that he was usually represented as a black man, as in this sandstone statue from Magdeburg Cathedral (ca. 1250). We have no idea why this change happened. (The Menil Collection)

politically independent, which gave them the right to hold legal courts, select leaders, and set taxes.

Townspeople also tried to acquire liberties, above all personal freedom, for themselves. It gradually developed that an individual who lived in a town for a year and a day, and was accepted by the townspeople, was free of servile obligations and status. Thus serfs who fled their manors for towns and were able to find work and avoid recapture became free of personal labor obligations. In this way the growth of towns contributed to a slow decline of serfdom in western Europe, although the complete elimination of serfdom would take centuries.

Merchants constituted the most powerful group in most towns, and they were often organized into merchant guilds, which prohibited nonmembers from trading, pooled members' risks, monopolized city offices, and controlled the economy of the town. Towns became centers of production as well, and artisans in particular trades formed their own **craft guilds**, including guilds of butchers, weavers, blacksmiths, bakers, silversmiths, and so on. Members of the craft guilds determined the quality, quantity, and price of the goods produced and the number of apprentices and journeymen affiliated with the guild. Formal membership in guilds was generally limited to men, but women often worked in guild shops without official membership.

Artisans generally made and sold products in their own homes, with production taking place on the ground floor. A window or door opened from the main workroom directly onto the street, and passersby could look in and see the goods being produced. The family lived above the business on the second or third floor. As the business and the family expanded, additional stories were added.

Most medieval towns and cities developed with little planning or attention to sanitation. Horses and oxen, the chief means of transportation and power, dropped tons of dung on the streets every year. It was universal practice in the early towns to dump household waste, both animal and human, into the road in front of one's house. The stench must have been abominable, as officials of the king noted in their order to the citizens of one English town in 1298:

> The air is so corrupted and infected by the pigsties situated in the king's highways and in the lanes of that town and by the swine feeding and frequently wandering about . . . and by dung and dunghills and many other foul things placed in the streets and lanes, that great repugnance overtakes the king's ministers staying in that town and . . . the advantage of more wholesome air is impeded. . . . [So] the king, being unwilling longer to tolerate such great and unbearable defects there, orders . . . the pigsties, aforesaid streets and lanes to be cleansed from all dung.[3]

> "The air is so corrupted . . . by dung and dunghills and many other foul things placed in the streets and lanes, that great repugnance overtakes the king's ministers staying in that town."
>
> **ROYAL ORDER TO THE CITIZENS OF BOUTHAM, ENGLAND**

Despite such unpleasant aspects of urban life, people wanted to get into medieval towns because they represented opportunities for economic advancement, social mobility, and improvement in legal status.

The Expansion of Trade and the Commercial Revolution

The growth of towns went hand in hand with a remarkable expansion of trade as artisans and craftsmen manufactured goods for local and foreign consumption. Most trade centered in towns and was controlled by merchants. They began to pool their money to finance trading expeditions, sharing the profits and also sharing the risks. If disaster struck the ship or caravan, an investor's loss was limited to the amount of that individual's investment, a legal concept termed "limited liability" that is essential to the modern capitalist economy.

Italian cities, especially Venice, led the West in trade in general and completely dominated trade with Asia and North Africa. Venetian ships carried salt from the Venetian lagoon; pepper and other spices from North Africa; and slaves, silk, and purple textiles from the East to northern and western Europe. Wealthy European consumers had greater access to foreign luxuries than they had earlier, and their tastes became more sophisticated. Merchants from other cities in northern Italy such as Florence and Milan were also important traders, and they developed new methods of accounting and record keeping that facilitated the movement of goods and money. The towns of Bruges, Ghent, and Ypres in Flanders were also leaders in long-distance trade and built up a vast industry in the manufacture of cloth, aided by ready access to wool from England, which was just across the channel. The availability of raw wool also encouraged the development of cloth manufacture within England itself, and commercial families in manufacturing towns grew fabulously rich.

In much of northern Europe, the Hanseatic League (known as the Hansa for short), a mercantile associa-

- **chivalry** A code of conduct that was supposed to govern the behavior of a knight.
- **craft guilds** Associations of artisans organized to regulate the quality, quantity, and price of the goods produced as well as the number of affiliated apprentices and journeymen.

tion of towns formed to achieve mutual security and exclusive trading rights, controlled trade. During the thirteenth century perhaps two hundred cities from Holland to Poland joined the league, but Lübeck always remained the dominant member. The ships of the Hansa cities carried furs, wax, copper, fish, grain, timber, and wine. These goods were exchanged for other products, mainly cloth and salt, from western cities. At cities such as Bruges and London, Hanseatic merchants secured special concessions exempting them from all tolls and allowing them to trade at local fairs. Hanseatic merchants also established foreign trading centers, which they called "factories," because the commercial agents within them were called "factors." (Later the word *factory* would be applied to centers of production as well.)

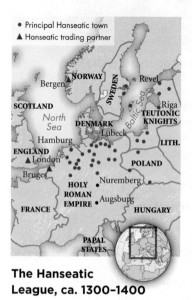

The Hanseatic League, ca. 1300–1400

These developments added up to what is often called the **commercial revolution**. In giving the transformation this name, historians point not only to an increase in the sheer volume of trade and in the complexity and sophistication of business procedures, but also to the new attitude toward business and making money. Some even detect a "capitalist spirit" in which making a profit was regarded as a good thing in itself, regardless of the uses to which that profit was put.

The commercial revolution created a great deal of new wealth, which did not escape the attention of kings and other rulers. Wealth could be taxed, and through taxation kings could create strong and centralized states. In the years to come, alliances with the middle classes were to enable kings to defeat feudal powers and aristocratic interests and to build the states that came to be called "modern." The commercial revolution also provided the opportunity for thousands of serfs in western Europe to improve their social position; however, many people continued to live hand to mouth on low wages. Also, it is important to remember that most towns remained small throughout the Middle Ages.

- **commercial revolution** The transformation of the economic structure of Europe, beginning in the eleventh century, from a rural, manorial society to a more complex mercantile society.

- **Scholastics** Medieval professors who developed a method of thinking, reasoning, and writing in which questions were raised and authorities cited on both sides of a question.

- **Gothic** The term for the architectural and artistic style that prevailed in Europe from the mid-twelfth to the sixteenth century.

Feudal nobility and churchmen continued to determine the preponderant social attitudes, values, and patterns of thought and behavior.

Learning and Culture

☐ What were the primary educational and cultural developments in medieval Europe?

The towns that became centers of trade and production in the High Middle Ages also developed into cultural and intellectual centers. Trade brought in new ideas as well as merchandise, and in many cities a new type of educational institution — the university — emerged, meeting the needs of the new bureaucratic states and the church for educated administrators. As universities emerged, so did other cultural advancements, such as new forms of architecture and literature.

Universities and Scholasticism

Since the time of the Carolingian Empire, monasteries and cathedral schools had offered the only formal instruction available. Monasteries, geared to religious concerns, were located in rural environments. In contrast, schools attached to cathedrals and run by the bishop and his clergy were frequently situated in bustling cities, where people of many backgrounds stimulated the growth and exchange of ideas. In the eleventh century in Bologna and other Italian cities wealthy businessmen established municipal schools, and in the twelfth century municipal schools in Italy and cathedral schools in France developed into much larger universities, a transformation parallel to the opening of madrasas in Muslim cities (see page 257).

The growth of the University of Bologna coincided with a revival of interest in Roman law. The study of Roman law as embodied in Justinian's *Code* (see page 208) had never completely died out in the West, but this sudden burst of interest seems to have been inspired by Irnerius (ca. 1055–ca. 1130), a great teacher at Bologna. Irnerius not only explained the Roman law of Justinian's *Code* but also applied it to practical situations, such as cases of inheritance and landownership.

At the Italian city of Salerno, interest in medicine had persisted for centuries. Greek and Muslim physicians there had studied the use of herbs as cures and had experimented with surgery. The twelfth century ushered in a new interest in Greek medical texts and in the work of Arab and Greek doctors. Ideas from this medical literature spread throughout Europe from Salerno and became the basis of training for physicians at other medieval universities. University training gave physicians high social status and allowed them to charge high fees, although their diagnoses and treatments were based on classical theories, not on interactions with patients.

Although medicine and law were important academic disciplines in the Middle Ages, theology was "the queen of sciences," so termed because it involved the study of God, who was said to make all knowledge possible. Paris became the place to study theology, and in the first decades of the twelfth century students from all over Europe crowded into the cathedral school of Notre Dame in that city.

University professors (a term first used in the fourteenth century) were known as "schoolmen" or **Scholastics**. They developed a method of thinking, reasoning, and writing in which questions were raised and authorities cited on both sides of a question. The goal of the Scholastic method was to arrive at definitive answers and to provide a rational explanation for what was believed on faith.

One of the most famous Scholastics was Peter Abélard (1079–1142). Fascinated by logic, which he believed could be used to solve most problems, Abélard used a method of systematic doubting in his writing and teaching. As he put it, "By doubting we come to questioning, and by questioning we perceive the truth." Other scholars merely asserted theological principles; Abélard discussed and analyzed them.

Thirteenth-century Scholastics devoted an enormous amount of time to collecting and organizing knowledge on all topics. These collections were published as summa (SOO-muh), or reference books. There were summa on law, philosophy, vegetation, animal life, and theology. Thomas Aquinas (1225–1274), a professor at the University of Paris, produced the most famous collection, the *Summa Theologica*, which deals with a vast number of theological questions.

In northern Europe — at Paris and later at Oxford and Cambridge in England — university faculties grouped themselves according to academic disciplines, or schools: law, medicine, arts, and theology. Students lived in privately endowed residential colleges and were considered to be lower-level members of the clergy, so that any student accused of a crime was tried in church, rather than in city, courts. This clerical status, along with widely held ideas about women's lesser intellectual capabilities, meant that university education was restricted to men.

At all universities, the standard method of teaching was the lecture — that is, a reading. With this method the professor read a passage from the Bible, Justinian's *Code*, or one of Aristotle's treatises. He then explained

> " By doubting we come to questioning, and by questioning we perceive the truth. "
>
> **PETER ABÉLARD**

and interpreted the passage. Students wrote down everything. Because books had to be copied by hand, they were extremely expensive, and few students could afford them. Examinations were given after three, four, or five years of study, when the student applied for a degree. Examinations were oral and very difficult. If the candidate passed, he was awarded the first, or bachelor's, degree. Further study, about as long, arduous, and expensive as it is today, enabled the graduate to try for the master's and doctor's degrees. Degrees were technically licenses to teach. Most students, however, did not become teachers. They staffed the expanding royal and papal administrations.

Cathedrals and a New Architectural Style

As we have seen, religious devotion was expressed through daily rituals, holiday ceremonies, and the creation of new institutions such as universities and religious orders. People also wanted permanent visible representations of their piety, and both church and city leaders wanted physical symbols of their wealth and power. These aims found their outlet in the building of tens of thousands of churches, chapels, abbeys, and, most spectacularly, cathedrals. A cathedral is the church of a bishop and the administrative headquarters of a diocese. The word comes from the Greek word *kathedra*, meaning "seat," because the bishop's throne, a symbol of the office, is located in the cathedral.

In the tenth and eleventh centuries cathedrals were built in a style that resembled ancient Roman architecture, with massive walls, rounded stone arches, and small windows — features later labeled Romanesque. In the twelfth century a new style spread out from central France. It was dubbed **Gothic** by later Renaissance architects who thought that only the uncouth Goths could have invented such a disunified style. The basic features of Gothic architecture — pointed arches, high ceilings, and exterior supports called flying buttresses that carried much of the weight of the roof — allowed unprecedented interior lightness. Stained-glass windows were cut into the stone, so that the interior, one French abbot exclaimed, "would shine with the wonderful and uninterrupted light of most sacred windows, pervading the interior beauty."[4] Between 1180 and 1270 in France alone, eighty cathedrals, about five hundred abbey churches, and tens of thousands of parish churches were constructed in this new style. They are testimony to the deep religious faith and piety of medieval people and also to the civic pride of urban residents, for towns competed with one another to build the largest and most splendid cathedral. In addition to marriages,

Notre Dame Cathedral, Paris, begun 1163 This view offers a fine example of the twin towers (left), the spire, the great rose window over the south portal (center), and the flying buttresses that support the walls and the vaults. Like hundreds of other churches in medieval Europe, it was dedicated to the Virgin Mary. With a spire rising more than 300 feet, Notre Dame was the tallest building in Europe at the time of its construction. (David R. Frazier/Photo Researchers, Inc.)

baptisms, and funerals, there were scores of feast days on which the entire town gathered in the cathedral.

Cathedrals served secular as well as religious purposes. Local guilds met in the cathedrals to arrange business deals, and municipal officials held political meetings there. Pilgrims slept there, lovers courted there, and traveling actors staged plays there. First and foremost, however, the cathedral was intended to teach the people the doctrines of Christian faith through visual images such as those found in stained-glass windows and religious statuary. In this way architecture became the servant of theology.

Troubadour Poetry

Educational and religious texts were typically written in Latin, but poems, songs, and stories were written down in local dialects and celebrated things of concern to ordinary people. In southern Europe, especially in

- **troubadours** Medieval poets in southern Europe who wrote and sang lyrical verses. The word *troubadour* comes from the Provençal word *trobar*, which in turn derives from the Arabic *taraba*, meaning "to sing" or "to sing poetry."
- **Black Death** The plague that first struck Europe in 1347, killing perhaps one-third of the population.

the area of southern France known as Provence, poets who called themselves **troubadours** wrote lyric verses celebrating love, desire, beauty, and gallantry and sang them at the courts of nobles and rulers.

Troubadour poets celebrated *fin'amor*, a Provençal word for the pure or perfect love a knight was supposed to feel for his lady, which has in English come to be called "courtly love." In courtly love poetry, the writer praises his or her love object, idealizing the beloved and promising loyalty and great deeds. Poetry in praise of love originated in the Muslim culture of the Iberian Peninsula, where heterosexual romantic love had long been the subject of poems and songs. Southern France was a border area where Christian and Muslim cultures mixed; Spanish Muslim poets sang at the courts of Christian nobles, and Provençal poets picked up their romantic themes.

Troubadours included a few women, with their poetry often chiding knights who did not live up to the ideal, as in this twelfth-century verse:

> I've suffered great distress
> From a knight whom I once owned.
> Now, for all time, be it known:
> I loved him — yes, to excess. His jilting I've regretted,
> Yet his love I never really returned.[5]

Crises of the Later Middle Ages

◻ Why have the later Middle Ages been seen as a time of calamity and crisis?

During the later Middle Ages, the last book of the New Testament, the book of Revelation, inspired thousands of sermons and hundreds of religious tracts. Revelation deals with visions of the end of the world, with disease, war, famine, and death — often called the "Four Horsemen of the Apocalypse" — triumphing everywhere. It is no wonder that this part of the Bible was so popular. Between 1300 and 1450 Europeans experienced a frightful series of shocks: climate change, economic decline, plague, war, social upheaval, and increased crime and violence. Death and preoccupation with death made the fourteenth century one of the most wrenching periods of history in Europe.

The Great Famine and the Black Death

In the first half of the fourteenth century Europe experienced a series of climate changes, especially the beginning of a period of colder and wetter weather that historical geographers label the "little ice age." Its effects were dramatic and disastrous. Population had steadily increased in the twelfth and thirteenth centuries, but with colder weather, poor harvests led to scarcity and starvation. The costs of grain, livestock, and dairy products rose sharply. Almost all of northern Europe suffered a terrible famine between 1315 and 1322, with dire social consequences: peasants were forced to sell or mortgage their lands for money to buy food, and the number of vagabonds, or homeless people, greatly increased, as did petty crime. An undernourished population was ripe for the Grim Reaper, who appeared in 1347 in the form of a virulent new disease, later called the **Black Death** (Map 14.3). The symptoms of this disease were first described in 1331 in southwestern China, part of the Mongol Empire (see page 334). From there it spread across Central Asia by way of Mongol armies and merchant caravans, arriving in the ports of the Black Sea by the 1340s. In October 1347 Genoese ships traveling from the Crimea in southern Russia brought the plague to Messina, from which it spread across Sicily and into Italy. From Italy it traveled in all directions.

Most historians and almost all microbiologists identify the disease that spread in the fourteenth century as the bubonic plague, caused by the bacillus *Yersinia pestis*. The disease normally afflicts rats. Fleas living

Procession of Flagellants In this manuscript illumination from 1349, shirtless flagellants, men and women who whipped and scourged themselves as penance for their and society's sins, walk through the Flemish city of Tournai, which had just been struck by the plague. Many people believed that the Black Death was God's punishment for humanity's wickedness. (Ann Ronan Picture Library/HIP/Art Resource, NY)

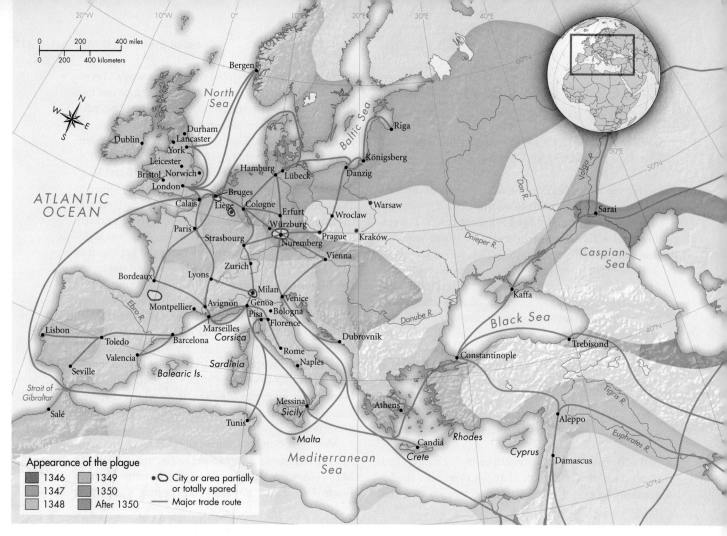

MAP 14.3 The Course of the Black Death in Fourteenth-Century Europe The plague followed trade routes as it spread into and across Europe. A few cities that took strict quarantine measures were spared.

Appearance of the plague

- 1346
- 1347
- 1348
- 1349
- 1350
- After 1350
- City or area partially or totally spared
- Major trade route

on the infected rats drink their blood and pass the bacteria that cause the plague on to the next rat they bite. Usually the disease is limited to rats and other rodents, but at certain points in history the fleas have jumped from their rodent hosts to humans and other animals. The fourteenth-century disease showed some differences from later outbreaks of bubonic plague; there are no reports of massive rat die-offs, and the disease was often transmitted directly from one person to another through coughing and sneezing. These differences have led a few historians to ask whether the fourteenth-century outbreak was some disease other than the bubonic plague — perhaps something like the Ebola virus. Debates about the nature of the disease fuel continued study of medical aspects of the plague, with scientists using innovative techniques such as studying the tooth pulp of bodies in medieval cemeteries to see if it contains DNA from plague-causing agents.

Whatever it was, the disease had dreadful effects on the body. The classic symptom was a growth the size of a nut or an apple in the armpit, in the groin, or on the neck. This was the boil, or *bubo*, that gave the disease

its name and caused agonizing pain. If the bubo was lanced and the pus thoroughly drained, the victim had a chance of recovery. The secondary stage was the appearance of black spots or blotches caused by bleeding under the skin. Finally, the victim began to cough violently and spit blood. This stage, indicating the presence of millions of bacilli in the bloodstream, signaled the end, and death followed in two or three days. Physicians could sometimes ease the pain but had no cure.

Most people — lay, scholarly, and medical — believed that the Black Death was caused by poisons or by "corrupted air" that carried the disease from place to place. They sought to keep poisons from entering the body by smelling or ingesting strong-smelling herbs, and they tried to remove the poisons through bloodletting. They also prayed and did penance. Anxiety and fears about the plague caused people to look for scapegoats, and they found them in the Jews, who they believed had poisoned the wells of Christian communities and thereby infected the drinking water. This charge led to the murder of thousands of Jews across Europe.

Viewpoints

Italian and English Views of the Plague

• *Eyewitness commentary on the plague includes the Italian writer Giovanni Boccaccio (1313–1375), who portrayed the course of the disease in Florence in the preface to his book of tales,* The Decameron, *and the English monastic chronicler Henry Knighton (d. 1396), who described the effects of the plague on English towns and villages in his four-volume chronicle of English history.*

Giovanni Boccaccio

"Against this pestilence no human wisdom or foresight was of any avail. . . . Men and women in great numbers abandoned their city, their houses, their farms, their relatives, and their possessions and sought other places, going at least as far away as the Florentine countryside—as if the wrath of God could not pursue them with this pestilence wherever they went but would only strike those it found within the walls of the city! . . . [A]lmost no one cared for his neighbor, and relatives hardly ever visited one another—they stayed far apart. This disaster had struck such fear into the hearts of men and women that brother abandoned brother, uncle abandoned nephew, sister left brother, and very often wife abandoned husband, and—even worse, almost unbelievable—fathers and mothers neglected to tend and care for their children as if they were not their own. . . . So many corpses would arrive in front of a church every day and at every hour that the amount of holy ground for burials was certainly insufficient for the ancient custom of giving each body its individual place; when all the graves were full, huge trenches were dug in all the cemeteries of the churches and into them the new arrivals were dumped by the hundreds; and they were packed in there with dirt, one on top of another, like a ship's cargo, until the trench was filled. . . . Oh how many great palaces, beautiful homes and noble dwellings, once filled with families, gentlemen, and ladies, were now emptied, down to the last servant!"

Henry Knighton

"Then that most grievous pestilence penetrated the coastal regions [of England] by way of Southhampton, and came to Bristol, and people died as if the whole strength of the city were seized by sudden death. For there were few who lay in their beds more than three days or two and half days; then that savage death snatched them about the second day. In Leicester, in the little parish of St. Leonard, more than three hundred and eighty died; in the parish of Holy Cross, more than four hundred. . . . And so in each parish, they died in great numbers. . . . At the same time, there was so great a lack of priests everywhere that many churches had no divine services. . . . One could hardly hire a chaplain to minister to the church for less than ten marks, whereas before the pestilence, when there were plenty of priests, one could hire a chaplain for five or four marks. . . . Meanwhile, the king ordered that in every county of the kingdom, reapers and other labourers should not receive more than they were accustomed to receive, under the penalty provided in the statute, and he renewed the statute at this time. The labourers, however, were so arrogant and hostile that they did not heed the king's command, but if anyone wished to hire them, he had to pay them what they wanted, and either lose his fruits and crops or satisfy the arrogant and greedy desire of the labourers as they wished. . . . Similarly, those who received day-work from their tenants throughout the year, as is usual from serfs, had to release them and to remit such service. They either had to excuse them entirely or had to fix them in a laxer manner at a small rent, lest very great and irreparable damage be done to the buildings and the land everywhere remain uncultivated."

Sources: Giovanni Boccaccio, *The Decameron*, trans. Mark Musa and Peter Bondanella (New York: W.W. Norton, 1982), pp. 7, 9, 12. Copyright © 1982 by Mark Musa and Peter Bondanella. Used by permission of W. W. Norton & Company, Inc.; Henry Knighton, *Chronicon Henrici Knighton*, in James Bruce Ross and Mary Martin McLaughlin, eds., *The Portable Medieval Reader* (New York: Viking, 1949), pp. 218, 220, 222.

QUESTIONS FOR ANALYSIS

1. How did the residents of Florence respond to the plague, as described by Boccaccio?
2. What were some of the effects of the plague in England, as described by Knighton?
3. How might the fact that Boccaccio was writing in an urban setting and Knighton was writing from a rural monastery that owned a large amount of land have shaped their perspectives?

Because population figures for the period before the arrival of the plague do not exist for most countries and cities, only educated guesses can be made about mortality rates. Of a total English population of perhaps 4.2 million, probably 1.4 million died of the Black Death in its several visits. In Italy densely populated cities endured incredible losses. Florence lost between one-half and two-thirds of its population when the plague visited in 1348. The disease recurred intermittently in the 1360s and 1370s and reappeared many times, as late as the early 1700s in Europe. (It still continues to infect rodent and human populations sporadically today.)

In the short term the economic effects of the plague were severe because the death of many peasants disrupted food production. But in the long term the dramatic decline in population eased pressure on the land, and wages and per capita wealth rose for those who survived. The psychological consequences of the plague were profound. (See "Viewpoints: Italian and English Views of the Plague," page 417.) Some people sought release in wild living, while others turned to the severest forms of asceticism and frenzied religious fervor.

The Hundred Years' War

While the plague ravaged populations in Asia, North Africa, and Europe, a long international war in western Europe added further death and destruction. England and France had engaged in sporadic military hostilities from the time of the Norman Conquest in 1066 (see page 398), and in the middle of the fourteenth century these became more intense. From 1337 to 1453 the two countries intermittently fought one another in what was the longest war in European history, ultimately dubbed the Hundred Years' War, though it actually lasted 116 years.

The Hundred Years' War had a number of causes. Both England and France claimed the duchy of Aquitaine in southwestern France, and the English king Edward III argued that, as the grandson of an earlier French king, he should have rightfully inherited the French throne. Nobles in provinces on the borders of France who were worried about the growing power of the French king supported Edward, as did wealthy wool merchants and cloth makers in Flanders who depended on English wool. The governments of both England and France promised wealth and glory to those who fought and manipulated public opinion to support their side in the war, with each country portraying the other as evil.

The war, fought almost entirely in France, consisted mainly of a series of random sieges and raids. During the war's early stages, England was highly successful, primarily through the use of longbows fired by well-trained foot soldiers against mounted knights and, after 1375, by early cannons. By 1419 the English had advanced to the walls of Paris. But the French cause was not lost. Though England scored the initial victories, France won the war.

The ultimate French success rests heavily on the actions of an obscure French peasant girl, Joan of Arc, whose vision and military leadership revived French

Suit of Armor This fifteenth-century suit of Italian armor protected its wearer, but its weight made movement difficult. Both English and French mounted knights wore full armor at the beginning of the Hundred Years' War, but by the end they wore only breastplates and helmets, which protected their vital organs but allowed greater mobility. This suit has been so well preserved that it was most likely never used in battle; it may have been made for ceremonial purposes. (Image copyright © The Metropolitan Museum of Art/Art Resource, NY)

◻ Picturing the Past

Siege of the Castle of Mortagne near Bordeaux This miniature of a battle in the Hundred Years' War shows the French besieging an English-held castle. Medieval warfare usually consisted of small skirmishes and attacks on castles. (© British Library Board, MS Royal 14 e. IV f. 23)

ANALYZING THE IMAGE What types of weapons are the attackers and defenders using? How have the attackers on the left enhanced their position?

CONNECTIONS This painting shows a battle that occurred in 1377, but it was painted about a hundred years later and shows the military technology available at the time it was painted, not at the time of the actual siege. Which of the weapons represent newer forms of military technology? What impact would you expect them to have on warfare?

fortunes and led to victory. Born in 1412 to well-to-do peasants, Joan grew up in a pious household. During adolescence she began to hear voices, which she later said belonged to Saint Michael, Saint Catherine, and Saint Margaret. In 1428 these voices told her that the dauphin of France — Charles VII, who was uncrowned as king because of the English occupation — had to be crowned and the English expelled from France. Joan went to the French court disguised as a male for safety and secured the support of the dauphin to travel, dressed as a knight, with the French army to the besieged city of Orléans.

At Orléans, Joan inspired and led French attacks, and the English retreated. As a result of her successes, Charles made Joan co-commander of the entire army, and she led it to a string of military victories in the summer of 1429; many cities surrendered without a fight. Two months after the victory at Orléans, Charles VII was crowned king at Reims.

Joan and the French army continued their fight against the English. In 1430 England's allies, the Burgundians, captured Joan and sold her to the English, and the French did not intervene. The English wanted Joan eliminated for obvious political reasons, but the primary charge against her was heresy, and the trial was conducted by church authorities. She was interrogated about the angelic voices and about why she wore men's clothing. She apparently answered skillfully, but in 1431 the court condemned her as a heretic, and she was burned at the stake in the marketplace at Rouen. (A new trial in 1456 cleared her of all charges, and in 1920 she was canonized as a saint.) Joan continues to be a symbol of deep religious piety to some, of conservative nationalism to others, and of gender-bending cross-dressing to others. Beneath the pious and popular legends is a teenage girl who saved the French monarchy, which was the embodiment of France. The French army continued its victories without her, and demands for an end to the war increased among the English, who were growing tired of the mounting loss of life and the flow of money into a seemingly bottomless pit. Slowly the French reconquered Normandy and finally ejected the English from Aquitaine. At the war's end in 1453, only the town of Calais remained in English hands.

The Great Schism, 1378–1417

Allegiance to Rome
Allegiance to Avignon
Official allegiance to Rome but with shifting local allegiances

The long war had a profound impact on the two countries. In England and France the war promoted nationalism — the feeling of unity and identity that binds together a people. It led to technological experimentation, especially with gunpowder weaponry, whose firepower made the protective walls of stone castles obsolete. However, such weaponry also made warfare increasingly expensive. The war also stimulated the development of the English Parliament. Between 1250 and 1450 representative assemblies from several classes of society flourished in many European countries, but only the English Parliament became a powerful national body. Edward III's constant need for money to pay for the war compelled him to summon it many times, and its representatives slowly built up their powers.

Challenges to the Church

In times of crisis or disaster people of all faiths have sought the consolation of religion, but in the fourteenth century the official Christian Church offered little solace. While local clergy eased the suffering of many, a dispute over who was the legitimate pope weakened the church as an institution. In 1309 pressure by the French monarchy led the pope to move his permanent residence to Avignon in southern France, the location of the papal summer palace. This marked the start of seven successive papacies in Avignon. Not sur-

prising, all these popes were French — a matter of controversy among church followers outside France. Also, the popes largely concentrated on bureaucratic and financial matters to the exclusion of spiritual objectives.

In 1376 one of the French popes returned to Rome, and when he died there several years later Roman citizens demanded an Italian pope who would remain in Rome. The cardinals elected Urban VI, but his tactless, arrogant, and bullheaded manner caused them to regret their decision. The cardinals slipped away from Rome and declared Urban's election invalid because it had come about under threats from the Roman mob. They elected a French cardinal who took the name Clement VII (pontificate 1378–1394) and set himself up at Avignon in opposition to Urban. There were thus two popes, a situation that was later termed the Great Schism.

The powers of Europe aligned themselves with Urban or Clement along strictly political lines. France recognized the Frenchman, Clement; England, France's historic enemy, recognized Urban. The rest of Europe lined up behind one or the other.

In all European countries the common people — hard-pressed by inflation, wars, and plague — were thoroughly confused about which pope was legitimate. In the end the schism weakened the religious faith of many Christians and brought church leadership into serious disrepute.

A first attempt to heal the schism led to the installation of a third pope and a threefold split, but finally a church council meeting at Constance (1414–1418) successfully deposed the three schismatic popes and elected a new leader, who took the name Martin V (pontificate 1417–1431). The schism was over, but those who had hoped that the council would also reform problems in the church were disappointed. In the later fifteenth century the papacy concentrated on building up its wealth and political power in Italy rather than on the concerns of the whole church. As a result, many people decided that they would need to rely on their own prayers and pious actions rather than on the institutional church for their salvation.

Peasant and Urban Revolts

The difficult conditions of the fourteenth and fifteenth centuries spurred a wave of peasant and urban revolts across Europe. In 1358, when French taxation for the Hundred Years' War fell heavily on the poor, the frustrations of the French peasantry exploded in a massive uprising called the Jacquerie (zhah-kuh-REE), after a supposedly happy agricultural laborer, Jacques Bonhomme (Good Fellow). Adding to the anger over taxes was the toll taken by the plague and by the famine that had struck some areas. Crowds swept through the countryside, slashing the throats of nobles, burning their castles, raping their wives and daughters, and killing or maiming their horses and cattle. Artisans, small merchants, and parish priests joined the peasants, and residents of both urban and rural areas committed terrible destruction. For several weeks the nobles were on the defensive, until the upper class united to repress the revolt with merciless ferocity. Thousands of the "Jacques," innocent as well as guilty, were cut down.

Taxes and other grievances also led to the 1381 English Peasants' Revolt, involving tens of thousands of people. The Black Death had dramatically reduced the supply of labor, and peasants had demanded higher wages and fewer manorial obligations. Parliament countered with a law freezing wages and binding workers to their manors. Although the law was difficult to enforce, it contributed to an atmosphere of discontent, which was further enhanced by popular preachers who proclaimed that great disparities between rich and poor went against Christ's teachings. Moreover, decades of aristocratic violence, much of it perpetrated against the weak peasantry, had bred hostility and bitterness.

In 1380 Parliament imposed a poll tax on all citizens to fund the Hundred Years' War, requiring rich and poor to pay the same amount and ordering sheriffs to collect it. This tax imposed a greater burden on the poor than on wealthier citizens, and it sparked revolt. Beginning with assaults on the tax collectors, the uprising in England followed much the same course as had the Jacquerie in France. Castles and manors were sacked; manorial records were destroyed; nobles were murdered. Urban discontent merged with rural violence. Apprentices and journeymen, frustrated because the highest positions in the guilds were closed to them, rioted.

The boy-king Richard II (r. 1377–1399) met the leaders of the revolt, agreed to charters ensuring the peasants' freedom from manorial obligations, tricked them with false promises, and then proceeded to crush the uprising with terrible ferocity. The nobility tried to use this defeat to restore the ancient obligations of serfdom, but the increasingly commercialized economy made that difficult, and serfdom slowly disappeared in England, though peasants remained poor.

Conditions in England and France were not unique. In Florence in 1378 the *ciompi*, or poor propertyless workers, revolted, and serious social unrest occurred in Lübeck, Brunswick, and other German cities. In Spain in 1391 massive uprisings in Seville and Barcelona took the form of vicious attacks on Jewish communities. Rebellions and uprisings everywhere revealed deep peasant and worker frustration with the socioeconomic conditions of the time.

Medieval Europe continues to fascinate us today. We go to medieval banquets, fairs, and even weddings; visit castle-themed hotels and amusement parks; watch movies about knights and their conquests; play video games in which we become warriors, trolls, or sorcerers; and read stories with themes of great quests, some set in the Middle Ages and some set in places that just seem medieval, with humble but brave villagers, beautiful ladies, powerful wizards, and gorgeous warriors on horseback. From all these amusements the Middle Ages emerges as a strange and wonderful time, when people's emotions were more powerful, challenges more dangerous, and friendships more lasting than in the safe, shallow, fast-paced modern world. Characters from other parts of the world often heighten the exoticism: a Muslim soldier joins the fight against a common enemy, a Persian princess rescues the hero and his sidekick, a Buddhist monk teaches martial arts techniques. These characters from outside Europe are fictional, but they also represent aspects of reality, because medieval Europe was not isolated, and political and social structures similar to those in Europe developed elsewhere.

In reality few of us would probably want to live in the real Middle Ages, when most people worked in the fields all day, a banquet meant a piece of tough old rooster instead of the usual meal of pea soup and black bread, and even wealthy lords lived in damp and drafty castles. We do not really want to return to a time when one-third to one-half of all children died before age five and alcohol was the only real pain reliever. But the contemporary appeal of the Middle Ages is an interesting phenomenon, particularly because it stands in such sharp contrast to the attitude of educated Europeans who lived in the centuries immediately afterward. They were the ones who dubbed the period "middle" and viewed the soaring cathedrals as dreadful "Gothic." They saw their own era as the one to be celebrated, and the Middle Ages as best forgotten.

□ CHAPTER REVIEW

□ How did medieval rulers overcome internal divisions and external threats, and work to create larger and more stable territories? (p. 394)

As Charlemagne's empire broke down, no European political power was strong enough to put up effective resistance to external attack, which came from many directions. Vikings from Scandinavia carried out raids for plunder along the coasts and rivers of Europe and traveled as far as Iceland, Greenland, North America, and Russia. In many places they set up permanent states, as did the Magyars, who came into central Europe from the east. From the south came Muslims, who conquered Sicily and drove northward into Italy. All these invasions as well as civil wars weakened the power of kings, and local nobles became the strongest powers against external threats. They established a new form of decentralized government, later known as feudalism. Common people turned to nobles for protection, paying with their land, labor, and freedom. By the twelfth century, however, rulers in some parts of Europe reasserted authority and began to develop new institutions of government and legal codes that enabled them to assert power over lesser lords and the general population.

□ How did the Christian Church enhance its power and create new institutions and religious practices? (p. 399)

The papacy also consolidated its power in the eleventh and twelfth centuries, though these moves were sometimes challenged by kings and emperors. Monasteries continued to be important places for learning and devotion, and new religious orders were founded. Meanwhile, Christianity expanded into Europe's northern and eastern regions, and Christian rulers expanded their holdings in Muslim Spain. On a more personal scale, religion structured people's daily lives and the yearly calendar.

□ What were the motives, course, and consequences of the Crusades? (p. 404)

A papal call to retake the holy city of Jerusalem led to the Crusades, nearly two centuries of warfare between Christians and Muslims. The enormous popular response to this call reveals the influence of the papacy and a new sense that war against the church's enemies was a duty of nobles. The Crusades were initially successful, and small Christian states were established in the Middle East. They did not last

KEY TERMS

vassal (p. 395)	**chivalry** (p. 410)
fief (p. 396)	**craft guilds** (p. 411)
feudalism (p. 396)	**commercial**
manorialism (p. 397)	**revolution** (p. 412)
serf (p. 397)	**Scholastics** (p. 413)
heresy (p. 402)	**Gothic** (p. 413)
reconquista (p. 404)	**troubadours** (p. 414)
Crusades (p. 404)	**Black Death** (p. 415)

very long, however, and other effects of the Crusades were disastrous: Jewish communities in Europe were regularly attacked; relations between the Western and Eastern Christian Churches were poisoned by the Crusaders' attack on Constantinople; and Christian-Muslim relations became more uniformly hostile than they had been earlier.

□ How did the lives of common people, nobles, and townspeople differ, and what new commercial developments increased wealth? (p. 408)

The vast majority of medieval Europeans were rural peasants who lived in small villages and worked their own and their lords' land. Peasants led hard lives, and most were bound to the land, although there were some opportunities for social mobility. Nobles were a tiny fraction of the total population, but they exerted great power over all aspects of life. Aristocratic values and attitudes, often called chivalry, shaded all aspects of medieval culture. Medieval towns and cities grew initially as trading centers and recruited people from the countryside with the promise of greater freedom and new possibilities. They also became centers of production, and merchants and artisans formed guilds to protect their livelihoods. Not everyone in medieval towns and cities shared in the prosperity; many residents lived hand to mouth on low wages.

□ What were the primary educational and cultural developments in medieval Europe? (p. 412)

The towns that became centers of trade and production in the High Middle Ages also developed into cultural and intellectual centers. Trade brought in new ideas as well as merchandise, and in many cities a new type of educational institution — the university — emerged from cathedral and municipal schools. Universities developed theological, legal, and medical courses of study based on classical models and provided trained officials for the new government and church bureaucracies. People also wanted permanent visible representations of their piety, and church and city leaders supported the building of churches and cathedrals as symbols of their Christian faith and their civic pride. Cathedrals grew larger and more sumptuous, with high towers and exquisite stained-glass windows. New types of vernacular literature arose in which poems, songs, and stories were written down in local dialects. The troubadours of southern France led the way with this new art form, using Arabic models to create romantic stories of heterosexual love.

□ **Why have the later Middle Ages been seen as a time of calamity and crisis? (p. 415)**

In the fourteenth century bad weather brought poor harvests, which contributed to an international economic depression and fostered disease. The Black Death caused enormous population losses and had social, psychological, and economic consequences. Additional difficulties included the Hundred Years' War, which devastated much of the French countryside and bankrupted England; a schism among rival popes that weakened the Western Christian Church; and peasant and worker frustrations that exploded in uprisings. These revolts were usually crushed, though noble landlords were not always successful in reasserting their rights to labor services instead of cash rents.

SUGGESTED READING

Allmand, Christopher. *The Hundred Years War: England and France at War, ca. 1300–1450*, rev. ed. 2005. Designed for students; examines the war from political, military, social, and economic perspectives and compares the way England and France reacted to the conflict.

Bartlett, Robert. *The Making of Europe: Conquest, Colonization and Cultural Change, 950–1350*. 1993. A broad survey of many of the developments traced in this chapter.

Bennett, Judith M. *A Medieval Life: Cecelia Penifader of Brigstock, c. 1297–1344*. 1998. An excellent brief introduction to all aspects of medieval village life from the perspective of one woman; designed for students.

Brooke, Rosalind, and Christopher Brooke. *Popular Religion in the Middle Ages*. 1984. A readable synthesis of material on the beliefs and practices of ordinary Christians.

Epstein, Steven A. *An Economic and Social History of Later Medieval Europe, 1000–1500*. 2009. Examines the most important themes in European social and economic history, with a wide geographic sweep.

Glick, Leonard B. *Abraham's Heirs: Jews and Christians in Medieval Europe*. 1999. Provides information on many aspects of Jewish life and Jewish-Christian relations.

Herlihy, David. *The Black Death and the Transformation of the West*, 2d ed. 1997. A fine treatment of the causes and cultural consequences of the disease that remains the best starting point for study of the great epidemic.

Janin, Hunt. *The University in Medieval Life, 1179–1499*. 2008. An overview of medieval universities designed for general readers.

Kaeuper, Richard W. *Chivalry and Violence in Medieval Europe*. 2006. Examines the role chivalry played in promoting violent disorder.

Madden, Thomas. *The New Concise History of the Crusades*. 2005. A highly readable brief survey by the preeminent American scholar of the Crusades.

Sawyer, Peter, ed. *The Oxford Illustrated History of the Vikings*. 1997. A sound account of the Vikings by an international team of scholars.

Shahar, Shulamit. *The Fourth Estate: A History of Women in the Middle Ages*, 2d ed. 2003. Analyzes attitudes toward women and provides information on the lives of a variety of women, including nuns, peasants, noblewomen, and townswomen.

Shinners, John. *Medieval Popular Religion, 1000–1500*, 2d ed. 2006. An excellent collection of a wide variety of sources that provide evidence about the beliefs and practices of ordinary Christians.

Tuchman, Barbara. *A Distant Mirror: The Calamitous Fourteenth Century*. 1978. A vivid description of this tumultuous time written for a general audience.

Wickham, Chris. *Framing the Early Middle Ages: Europe and the Mediterranean, 400–800*. 2007. A massive yet accessible survey of economic and social changes in many regions, with great attention to ordinary people.

NOTES

1. D. C. Douglas and G. E. Greenaway, eds., *English Historical Documents*, vol. 2 (London: Eyre & Spottiswoode, 1961), p. 853.

2. Fulcher of Chartres, *A History of the Expedition to Jerusalem, 1095–1127*, trans. Frances Rita Ryan, ed. Harold S. Fink (Knoxville: University of Tennessee Press, 1969), pp. 121–123.

3. H. Rothwell, ed., *English Historical Documents*, vol. 3 (London: Eyre & Spottiswoode, 1975), p. 854.

4. Erwin Panofsky, trans. and ed., *Abbot Suger on the Abbey Church of St.-Denis and Its Art Treasures* (Princeton, N.J.: Princeton University Press, 1946), p. 101.

5. Quoted in J. J. Wilhelm, ed., *Lyrics of the Middle Ages: An Anthology*. Copyright 1990. Reproduced with permission of TAYLOR & FRANCIS GROUP LLC in the format Textbook and Other Book via Copyright Clearance Center.

For practice quizzes and other study tools, visit the **Online Study Guide** at bedfordstmartins.com/mckayworld.

For primary sources from this period, see *Sources of World Societies*, **Second Edition**.

For Web sites, images, and documents related to topics in this chapter, visit **Make History** at bedfordstmartins.com/mckayworld.

in Pacific Ocean region, 360
Paleolithic, 2, 8(m)
population growth of, 13–14
Human sacrifice. *See also* Sacrifices
　Aztec, 315, 316, 316(i)
　in China, 96, 97
　Maya, 308
Hunayn ib Ishaq (Islam), 241
Hundred Schools of Thought (China), 103, 111
Hundred Years' War, 418–420
Hungarians, Magyars as, 394
Hungary, 224, 332, 395. *See also* Magyars
　Christianity in, 403, 404
　German settlers in, 404
　Rome and, 159
Huns, 181, 207, 224–225, 333, 347. *See also* Xiongnu people
　Gupta Empire and, 348
Hunting
　gathering and, 6, 11–14, 117, 271
　horticulture and, 21
　by Mongols, 336
　Paleolithic, 9
Husbands, in Mesopotamia, 43
Hydaspes (Jhelum) River, 82
Hydrostatics, 138(b)
Hygiene. *See* Sanitation
Hyksos people, 47
Hyphasis River, Alexander the Great at, 131

Iberian Peninsula, 224. *See also* Portugal; Spain
　Christianity in, 261, 404
　Muslims in, 230, 261
Ibn al-'Arabi (Sufi), writings of, 260–261
Ibn Al-Athir, on Crusades, 406–407(b)
Ibn al-Razzaz al-Raziri, inventions of, 257(i)
Ibn Battuta, Abu 'Abdallah, 254(b), 254(i), 277
　on Delhi sultanate, 352
　on spice trade, 357(b)
　on Timbuktu, 282
　on trans-Saharan trade, 275
Ibn Muhammad al-Diruti al Mahalli, Ali, daughter of, 258
Ibn Rushid. *See* Averroës
Ibn Sina of Bukhara. *See* Avicenna
Ibo people (Nigeria), 274
Ice Age, 301
Iceland, 394, 395
Iceman, 25(b), 25(i)
Iconoclastic controversy, 213–214
Identity, in Paleolithic kin groups, 14
Ideograms, 39, 46, 52
Ideologies. *See* Intellectual thought; Philosophy; Religion(s)
Idolatry, 213
Ife people, ruler of, 266(i)
Igbo people, 273–274
Ikhwan al-Safa, on Jesus, 262
Iliad, 118
Il-Khanate (Mongols), 245, 345

Illness. *See* Diseases; Epidemics; Medicine; specific conditions
Imam (leader), 240
　in Ghana, 279
Immigrants and immigration. *See* Migration
Imperator (Rome), 154, 157, 158(i)
Imperialism. *See also* specific regions
　Athenian, 123
　Inca, 321–323
Incas, 302(i), 304, 320–327, 321(m)
　imperialism of, 321–323
　khipu and, 37, 304, 305(i), 322
　lifestyle of, 324–325(b), 325(i)
　potato farming by, 19(i)
　society in, 323–327
　ten paths in, 324–325(b), 325(i)
　textiles in, 326(i)
Inca Yupanque. *See* Pachacuti Inca
India. *See also* Asia; Gandhi, Mohandas; Mughal Empire (India)
　agriculture in, 66, 71, 82, 353
　Alexander the Great in, 81–82
　ancient civilizations, 65, 66–69
　army in, 82
　arts in, 69(i), 81(i), 86, 350–351
　Aryans in, 65, 69–74, 71(i)
　Bactrian armies in, 134
　Buddhism and, 64(i), 188
　castes in, 354
　cities and towns in, 68–69, 69(i), 74
　culture(s) of, 86, 347–355, 360
　division of, 347
　families in, 355
　geography of, 66
　government of, 71, 81, 82, 86
　Greek culture and, 86
　Gupta Empire in, 347, 348–352
　Harappan civilization in, 65, 66–69, 67(i)
　Hellenistic trade with, 134
　Homo sapiens spread across, 9
　Huns in, 348
　Indo-European migrations and Vedic Age, 70(m)
　intellectual thought in, 348
　Islam and, 238, 348, 349–350
　languages in, 69–70, 348
　lifestyle in, 71–73, 353–355
　Mauryan Empire in, 65, 75, 81–85, 347
　medieval, 348–352, 353–355
　Mongols in, 353
　Mughal Empire in, 353
　Neolithic, 66
　Persia and, 71, 81
　religions in, 65, 74–81, 84–85, 348–355
　slaves and, 291
　society in, 354–355
　Southeast Asia and, 355
　Srivijaya and, 359–360
　states in, 86–87
　textiles in, 353
　trade and, 67, 68, 86–87, 182
　Turks in, 334
　wars in, 353
　women in, 72–73, 355

workers in, 353, 354
writing in, 66, 74, 87(i)
Indian, 301. *See also* American Indians; Amerindians; India
Indian elephants, ivory and, 291
Indian Ocean region, 286. *See also* Southeast Asia
　Chola people in, 348
　shipping in, 253
　slave trade in, 291
　trade in, 163, 253
Indigenous peoples, 301. *See also* specific groups
Individual, in species, 4
Indo-Aryan period, in India, 70
Indochina, Funan and, 355
Indo-European language family, 49, 58, 69
Indo-European people
　migrations and Vedic Age, 70(m)
　as nomads, 58–59
Indo-Greek states, 86, 134
Indonesia
　hominid remains found in, 10
　spice trade and, 357(b)
　Srivijaya in, 359
Indra (god), 73
Indus River region, 65, 66, 81, 82, 86, 238, 348, 349. *See also* India
　crops in, 20
　Islam in, 350
　Mesopotamia and, 42, 43, 71
Industry. *See also* specific industries
　in China, 370
　in Rome, 163
Infanticide, Paleolithic, 14
Infants, hominid development and, 9
Inferno (Dante), Muslims in, 263
Inflation, in Rome, 170
Influenza, 22
Infrastructure
　Hellenistic, 134
　in Vietnam, 197
Inheritance
　Aztec, 319
　gender and, 26–27
　mitochondrial DNA and, 7
　of property, 27
　in Rome, 158
　of serfdom, 409
Inland Sea, Japan and, 198–199
Inner Asia, 180–182
　China and, 92
　Turks from, 333–334
Inner Mongolia, 92
Innocent IV (Pope), 345
Inscriptions, 35–36
Institutes (Justinian), 208
Intaglio process, 139(i)
Intellectual thought. *See also* Education; Philosophy; Renaissance; Scholarship; Writing
　Byzantine, 208–209
　Carolingian Renaissance and, 228–229
　in China, 103–111, 178–180

□ TIMELINE | A History of World Societies: An Overview

Africa	The Americas
10,000 B.C.E. *Homo sapiens* evolve, ca. 250,000 years ago Farming begins in Nile River Valley, ca. 9000 Domestication of cattle; plow agriculture, ca. 7000 Unification of Egypt, 3100–2660	Possible migration into Americas begins, ca. 20,000–30,000 Farming begins, ca. 8000 Maize domesticated in Mexico, ca. 3000
2500 B.C.E. Egypt's Old Kingdom, 2660–2180 Egypt's Middle Kingdom, 2080–1640 Hyksos migrate into Egypt, 1640–1570	First cities in Peru; earliest mound building in North America, ca. 2500 Textiles become important part of Peruvian culture, ca. 2500 Farmers in southwestern North America grow maize, ca. 2000
1500 B.C.E. Egypt's New Kingdom, ca. 1550–1070 Ironworking spreads throughout Africa, ca. 1500 B.C.E.–300 C.E. Akhenaten institutes monotheistic worship of Aton, ca. 1360	Olmec civilization in Mexico, ca. 1500–300 Earliest cities in the Andes built by Chavin people, ca. 1200
1000 B.C.E. Political fragmentation of Egypt; rise of small kingdoms, ca. 1100–653 Bantu migrations across central and southern Africa, ca. 1000 B.C.E.–1500 C.E. Persians conquer Egypt, 525	Olmec center at San Lorenzo destroyed; power passes to La Venta, ca. 900
500 B.C.E. Ptolemy conquers Egypt, 323	
250 B.C.E. Scipio Africanus defeats Hannibal at Zama, 202 Meroë becomes iron-smelting center, ca. 100	Hopewell culture flourishes in North America, ca. 200 B.C.E.–600 C.E.

Asia and Oceania	Europe	Middle East
Farming begins in Yellow River Valley, ca. 9000 Domestication of cattle; plow agriculture begins, ca. 7000	Farming spreads to Greece, ca. 6500 Smelting of copper in Balkans, ca. 5500 Farming spreads to Britain, ca. 4000	Farming begins; domestication of goats and sheep in the Fertile Crescent, ca. 9000 Invention of pottery wheel in Mesopotamia, ca. 5000 First writing in Sumeria; city-states emerge, ca. 3500
Harappan civilization, ca. 2800–1800	Minoan culture emerges, ca. 2000 Arrival of Greeks in peninsular Greece; founding of Mycenaean kingdom, ca. 1650	Smelting of iron begins in Mesopotamia, ca. 2500 Akkadian empire, ca. 2331–2200 Hammurabi's law code, ca. 1790
Shang Dynasty; first writing in China, ca. 1500–1050 Vedic Age: Aryans dominate in North India; caste system develops; the *Rigveda*, ca. 1500–500	Mycenaeans conquer Minoan Crete, ca. 1450 Greek Dark Age; evolution of the polis, ca. 1100–800	Hittites expand empire in Mesopotamia, ca. 1600 Moses leads Hebrews out of Egypt, ca. 1300–1200 United Hebrew kingdom, ca. 1020–930
Early Zhou Dynasty, ca. 1050–400 *Upanishads*, foundation of Hinduism, 750–500 Life of Confucius, 551–479 Persians conquer parts of India, 513 Founding of Buddhism and Jainism, ca. 500	Fall of Minoan and Mycenaean cultures, ca. 1000 Rise of Sparta and Athens, 800–500 Roman Republic founded, 509	Assyrian Empire, ca. 800–612 Spread of Zoroastrianism, ca. 600–500 Babylonian captivity of Hebrews, 587–538 Cyrus the Great founds Persian Empire, 550
Warring States period; golden age of Chinese philosophy, 403–221 Brahmanic religion develops into Hinduism, ca. 400 B.C.E.–200 C.E. Zhuangzi and development of Daoism, 369–268 Alexander the Great invades India, 326 Seleucus establishes Seleucid Empire, 323 Mauryan Empire, ca. 322–185 Reign of Ashoka; Buddhism spreads in central Asia, 269–232	Flowering of Greek art and philosophy, 500–400 Persian wars, 499–479 Peloponnesian War, 431–404 Roman expansion, 390–146 Conquests of Alexander the Great, 336–323 Punic Wars; destruction of Carthage, 264–146	Persian Empire falls to Alexander the Great, 330 Alexander the Great dies in Babylon, 323
Qin Dynasty unifies China; construction of Great Wall, 221–206 Han Dynasty, 206 B.C.E.–220 C.E. Han government controls Silk Road across central Asia, 114 Chinese armies conquer Nam Viet, 111 *Bhagavad Gita*, ca. 100 B.C.E.–100 C.E.	Late Roman republic, 133–27 Julius Caesar killed, 44 Octavian seizes power, rules imperial Rome as Augustus, 27 B.C.E.–14 C.E.	

	Africa	The Americas
1 C.E.	Expansion of Bantu-speaking peoples into eastern and southern Africa, ca. 100	Moche civilization flourishes in Peru, ca. 100–800
200 C.E.	Aksum (Ethiopia) controls Red Sea trade, ca. 250	
300	Christianity comes to Ethiopia from Egypt, 328 Aksum accepts Christianity, ca. 350	Hohokam use irrigation to enhance farming in southwestern North America, ca. 300 Classical era in Mesoamerican and North America; Maya and other groups develop large advanced states, 300–900 Peak of Teotihuacán civilization in Mexico, ca. 450
500	Political and commercial ascendancy of Aksum, ca. 500–700 Christian missionaries convert Nubian rulers, ca. 600 Muslim conquest of Egypt; Islam introduced to Africa, 642 Height of African Mediterranean slave trade, ca. 650–1500	Peak of Maya civilization, ca. 600–900
700	Expansion of Islam into Ethiopia weakens state, 700–800 Berbers control trans-Saharan trade, ca. 700–900 Islam spreads across Sahara, 800–900 Kingdom of Ghana, ca. 900–1300	Teotihuacán destroyed, 750 Period of crop failure, disease, and war in Mesoamerica; collapse of Maya civilization, 800–1000 Toltec hegemony, ca. 980–1000
1000	Islam penetrates sub-Saharan Africa, ca. 1000–1100 Great Zimbabwe built, flourishes, ca. 1100–1400	Inca civilization in South America, ca. 1000–1500 Peak of Cahokia culture in North America, ca. 1150 Toltec state collapses, 1174
1200	Kingdom of Mali, ca. 1200–1450 Mongols conquer Baghdad; fall of Abbasid Dynasty, 1258	Cahokia's decline begins after earthquake, ca. 1200

Asia and Oceania	Europe	Middle East
Shakas and Kushans invade eastern Parthia and India, ca. 1–100 Maritime trade between Chinese and Roman ports begins, ca. 100 Roman attacks on Parthian empire, ca. 100–200 Chinese invent paper, 105	Roman Empire at greatest extent, 117	Life of Jesus, ca. 3 B.C.E.–29 C.E.
Buddhism gains popularity in China, Japan, and Korea, ca. 200–600 Age of Division in China, 220–589 Fall of the Parthian empire; rise of the Sassanid, ca. 226	Life of Diocletian: reforms Roman Empire; divides into western and eastern halves, 284–305	Sassanid dynasty in Persia, 226–651
Three Kingdoms Period in Korea, 313–668 China divides into northern and southern regimes, 316 Gupta Empire unites northern India, ca. 320–480 Huns invade India, ca. 450	Life of Constantine: legalizes Christianity; founds Constantinople, 306–337 Christianity official state religion of Roman Empire, 380 Germanic raids on western Europe, 400s Clovis rules Gauls, ca. 481–511	
Sui Dynasty restores order in China, 581–618 Prince Shōtoku introduces Chinese-style government in Japan, 604 Tang Dynasty in China; cultural flowering, 618–907 Korea unified, 668	Reign of Justinian; *Code* and *Digest*, 527–565 *Rule* of Saint Benedict, 529	Life of Muhammad, 570–632 Publication of the Qur'an, 651 Umayyad Dynasty; expansion of Islam, 661–750
Creation of Japan's first capital at Nara, 710 Islam reaches India, 713 Heian era in Japan, 794–1185 Khmer Empire of Cambodia founded, 802 Koryŏ Dynasty in Korea, 935–1392 North Vietnam gains independence from China, 939 Song Dynasty in China; invention of movable type, 960–1279	Muslims defeat Visigothic kingdom in Spain, 711 Christian reconquest of Spain from Muslims, 722–1492 Carolingians defeat Muslims at Poitiers, 732 Viking, Magyar invasions, ca. 800–950 Treaty of Verdun divides Carolingian Empire, 843	Abbasid caliphate; Islamic capital moved to Baghdad, 750–1258 Height of Muslim learning and creativity, ca. 800–1300
Construction of Angkor Wat, ca. 1100–1150 Muslim conquests lead to decline of Buddhism in India, ca. 1100–1200 China divided into Song and Jin empires, 1127 Kamakura Shogunate in Japan, 1185–1333	Latin, Greek churches split, 1054 Norman Conquest of England, 1066 Crusades, 1095–1270 Growth of trade and towns, ca. 1100–1400	Seljuk Turks take Baghdad, 1055
Easter Island's most prosperous period, ca. 1200–1300 Turkish sultanate at Dehli, 1206–1526 Peak of Khmer Empire, 1219 Mongol's Yuan Dynasty in China, 1234–1368 Mongols invade Japan, 1274, 1281 Marco Polo travels in China, ca. 1275–1292 Mongol conquest of Song China, 1276	Magna Carta, 1215 Life of Thomas Aquinas; *Summa Theologica*, 1225–1274 Mongol raids into eastern Europe; Mongols gain control of Kieven Russia, 1237–1241	Mongols conquer Baghdad, 1238 Ottoman Empire, 1299–1922

Africa	The Americas
1300	
Height of Swahili city-states in East Africa, ca. 1300–1500	Construction of Aztec city Tenochtitlán begins, ca. 1325
Mansa Musa rules Mali, ca. 1312–1337	
Ibn Battuta's travels, 1325–1354	
1400	
Songhai Empire, ca. 1464–1591	Height of Inca Empire, 1438–1532
Arrival of Portuguese in Benin, 1485	Reign of Montezuma I; height of Aztec culture, 1440–1467
Da Gama reaches East Africa; Swahili coast enters period of economic decline, 1498	Inca city of Machu Picchu built, 1450
	Columbus reaches Americas, 1492
1500	
Portugal dominates East Africa, ca. 1500–1600	Portuguese reach Brazil, 1500
Era of transatlantic slave trade, ca. 1500–1900	Atlantic slave trade begins, 1518
Muslim occupation of Christian Ethiopia, 1531–1543	Cortés arrives in Mexico, 1519
Height of Kanem-Bornu, 1571–1603	Aztec Empire falls, 1521
	Pizarro conquers Inca Empire, 1533
	First English colony in North America founded at Roanoke, 1585
1600	
Dutch West India Company founded; starts to bring slave coast of West Africa under its control, 1621	British settle Jamestown, 1607
Jesuit missionaries expelled from Ethiopia, 1633	Champlain founds first permanent French settlement at Quebec, 1608
Dutch East India Company settles Cape Town, 1652	Caribbean islands colonized by French, English, Dutch, 1612–1697
Importation of slaves into Cape Colony begins, 1658	English seize New Amsterdam from Dutch, 1664
1700	
Major famine in West Africa, 1738–1756	Silver production quadruples in Mexico and Peru, ca. 1700–1800
	Colonial dependence on Spanish goods, ca. 1700–1800
1750	
Peak of transatlantic slave trade, 1780–1820	Seven Years' War, 1756–1763
Olaudah Equiano publishes autobiography, 1789	Quebec Act, 1774
British seize Cape Town, 1795	American Revolution, 1775–1783
Napoleon's army invades Egypt, 1798	Comunero revolution in New Granada, 1781
	Haitian Revolution, 1791–1804

Asia and Oceania	Europe	Middle East
Ashikaga Shogunate, 1336–1573 Mongols defeated in China, 1368 Ming Dynasty in China, 1368–1644 Timur conquers the Delhi sultanate, 1398	Hundred Years' War, ca. 1337–1453 Black Death arrives in Europe, 1347 Great Schism, 1378–1417	
Maritime trade and piracy connects East Asia and Southeast Asia with Europe, ca. 1400–1800 Zheng He's maritime expeditions to India, Middle East, Africa, 1405–1433 Reign of Sultan Mehmed II, 1451–1481	Development of movable type in Germany, ca. 1450 Italian Renaissance, ca. 1450–1521 Age of Discovery, ca. 1450–1650 Ottomans capture Constantinople; end of Byzantine Empire, 1453 Unification of Spain; Jews expelled, 1492	Ottoman Empire conquers Byzantine Empire under rule of Sultan Mehmet II, 1451–1481
Increased availability of books in China, 1500–1600 Barbur defeats Delhi sultanate; founds Mughal Empire, 1526 Japan unified under Toyotomi Hideyoshi, 1537–1598 First Christian missionaries land in Japan, 1549 Akbar expands Mughal Empire, 1556–1605 Spain founds port city of Manila in the Philippines, 1571	Michelangelo paints Sistine Chapel, 1508–1512 Luther's Ninety-five Theses, 1517 English Reformation begins, 1527 Scientific revolution, ca. 1540–1690 Council of Trent, 1545–1563 Peace of Augsburg ends religious wars in Germany, 1555 Netherlands declares independence from Spain, 1581	Safavid Empire in Persia, 1501–1722 Peak of Ottoman power; cultural flowering under Suleiman, 1520–1566 Battle of Lepanto, 1571 Height of Safavid Empire under Shah Abbas, 1587–1629
Tokogawa Shogunate in Japan, 1603–1867 Japan closes its borders, 1639 Manchus establish Qing Dynasty in China, 1644–1911 Dutch expel Portuguese in East Indies; gain control of spice trade, ca. 1660 French arrive in India, ca. 1670	Thirty Years' War, 1619–1648 Growth of absolutism in Austria and Prussia, 1620–1740 English civil war, 1642–1649 Habsburgs expel Ottomans from Hungary, 1683–1718 Revocation of Edict of Nantes, 1685 Glorious Revolution in England, 1688–1689 The Enlightenment, ca. 1690–1789	Shah Abbas captures much of Armenia from the Ottomans, 1603
Height of Edo urban culture in Japan, ca. 1700 Christian missionary work forbidden in China, 1715 Persian invaders loot Delhi, 1739 French and British fight for control of India, 1740–1763	Growth of book publishing, ca. 1700–1789 War of the Spanish Succession, 1701–1713 Peace of Utrecht, 1713	Afghans seize Isfahan from Persians, 1722
Treaty of Paris gives French colonies in India to Britain, 1763 Cook claims land in Australia for Britain, 1770 East India Act, 1784 First British convict-settlers arrive in Australia, 1788	Watt produces first steam engine, 1769 Industrial Revolution in Great Britain, ca. 1780–1850 French Revolution, 1789–1799 Romantic movement in literature and the arts, ca. 1790s–1890s National Convention declares France a republic, 1792	Ottoman ruler Selim III introduces reforms, 1761–1808

	Africa	The Americas
1800	Muhammad Ali modernizes Egypt, 1805–1848 Slavery abolished in British Empire, 1807	Latin American wars of independence, 1806–1825 Brazil wins independence, 1822 Political instability in most Latin American countries, 1825–1870 U.S.-Mexican War, 1846–1848
1850	Suez Canal opens, 1869 Western and central Sudan unite under Islam, 1880 European "scramble for Africa"; decline of slave trade, 1880–1900 Battle of Omdurman, 1898 South African War, 1899–1902	U.S. Civil War, 1861–1865 Dominion of Canada formed, 1867 Latin American neocolonialism, ca. 1870–1929 Diaz controls Mexico, 1876–1911 Immigration from Europe and Asia to the Americas, 1880–1914 Spanish-American War, 1898
1900	Union of South Africa formed, 1910 Native Land Act in South Africa, 1913 Du Bois organizes first Pan-African congress, 1919	Mexican Revolution, 1910 Panama Canal opens, 1914 Mexico adopts constitution, 1917
1920	Cultural nationalism in Africa, 1920s Gold Coast farmers organize cocoa holdups, 1930–1931	U.S. consumer revolution, 1920s Stock market crash in U.S.; Great Depression begins, 1929 Revolutions in six South American countries, 1930 Flowering of Mexican culture, 1930s New Deal begins in United States, 1933
1940	Decolonization in Africa, 1946–1964 Apartheid system in South Africa, 1948–1991	"Mexican miracle," 1940s–1970s Surprise attack by Japan on Pearl Harbor, 1941 United Nations established, 1945
1950	Egypt declared a republic; Nasser named premier, 1954 French-British Suez invasion, 1956 Morocco, Tunisia, Sudan, and Ghana gain independence, 1956–1957 France offers commonwealth status to its territories; only Guinea chooses independence, 1958 Belgian Congo gains independence; violence follows, 1959	Cuban revolution, 1953–1959 Military rule ends in Venezuela, 1958 Castro takes power in Cuba, 1959

Asia and Oceania	Europe	Middle East
British found Singapore, 1819	Napoleonic Europe, 1804–1814	Ottoman Empire launches Tanzimat reforms, 1839
Java War, 1825–1830	Congress of Vienna, 1814–1815	
Opium War, 1839–1842	European economic penetration of non-Western countries, ca. 1816–1880	
Treaty of Nanjing; Manchus surrender Hong Kong to British, 1842	Greece wins independence, 1830	
	Revolutions in France, Austria, and Prussia, 1848	
Taiping Rebellion, 1851–1864	Unification of Italy, 1859–1870	Crimean War, 1853–1856
Perry opens Japan to trade; Japan begins to industrialize, 1853	Freeing of Russian serfs, 1861	Ottoman state declares partial bankruptcy; European creditors take over, 1875
Great Mutiny/Revolt in India, 1857	Unification of Germany, 1866–1871	
Meiji Restoration in Japan, 1867	Massive industrialization surge in Russia, 1890–1900	
Indian National Congress, 1885		
French acquire Indochina, 1893		
Sino-Japanese War, 1894–1895		
U.S. gains Philippines, 1898		
Boxer Rebellion in China, 1900	Revolution in Russia, 1905	Young Turks seize power in Ottoman Empire, 1908
Commonwealth of Australia, 1901	World War I, 1914–1918	Turkish massacre of Armenians, 1915–1917
Russo-Japanese War, 1904–1905	Bolshevik Revolution and civil war in Russia, 1917–1922	Sykes-Picot Agreement divides Ottoman Empire, 1916
Muslim League formed, 1906	Treaty of Versailles, 1919	Balfour Declaration establishes Jewish homeland in Palestine, 1917
Korea becomes province of Japan, 1910		
Chinese revolution; fall of Qing Dynasty, 1911		
Chinese republic, 1912–1949		
Amritsar Massacre in India, 1919		
Gandhi launches nonviolent campaign against British rule in India, 1920	Mussolini seizes power in Italy, 1922	Large numbers of European Jews immigrate to Palestine, 1920s–1930s
Jiang Jieshi unites China, 1928	Stalin takes power in U.S.S.R., 1927	Turkish republic recognized; Kemal begins to modernize and secularize, 1923
Japan invades China, 1931	Great Depression, 1929–1933	Reza Shah leads Iran, 1925–1941
Mao Zedong's Long March, 1934	Hitler gains power in Germany, 1933	Iraq gains independence, 1932
Sino-Japanese War, 1937–1945	Civil war in Spain, 1936–1939	
Japan conquers Southeast Asia, 1939–1942	World War II, 1939–1945	
Japan announces "Asia for Asians"; signs alliance with Germany and Italy, 1940	Marshall Plan, 1947	Arabs and Jews at war in Palestine; Israel created, 1948
United States drops atomic bombs on Hiroshima and Nagasaki, 1945	NATO formed, 1949	
Chinese civil war; Communists win, 1945–1949	Soviet Union and Communist China sign 30-year alliance, 1949	
Philippines gain independence, 1946		
Independence and separation of India and Pakistan, 1947		
Japan begins long period of rapid economic growth, 1950	Death of Stalin, 1953	Turkey joins NATO, 1953
Korean War, 1950–1953	Warsaw Pact, 1955	Suez crisis, 1956
Vietnamese nationalists defeat French; Vietnam divided, 1954	Revolution in Hungary, 1956	
Mao announces Great Leap Forward in China, 1958	Common Market formed, 1957	

	Africa	The Americas
1960	Mali and Nigeria gain independence, 1960 Biafra declares independence from Nigeria, 1967	U.S. Alliance for Progress promotes development and reform in Latin America, 1961 Cuban missile crisis, 1962 U.S. Civil Rights Act; United States starts Vietnam War, 1964 Military dictatorship in Brazil, 1964–1985 Military takeovers lead to brutal dictatorships in Argentina, 1966, 1976
1970	Growth of Islamic fundamentalism, 1970s to present	U.S. Watergate scandal, 1972 Nixon visits China; reconciliation between U.S. and China, 1972 Military coup in Chile, 1973 Revolution in Nicaragua, 1979
1980	Blacks win long civil war with white settlers in Zimbabwe, 1980 AIDS epidemic, 1980s to present South African government opens talks with African National Congress, 1989	Democratic wave gains momentum throughout Latin America, 1980s Nationalization of Mexico's banking system, 1982 Argentina restores civilian rule, 1983 Brazilians elect first civilian government in twenty years, 1985
1990	Nelson Mandela freed in South Africa, 1990 Rwandan genocide, 1994 Second Congo War, 1998 to present	Canada, Mexico, and United States form free-trade area (NAFTA), 1994 Haiti establishes democratic government, 1994 Socialist "Bolivarian revolution" in Venezuela, 1999
2000	Civil war and genocide in Darfur, 2003 to present Mugabe increases violence against opponents after losing Zimbabwean election, 2008 Populist uprisings and protests break out in Tunisia, Egypt, and elsewhere in North Africa, 2010–2011	Terrorist attack on United States, 2001 Economic, social, and political crisis in Argentina, 2002 Formation of the Union of South American Nations, 2008 Raúl Castro succeeds his ailing brother Fidel as president of Cuba, 2008 Catastrophic earthquake in Haiti, 2010 U.S. begins troop drawdown in Afghanistan, 2011

Asia and Oceania	Europe	Middle East
Sino-Soviet split becomes apparent, 1960	Building of Berlin Wall, 1961	OPEC founded, 1960
Vietnam War, 1964–1975	Student revolution in France, 1968	Arab-Israeli Six-Day War, 1967
Great Proletarian Cultural Revolution launched in China, 1965	Soviet invasion of Czechoslovakia, 1968	
Bangladesh breaks away from Pakistan, 1971	Helsinki Accord on human rights, 1975	Revival of Islamic fundamentalism, 1970s to present
Communist victory in Vietnam War, 1975	Soviet invasion of Afghanistan, 1979	Arab-Israeli Yom Kippur War, 1973
China pursues modernization, 1976 to present		OPEC oil embargo, 1973
		Civil war in Lebanon, 1975–1990
		Islamic revolution in Iran, 1979
		Camp David Accords, 1979
Japanese foreign investment surge, 1980–1992	Soviet reform under Gorbachev, 1985–1991	Iran-Iraq War, 1980–1988
Sikh nationalism in India, 1984 to present	Communism falls in eastern Europe, 1989–1990	Palestinians start the intifada, 1987
China crushes democracy movement, 1989		
Collapse of Japanese stock market, 1990–1992	Conservative economic policies, 1990s	Persian Gulf War, 1990–1991
Economic growth and political repression in China, 1990 to present	End of Soviet Union, 1991	Israel and Palestinians sign peace agreement, 1993
Congress Party in India embraces Western capitalist reforms, 1991	Civil war in Yugoslavia, 1991–2001	Assassination of Israeli prime minster Yitzak Rabin, 1995
Kyoto Protocol on global warming, 1997	Maastricht Treaty creates single currency, 1992	
Hong Kong returns to Chinese rule, 1997	Creation of European Union, 1993	
China joins World Trade Organization, 2001	Resurgence of Russian economy under Putin, 2000–2008	Israel begins construction of West Bank barrier, 2003
India and Pakistan come close to all-out war, 2001	Euro note enters circulation, 2002	Wars in Iraq and Afghanistan, 2003 to present
North Korea withdraws from 1970 Nuclear Non-Proliferation Treaty, 2003	Madrid train bombing, 2004	Hamas establishes Palestinian Authority government, 2007
Tsunami in Southeast Asia, 2004	London subway and bus bombing, 2005	Populist uprisings and protests across the Middle East, 2010–2011
Terrorist attack in Mumbai, India, 2008		
Massive earthquake in Japan, 2011		
Al-Qaeda leader Osama bin Laden killed in Pakistan, 2011		

◻ ABOUT THE AUTHORS

JOHN P. McKAY (Ph.D., University of California, Berkeley) is professor emeritus at the University of Illinois. He has written or edited numerous works, including the Herbert Baxter Adams Prize–winning book *Pioneers for Profit: Foreign Entrepreneurship and Russian Industrialization, 1885–1913.*

BENNETT D. HILL (Ph.D., Princeton University), late of Georgetown University, published *Church and State in the Middle Ages* and numerous articles and reviews, and was one of the contributing editors to *The Encyclopedia of World History.* He was also a Benedictine monk of St. Anselm's Abbey in Washington, D.C.

JOHN BUCKLER (Ph.D., Harvard University), late of the University of Illinois, authored *Theban Hegemony, 371–362 B.C., Philip II and the Sacred War,* and *Aegean Greece in the Fourth Century B.C.* With Hans Beck, he most recently published *Central Greece and the Politics of Power in the Fourth Century.*

PATRICIA BUCKLEY EBREY (Ph.D., Columbia University), professor of history at the University of Washington in Seattle, specializes in China. She has published many journal articles and *The Cambridge Illustrated History of China* as well as numerous monographs. In 2010 she won the Shimada Prize for outstanding work of East Asian Art History for *Accumulating Culture: The Collections of Emperor Huizong.*

ROGER B. BECK (Ph.D., Indiana University) is Distinguished Professor of African and twentieth-century world history at Eastern Illinois University. His publications include *The History of South Africa,* a translation of P. J. van der Merwe's *The Migrant Farmer in the History of the Cape Colony, 1657–1842,* and more than a hundred articles, book chapters, and reviews. He is a former treasurer and Executive Council member of the World History Association.

CLARE HARU CROWSTON (Ph.D., Cornell University) teaches at the University of Illinois, where she is currently associate professor of history. She is the author of *Fabricating Women: The Seamstresses of Old Regime France, 1675–1791,* which won the Berkshire and Hagley Prizes. She edited two special issues of the *Journal of Women's History,* has published numerous journal articles and reviews, and is a past president of the Society for French Historical Studies.

MERRY E. WIESNER-HANKS (Ph.D., University of Wisconsin–Madison) taught first at Augustana College in Illinois, and since 1985 at the University of Wisconsin–Milwaukee, where she is currently UWM Distinguished Professor in the department of history. She is the coeditor of the *Sixteenth Century Journal* and the author or editor of more than twenty books, most recently *The Marvelous Hairy Girls: The Gonzales Sisters and Their Worlds* and *Gender in History.* She is the former Chief Reader for Advanced Placement World History.

ABOUT THE COVER ART

Egyptian Mummy Mask This Egyptian mummy mask from the era of the New Kingdom (ca. 1295–1069 B.C.E.) shows a young woman with lively eyes and a slight smile. Mummy masks — made of cloth glued together in layers like papier-mâché and then painted — were placed over the wrapped heads of mummies to protect them during the journey to the afterlife. Like much Egyptian art, they were idealized portraits, depicting individuals as they wished to be seen.